A HISTORY OF MODERN TIMES

FROM 1789 TO THE PRESENT DAY

BY

D. M. KETELBEY M.A. F.R.Hist.S.

EDITOR OF "EUROPEAN HISTORY FROM THE FALL OF ROME
TO THE EVE OF THE FRENCH REVOLUTION" ETC.

NEW EDITION REVISED

GEORGE G. HARRAP & CO. LTD.

LONDON   TORONTO   BOMBAY   SYDNEY

First published September 1929
by GEORGE G. HARRAP & CO. LTD.
182 *High Holborn, London, W.C.* 1

Reprinted: October 1932; October 1935; November 1937

New Edition, revised, published March 1940

Reprinted November 1941

Made in Great Britain. Printed by Neill & Co. Ltd., Edinburgh

PREFACE

I HAVE no need to emphasize the difficulties and dangers that beset an author who attempts to give, in small compass, a comprehensive survey of the vast developments of modern history. His omissions will be prejudicial, his emphasis arbitrary, his condensations biased. While on the one hand he is conscious, as Professor Alison Phillips has expressed it, that "as a student of modern times, he is labouring largely in darkness," on the other he is fully aware that it is beyond his human capacity independently to examine all the evidence that already exists. In every sentence he is exposed to the criticism of the specialist.

I have tried to give in fair outline—except where I considered myself justified in dwelling rather more fully on one or two matters of which I have made a special study—the chief movements of the Age of Democracy, and an analysis, where I could, of the factors which produced them. As I approached the present day I have naturally felt more restricted in my comments and hampered in my judgments. With this modification, however, I have attempted to give an interpretation as well as a narrative of the sequence of events. I have not ignored either detail or personality where the one seemed significant or the other illuminating. It is my hope that both the student and the general reader will find in this book, in language which does not suggest to him that the reading of history is wholly divorced from the writing of English, a starting-point for further inquiry and a stimulus to thought.

In the European chapters I have been driven by exigencies of space to concentrate mainly on the greater countries, and it is with real regret that I have often relegated the smaller nations to the realm of reference or illustration. This book is distinguished, however, from a history of Europe by three sections, on colonial expansion, on the United States of America, and on the Far East, subjects which no student, either of history or of politics, can afford any longer to ignore. As never before, Europe is hinged with the rest of the world.

5

I have considered it inadvisable to equip this book with an exhaustive bibliography, from which the average reader is often unable to make a selection. The list of books therefore consists of a certain number of recommended volumes, easily accessible, which will advance the inquirer many stages in the chief subjects in which he is likely to be interested. The books mentioned, or a work of reference like *The Cambridge Modern History* or the *Encyclopædia Britannica*, will give him a larger bibliography if he should desire it.

I should like to express my sense of indebtedness to my friends H. M. W. and M. L. K., who have helped me immeasurably throughout the whole production of the book.

D. M. K.

June 1929

NOTE TO THE NEW EDITION

In the ten years that have passed since the publication of this book some obscure matters have been clarified, especially by the continued publication of the volumes of *British Documents on the Origins of the War* (1898–1914), and some startling and tragic developments have taken place in international affairs. I should like to thank the Publishers for giving me in this edition an opportunity of incorporating, to the utmost limits of its pages, some of this new knowledge and of these recent developments. The original text is able to stand, however, without serious modification; some corrections of detail have been made, some doubts have been resolved, some paragraphs have been added to the later chapters.

A history of our own times must inevitably lag behind events, but it is clear that the great age which this book attempts primarily to describe is closing, rounded by despotisms. The world which opened to the cry of "Man is born free" is yielding to the pressure of new totalitarian organizations and to the manifestations of new tyrannies. Democracy, its dominant inspiration, is in eclipse; the British Empire and post-Revolutionary France, the keystones of its political and economic systems, are on the defensive. The age passes, bequeathing a rich heritage, whose value has yet to be tested in the assay of history.

D. M. K.

February 1940

CONTENTS

CONTENTS

MAPS

A HISTORY OF
MODERN TIMES

CHAPTER I

INTRODUCTION

THROUGHOUT the course of European history there seems to be from time to time an outburst of unusual activity, a display of excessive energy. Such a period was the nineteenth century, shaped by the mighty whirlwind forces set in motion by the French and Industrial Revolutions. In the midst of these two vast movements the eighteenth century found its dissolution and the nineteenth century its birth. Falling together in time, their combined influence has been greater and more direct than that of the Renaissance or the Reformation, than the fall of Rome or the martyrdom of St Peter. They have created a chasm between the centuries, and transformed the world. It would be easy to present so startling a contrast between the eighteenth century and the world of to-day that they would seem to have little in common save human nature and a continuous history. But the French and Industrial Revolutions are only the products of what went before; they are indigenous movements; they have not been imposed from outside by an alien civilization, as Rome was Teutonized, or the East Westernized; nor brought in the train of conquest, as Spain received the ideas of the Arabs, Mexico in her turn those of Spain, Russia those of Tartary, or India those of England. They are the spontaneous expression of an innate energy and a native culture; and in the eighteenth century, which is the last fruit of a vanished world, may be found the germ and many of the formative influences of the new world that has taken its place. It is the grave of one epoch and the cradle of another.

The discoveries of Copernicus had by the eighteenth century long destroyed the geocentric theories of the universe, although the pure science of astronomy was still muddied by infiltrations of astrology. Geographical knowledge, on the other hand, was in the eighteenth century only arriving at its modern fullness. Most of America was still exclusively inhabited by its own natives; the interior of the Dark Continent of Africa was still unexplored;

The eighteenth century.

One civilization dying; another being born.

Geographical knowledge.

15

a North-west Passage was looked for; New Zealand was barely circumnavigated; New South Wales, the new deportation ground for British convicts, whom, after 1783, the United States were in a position to reject, still comprised the greater part of what was known of the "Terra Australis Incognita"; but the position, size, and shape of the chief territories of the world had been investigated; something of the southward extent of the Pacific Ocean had been ascertained; and Bering had already discovered that Asia and America were separate continents. Large areas of the world were not yet appropriated, but they had become permanent factors of political and economic value. The eighteenth century had completed the foundation of geographical knowledge on which the nineteenth century was to build.

Communication between the continents, especially between East and West, was slight, but it was well established, and from the eighteenth century it became continuous. Most inter-

Inter-continental communications small in quantity, but fully established.

course was confined to local areas; the Isthmus of Panama was still a barrier between the oceans, and camels carried the grain of the Nile to Arabia across the desert which is now intersected by ships steaming on their passage to India; the East still turned its back upon the West, and Captain Cook was first worshipped and then murdered in a conflict of civilizations in the island of Hawaii; the great Mohammedan world lying round the Indian Ocean had not yet surrendered its independence to Europe; there were no "Treaty Ports" and no Pacific Question, and only one Englishman was reputed to know Chinese; and yet the characteristic features of to-day may be found in embryo, and sometimes in a more advanced state. England had a firm hold upon India; the isolation of China was already being penetrated by the Muscovite agent by land in the north and by the Anglo-Indian opium-trader by sea from the south; already she had begun to look askance upon the "foreign devil," and to persecute the Jesuit missionaries who had been with her for two hundred years for seeking to overturn her empire. Rival East Indiamen of England and Holland traded among the Spice Islands; Dutch commercial companies quarrelled over tariffs with the customs officials of Japan, whose people of both sexes and all ages smoked tobacco introduced by the Portuguese. In all directions there were signs of activity and expansion. In the Arctic regions, along the shores of Japan and Tartary, in the unfamiliar South Sea Islands, on the coasts of Africa and the banks of the Niger, might be found pioneers of science and exploration; Russians, Danes, Norwegians, French, Dutch, and British travellers, looking for specimens for the Botanical Society of Amsterdam, making observations for the English Royal Society on the planets of the Southern Hemisphere, seeking a North-west

Passage, pursuing wealth, founding empires, adding to the treasury of knowledge which the nineteenth century has received.

In the sphere of international politics there has been since the eighteenth century some modification of the methods of diplomacy and some readjustment of the relative position of states, but in spite of the interruption of the Napoleonic wars the political history of the last two hundred years has been remarkably continuous. The path of diplomacy no longer lies through the heart of a king or the pockets of his mistress; the League of Nations has furnished the idea of the Concert of Europe with a permanent secretariat; but wars have not ceased with the advent of democracy, and the economic and colonial rivalry which disturbed the peace of the eighteenth century has only been magnified in the nineteenth. Of the five great political achievements of the last hundred years —the ascendant democracy of America, the German, the Russian, and the British Empires, and the Kingdom of Italy—four were already foreshadowed before the French Revolution. *International politics.*

Five main achievements of the nineteenth century.

'Germany' was merely a territorial expression covering three hundred separate states, but a King of Prussia had made a hobby of collecting soldiers, and the German Empire of 1871 was won as much on the fields of Rossbach and Minden as on those of Sadowa and Sedan. *The German Empire.*

Russia was a *parvenu* among Western states, and St Petersburg was not a hundred years old when the Bastille fell, but Catherine II had already laid her heel upon Poland, ousted the descendants of Tamerlane from the Crimea, and scattered her agents throughout Siberia and Central Asia. *Russia.*

Although in 1763 the conquest of Canada was held in some quarters to be less valuable than that of a West Indian island, it was on the Heights of Abraham and the plains of Plassey that the British Empire was won; it was the challenge which the revolt of the American Colonies gave to the colonial theory that has led to the evolution of Dominion self-government and federation, which has held that empire together; and it was the Irish questions raised by Grattan and Wolfe Tone that have led to the only important break in Imperial unity since 1783, for Ireland too by the end of the eighteenth century was set on that path of progression described in the words of her own orator [1] as "from injuries to arms and from arms to liberty." *The British Empire.*

The growth of the United States, the nation of exiles, is more strange. In 1789 it was a fringe of scattered settlements on the east coast of America, but their union and independence, though newly won, had been baptized in blood, and the most civilized people in Europe was proud to count them allies. *The United States of America.*

[1] Henry Grattan.

Italy alone gave small promise of her future.[1] She was divided among Bourbon and Habsburg, Church and city-state, and many princely families. But among these latter was one cradled in the mountains, the royal house of Savoy, which was slowly increasing its power and adding to its prestige.

Italy.

Prophecies of decay as well as those of achievement may be found in the eighteenth century. The house of Habsburg was, when the Bourbons fell, the most honoured dynasty in Europe, but even before the humiliations inflicted upon Austria by Napoleon she had been defeated by Prussia and defied by Belgium; her composition was mediæval, her prestige intimately linked with the Holy Roman Empire, whose somewhat belated epitaph Voltaire had already pronounced;[2] like the temporal Papacy, she was an anachronism.

The decay of Austria

Turkey in Europe, although her power stretched beyond the Danube, was a declining empire, and her evident weakness had considerably excited the cupidity of Catherine II. The submerged Christian states were beginning to revolt, Russia and Austria had declared themselves her enemies, and it was only the distraction of other European problems that delayed her partition.

and Turkey also foreshadowed.

As for the other states, the independence of Poland, flickering through the last twenty-five years of the century, was extinguished in 1795; Denmark, Sweden, and Spain had already become minor Powers, although Denmark owned Norway, although Sweden was still illuminated by the setting sun of the house of Vasa, although Spain could still alarm England by her enmity.

Poland. Denmark, Sweden, and Spain.

It is rather in matters of social and economic equipment, in method and technique, in the mechanism of finance, and in the personal relationship of human beings to each other that the greatest contrast exists between the eighteenth century and the world of to-day; between the ceremonious, brightly coloured column and line engagements of Fontenoy and the long-extended trench warfare of Ypres; between the European serf of 1789 and the emancipated proletarian of to-day; between a world of benevolent, or malevolent, despotisms, monarchies, aristocracies, and squirearchies, where a peasant might with impunity

Great social, economic, and financial changes,

---

[1] An anonymous writer of the year 1763, forecasting *The Reign of George VI*, 1900–1925, prophesies, however, the union during the nineteenth century of all Italy, except Venice, under the Neapolitan Bourbons. He anticipates also that Russia by 1900 will have swallowed not only Poland, Finland, and the Crimea, but the Scandinavian kingdoms as well. This small book, of much general interest, was edited by Professor Oman, and republished in 1899.

[2] " Neither Holy, nor Roman, nor an Empire."

be ridden down by a nobleman, and even in England a young man publicly hanged for "robbing one of his Majesty's messengers of a watch on the highway"; a world of sailing-ships and hand-looms and stage-coaches,[1] of great East Indiamen and fast, full-rigged tea-clippers, of pirates and smugglers, slave-traders and press-gangs, of curfews and hustings, plagues and fires; a world of elegance and leisure, drunkenness and coarseness, of picturesque externals and lost causes, of Hogarth and Watteau, of Chesterfield and Voltaire, of Dr Johnson and the Young Chevalier; between all these on the one hand, and on the other the familiar features of modern life, the large industrial towns and the great mechanical inventions; aeroplanes, motor-cars, and ironclads, factories and cinemas, gramophones and the modest wireless poles in the back gardens of Suburbia, paved roads and lucifer matches, international loans and propaganda, policemen and station bookstalls, the whole paraphernalia of democracy, with its majority rule, its emancipated women, its popular Press, its national education.

And yet even in science, industrialism, and humanitarianism, which have dominated the nineteenth century, great strides had already been made by the end of the eighteenth. *but considerable anticipations of them may be found in the eighteenth century.* When in 1758 Frederick the Great formulated the doctrine that "battles are won by fire superiority" he had proclaimed the fundamental principle of modern warfare, from the full recognition of which has followed the decline of the cavalry arm and the bayonet charge, the extension of long-range fire, trench defence, and all the ensuing characteristics of modern military technique. *War.* Jews, Catholics, and atheists were excluded from the English Parliament, a witch was burnt in Scotland in the year of the Forty-five, and as late as 1780 London was for three days at the mercy of a mob of Protestant fanatics; *Religious toleration.* nevertheless, the eighteenth century was a reasonable age: religious passions were running low and ideas of toleration gaining ground. *The slave-trade.* Although the slave-trade flourished and prison conditions were barbarous, Wilberforce, Howard, and Elizabeth Fry were not working in vain. *Prisons.* The periodicals of to-day, though different in content and style, are the lineal descendants of *The Gentleman's Magazine* and *The Annual Register*;[2] even the *Encyclopædia Britannica* had run through three editions before the French Revolution; *The Press.* for the Press, in its distinctive sense, as a medium of information and

[1] A great outcry was raised against fast driving because of a journey from London to Edinburgh which took 40 hours.

[2] It is an interesting comment on the development of journalistic literature to read the apology in the first volume of *The Annual Register* (1758), which, " though the learned may censure," is intended " for readers of another order. For such

communication for the people, was born in the eighteenth century. Many a scribbler of the day starved because the habit of literary patronage was dying out, and it had become necessary for an author and a publisher to satisfy the needs and appeal to the taste of a wide reading public. The *clientèle* may have changed, but the principle is a fundamental pre-requisite of the modern Press.

In an age, too, when women no longer sought from predilection, nor were compelled by the need of personal security, to enter a con
Women.   vent, they were able to play a much larger part in the social and mental life of the community, and in the days of Hannah More and Fanny Burney, of the great French *salons* and the "Society of Blue Stockings," however unpopular "the character of a learned lady" may have been, the intellectual status and the secular professionalism of women were marching with rapid strides.

So, too, the English countryside and the British character bore many familiar features; the chess-board hedges were springing up
General   with the second period of enclosures; the towns of to-day,
appearance   though unrepresented in Parliament, were developing on
of England.   the site of the coalfields; the huntsman was a more familiar sight then than now, and the cock-fight and the bruising contest [1] drew the ancestors of those who now watch the football or cricket match; but Protestantism had already laid its hand upon British games, upon the British Sabbath and the national temperament. [2] Had not Voltaire already written that "Philosophy, liberty and the climate conduce to misanthropy in London"?

Many fundamental principles also of mathematics, medicine, engineering, chemistry, and philosophy were already well known.
Science.   Napier's logarithms and Leibnitz's calculus were nearly two hundred years old; the circulation of the blood was discovered by Harvey, physician to Charles I. Modern dynamics is based on Newton's laws of motion, Lavoisier, the father of modern chemistry, was guillotined in the French Revolution, and Kant died, an old man of eighty, in the year that Napoleon was crowned emperor. The first submarine was used against an English ship in the American War of Independence, and early steam engines were being invented in Holland, France, and England before the century was out.   Experi-

readers it is our province to collect matters of a lighter nature, that please even by their levity, by their variety, by their aptitude to enter into common conversation"; so, the editor continues, "we may insinuate a taste for knowledge."

[1] In the great match between Humphreys, the Christian, and Mendoza, the Jew, £20,000 was taken in bets.

[2] In the eighteenth century lotteries were a common means of raising money. They were offered promiscuously by the State and by individuals, alike by bishops and the common oyster-stall keeper or the "snuff- and pigtail-maker." Lotteries are now abolished in England.

ments in the culture of plants by magnetic electricity were also being made about the same time.

In the realm of art, if the race of artists and men of letters had perished in the French Revolution, the world would still have possessed Shakespeare and Dante, Cervantes and Corneille, Leonardo, Rembrandt, Velasquez, and Bach. It would still have **Art.** treasured Stradivarius violins, Dutch marquetry, and French colourprints. For the eighteenth and nineteenth centuries have this in common, that both received the heritage of the Renaissance **A common** and the Reformation; and this common heritage is at the **heritage.** same time the cause of the difference between them. For the ideas of these two great movements, nurtured in the comparative peace and prosperity of the eighteenth century, developed with such remarkable rapidity that they seem to have cut off rather than joined the **The real** world which came after from that which went before, to **difference.** have made, as Pitt said of the French Revolution, "a schism with the universe." It is exactly this characteristic, the acceleration at the end of the century of the growth of these ideas, which has brought about what is justly termed a "revolution," for in spite of the real continuity of the history of the last two hundred years it is still true that a fundamental change has taken place, which has impressed an ineradicable mark upon the life of the community and the souls of men. In our habits of life and conventions of thought, in our attitude to God, our parents, our children, our servants, **The French** our employers, in our conception of duty and our scale of **Industrial** values, in our professions, our interests, our tastes, in most **Revolutions** things that make for sympathy between mortals, we are **the** strangers to our ancestors of the eighteenth century. We **centuries.** have knowledge and powers that would then have been held divine; and where they saw the hand of God we see only a natural phenomenon or a human device.

For the French and Industrial Revolutions have intervened, and a world has passed away, never to return—a world dominated by old Europe and old traditions; with a mediæval empire, a feudal aristocracy, and for the privileged a life unsurpassed in its amenities. A new era has come into existence to the tune of *Yankee Doodle* and the *Marseillaise*. New standards, new values, and new voices have arisen. Old Europe has seen the new world grow up and take authority. The isolation of states has vanished, individuals and communities have come to depend upon each other all over the world. A strike in Birmingham may deprive a Hottentot beauty of her adornments, or an earthquake in Los Angeles spoil the amusement of a village in Caithness. A murder in Serajevo ruins half the fundholders in Europe and introduces a world war. For wars have not ceased; like our manufactures, our finances, our fashions, our arts, they are produced on a larger scale and with the aid of more elaborate and costly machinery.

Western civilization is everywhere prevailing, and if in the conflict of races the West is destroyed, it will be by the instruments of death and destruction it has itself perfected.

For Science, Industrialism, and Democracy have come hand in hand and triumphed. They have encompassed the whole world, and prevailed over the reluctant East. They have broken down the aloofness of nations, the monopolies of races and castes, and the dominance of tradition. They have freed the slave and emancipated the serf, exalted the humble and protected the weak, but, like the aristocracy of old, they have been bought at a price. They have given us speed and robbed us of leisure; they have given us mechanical powers and robbed us of handicraft. The Press has tended to supplant literature, multiple diversions to curtail enjoyment, the professional to drive out the amateur. Powers have outgrown experience; the destinies of mankind are entrusted to the multitudes, or to those who, by economic pressure or the arts of demagogy, can control them.

POSTSCRIPT

The preceding paragraphs have been allowed to stand, though the world has moved fast in the decade since they were written. The "modest wireless poles in the back gardens of Suburbia" have given way to the radio-diffused loud-speakers in the blocks of ideal workmen's flats; the banished curfew has been restored, and cruelties have been revived that the eighteenth century had relegated to a remote barbarism. Democracy seems to have forgotten the fundamental principle that gives it value—the belief in the dignity of the individual which demands from each citizen an educated sense of responsibility in himself and a cultivated respect and consideration for his neighbour; so European peoples have allowed themselves to be swayed, bullied, drilled, tortured, or herded at the commands of their masters. Individualism has become submerged in collectivism, a man has become a "unit of power," democracy has receded before proletarianism, and proletarianism has raised up, for its own chastisement and to trouble the world, despotisms of a crudity, barbarism, ruthlessness, and might hitherto unexampled.

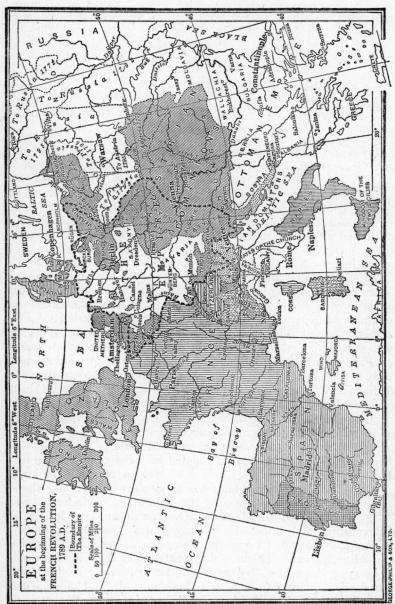

EUROPE
at the beginning of the
FRENCH REVOLUTION,
1789 A.D.

Boundary of
The Empire

Scale of Miles
0 50 100 200 300

From "European History," by Hutton Webster (D. C. Heath and Co.)

CHAPTER II

THE LAST YEARS OF THE ANCIEN RÉGIME

I. THE STATE OF FRANCE

IN May 1774, fifteen years to a month before the meeting of the States-General which was to inaugurate the French Revolution, Louis XV, *roué* and reprobate, was dying of smallpox and his vices in the *château* of Versailles. The royal sins were confessed and absolved; the customary rites of the Church administered; the Court fled from infection, the Dauphin was hurried into quarantine, and during the night of the 12th to the 13th, a *cortège* of three hunting coaches, lighted with torches and escorted by guards, bore the mortal remains of the one-time "Well-beloved" to Saint-Denis. It was the last royal funeral which was to issue from Versailles. It is reported that the mob hooted and drunkards sang ribald songs. None mourned save Mesdames the late King's daughters, who had alone brought to their father's death-chamber an honourable devotion, and those—mistresses and ministers —who saw in his demise their own downfall. With acclamation and hope France turned to the young monarch of twenty, who seemed already to have inaugurated a reign of virtue and enlightenment. He had dismissed that all-important officer of his grandfather's Court, the Steward of the Royal Pleasures, and he had suffered himself, in company with his brothers, to be inoculated against smallpox—a precaution which, though regularly practised in the Northern Courts, was regarded with alarm and even censure in Paris.

The death of the reprobate Louis XV.

Some apprehension, however, mingled with the general congratulation, for the accession of Louis XVI was of no ordinary kind. The generation which was to destroy France and shape her anew was growing to manhood. Condorcet was thirty-two, Mirabeau twenty-six, a dozen other leaders of the Revolution at an impressionable age round about the twenties— Brissot, Mme Roland, La Fayette, Robespierre, Vergniaud, Camille Desmoulins, Barnave. One of the spectators of the King's coronation in 1775 was a boy of sixteen who had run away from school, seventy miles distant, "to see how a king was made." His name was Jacques Danton, and eighteen years later he was to unmake that same king.

A portentous accession.

Hardly a man, of course, saw at the King's accession the shadow of the scaffold upon the throne, but many were aware of the insistent temper of the time, of ripening impulses toward reform, redress, and even revolt. They knew that France demanded in Louis not only a monarch, but a saviour, and they feared that neither he nor any man could play the part. "My dear Abbé, far worse is yet to come," replied Mlle de Lespinasse when she heard that the reign of Louis XV was at last at an end. It is true that she spoke from a heart bitter with personal disappointment, but she was the friend of d'Alembert, and the patroness of the Encyclopædists, and her pessimism was prophetic.

For all the brilliance of the *ancien régime* could not conceal a gross and ominous disorder. The kingdom of the " Roi Soleil " still out-shone every state in Europe,[1] his Court was the model of princes, his language and literature more familiar to them than their own. French Academicians, and French dancers, were honoured as much at St Petersburg as at Paris. The society of the capital was the flower of European civiliza-tion. There Mme du Deffand presided over an inter-national circle of celebrities, and, even at the age of seventy, could command the illustrious homage of Horace Walpole, Burke, and Gibbon. The drawing-room of Mme Necker was a school of political economy, the flat of Mlle de Lespinasse a symposium of philosophers. To be admitted to those charmed circles was the am-bition of social and intellectual aspirants all over Europe.[2] There might be found all that made perfect the ease and elegance of social intercourse, the glamour of great names, the sparkle of great wit, variety of entertainment, fertility of discussion and theme, and the friendly consciousness of common interest.

The flowers of the ancien régime "blossomed on a dunghill."

There is, however, another side to the picture. The Voltaire who was the intellectual god of Europe lived in exile at Ferney; the Encyclopædists who furnished the ideas of the world were under-mining the traditions of their own country; the *Nouvelle Héloise*, which could move to tears the sympathetic sensibility of the day, was the precursor of the *Contrat Social*, which was to become the text-book of a revolution. In a darkness deepened by contrast with such radiance might be perceived a monarchy at once despotic and weak, a corrupt and worldly Church, a nobility growing increasingly parasitical, a bankrupt exchequer, an irritated *bourgeoisie*, an oppressed peasantry,

[1] The population of 25 millions was more than twice that of England or Prussia, and as great as Germany, Austria, and Hungary together.

[2] An introduction to Parisian society was a necessary part of the education of any Englishman of position. On the other hand, it must be remarked that during the two generations which elapsed between the death of Louis XIV and the French Revolution there was hardly a Frenchman of eminence who did not either visit England or learn English, while many did both.

financial, administrative, and economic anarchy, a nation strained and divided by misgovernment and mutual suspicion—all the factors, as Chesterfield pointed out, which lead a country to revolution.[1]

It must not be forgotten, however, that the high standard of French civilization was no less a factor in the Revolution than these abuses.

Peculiar combination of stimulus and oppression. The *bourgeoisie*, though discontented, was prosperous and enlightened. The freedom of the peasants compared favourably with the comprehensive serfdom of their neighbours in Prussia, Austria, Poland, or Russia. Only a nation sensitive to ideas and culture could have produced Montesquieu, Voltaire, Rousseau, and the Encyclopædists, or, having produced them, listened to them. France presented, indeed, that combination of grievance and independence, of obscurantism and enlightenment, of irritation and incentive, which makes the best material for revolution.[2]

The most striking characteristic of the *ancien régime* was its disorder. "A prodigal anarchy," a "*débris* of powers," are the terms

Disorder and confusion. which have been used to describe that interweaving confusion of tradition, edict, law, and privilege, of provincial independence, feudal rights, and royal power, which constituted pre-Revolutionary France. It is difficult and perhaps confusing to follow paths in such an historical jungle, but on the whole two main

Two main ideas. ideas may be traced in the moulding and development of the complicated conditions which had arisen by the end of the eighteenth century.

The first may be expressed in the ancient French maxim: "The nobles fight, the clergy pray, the people pay." This was essentially

(1) The feudal idea a feudal idea, and implied that separation of functions, responsibilities, and classes whose influence pervaded the whole of French society. From it was derived the social superiority of the nobles; that touch of caste which made a 'nobleman' even of

pervaded society, law, the distribution of offices, younger sons, who in England would rank as commoners; which reserved for men of high birth commissions in the army and the higher offices of the Church; which made it difficult for an impoverished lord to recruit his fortunes by marrying into the industrial wealthy classes; which extended even to the scaffold, entitling a nobleman to be beheaded for a crime for which a commoner was hanged. It explained also that glaring financial inequality which, directly

---

[1] A prophecy only slightly marred by the fact that he foresaw the same end for England too.

[2] To attribute the Revolution to "the ambitious absurdities of the monarchy," as Mr H. G. Wells has done in his *Outline of History*, or to any other single cause, is manifestly inadequate. It seems as if the character of the Revolution, its violence and irresistible pressure, have, by suggesting inevitability, paralysed analysis.

and indirectly, was primarily responsible for the Revolution. For nearly the whole of the revenue of the Crown was contributed by the Third Estate, the "people," the non-noble and **and** non-clerical class, and the rural section provided most of **finance.** the income of the Church and nobility as well. Thus the peasants paid three times over. To the State they paid taxes, to the Church tithes, and to the nobles feudal dues.[1]

The nobles, on the other hand, who "fought," and the clergy who "prayed," contributed an insignificant proportion of the revenue. The nobility was assessed for a part of the *vingtième* and a capitation tax, both originally war impositions, but they usually managed to evade payment. The clergy had compounded in 1710 for total immunity in return for an occasional "free gift," and whenever it was proposed to tax them they replied solemnly: "Do not make us choose between God and the King, for you know what our answer will be."

The taxes were thus distributed in such a way that the bulk of them fell on the classes least able to pay them; for, besides a large number of offices and administrative posts which carried with them exemption from taxation, all who could afford it had secured a similar privilege by buying patents of nobility. "While every noble is by no means rich, every rich man," wrote Malesherbes, "is noble." In one way or another the wealthy classes paid the smallest share of taxation.[2]

[1] *Note on Finance.*—The peasants paid :

(1) To the State

   (a) indirect taxes, like the " vile salt tax " and other *aides* ;
   (b) direct taxes, like the *taille*, which in some provinces was a property tax, in others a poll tax. It was sometimes as high as 53 out of 100 livres.

(2) To the Church they paid tithe, which varied from one-twentieth to one-twelfth of the farm produce and was a charge on all land, noble or non-noble. It was evaded as often as possible, and when the Revolution broke out there were 400,000 lawsuits pending on this matter alone.

(3) To the nobles they owed feudal dues, which varied on each estate. They included a *corvée*, or forced labour, of two or three days, contributions in kind, and numerous tolls on every agricultural operation or commercial transaction in which they were engaged ; while the very produce which must pay their tax and yield their livelihood was exposed to the birds or boar or deer which, under the protection of game laws, throve at their expense.

The chief feudal rights of the nobles were

   (a) *Corvée seigneuriale* =right to unpaid labour.
   (b) *Banalités.* The noble had the right to compel his tenants to send their grapes to his wine-press, and their corn to his mill, their bread to his oven, etc. ; of course, tolls were charged for use.
   (c) *Banvin* =the lord's monopoly of wine in his district.
   (d) *Péages* =tolls on roads, fords, and bridges.
   (e) *Terrage* =special harvest dues.
   (f) *Droits de colombier et chasse* =rights of dovecot and hunting. The game rights were the most hated of the feudal rights.
   (g) Various other dues and payments.

[2] It has been computed that as much was collected in taxes from one class in 1785 as was raised by the whole population of France, then a third greater, on the eve of the 1870 war.

The taxes were not only oppressive; they could be arbitrarily increased in a secret session of the Royal Council, for the mediæval idea still persisted that the State revenue was part of the king's private accounts. They were unfairly distributed even among those who paid them; the indirect taxes, which were farmed, were often unscrupulously extorted; the direct taxes, for which the peasants themselves were responsible, were collected with great difficulty and inconvenience.

In the social, financial, and economic structure of France may thus be seen remnants of the feudal idea, but cutting across it was another conception, the monarchical, which may be summarized in the historic phrase of Louis XIV: "*L'État, c'est moi.*" In this is expressed the undoubted and instinctive alliance of king and people against the risk of a rampant feudalism. The people had given support to their sovereign that he might preserve the unity of the nation and keep down the power of the nobles. But there had arisen an excessive concentration of political and administrative power in the hands of the Crown at the expense of all the other orders of the realm. The Conseil du Roi was more important than the Privy Council under the Tudors. It was solely dependent upon the sovereign; it possessed a monopoly of executive power and an undefined legislative and judicial authority. Its control was so extensive that it could declare war, fix taxes, make laws, or try important lawsuits, and so minute that a village steeple could not be repaired without its permit. It appointed the Intendants, who governed the provinces; they were men of non-noble birth, who were the sole administrative agents of the district. They regulated the rural police, apportioned the militia, supervised the collecting of the *taille*, and, armed with powers of death, tried most of the civil and criminal cases within the area. They were the real rulers of provincial France, in spite of the obscurity in which they worked, overshadowed, as they were, socially by the nobles and politically by the nominal governorships, *bailliages*, *sénéchaussées*, and other remnants of old administrative divisions, which concealed but did not limit their powers. "Do you know," wrote Law in surprise, "that this kingdom is governed by thirty Intendants?" They were as powerful as Napoleon's prefects, who were their historical successors.

A hierarchy of royal functionaries had thus appropriated administrative power; the legislative power had also disappeared; it had once resided in a States-General of clergy, lords, and commons, but no such body had been called in France since 1614; national laws had been replaced by royal edicts. The judicial functions of the Crown,

(2) The monarchical idea.

Excessive concentration of administrative, political, and judicial power in the hands of the Crown.

which had once been limited to the modest dimensions of the oak of Vincennes, had by the eighteenth century also superseded those of nobles, Church, and town. Save for a few lingering feudal courts, the power of justice was in the hands of the King's courts, the King's Council, and the thirteen royal *parlements* (law-courts) of the chief towns—although they proved almost as troublesome to him as if they had not been royal.[1]

With the creation and maintenance of such a vast centralization, administrative, legislative, and judicial, the energy of the Crown was exhausted. Though it could dispense with the States-General, spasmodically intimidate the law-courts, draw the life from the local government of noble or provincial assembly, leaving merely encumbering ruins, it could The energy of the Crown exhausted. neither initiate necessary social or judicial reforms nor touch the great feudal and financial privileges of the nobility and the Church. Even under pressure of bankruptcy it was unable to abolish the exemptions from taxation. Rather it adopted ignominious and unscrupulous expedients—sold offices, titles, honours, municipal rights, all of which carried immunity from taxation, and after giving the Treasury a temporary relief served further to embarrass it. Royal and official ingenuity employed itself in creating a "beer-tastership" of Paris, a "controllership of wigs," an "hereditary jury in charge of burials," and thousands of administrative or semi-administrative posts. Many were frankly sinecures; others with some shadow of claim to usefulness duplicated and multiplied each other.[2] When the royal ingenuity and the Treasury were again exhausted, honours and municipal rights which were granted by the last king could always be revoked by the next, and then resold—"the necessity of our finances," the royal edict explained.

Thus there existed side by side two political ideas, feudal and monarchical, mutually limiting, the latter superimposed upon the former, sometimes destroying it, sometimes giving way before it. The result was a combination of inequality and despotism, and an unparalleled confusion only magnified by the sale and resale of offices, by the accumulation of Two ideas side by side, mutually limiting.

Confusion.

[1] By the seventeenth century the *parlements* had become powerful legal bodies of hereditary officials. There was no clear division, as in England, between the judicature and other departments of State. The King tried to weaken the power of the *parlements* by 'evoking' cases from the Courts to the Council and Intendants ; the *parlements*, on the other hand, strove also to enlarge their powers—notably the Parlement of Paris, which sought to turn its function of registering the King's edicts into that of making laws, especially in the absence of the States-General. As a legislative body it failed, but from the days of the Fronde to those of the Revolution it adopted a factious and intransigent policy, in which it is difficult to see any consistent feature save that of hostility to the Crown.

[2] The clerks of the Gabelle office performed their duties in rotation for a year at a time.

arrears of work, and by a fussy, capricious spirit which so often appeared at headquarters.[1]

The confusion was further increased by the privileges and claims of provinces which had been successively annexed, some by con-
Provincial quest, some as a marriage-dower, some by treaty, each
privileges. with its own laws and traditions, instinct with ancient history, and conscious of its own identity before that of France. The *pays d'état* of Languedoc and Brittany had retained active local assem-
Economic blies and a measure of real self-government. Finally, the
regulations. whole country was honeycombed with economic restrictions—gild regulations, town regulations, provincial customs duties, feudal customs duties, conflicting or overlapping, multiplying confusion and hampering commerce.

Under such conditions it was easy for inequality to arise, and for the authority of the Crown—where it could be exercised amid the impeding growth of local powers—to be despotic. There was no
No check. check upon the Government such as exists in publicity
and a representative system. There was no statement of accounts, no Parliamentary criticism, the Press was far from free, and any attack upon a Government measure liable to be punished. There was no uniform code of laws, but 384 different customs; there was no guarantee of personal liberty, no Habeas Corpus Act; and *lettres de cachet* [2] were so common that "no one was so exalted that he was safe from the ill-will of a minister, or so insignificant that he might not incur that of a clerk." The secrecy covering the administration favoured corruption and suspicion, and the Government was often credited, or debited, with actions of which it had not been guilty. "People often complain," wrote de Tocqueville,

that Frenchmen despise the law; alas, where could they have learned to respect it? We may say that among the men of the *ancien régime* the
No sense of place which the law ought to occupy in the human mind
law. was vacant. Every suitor demands a departure from the established rule with as much insistence as if he were demanding its observance; in fact, the rule is hardly ever upheld against him, save when it is desired to evade his request.

Privilege, concession, exemption—not law—was the basis of French society; expedient, not principle, the policy of its rulers. It is not to

[1] "The Government seldom undertakes," wrote de Tocqueville, "and soon abandons the most necessary reforms which demand a persevering energy, but it constantly changes particular regulations. In the sphere which it inhabits nothing remains an instant in repose. New rules succeed one another with a rapidity so strange that the agents of the State do not know how they are to obey. Municipal officers complain to the Controller-General himself. The variation of the financial regulations alone, they say, is such as not to allow an officer, were he irremovable, to do anything else but study the new regulations as they appear."
[2] Warrants for arrest without trial.

be wondered at that the earliest demand of the Revolutionaries was for a "constitution," by which they meant a system, an organization.

The effect upon the people was to create distrust, suspicion, and discontent.   Class was divided against class, group against   Effects upon group; not one was satisfied; each maintained itself in as   the people. great an isolation as possible, distrusting the class above, despising the one below.

The oppression of the peasants was patent, even though they were not the troglodytish brutes pictured by La Bruyère,[1] nor such spirit-less victims of unmitigated tyranny as Arthur Young's   The generous sympathy for a race less fortunate than his own   peasants. painted them.[2]   They were not serfs,[3] they could buy and sell, go and come, choose a trade or a bride at will, and a large proportion of them were by a remarkable thrift acquiring land.[4]   As much as one-third of all the land of France was held by peasant proprietors.   But what future lay for them in the opportunities of an obsolete feudalism? Their estates were burdened, if not their persons; their agricultural profits were reduced to a minimum, their ambitions checked.   For agriculture, as a source of food, as a source of profit, as a national enterprise, was in the hands of the nobles, and the consequences were, first, to prevent the growth of that most stable element of a com-munity, an agrarian, yeoman class, and, secondly, to keep town and country perpetually on the verge of starvation.[5]

The *bourgeois*, the industrial and professional middle class of the towns,[6] were more prosperous, often highly enlightened, less bur-dened by tithes and feudal dues, or the irritating militia   The indus-service, but they were more roused by religious intolerance   trial and and the judicial abuses of torture during trial, by arbitrary   professional imprisonment, and cruel and unequal punishments.   They   classes. resented more the social superiority and the degenerate extravagance

[1] See La Bruyère's *Characters*.

[2] See Arthur Young's *Travels* (July 12, 1789).   Arthur Young, whose travels in France were popularized by the Convention, published in 1793 a recantation en-titled *The Example of France*.

Jefferson's impression is worth noting : " I have been pleased to find among the people a less degree of physical misery than I had expected " (*Correspondence*, April 11, 1787).

[3] A few serfs only remained in ecclesiastical territory.

[4] It must be remembered that the peasants paid no rent for their land.   More-over, since they were assessed for taxation according to the external appearances of their wealth, it was to their interest to conceal as far as possible evidence of their possessions and to cultivate a semblance of poverty.

[5] There is no more serious indictment of the feudal control of agriculture in France than that a poor harvest, or a corner in wheat, brought her, for all her fertility, to the edge of starvation.   And the first to feel it was the easily inflamed, submerged class of poor artisans.

[6] There was undoubtedly during the second half of the eighteenth century a strong drift of the more prosperous peasants to the towns.

of noble or wealthy cleric, and they were more susceptible to the influence of the democratic literature of the day. From this class came the chief leaders of the Revolution, but, in Napoleon's phrase, it was "vanity rather than liberty" that was the stimulus.

There was discontent also in the army and in the Church, and but for the support of the soldiers and the lesser clergy in 1789 the people's cause might have been then defeated. Among all ranks **The army.** of the army freemasonry and the fashionable philosophy had infused democratic ideas; the soldiers resented the harsh discipline, the poor food and low pay; they could not rise to commissioned rank themselves, and they had little respect for the incompetent appointments of a Mme de Pompadour. But many of these conditions existed all over Europe. In Prussia, whose military reputation was the highest in Europe, the discipline was harsher; in England babies in their cradles were made into majors; in Russia alone could an officer rise from the ranks.

There was the same cleavage in the Church as in the army. To a man like Voltaire, and to the thousands of Frenchmen who shared **The Church.** his opinions, the Roman Catholic Church in France was an intolerable despotism, unrelieved even by the faith that might have redeemed it. It was discredited by quarrels between Jansenists and Jesuits, dishonoured by worldliness and corruption, sapped by wealth, privilege, and monopoly, undermined from within and without by scepticism and atheism. "Let us at least have an Archbishop of Paris who believes in God," Louis XVI is said to have remarked when he rejected Brienne, Archbishop of Toulouse, as a candidate. There was little in common save common sin between the wealthy beneficed clergy and the parish priests; the one, aristocrats by birth, distinguishable from the lay nobility more by their dress than by their manners; [1] the other hardly less ignorant and rude than the peasants from whom they had mostly sprung; the former with their revenues of thousands, or hundreds of thousands, of livres; the latter so poor that their stipends had to be raised to £25 per annum. But it was the lesser clergy, notably those of the towns, who were themselves to help to pull down the Church; many of them were alive to the reforming movement of the day; they had subscribed to the *Encyclopædia*; they read Plutarch and Rousseau and turned democrat; and when the priests joined the representatives of the people in the hall of the Menus Plaisirs on the June day of 1789, the Church of the *ancien régime*, in all its glory and corruption, the wealthiest political institution in France, fell, like the Renaissance Papacy, for ever.

---

[1] The Abbé Sicardé could find only fifteen virtuous prelates out of a hundred and thirty—enough to have saved Sodom, but not the Church of France.

There was in a sense no greater victim of the *ancien régime* than the nobility which seemed to profit so highly from it. It was privileged, but powerless. The jealousy of the Crown *The nobility.* had excluded it from political life, rendered it effete, obnoxious, and helpless. Louis XIV had made the nobles into courtiers, cut them off from their own estates—which they had come to regard as a place of exile—deprived them of the natural leadership of the people which should have fallen to them, and robbed them of the administrative experience and training which might have saved them, and France, in time of trouble. They were severed from the soil which was the real source of their strength. They came to be hated by the peasant tenantry, whom they neither governed nor knew, but only taxed. Their only weapon was Court intrigue, their only refuge class privilege; and when the Revolution broke out they found themselves, laymen and clerics alike, without allies anywhere in the State, dependent upon a king even weaker than they, inexperienced, discredited, without defences, insidiously disarmed by their sympathy with the very philosophy which was directed against them.

The Crown too was, by the end of the eighteenth century, more the slave than the lord of its own despotism. The king could no longer modify a system of which he might disapprove, and for which he would certainly be held responsible. If *The Crown.* he tried to reform an abuse or introduce an economy the Court compelled him to abandon it—it was the nobles' revenge. He no longer led the army to battle, nor, it was believed, guided the counsels of the nation with wisdom. He had become a *roi fainéant*, shorn, since the days of Louis XV, of much of his sanctity. The old alliance between king and commons, to which Louis XVI, in summoning the States-General, sought to appeal, was broken, and there was no body of civilians or soldiers on whom he could rely. And yet there was undoubtedly a good deal of monarchical feeling in the country even up to 1791, and a Henry IV might still have saved the Crown.

Within this society of malcontents, working upon them and among them like leaven, were writers, stimulating them, pointing their discontent, dissolving the traditions which alone held them together, voicing their grievances, giving them a leader- *Literature.* ship and a faith; for in a land of no Parliament the men of letters had come to be the politicians.[1] In innumerable ways they demonstrated the rottenness of French institutions—by satire and wit, criticism and comparison, analogy and innuendo, by scientific exposition, by sociological theory, by downright abuse—but with caution, for did not eloquence consist in "the art of saying everything without being sent to the Bastille"? For this reason, and

---

[1] *Cf.* Bolingbroke and the *Craftsman.*

C

because those who wrote were seldom hampered by experience of the practical difficulties of administration, the literature of this new democracy came to be dominated by generalization and emotionalism, abstract theory and extreme logic, by formulæ and sentimental analogy, which proved as poor a basis for constitution-making in France of 1791 and 1793 as in Germany of 1848 or Russia of 1917. All the more, however, did it make excellent gunpowder for destroying the State, and never before was a revolution so armed with words and phrases. The religious democracy, emanating also from Geneva, which washed over Europe in the sixteenth and seventeenth centuries had its literature; but the pamphleteers of Puritanism, both in scope and effect, played an altogether different *rôle* from the journalists of the political gospel of Rousseau. The former were secondary and interpretative, harnessed to religion; the latter, having free play among unfettered ideas of natural freedom and original virtue, quickened and took possession of the movement which had fathered them. They gave to it power and direction and character, whence arose many of the differences between the English and the French Revolutions.

Writers of all kinds prepared the French Revolution. Early in the century there was Montesquieu, fortunate in his birth and ambitions, of wide travel and a serene temperament, a man who had known not an hour's boredom in his life, and hardly a misfortune. He had neither the views nor the attitude of a Revolutionary, and he was both a Catholic and a Monarchist; but in a moderate, Whiggish way he criticized the abuses of the Church and the despotism of the State—was not despotism like cutting down a tree to get at the fruit? He criticized by satire—by mordant comments on French manners and customs from pretended Persian visitors; he suggested by comparison—in England there were Liberty and Equality, and institutions which were safeguards of freedom; he exposed by implication, in the most famous of all his books, *L'Esprit des lois*, in which he analysed the principle of government and traced the evolution of laws and constitutions.

Montesquieu's reputation has grown dim, but though he was neither the first philosopher nor the first political thinker, he may be said to have founded the scientific study of historical evolution. He amassed and co-ordinated historical facts; he deduced from them general conclusions. He interpreted history in the light of a consistent and unfolding idea and viewed laws and Governments as products of inherent natural forces. He anticipated Hegel as the exponent of a philosophy of history, and all with a wit and eloquence which raised jurisprudence to the rank of literature.

A contrast to Montesquieu in method and temperament was his

more famous junior contemporary, François-Marie Arouet, better known as Voltaire. He was the most honoured man in Europe in the middle of the eighteenth century, but "every circum- stance about him recalls tumult and contention." His health was poor, and his temper irritable. He imbibed in *Voltaire (1694–1778).* infancy from his godfather, a cynical *abbé*, the language of infidelity; his library was founded by a bequest from Ninon de l'Enclos. He pursued his chosen profession of letters at the price of a prolonged quarrel with his father, a provincial notary. He gained coveted admission to the aristocratic literary circles of Paris, but a satire threw him into the Bastille, and a repartee brought him a thrashing from a nobleman's lacquey. He was the pensioner and honoured guest of Frederick the Great, but he left the Prussian Court with rage in his heart and a volume of his patron's poems in his pocket— for which theft he was seized and imprisoned at Frankfort by Frederick's orders. He settled as a *grand seigneur* on the shores of Lake Geneva with a niece, and a fortune that he had accumulated largely by successful speculation, but he spent his twenty years of retirement in discharging upon Europe the gibes and challenges and denunciations of his pen. He returned at last to his own country, from which he had so long been exiled, but he died in the hour of his triumph, and the *abbé* who, on the strength of a death-bed confession, buried him in consecrated ground was deprived of his office for the action. Twelve years later the Revolutionaries trans- ferred his remains, with those of Rousseau, to the Panthéon, thereby doing honour to their mighty collaborator.

Voltaire was an indefatigable writer—poet, historian, philosopher, dramatist, correspondent, lampoonist, and, pre-eminently, satirist. He was inspired by a wide philanthropy, a caustic wit, and a bitter hostility to the Church. *"Écrasez l'infâme"* recurs like a refrain throughout his letters, and the destruction of ecclesiastical despotism was to him the beginning—and perhaps the end—of justice and enlightenment. Much, however, as Voltaire derided Christianity and struck at the fetters of the Church, he was no atheist. *Deo erexit Voltaire* ran an inscription over the village church which he restored at Ferney, for "if God did not exist, it would be necessary to create him."

Nor can he be called a democrat. To attack the Altar was ulti- mately to undermine the Throne which rested on it, but Voltaire never consciously aimed at the monarchy, and he was fully aware of the dangers of popular government. "Why do you not stop where Voltaire did?" said the Duc de Choiseul in 1764 to the new philosophers. "Him we can comprehend. Amidst all his satires he respected authority."

The authority which Voltaire respected was destroyed by Jean-Jacques Rousseau, to whom in early life he was an inspiration. **Rousseau (1712–78).** Later there grew up between them the enmity which so often exists between those who, in the eyes of posterity, seem to have worked for the same cause. It was a natural expression, however, of their different aims and temperaments. Rousseau began where Voltaire left off; the latter harnessed the horses of reason, the former unchained the tigers of emotion.

The story of Rousseau's life is told in full in his own *Confessions*; and there is little of it that does not afford greater interest to the student than satisfaction to the moralist. He was the son of a disreputable Genevan watchmaker, and his education was such as is derived from a wandering life, an assortment of occupations, and an ardent, varied, but desultory private reading. He roamed from country to country, abandoning friend for friend and one interest for another. He served as a footman, a tutor, a secretary. He made lace, he copied music, he gave lessons, wrote articles for the new *Encyclopædia*, gambled, wooed countess and kitchen-maid. He composed a successful opera and produced half a dozen literary works. Of these one, the *Nouvelle Héloïse*, was the best-selling novel of the age; *Émile* was an essay on education that is still a text-book of pedagogy—though Rousseau's own children were abandoned to a foundling hospital; a third, the *Contrat Social*, written largely amid the English woods of Nuneham Courtney, produced a revolution.

Rousseau's last days were haunted by a suspicion and fear of persecution which alone would condemn him to-day as insane. His life betrayed, indeed, not only touches of cowardice and treachery, but irresponsibility, irritableness, and uncontrolled passion that amounted almost to mental derangement. "Jean-Jacques is a wild animal, and should be regarded only through the bars of a cage," wrote d'Alembert. On the other hand, he revealed imaginative genius, susceptibility, fervour, and sympathy with the oppressed, and for many people he possessed an irresistible personal fascination.

The political influence of Rousseau's works, especially of the *Contrat Social* and the *Discours sur l'inégalité*, was incalculable, **The "Social Contract" (1762).** not only in France, but in all Europe. His fundamental theory was that of the inherent virtue of the "natural man," whom civilization and institutions had corrupted and deprived of his natural rights to liberty and happiness. "Man is born free, but everywhere he is in chains." He should return, then, to his primitive innocence and happiness, and destroy the institutions that had enslaved him. Laws should be the expression of the "general will," of the deep, instinctive conscience of society. Kings were the creations of an original contract framed by the people for the promotion of their welfare, and a sovereign's title was dependent upon his guardianship of the rights of his subjects. The people of France had lost their rights, the contract had been violated, the Crown had forfeited the allegiance of the nation. Much of Rousseau's theory was hardly intended to apply to communities larger than a Swiss canton, but it was destined to destroy the monarchy of France. For revolt was the tenor of his writings, of his conduct, of his turgid eloquence—"revolt, in the name of nature, against the vicious and artificial social system of his time."

The unproved assumptions and the sentimental generalizations carry little conviction to moderns who live after the Revolution and have forgotten that what may seem sophisms contained a burning protest against the real evils of the day. The theory of the social contract may be historically untenable, but it was only another way of saying that those who govern must recognize their responsibilities. The people of France were suffering because the interests of the Crown were divorced from those of the State, because the nobles no longer fought, and the clergy no longer prayed—because the social contract was broken. It was a reversion to the ancient maxim, and whatever penalties France has had to pay for Rousseau's eloquence, he conferred on her two benefits which can be summarized in Lord Morley's words:

In the first place he spoke words that can never be unspoken and kindled a hope that can never be extinguished; he first inflamed man with a righteous conviction that the evils of the existing order of things reduced civilization to a nullity for the great majority of mankind . . .; second, by his fervid eloquence and the burning conviction which he kindled in the hearts of great numbers of men, he inspired energy enough in France to awaken her from the torpor as of death which was stealing so rapidly over her.

Montesquieu, Voltaire, and Rousseau were the giants of the age. There were writers of smaller stature: Diderot, d'Alembert, and the group of editors and contributors of the influential Other *Encyclopædia* [1] which appeared in the fifties—most of writers. them sceptics in religion and rebels in politics; there were the Physiocrats, of whom Quesnay was a pioneer and Turgot an illustrious member, who criticized the economic conditions of France and advocated freedom of labour and barter and the more profitable use of land; Beaumarchais, who turned the stage to social satire, and others known only perhaps to the historical student—Helvetius,

[1] *Encyclopédie ou dictionnaire universel des arts et des sciences,* one of the most celebrated works of its kind, edited mainly by Diderot, but containing contributions from the most notable men of the day. The first edition of the *Encyclopædia Britannica* was published in Edinburgh between 1768-71.

d'Holbach, the Abbé de Raynal, who wrote a *Philosophical History of the Two Indies*, and the Socialist-publicist Abbé de Mably, with whom every good revolutionary was familiar.

The ideas inculcated by the writers and pamphleteers permeated all classes. The bloods of Paris rode their horses *à l'anglaise*, Revolutionary ideas rising in their stirrups after the manner of English spread jockeys. Society played whist and wept over *Clarissa* through all *Harlowe*, which for true sensibility was the only rival of classes. the *Nouvelle Héloise*. First David Hume, and then, when Anglomania had paled before the rising sun of America, Benjamin Franklin became the most popular man in Paris. The simple life became the cult of the day; the artificial gardens of the seventeenth century were replaced by 'natural' brooks and ponds. Marie-Antoinette fled from the elaborate etiquette of Versailles and played the shepherdess in the Petit Trianon; she reduced her baby daughter's retinue to eighty lest she should be brought up with unsuitable ideas of royal state. There was a symbolical change in dress and art. Noblemen were hardly distinguishable from commoners, and ladies, catching the mode from Mme Berthin, the Queen's dressmaker, abandoned the elaborate gowns of Louis Quinze for the simple Greek style. The pastoral pose of Watteau gave way before the classical pose of David.[1] In religion Christianity was supplanted by alternating fashions of atheism and occultism. There were, naturally, critics of the Encyclopædists and their ideas, but such criticism was often merely an incident in the rivalry of *salons*, like the musical quarrel between the supporters of Gluck and those of Piccini.

The King read Rousseau and believed that man was good, and none enjoyed more than the nobles themselves the caricatures against their order in the *Mariage de Figaro*, Beaumarchais's play, which after a long suppression ran for eighty nights in 1784. "What has a noble done for all his privileges," asks Figaro, "except give himself the trouble of being born?" The nobles thought it a good joke, and when the King protested that such jokes were dangerous they improved on the humour by replying with Figaro, "It is only little minds that fear little writings."

Thus the gospel of the oppressed became the fashionable diversion of their oppressors, and polite society was taught to repeat the formulæ of democracy. On many of their adherents these made little impression, and they were abandoned as soon as the practical

---

[1] The following are some of the titles of David's pictures (1748–1825): *Date obolum Belisario* (1780), *The Grief of Andromache* (1782), *The Oath of the Horatii* (1785), *The Death of Socrates* (1788), *The Love of Paris and Helen* (1788), *Brutus* (1789).

application of them threatened estates or position. To some few they became real articles of faith, leading them either to the ranks of the Revolutionaries, or to that troublous state where interest is at war with conviction, enabling men neither to protect the one nor follow the other.

II. "REPENTANT DESPOTISM"

Louis XV, indolent, self-indulgent, profligate, and irresponsible, had turned a blind eye to the gathering clouds, of whose existence he had been well enough aware, and the storm passed him by and fell upon his comparatively innocent successor. Louis XVI was twenty years old at his accession. "It seems as if the universe is falling on me," he cried. "God, what a burden is mine, and they have taught me nothing!" For he was serious, alive to his responsibilities, not without intelligence, well-intentioned, amiable, virtuous, and kind. But the times required of him other qualities. "When men call a king a kind man his reign has been a failure," remarked Napoleon. Louis was slow of sense and mind; "he is uninformed matter," wrote his brother-in-law, Joseph II, "the *fiat lux* has not yet come." He was moved to action not by some innate force, but by strong pressure from outside—the tears of his wife, the demands of his ministers or courtiers. "No one trusts him," wrote a Revolutionary of 1789, "for he has no will of his own." It was known that his hand could be forced, and that was one of the vital factors of the Revolution. "Speak out freely," cried Louis's aunt, the Princesse Adélaïde, "shout, scold, make an uproar like your brother d'Artois, knock down my china and break it, make some noise in the world." Louis was of no account because he made no noise in the world; he could not even simulate wilfulness, which might have been taken for will. Marie-Antoinette called him her "poor man" and put on the clock at nights so that he should go to bed earlier and enable her to get out her faro table the sooner.

Fundamentally Louis was uninterested in the art of governing and had not enough histrionic talent to play the King. "How fortunate you are!" he said to Malesherbes, on the latter's resignation. "I wish I could resign too." And the happiest period of his life, save for the fact that he was deprived of his hunting, was probably that which he spent in the Temple as a prisoner. His diary was a huntsman's record, and a passion for the chase and a large appetite seemed to be the only Bourbon characteristics that he inherited; his chief hobby was a private forge which he kept half hidden from his wife in an upper room of Versailles; his intellectual tastes were mainly geographical and astronomical. But he cared for his people; he had studied Fénelon on the duties of a king, and his comments on Necker's scheme for Provincial Assemblies showed that he was not devoid of political foresight.

Marie-Antoinette, who was nineteen in 1774, had a far more vigorous and decisive personality, and came to exercise a great deal
Marie-Antoinette. of influence over her husband. "The King has only one man about him—his wife," wrote Mirabeau. Unfortunately the Queen, though gracious, regal,[1] and sympathetic to certain obvious types of suffering, had no political experience, little political sense, and a narrow view of life that was all the more dangerous as she came to have real power. In matters of statesmanship she was an unworthy daughter of the great Maria. Even more than her husband, she would have adorned a private station; unlike Elizabeth Tudor, she never realized that her personal tastes, virtuous as they might be, and her personal preferences and standards, however loyal and honourable, should not become the rule of the State. Her very qualities led her to harm. She was staunch to friends who deceived her, and her sympathies made her the innocent tool of ambitious factions and Court intrigue. Her gaiety and dislike of etiquette gave excuse for scandal; her extravagance cause for criticism, ignorant though much of it was.[2] Her acts of real self-denial were obscured by her carelessnesses and her mistakes. It was forgotten that she had given of her personal allowance for the relief of the poor, and remembered that she had revived an important post in her household for the young widow, the Princesse de Lamballe. Her brother, the didactic Joseph, who found it easy to criticize his relatives, pointed out to her the unwisdom of her course. "Why do you interfere,

---

[1] Cf. the pictures of Marie-Antoinette by Horace Walpole and Burke :
"She is a statue of beauty when standing or sitting. . . . Grace itself when she moves. . . . They say she does not dance in time ; but if so, it is certainly the time itself which is at fault."—HORACE WALPOLE.
" It is now sixteen or seventeen years since I saw the Queen of France, then the Dauphiness, at Versailles ; and surely never lighted on this orb, which she hardly seemed to touch, a more delightful vision. I saw her just above the horizon, decorating and cheering the elevated sphere she had just begun to move in ; glittering like the morning star, full of life and splendour and joy. Oh, what a revolution ! Little did I dream when she added titles of veneration to those of enthusiastic, distant, and respectful love that she should ever be obliged to carry the sharp antidote against disgrace concealed in that bosom, little did I dream that I should have lived to see such disaster fallen upon her, in a nation of gallant men and in a nation of honour and of cavaliers. I thought ten thousand swords must have leapt from their scabbards to avenge even a look which threatened her with insult. But the age of chivalry is gone ; that of sophists, economists, and calculators has succeeded, and the glory of Europe is extinguished for ever."—EDMUND BURKE (written in 1790).
[2] Stories of her extravagance were widely spread. When the deputies of the Tiers État arrived at Versailles in 1789 they demanded to be shown a room in the Trianon which, according to them, " was wholly ornamented with diamonds, and with wreathed columns studded with sapphires and rubies " (Mme de Campan).

dismissing ministers, sending one back to his estates, giving office to this or that, helping another to win his case, and creating a new expensive post at Court? Have you ever asked yourself by what right you interfere in the affairs of the French Government?" She remained to the end *l'Autrichienne*, understanding little either the country or the times in which she lived. As misfortunes fell upon her her helplessness drove her to duplicity. She played a double and underhand game, which France called treason. Hatred and malice pursued her, coupling her name with slander, making her responsible for every unpopular action.[1] She found herself without supporters in any class, and sought refuge increasingly in the affection of her family and the defence of a proud and haughty spirit.

The ironic spirit plays about revolutions. The King and Queen who within twenty years were to die at the hands of their own people ascended the throne with the best intentions. They responded readily to tales of popular suffering, and gave up gratuities to which they were entitled that they might not increase the burden of the taxpayers. Because the people wished it, Louis summoned back the Parlement of Paris from exile, thus recalling an old enemy, and, as it was to prove, giving in to a new one at the same time. Of the new ministers, Turgot and Malesherbes might have been nominated by the reformers themselves. "We are governed by philosophers," wrote Mme du Deffand.[2] In fact, for the first seven years of his reign Louis made through his ministers a consistent and courageous attempt to initiate a policy of reform and to remove the afflictions of the people.

The first seven years were years of reform.

Not in the years of Sully or Colbert had France possessed a statesman with so vast a programme of internal reforms as Turgot. During his short ministry of twenty months he materially improved the finances of the State by a careful economy and a scrupulous administration; without raising fresh loans or imposing new taxes he balanced the revenue and the expenditure; he proclaimed and upheld against opposition the free circulation of grain within the country, and, by an exercise of royal privilege, he forced through the Parlement of Paris six edicts, one of which freed the peasants from the royal *corvée*, substituting for it a tax on property, and another relieved the artisans by abolishing the monopolistic

Turgot (1774-76).

[1] In *L'Orateur du Peuple* of June 22, 1791 (after the royal flight), she was described as " This accursed queen, who unites the profligacy of Messalina with the bloodthirstiness of the Medici. Execrable woman, Fury of France, thou wert the soul of the plot."

[2] Not that Mme du Deffand liked philosophers, too many of whom patronized the *salon* of her rival, Mlle de l'Espinasse. She describes them as men with " plenty of brains, a trifle of talent, and no taste at all."

trade guilds and wardenships of the towns.[1] Turgot was supported in his reforms by Malesherbes, Minister of the Interior, a modest, sincere man who confined himself to the humbler measures of reducing the number of *lettres de cachet* and of mitigating harsh sentences of imprisonment. In the War Office the Comte de Saint-Germain, an old soldier of rigid, intractable views, set himself to cut down the expenses of the French army, to abolish many of its supernumerary offices, to reduce the household troops, and to tighten up discipline.

When Turgot fell he was replaced after an interval by another reformer, Necker, a Swiss Protestant, a practical banker of great **Necker** repute rather than a statesman. He practised economy **(1776–81).** more stringently than Turgot, even to such details as renewing the linen of the royal household every seven years instead of every three, while he himself refused the emoluments of office. The costly, though successful, war with England, on which France embarked during his ministry, drove him, however, to fresh borrowings, direct and indirect.

Necker introduced other reforms in a somewhat piecemeal fashion. He induced the Crown to set free the royal serfs and forgo certain feudal rights; he took steps toward setting up Provincial Assemblies; he carried on Turgot's economic reforms and restricted the use of torture, and he proposed full civil rights for Protestants, a measure of equity which was granted in 1788.

But he too fell soon from office, and with his fall the first period **The failure** of voluntary reform on the part of the Crown came to an **of the first** end. The attempt had failed. Despotism had repented **period of** of its past, but too late and in vain; it was chained to its **royal reform.** own misdeeds and could not escape their consequences.

The causes of failure are many, some of them matters of principle, some of long dominant forces, some of mere accident. Neither Turgot nor Necker was a tactful advocate of reform. Turgot was too frigid, not suave enough; he had too little sympathy with the infirmities of men; he would make no compromise with their self-interestedness. He pressed through his reforms in too great a hurry. "The needs of the people are immense," he pleaded, "and in my family gout carries us off at fifty." Necker, on the other hand, was irresolute, vain, and self-conscious, and socially he was a bore. He

[1] Had Turgot remained longer in office he would have anticipated many of the constructive measures of the Constituent Assembly; he proposed to free the land from tithe and feudal burdens, to break down the restrictions that hampered trade and manufacture; to set up Provincial Assemblies, reduce the wealth of the Church, nationalize some of its property, and abolish many of its monasteries. He would have codified the laws, thrown open professions to all classes, and established national education, a free worship, and a free Press.

helped to discredit the work of reform by publicly criticizing Turgot, and though the appointment of a foreigner and a Protestant showed Louis's toleration it in no way served to reconcile the courtiers to the loss of their pensions and their privileges. Both Turgot and Necker had to work against the intrigues of their own colleague, Maurepas, Minister President, who had practically been forced upon Louis by a managing aunt, the Princesse Adélaïde. Maurepas was old, too anxious to commend himself to the Court, and too much inclined to think that all problems could be solved—or shelved— by an epigram.

Ministers are subordinate officers, however, and removable; behind them was the King. Fundamentally Turgot and Necker failed not from their own incidental demerits, but because of the character of the King and the strength of the opposing interests leagued against them. Had the King supported them firmly some measure of success would have fallen to them, and when in May 1776 he gave in to the clamorous Court and dismissed Turgot, the Revolution—that is, reform not by, or with, but in spite of the King—became inevitable.

For combined against reform were the courtiers, the Church, the members of the Parlement, the financiers, the farmers of revenue, the merchants, and the tradesmen. It was to be expected that they should resent innovations which deprived them of privileges or profits and upset the calculable order which suited them so well. "Why make innovations?" cried one. "Is not all well with us?" It is natural, too, that they should put pressure on the Queen, and through her on the King. How should she withstand not only the persuasions of her friends, the Polignacs, but also the arguments of her tutor, and of Choiseul, the renowned minister of Louis XV, to whom she owed her position as Queen of France? Even the people rose up against Turgot's measures to help them; were they worked upon by agitators, agents of secret revolutionary organizations, of grain monopolists whose interest lay in preventing freedom of transport, or was it the English, or the Freemasons, or the Duc d'Orléans, cousin and potential rival to the King? All these influences were and are suspected. Open and secret forces, private interest, misguided conservatism, misplaced generosity, and weakness—all succeeded in creating a mist before the pit into which France was rushing, and from which Turgot and Necker—perhaps Turgot alone—might have saved her.

The attempted reforms and their failure hastened the Revolution. "It is not always by going from bad to worse," says de Tocqueville, "that a state falls into revolution." The Crown had pointed the way to better conditions; it had accustomed the people to the idea of reform; it had weakened the links which had bound them to the old *régime*; it had shown up in a high light its own uselessness and the incorrigible obscurantism of the privileged classes. It had succeeded, in fact, in weakening the connexion between the monarchy and all other classes of the State—both because reforms had been attempted and because they had failed. The army, on which the King should in the last resort have relied, was left rebellious by Saint-Germain's measures, and the household troops, the most loyal of the regiments, had been reduced. It is one step from the dismissal of Necker in 1781 to the calling of the States-General in 1789.

The failure of reform hastened the Revolution.

The history of that step can only be sketched in outline. For a time the French monarchy seemed more brilliant than ever. Vergennes's foreign policy had raised France to a height not reached since the days of Louis XIV. She had checked the Emperor and inflicted upon England a humiliation greater than any she was to suffer under Napoleon. She had for a time won the mastery of the seas; she had threatened the shores of Britain with invasion and launched the republic of America.

At home there was for a time prosperity, artificially created by the war, and there was gaiety and activity. The King bought a new palace for himself at Rambouillet, and another at Saint-Cloud for the Queen. There were masqued balls, *fêtes*, Beaumarchais's play at the theatre, marvellous magnetic *séances* in Mesmer's rooms. There were wonderful inventions, speaking animals, flying birds, an air balloon in which a Frenchman crossed the Channel and waved the French flag over England, and there was an alchemist, Cagliostro, guaranteed by no less a person than the Cardinal de Rohan himself to have found the secret of making gold.

But revolution was preparing. England was to have ample revenge for the help which France had given to her rebellious colonies, for the distant thunder of the American War of Independence echoed through France like a trumpet-call. Frenchmen had fought for the young republic; democrats had seen the theories of Rousseau put into practice and freedom established in a land of innocence; they had seen revolution succeed; and they came back—men like La Fayette, who had gone forth to America like a Crusader to a Holy War—fired with the inspiration of a practical example.

Their opportunity lay in the King's need, for the financial question had come to swallow up every other. The three years before the meeting of the States-General should be studied in detail to understand how the King was driven from one expedient to another until at last he was forced to summon the representatives of the people. The country was rushing downhill to bankruptcy, impelled by the war with England, which was in more ways than one a costly undertaking for France, impelled also by the policy of bluff adopted by Calonne, the "golden-mouthed," a charlatan who had been made Finance Minister in 1783. He conducted the finances of the State on the same principle on which he conducted his own—"If a man wants to borrow he must appear to be rich; to appear rich he must spend profusely." He embarked upon a mad prodigality of expenditure, and contracted fresh debts. The time came, however, when the finances were exhausted. The Parlement demurred at registering repeated loans, and by no fresh device could Calonne raise money. Necker published a criticism, *The Administration of the Finances of France*, of which 12,000 copies were sold. Necker was exiled, but the situation was not improved. There was only one remedy—there must be more taxation. But of whom? Calonne proposed an "Assembly of Notables." It was a magnificent piece of bluff, in the best tradition of Henry IV, but it failed. The Notables, though many a prince among them Calonne had "obliged with millions," were refractory, and would not vote the taxes. La Fayette demanded a States-General. Calonne retired, leaving the problem to his successor, Brienne. But Brienne, in spite of the fact that he had "all his life felt a predestination for the highest offices," could do no better.

The financial question forces the situation.

The Notables were dissolved, but the Parlement of Paris took up their cry for a States-General. The Parlement was banished, then recalled, forced to register the edicts of taxation, then permitted to cancel them. The Parlements of the provinces sent petitions, and the excitement of the people grew; then the Parlements were abolished and new courts set up, which proved a farce; *lettres de cachet* were prepared, the Duc d' Orléans exiled to his estates.

All these panic measures, however, brought in no money, and the financial pressure was relentless. The Protestants were given civil rights, in the hope of raising a fresh loan; Necker was recalled to the ministry; an appeal was made to the clergy, to the philosophers, to the Queen—and at last, so were Louis and his ministers harried from one device to another, to the people.

In January 1789, in the midst of an unsurpassed excitement, elections began to take place for a meeting of the States-General of France, called at last after a hundred and seventy-five years' abeyance.

CHAPTER III

THE FRENCH REVOLUTION (1789-95)

I. The Constituent Assembly (May 1789–September 1791)

The States-General met at Versailles, ten miles or so from Paris, on May 5, 1789. It consisted of 285 nobles, 308 clergy, of whom two-thirds were parish priests, and 621 representatives of the Third Estate, elected by all men of twenty-five and over who were on the tax The States- register. Something of a mediæval character still remained General. to the States-General, and the deputies tended to regard themselves less as legislators than as petitioners presenting griev-ances to the King. Each member had brought with him a *cahier*, or list of complaints from his constituency. These covered a multi-tude of subjects, but a certain uniformity among them reveals some attempt at organization—not on the part of the King, who did not make the slightest effort to manage the election, but on the part of revolutionary and democratic agencies already in existence.

There was no expression of dissatisfaction either with monarchy itself or with the reigning dynasty, but there was a general demand for The cahiers. a 'constitution,' for improvements in prisons and hospitals, and for reforms in economic, ecclesiastical, and political matters. Some requests were contradictory, others merely local. Some quoted Cicero and some Rousseau. Some were essays on the liberty of the individual, others humble petitions—to be allowed to keep a cat, to light a fire without payment of a due, that trespassing dogs might be killed rather than hamstrung, that wine might be freely sold, that marriage and burial fees and the "vile salt tax" might be reduced, that the ponds might be kept cleaner, or Paris have more lamps.[1] These were intended partly as instructions to the deputies, and they were later used as material, though not very largely, for the new constitution.

The immediate need of the deputies, however, was for a practical programme. They had first to define their procedure, test their powers, and discover their leaders. They were unknown to each

---

[1] Out of 50,000 or 60,000 *cahiers* only about 400 have been published. It must be remembered that these are lists of grievances, and give only a one-sided picture of the state of France. It would be easy in any country and under any Govern-ment to draw up an imposing list of complaints.

other, inexperienced, without traditions adequate to so momentous an occasion. The Third Estate, conscious of its responsibilities and somewhat embarrassed by social affronts it had already received, was on its guard, suspicious of the King and the privileged orders, watchful of encroachments, loyal, but nervously defiant. The King, too, had as little experience of popular government as the deputies, and the course of French history might have been very different if Louis XVI had taken lessons in Parliamentary management from an English minister. He had no programme to put before them, nor any plan by which he might have guided their deliberations. He opened the proceedings with a brief speech—keeping his plumed hat on the while—in which, in a loud voice, he set forth his rights and gave vague assurances of his "sentiments." Then after a few more promising remarks from a minister, Barentin, most of which could not be heard, and a disappointing financial statement from Necker, he withdrew together with the Queen and the royal party. He had retired without throwing any light on the problem which chiefly concerned the Commons—how was the States-General to be constituted, in one house or three, and what was the order of voting, by heads or houses? The clergy and nobles followed the King, withdrawing to separate apartments and leaving the Third Estate to discuss their problems alone. "The battle has begun," wrote a deputy from Lorraine.

It was, then, in the Hall of the Menus Plaisirs (the King's Diversions), where the next day the Commons reassembled, that the first scene of the Revolution was to be played. In all it lasted eight weeks, from this day of May 5 to another day, June 30, when men ran about with torches in the streets of Versailles and Paris, shouting and rejoicing because the King had given way. *The first encounter.*

Louis had allowed to the Third Estate twice as many deputies as to the Nobility or to the Clergy, but if the States-General sat as three houses and voted as orders the Third Estate would lose the advantage of its double representation. Surely, then, argued the Commons, he meant them to sit as one house. But why in that case did he not give definite orders, and why had he assigned separate apartments? The Commons at any rate determined to fight for the single house. It was the duty of each order to "constitute itself" to verify the election of the deputies and appoint officers. The Commons refused to do so until the other two orders had joined them. They adopted a masterly policy of inaction; for five weeks they waited and negotiated and waited again, ignoring the refusals which from time to time they received from the other houses. On May 28 their determination was enforced by the Paris deputies, who arrived late but full of zeal. They included the astronomer Bailly, who was to *The action of the Commons (May–June 1789).*

become their President and Mayor of Paris, and the renegade Abbé Siéyès, who as the author of the widely read pamphlet on the Third Estate [1] had already an aureole round his head. On Siéyès's motion a final summons was sent to the other two houses on June 12, and on the 13th, as the benches reserved for the nobles and clergy were still empty, the Third Estate determined at last to "constitute itself" without them. Suddenly there entered the house three *curés* whose names deserve to be recorded, Lecesve, Ballard, and Jallet. "Preceded by the torch of reason, led by our love for the public weal,

Three curés join the Commons. and by the cry of our consciences, we come to join our fellow-citizens and brothers." Thus spoke Jallet. It was a pretty speech, in the manner of the day, and the three priests were received with tears and embraces and wild rejoicing. The next day came nine more ecclesiastics, who were as cordially embraced. The numbers were small, but they were harbingers of the surrender of the privileged orders. The Third Estate was now emboldened to further steps. On the 17th, without waiting for the sanction of the King—"had the United States asked for the sanction of the King of England?"—it declared itself to be the sole representative body of France, and took the title of the

The Third Estate constitutes itself the National Assembly. "National Assembly." Then it charged the country that from the day when the Assembly should be broken up all taxes "not specifically, formally, and freely voted by the Assembly should at once cease in every province in the Kingdom." For with all its apparent boldness the new National Assembly was heartily afraid of dissolution. "We shall soon be back in our provinces," wrote a deputy.

In the meantime the clergy and nobles in their separate houses had been discussing the question of joining the other order. On June 19 the clergy decided to do so after a heated debate, and by a majority of 149. It is reported that "a noise like thunder" went up, reaching the Palace itself, when the decision was known. The nobles, on the other hand, having come to threats and challenges and the drawing of swords, broke up in confusion, and the anti-popular section appealed to the King. It was at this point that Louis, yielding to the reactionary arguments of the Court and of his brother d'Artois, determined to interfere, and to embark, on behalf of the nobles, upon a policy of repression, which six weeks before might have been effective, but which, now that the Commons were fortified by the adherence of the clergy, was merely to lead to defiance. He fixed a "royal sitting" for June 23, and in the mean-

---

[1] The pamphlet contained the following famous questions :
    Question : What is the Third Estate ?   *Answer:* Nothing.
    Question : What should it be ?   *Answer:* Everything.

time closed the hall of the Commons that the incidents of the last few days should not be repeated. Accordingly when the deputies arrived on the 20th they were told that the upholsterers were making preparations in the hall for the 23rd. The Commons stood dismayed in the drizzling rain until, on a sudden motion, they turned into a neighbouring covered tennis-court. There the painter David has depicted them (with one or two historical inaccuracies)—six hundred deputies surging round Bailly, their president, whom they had lifted on to a table, and taking, with right hands stretched out to heaven, the oath which was to shake the monarchy, an oath never to allow themselves to be dissolved "until the constitution had been established and set on a firm foundation." It was proposed by Mounier, a man whose subsequent history should be remarked, and only one deputy refused to take it. Him they accounted mad.

The King determines to interfere.

Mounier proposes the Tennis-court Oath (June 20).

Such men were not to be intimidated, not by the Comte d'Artois, who drove them from the tennis-court to the church of Saint-Louis under pretence of reserving the court for a match, not by the Royal Session itself on the 23rd.

The King was sad and gloomy, the nobles confident of victory, the Commons grim, silent, and apprehensive. There was a grant of some constitutional concessions, then came the royal order. The Estates were to deliberate in their separate chambers and merely on questions of taxation; they were not to discuss the form of the Constitution, feudal property, or the just rights and titles of the first two orders. *Cy veult le Roi.* It was the King's will. It was also his will that the Commons should depart. The King left the hall, the nobles followed, then the clergy. The Commons remained behind "in gloomy silence." Deux-Brézé, the King's Grand Master, appeared in full Court dress. There were Gardes Françaises [1] at the door. "The King requests that the deputies of the Third Estate retire." Then Mirabeau, who from this moment was to become their leader, threw himself forward, his heavy shoulders charged with defiance, his pock-marked face and bloodshot eyes afire. "Sir, go tell your master that we are here by the will of the people and nothing but bayonets shall drive us out." Deux-Brézé went; the message was given. "They mean to stay?" repeated Louis wearily. "Very well, let them stay"—for he knew he could not count upon the Gardes Françaises.

The Royal Session (June 23).

The King is defied with impunity.

[1] An infantry corps of the regular army, entrusted with the special care of the royal family. In time of peace it policed the districts round the royal residences, and thus, coming into contact with the people, it was more infested by revolutionary ideas.

D

The King's hand had been forced; the Commons had triumphed. Siéyès was ready with an appropriate speech. Four days later Louis wrote that he desired the union of the Three Estates, already an accomplished fact. "The Revolution is over," wrote a Frenchman. In truth, it was only the first scene of it, and the victory was with the people's representatives. The Commons had defied the King

The union of the Three Estates. and the privileged orders, and they still lived. They had more than preserved their existence; they had proclaimed their authority and proved it. They had unfurled their standard and organized their forces. The royal mantle had been rent and the foolishness of the King revealed.

The Commons were still afraid of him, however, and when at the beginning of July troops began to be concentrated in the neighbour-

The action of Paris. hood of Versailles they saw their corporate existence, even their personal safety, seriously threatened. It is this which explains the attitude of the National Assembly toward the events of July 11–14.

The next scene of the Revolution was laid in Paris. In the capital revolutionary organizations, secret and open, foreign agents, public agitators, and all who were interested in embarrassing the Bourbon monarchy found an excellent sphere for their operations. There among the not too reputable populace which lounged in the gardens of the Palais Royale—the town house of the King's cousin, the Duc d'Orléans—democratic orators found a ready and inflammable audience. There too congregated bands of ruffians, "of terrifying appearance, with knotted sticks and disfigured faces," who ever since April had held Paris in the grip of a hysterical fear. Some were the hooligans which every capital possesses and any time of discord produces; some were peasants from the countryside, attracted by the largesse which had been distributed to the poor; others again were "hot-blooded" brigands from the South, tempted by the hope of plunder or deliberately invited by agents in Paris. Among others it is certain that the Duc d'Orléans, Philippe Égalité, hoping to turn the revolutionary enthusiasm to his own account and to transfer the Crown from his cousin's head to his own, was importing into Paris hired ruffians who at any propitious moment would be ready to serve his purpose.[1] And the respectable citizens, on edge with fear, and dreading continually a repetition of the *Affaire Réveillon*,[2] or they hardly knew what violence or pillage, had formed among themselves a citizen militia and set up at the Hôtel de Ville an informal committee.

It was this mixed population of the Palais Royale gardens which Camille Desmoulins, the greatest of the street orators of the day, in-

[1] For the discussion of the evidence see N. H. Webster, *The French Revolution.*
[2] An affray in Paris on April 28.

cited to revolution and to class warfare. "The beast has fallen into the snare; let us strike it down. Never have victors been offered a richer prey; forty thousand palaces, town houses, and country mansions will be the reward of valour." All through July the popular excitement was fostered by the massing of the troops and the growing fear of famine. On the 11th the opportunity which the leaders were seeking seemed to have come. The King dismissed Necker, who, unsatisfactory as he was, had come to stand in the eyes of the people as the advocate of their cause at Court. On Sunday, July 12, Camille Desmoulins, rushing into the Palais Royale gardens and leaping on to a table in front of one of the *cafés*, raised the cry, "To arms, to arms! Not a moment must be lost! Monsieur Necker has been dismissed! His dismissal sounds the tocsin of the St Bartholomew of patriots. To-night all the Swiss and German battalions in the Champ de Mars will come out and slaughter us. We have but one chance left, to fly to arms." The mob swarmed out of the gardens, plucking leaves from the chestnut-trees as badges. Seizing busts of Necker and Orléans from a gallery of wax portraits, they marched with these at their head. In the Place Louis XV they met and stoned a regiment of German dragoons, who pursued them to the Tuileries gardens, and who would probably have suppressed the mob at this stage but for the arrival of numbers of Gardes Françaises, who deserted to the mob. The commander of the troops, loth July 12. to shed blood, ordered them to retire. Their retreat handed over the city to insurrection.

That night, at the signal of insurrection, twenty to forty thousand bandits entered the city, pillaging and terrorizing as they came, so that "none but the children slept." The next day the mob,[1] stimulated by the sacking of bread-shops, prisons, the house of the lieutenant of police and the convent of Saint-Lazare, where wine was found, swarmed round the Hôtel de Ville clamouring for arms. Good citizens were there too, in response to the July 13. tocsin, which was calling upon Paris to defend itself from the long-expected danger which had at last come upon it. De Flesselles, the Provost of the Merchants, in the meantime temporized. The mob he sent off looking for arms on false scents, a ruse that was to cost him his life; to the citizens he feared to give arms, but he sent for instructions to Versailles.

By the 14th the mob had secured arms of many kinds; Saracen weapons from the King's Garde-Meuble, two cannon mounted on

---

[1] The mob had abandoned green as it was the colour of the Comte d'Artois and had adopted the tricolour, the red and blue of Paris with the Bourbon white slipped in between—but was it not significant that these were the colours of the Orléans livery?

silver, a present from the King of Siam, thirty-two thousand muskets from the Invalides, which had been raided, and fifty thousand pikes which had been forged during the night. The rumour spread that there was gunpowder at the Bastille. Casual as it seemed, the move had been planned the night before by the leaders. The people had little to do with the Bastille,[1] but its eight grey towers, frowning on the Faubourg Saint-Antoine, could be made to serve as the grim, mysterious symbol of despotism. Delaunay, the governor, with a garrison of ninety-five pensioners and thirty Swiss Guard, and with a few guns which were used for firing salutes, could put up only a poor defence. Attempts at negotiations were over-ridden by the crowd, the trained soldiers having cut the chains of the drawbridge, and the mob, led by the Gardes Françaises, rushed into the courtyard. There was a flash of fire, then Delaunay surrendered to a sergeant of the guard, "on the faith of a French soldier that no harm should be done to any person." The prisoners of the Bastille were ostentatiously set free—four coiners, two madmen, and a murderer—and Delaunay was dragged triumphantly back to the Hôtel de Ville. On the way the crowd, getting out of hand, fell upon the governor and hacked him to pieces. A cook's apprentice cut off his head. It was set upon a pike together with the heads of some of the defenders, and with these grisly trophies the mob riotously entered the Hôtel de Ville. Soon the head of de Flesselles joined the others, and "women and children danced round them." The mob had tasted blood. A few days later two ministers, Foulon and Berthier, who had entered the Government on Necker's fall, were as brutally murdered, and in memory of an impatient remark[2] Foulon's head was borne aloft with hay in its mouth.

The taking of the Bastille was hailed by contemporaries as an event of the first magnitude,[3] and such it proved to be; but it was the Assembly that gave to it its political consequences, and created out of an act of brigandage the legend of a glorious and spontaneous uprising of the people against oppression. Full of bitterness and fear toward the Court, anxious to recover favour with the people, who had lately been expressing dissatisfaction,[4] and not unrelieved that the dreaded fortress no longer existed for their own reception, the Assembly showed approval

July 14.

The taking of the Bastille.

How the event was received.

---

[1] The Bastille was the aristocrat's prison ; the common offender was usually imprisoned in the Bicêtre.
[2] " Let the people eat grass."
[3] " How much is this the greatest and best event that has ever happened."—C. J. Fox.
[4] " When there was one king we had bread ; now that there are 1300 we have none."

of the events of July 14. Thereupon the Committee of the Hôtel de Ville and the National Guard began to claim credit for what they had been unable to prevent, and attributed any regrettable incidents to the treachery of Delaunay. An amicable agreement between the Assembly and Paris was made. La Fayette was made commandant of the National Guard and a 'mayoralty' of Paris was created for Bailly, while the Archbishop of Paris, a deputy who only a week before had objected to the union of the three orders, offered up a *Te Deum* in Notre-Dame, where a "sublime discourse" was pronounced, exalting the mutinous behaviour of the Gardes Françaises.

Then the King, who had already agreed to recall Necker and dismiss the foreign troops, was called in "to set his seal" on the reconciliation. Accordingly on the 17th he went to Paris, followed by three-quarters of the Assembly, and preceded by fishwives and market-women, who danced before him waving branches adorned with ribbons. He was met by the Mayor and the electors at the Hôtel de Ville, and, with a foolish smile, he put on a tricolour cockade. "Well done! He belongs to the Third Estate!" cried the populace, while some demanded, with the brutality of truth, "Has the King signed his capitulation?"[1] A little later, though his ministers had been murdered in the interval, Louis agreed that a statue of himself should be erected on the site of the now demolished Bastille. At this fashionable ladies, not to be outdone, bought the stones of the old fortress at so much a pound, "like good meat," and had them set up as ornaments.

July 17.

Thus "out of a mighty lie, a new era sprang into life. Liberty was smirched at the very moment of her birth."[2] A factious proceeding was given the seal of national approval and royal patronage, and the consequences were to be fruitful of anarchy.

It was to be expected that the example of Paris should lead to the outbreak of disorder in the provinces, where forty thousand *châteaux*, the 'Bastilles' of the villages, remained to be destroyed. The long-standing hostility to the nobles, which could now be indulged with little fear of punishment, was embittered by the growing fear of famine. As in Paris, brigands too played their part, and created all over the country a "great panic," hardly to be accounted for, but real enough to prompt the wildest actions, and to cause the peasants to arm themselves in self-defence. Once armed, it was easy enough to turn the peasants against the aristocracy. Deliberate agitators multiplied malicious and slanderous rumours that the *seigneurs* were holding up the grain, or the bishops

The action of the provinces.

---

[1] *Cf.* Bailly's speech: "Henry IV conquered his people, and here are the people conquering their king "—and he might have added " and their Parliament."
[2] L. Madelin, *The French Revolution.*

poisoning the wells. They even asserted that the King himself had asked for the help of the peasants in the destroying of the nobility. So tax-collectors and financial agents, bishops and *abbés*, mayors and even peasants who refused to join the rioters, were seized and ill-treated and their houses despoiled. *Châteaux* and granaries were burnt, records of dues destroyed, religious houses pillaged, woods devastated, game mutilated, crops trampled down; famine, against which the peasants warred, increased; nobles were smoked out of the country; officials went into hiding; all authority was paralysed, and 'spontaneous anarchy' was added to organized disorder. In the villages and towns, as in Paris, informal 'communal' governments were set up, but, often revolutionary in sympathy and always illegitimate in origin, they had as yet little power to stem the prevailing lawlessness.

And the Assembly? Many of the more moderate deputies were distressed by the reports that reached them. A few extremists rejoiced, and attempted even further to excite their constituents.[1] Several believed, with Mirabeau, that "the nation must have its victims," or, being unsatisfied, it would destroy everything. Suddenly, in the midst of their deliberations, about eight o'clock on the night of August 4—to be recalled henceforth as the "night of dupes"

The Assembly's answer. —the Vicomte de Noailles, a penniless noble known to his familiars as "Jean Sans Terre," and, as some allege, an Orléanist agent, rose to speak. The cause of the trouble, he said, was the odious burden of feudal dues; they must be done away with. These words unloosed a delirium of competitive generosity and a legislative hysteria which was to make that session the most momentous in the history of the Assembly. All gave away what they could, either of their own or of their neighbours. Nobles renounced their dues, bishops their tithes, *seigneurs* their sporting rights, provinces their privileges, towns their immunities. All through the night decree after decree was passed, to the number of thirty, abolishing serfdom, feudal jurisdiction, manorial rents, tithes, game laws, saleable offices, clerical fees, unequal taxation, pluralities, and municipal and provincial rights. By the morning, amid tears and embraces, cheers and applause, a social revolution had been accomplished.[2] Two nobles proposed a vote of thanks, which was hailed with acclamation, to Louis XVI as the "restorer of French liberty," and the Archbishop of Paris concluded with a *Te Deum*.

This was the answer of the Assembly to the provinces. Thus the

[1] See Arthur Young's *Travels*, July 24, 1789 : " Thus it is in revolutions, one rascal writes and a hundred thousand fools believe."
[2] In spite of the fact that many feudal burdens still remained to be subsequently abolished in 1792 and 1793.

people thought they could do what they liked, and anarchy became triumphant.

The deputies had in the meantime begun to consider the new constitution for which France had been looking ever since their election. They determined on the motion of La Fayette to publish, by way of preface, a statement of general principles, after the example of the American Colonists. On August 12, therefore, was issued a Declaration of the Rights of Man, which, inspired by Geneva and Philadelphia, proclaimed "for all men, for all times, for every country, and as an example to the whole world," that "all men being born equal should have equal rights." This declaration was not only an assertion of defiance against the King. It provided what all faiths and all political parties need, and what the monarchists conspicuously lacked—a definition of creed, a programme round which the supporters of revolution could rally. But the cause of democracy was to suffer dearly for the comprehensiveness of its claims, and for this reason it was a mistaken measure of policy. In the first place, as Mirabeau pointed out, it would have been better to have reminded the people rather of their civic duties than of their rights. Secondly, it raised expectations which the Assembly afterward found it impossible to fulfil, and problems which they could not solve. The rights of man were "a secret which should be concealed until a good constitution had placed the people in a position to hear it without danger." Or again, as Malouet demanded, "Why should we carry men up to the top of a mountain and thence show them the full extent of their rights since we are forced to make them descend again and assign them limits and cast them back into the world as it is, in which they will come on boundary marks at every step?" There was rendered inevitable a contradiction between the Declaration and the new constitution which was to lead to conflict for five years. In the Declaration the Assembly "lifted the curtain which veiled an impossible liberty only to drop it again in the constitution."

The making of the new constitution (July-December 1789).

The Declaration of the Rights of Man (August 12, 1789).

The political framework of the new constitution was completed by the end of 1789. The legislative power was to be vested in a single chamber, chosen for two years, not by universal suffrage, but by a tax-paying electorate of a little over four millions.[1] Only men who

---

[1] The question of equality was evaded in this way : all men are citizens, but there are passive citizens, the poor, and active citizens, taxpayers. Only active citizens should vote. All who paid taxes equivalent to three days' work voted for the electors ; the electors, who must pay taxes equivalent to ten days' work, voted for the deputies. Thus was the curtain immediately dropped upon the equal rights of man. Universal suffrage was of course proposed, so was women's suffrage, by Condorcet.

paid at least fifty livres (a *marc d'argent*) in taxes and were landed proprietors could be candidates for election. The same civil rights were extended to Protestants, Jews, and the mulattoes of the colonies, and along with the abolition of titles all careers were thrown open to commoners.

The hereditary monarchy was retained, and the King, who was to adopt the title of "King of the French," was to be head of the army and the administration. He could nominate the highest functionaries and choose and dismiss ministers. He could coin money, direct the military forces, and if authorized by the Assembly he could declare war. By a suspensory veto he could hold up legislation for six years, during three successive Assemblies, but he could not dismiss the Assembly, nor could he overcome it by force, for the troops were forbidden to approach within sixty thousand yards of the Assembly. In spite of these limitations the King retained as head of the executive a certain measure of power. In practice it was difficult for him to exercise it. He had no taxing power; he could hardly initiate legislation, or co-operate with the legislature, for none of his ministers could be a member of the Assembly—a check upon the executive inspired by Montesquieu's theory and America's example. His appointments were to be called in question, his right of veto was to be challenged by the mob. The whole question of the veto and its discussion, totally misapprehended by the people,[1] had been used by those interested to work up a second demonstration of popular violence. The Breton deputies, the Duc d'Orléans, Mirabeau, who

An interruption. hoped to win power from the issue, and the most violent section of revolutionaries, who thought that "a second fit" of revolution was necessary, all these contributed in some measure to produce the "March of the Women" from Paris to Ver-

The "March of the Women" (October 1789). sailles. A loyalist demonstration at a regimental supper on October 1 gave them their opportunity, the scarcity of grain their rallying cry. For three days, from October 4 to 6, Versailles—the Assembly and the Palace—was given over to the mob of women, and men dressed as women, who had marched from Paris to clamour for bread. They swarmed through the Palace, seeking like ravenous beasts to tear the Queen to pieces, and would perhaps have done so on the night of the 5th but for the loyalty of her bodyguard. Once again the Assembly, fearing the scheming of the Queen more than the violence of the mob, lent itself to disgraceful scenes and became the

[1] " Do you know what ' veto ' means ? " cried the demagogues. " Listen. You go home ; your wife has cooked your dinner. The King says ' Veto '—no more dinner for you." The growing famine was attributed to ' suspensory vetoes ' which had been bought by the aristocracy to hold up bread. (Quoted by L. Madelin, *The French Revolution*.)

tool of the rioters. La Fayette, who had arrived from Paris with the National Guard, played also, whether from duplicity or weakness, into their hands, and it was on his suggestion that when the 'women' surged back to Paris on the 6th they were accompanied by the royal family—"the baker, the baker's wife, and the baker's son." A joker put up a notice, "Versailles to let," and from that day the King was to live in an ever-narrowing imprisonment in the midst of "his people" of Paris. The Assembly too followed their king to the capital, thus placing themselves more directly under the influence of the populace, whose 'pike' methods were as direct as they had proved efficacious.

After the new constitution had been drawn up the Assembly proceeded to administrative reorganization. The Intendants were abolished; the old provinces dismembered, and eighty-five new departments with elective councils were established. The old **Adminis-** Parlements were superseded by graded courts with judges **trative** elected for short periods. The old corporations and the new **measures.** Provincial Estates were alike suppressed. There was much criticism of this wholesale replacement of existing administrations. "The disorganization of the kingdom could not have been better planned," said Mirabeau. The result was, in fact, so considerably to weaken the executive authority throughout the country as to prepare the way first for the local tyrannies of the informal communes and National Guards which were springing up all over France, secondly for the Terror of '93, and thirdly for the dictatorship of Napoleon.

In the meantime the financial question was becoming urgent, and no adequate effort had as yet been made to deal with it. Two loans for a hundred and thirteen million livres which were issued on the authority of the Assembly had yielded only twelve millions; the taxes could no longer be collected; "patriotic offerings" had produced only seven millions, and again "bankruptcy was at **Financial** the door." The Assembly was face to face with a problem **measures.** which could no longer be postponed. Scheme after scheme was proposed only to be abandoned—all save one. There still remained one source of wealth—the coffers of the Church. The tithe had been abolished, why should not the property of the Church be seized? Anti-Catholic prejudice gladly supported the financial argument for the despoiling of the Church, and "obliging theorists" contended that its accumulated wealth had really only been left to it "in trust for the people." On October 10 the Bishop of Autun, the cynical, shrewd "goat-footed" Talleyrand, proposed that the property of the Church should be placed at the disposal of the State. It was immediately supported by Mirabeau, and after a long and passionate debate was carried by 368 votes to 346, forty members refraining from voting, and 300, nearly all belonging to the Right, being absent.

It was, however, no easy thing to turn into money so large an amount of real estate, and the acquisition of the property of the **Assignats.** Church was at first an embarrassment rather than a help. It was therefore decided, with the help of the municipalities who were willing to buy up some of the Church lands, to issue notes on the security of the ecclesiastical estate. These were the famous *assignats*, which, originally a form of mortgage on the Church property, soon became a regular paper currency. They passed into every one's hands, and so helped to establish the permanence of the new settlement even more widely than the transference of the English monastic lands to the new nobility by Henry VIII had secured the English Reformation. Thus politically the *assignats* were a success. Financially they led to bankruptcy. The original intention of issuing notes only to the value of half the lands was, under growing financial pressure, abandoned, and as issue succeeded issue, and the four hundred millions of 1790 grew to the forty-five thousand millions of 1796, the value of the *assignats* deteriorated until they became worthless.

The nationalization of ecclesiastical property had brought two other problems in its train. The dissolution of many religious houses **Social con-** which accompanied it had thrown upon the country, as **sequences.** in England of the sixteenth century, the care of the poor. In place of the "barren and dangerous charity" of the Church, "calculated to encourage idleness and fanaticism," the National Assembly decided therefore to set up workhouses "which will be useful to the State and in which the poor man will find a subsistence thanks to his own labour. Thus there will be no more poverty-stricken people save those who choose to remain so." The argument is familiar. By May 1790 11,800 artisans were being kept in the charity workshops; by October the number was 18,800, and more than fifteen million livres had been spent on their upkeep.

Secondly, there remained the question of provision for the clergy, who no longer had endowments to support them. This was to lead **Religious** to the Civil Constitution of the Clergy, a reorganization of **con-** the Church of France which was to complete the alienation **sequences.** of that body already set on foot by the appropriation of their property, which was also to estrange a large section of the French people, and to drive the King into opposition. Although **The Civil** the clergy of all ranks had so far proved invaluable allies of **Constitu-** the Revolution, the debates on the "Budget of Public **tion of the** Worship" aroused and revealed antagonisms older than **Clergy** 1789. "The dead spoke"; persecuted Huguenots, Jansenists, and Gallicans of the sixteenth and seventeenth centuries, as well as sceptics and deists of the eighteenth, framed the Civil Constitution of the Clergy. By this all officers of the Church were to be paid servants of the State. The new departments were substituted for the irregular dioceses, and to the departmental civil authorities, who were not necessarily Catholics, the election of bishops and priests and a large measure of control over them was entrusted. The Civil *creates for the Revolution its most serious enemies.* Constitution was therefore an administrative reform on the fashionable geometrical lines, a political measure, for it abolished the Concordat of 1516 between France and the Papacy, and, in respect of the principle of election, an evangelical reversion to the Primitive Church.

Its result, however, was to turn the Church of France into a State department, and to arouse throughout the Catholic population a general resistance. The King sanctioned the decree in anguish fifteen days after it had passed the Assembly and then fell into a fever of remorse. In the provinces an attempt to dissolve the chapters led to disorder. It was, however, the decree of November, compelling all the clergy to take an oath of allegiance to the State and the Constitution, which forced the issue and flung down the challenge in the face of Catholic France and of Catholic Europe. About half the priests refused to take the oath, and all the bishops except four, two of whom were Talleyrand and Brienne, the late minister of Louis. In March and April 1791 the Pope condemned the Civil Constitution, and when the Head of the Church spoke the King, the clergy, and half of France were prepared to obey, and, in doing so, to defy the Assembly. The Civil Constitution had at last brought the Revolution face to face with its enemies.

It precipitated the second period of crisis through which the Assembly was to pass.[1] On all sides there were dangers and difficulties. Necker had resigned his ministry and left the country in despair. Many classes of the state were alienated and discontented. The Parlements were petitioning against their abolition; the commercial classes were thrown into confusion by the new regulations; the provinces were everywhere disturbed, the Church in revolt; half the shops and a third of the factories were closed, poverty and economic disorder were increasing; the *Critical months (January– July 1791).* country, tired of politics, wished only to resume its ordinary business, and already elections were being left to the 'societies.' Camille Desmoulins was exciting sedition in his paper, *Les Révolutions de Brabant et de Flandres*, and Marat was demanding heads through his journal, *L'Ami du Peuple*, while *General dissatisfaction.* from all quarters of France came complaints against the Assembly,

[1] The first having been in May and June 1789.

that it had gone too far, or not far enough, that it had neglected the *cahiers* and failed to bring the millennium to earth.

The Assembly, weary and unpopular, was divided within itself. On the left the Breton deputies were pressing extreme measures **The Assembly.** and tending increasingly to look outside the House to the Jacobin Club for their instructions. This society of extremists, the best political organization in France, formed from the original Breton club, and taking its name from an old Jacobin or Dominican monastery in the Rue Saint-Honoré, where it was housed, was, with its eleven hundred members in the capital and its four hundred branches in the provinces, rapidly becoming the chief factory of public opinion both in Paris and in the country. The conservative and moderate members of the Assembly were withdrawing from its deliberations. As early as October 1789 Mounier—the ardent, high-souled revolutionary of May and June, proposer of the Tennis-court Oath, President of the Assembly during the October 'days'—had resigned his seat, called on his colleagues to follow his example, tried vainly to raise a rebellion in his native province of Dauphiné, and finally emigrated as a protest against the "rule of the pikes." In April 1791 the Assembly suffered a still more serious loss by the death **Death of Mirabeau.** of its president, Mirabeau. He of the bull neck and the "black *chevelure*," the man of "instincts and insights," of duels, storms, prisons, debts, disease, and vices, whose "very ugliness was a power," died at the age of forty-two, worn out by his activities and his passions. "Sinned against and sinning," indomitable son of a tyrant father, author of political attacks and obscene satires, unscrupulous, cynical, ambitious, eccentric, venomous, violent, he was the greatest man the Revolution had produced. He was no theorist, no slave of a formula, not even the leader of a regular party, but a practical, clear-sighted, far-seeing man, with a "brain and heart of fire," supporting this measure or that, paid but not bought by the Court, willing to flatter mob or Queen for his own power; denouncer of despotism, but upholder of monarchy, supporter of constitutional liberty, but advocate of a strong executive, "adventurer of genius in a dissolving society," but the only man who could have led the "wild asses" of the Assembly and the "royal cattle" of the Court into the paths of harmony. "He it was who shook old France to its basis, and as if with his single hand held it toppling there, still unfallen." The jealousy of the Assembly had excluded him from the ministry, and the suspicion of the Court had kept him from the royal councils, but he seemed at the end to have overcome them both. When he died Paris enjoined a three days' mourning, deputies wept, and representatives of the King walked side by side with those from the Jacobin Club in the funeral procession, three leagues long, which bore him to the

Panthéon. Old France was buried with him. "I carry the last rags of the monarchy with me." New France lost a far-seeing pilot. "I see so clearly that we are in the midst of anarchy, and sinking deeper into it every day." Like Mounier, his own part in it filled him with remorse. "I am overwhelmed by the thought that all I have done has been to help on a huge destruction." Had he lived he might have saved the monarchy and diverted the Revolution to constitutional paths.

"Mirabeau thought himself an Atlas," was Mme de Campan's sarcastic comment, and it is true that after his death there were no shoulders broad enough to bear his burden. La Fayette, a compound of chivalry, idealism, and indecision, was defied by the National Guard that he commanded. The regular troops were in mutiny. From October 1789 an orgy of insubordination had broken out among them, culminating in the insurrection of Nancy. Ambitious young officers, democratic sergeants, had led revolt after revolt, throwing their superiors into prison, rescuing comrades, seizing regimental funds, insulting officers, and generally defying authority. The Assembly adopted a policy of supineness which only encouraged the mutineers. In the hope, which proved vain, of arousing in the soldiers loyalty to a new and acceptable ideal the Assembly had invited them to send representatives to the Festival of the Federation, held in July 1790, to celebrate the first anniversary of the fall of the Bastille. It was a debauch of magnificent sentiment. Sixty thousand delegates from the 'federated' branches of the National Guard all over France assembled in Paris. A mighty earthen amphitheatre was raised in the Champ de Mars by the ardent labour of volunteers, by the busy shovels of priests, soldiers, and elegant ladies. In the midst was a towering altar to *la Patrie*. There were processions, military displays, banners, flowers, and the Bishop of Autun, Talleyrand of fame, assisted by four hundred priests in white surplices and tricoloured stoles, celebrated Mass to the singing of choristers and the roar of cannon. The King swore to defend the constitution, the Queen, carried away by the buoyant enthusiasm of the hour, held forth the baby prince to the cheers of the multitude. It was a day of triumph—not for the King, who was quite eclipsed, but for La Fayette, who, amid waving banners and gleaming swords, stood at the altar with the text of the oath in his hand, the rock and the defence of the Revolution. Or so it seemed. The representatives of the regular troops, having fraternized with the National Guard, returned to their regiments more mutinous than ever. Even Bouillé's troops on the Metz frontier, the last loyal regiment of the line, were infected. The army had become completely demoralized, useless to the King, troublesome to the Assembly, so that men

The Festival of the Federation (July 14, 1790).

began to ask whether a foreign war would not be a useful means of restoring discipline.

For though the Assembly was resolutely refusing to have a foreign policy it had become involved without its will in foreign problems, Foreign   and the intervention of Europe was becoming every day affairs.   more of a possibility. The preoccupation of the Powers on the one hand and the triumphant pacifism of the Assembly on the other were to postpone the outbreak of war for another year,[1] but the seeds were already sown. The abolition of the feudal rights of German princes who held land in Alsace had embroiled France with the Empire, the Civil Constitution and the annexation of Avignon had alienated the Papacy. The French nobles, grown tired of parrying their injuries with jests, were fleeing from France in increasing numbers. Grouped round the Comte d'Artois, who had early transferred his meddlesomeness from Versailles to Turin and thence to Coblenz, they formed on the frontiers of France a dangerous band of *émigrés*, who divided their time between amusing themselves and intriguing with foreign Courts for help against the Revolution. Their behaviour excited, it is true, more ridicule than sympathy, but the Assembly was only too well aware that a word from the King or Marie-Antoinette would turn an undignified farce into a serious menace.

Thus from all quarters the arrows of the Assembly were returning to it again, barbed and poisoned. But the greatest danger was to come from the Court, where after long delays a plan was being put into execution on whose success or failure hung the fate of the Revolution.

The King, after one or two diffident and vain attempts to oppose the Revolution in the summer months of 1789, had let it run its course with an amiable docility which, although it arose partly from a conscientious desire to consult the wishes of his subjects, seemed to most people only contemptible. He had smiled, when requested, upon the taking of the Bastille in July. He had amiably The flight of the royal   acceded to the demands of the 'women' who dragged him family   to Paris in October; and he had withdrawn at the Tuileries (June 1791).   into a political retirement from which, from time to time, the Assembly called him forth to appear at revolutionary shows, to stimulate the flagging populace to enthusiasm and to give to the national decrees a royal sanctity. On these occasions Louis was often greeted with warmth and enthusiasm, hailed as the "best of kings," but he never succeeded in turning an effusive outburst of loyalty to his own advantage.

The more active mind of Marie-Antoinette, however, was em-

[1] See Chapter III, section II (p. 66 *et seq.*).

ployed in considering schemes. Mirabeau and La Fayette she could
not bring herself to trust, though either might have helped her; the
troops could not be relied upon. There seemed to her, therefore
only one resource—her brother the Emperor. But the cautious
Leopold refused, as he naturally must, to take any step without a
direct appeal from Louis, who had apparently accepted the Revolution. It was not until the Civil Constitution of the Clergy threw
him into real conflict with the Revolution that Louis made the Queen's
plan his own, and appealed for help to the Emperor. Neither the
King nor Marie-Antoinette anticipated a regular invasion of France.
The King primarily desired his freedom, upon which every day
encroachments were being made, and toward which the plans and
preparations of the Court now began to be directed. But everywhere were spies and enemies. Louis's own valets wore the uniform
of the National Guard; the Mistress of the Wardrobe betrayed the
Queen's preparations. The royal pair were prisoners in their own
palace. The mob watched their movements with an offensive
closeness. The National Guard obstructed them. The Assembly
bullied them. The King must take his Easter communion from a
'constitutional' priest; he must write a circular letter to the Courts
of Europe affirming his freedom; and Louis, determined now only
upon escape, dissembled and gave in to every request. He seemed
to onlookers to have reached the depths of humiliation. There was
to be a lower level.

On the morning of June 20 a *valet de chambre* raised the alarm.
The royal bedchamber and the rooms of the Queen and her children
were deserted. The tocsin was immediately sounded, and while
Paris was giving itself over to terror, indignation, rage, and ribaldry,
and flower-women and street-boys were pouring with impertinent
curiosity into the Tuileries, a huge coach containing the Baroness
de Korff, her family, waiting-maid, travelling-companion, and
steward was rolling eastward along the dusty white roads of Champagne.[1] The royal family was fleeing to the frontier. Châlons was
passed and safety seemed in sight, for an escort of dragoons was
expected from Bouillé's regiment, which lay near Montmédy. With
Bouillé's troops at his back Louis would dictate his own terms to
the Assembly. The dragoons were dispatched, but, already half-

[1] The coach contained the Baroness de Korff (Dame de Tourzal, governess to
the royal children), two children, a waiting-maid (the Queen in a gipsy hat), a
travelling-companion (Mme Elizabeth, the King's sister), and the steward (the
King). The Comte de Provence, the King's brother, fled from Paris the same
night and reached the frontier successfully by a different route. Had the flight
of the royal family been put into competent hands, and had the members agreed
to travel separately and without troops and an elaborate equipment, it might have
been successful. The Comte d'Artois had left with the troops after the taking of
the Bastille, 1789. The King's aunts had departed in the beginning of 1791.

mutinous, they were seduced before they met the King by the people of the villages through which they passed. The lumbering royal coach aroused suspicion, and as it drove eastward along the road out of Sainte-Menehould, young Drouet,[1] the postmaster's son, spurred through the night across the Argonnes, in a ride that was to become famous, for the fate of France and the Revolution hung upon it. He arrived at Varennes in the early morning, roused the inhabitants from their beds, and when the King reached the turning to Montmédy, just outside the village, to the right, twenty miles only from the frontier, he found an improvised barrier of carts drawn up against him. There were a few royal troops in the town, and a show of force might still have won the day. But Louis, averse as ever from measures of violence, gave himself up immediately, and almost, it seemed, with relief. With tears in his eyes he embraced his accuser before the half-dressed crowd. On the road back to Paris the rabble collected about them, mocked the Queen, and spat upon the King. Half-way the deputies from the Assembly crowded in upon them. Pétion ate sandwiches in a democratic manner, and talked of the time when France would be "fortunate enough to be ripe for a republic." In the streets of the capital not a cheer was raised nor a head uncovered; the National Guard carried their arms reversed as if for a funeral. The next day the King was suspended from his functions by the Assembly.

Whatever might have been the consequences of the royal flight if it had succeeded, nothing but disaster could follow its failure. The prestige of the monarchy had, with the dignity of the King, been dragged through the mud, and the republic of September 1792 was the direct answer to the flight of June 1791. The King had been

The beginning of practical republicanism. revealed at best as a deserter, at worst as a traitor to the Revolution—for he had left behind a letter repudiating all Acts passed since he had lost his freedom. The Assembly had in the crisis acted with promptness and decision, and the nation had learnt that the removal of the King had not wrecked the State. Hitherto the destruction of the French monarchy had belonged to the realm of constitutional hypotheses; the "electric shock" of June 21–22 transferred it at one blow to that of practical politics. It was debated in the clubs; it

[1] Drouet was, of course, the hero of the episode. He was borne high in the returning procession, lost his hat, belt, and scabbard and nearly his clothes in the enthusiasm with which he was received in Paris. He was given a grant of £1200 and was elected in 1792 to the Convention. He was taken prisoner by the Austrians and exchanged for a king's daughter. Napoleon gave him the Legion of Honour, made him sub-prefect at Sainte-Menehould, and was his guest at Valmy. After the Hundred Days he disappeared. On his death in 1824 he was discovered to have been living in obscurity under a false name.

was openly talked of in the streets, where men had already torn off the lilies from the royal palace.

The republic was not to come yet, however. On the contrary, a distinct reaction toward the Crown was marked both in and out of the Assembly. The Jacobin Club was riven by the question; and Lameth and Barnave at the head of the Moderates seceded and formed the new club of the Feuillants. Reactionary clauses were inserted into the constitution; and a demonstration on the Champ de Mars on July 17 in favour of a republic was dispersed by troops on the authority of Bailly and La Fayette—an unprecedented measure of firmness against the populace which was later to cost Bailly his life but which revealed how much the former leaders of the Revolution had ceased to fear the monarchy which they could now afford to protect. *A temporary reaction in favour of the Crown.*

By September a perfect reconciliation seemed to have been effected between the King and the Revolution. Louis gave his adherence to the Constitution. The Assembly reinstated the King in his functions, issued a pardon to the *émigré* nobles, who began to return, and, having made provision for a new legislature, dissolved itself. A magnificent festival, according to custom, was held to celebrate the proclamation of the constitution. There were fireworks and illuminations and tricolour flags, and the King, walking about among his people in the Tuileries gardens, was greeted on all sides as *notre bon roi*. Royalist pieces were played in the theatre. "Let the nation revert to its own cheerful nature," cried the King, "for the end of the Revolution has come." There was universal rejoicing. One and all echoed the royal sentiment. *The end of the Constituent Assembly.*

At five o'clock a balloon surmounted by an eagle with outstretched wings was sent up into the clouds. A car was attached "in which two intrepid voyagers flew up to visit the ethereal spaces where thunderstorms are formed." "The simile was exact," says M. Madelin. "The constitution was in the clouds, and the poor globe was to be torn to pieces. The eagle alone was to hover over storm-ravaged France and bide his time."

As to the Assembly, its work was done; it had passed twenty-five thousand decrees and made a new constitution. In utter weariness the deputies laid down their burdens, enacting before they separated that no member of the Constituent Assembly should be elected to the new legislature.

It is easy to criticize the work of the Assembly. It left a heritage of problems at home and abroad; it had destroyed wholesale a system of administration; it had opened the way to mob rule; it had enunciated dangerous theories; it had created a religious schism

E

and defied international law; it made the mistake—to a British mind—of divorcing the legislature from the executive, and, what was more serious, by its final decree it cut off the new Assembly from the experience of the old one. Much of its work was subsequently undone, but much remained permanent, and it must be remembered that most of its mistakes were committed in fear of the Crown, and arose from the corporate and individual insecurity that haunted all its actions.

It had made the initial act of defiance and cleared away the accumulations of history. It had secured the unity of France and set up in a new political structure a monument to democracy; it had let loose the energy of the people and made an honest attempt to inaugurate a common system of laws and an equitable division of burdens. It had created a civil and social revolution and established in the will of the people a new criterion of public policy. For all time and for all the world it had proclaimed a new gospel, that of the personal dignity of the common man.

II. The Legislative Assembly (October 1791–September 1792)

The Legislative Assembly, which met the day after its predecessor was dissolved, was full of untried men, with plenty of ideas and an

The Legislative Assembly. abundance of eloquence, but new to experience and new to glory. There was a preponderance of lawyers, many of whom had won a local reputation for revolutionary ardour and were ambitious to play a part on a larger stage. It was a new generation of young revolutionaries dazzled by dreams of unprecedented opportunities, lured by the glamour of Paris, and not indifferent to the eighteen francs a day which they received as deputies.

On the Right sat the Feuillants and Constitutionalists, friends of Barnave and Lameth, who had formed the Left of the old Assembly; thus showing at once how the Revolution had advanced and the centre of political gravity shifted. For the Left of the new Assembly was composed of Jacobin extremists and revolutionaries, who, in the preliminary debates on procedure, on the revolt in San Domingo and the disorder in Avignon, showed themselves to be the most effective party. From these a group gradually distinguished itself, known alternatively as the Girondists from the number of its leaders who represented the Gironde, or as the Brissotins, after the Norman, Brissot, who guided its policy. It came to dominate the Assembly,

The Girondists. to capture the ministry and mould the fortunes of France at a critical time in its history. Within a year it had brought about the fall of the monarchy and provoked a foreign war which with few intermissions was to last for more than twenty years. Finally in its weakness it handed over the Revolution to Paris, the populace and the clubs.

The Girondists were therefore one of the most important sets of political experimentalists in the history of France, and they are one of the most interesting, whether one regards them, with Lamartine, as tragic idealists or, with more iconoclastic historians, merely as sentimental windbags. They were primarily passionate enthusiasts, full of theory and zeal, and possessed of a marvellous eloquence, dangerous to themselves and to France. They loved to stage effects and to behold themselves as kin to the heroes of antiquity. Their gods were Brutus and Aristides, and their evangelist Plutarch. They were humane, and they died well, but they did not scruple to use the arts of demagogy, and they were without prescience. Nor could they control the passions they aroused. They were 'idealogues,' and there was not a practical statesman among them, for all that they owned the learning of Condorcet, Academician and Encyclopædist, and the Ciceronian eloquence of Vergniaud. Charlotte Corday, who murdered Marat that she might be "with Brutus in the Elysian Fields," was their martyr, and that incurable romantic, Mme Roland, their inspiration. Their hero was Pétion, weak and handsome, virtuous and vain, who was Mayor of Paris and for a time the adored 'Christ' of a new gospel. And their leader was Brissot, who dressed like a Quaker and talked like a communist, who had been a journalist and thought himself omniscient, a man of exhaustless activity, who displayed his zeal in a sequence of grudges. This man of words, in spite of his immeasurable inferiority, his lack of perspicacity and organizing ability, stood between Mirabeau on the one hand and Danton on the other as arbiter of the fortunes of France.

The Girondists were full of ambition for themselves and their cause. They wanted "to strike a blow for the Revolution," which in practice meant to pull down some part of the old edifice Their that had been left standing. And what of the *ancien régime* policy. was still left to be destroyed, save the Crown? The Girondists had already supported the Jacobins in throwing open the debates of the Assembly to the populace and in introducing the *appel nominal*, by which each deputy was called upon by name to register his vote.[1] By these measures they gained strength in the house and a following outside. Then they embarked upon a bold and ingenious policy of provocation. The two most prominent enemies of the Revolution were the *émigré* nobles outside France and, within, the priests who would not take the oath to the constitution. These the

[1] It was reckoned that this made a difference of at least a hundred votes, owing to the fear inspired by the populace.

Girondists heartily denounced as fomenters of disturbance and friends of the King. They passed decrees sentencing to death all the *émigrés* who had not returned to France by January 1, 1792, and ordering all priests to take the oath within a week under penalty of forfeiture of their livings or pensions. But these decrees were bait to catch a larger fish, and behind the *émigrés* and the non-juring priests the Girondists aimed at the throne. The question of the Church touched the King's conscience, and although Louis had little reason to love the *émigrés* whose intriguing had embarrassed him both at home and abroad he could not sentence his brothers to death. He therefore vetoed both sets of decrees. This was exactly what the Girondists desired and had anticipated. The King stood self-revealed as the enemy of the Revolution and in league with traitors, and what popularity was left to him began rapidly to ebb away. But the Girondists went farther; they wished to make a traitor of the King himself, and to do this a foreign war was necessary, which would place Louis in an impossible position of sympathizing with his enemies and fighting against his friends. Then would all treasons be unmasked and all divisions merged in one great purpose. The Revolution militant would become the Revolution triumphant; it would lay the Crown at the feet of the people; it would carry the democratic creed into foreign countries; and, not the least of its results, it would put the Girondists into office on the wave of an ensuing patriotism. Therefore the Girondists deliberately set themselves to provoke a foreign war, while Condorcet the pacifist dreamed dreams of a United States of Europe.

Decrees against the émigré nobles and the non-juring priests (November 1791).

The intervention of foreign Powers in the affairs of France was rapidly becoming little short of inevitable. First, because the revolutionaries themselves were growing increasingly propagandist. The French Revolution had never held itself to be a purely national movement. The Rights of Man had already been proclaimed in Warsaw and Philadelphia, and universal brotherhood could not be confined to the boundaries of France. Revolutionary democracy was a new creed based on a new philosophy and a new theory of ethics, and, like a new religion, could be preached throughout the world. The Constituent Assembly had resolutely refused to have a foreign policy; the Legislative Assembly as resolutely determined to have a vigorous one, and to turn a political faith into a fighting force, which, like Islam, should make political and spiritual conquests at one and the same time. The cause of France became the "cause of all peoples against all kings." Thus the potentates of Europe saw revolution rising up like a hydra-headed monster, and found themselves compelled to war against France, in

The growth of foreign intervention

order to crush the enemy who would otherwise destroy them in their own capitals.

Moreover, owing to the weakness and obstinate conscientiousness of the King, foreign Powers had become by a logical result the only rallying-point for those who were opposed to the Revolution. Had Louis followed Mirabeau's advice, and that of all those who were on his side, and set up a standard of revolt anywhere in France outside Paris, as Charles I did at Nottingham, had he even, as Napoleon said, "mounted his horse," he would have provided just such a focus of opposition to the Revolution as was so conspicuously lacking. He had fled, on the contrary, to the eastern frontier as a fugitive, thereby openly recognizing that the only real and effective source of opposition to the Revolution lay in the foreign Powers to whom the dispossessed nobles had already turned. And so the whole course of the Revolution was modified; royalism looked beyond the frontier and became treason; democracy became fired with patriotism, reckless with panic, identical with an aggressive militarism, and there followed the Terror and the Empire, which embittered the issues and drove the history of France and of Europe pendulum-wise for a century.

in a sense become inevitable,

It is not therefore to be wondered at that foreign Powers should have intervened, but rather that their intervention should have been tardy and, when it came, ineffective. It was because the French Revolution fell upon a Europe preoccupied with its own problems and divided within itself. Wordsworth and Coleridge might acclaim the dawn of a new era, and Fox hail the fall of the Bastille as the greatest event in history; cosmopolitans in St Petersburg might receive the good news with mutual embracings, and *illuminati* and enthusiasts all over Europe might plant trees of liberty and greet each other heartily as 'citizens,' but the Courts of Europe saw in the French Revolution only another factor in international diplomacy. They were neither shocked nor, at first, alarmed by it; revolts were misfortunes to which states were liable, and they looked only for its effects on the Balance of Power. They saw in the weakness of the monarchy the impending dissolution of France, and, congratulating themselves on the enforced inaction of a hitherto powerful neighbour, they turned with greater security to their mutual rivalries and their own national ambitions. Thus Pitt, not unfriendly, like many Englishmen of Whig traditions, to what seemed at first a flattering compliment to the Glorious Revolution of 1688, welcomed with relief the embarrassment of England's old enemy; with an easier mind he addressed himself to reforms at home and to the recuperation of the national prestige and finances after the American war, and he

but long delayed.

Europe preoccupied.

England.

maintained a resolute neutrality until his own country's interests should be involved. Frederick William of Prussia saw in the Revolu-

Prussia. tion the rupture of the Bourbon-Habsburg alliance made by Choiseul, and opened formal relations with the leaders of the Assembly. Gustavus III of Sweden, although deeply concerned as a chivalrous knight for the distressed Queen of France, was too

Sweden. remote and too much occupied with a nearer issue to take effective action on her behalf. For there was in the East of Europe a far more absorbing problem than the one which had arisen in the West.

Russia, the creation, as a Western Power, of that enterprising barbarian Peter the Great, was rapidly becoming one of the most

The Eastern formidable states of Europe. Her continual expansion
problem. under Catherine II, a German woman of masculine ambition and royal immorality, was the leading question of European diplomacy. It threatened the safety of her weaker neighbours, Sweden, Poland, and Turkey, and the peace of the more powerful and distant states, Prussia and Austria. With the participation of these last two Powers Catherine had already seized part of Poland in 1772, and when the French Revolution broke out she was engaged in a scheme for the partition of Turkey. She had secured as her ally the Emperor Joseph II—although subsequent history has proved the real opposition of the Balkan interests of Russia and Austria. For Joseph was anxious to destroy the existing understanding between Prussia and Austria, and he wanted Catherine's support for his own schemes of aggrandizement in Central Germany.

Thereupon Sweden seized the opportunity of Russia's engagement in the Balkans to declare war upon her, while Prussia stirred up the Poles, supported the Belgians in a revolt against Joseph, and replied to the Austro-Russian agreement with a diplomatic counter-move in the Triple Alliance of England, Prussia, and Holland. The chief European Powers were therefore fully occupied.

But in February 1790 Joseph II died, the didactic and ambitious Emperor, the "crowned *philosophe*," who believed that good inten-

Death of tions were a sufficient qualification for ruling a state. He
Joseph II was succeeded by his brother Leopold II, who had already
(February proved himself in Tuscany a tactful reformer and a cautious
1790). statesman. He set himself immediately to allay the storms which his predecessor had aroused. He pacified Hungary, suppressed the Belgian revolt, made peace with Turkey, and frustrated

Leopold II the enmity of Prussia by an understanding with Frederick
reverses his William at Reichenbach. The rupture of the Austro-
policy. Russian alliance consequently induced Catherine, already perturbed by hostile movements in Poland and checked in Turkey

by protracted sieges, to come to terms with Sweden, the more serious of her enemies. And Gustavus III on his part, although his guns had been heard in the imperial palace of St Petersburg, was equally ready for peace, for he was harassed by rebellious nobles within his kingdom and by Danish attacks without.

The Peace of Verela accordingly inaugurated a close alliance between Russia and Sweden, and a new stage in the history of Europe, for from its conclusion Catherine II began consistently and ardently to advocate the cause of the Bourbons. The bust of Voltaire was relegated to the attic; Gustavus III was encouraged to support Louis's flight, and Leopold *The Peace of Verela (August 1790).* and Frederick William were urged to put down Jacobinism in France while Catherine crushed it in Poland and Turkey. For though Catherine's hatred of the fruits of the French philosophers—whom to advertise herself in the West she had once affected to admire— was partly genuine it was largely dictated by her own ambition to repartition Poland. If the German Powers were winning compensation for themselves on the Rhine, she would have a freer hand on the Vistula and the Danube. *Catherine II turns to the Bourbon cause.* She made every effort therefore to involve her rivals in French politics, and at last succeeded. But for all her professed zeal for the Bourbons she was not to put into the field a single soldier of her own in their cause, and when the coalition against the French Republic was at last formed it was she who was to break it up.

Leopold was, however, in no hurry to promote a crusade on behalf of the French king. He was fully aware of Catherine's Polish intentions, and did not take very seriously the appeals either of the *émigrés* or of Marie-Antoinette. The stream of fugitives who through the winter of 1790 flocked to Paris to offer German or Swiss or Italian lands to Liberty and France did not move him to action; nor the eloquent warnings of Burke, who had become far too much the spokesman of the *émigrés*, nor the infringement of the Alsatian rights of German princes, nor the actual annexation of Avignon [1] to France. He allowed his apprehensions to be lulled by the pacific protestations of the National Assembly, and merely offered to help Louis in his flight from Paris. "We must declare," cried Robespierre, "that France renounces all thoughts of conquest, that she considers her

---

[1] Since the fourteenth century Avignon and the surrounding county of Venaissin had been subject to the Papacy, by whom it had been governed in a spirit of mildness. On the outbreak of the French Revolution the citizens had demanded union with France, but the Constituent Assembly had hesitated to commit such a breach of international law as annexation would involve. The Avignonese had thereupon overthrown the Papal Government on their own account, and a period of wild disorder had followed. The Constituent Assembly therefore voted for annexation at the end of its session ; the town and county were occupied by French troops in November 1791, and formally incorporated in September 1792.

limits to be fixed by an eternal destiny." The sentiment, which in 1791 was not in any way ironical, was incorporated into the constitution to secure its permanence. It succeeded in postponing the European war for nearly a year.

Even the failure of the King's flight, which resulted in humiliation and imprisonment for Louis, did not bring about the final act of

Effect of the King's flight. intervention, though it brought it several stages nearer realization. Leopold issued a manifesto from Padua in July calling on all the sovereigns of Europe to support the French king's cause as their own, and in August he met the Prussian

The Manifesto of Padua (July 1791). king at Pillnitz. But all the zealous importunity of the émigré princes who were allowed to be present could produce nothing more than a declaration expressing the willingness of the Emperor and the King of Prussia to undertake armed intervention if the other monarchs of Europe would join them. Concerted action was, however, out of the question; there

The Declaration of Pillnitz (August 1791). were guarantees to be given, and Catherine pleaded the lateness of the season. Thus the Declaration of Pillnitz seemed rather to delay than hasten intervention, and when in September Louis accepted the constitution Leopold abandoned all hostile designs.

The Declaration of Pillnitz, however, and the Manifesto of Coblenz, a violent denunciation of the Revolution which the émigré nobles had attached to it, served the cause of the Girondists in the new Assembly. They irritated without really alarming France, and together with the "army of Condé," a corps of émigrés savouring of comic opera, they gave a pretext for aggravating the war fever, which famine and the recklessness bred by social and financial disorder were already stirring up throughout the country. Nearly all parties in France had come to desire war, the Girondists for the reasons already given, the Feuillants and Monarchists because they believed that it would strengthen the executive; they thought that a successful war would rouse latent royalism, obscure other issues, and restore to Louis at the head of his army the power and popularity which he had lost as "chief clerk of the State." The Queen hoped by foreign arms, or at least by a parade of foreign arms, to reimpose Louis upon his people. Only the extreme Jacobins, who now broke away from the Girondists, opposed a war, for the very reason for which the Monarchists desired it. They feared that from a war would emerge either a regenerated monarchy or a dictatorship. In the long run they were right. The first answer to the war was the Republic of September 1792, and the second was Napoleon.

With the exception of the extreme Jacobins under Danton and Robespierre, all parties then began to prepare for war during the winter of 1791 and the spring of 1792. Brissot made inflammatory speeches in the Assembly, full of classical allusions; the Girondists passed peremptory decrees which they compelled the King to transmit, requesting the Elector of Trier to disperse the *émigrés* and fixing the amount of compensation to be given to German princes. The Queen begged her brother the Emperor to call a European congress and take up arms on behalf of the Crown. Narbonne, the King's minister, who was determined to steal the thunder of the Girondists and to turn the war into the King's war, outdid them in bellicosity. He sent three armies to the frontier, he demanded a war grant, which was raised largely from the confiscated estates of the *émigré* nobles, he made a personal tour of inspection, and reported that armies and fortresses were all in readiness for war. All through the winter volunteers poured in—peasants, clerks, artisans, and a few nobles. *Decrees against the Elector of Trier.*

In the meantime the Emperor Leopold, who had known so long how to wait, was at last roused to a firm and retaliatory mood. He declared his intention of supporting the Elector of Trier and the German princes; he demanded the restoration of Avignon and of the estates of the Imperial princes; he concluded an offensive and defensive treaty with Prussia, and to an imperious demand from the Assembly that he should not interfere in the affairs of France he replied by a censure of the Revolution and a denunciation of Jacobinism. But on March 1, the day that his reply was read in the Assembly, Leopold died, and for a moment the Austro-Prussian understanding was shaken by the death of the statesman-Emperor, wisest of the children of the great Maria Theresa. He was succeeded by his son, Francis II, who was, however, a more violent enemy of the Revolution than his father; the Girondists renewed their hostility; Catherine removed Frederick William's last scruples by offering Prussia a share in the partition of Poland, and the anti-French party triumphed again in Vienna and Berlin.

It was, however, to be a Girondist war after all, for at the beginning of March Narbonne fell from office, and on the 23rd a ministry, drawn up over the breakfast-table of Brissot and appointed by the King as a measure of despair, succeeded to power. Dumouriez, the new Minister for Foreign Affairs, who was not a genuine Brissotin, but an adventurer with ideas of foreign policy belonging to the old school, made a vain attempt to detach Prussia from the Austrian alliance. Then yielding himself to the prevailing militancy, he appeared in the Jacobin Club in a red cap and a general's uniform, and on April 20 the King, dull-eyed and helpless, read the declaration of war against the King of Hungary and Bohemia. "The people desires *The "Great" or Girondist Ministry (March 23). War, April 20, 1792.*

war," cried a Girondist orator. "Make haste to give way to its just and generous impatience. You are perhaps about to decree the liberty of the whole world." There were only seven dissentient voices, and in the streets the people acclaimed the declaration with delight.

And so, singing *Ça ira*, the French nation went to war, and plunged into a five months' story of defeat, humiliation, and invasion. Its army was disorganized, small, and disaffected. The old troops were mutinous, the volunteers insubordinate and inexperienced; two-thirds of the officers had deserted; there was no cohesion in the command or confidence between the officers and men. Rations were inadequate, fortresses in disrepair, for all Narbone's report, and the French plans were betrayed by the Queen. The three columns which invaded the Austrian Netherlands were defeated and routed. La Fayette was forced to retreat and Théobald Dillon was murdered by his own men. The French could not face the fire of the white-coats. The spectacle was ludicrous, humiliating, and vastly important.

Five months of defeat and humiliation, April–September.

The Austrians laughed. "We need not swords, but whips," they said. They despised their enemy and lingered, thinking the victory certain. They did not even attempt to seize the frontier fortresses, but looked back suspiciously at Catherine, who had invaded Poland on May 1, and waited for Prussia, who did not declare war until July 25. The combined troops were put under the command of the Prussian generalissimo Brunswick, who was persuaded by the *émigrés* to issue on July 28 a manifesto drawn up by one of them, threatening with "all the rigours of war" those "who should dare to defend themselves." Then after a short interval, during which his challenge had produced in Paris the disastrous attack on the monarchy of August 10, he invaded France on August 19 with 20,000 Austrians, 42,000 Prussians, and 8000 *émigrés*. It was to be merely a parade. On the 22nd Longwy fell, and on September 2 Verdun, the French commander having blown out his brains. Not a fortress stood between the Austro-Prussian troops and Paris, and they were only a fortnight's march away. But their rapid advance had been preceded by three months' inactivity which bore in France momentous results.

The invasion of France (August 19).

The five months from the declaration of war on April 20 to the capture of Verdun by the Prussians, covering in time the initial defeat, the suspended attack, and finally the invasion at the end of August, were at home the turning-point of the Revolution. They were a period of highly critical struggle between on the one side royalism and all that was allied with it, and on the other republicanism and all that it put into power. In April France was a

The five months in Paris. The turning-point of the Revolution.

constitutional monarchy, based on a middle class, with a Parliament which was still looked to for authority. By September the
France of April was hardly to be found; the last scaffolding of

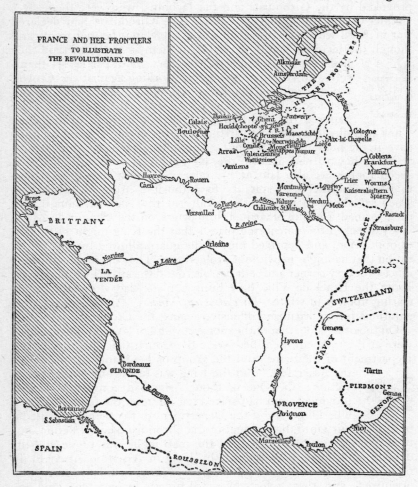

the monarchy had fallen, the black-breeched middle class was at
the mercy of the red-capped *sans-culottes*, the Parliament in bondage
to an insurrectionary Commune, the Girondists superseded by the
Jacobins, Brissot and Roland by Danton. Old problems had vanished
and new ones arisen, and between them were blood and panic and
inextinguishable memories.

The new situation was partly the psychological consequence of a hysteria of panic caused by war and defeat, which paralysed the legislature and maddened the populace. But it was partly deliberately provoked by the Girondists and the Jacobins, who were themselves victims of the prevailing emotions. The Girondists had declared war in April with the indirect object of attacking the monarchy, and though the Jacobins had disagreed with them as to the method they had been in accord as to the aim. Both parties set themselves to stimulate the forces working against the Crown, to undermine its defences, to provoke assaults upon it, and foster disorder which best served their cause. They flattered the mob, and gave servile homage to its panic. They had already opened to it the galleries of the Assembly; they gave it the honours of a sitting. The outcry against profiteers and traitors they turned against the King; bread riots and financial speculation were also laid at his door. They invited desperadoes to Paris and offered hospitality to enthusiasts from the provinces. They set about to weaken the loyalty of the National Guard, and they formed a camp of armed supporters on the Champ de Mars They attacked the non-juring priests that the King might be incited to opposition, and deprived him of the guard allowed by the constitution that he might be without protection. They opened recruiting-offices at every corner and sent patrols round the streets with fanfares. From the Hôtel de Ville they hung a black flag with four words staring upon it in white—*La Patrie en Danger*. All these were preparations for an organized offensive against the Crown.

The deliberate policy of the Girondists and Jacobins.

On the other side, that of the monarchy and of law and order, which were at the moment identified, were the Court, the Directory of the Department of the Seine, and the group of Feuillants in and out of the Assembly. But the King was feeble and without conviction; the Queen, though she had conviction, lacked judgment, and had staked her all upon the foreign armies. The Directory of the Department of the Seine instituted a belated inquiry into the conduct of the Girondist Mayor, Pétion, but its authority over the officials of the metropolis was vague and ill-defined, and, unsupported either by King or Assembly, it could do nothing to stem the growing disorder. The Feuillants were disorganized, and their efforts were ill-timed, inconsistent, and ineffectual. When the Girondists gave a *fête* to the Swiss convicts they counterposed with a *fête à la loi*, but coming after the other their celebration fell flat. La Fayette offered the only serious resistance to the Girondists and the Jacobins, and he might have succeeded but that the King, who could not bring himself to trust one who had done so much for the Revolution, betrayed him. It is part of the irony in

The failure of attempts to save the monarchy.

which the French Revolution abounds that the immediate career of
La Fayette, a true knight of the Revolution, should have come to an
end in attempts to save the Crown. The first occasion was after
June 20, when La Fayette returned to the capital with the avowed
intention of closing the Jacobin Club and of leading the monarchical
reaction which had shown signs of setting in. But he was forced to
return unsuccessful to his army. Again after August 10 he tried to
lead his troops to Paris in defence of the King, and it was after their
refusal to follow him that, twice defeated, he crossed the frontier and
gave himself up to the enemy. Thus inopportuneness, disorganization, accident, and the King's own distrust ruined all attempts to save
the monarchy.

Three outstanding events marked the progress of the policy of the
Jacobins and the Girondists—those of June 20, August 10, **Three**
and September 2–6.   **events.**

June 20 was a 'day' organized by the Girondists in revenge for
their dismissal from the ministry. That and the King's veto of the
decree against the non-juring priests served as excuse.
But though the mob broke into the Tuileries, swarmed **June 20.**
about the King all day, pressed him into an embrasure, forced him
to drink sour wine, and put a red cap upon his head, the object of
the revolt was not attained. The King's courage saved his head, nor
was he persuaded either to recall the ministers or withdraw the veto.
The riot dwindled into failure, but a beginning had been made, and
Jacobins and Girondists set themselves to instigate another attack,
which after some abortive outbreaks finally took place on August 10.

August 10 was the last day of the old monarchy and the crucial
date of the period. On July 28 the publication of the Brunswick
manifesto had given an invaluable fillip to the temper **August 10.**
of the people, and the arrival of a band of Marseillais in
Paris on the 30th, singing their now renowned hymn to the Revolution, had brought reinforcements to the assault.

The incidents of the day itself cannot be told here; only a scene
or two of the picture can be isolated—the heavy apprehensiveness of
the sleepless night while the tocsin sounded from the churches and
the public places; Mme Elizabeth commenting to the Queen on
the brilliant dawn as she rose that morning; the King, fearful and
hopeless, his "curls all flattened," reviewing the National **The taking**
Guard; the Queen's brave gesture of the pistols and her **of the**
husband's rejection of them; then the royal retreat to the **Tuileries**
Manège,[1] the Dauphin kicking up the fallen leaves in the **and the**
gardens through which they passed; the brave defence of **fall of the**
the Tuileries, the mistaken order, the massacre of the Swiss Guard, **monarchy.**

[1] The hall where the Assembly was sitting.

the rush of the mob into the Palace, the enfilading of the rooms, the smashing of the Queen's mirror, and the doing to death of all the royal servants.

Amid such scenes the old French monarchy came to an end, amid treachery and brutality, pathos and heroism, the helplessness of the King, the blood-lust of his people, and the fidelity of mercenary troops, while, contemptuous alike of King and people, a Corsican lieutenant stood looking on.

And while the King, huddled with his family, sat eating a roast chicken in a stenographer's box, the Assembly debated upon his fate. More than 450 members out of 750 stayed away, the rest, "under the orders of the galleries," unwilling to vote his deposition and afraid not to do so, shifted the problem on to others' shoulders. They 'suspended' him from his functions, handed over his person to the new power that had arisen—the insurrectionary Commune of Paris— and summoned a National Convention to decide on his deposition.

For more than the monarchy fell on August 10. The Legislative Assembly, the executive, the Girondists, the middle class, the Revolu-

The triumph of the Jacobins and of the people.
tion itself, received on that day a new master, the People, and with the People the Jacobins, who worked through it and by it. During the preceding months the rift between the Jacobins and the Girondists had widened. The former had the better organization in the club which they commanded, the keener convictions, and above all they had in Danton the only practical statesman of the day at their head. The Girondists were humane enough to be somewhat afraid of the rule of pikes, and were at heart willing even to make terms with the King if he would have put them into power. But the King scorned their approaches as he had scorned those of so many who had sought to save him, and the Girondists laboured on after the Jacobins, endeavouring not to be outdone by them in professions of zeal. But though they did not finally fall until June 1793 they were in fact beaten on August 10, 1792. The real victory of that day was with the Jacobins. They forced the Girondists to share the ministry with them; they secured the persons of the King and his family. Above all, they captured the municipality of Paris, turning out by a *coup d'état* the legal Girondist Council, and setting up in its place an insurrectionary Government, to be known in history as "the Commune." Jacobinism, however much in practice the dominance of a minority, stood in theory for direct democracy, for the 'People in revolution' as the phrase went. "When the People puts itself in a state of insurrection it withdraws all powers and takes them to itself." It was in that theory that the Commune became master of Paris, of the Assembly, of France and the Revolution. And the great figure which repre-

sented this triumph was Danton, the Mirabeau of the People. "I came in," he said himself, "through the breach in the Tuileries."

August 10 had its effect upon the People itself and led to the third set of events in early September. Nine days after the fall of the monarchy the Prussians and Austrians invaded France, and within a fortnight they had taken every fortress between them and Paris. Roland and Brissot in the ministry seemed paralysed, pro- The posed to leave Paris, and chose this mistaken moment for massacres the humane acquittal of Montmorin, the 'traitor.' The of Septem- people were in a panic, volunteers poured in. Treason ber 1792. was the cry of the day, treason in the Court, treason in every house. Danton ordered house to house visits "to look for arms," and the prisons were soon filled with aristocrats and suspects, friends of the King, friends of the enemy, priests and relatives of émigré nobles and those who had not approved of the incidents of August 10. And while the brave recruits were sent to the front, should traitors remain behind immune? The people had learnt its strength on August 10, the spirit of lynching had gripped them, and "no human power," said Danton, "could have stopped them." On September 2 Verdun fell. That day a band of murderers—not more than 150 strong, but they had the people behind them—went from prison to prison, dragged out the inmates, mocked them by a form of trial, and then "executed Justice" upon them. Altogether about 1600 were murdered.

Danton, who alone could have saved them, looked on, said the prisoners could "save themselves," talked later of the "just anger of the People." There is evidence that with Marat he instigated the murders, and even tried to induce the provinces to follow the ex- ample of Paris. In any case they were an incident of his political tactics. The power of the people was one of his weapons in the defence of France. It was useful too at home as well as against the enemy, for during those days of September the elections to the Convention were taking place, not on the limited suffrage of 1791, but on a fresh basis of universal manhood suffrage.

III. THE CONVENTION (SEPTEMBER 1792–OCTOBER 1795)

With the dissolution of the Legislative Assembly the Revolution in one sense came to an end, as a battle with the *ancien régime*, as a struggle for liberty. A series of progressive, if spasmodic, attacks A change upon the old order had been made; the nobility had been in the scattered, the Church humiliated, the administration character dispersed, the monarchy destroyed. Democracy had Revolution. triumphed in destruction, but it had at the same time brought the very existence of the State into mortal peril. The safety and integrity of France was already assailed by foreign enemies; it was to be further threatened by civil war. The Republic was endangered in the hour of its birth.

A new need therefore arose, that of preserving the State and the Republic, and of building up another power to replace that which had been destroyed. From September 1792 the course of the Revolution was relentlessly determined by that urgent practical impulse which, taking precedence of all others, drove theory aside, and liberty, and Salus populi mercy, and humanity itself, until a new executive and a suprema lex. national defence had been organized. The *ancien régime* was destroyed in the name of the rights of man; in the name of the public safety the new State was consolidated out of its ruins, and for a time a despotism framed far greater than the one it had superseded.

For it is natural that an edifice built in sight of the enemy should bear peculiar features; that it should give security against the invader rather than liberty to the inmate, especially where hostility without was reinforced by treason within. There grew up, therefore, on the foundations of the public safety one of the greatest tyrannies of history; democracy turned dictator and then persecutor, and the Republic of '92 became the Terror of '93 and '94.

The building up of a national defence demanded by the exigencies of war was therefore the first motive in the complicated history of the years 1792–95. Entangled with it, running sometimes across it and sometimes side by side, was another, the struggle between the factions to win control of the new power and the new machinery which was being created. Thus, while on the one hand there was established an unparalleled despotism over the nation, there existed on the other a continuous struggle for supremacy among the possessors of authority.

The Convention met on September 20, 1792, and voted the next day the deposition of the King. It was a foregone conclusion. But Valmy on the day of the assembling there occurred behind the (September defiles of the Argonnes, round about the mill of Valmy, a 20, 1792). small engagement, with unexpected result, between the French and Prussian troops. The affair was extremely slight, a mere cannonade in the drizzling rain, but the soldiers of the Republic for the first time stood firm to the enemy's fire, and the incredible thing happened. The advance of the enemy was checked. "On that day," says Goethe, who was present, "we entered upon a new The enemy world." France, which had seemed on the verge of is turned. national disaster, was saved. Danton, ignoring the lofty arrogance which was aroused in the Convention, negotiated feverishly for a retirement, and at the end of September the Prussians, after a slow retreat, crossed the frontier out of France. They had lost as good a chance as they were to have for twenty years; but the King

of Prussia was half-hearted, his general, Brunswick, afraid of losing
his reputation, and the troops had dysentery. The King of Prussia was
jealous of Austria, concerned about Russian ambitions in Poland, not
very friendly to the *émigrés*, and inclined to suspect that he was pulling
other people's chestnuts out of the fire. For Louis XVI the departure of the Prussians was as ill-timed as their invasion had been. One
had precipitated his downfall, the other was to hasten his death.

The check of Valmy was only a prelude to a series of revolutionary
successes which were to prove, nevertheless, as insecure as they were
rapid. The Sardinian possessions of Savoy and Nice were Two months
occupied without a blow by Montesquiou, who was hailed of victory.
as a liberator. On the invitation of the Rhenish patriots Custine
made a dash into Germany and seized Spires, Worms, and Mainz,
and held Frankfurt to ransom. The Convention even threatened
Turin, Genoa, and the "Pope of Rome," and in November Dumouriez
began to advance upon Belgium. On the 6th, at Jemappes, he won
the first real victory of the Republic. The next day Mons was entered
amid the welcome of the people, and afterward Brussels. Dumouriez
established his headquarters at Liége; Antwerp admitted his lieutenant, Miranda, and the Austrian Netherlands lay at the feet of the
French.

Upon France the effect of the victories was as an intoxication,
and republican faith and national ambitions grew alike exultant.
The boldest territorialism of the fallen Bourbons was revived and
proclaimed side by side with the aggressive altruism of the new
democracy. On the one hand the Republic removed the restrictions
upon the trade of the river Scheldt and offered armed help to the
struggling democracies of Europe—provided they paid her expenses;
on the other she would have for herself her natural frontiers of the
Rhine, the Alps, and the Pyrenees. She therefore annexed The
Nice, Savoy, and Belgium. The Jacobins, strong in the November
Gallic assertiveness which, whether under monarchy or decrees.
republic, appears from time to time in the history of France, flaunted
triumphs and decrees in the face of Europe. At last, as a superlative
gesture, they flung to the anointed monarchs of the old world the
head of its most sacred king. On January 21, 1793, Louis Capet,
martyr to an outworn faith and his own ineffectual goodwill, was
guillotined in the Place Louis-Quinze. It was the will of the Jacobins.
The Girondists could not prevent it; the Convention dared not. "It
required more courage," wrote a deputy, "to absolve than
to condemn." If Louis XVI is not so heroic a figure as The King's
Charles I, he died with a kingly courage, protesting his death
innocence and trusting that his death would consolidate the (January 21,
happiness of his people. They beat up the drums to drown his voice, 1793).

F

and afterward only a few shouts of "Long live the nation" broke the deep disquietude which fell upon the crowd. "We have broken up the roads behind us," cried a revolutionary. The King's death was a final act from whose consequences there was no release, no looking back, only an incessant going forward until a power arose—in Napoleon—strong enough to protect the nation from reprisals.

The execution of Louis XVI precipitated the European war which other causes had already brought within sight. Every state felt its own security threatened by the proclamations and victories of France, which stimulated its own malcontents. England, whose interest has always lain in the preservation of the independence of the small states opposite the Kentish coast, saw her commercial supremacy threatened by the opening of the Scheldt and the annexation of Belgium. Holland was in immediate danger. French troops were at her door. The doctrine of the natural frontiers, by pushing the French boundary up to the Rhine, would cut her territory in two. Her invasion was openly discussed in the Convention, and on January 29 definitely ordered. By the end of March, therefore, France found herself at war with the greater part of Europe, with Austria and Prussia, England and Holland, Spain and Sardinia, Portugal, Naples, Tuscany, and the states of the Empire. Catherine II of Russia offered the hospitality of St Petersburg to the late King's brother, the Comte d'Artois, and, like Elizabeth of England after the massacre of St Bartholomew, she put her Court into mourning, but she did not go to war. The war in the West gave her too good an opportunity of realizing her ambitions in Eastern Europe, and two days after the death of the King, whom she pretended to mourn, she arranged with Prussia the second partition of Poland. Even America, whose own revolt had been so powerful an example to France, was shocked by the King's execution. Only Switzerland was friendly.

The Convention did not shrink from war. Dumouriez, who in the crisis of '92 had advocated a similar bold offensive, opened the campaign by the invasion of Holland. He was, however, beaten back before Maestricht, and then recalled by the Convention to defend the Austrian Netherlands. But Dumouriez had ambitions of his own, and, perhaps proposing to himself the *rôle* of a second Monk, had already resolved to overthrow the regicide Government of Paris. He determined upon a pitched battle with the Austrians that he might be crowned with victory before he marched upon Paris. It was the policy of a bold adventurer such as Dumouriez was. He staked everything and lost. He was defeated at Neerwinden on March 21. For France the issue of the battle meant the recovery of Belgium by the Austrians. For Dumouriez, his plans revealed and his prestige destroyed, it meant disgrace. Commissioners were sent to arrest him. He seized them and handed them over to the Austrians as hostages for the life of Marie-Antoinette. Then, having failed to induce his army to follow him, he gave himself up to the enemy. With him there crossed over one who was to be heard of again—Louis-Philippe, Prince Égalité, son of that Philippe Égalité, Duc d'Orléans, who as a member of the Convention, out of a care, which proved vain, for his own safety, had just voted for the death of his cousin, Louis XVI. invasion (March– July 1793).

The loss of Belgium was followed by the invasion of France. The English besieged Dunkirk. The Austrians, advancing slowly, took Condé and Valenciennes in July and threatened Lille. Elsewhere too France suffered defeat and invasion. Prussian and Imperial troops had won back Frankfurt and Mainz, and were on the point of entering Alsace. In the South the Spaniards had crossed the Pyrenees, conquered Roussillon, and forced the Bidassoa.

In the meantime a civil war of a spasmodic nature, but of considerable proportions, had broken out in France. In the West, in Brittany and La Vendée, both the Catholic Church and the old nobility—most of whom, too poor to go to Court, had lived on their own estates—had a greater hold upon the people than in any other part of France. The King too was honoured there. When, therefore, the decree of February was published, by which conscripts for the Republican armies were to be raised by lot among them, the peasants rose in revolt, resolving that if they had to fight it should be against and not on behalf of the regicides. The first outbreak was easily suppressed. The second, which occurred after Easter, was more serious. It received the adherence of many of the gentry, and was led by some men of interesting and ardent personality. It proclaimed Louis XVII king, and at one time sought—in vain—the help of England. It resisted the two armies of Brest and La Rochelle created to put it down, and defeated Westermann and his troops in July. Against heavy odds it held out until the autumn, and it was not until regular soldiers, released by the fall of Mainz, were dispatched against them that the rebels, their spirit and strength broken by many vicissitudes, were beaten down in September. Civil war. La Vendée (March– September 1793).

Contemporary with the later stages of the Vendéan rising, though distinct from it, was a second rebellious movement. This was composed of a number of entirely civic revolts which broke out in many towns in all parts of France. It came later in the year, and was aimed against the tyranny of the Jacobins and of the Commune of Paris and accentuated by the overthrow of the Girondists in the *coup d'état* of June 2. It was therefore a separatist or federalist movement, but no town received any help The revolt of the cities (June– December 1793).

from the peasants of its own neighbourhood or established any concerted military action with any other city. Many of the Girondists who fled from Paris in June joined the insurgents, especially at Caen and Bordeaux; but they proved themselves poor men of action and indifferent leaders. It was easy, therefore, for the Jacobins to suppress the disconnected and ill-organized insurrections one by one. Marseilles, weakened by Jacobin sympathies within the city, surrendered at the end of August; Bordeaux and Lyons were taken during October. Toulon, which had admitted an English garrison, was only recovered in December by the aid of a young Captain Buonaparte. In all these towns severe reprisals were taken by the Jacobins. Local 'Terrors' were set up all over France, and Lyons, condemned for its desperate resistance to change its name to Commune Affranchi, was struck off the Revolutionary roll of French towns.

At Caen, however, to which the presence of seventeen fugitive Girondists gave a greater importance, the Jacobin Commissioner, Robert Lindet, behaved with clemency. His conciliatory policy did much to cause the failure of the movement, and after the publication of the new Constitution of 1793, which contained such democratic devices as annual legislatures, manhood suffrage, and a referendum, the rebellion dwindled away. Its only important incident was the murder of Marat in Paris by Charlotte Corday, a young Norman girl.

This revolt was the last tragic stage in the history of the Girondists. All through the autumn of '92 they had lost ground to the Jacobins. They had been out-voted on the question of the annexation of Belgium in November; they had opposed step by step the trial and execution of the King in January '93. They had been defeated on economic matters and on the question of conscription; they had been excluded from the Committee of Public Safety in April, for after the desertion of Dumouriez, their general, their last prop was removed. In June they were turned out of the Convention by a popular rising. Some were imprisoned, to be guillotined the following October. Others, already mentioned, fled to the provinces and stirred up civil war.

The end of the Girondists.

It was a last unwise step in a consistently inexpedient policy. In France's great need, in the crisis in the history of their own party, they had never been able to put forward a vigorous and effective programme. They had remained hidebound by their theories of individual liberty and local autonomy. To avert the growing danger they offered drafts of a new constitution and eloquent phrases. They expended their energies in violent invective, in denunciation of the Jacobins, in outcries against Paris. "Let Paris be reduced to her eighty-third share of influence," they demanded at one time. At another they threatened that the capital should be reduced to ashes

so that "posterity shall ask on which side of the Seine she stood."
Not even when Danton sought a reconciliation with them could they
forgo their hatred. "You know not how to forgive!" cried Danton.
It was their undoing, and when, with the Austrians in their country,
they took up arms against the Jacobins they committed in the eyes
of Frenchmen the unforgivable sin. But they deserved a better fate,
for all their weakness and blindness, their vacillation and theoretical
rigidity.

So the brilliant company of unpractical idealists went out of
history, leaving imperishable memories of tragedy and pathos—of
twenty men on a Paris scaffold chanting the *Marseillaise* until, one
by one, death stilled their voices—of Vergniaud scorning the guillotine prepared for him by his own countrymen—of Mme Roland's
cry, "Oh, Liberty, what crimes are committed in thy name!"—of
the band of fugitives hunted down through the months from one
refuge to another, until one by one they succumbed to capture or
despair—of a wood near the Garonne where the dogs quarrelled over
the bodies of Buzot, the lover of Mme Roland, and Pétion, whom
Paris once adored as Christ.

Thus during the greater part of 1793 the plight of France was
considerably worse than it had been in 1792. The invasion of Holland had failed; Belgium and the Rhine conquests were lost. France
was invaded by enemies with whom the idea of partition was rapidly
replacing that of the restoration of the Bourbons. Civil war was
draining her strength and employing her armies, and her most
renowned general had deserted to the enemy.

The Jacobins took every advantage of France's desperate need and
of the feebleness of the Girondists. They were a party of action,
essentially practical and fortunate in that their own interests were
identifiable with an ardent patriotism. They had become converts
to the war, for they saw that in a "state of siege" their own The policy
aims could best be realized together with the welfare of the of the
country. Thus while they strove to strengthen the unity Jacobins.
of France, build up a new executive and organize an effective defence
against the enemy, they were working also to increase their own
power and to secure themselves a following. They embarked upon
a vigorous campaign against the foreign enemy, against the Girondist
and the internal rebel, against the non-juring priest and the *émigré*
noble. They took in hand the conscripting of new armies to supple-
ment the volunteers of '91 and '92. They bought popularity by
adopting the economic programme of the streets; they taxed the
rich, guaranteed the right to work, which meant in practice the right
to receive wages, fixed a maximum price for bread, and regulated
industry and trading in the interests of the people. They undertook

the feeding of Paris. They strengthened their own party there by emphasizing the power of the capital, thus at the same time seeking to cement the unity of France. "Paris is the centre of light. Paris has made the Revolution, and when it shall perish there will no longer be a revolution." That was Danton's answer to the threats of the Girondists. Yet it would be erroneous to regard Jacobinism as a policy of deliberate self-seeking. Jacobinism was the fruit neither of ideology nor of self-interest, but "an instinctive reaction of a half-practical, half-fanatical type of mind to special circumstances, the circumstances of war." [1]

Out of that reaction the Jacobins built up the Committee of Public Safety, the first real executive to govern France since the fall of the monarchy. It was developed by slow degrees during the first half of 1793, and new powers were added as the national dangers increased. On March 9 a Revolutionary Tribunal was set up, and on the 21st Revolutionary Committees with executive powers were established in every commune. After the battle of Neerwinden the first Committee of Public Safety was formed of twenty-five members, some of whom were Girondists, but after Dumouriez's desertion on April 5 the Girondists were turned out of the Committee, which was reduced to nine.

The Committee of Public Safety.

Revised in April (Danton)

Thus by April the machinery was completed which was in Danton's words to establish "that momentary despotism of liberty," which was "indispensable to crush the despotism of kings." But the policy of terror which accompanied it was not fully enforced until July, when Robespierre reconstructed the Committee, excluded Danton from it, and a little later added himself to it. Danton was the greatest statesman since Mirabeau, but he was not able nor industrious nor persistent enough to keep in his hands the threads of power. A great crisis called forth in him an ardent energy, and he seemed the embodiment of audacity and courage. On such occasions he showed neither hesitation nor scruple in achieving his aim or sweeping aside his enemy. But when the crisis was past the impulsive energy faded, and he relapsed into a laziness and lethargy fatal to his own supremacy. Never vindictive, he failed to guard himself against his enemies, ceased to be ambitious, grew "sick of men." So he was first superseded in the Committee in July 1793, and then put to death in April 1794, by Robespierre, whom he despised, who, in his opinion, had not "wits enough to cook an egg." The "sea-green incorruptible" [2] was a man of unsleeping ambition, cautious and calculating, a man of virtue, impervious to bribes, a hater of women, a narrow-minded

and again in July (Robespierre).

Danton.

Maximilien Robespierre.

[1] G. Elton, *The Revolutionary Idea in France, 1789-1871.*   [2] Carlyle.

egoist, an unimaginative fanatic, a rigid, inhuman theorist, who sent friend or foe impartially to the guillotine for the sake of his mission. From the days of the Constituent Assembly this apostle of Rousseau had kept his name before the people and slowly worked up his power until he became ruler of the Committee of Public Safety, dictator of France, and, after June 1794, when he set up the worship of the Supreme Being, arch-priest of her new religion. This unrivalled supremacy, won by faith and caution, he kept only by a policy of increasing terrorism. From July 1793 to July 1794 he maintained his power by violence and fear, alike in the provinces and in Paris. The toll of victims was long. Throughout the country from east to west, from Nantes to Lyons, the Government's agents were urged on to their work, and eighteen hundred persons were shot in the quarries of Gigandet and the fields of Mauve, another eighteen hundred thrown into the Loire; Le Bon did "good butchery" at Arras, Fréron in Provence, Fouché at Lyons. In Paris "heads fell like slates," over 2600 of them, strangely mingled in a common fate. Mme Roland, Mme du Barry, Mme Elizabeth, Charlotte Corday, and Marie-Antoinette; the followers of Hébert, because they were atheists and established the worship of Reason; [1] Danton, Camille Desmoulins, and Fabre d'Eglantine, because they pleaded for indulgence at home and peace abroad and were not "true patriots"; Girondists and Feuillants; Malesherbes, who had pleaded for the King's life, and Philippe Égalité, who had voted for his death; good men of '89, Bailly and Barnave, the generals Westermann and Custine, André Chénier the poet, Lavoisier the chemist, Royalists and Republicans, atheists and Roman Catholics, depravers of morals and breakers of economic laws, deputies and unsuccessful generals, farmers, speculators, and shopkeepers—all suffered alike in this joint reign of Virtue and Terror. "To be safe you must kill all," Hébert himself had said. Trials grew shorter and executions more numerous, from one every two days to 65 a month, then 116; from 155 to 381, and after the law of suspects was passed, by which men were to be arrested on suspicion, 1366 were put to death in forty-seven days. At last the Convention, led by members of the Committee who were themselves doomed, rose up against Robespierre in July 1794, and with ninety-two of his followers he was guillotined. In the *mêlée* he had been shot in the jaw, perhaps by his own hand, but they hurried him to the scaffold, fearful of the man who had himself sent so many there before him; the same man who in his early manhood as a criminal

The Terror (July 1793–July 1794).

---

[1] The worship of Reason was inaugurated in Notre-Dame in November 1793. In the same mood of ' reason,' during which Hébert's influence was supreme, a new Revolutionary calendar was adopted to date from the proclamation of the Republic, September 21, 1792. The Christian significance of the old calendar was destroyed.

judge at Arras had resigned his post rather than pass a sentence of
The end of the Terror. death. He wore the same sky-blue coat in which he had presided over the Festival of the Supreme Being. With Robespierre's fall the Jacobin organization was destroyed and the Terror came to an end.

But it must not be forgotten that nine other members of the Committee of Public Safety must share with Robespierre the praise and some of the blame of what was done during the Terror. It was **The work of the Committee of Public Safety.** Saint-Just who managed the police, who opened correspondence and organized the spy system. Hérault de Séchelles was responsible for diplomacy, Saint-André for the navy, and Carnot, the "organizer of victory," for the "fourteen armies of the Republic." For all business was centralized in the Committee and all machinery directed by it. It had ample secret service funds; it controlled the Convention; it planned campaigns, it appointed generals; it governed the provinces and chose the civil officials; it conscripted soldiers; it regulated commerce and the price of bread; it even had a department for education, religion, festivals, and fine arts. By a tireless activity it established over France an absolute dictatorship.

Napoleon admitted that he owed to the Committee of Public Safety a great debt, for out of its rule, or the activity of Samson the executioner, emerged unity and victory. The rebellion at home was **Unity and victory.** suppressed, the foreign enemy expelled, and a course of conquest resumed. The allies, hampered by a diversity of aims, by mutual jealousies, and distracted by the Polish Question, were already beaten back by the end of 1793, the English at Dunkirk and Toulon, the Austrians at Wattignies, the Prussians at Weissenburg, while Kellermann occupied Savoy. Only in the Pyrenees did the French experience failure.

In 1794 the victories were continued. The battle of Fleurus put Belgium into French hands; Kaiserslautern gave them the Rhine. Except for the naval defeat of June 1 at the hands of Great Britain, the French were universally successful. In January 1795 Holland was overrun, and in April Prussia and Spain made peace at Basel. Thus before the Convention was dissolved the missionary spirit of the Republic and the magnificent organization of the Committee of Public Safety had broken up the First Coalition.

After the fall of Robespierre and the end of the Terror the Centre party in the Convention asserted itself. The Commune of Paris, the Jacobin Club, the Revolutionary Tribunal, and the Committee of Public Safety were suppressed. The democratic constitution of 1793, which had lain in a box since its publication, was annulled, and a new constitution, embodying a reaction against sansculottism and a return to a property qualification, was imposed upon France.   It set up an executive and a twofold legislature which for four years guided the country—or rather held the reins while the The country and a young, ambitious artillery officer guided them- Directory. selves.   It achieved the greatest measure of stability yet attained by any revolutionary Government, not so much because of its strength as because the forces that were to overthrow it were not yet collected, because—with the exception of the young artillery officer—the whole nation, people and Government alike, seemed to be inhabited by a spirit of uncertainty, of indecision, almost as of expectation; and in retrospect it is impossible to see the years 1795–99 except as an interim period between the Revolution and the rise of Napoleon.

CHAPTER IV

NAPOLEON

I. "To Destiny" (1769-99)

"I HAVE a presentiment that this little island will some day astonish Europe," wrote Rousseau in 1762, as he contemplated the struggles of Corsica for independence. Seven years later, on August 15, 1769,

Origin. there was born the boy Napolione Buonaparte, who was to justify the prediction and raise to immortality the island story which but for him would have been buried in the obscurity of historical minutiæ. His inheritance was a patrician name, a foreign ancestry from the land of Machiavelli and, as he sometimes liked to remember, of Julius Cæsar, the poetic, imaginative versatility of his father, Carlo Buonaparte, the pride, Amazonian courage, and calculating thrift of his mother, Letizia. His upbringing amid penury and hardship and the associations of recent and unsuccessful national and family struggles was in the spirit of the rocks and rugged mountains of his birthplace, of its independence and insular self-sufficiency, its vendettas, its clannishness, its close family life. His education, which he received free at the École Militaire of Brienne, was the fruit of Corsica's failure and of the submission of his father to France and the prize of an alleged title of nobility. So, ironically, were the foundations of his career laid at the expense of the King of France and based on the privileges of birth.

At school the young Napoleon was marked by a preternatural seriousness, by a precocious sense of responsibility toward his work

School. and his family, by a capacity for endurance, by moodiness, reserve, and occasional outbreaks of temper, by a growing contempt for his fellows, who despised his poverty and laughed at his foreign accent and name. "The youngster is made of granite, but there is a volcano inside," said one of his masters.

As a sub-lieutenant at Valence, forced to economize in food and clothes and hating "the multicoloured young French popinjays" who

Youth. were his brother officers, he talked with burghers of the ideas of Voltaire and Montesquieu and the theories of Rousseau and Raynal; in his *café* lodgings, to the click of the billiard-balls in the next room, he read history and mathematics, Plutarch and Plato; he studied the campaigns of Frederick the Great and the constitutions of England, Switzerland, Sparta, Egypt, and Turkey; he drew up plans for the fortification of Corsica; he even drafted a novel on the island theme; he composed essays on such subjects as monarchical authority, human inequality, and suicide. Moods of despair induced by his own or his country's misfortunes, or by the slowness of military promotion, alternated with heroic dreams of personal ambition or Corsican independence. Always Corsica, and mingled with Corsica his family, were in his mind, and the Revolution, when it dawned in France, came to him as a dazzling gleam across the night of his country's servitude, as a promise of that liberation which might be snatched for Corsica from the disputes of the hated foreigner.

From 1789 to 1793 Lieutenant Buonaparte's best efforts and most of his time—for presuming on the disorganization of the French army he continually outstayed his leave—were spent in Corsica. Corsica. In some features the course of the French Revolution was reproduced in miniature in the island. At first, as a revolutionary, Napoleon was at war with the French monarchical Governor. Then when Corsica had been granted the full political rights of a French department by the National Assembly, when Paoli the national leader had returned with the survivors of his band of exiles, Napoleon found himself fighting as a Frenchman and a Jacobin against his former hero, who had espoused the Moderate cause, and was on the Failure and point of admitting English help. He was, moreover, de- flight. feated, outlawed, and banished by his own compatriots, and in June 1793 he fled with his family under French protection to France, thus seeking refuge as an exile from his native land in the country which he had hated most of his life as the soil of the tyrant foreigner.

While his family sheltered on the fourth floor of the confiscated home of a guillotined nobleman of Marseilles, and applied as "persecuted patriots" for rations from the Commandant, Napoleon lived and moved about with his regiment. In the struggle which was proceeding between the Girondists and the Jacobins Napoleon announced his adherence to the Jacobin side in a pamphlet entitled *Le Souper de Beaucaire*, and when in August 1793 Toulon, one of the rebellious cities, admitted an English garrison, Buonaparte was appointed to the command of the artillery in the French army that went to its recapture. By a brilliant disposition of guns on the tongue Toulon. of land which divides Toulon into twin harbours he drove the English from the town in December. It was his first victory, the presage of his future. He was given the rank of brigadier-general and sent on a commission to examine the fortifications of the coast from Toulon to Nice. Men began to feel his power; two young officers, Marmont and Junot, who were to follow him through most of his career, attached themselves to his fortunes; his 'star,' of which he spoke so often, had begun to rise in the heavens.

In less than a year, however, he was involved in the fall of Robespierre, and he spent his twenty-fifth birthday in the prison of Fort **Prison.** Carré, near Nice, counting the catastrophes which dogged his career. But as he had done nothing to compromise himself he was speedily liberated.

Napoleon's genius had hitherto but flashed for a brief and brilliant moment before the mirror of France. October of 1795, or, in Revo-**The coup d'état of Vendémiaire (October 5, 1795).** lutionary parlance, Vendémiaire III, introduced the identification of his personal career with the national fortunes which was to last for twenty years. It is not without significance that he should have entered history as "General Vendémiaire" with his guns trained on the people. As a spectator of the attack on the Tuileries in August 1792, Napoleon's soldierly instincts had already been shocked by the feeble resistance offered to the mob. Three years later, when the tottering and panic-stricken Convention [1] sought his protection against a threatened attack of the Royalists and Parisians, neither his sense of discipline and orderly government nor his will to power could resist the appeal. After half an hour's deliberation he accepted, and he was strong enough to stipulate that he should be absolutely free from supervision.

And so for the first time for seven years the Parisian mob was met by an organized opposition. The approaches to the Tuileries were covered by forty big guns under Murat, who that day was to link his name with that of Buonaparte. Even the lawyers of the Convention were supplied with weapons. In two hours the streets were cleared, the Convention was saved, and the power of the mob was buried with the four hundred corpses which were the result of the morning's conflict. The successful demonstration of military force may be said to have put an end to the Revolution, though it preserved the regicide republic and the "career open to talent." The "whiff of grape-shot" which dispersed the rudiments of a restoration of royalism cleared the ground for the dictatorship of genius.

Napoleon was rewarded with the command of the Army of the Interior, but from the days of '94 his heart had been set upon the Army of Italy. Besides, political favour was uncertain and Paris not the safest of residences. The Directors who were then ruling France **The Italian command.** were also for their part by no means disinclined to remove from the centre of influence a dangerous young man who had already proved his ambition, his ability, and his independence. Carnot was genuinely impressed by his military power, and the

[1] The Convention dissolved itself on October 26, 1795, after the appointment of the first Directors.

others were persuaded that the Army of Italy, which had lingered for three years, inactive, half starved, wasted by disease, on the slopes of the Alps, would swamp his energies and divert his ambitions. When therefore the Commander-in-Chief of the Italian army, to whom Napoleon's own plan of campaign had been sent, suggested that the "imbecile" who drafted it should try his own hand at executing it the Directors took him at his word and replaced him by Napoleon.

Two days before Napoleon set out for the Army of Italy he married a wife. Josephine Beauharnais was by birth and previous marriage of noble rank. Her husband, the Vicomte de Beauharnais, an early revolutionary, and President of the National Assembly Josephine. at the time of the King's flight in 1791, had been subsequently guillotined. His wife had been saved only by the fall of Robespierre, and the same day in 1794 which saw the incarceration of Napoleon saw also the liberation of Josephine. She was poor and the mother of two children, Eugène and Hortense, and her reputation was not of the highest, but Napoleon rapidly fell under the spell of her grace and elegant distinction, of the languorous softness of her Creole nature, of her tact and kindliness. Her rank flattered him, her social charm would strengthen his position, and the vehement ardour of his volcanic nature was aroused. On her side there was admiration of his genius, the susceptibility and complaisance of a weak nature before his compelling force, some calculation, wonder at his self-confidence —or was it only "immeasurable conceit"?—as well as apprehension of an affection "so stormy that it bordered on madness." A different woman, or a faithful return of his devotion, might possibly have altered the course of his life and the scale of his values, but the imaginative yearning which coloured his devotion toward her, perhaps in any case doomed by its own insatiableness to disappointment, could in no wise find fulfilment in what at that stage was all she had to offer him—skill in the arts of a facile amorousness. How far Josephine's influence with the Director Barras secured for Napoleon the Italian command lies on the doubtful borderland between scandal and history. In point of time the marriage and the Italian command practically synchronized at the beginning of March 1796, and the legend "To Destiny" which was engraved in fateful superstition inside the wedding-ring came to be the verdict of history.

There was a lyrical quality about the first Italian campaign which was not present in the same degree in any subsequent one. The first For the first time the young general of twenty-seven, romp- Italian ing from victory to victory, snatched, as at Arcola, from the campaign very jaws of defeat, was to show the stuff of which he was 1796–October made. For the first time the Corsican was to sleep in the ber 1797). palace of kings, negotiate with foreign potentates, and declare his will to the Pope. For the first time, in the vigour of youthful health and eagerness and in the inspiration of a passion which had not yet found disillusionment, he was to prove his strategical skill, his perfect mastery of the comparatively new science of artillery, and to display that boundless activity which was the amazement and undoing of his opponents. How could half a dozen old gentlemen, some of whom were in addition deaf or gouty or royal, hampered by a rigid Imperial Council, cope with the hardy Corsican who never allowed himself to be impeded by instructions from home, who on the third day of his arrival "sent a hundred and ten workmen to make a road, suppressed a mutiny in a brigade, quartered two artillery divisions, gave orders in a case of horse-stealing, and answers to the requests of two generals concerning commands, an order to a general to call up the National Guard of Antibes, another order to find the most efficient officer in the mutinous brigade, addressed the general staff, reviewed the troops and gave the orders of the day"? Could they match themselves with a general who side by side with a military campaign conducted also an epistolary one to the Directors at home and then had energy to write a love-letter from every halting-place?

Here too Buonaparte revealed his power over men, of inspiration, of discipline, his ability to touch the emotions. "I will lead you into the most fertile plains of the world. . . . There you will reap honour and glory and wealth." He who fulfilled that promise turned cabin-boys into generals, a mutinous, tatterdemalion army into regiments of heroes, and made a name as the "little corporal" of Lodi which men were to follow for two decades.

He discovered the magic of phrases and the power of ideas. He who could rouse with a battle-cry and send home a report that might be the envy of a newspaper correspondent, could with 'liberty' and 'friendship' and heroic names upon his lips make a conquered people hail him as deliverer. He received his initiation into affairs of high international policy, he disclosed his capacities for statesmanship, his real understanding of the Italian situation—for all that he dropped the *u* in 'Buonaparte' that he might be more the Frenchman—and in the partition of Venice he made his first important essay in political realism.

He learnt, too, to distribute bribes and threats in the governing of men, to mingle bluff, ingenuousness, and peremptoriness in the practice of diplomacy, and how effective was the gesture, "At two o'clock my troops have orders to attack!"

In all directions there was the dawning of vast ambitions, the awakening of great powers, of the sense of immense possibilities, of the growing consciousness that he had begun to live in the eye of history. As yet "my record will not occupy more than half a page," but "I feel that deeds await me of which the present generation has no inkling."

On March 27, 1796, Napoleon took over the Italian army at Nice. Within a month he had led his army round the Alps into Piedmont through the gap where the Alps and the Apennines converge, driven

NAPOLEON'S ITALIAN CAMPAIGNS

the Austrians, who held one road, across the Po, defeated the Sardinians, who held the other, in a series of skirmishes and forced them to a truce at Cherasco on April 28. He showed prudence in the terms—recognition by Sardinia of the French annexation of Savoy and Nice in 1792, three fortresses and the control of the roads through Piedmont—as he had shown caution in not marching upon Turin, the Sardinian capital. After the truce he advanced eastward against the Austrians; on May 10 he forced the bridge of Lodi on the Adda River, and on the 15th he entered Milan in triumph like a Roman general. He was welcomed as a liberator with enthusiasm and flowers; he gave the Milanese freedom from Austrian domination; **Milan.** he set up councils and a National Guard; he patronized their artists and men of letters. A few days later he imposed a levy of twenty million francs, and dispatched wagons of their works of art and precious manuscripts to France.

Napoleon next advanced to the siege of Mantua, whither the Austrians had retired. Four attempts were made to relieve it, all of which were repulsed by the French—the first in August at Castiglione, the second a month later at Bassano, the third in November, **Mantua.** in the hardly won battle of Arcola, in which Napoleon himself was saved only by the heroism of his adjutant Muiron, who, covering the general with his own body, was killed in his place; the fourth attempt, which was made in the following January, was defeated at Rivoli. On February 2, 1797, Mantua surrendered. Marching eastward and northward, Napoleon proceeded toward Vienna. On April 7 his vanguard reached Leoben, not a hundred miles from the Austrian capital.

After Bassano Napoleon had already turned aside to set up the Transpadane Republic. The democratic and nationalist aspirations **The Transpadane Republic.** of oppressed, misruled, and divided Italy had turned to him for championship, and out of Modena and Reggio and the Papal cities of Bologna and Ferrara he formed a small new republic on a popular basis, with representative Assembly and National Guard.

Again, after Mantua had fallen Napoleon proceeded to settle an account with the Pope. At the command of the Directory, whose anti-Catholic policy had confirmed the alienation of the **The Papacy.** Papacy, Napoleon had already invaded the States of the Church. He had been wise enough, even against the wishes of the Directors, not to antagonize Catholic Europe by an attack on Rome. It had, moreover, not been necessary, for the general's reputation and a trifling show of force had brought the timorous cardinals to terms. A tendency to prolong the negotiations, however, and demonstrations of hostility to the French when the Austrians seemed likely to be victorious, convinced Napoleon that the Pope needed another lesson. For the second time he invaded Papal territory in February 1797, concluding on the 19th the Treaty of Tolentino. By this the Pope was forced to grant the exclusion of the English from Papal ports, the recognition of the Transpadane Republic, and the French occupation of Avignon, thirty millions of francs as tribute, five hundred manuscripts, and one hundred pictures and works of art, including especially "the bronze bust of Junius Brutus and the marble bust of Marcus Brutus." There was no reference to the religious issues between France and the Church; already General Bonaparte recognized the power of the idea of Catholicism which as Emperor Napoleon he was first to enlist and then to defy.

By April 1797, with Napoleon within a hundred miles of Vienna, both sides were ready for peace. The victorious French general in Italy could expect no more reinforcements, which were needed by the defeated generals in Germany; he was aware of discontent in his rear and conscious that the *rôle* of peacemaker was become in France more popular than that of conqueror. The Directory wanted peace before the elections, had already, in fact, made overtures after Arcola; their armies under Jourdan and Moreau had been defeated and driven back in Germany; their naval policy had resulted disastrously in the destruction of the Dutch fleet by Duncan at Camperdown and of the Spanish fleet by Jervis at Cape St Vincent; they were unwilling to be committed to a permanent military or political defence of Italy, and anxious to cut short the career of a general who might at any moment turn *condottiere*, set himself up as King of Italy, and even direct his troops against France.

As for Austria, she had a war to conduct on two frontiers; she had been decisively defeated in Italy, and could spare no men from Germany, even though she was temporarily victorious there. Her allies, too, were failing her. The Tsarina Catherine II had died in the previous November, and her successor, Paul, showed no disposition to further Austrian schemes of aggrandizement; England, having abandoned Corsica and withdrawn from the Mediterranean, had left open the communications between France and Italy, while Prussia seemed likely to make a bid for German hegemony by an alliance with the Republic. On the other hand the victories of the Archduke Charles, which fixed for the moment the wavering allegiance of the Southern States, might be used to advantage in the negotiation of terms.

Thus Napoleon was able to crown his victories with peace and add the reputation of a diplomatist of the first order to that of a general. The preliminaries of Leoben, embodied later in the Treaty of Campo Formio (October 1797), put an end to the war, five years long, which the Girondists had inaugurated with rejoicing in the April of 1792. Austria was to recognize the French frontier of the Rhine, which meant the loss of the Austrian Netherlands and of the Imperial Electorates of Trier, Mainz, and the Palatinate; she was to cede Lombardy and receive in return part of the once grand republic of Venice, which during the war had been struggling to preserve a miserable and defenceless neutrality between France and Austria.

G

While the negotiations were being continued during the summer of 1797 Napoleon continued his work of settling and reorganizing Italy, holding court the while with his wife and mother, three brothers, three sisters, and a maternal uncle, at the castle of Montebello. There was Verona to be punished for the murder of French prisoners, Venice to be conquered as a bait for Austria, and there were political schemes in view. Venice fell easily; she was first goaded by Napoleon into abandoning her neutrality, then betrayed by a deliberately fostered revolution within, then insulted by a profusion of protestations respecting liberty and democracy, and then occupied without a blow, for her fortresses were at anyone's mercy. Thus Napoleon was able to secure for France the Ionian islands, and to hand over to Austria the city of St Mark and all the Venetian territories in Istria and Dalmatia and up to the Adige. But Napoleon never forgot that the Doge fell down dead when he was taking the oath of allegiance to Austria.

The oligarchy of Genoa was also deposed and replaced by a moderate democracy which was subjected to France, but it was in the Cisalpine Republic, composed of Lombardy, the Transpadane, and parts of Venetia and Switzerland, that Napoleon set up a monument to his statesmanship as permanent as was the battle of Arcola to his generalship. As a new political unit transcending dynastic interests and local Italian divisions, it was the first triumph of the Risorgimento, the first step toward that national unity which, two generations after Napoleon's empire had fallen, was to be built on the foundations of the Cisalpine Republic.

Genoa.

The Cisalpine Republic.

It would seem as if General Bonaparte was clearly advancing toward that dictatorship of France which he afterward achieved. In September the civil Government had again been saved from a Royalist restoration by troops which he had dispatched. When the victor of Arcola and the author of Campo Formio himself returned to Paris—by way of Rastadt, where an Imperial Conference had been summoned to discuss problems arising out of French occupation of the left bank of the Rhine—he was greeted as a national hero. The Directors, uneasily effusive, gave him a public reception in the Luxembourg and appointed him to the Army of England. "Go," said Barras, embracing him before the people, "go and capture the giant corsair that infests the seas."

Napoleon's return to Paris.

But Napoleon was to suffer another set-back to the realization of his destiny, one created partly by the fantasy of his own genius.

England, the solitary survivor of the Coalition of '93, was France's most hated enemy. She was the centre of Royalist plots, the soul and the purse of the Continental opposition, and, strong in her naval supremacy and her island position, she forced the Republic to encounter her on an element where France was most weakened by the Revolution. The French Directors had already pressed the fleets of Spain and Holland into their service, but the former, as we have seen, had been defeated by Jervis off Cape St Vincent, and the latter by Duncan off Camperdown in the same year of 1797. French attempts to stir up a rebellion in Ireland had also failed as yet. "He who should conquer England would have Europe at his feet." Nevertheless Napoleon quickly realized that no invasion of the island was practicable without a considerably stronger fleet. But with that vision which always illuminated his statesmanship Napoleon saw England not as an island, but as an empire of far-flung provinces, of which India was the richest. To the Mediterranean islander the East was an alluring dream, to the emulator of Alexander Egypt was an inexhaustible field, and Napoleon, who had already looked eastward from the Adriatic and contem- *The Egyptian expedition.* plated the destruction of the crumbling Turkish Empire, who had already complained that the "molehill" of Europe was too small for him, determined upon the conquest of Egypt. It would give him an invaluable base for operations, either against India or against Turkey, should he decide to "take Europe in the rear," or a foundation for a new empire, should he determine to play the Alexander.

And in Paris there was nothing for him to do; the "pear was not ripe." He was not old enough nor willing enough to join the Directory; he was not ready to overthrow it. The people of Paris had short memories, which needed to be constantly refreshed with new exploits. "Were I to remain here long, doing nothing, I should be lost. In this great Babylon everything wears out; my glory has already disappeared. This little Europe does not supply enough of it for me. I must seek it in the East; all great fame comes from that quarter."

The Directors were delighted by a project which would remove a dangerous man so far. France was unfortunately bankrupt and two-thirds of the National Debt had just been cancelled, but Switzerland and Rome were invaded and forced to pay tribute. Josephine, who enjoyed her husband's reputation more than his presence, was no less relieved by his departure and by the reflection that she would not this time, as in the Italian campaign, be asked to abandon the Paris season to join him.

In May 1798 four hundred ships carrying an army and a staff of scholars set out from Toulon—thirty-eight thousand troops and a hundred and seventy-five learned civilians, "astronomers, geometricians, mineralogists, chemists, antiquarians, bridge-builders, road engineers, Orientalists, political economists, painters, and poets."

For this was to be no mere military conquest; it was to be the ravishing of a civilization.

An English fleet under Nelson was cruising in the Mediterranean, but the storm which delayed Napoleon's departure for twenty-four hours dispersed it. The French were thus able to proceed without hindrance, first to Malta, which they seized on their way, and then to Alexandria. Thither Nelson had hurried, preceding them by three days, but, having vainly scoured the Eastern Levant for the French fleet or news of it, he had turned back for further tidings of its destination. Thus an encounter was lost, which all subsequent history must deplore, between the greatest general and the greatest admiral of modern times.

Malta.

After taking Alexandria Napoleon advanced through the desert toward the Nile, utterly routed a force of Mamelukes at the Battle of the Pyramids, and entered Cairo. There he set himself to enlist the moral support of the Moslem races. He could not—alas, that he had not lived two thousand years or so before!—like Alexander declare himself the son of Jupiter, but he could honour the native religion with his patronage. He could flatter the divan of Cairo, quote from the Koran, argue that atheist France, being less Christian, was more Mohammedan, imply his own imminent conversion, draw up plans for a mosque for the French army, which, he suggested, was held back from accepting Allah and his Prophet only by the necessity of circumcision and the prohibition of wine.

The Battle of the Pyramids.

"Forty centuries are looking down on you."

Suddenly on August 1 the whole scheme of Napoleon's ambitions was transformed by Nelson's victory at the mouth of the Nile. All but four of the French ships were taken or destroyed, and he found himself cut off in Egypt in the midst of a fanatical and hostile population, under physical conditions of heat, thirst, and disease almost unendurable, and with an army that was growing mutinous. No less than in his victories and successes, however, Napoleon showed his genius at times of reverse, and his marvellous power of adaptation to changed conditions. The weeks of waiting for news from France he turned to account in scientific and archæological activity which has made him the greatest benefactor of modern Egyptology. Vineyards and cornfields were planted to relieve the embarrassment of his army; bakeries, windmills, foundries, bootshops, and gunpowder works were established. The minerals of the Nile and the natron lakes were explored, astronomical and geological surveys were made; physicians made researches into the causes of Oriental diseases, archæologists discovered the temples of Memphis and the wells of Moses. An engineer found at Rosetta a stone with a trilingual inscription which solved the riddle

Nelson's victory of the Nile.

of the hieroglyphs. The general himself visited Suez, traced the course of the old canal, planned that of a new one which fifty years later was confirmed by De Lesseps.

News came at last that Turkey had declared war against France, and that a Turkish expedition was advancing through Syria into Egypt. A revolt broke out in Cairo which Napoleon suppressed with Oriental cruelty. With a rapid reconstruction of plans he determined to invade Syria. From Acre *The Syrian campaign (1799).* to Damascus, thence through Persia, where the Shah was friendly, to the Indus, there to co-operate with Tippoo Sahib—his imagination did not falter before so giant a conception. Or he would take Constantinople, put an end to the Turkish Empire, and perhaps make his way home through Vienna after annihilating the house of Habsburg.

The advance into Syria was made under great difficulties, through Jaffa, where three thousand prisoners had to be slaughtered because they could not be fed, as far as Acre. There Napoleon was forced to a halt by a Royalist engineer, Phélipeaux, and an English admiral, Sir Sydney Smith. He had neither the *Acre (April–May 1799).* time nor the temperament to undertake a long siege. There was ominous news from Paris, murmuring from his troops. He had no choice but to order a retreat to Egypt—a terrible retreat, on foot, for there were not enough horses, with every four men carrying a sick comrade, with plague and thirst as companions. But he was still able in August to achieve the complete annihilation of a Turkish army which landed at Aboukir Bay. Then news came to him that while he had been cut off in Egypt another coalition had been formed against France, that she had lost Italy, that the Directors were powerless. "Should France need me," he had written to his brother before the Egyptian campaign, "I shall come home."

Like an unsuccessful adventurer Napoleon stole away from Egypt, through the British fleet, back to France. The army, which he left to Kléber—by letter, lest there should be a mutiny—lingered trapped for two more years until it was defeated by British troops, and returned, what was left of it, in British ships. As a magnificent political enterprise, the Egyptian venture had failed. British power in India was unimpaired. Not even a new French colony was founded, and Malta, whose mediæval peace Napoleon had so rudely disturbed, was captured by Britain in 1800. At the beginning, as throughout Napoleon's career, the sea and the Mistress of the Sea daunted him. Extensive as were his interests, his power of control, his expert knowledge, his technical efficiency, they stopped short of a sphere where he remained always an outsider.

The Directors were panic-stricken at his return. They had believed him as good as dead. So had Josephine, whose infidelities and frivolity had killed the fine faith of his first devotion. "Only one resource is left to me—to become an absolute egoist," remarked the general of thirty in a cynical mood. But the people embraced one another in the streets for joy at his coming. "It looks as if every one had been waiting for me. A while back would have been too soon. To-morrow would have been too late. I have come at the right moment." The pear was now ripe.

Return to Paris.

"I have come at the right moment."

II. MASTER OF FRANCE (1799–1804)

There is nothing heroic about the *coup d'état* of Brumaire which, three weeks after Napoleon's return from Egypt, made him master of France. "At no time of my life have I behaved with greater skill," Napoleon is reported to have said to Mme de Rémusat in 1803. But the skill lay in the planning of the intrigue, and in the choosing of confederates—principally Siéyès and Talleyrand, men of '89, one of whom was a Director, and the other Foreign Minister. As the inauguration of a dictator, the execution of the plot was ignominious.

The coup d'état of Brumaire (November 9–10, 1799).

Ostensibly the Government was to be overthrown with every appearance of legality. The five Directors were to resign, and the two legislative councils—the Ancients and the Five Hundred—were to vote, in a thoroughly constitutional manner, a revision of the constitution. Precautionary measures were, of course, to be taken—one Director to be bribed, another to be intimidated, a third to be invited to breakfast by Josephine ("Was Brutus' mood so paltry?" thought Bonaparte), a few trusted generals with troops were to be handy, and fortunately Napoleon's brother Lucien was for that month President of the Five Hundred.

But the attempt to preserve an ostensible legality broke down. The Directors were easily disposed of, but the councils proved refractory. The Ancients refused to be convinced that Napoleon was the saviour of the State, and in the hall of the Five Hundred he was received with cries of "Down with the tyrant!" "Outlaw him!" To save himself from outlawry Napoleon called on the troops. They cheered, but did not move. He began to make a speech. "For heaven's sake, hold your tongue!" cried his brother Lucien, and it was not until the latter, drawing his sword, vowed to run Napoleon through the body "should he ever dare to threaten the liberties of France" that the soldiers entered the hall and sent the toga'd councillors skeltering through doors and windows. About midnight a few of the deputies returned and voted a revision of the constitution, entrusting it to three provisional Consuls, Bonaparte, Siéyès, and Ducos.

Thus Napoleon from the very brink of outlawry was raised to power by the gesture of a younger brother who had told him to "hold his tongue." Neither brother forgot the indebtedness. But the real strength of his position lay in the overwhelming popular vote which a month later was given for the new constitution drawn up by Siéyès and modified by Bonaparte. The adoption of classical republican titles and the apparent division of executive power between three officers did not disguise the fact that supreme power had been placed in Bonaparte's hands. As First Consul, "with plenary powers and plenty of work," he had virtually been made dictator. He named the ministers and the officials of the administration, and most of the judges. He was commander-in-chief of the army, and supervized local government; he controlled foreign affairs and the diplomatic service. He was president and nominator of the Council of State, which initiated legislation, and resembled in its functions and scope the *Conseil du Roi* of the Bourbon kings. The Consulate was, in fact, a restoration of the despotism of the late dynasty, but with a difference. It was a despotism based on efficiency and popular support, and it was associated with no privilege of birth. In Napoleon's opinion France loved not liberty, but equality, and under his *régime*, with the unfortunate exception of his own family, there was no passport to office save merit.

Napoleon First Consul (1799–1804).

The people of France willingly accepted this despotism, because they were used to changes of Government, because they wanted and recognized a strong ruler, independent of party, because they were tired of the Directory and its intrigues and incompetence, which could keep the country neither solvent nor free from brigandage, rebellion, and foreign defeat. "Citizens, the revolution has returned to the principles with which it began. It is at an end." With these words Napoleon commended the constitution to the people. Eight years before Louis XVI had also proclaimed a new constitution, and pronounced the end of the Revolution. In the interval, through disorder, terror, war, and weariness, France had progressed from a constitutional monarchy to that dictatorship which is no uncommon ending of revolution.

Napoleon devoted himself immediately to the restoration of order within France. He suppressed the revolts in La Vendée and Brittany; he laid the foundations of financial stabilization. He showed the comprehensiveness of the new dictatorship by making appointments from all parties, excluding only irreconcilables. At the Foreign Office was Talleyrand, the ecclesiastical noble of the *ancien régime*; Fouché, the Jacobin regicide, was his Minister of Police. He invited the *émigrés* back to France, demanded merely a promise of allegiance from the priests, and allowed the non-jurors to officiate where no opposition was thereby aroused.

With the opening of the new campaigning season of 1800 Napoleon turned against the external enemies of France. A Second Coalition had in the previous year been formed against her, consisting of Russia, Austria, England, Naples, Portugal, and Turkey. An Anglo-Russian expedition under the Duke of York had invaded Holland, and in Italy an Austro-Russian army had captured Mantua, in Lombardy, and Alexandria, in Piedmont, while a Russian force under Suvaroff had defeated the French at Novi and driven them upon Genoa, which was all that was left to them of Napoleon's conquests. But the Allies' successes were already checked before Napoleon returned from Egypt. In September Masséna defeated the Russians at Zürich and sent Suvaroff retreating through Switzerland; in October Brune had forced the incompetent Duke of York to capitulate and to agree by the Convention of Alkmaar to the withdrawal of his troops. The Tsar Paul determined to participate no longer in the land campaign, and to confine himself to operations in the Mediterranean. What the arms of the French had begun the mutual jealousies of the Allies continued. Partly to provoke these jealousies and partly to gain time, Napoleon had sent, in December 1799, a letter to George III and the Emperor Francis, expressing his desire for peace. It was rejected by Pitt on the ground that the restoration of the Bourbons was a *sine qua non* of any negotiations. But as Napoleon had made no definite proposals, as he was known to desire the return of the French domination of Italy, and as he was acute enough to realize that his domestic position would be strengthened by fresh adventures in a field where he was as yet undefeated, it is difficult to believe he was sincere.

In the spring of 1800 Napoleon took the field (see map, p. 95). He had at first intended to campaign in South Germany and strike at Vienna from that side, but the difficulty of working with the French general Moreau caused him to abandon that intention and led him once again into the valley of the Po. But he approached it not, as before, round the Alps, but over them, a second Hannibal, and the bravest spectacle that the monks of St Bernard have ever seen was the seven days' transit of the French army through the Pass, with ammunition and artillery. A distance of five leagues was impracticable for vehicles, and the guns, taken from their carriages, and laid inside the hollowed-out trunks of pine-trees, were dragged with ropes by peasants or soldiers.

The campaign which was thus brilliantly entered upon was a masterpiece of bold design and rapid adaptation. It reached its climax in the overwhelming victory of Marengo in June 1800. But

Marginal notes:

Foreign affairs.

The second Italian campaign (1800).

like the *coup d'état* of Brumaire it was a victory won in its last stages by another. The battle which at three o'clock Napoleon had lost was won at seven by Desaix and his reinforcements, and *Marengo* by Kellermann's cavalry charge. "The battle is lost, *(1800).* but there is time to gain another," Desaix was rumoured to have said, and the sentence would form a worthy epitaph, for he fell on the field of Marengo.

After a brief visit to Milan Napoleon hurried back to Paris. He had been absent for two months, during which he had recovered almost all that had been lost in Italy. In Germany Moreau supplemented Napoleon's Italian campaign by the victory of Hohenlinden in December, and advanced to within seventy-one miles of Vienna. When in the same month the fortresses of the Mincio were turned by the arrival of another French army under Macdonald, which, outmatching the transit of the St Bernard Pass in May, had entered by the Splügen in December, Austria agreed to terms.

The Peace of Lunéville (February 1801) practically repeated the terms of Campo Formio with a few modifications unfavourable to Austria; once again Austria recognized the Batavian, Helvetic, and Cisalpine Republics, the French occupation of *The Peace* Belgium and the left bank of the Rhine. But whereas the *(February* first Italian campaign was the measure of the triumph of a *1801).* mere general and diplomatist in the service of the Republic, the second was part and prelude of a vast scheme of Continental and colonial ambition nursed by the ruler of France. Napoleon never stood still; such a static conception as a mere restoration to a *status quo* was utterly alien to his nature. His outlook had expanded with his responsibilities and opportunities. The Egyptian expedition had shown on what scale he was prepared to encounter England. After Lunéville his dynamic imagination had soared beyond the defeat of Austria and the break-up of the Coalition. He began already to shape the idea, which he was later to strain himself and France to the *Continental* utmost to realize, of a great league of European states which *ambitions.* he should direct against that arch-enemy whom he could not meet on land or crush at sea.

And outside Europe he envisaged—what he was never able to construct—a French colonial empire surpassing that of his island rival. He tried to re-establish French authority in the West Indian *Colonial* island of San Domingo [1]—with the loss of thirty thousand *schemes.* men and twenty generals, including his brother-in-law, Pauline's

[1] The central figure in the story of Haiti (or San Domingo) was the ex-slave Toussaint l'Ouverture, who showed real powers of leadership and government, "the only negro of unmixed blood," says Dr Fisher, " who has ever exhibited the qualities of a statesman." He brought the island under his control, introduced order, government, and commercial measures; he framed a constitution giving

husband, Leclerc. He forced Spain to cede Louisiana, only to sell it
almost immediately, on American protests, to the United States. He
sought an alliance between native and French interests in India, and
stirred up hostility to Britain. He sent a politico-scientific expedition to Australia. But Napoleon was never sufficiently free from
European preoccupations to realize his projects in this sphere.

In the meantime, within two and a half years from the *coup d'état*
of Brumaire, Napoleon was able to sign the first peace with England
that had been made since the outbreak of war in 1793.

In 1800 the Tsar Paul, having fallen out of the Second Coalition,
had quarrelled with England and formed, as a protest against her
Peace with   naval supremacy, the second Armed Neutrality.[1] This had
England.   been dissolved, however, by his assassination in March
1801, and by the destruction of the Danish fleet by Nelson at Copenhagen. Nevertheless England was tired of the war, and the inferior
Addington ministry which succeeded that of Pitt had no longer the
will to prolong it. Napoleon too, much occupied with home affairs
and overseas schemes, desired a respite in which to construct a navy
which might prove a match for that of Great Britain. In March 1802,
therefore, there was signed at Amiens that peace of which it was said
in England that "everybody was glad and nobody proud." Great
Britain surrendered all her colonial conquests save Ceylon and Trinidad, agreed to restore Malta to the Knights of St John and Minorca
to Spain, and to abandon the royal title of France—a mere anachron-
istic survival from the days of Edward III. Napoleon for his part
was to evacuate Egypt, where Abercromby had just defeated his army,
and Naples and Portugal, both easily recoverable by the man who
controlled the larger part of the peninsulas to which they belonged.

More important at this time, however, than foreign policy, and more
permanent than all the political conquests which Napoleon was ever
The organi-   to make, were the measures he introduced for the internal
zation of   government of France. The efficiency, industry, and in-
France.   corruptibility of which he was himself an example he demanded and instilled throughout the administration. "The gigantic
entered into our very habits of thought," wrote one official. Like

himself life powers and reducing French authority to a shadow. He would be,
in fact, the " Bonaparte of San Domingo." Napoleon, resolved to chastize his
insolence, sent 25,000 men under Leclerc and fifty warships to restore slavery and
the authority of France. Toussaint was taken prisoner by an ingenious ruse and
sent to France, where he died of ill-treatment and the climate. But the West Indian
climate took its toll of the French army ; Leclerc died, and within twelve months
there were no more than 8000 troops left, who could not, even with reinforcements,
hold their own against Toussaint's lieutenants and the English. In December
1803 the island was evacuated, and at St Helena Napoleon admitted that the
expedition had been an error in policy.
    [1] The first had been formed in 1780, during the War of American Independence.

Pitt, Napoleon strove to abolish the undue profits of contractors and frauds on the public service. He checked speculation in the depreciated currency, regulated the Stock Exchange, and founded the Bank of France. He established a national system of education, with graded schools and free scholarships.

Finance.

Education.

He drew upon both royal and revolutionary experience. In the new bureaucratic local government he restored the centralization of the *ancien régime*. From the mayor of the commune to the prefect of the department, the agents of local administration were as much the creatures of the central Government as the *intendants* of the Bourbon kings.

Local government.

But as he did not restore the monopolistic trade guilds which had been abolished by the National Assembly, so he did not disturb the multiple small vested interests created by the Revolutionary land settlement. He called for no surrender by the peasants of the land which they had bought, often at ludicrously small prices, from the estates of Church and nobility.

Land settlement.

He did his utmost to provide work for the unemployed. "There are many out-of-work shoemakers, hatters, tailors, and saddlers. See to it that five hundred pairs of shoes are made every day." And again: "Issue an order that two thousand of the Saint-Antoine workmen are to supply chairs, chests of drawers, etc." It was partly for this reason that he undertook great town-planning schemes in Paris. "We must provide work. . . . Get on with the cutting of the Ourcq Canal, with the construction of the Quai Desaix, and the paving of the back streets." It was also partly that Paris might become the artistic centre of Europe, that Frenchmen might find in their capital satisfaction for their instincts of pride and beauty. Therefore had he already spoiled Italy of her treasures. Therefore, too, did he encourage literature and art. Lists were to be made of "the ten best painters, sculptors, composers, musicians, architects, and other artists whose talents make them worthy of support. People complain that we have no literature. That is the fault of the Minister of the Interior." Painters were summoned to seek inspiration in the pageantry of French victories, and poets a theme in the mission of her history, but Napoleon intended, as much as the Bourbons before him, that art should prove a tractable handmaid to politics. It is a sufficient commentary that while England and Germany were producing a great and fertile literature France, for all the encouragement she received, could add to her literary roll only the names of Châteaubriand and Mme de Staël, both of whom suffered Napoleon's displeasure.

The beautification of Paris.

From a somewhat similar motive Napoleon founded the Legion of

Honour. "The French are accessible to only one sentiment—love of honour. . . . Soldiers must be allured by fame and pay. . . . Here **The Legion of Honour.** is a new kind of money assessed at a different valuation from current coin—and inexhaustible." Baubles? Yes, but "men are led by baubles."

The two greatest monuments to his statesmanship and political grasp are, however, the Code Napoléon and the Concordat. One of the greatest evils of the *ancien régime* was the lack of a uniform code of law, and although five drafts had been prepared by revolutionary assemblies none of them had been put into execution. The first task that Napoleon set himself was to remedy that defect. The **The Code Napoléon.** Code Napoléon, which came into effect in 1804 and is still the law of France, was a brief, clear collection of legal principles. It was based on common sense and experience rather than on theory, and it was animated by no political or religious prejudice. It granted religious toleration and equity, enjoined civil marriage, and permitted divorce; on the other hand it upheld strongly the value of family life, the authority of the father, the sanctity of private property, and—as was to be expected from a legislator who held that "all women are slaves"—the subjection of women.

The Concordat, further testimony to Napoleon's freedom from ideology, healed that breach with the Roman Church which had **The Concordat.** been the chief stumbling-block of the Revolution. Apart from a vague susceptibility to church-bells and a sense of the wonder of the starry universe "and all that," Napoleon himself had no religion. "People will say that I am a Papist. I am nothing. I was a Mohammedan in Egypt; I shall be a Catholic here for the good of the people."

In the metaphysical and philosophical regions of thought Napoleon's limitations were clearly marked. Religion was to him only a useful political instrument, a national imaginative focus, a social cement, a safety-valve. "The people must have a religion, and the religion must be in the hands of the Government." As it was, the religion of France was in the hands of the enemies of the Government. "Fifty *émigré* bishops in English pay are the present leaders of the French clergy," observed Napoleon. The altars were therefore 'restored' to France. An agreement with the Pope was reached by which, while Napoleon conceded the celibacy of the priests, the investiture of bishops by Rome, and the re-establishment of canon law, the Pope accepted the payment of stipends by the State and the Revolutionary land settlement.

Napoleon's work has been traced back in part to the *ancien régime*, in part to the Revolution. He "organized the *ancien régime*"; he "consolidated the Revolution." Both statements are true, because there was a real continuity between the two periods, because he embodied fundamental national instincts evident in both. Napoleon perpetuated the destruction of feudalism; he stabilized an equitable finance; he guaranteed the "career open to talent"; he left the peasant in possession of the land of noble and ecclesiastic, and he gave to the middle class social and civic equality. That is, in all that was essential he conserved the work of revolution, and confirmed to the co-heirs of revolution—the peasants and the *bourgeois*—the heritage they had won. But he did more; he personified the unity of the nation as the *Roi Soleil* had done; and he satisfied that fundamental instinct for order which, thwarted by the historical chaos of the *ancien régime*, had been the chief end of revolution. Because in foreign affairs he gave them glory, and in home affairs national organization, both of which they ardently desired, Frenchmen readily forgave him that he deprived them of political liberty, which they had never wanted.

After the *coup d'état* of Brumaire there were many who believed that Napoleon would play the part of Monk and bring back the Bourbons to France. The future Louis XVIII three times made overtures to him, and received only the reply, "I shall be happy to do all in my power to contribute to the welfare and happiness of your retirement." Napoleon despised the royal princes who remained in their hiding-places. "They should have come back to France in the first fishing-smack" scornfully declared the man who had sailed back to France through the English fleet in 1799.

Royalist disappointment began to express itself in Royalist plotting. On Christmas Eve, as Napoleon was driving to the Opéra to hear Haydn's *Creation*, a bomb exploded in the street and killed twenty people. But Napoleon visited the attempt not on the Royalists, but on the Jacobins. It was a measure of statecraft; the latter he feared, the former he wished to conciliate. "I am not afraid of the sort of conspirator who gets up at nine o'clock and puts on a clean shirt." He banished a hundred and thirty Jacobins and suppressed sixty newspapers.

Plots.

Nevertheless a little later reports reached him from his spies that a conspiracy had been formed on a larger scale to seize the First Consul and restore the monarchy. The Comte d'Artois seems to have been the centre of it, and Pichegru, the conqueror of Holland, Moreau the Jacobin, victor of Hohenlinden, and Georges Cadoudal, the Chouan hero, were involved in it. Upon the discovery of the plot Cadoudal and twelve accomplices were put to death. Pichegru died in prison, probably by his own hand, and Moreau was banished to the United States.

Napoleon then followed up the punishment of the conspirators

with a flagrant injustice.   Reference had been made in the evidence
to a young Bourbon prince, whom the police thought to be the young
Duc d'Enghien, son of the Prince de Bourbon, a scion of the house
of Condé, who was living just over the Rhine frontier.   With no
proof whatsoever of his guilt, Napoleon thereupon had him kidnapped
upon foreign soil, brought to Vincennes, and put through a form of
Execution   trial.   At 2.30 in the morning, not four hours after his
of the Duc   .arrival, he was shot and thrown into a grave which had
d'Enghien.   been already prepared for him.   Whether it was a severe
object lesson to the royal family, or a measure of panic, or committed
at the instigation of Talleyrand in the hope of bringing about
Napoleon's downfall, it was a crime and a blunder.   It was a shock
to Europe and an excuse to his enemies.   The Court of St Petersburg
went into mourning, Prussia turned toward Russia; Austria added
another item to the count against France, England began to form the
Third Coalition.

There was another result.   "They seek to destroy the Revolution
in my person. . . . I am the French Revolution, and I must defend
it," Napoleon had remarked, with all the egotism of the *Roi Soleil*.
In preserving the Revolution he put an end to the Republic, and the
Royalist plotters who hoped to give France a king succeeded only in
giving her an emperor.   In 1802 he had already been made Consul
Napoleon   for life and empowered to nominate his successor.   In
becomes   March 1804 he took the title of Emperor of the French.
Emperor.   "The name of king is outworn.   It carries with it a train
of obsolete ideas, and would make me nothing more than the heir of
dead men's glories. . . . The title of emperor is greater than that
of king.   Its significance is not wholly explicable, and therefore it
stimulates the imagination."   Like the Concordat with the Church,
the imperial title was a political instrument to be used in the governing of men.   Even the Pope was summoned to Paris to give his blessing, but at the last moment the Emperor placed the Crown upon his
head with his own hands, thus flouting his Holiness in the very act
of coronation.

France accepted the Empire as she had accepted the *coup d'état*
of Brumaire, with almost unanimous acclamation.   "You French
love monarchy," said Napoleon, speaking as the foreigner that he
was.   There were only a few protests.   Carnot, the only surviving
revolutionary general who did not bend before Napoleon, went into
voluntary exile; and the night before the coronation a poster appeared on the walls of Paris announcing, "The Last Representation
of the French Revolution—for the benefit of a poor Corsican family";
and in Vienna the greatest of musicans tore off the dedication of the
Symphony Eroica.

More than a new title was introduced with the Empire. Napoleon was, indeed, master of France, anointed heir of Charlemagne and of the Grand Monarch, incarnation of the larger despotism which democracy in its inexperience and incapacity had raised up for itself. But a new stage in the history of his own career was ushered in, and with it new problems and a new setting. To the picture of the general exhorting his troops to battle, poring over the map of his campaigns, resting beside the camp-fire with his grenadiers; to that of the President of the Council of State, dictating, arguing, analysing, working indefatigably and with a marvellous expert knowledge on a host of subjects, must be added that of an unamused emperor amid an embarrassed Court and a quarrelling family that was a butt of the caricaturists of Europe. Who can doubt which was the bravest picture, or upon what title Napoleon's power really rested?

An emperor must have a Court. Mme de Campan was brought from her academy for young ladies to arrange the Empress's train after the fashion of her late Majesty the Queen of France. Mme de Rémusat, to whose *Memoirs* a grateful posterity is indebted, was to be chief lady-in-waiting. The generals of the Republic became marshals of the Empire. The Corsican brothers became Grand Dignitaries, the sisters Imperial Highnesses. There were disputes as to precedence and the question of an heir. Perhaps the Empress would have to be divorced, but meanwhile Napoleon's brother should marry Josephine's daughter, although the affections of both were placed elsewhere. Lucien, who had married a woman of no repute whom he obstinately refused to renounce, was exiled, and Jerome, who had allied himself with a Miss Patterson, of Baltimore, was bullied into a proper sense of the family position. Josephine delighted in the new *rôle*. With her two hundred and fifty hats and seven hundred dresses she spent more than the late Queen of France in trying to regain her husband's affection, and keep up the imperial state. Perhaps the wisest of them all was Madame Mère, the thrifty Corsican mother, who only remarked in her foreign accent, "*Pourvou que cela doure*," and saved what she could for the day of misfortune.

III. The Bid for the Mastery of Europe (1804–9)

The renewal of war between England and France in May 1803 has been called "the greatest event of the century."[1] It not only involved Napoleon in a struggle with Europe which did not end until his defeat, but it influenced the course of history in America, Africa, India, and even Australia.

The renewal of war (1803)

France already stretched to the Rhine, and in 1802 she had

[1] Dr Holland Rose, *Napoleon*, vol. i, Chapter XVII, p. 429.

incorporated Piedmont, Parma, and Elba. Holland and Switzerland were little more than subsidiary states, Spain was tributary, and Portugal and Naples too weak to be independent. Louisiana

breaks in upon some of Napoleon's greatest enterprises.

and various West Indian islands gave her promise of the control of Central America ; a peaceful development of Australian enterprise might have brought a large part of the southern continent under the French flag. The Cape of Good Hope and Mauritius provided her with bases whence she could threaten India, while astute diplomatic intervention in the crumbling Turkish Empire would almost certainly have given her the Morea or Syria or Egypt. The foundations were laid of a colonial empire and of world-markets which might well have been developed to crush Great Britain. Napoleon was Consul for life and President of the Italian Republic; in a little more than a year he was to become Emperor. What could he hope to gain by war that he could not win better from peace, except the satisfaction of an immediate military and political victory over the country which had consistently thwarted his will to power? For this he was to sacrifice the substance of his gains and the promise of his transoceanic schemes.

The Peace of Amiens was little more than a truce, and constituted no check upon French aggrandizement. The deep-seated rivalry between the two countries was undiminished, and England's suspicions of Napoleon were only confirmed by the growth of his power

Causes.

during 1803, by the Italian annexations, the Swiss intervention—although that was as brilliant a piece of statesmanship as it was self-interested. She was irritated by the exclusion of British goods from French ports; she distrusted the continued military occupation of Holland, the San Domingo exploit, the acquisition of Louisiana; she was alarmed by the equipment of a French expedition to India, by Napoleon's evident designs upon Turkey, and his Mediterranean ambitions, by his political conversations with the Tsar, and by the deliberate publication in January 1803 of the bellicose report of Colonel Sebastiani's mission to Algiers, Egypt, Syria, and the Ionian islands, which described the popularity of the French in the Levant and the ease with which Egypt might be reconquered. As a set-off to this unexpected aggrandizement, as a defence against the French domination of the Mediterranean, as a safeguard of Egypt and the route to India, and on the petition of Turkey, England resolved not to give back Malta until she was reassured as to Napoleon's intentions. Napoleon immediately charged her with violating the Treaty of Amiens, and insisted upon making the retention of Malta a *casus belli.* He had already complained that England was countenancing libellous attacks upon him in the British Press, that she was sheltering the Bourbons and other French *émigrés.* He was undoubtedly inclined to war by the news of the miscarriage of the San Domingo expedition, and by the desire to cover up the somewhat unheroic surrender of Louisiana to the United States, which had been largely forced by the fear of an Anglo-American alliance. He was influenced by the conviction, which assails many *parvenus*, that war was necessary to the stability of his government. "Within and without, my dominion is founded on fear." In addition it is impossible not to see during the negotiations a deterioration in Napoleon's character, an impatient irritation at resistance which denoted the wavering of his political balance and the weakening of his political insight.

The actual declaration of war came prematurely for his plans on May 16, 1803. After a vain attempt to postpone it he occupied Hanover, quartered troops upon Naples, and with money from the sale of Louisiana, tribute from the Ligurian and Italian republics, and exactions from Spain to defray the costs of war, he threw himself into what was one of the most interesting and inscrutable of his schemes —the invasion of England. He stationed troops at Boulogne and along the Northern coast, conscript troops which were drilled and trained until they became the best fighting material in Europe. He hurried on with naval preparations, collected craft of every type, set the dockyards of France and Holland astir with the con-   Attempted struction of a flotilla of flat-bottomed boats for the convoy   invasion of of troops across to England. He widened the harbour of   England Boulogne, pressed the Dutch and Spanish navies into his service, and planned an elaborate naval strategy by which the French fleets might be brought into the Channel and the British fleet manœuvred out of the way by feint attacks upon Egypt, upon Ireland, and upon the West Indies.

On the other side of the Channel a patriotism hardly known in England since the Armada was animating the country. Volunteers enlisted, troops and guns were posted along the coast, defences strengthened, and the Martello towers, which still add to the interest of the shores of Sussex and Kent, were built. Arrangements were made for clearing the southern counties of food, for removing the royal family to Worcester, and the ammunition from Woolwich to the Midlands, while the British Navy blockaded the fleets of Brest and Toulon, seized enemy ships, French islands, and Dutch colonies.

For eighteen months the two armed opponents stood face to face across the Channel, "a ditch that it needs but a pinch of courage to cross." At length in August 1805 the 'Army of England' moved, but it was not against Britain. A sudden renunciation and a new offensive had been decided upon; Napoleon had faced about and was marching against Austria, and his army was over the Rhine before news came of its first movement. And so the 'ditch' was not to be

H

crossed by Napoleon until, ten years later, the *Bellerophon* was to
bear him to Plymouth, a voluntary captive awaiting sentence. The
invasion of England had been abandoned. Whatever measure of
seriousness it contained, whatever its chances of success, or however
much it was a piece of quixotry on the part of him whom the wits of
Paris called the "Don Quixote de la Manche," its abandonment was
foiled by   in the last resort due to the British Navy. Command of
naval   the sea, if only for a short time, was essential to a successful
inferiority.   invasion, and for this Napoleon manœuvred in vain. His
naval inferiority consistently foiled him, an inferiority not so much of
numbers, which were swelled by the Spanish and Dutch contingents,
as of technique, training, and command. Villeneuve was a poor
match for Nelson, but even Villeneuve was not allowed a free hand.
The service where success was contingent not only upon tides and
varying winds, but upon technical experience, was controlled in the
last resort by a layman. The French navy was ruled not by a sailor,
but by a soldier, Napoleon himself.

The last strategical effort by which Villeneuve, having decoyed the
British fleet to the West Indies, was to double back, join the Brest
fleet, which was also to elude a blockading squadron, and then make
its way in strength up the Channel, was defeated on August 15, when
the French admiral was forced by Nelson's vigilance and an encounter with Calder to put into Cadiz harbour. It was on this news
that Napoleon set on foot his new campaign, and turned the 'Army
of England' into the 'Grand Army.'

In the meantime Pitt, who had returned to office in April 1804, had
formed against France a Third Coalition, consisting of England,
The Third   Austria, and Russia, and in the second line Sweden and
Coalition   Naples. Napoleon had already given ample provocation.
(1805).   The death of the Duc d'Enghien had roused the new
idealist Tsar, Alexander I. The assumption of the Imperial title had
challenged the prestige of the Holy Roman Emperor. An osten-
tatious visit to Aix-la-Chapelle, the ancient Carolingian capital, had
A second   shown the direction of Napoleon's thoughts, and recalled
Charle-   memories of him who had ruled from Calais to Rome, from
magne.   the Bay of Biscay to the Danube. The analogy was emphasized when in June 1805 Napoleon, having annexed Genoa to
France and abolished the Cisalpine Republic, crowned himself with
the Iron Crown of Lombardy and the title of King of Italy. Austria
and Russia thereupon, on the promise of English subsidies, declared
war against France. Prussia remained nervously neutral.

The campaign against Austria was swift and decisive. Two
Austrian armies were put into the field, the larger under the Archduke
Charles in Italy, the smaller under General Mack in Germany.

Napoleon, however, leaving the Italian campaign to Masséna and his own stepson Eugène, adopted the plan he had formed in 1800, of striking across the south of Germany to Vienna. On October 20, three weeks after he had crossed the Rhine, he encircled Mack's army at Ulm and forced it to surrender. The Archduke Charles, who had also been defeated, was hurriedly recalled to protect Vienna; but he arrived too late, and by the middle of November the Austrian capital, for the first time in modern history, had surrendered to a foreign foe. Francis II fled to join the Tsar, for the resistance of the Allies had received a fresh fillip in the news of the victory of Trafalgar, which took place the day after the capitulation of Ulm. The French and Spanish fleets were crippled, and any hope that Napoleon may have entertained that he might win the supremacy of the sea was finally defeated. Nelson fell in the battle, but he had not left his work unfinished.

Campaign against Austria.

Ulm (October 1805).

Trafalgar (October 21, 1805).

Austria was therefore stimulated to further resistance; there was a Russian army in the field, and the Tsar Alexander was ardently desirous of defeating the unvanquished Corsican. The encounter took place on the field of Austerlitz, in the plain of Moravia. The three emperors were present; the day was December 2, the anniversary of the crowning of the newest of them. It was a victory for Napoleon such as Europe had not seen since Marlborough cut the Franco-Bavarian army in two at Blenheim. The Tsar retreated eastward with his army, and the Emperor Francis submitted for the third time to the conqueror. The Peace of Presburg, which was signed before the end of the year, after barely a four months' campaign, marked a further stage still in the history of the new Charlemagne. Austria was naturally to be weakened; in Italy by the loss of her possessions in Venetia and Dalmatia, in Germany by the cession to Bavaria of the Tyrol and part of Swabia. For it was part of Napoleon's deliberate policy to strengthen the South German states, and to create a dependent relationship between them and him which would form a complete check to Austria. Bavaria and Würtemberg were made into kingdoms, and Baden became a Grand Duchy. Three dynastic marriages cemented the arrangements; between Eugène Beauharnais and a daughter of the Bavarian house of Wittelsbach; between Jerome Bonaparte, who had put away his wife from Baltimore, and a princess of Würtemberg; between a niece of Josephine and a Badenese prince.

Austerlitz (December 1805).

Peace of Presburg (December 1805).

The most important consequence of the Peace of Presburg was, however, the reconstruction of Germany. Francis II had already discarded the elective Imperial title, which had been held by the

Habsburgs for nearly four hundred years, in favour of that of 'Hereditary Emperor of Austria.' Napoleon, proceeding farther, abolished that enfeebled and enfeebling institution the Holy Roman Empire, "neither Holy, nor Roman, nor an Empire," though venerable with age and history. Some of the smaller states were wiped out as independent principalities. Sixteen in the south and west of Germany, formed into a league known as the Confederation of the Rhine, became tributary vassals of the French Emperor.

The end of the Holy Roman Empire.

"Roll up the map of Europe," Pitt is said to have remarked after Austerlitz, "it will not be wanted these ten years." The prophecy was almost too accurate to be authentic, though Pitt barely lived to see the beginnings of its fulfilment. Napoleon, become Charlemagne indeed, had lent himself to the vision of a Western Empire, to the policy of a federated Europe under his protection and rule—for he never considered Russia as other than an Eastern nation. "There will be no peace in Europe," he had observed at Aix-la-Chapelle, "until the whole continent is under one suzerain."[1] It is never wise to interpret Napoleon's *obiter dicta* as statements of deliberate policy, but the year 1806 and the distribution of states and kingdoms which followed it brought progressively nearer realization the design of a "whole continent under one suzerain." Eugène Beauharnais was already viceroy for Napoleon in the Kingdom of Italy, and General Marmont his agent in the new provinces of Illyria. A display of political ruthlessness turned Ferdinand of Bourbon and his wife Caroline,[2] sister of Marie-Antoinette, out of Naples for harbouring English ships, and gave the sovereignty to Joseph Bonaparte in their place. Another brother, Louis, was 'bestowed' upon Holland, which had passed like France through successive stages from a republic to a monarchy. Sister Élise became Grand Duchess of Tuscany, Murat (Caroline's husband) Duke of Cleves. Talleyrand, Berthier, and Bernadotte (Joseph's brother-in-law, who had more than once to be conciliated) were given imperial fiefs. The intractable Lucien, who would not give up his wife and his independence, received nothing, for all that he had rendered Napoleon good service on the Nineteenth Brumaire. "Those who will not soar with me shall no longer be of my family. I am making a family of kings attached to my federative system."

A federative system and a family of kings.

The federation of Europe was to serve another purpose. It was to be turned into a powerful economic weapon with which to strike at England. The battle of Trafalgar had driven Napoleon farther

[1] This is partly the defence of the Hitlerian projects for a German hegemony.
[2] See genealogical table, p. 603.

toward that idea of a vast European blockade of Great Britain which later came to be called the Continental System.   From the heel of Italy to the mouth of the Elbe he sought to close the ports of Europe to English goods.   The satellite states were, of course, obedient.   The Pope could be bullied into compliance.   "Tell him that I am Charlemagne, the Sword of the Church, his Emperor, and as such I expect to be treated." Portugal also would not dare to stand out alone.

The economic blockade of England.

But to extend the blockade into the Baltic Prussia too would have to come within Napoleon's orbit.   For ten years, since the Peace of Basel in 1795, Prussia had remained neutral in the struggles against Napoleon.   She had not joined the Second Coalition, and although she had been pressed by Austria and Russia to become a member of the Third she had, after much vacillation, still refused.   Neither the French occupation of Hanover, nor the violation of Prussian territory by Napoleon's troops, nor the defeat of Austria, had moved the pacific Frederick William III from a neutrality which neither showed dignity nor won respect.   For Napoleon was bent upon securing Prussia's complicity in the economic campaign against England, either by an alliance with him, or by involving her in open war with Great Britain.   He therefore offered her as a bait George III's electorate of Hanover, which was partially in French occupation.   After some hesitation Prussia accepted it and dispatched her troops into the electorate, whereupon England retaliated by seizing Prussian merchant ships.   But Prussia had no real quarrel with England, and the prospect of war aroused irritation only against the dictator and the francophile party which had brought her to that pass.   When it at length leaked out that during some abortive peace negotiations with Fox Napoleon had proposed to restore Hanover again to the English royal family, the end of Prussian endurance came, and war was declared against France.   It was, however, an ill-timed moment, part of the inopportuneness which at this time dogged the resistance to Napoleon.   Had Mack waited at Ulm for a Russian army, and Alexander at Austerlitz for an Austrian force, had Prussia joined the Third Coalition when her alliance would have been of use, instead of at a time when she could neither give nor receive help, the enemies of Napoleon might have been able to measure themselves more effectively against him.

War with Prussia.

It was the first encounter between Napoleon and the army which Frederick the Great had trained, but the defeat of Prussia was even swifter and more disastrous than that of Austria. Two victories in one day gave her into Napoleon's hands —at Jena, won by the Emperor himself against the army of Prince Hohenlohe, and at Auerstadt, where Davout defeated a

Jena and Auerstadt (October 14, 1806).

superior force under Brunswick, who fell mortally wounded, so ending a career already somewhat tarnished in the earlier campaigns against the revolutionary Republic.

The "defeat of Rossbach [1] had been avenged," and at the same time the Manifesto of Coblentz; several Prussian fortresses capitulated to French troops, and on October 25 the conqueror entered Berlin and seized the sword of Frederick the Great as his prize. From the Castle of Charlottenburg he issued the famous Berlin Decrees, declaring the British islands to be in a state of blockade and subjecting to confiscation British goods and all ships which touched at a British port or one of her colonies.

Upon Prussia he levied a heavy tribute, but as she refused, like Austria, to give up the alliance with the Tsar, Napoleon proceeded against Russia before making terms of peace with Prussia. Benningsen, the Russian general, refused, however, to let himself be caught, and Napoleon was compelled to winter in Poland. It was not until February 1807 that the battle of Eylau took place between the Russians and the French. Napoleon remained upon the field and therefore claimed the victory, but he lost more than half his men, 35,000 experienced soldiers of the Grand Army. Already might he have found warning in this, his first campaign against Russia. There were no roads and little food; his forces were discontented and starving, so that the soldiers rifled the potato dumps and the horses tore straw from the roofs. Suicides were reported. "I know my Frenchmen," said Napoleon. "It is difficult to march them on distant expeditions. France is too beautiful."

Campaign against Russia.

Eylau (February 1807).

Any hopes which had been roused among the Allies by the battle of Eylau were, however, rudely crushed by the Russian defeat at Friedland in June 1807. A single battle could not bring about the fall of the Russian Empire, as Austerlitz and Jena had destroyed Austria and Prussia, but it was nevertheless decisive. It justified Alexander in negotiating with Napoleon. For the French emperor was conducting a diplomatic campaign as well as a military one. He had concluded an armistice with Sweden, which was threatening his rear, pacified Austria upon his flank, stimulated the national aspirations of Poland, made a treaty with the Shah of Persia—all this while from afar he ruled his own dominions with an astonishing attention to detail—five pages of instructions to the King of Holland, orders to Joseph and Jerome, arrangements to the French bishops for a public thanksgiving service, instructions to the Press as to the suitable reporting of foreign affairs, police orders to Fouché regarding among other things the exile of Mme de Staël, inquiries as to the state of two

Friedland (June 1807).

[1] Frederick the Great's victory over France in the Seven Years War, 1757.

Parisian theatres, plans for building the Stock Exchange and the Madeleine, drafts for a new university.

On a raft on the river Memel as it flows past Tilsit a conference between the two emperors was staged to discuss the preliminaries of peace. Subsequent meetings were held in the town itself, whither came also Frederick William III of Prussia and the spirited Queen Louise to plead for her country. Over the impressionable, mutable Tsar, a "hero of romance," but a "pleasant, amiable fellow," with whom "if he were a woman," remarked Napoleon, "I should fall in love," the French Emperor was quickly able to establish an **The Treaty** ascendancy. Alexander surrendered himself as easily to the **of Tilsit** ideas which Napoleon artistically presented to him as he **(July 1807).** was later to depart from them, and a double treaty, part public, part private, was signed.

The public treaty mainly confirmed the mutilation of Prussia and certain new political creations set up by Napoleon. Out of the ceded western provinces of Prussia, together with Hanover and some small German states, there was made for Jerome Bonaparte the kingdom of Westphalia, as a sort of experimental ground for French democracy. The eastern provinces, mainly Prussian Poland, were joined with Austrian Galicia to form the Grand Duchy of Warsaw, which was placed under the King of Saxony. But Napoleon went no farther toward fulfilling his somewhat indefinite promises [1] of Polish independence. He sacrificed Poland, while Alexander for his part sacrificed the integrity of Prussia, which he had promised Queen Louise to uphold.

The secret clauses of the treaty were indications of intention rather than of fact. Napoleon was to have Russia's support in the economic war with England, while in return he was to aid Alexander in seeking compensation in Sweden and Turkey for French aggrandizement. But the French Emperor would not admit Russia's claim to Constantinople. "That would mean the mastery of the world." For the negotiations with Alexander revealed again the incessant activity of Napoleon's imagination. Always, to his undoing, was he lured on to new visions. Thus after Tilsit his thoughts were again upon the East. "I shall not be master until I have signed the peace of Constantinople." Again, as he wrote later to the Tsar: "An army of fifty thousand Frenchmen and Russians, with perhaps a few Austrians, could march to Constantinople and thence hurl itself upon Asia. Once it had reached the Bosporus, England would lie at the feet of the

---

[1] The following is an illustration of the non-committal character of his manifestoes : " Shall the throne of Poland be re-established, and shall this great nation resume its independence ? God only, Who holds in His hands the issues of all events, is the Arbiter of this great political problem."

Continent." Once again Napoleon proposed to strike at the island through the Empire, and reach Great Britain by way of the East. There is no greater tribute to England's mastery of the sea than that Napoleon should have thought it "easier to send troops from Paris to Delhi than from Boulogne to Folkestone."

More than once England was to recall Napoleon from his world-embracing visions to the fact that the victory over the West was not yet complete. Between England and France the issue was growing more acute. Each combatant threw ever-increasing effort into the struggle, which was turning into a mutual economic strangulation. To the Berlin Decrees England had replied with her Orders in Council of 1807, closing the ports of France and her Allies, and threatening the ships of neutrals who touched there with seizure. To neutrals the economic war presented a difficult problem. In September of the same year England went to the length of destroying or appropriating the Danish fleet at Copenhagen as a desperate remedy against growing French aggression in the Baltic. Napoleon thereupon retaliated with the more stringent regulations of the Milan Decrees of December 1807. Already, however, the Continent was beginning to feel the pinch of the commercial blockade. There were complaints of the loss of ships, demands for permits of exemption, and reports of smuggling, and when Bourienne, Napoleon's agent at Hamburg, was ordered to buy fifty thousand overcoats for the French army during the Eylau campaign he was unable to get them except from England.

The Continental System.

In France, where the news of Marengo six years earlier had aroused a delirium of excitement, the news of Jena had hardly raised a cheer. Napoleon had been away from his capital for ten months, and there were rumours and complaints. Discipline had to be tightened, a more rigid censorship of the Press established. An imperial university should mould the thought of the *intelligentsia*, public grammar schools should teach the catechism of an emperor made in God's image; a new hereditary nobility should anchor the military classes. The dynastic idea was developing, but Napoleon still had no direct heir and there was increasing discussion about the divorce of Josephine.

In two other quarters of Continental Europe obstacles were forming to Napoleon's dominance which were to grow into millstones about his neck. He was to antagonize the Catholic sentiment of Europe; he was to raise against himself the spirit of nationality.

Pius VII entered upon his ill-fated pontificate in 1800, barely a year after the *coup d'état* of Brumaire. One of his first acts was to sign the Concordat with Napoleon in 1801, and one of his first disappointments to see it curtailed by the Articles of 1802. He had reluctantly

attended the Emperor's coronation in 1804, but he found that concessions had only been followed by renewed exactions. In 1806 had
come a demand that the Papal ports should be closed against
British ships, to which the Pope replied with assertions of The Papacy.
his neutrality. Napoleon only grew more insistent. "No doubt your
Holiness is sovereign in Rome, but I am Emperor, and my enemies
shall be your enemies." When he threatened to "revoke the gifts of
Charlemagne" and reunite the lands of the Church with the Empire
Pius broke off negotiations. In April 1808, therefore, the Papal
States were seized by French troops and Rome was occupied. A year
later, in May 1809, they were formally annexed to the French Empire.

The Pope had recourse to spiritual arms. He issued a Bull of
Excommunication. "Does he think," cried Napoleon, "that my
soldiers' weapons will drop from their hands?" On the morning of
July 6 the Quirinal was broken into and the Pope carried off.

Ten years before Napoleon had written that "the influence of
Rome is incalculable. It was an error [of the Directory] to break
with this power." He was to prove the wisdom of his earlier fore-
sight and the folly of departing from it. If Napoleon's own remarks
at St Helena are to be trusted, something of a Caliphate of the West
which would combine spiritual and temporal jurisdiction seems to
have been in his mind. If a docile Pope could have been kept in
Paris (as he was from 1812 to 1814), then "Paris would have become
the capital of Christendom, and I should have directed the religious as
well as the political world."

Before the quarrel with the Papacy had reached its height the
Emperor had embarked upon a new scheme. There were in
Napoleon certain characteristics which might to-day have made him
a financier on a large scale, and many of his enterprises, prompted
by an instinctive 'drive' more than by political need, partake of that
mixture of wide vision, unscrupulousness, calculation, and Portugal
speculativeness which exactly marks some kinds of modern and Spain.
financial transactions. In such a category may be placed the assault
on Spain. That Napoleon should attempt to coerce Portugal into his
comprehensive economic system was the fruit of a fanatical but com-
prehensible political conception. That he should seek to justify the
seizure of Spain on the ground that her existence as an independent
country endangered his flank when he was engaged in war with
Germany indicated only defective political analysis, as he himself
recognized afterward. Nor did the certain intention of reforming the
appropriated country excuse Napoleon any more than bequests to a
hospital exonerate a shady speculator.

The Regent of Portugal had agreed under pressure to close his ports
to Great Britain, but upon his refusing further to sequestrate British

merchandise Napoleon determined upon the immolation of a country whose size, like that of Denmark, made it an easy prey to a large Power. Napoleon's interference in Portugal was, in fact, the alleged reply to Britain's intervention in Danish affairs.

With the design against Portugal, however, there was ingeniously entangled a larger scheme for the enslavement of Spain. Since the Peace of Basel in 1795 Spain had been a tractable dependant of France. She had sent money and men to Napoleon's wars and sacrificed colonies and ships in his service. But in 1806 at the beginning of the Prussian campaign Godoy, the favourite of the Queen and the real ruler of Spain,[1] had ordered, out of personal annoyance it seems, the mobilization of the Spanish troops, an order which upon the Prussian defeat at Jena he hastily cancelled. Behind this act, however, Napoleon saw a "hostile dynasty" that was a menace to his safety. He determined upon the destruction of another branch of that Bourbon family which had already been driven out of France, Naples, and Parma, a branch so corrupt and so effete that it could put up neither a moral nor a political defence.

A beginning was made by denuding Spain of 15,000 troops,[2] which were demanded for service on the Danish frontier. Then under cover of a joint Franco-Spanish arrangement for the partition of Portugal, which was made at Fontainebleau in October 1807, French troops crossed the Pyrenees. A contingent of 25,000 men under Junot marched to Lisbon to seize the Portuguese navy and treasure, to find that the fleet had sailed with the treasure and the royal family under a British convoy. Portugal was then held in French occupation.

Nevertheless French troops continued to pour into Spain during February and March 1808, until there were nearly 100,000 men in the Peninsula. They took possession of the four most important Spanish strongholds, they poured into Madrid, producing upon the Spanish royal family "the benumbing effect of a boa-constrictor upon its prey." At last in alarm Charles IV and Marie-Louise and Godoy made preparations for flight, but were checked at Aranjuez by an insurrection of the Spanish people, who forced the King to abdicate in favour of his son Ferdinand. Ferdinand was a national hero simply by virtue of his opposition to his mother and her paramour, for he was pusillanimous and vacillating by temper, and surrendered to Napoleon with hardly an attempt at sustained protest. An interview was held at Bayonne in May 1808 between the rival Spanish monarchs and Napoleon, who by a mixture of guile and threat in-

---

[1] Perhaps his best title to fame is that he was patron of the famous painter Goya (1746–1828).

[2] Many of them, it is worth noting, returned to fight against the French in Spain.

duced them both to renounce their claims to the throne. Joseph Bonaparte was called from Naples to be King of Spain and the Indies, and Murat was sent to Italy to replace him.

Thus Napoleon was in possession of the whole peninsula. There arose against him, however, an unexpected enemy. "A country as full of monks as yours is easy to subdue," he had remarked, ignoring entirely a factor of which the history of France should have reminded him—the people. The very incompleteness of the national amalgamation showed the tenacity of the national and provincial character. It was a proud people with dogged attachments, entirely uninfluenced by the doctrines of the French Revolution, and not yet susceptible to promises of reformed constitutions. It saw in Napoleon only the enemy of the national religion, invader of the national integrity, and despoiler of the crown. Led by Asturias, province after province rose against the French in a resistance which was at once "national in its spontaneity and local in its intensity." In June 1808 the world saw the unfamiliar spectacle of the surrender at Baylen of a French army to the comparatively ill-organized Spanish forces. Baylen (June 1808). What Valmy was in the war of the French Revolution against Europe, Baylen was in the war of Europe against Napoleon— the dawn of a new era. Joseph withdrew from Madrid, and Napoleon, furious to the length of ordering the imprisonment of Dupont and the other officers who had capitulated, found himself unexpectedly confronted with the necessity of conquering a land which gave all the advantages to the defence. The geographical conformation favoured the type of guerrilla warfare in which the Spaniards excelled, and its peninsular situation gave easy accessibility to the British fleet and British resources. For the Spanish appeal to England was quickly answered; in August troops were landed in Portugal which under Sir Arthur Wellesley, a young general who had already distinguished himself at the battle of Assaye,[1] defeated Junot and his army at Vimeiro. It was followed by the Convention of Cintra, signed by Sir Hew Dalrymple, by which the French forces were to withdraw from Portugal. They were to be conveyed in British ships and allowed to retire with their spoil. Although these last two clauses were severely condemned in England they could not dim the importance of the French withdrawal or the larger significance of the fact that Napoleon's troops had been defeated twice within three months.

But the master could still be victorious. In a brief campaign snatched at the end of the year 1808 between the political scheming of Erfurt and a new war against Austria Napoleon, at the head of 150,000 men, routed the Spanish forces, reinstalled his brother in

---

[1] 1803, against the Mahrattas ; " the severest engagement hitherto fought in India."

Madrid, introduced such reforms as the abolition of feudal laws and the Inquisition in a vain attempt to conciliate the natives, and drove

Napoleon in Spain. to the coast a small force of 26,000 British which had penetrated into the north of Spain. There General Sir John Moore achieved all that he could. He had drawn off the Emperor from Southern Spain; he conducted a masterly retreat, and he secured the embarkation of his troops by the battle of Coruña against Soult, though he himself fell on the field. For Napoleon, already called from Spain by intrigue in Paris and the rumours of a new war brewing in Europe, had left the end of the campaign to his marshal.

It was characteristic of Napoleon that he should dally with schemes of Eastern and overseas enterprise while he was still engaged in the subjugation of the Pope and the kingdoms of Spain and Portugal. Proposals both for the partition of Turkey and for a joint expedition to India were made to the Tsar, but they may have been little more than political devices to hold his wavering allegiance. For not only were the harmonies of Tilsit growing faint, but all Europe was conscious that the Spanish rising had caused profound changes in the political situation. Napoleon, realizing that only by a firm alliance with Alexander could he maintain his hold over Central Europe, invited the Tsar to a conference at Erfurt in September 1808. There

Erfurt (September 1808). he hoped to re-establish his ascendancy, and the meeting was in truth graced with pretty scenes. There were the resplendent equipages of four kings and thirty-four princes to lend dignity to Napoleon's suite; there was the affecting incident at the theatre when both Emperors stood up and clasped hands at the words, "The friendship of a great man is the gift of the gods"; there was talk of a new marriage between the Bonaparte and a Romanov princess. Nevertheless Napoleon achieved little by the conference except a social effect and a little reflected glory that came from the homage of Wieland and Goethe. From Alexander he extracted, before he left for the Spanish campaign, only a secret promise that he should have Russia's support if Austria should strike first against France. Perhaps Alexander was weighing the treacherous suggestions of Talleyrand: "Sire, what do you do here? It is for you to save Europe, and you will only succeed in that by resisting Napoleon. The French people are civilized, their sovereign is not. The sovereign of Russia is civilized, her people are not. Therefore the sovereign of Russia must be the ally of the French people."

Six months later, in April 1809, Austria, impelled by one of those

Austria again makes war, national impulses which, inspired by the example of Spain, were beginning to make themselves felt in Central Europe, declared war against France for the fourth time in two decades. And for the fourth time Austria was to be beaten by Napoleon.

With marvellous rapidity Napoleon advanced into Bavaria, conducted a fine piece of military manœuvring, won a five days' battle
round Ekmühl on the Upper Danube, and three weeks and is
later entered Vienna.   Although in an attempt to force the defeated.
Danube he was compelled to withdraw at Aspern Essling, he wiped
out the defeat and gave a decisive blow to the war in the hotly contested battle of Wagram in July.   The Emperor Francis
was forced reluctantly to make peace.   The promised help Wagram.
from England had resulted only in the mismanaged expedition to
Walcheren, which though "it gave Napoleon one of the worst frights
of his life " had failed in its object of seizing Antwerp; news also
arrived that Wellesley had retired on Portugal after the battle of
Talavera; [1] the Tsar had been bribed with the offer of Galicia to
maintain his alliance with France; the Pope was a prisoner in
the Emperor's hands; other risings in Germany had all been suppressed.

Austria lost by the terms of peace three and a half million subjects
and territory on the German, Polish, and Italian frontiers. Treaty of
She was forced to pay a heavy indemnity, to join the Con- Schönbrunn
tinental System and recognize the new Spanish kingdom. (October
A few months later she gave a princess to the con- 1809).
queror. For dynastic reasons the much-talked-of divorce Divorce of
of Josephine had at last been arranged and Napoleon had Josephine
asked and received in marriage a daughter of the Habs- riage with
burgs, that to carry on the name of the royal *parvenu* there Marie-
might be a son who should have the proudest monarch in Europe Louise.
for a grandfather.

IV. THE DOWNFALL (1810–15)

Napoleon's second marriage marked the measure of his triumph
over old Europe; it marked too the measure of old Europe's triumph
over him, the victory of the dynastic idea over the Revolution, the
power of royal entail upon the career of individual genius.   When
in 1811 an heir was born the pledge of perpetuance seemed to have
been given to his greatness, and the proudest of Imperial memories
was recalled in the title of the King of Rome.   The Napoleonic
empire was at its height.   Austria was subdued and allied The
in marriage, Spain and Portugal were cowed, the Pope height of
humbled, Sweden submissive, the rupture of the Franco- power
Russian alliance had been averted; England was suffering (1810–11).
heavily from commercial distress, and was, furthermore, drifting into

[1] It was after the battle of Talavera that Wellesley was created Viscount
Wellington.

war with the United States of America. Napoleon's word was
law from the Baltic to the Mediterranean, from the Tagus to the
Niemen.

But already the forces were collecting which were to bring about
the destruction of the Imperial edifice. The building was, in fact,
never completed, never made storm- and weather-proof before it
began to crack and crumble, to show a fissure here or a breach there

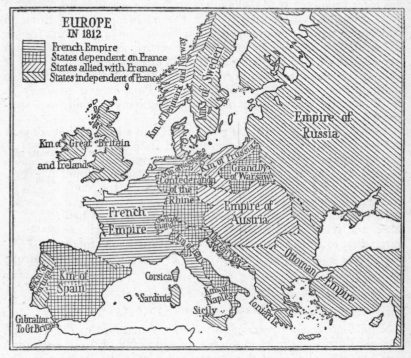

where England directed her battering-rams. In Italy Sicily and
Calabria held out against the conquest of the kingdom of Naples,
in the Iberian peninsula resistance had only been dispersed to the
hills to be mobilized again by an English general; the civil and
military reforms of Stein and Scharnhorst were regenerating Prussia,
and a new age began for Germany when Fichte gave his *Addresses
to the German People*. Popular exasperation under the economic,
financial, and military pressure of France was everywhere stirring
a new spirit of offensive. At Schönbrunn a young Tyrolese had
tried to kill the tyrant. In France the people were growing weary of
glory and of the unceasing drain upon their manhood. There was

treachery in Paris; Fouché and Talleyrand could not be trusted;
twenty-seven vacant bishoprics showed the temper of the Church.

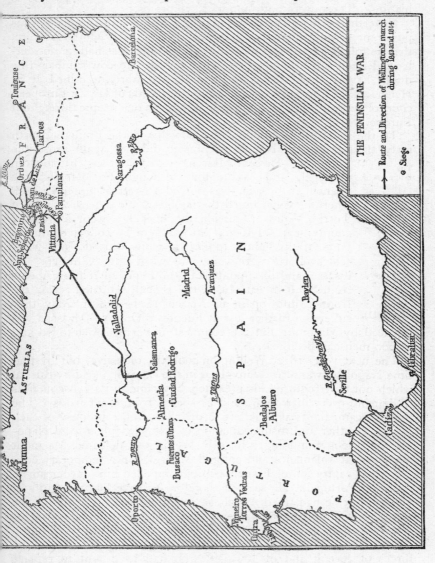

Even the Emperor's brothers were ungrateful, and Louis Bonaparte
talked of his "divine right" to the kingdom of Holland.

As for Napoleon, he had lost a battle, and he had begun to talk of the "nature of things," of an impalpable destiny which was guiding his life. These were both ominous symptoms.

Nevertheless, so great was Napoleon's genius and so effective his power of organization, so weak the inherent parts of the Empire, that he might have overcome his existing difficulties had he not embarked upon a fresh enterprise. But for the Moscow campaign he might have realized the conception he afterward described at St Helena, of "a European system, a European code of laws, a European court of appeal. There would then have been one people throughout Europe."

To the relief of Wellington, who considered the Emperor worth forty thousand men, Napoleon himself did not again cross the Pyrenees. He sent Masséna to drive out the British from Portugal, and Wellington, although he defeated the French at Busaco, was forced to retreat upon Lisbon, where he constructed the famous triple defensive lines of Torres Vedras. Outside the lines he swept a tract of country bare of food; within them he collected inhabitants, troops, and supplies. Against this defence Masséna's efforts were vain, and worn out by hunger and disease, and disappointed in the hopes of reinforcements from Soult in Andalusia, the French returned across the frontier into Spain in March 1811, and in May they suffered a further loss at Fuentes d'Onoro. Masséna was replaced by Marmont, but the conquest of Portugal was foiled and 35,000 men had been lost.

The Conquest of Portugal fails.

Busaco (September 1810).

Lines of Torres Vedras (October–November 1810).

Fuentes d'Onoro (May 1811).

The next year, 1812, Wellington took the offensive, but by that time Napoleon was already involved in the campaign against Russia, which not only required his presence, but came in its consequences to demand every man that could be spared from other fields. The Spanish campaign was thus left to marshals whose jealousy of each other and insubordination to King Joseph proved Napoleon's undoing. In July Wellington defeated Marmont at Salamanca and entered Madrid, but a temporary concentration of French armies compelled him once again to retire on Portugal. He seemed therefore to have lost the fruits of victory, but he had freed Andalusia and preserved his army for the triumphant campaign of 1813, conducted in real co-operation with the Spanish armies. In May Wellington advanced to Valladolid, and thence to Vittoria, where he defeated the forces of Joseph and of Jourdan, who had been sent to replace Soult. Joseph, to his brother's disgust, abandoned the struggle and fled to Saint-Jean-de-Luz, but though Napoleon hastily sent back

The Spanish war.

Salamanca (July 1812).

Vittoria (May 1813).

Soult to Spain he was unable to recover a country which was irretrievably lost, and the only result was to tie up 150,000 men who were by that time badly needed to save Napoleon himself in Saxony.

Wellington had nevertheless a stupendous task, not only in the encountering of such difficulties as arose from the defection of his allies and the obstinate indiscipline of his own troops, but still more in the conduct of intricate campaigns in what was becoming, as he advanced north, country of almost insuperable geographical difficulty. He could count only upon one advantage—the infinitely greater demoralization of the French troops.

The fights of the Pyrenees.

Slowly and relentlessly he forced his way across the Pyrenees, pushing the French army before him. His passage consisted of a series of severely contested fights, many of which gave him only a slight advantage of position, some of which seemed to be almost defeats. It was in the end the Iron Duke's rigid discipline, his invincible will and "transcendent common sense," that triumphed, together with the fact that Napoleon himself had been beaten in another quarter.

In June Wellington invested San Sebastian on the coast and the old walled city of Pamplona; the former was taken by storm in August, but it was not until October that the latter fell. Then, crossing into France, Wellington forced Soult from his position on the Nivelle and advanced to the investing of Bayonne, which he established by the hard-fought battles of the Nive and Saint-Pierre, and by the passage of the Adour. Leaving Bayonne invested, Wellington in February 1814 began to pursue Soult's army, which was retreating eastward across the low spurs of the Pyrenees. There were encounters at Orthez and Tarbes, and a contest before Toulouse that was by no means victorious for Wellington. But by this time the French cause was already lost; the Allied armies in the North had entered Paris. On April 11 Napoleon himself abdicated; on the 12th Toulouse and Bayonne surrendered, and the Peninsular War was at an end.

The Spanish imbroglio was one of Napoleon's most serious mistakes, and one of the principal causes of his fall. He entered upon it unscrupulously, counting upon the absence of opposition. When resistance came he underestimated its strength. Great Britain made a wise departure from her previous policy in undertaking a sustained land campaign in the Peninsula, and the endurance and generalship of Wellington were factors omitted from Napoleon's calculations. Once the Emperor had embarked upon war he could not draw back without acknowledging defeat, and yet, though he recognized this, he threw neither the full power of his genius nor all his resources into its successful conclusion. He hurried away in 1809 before he had himself completed the conquest of Spain; he did not support Masséna

I

in 1810; he withdrew Soult in 1812, and in 1813 he wasted men in trying to recover what was lost. His own faults were aggravated by the mediocrity of Joseph and the jealousies of his generals, and 300,000 Frenchmen were lost in the Peninsula without securing anything but the hatred of the Spanish nation.

Most serious of all was the entering upon fresh Continental commitments before the Spanish issue was decided. The "Spanish Ulcer" then became a prolonged drain upon Napoleon's resources, and the Spanish resistance a continual inspiration to the peoples of Europe. In Spain itself the struggle led to an awakening which the ideas of the French Revolution had stirred elsewhere but had utterly failed to achieve in the Peninsula. It struck the death-blow to the *ancien régime*; and, as a French historian remarks, "after having fought against France for six years Spain proceeded to fight for sixty years to impose French ideas upon its restored dynasty."

During 1810 and 1811 Napoleon himself was engaged in the administration of his empire and the pursuit of the economic blockade against England. He built canals and roads, encouraged manufactures, codified laws, constructed public monuments and works, and gave an impetus to the material development of his dominions which has only gathered force throughout the nineteenth century. He stimulated also certain kinds of liberal movements in the newly annexed provinces, but in France he hung heavier chains about the neck of freedom.

Much of the material benefit which Napoleon's subjects derived from his social legislation was undone by the rigorous economic measures which he tried to enforce against England, most of which recoiled upon his own empire. Napoleon, who despised the ideology of the French Revolution, approached political economy in much the same empirical spirit with which he regarded religion. He held the view of Louis XIV and Colbert that the commercial prosperity of a country depended upon its exports, and he pursued a policy not dissimilar to that of the Grand Monarch. In every possible way he sought to keep out of Europe the exports of England and her colonies. He imposed prohibitive duties; he appointed an army of customs officers from whom he demanded superhuman vigilance and technical knowledge. He ordered warehouses of colonial produce to be destroyed. By these means he dealt heavy blows at English commerce, but as long as he allowed her to import Continental and even French wheat he averted the only danger which would necessarily bring her to her knees—fear of starvation, which with poor harvests and a growing population was no imaginary contingency. While England maintained her naval supremacy there was little chance of any other country seizing her

The Continental System enforced.

export trade, and increasing quantities of British-borne goods made their way into the Continent, through Spain and Portugal, up the Danube, under cover of special permits, by means of the inevitable smuggling. Devices of all kinds were adopted; there was a startling advance in the number of funerals, until it was found that the hearses were filled with sugar. And the enhanced prices of sugar, tobacco, coffee, cotton, and other commodities taxed the suffering peoples of the Continent without always harming Great Britain. Holland, which was almost entirely a commercial nation, was so seriously affected that its king, Napoleon's brother, refused to promulgate the Imperial decrees. Napoleon therefore annexed the country to France, along with the Duchy of Oldenburg and the Valais. Thus in 1812 enlarged France stretched from Lübeck on the Baltic to a point several miles south of Rome.

It was the commercial question which precipitated the break with Russia. It was evident that the alliance between the Emperors of the East and West was weakening under increasing strain. Napoleon, irritated by Alexander's lukewarm assistance in the war against Austria and offended by the rejection of his offer of marriage to the Tsar's sister, regarded the growing estrangement with a mixture of fatalism and reckless defiance.

The Tsar's francophil policy had arisen partly out of temporary annoyance with England, partly out of surrender to Napoleon's personality, and partly out of a desire to serve the ambitions of Russia, but there had always existed in Russia a party strongly opposed to it. Alexander himself was growing ever more conscious of the barrenness of its results. Russia was at the time involved through her own ambition or Napoleon's interests in five wars—with Persia, Turkey, Sweden, England, and Austria. Napoleon had failed to give the promised support in Turkey, and it was evident that the Peninsular War had deferred the partition of that country indefinitely. From Sweden Russia had, indeed, won Finland, but the acquisition lost some of its attractiveness by appearing to have been received at Napoleon's hands. As for the conflict with England and Austria, commercial distress was a serious result of the former, and Galicia a poor reward for the latter.

Alexander further took umbrage at Napoleon's seizure of Oldenburg, whose duke had married the Tsar's sister. Already he regarded as a dangerous menace the enlargement of the Grand Duchy of Warsaw in 1809, and the consequent encouragement of Polish nationalism. He demanded from Napoleon a public pledge that he would never revive the Kingdom of Poland, but this Napoleon refused to give.

Thus every measure betrayed or fostered suspicion between the two Emperors. Napoleon resented Alexander's growing power and independence; the Tsar was alarmed by the indefinite extension of the French Empire.

It was, however, a tariff revolution in Russia which finally led to war. For local reasons Alexander was unable to adhere any longer to the blockade of British exports. In October 1810 Napoleon requested him to lay an embargo on all neutral ships in Russian waters, on the plea that British merchandise made its way into the Continent under cover of forged certificates of origin. Alexander refused the request and issued a *ukase* in December facilitating the entrance of neutrals and putting a heavy duty on articles of luxury such as wines and silks, which were French exports. Napoleon regarded this as equivalent to a declaration of hostility—although he tried to shift the ground of dispute to Poland—and war followed in April 1812.

Napoleon seems to have undertaken the Russian campaign almost in the spirit of a welcome adventure. "Moscow," he said, "is the half-way house to India." He collected a new Grand Army, half of French troops, the rest, since many of his best French soldiers were in Spain, Germans, Italians, Poles, Illyrians, Swiss, Dutch, and a few Spaniards and Portuguese, a motley host of 600,000 men, with ammunition and supplies on the same colossal scale. There were contingents from Austria and Prussia; Polish patriotism furnished 60,000 soldiers against the Moscovite; but the refractory Bernadotte, who had been chosen heir apparent of Sweden, made terms with Alexander. Neither did Turkey support Napoleon.[1]

The expedition to Moscow was the first act in the great tragedy of Napoleon's fall.[2] It was preceded by a magnificent reception held by the Emperor at Dresden. There all the leading sovereigns of Germany, the Emperor of Austria, and the King of Prussia assembled to meet him; there Napoleon played the host in the capital of his Saxon vassal, "inviting his Imperial father-in-law to dinner every day, but the King of Prussia and the Master of the Castle, as people of inferior rank, only every other day."

The campaign opened with a rare testimony to one man's might as, in the early hours of midsummer morning, the central column of the great army of nations filed across the bridge of the Niemen at Kovno and debouched into the sandy wastes of Lithuania. It developed into a contest with forces before which the greatest genius retired broken —the religious patriotism of a people, the elements of nature, the inhospitable steppe, the trackless waste, cold, hunger, and disease. The strategy of Napoleon in penetrating into a country where even more than in Spain "small armies are beaten and large armies starve,"

The Russian campaign (June–December 1812).

[1] Peace was made between Russia and Turkey in May 1812.
[2] It has received the epic description it deserves in Tolstoy's *War and Peace*.

has often enough been criticized, and a Russian prisoner even pointed to the warning of Charles XII. But, as in Spain, Napoleon did not anticipate a sustained resistance; he proposed that an early battle would bring the Tsar to his feet. And possibly on one occasion an early battle might have been forced upon Russia but for the dilatoriness of Jerome Bonaparte, who was afterward cashiered. But in the face of more than half a million men what could the Russian armies do but retreat? And what timidity at first dictated policy came to advise. As Napoleon pushed farther into the country through Vilna to Smolensk peasants and soldiers alike retired before him, burning their

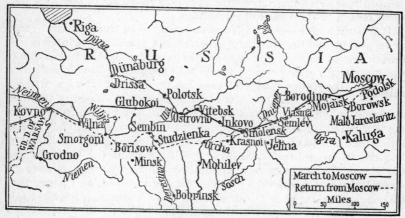

NAPOLEON'S RUSSIAN CAMPAIGN

food stacks and their towns. At Smolensk the Emperor, who ever found it difficult to turn back, resolved to press on to Moscow, although transport was difficult, food scarce, provisions and equipment, some of which came from England, had not arrived, although the men were dying of dysentery and the horses of the rank fodder, and the troops had fallen to marauding, although news had arrived of the defeat at Salamanca. At Borodino Kutusoff's army, which threw itself at last across his path, was defeated on a field of carnage where 100,000 men were slain. The victory gave "the beautiful and magical city" into Napoleon's power—Moscow, and, as he thought, Russia. Napoleon felt almost tenderly toward it—"a city that has been occupied by the enemy is like a woman that has lost her honour." He prepared to be magnanimous, to set free the serfs, to protect Mother Church as he had protected Catholicism in France and patronized Mohammedanism in Cairo. He entered Moscow on September 14 to find it abandoned, "that the

Borodino.

Moscow.

wolf might fall into the trap," the ancient and holy capital of Russia destroyed by a fire that might have been deliberate but could in any case hardly have failed to break out among its deserted wooden houses.   In Moscow Napoleon awaited expected overtures of peace from Alexander, occupying himself the while with the reorganization of the Comédie Française in Paris.   But from St Petersburg no word came, for two men were at hand fortifying the Tsar's resolution.   One was Bernadotte, elected Crown Prince of Sweden, who had been jealous of Napoleon from the days of Brumaire; the other was the indomitable German patriot Baron von Stein, reorganizer of Prussia, whom Napoleon had driven by an act of outlawry four years before to the Court of Alexander.

It was then October, and Napoleon, fearful of treachery in France or of a new coalition in Europe, dared not spend the winter in the remoteness of Russia.   He ordered the retreat.   And so began one of the most tragic marches in history.   Through the November snows **The retreat.** the troops trudged westward, their clothes in rags, without food or shelter, abandoning their loot, blowing up their ammunition, flinging away their weapons as the hardships of nature made them indifferent to defence against man; those who had horses killed them for food, and proceeded on foot.   Discipline broke down, and the troops robbed each other.   All the while the Cossacks and the Russian soldiers preyed upon their flanks and rear, cutting off stragglers; and as the men fell they died of the cold, and where they bivouacked at night a hundred little snow-covered hillocks would mark their frozen corpses in the morning.

The passage of the Beresina in the face of the enemy was bravely though barely effected, and when the floods abated 12,000 bodies told what price had been paid.   At length in the middle of December 20,000 men recrossed the bridge at Kovno, of all the host who had set out six months before.   There were stragglers and a contingent or two higher up the river and more than 100,000 men were distributed through Russian prisons.

"The Grand Army is destroyed.   His Majesty's health has never been better."   So ran the 29th Bulletin.   Leaving his army near the frontier, Napoleon hastened unknown through Germany back to Paris, to falsify reports of his death, put down conspiracy, and raise fresh troops.   In some ways the scenes of thirteen years before seemed to be repeated.

The retreat from Moscow aroused among Napoleon's enemies such **The War of Liberation (1813).** a mood as had not been seen in Europe since the Crusades. First the Spanish peoples had spoken, then the Russians, and now the Germans.   Yorck, the Prussian general commanding the Prussian contingent in Napoleon's army, signed on his own responsibility a convention with the Tsar, who was resolved to liberate Europe. The Estates of East Prussia sent resolutions demanding war, and when at length Frederick William III, urged by Stein and driven by the overwhelming national impulse, determined to join Alexander, and issued in February an unprecedented "Appeal to my People," there was an immediate and spontaneous response. Volunteers flocked to the colours until one in seventeen of the inhabitants was under arms—old soldiers, students, professors, schoolboys, miners, princes; "the peasant left his farm, the artisan his workshop." Poor women gave their gold wedding-rings as a national offering. Poets burst into song, the Germans marched to the War of Liberation with the verses of Arndt upon their lips, as the Frenchmen of '92 had marched to the *Marseillaise*.

Napoleon was now fighting against the very spirit he once had turned to his service, and the weapons he had employed against the ancient dynasties of Europe were now turned against its newest tyrant. By heroic efforts he managed to put 200,000 men into the field, mostly reserves and young recruits called up before their time. It was in Saxony that the campaign was fought, and the second act played in the tragedy of Napoleon's downfall. The Saxon campaign. Two victories at Lützen and Bautzen in May 1813 seemed to give the Emperor once again the assurance of ultimate triumph, but in reality they bore little fruit save to determine the wavering King of Saxony to adhere, to his own ultimate misfortune, to Napoleon's side. They were followed by a truce. Lützen and Bautzen.

Much depended upon the attitude of Austria, who had hesitated to join the coalition formed by Russia, Prussia, Sweden, and England against Napoleon. Napoleon refused, however, to concede her former Illyrian provinces in order to secure her support, and in August Austria declared war. When the campaign reopened, therefore, there was a Russo-Prussian army under Blücher in Silesia, a Swedish force approaching from the north, and Austrian troops advancing from the south upon Dresden. Outside the Saxon capital Napoleon won against the Austrians his last great victory. But he had not the men to pursue his advantage, and on all sides news arrived of the defeat of his lieutenants, at Grossbeeren, at Katzbach, at Dennewitz. The odds were too heavy against him, and were continually increasing; no single victory could stay the swelling tide which threatened to engulf him. Slowly the Allies closed in upon him; his garrisons capitulated, his detachments surrendered; he was forced back upon Leipzig. There in a four days' battle in the middle of October the campaign was forced to a decisive issue; there the greatest military conqueror of Europe The Fourth Coalition. Dresden (August 1813). Leipzig, "the Battle of the Nations" (October 1813).

was defeated in what was justly called "the Battle of the Nations." The French army, worn and diminished, was gradually overpowered by an enemy which was continually being strengthened during the struggle by fresh reinforcements. Even the Saxon regiments in Napoleon's army deserted to the enemy. The scales were too heavily weighted, the result could not be other than defeat, and at four o'clock in the afternoon the Emperor ordered the retreat. It is told that at nine o'clock a little man "in a peculiar dress" stood deep in thought, whistling *Malbrouck s'en va-t-en guerre*, and watching the rout of his army.

With the defeat of Leipzig the whole Napoleonic edifice collapsed. Bavaria and Mecklenburg had already seceded to the Allies; the Confederation of the Rhine and the kingdom of Westphalia fell to pieces, the Rhenish provinces were occupied by Prussia, the last garrisons surrendered, and the cities of the Baltic shook off the yoke of the conqueror. States opened their ports to Great Britain and the Continental System perished. Denmark concluded peace with the Allies, the princes of Germany hastened to make terms for themselves. The Dutch rose in revolt and formed a provisional Government under the Prince of Orange, Jerome Bonaparte fled, Murat, King of Naples, and his wife Caroline, sister of Napoleon, deserted to the enemy. Eugène alone, whose mother Napoleon had divorced that he might found a dynasty, remained faithful in Italy.

Not yet, however, was Napoleon's indomitable will bent to submission. Although the French legislature and Council of State demanded peace, although the Allies offered from Frankfurt terms which included the retention by Napoleon of his throne and by France of Belgium, Savoy, and the Rhine frontier—terms which in the light of later history were highly favourable—the Emperor could not bring himself to accept them. He had conducted a skilful retreat, and "by next May," he exclaimed, "I shall have a quarter of a million of men on the Rhine." He would not acknowledge defeat, convinced as he was that to do so meant the ruin of his power. "I will die," he had said to Metternich in August, "rather than cede a hand's-breadth of soil. Your born kings can accept defeat twenty times over and still go back to their palaces. I am the child of fortune, and I cannot do this. My power will not outlast the day on which I cease to be strong, on which I cease to be feared." From the first year of his empire the sentiment had been in his mind, spurring him on to fresh wars and at the end to a last obstinate resistance.

The defensive campaign in France.

Thus the Allies had still to fight their way to Paris through a third campaign in the valleys of the Seine and the Marne. It was an heroic struggle, demonstrating once again Napoleon's brilliant generalship, his resourceful strategy. In addition to Wellington's army, which crossed the Pyrenees, three armies invaded France from the north and east—Bülow from Belgium, Blücher with a combined Russo-Prussian army from the Rhine, and Schwarz with the Austrians from Switzerland and Basel. With the advantage of interior lines Napoleon dashed from one army to another. In February Blücher defeated him at La Rothière, and for a moment he came near to accepting peace on terms which would still have left him his throne, But the next morning he rallied, resolved to avenge himself on Blücher, and inflicted within a few days three such rapid blows upon the Austrian and Prussian armies as seemed almost to promise him a victory in the last ditch. The Austrians wavered, but Blücher's dogged patriotism pushed on, and Napoleon's small army, worn out by forced marches, diminished by repeated battles, could not prevail against the weight of the numbers which accumulated against it. Napoleon determined upon a last bold move—to strike across to Lorraine, cut off the enemy's communications, and draw off and perhaps divide his forces. The manœuvre failed, for the Allies replied with an equally bold counterstroke against Paris. On March 30 the heights of Montmartre were taken, and the French capital surrendered to the Tsar.

Napoleon hurriedly returned to Fontainebleau, but the Senate and the legislature were demanding his abdication; the Empress, ignoring the courageous counsels of her predecessor, Josephine, had fled to Blois with the King of Rome; Talleyrand was preparing with the Allies' ambassadors a restoration of the Bourbons. Fouché, who with Talleyrand contrived to put himself at the head of the new order, suggested deliberately that Napoleon should go to America. The marshals were deserting one after another—Marmont, who had been with him from the days of Toulon, Augereau, victor of the Italian campaign, Ney, who had valiantly held the rearguard in the retreat from Moscow, even Berthier surrendered to the Provisional Government. On April 11 the Emperor signed away the throne for himself and his son. On the 20th he bade farewell to his Guard, kissed the Imperial eagles, and amid the

Napoleon's first abdication (April 11, 1814).

tears of his soldiers set out through a by no means friendly France to that island of Elba which was allotted to him for empire, while a portly gentleman from Buckinghamshire proceeded to take his place upon the throne of France.

For ten months Napoleon ruled in Elba, organizing his miniature kingdom, and watching the course of affairs in France and Europe. He saw the Allies quarrelling over the division of spoils and the *émigré* and clerical party leading reaction in France.

Elba.

He saw the army growing restive beneath severe retrenchment and deliberate slights, and the peasantry regarding with apprehension a restoration of their lands to their pre-Revolutionary owners. He saw a people bored with its *grospapa*, who held no place in its heart or imagination.

On March 1 Napoleon, having escaped from Elba, landed with 1100 men near Cannes. Avoiding the route through the Royalist Provence, where in 1814 he had been received with execra-
The Hundred Days (March–June 1815).
tion and had been compelled to disguise himself in an Austrian uniform and don the white cockade of the Bourbons, he crossed the spurs of the Alps and advanced to Paris. His progress became a triumphant procession. The peasants flocked to his support, and the troops sent to oppose him were won over near Grenoble by a characteristic gesture. Opening his coat, he stepped in front of them. "Which of you will fire upon his Emperor?" Then without a shot fired he entered the capital, Louis XVIII and the Comte d'Artois fled, ministers and marshals shamefacedly returned to him. With promises of peace and liberty he took over the Government, persuading the staunch republican Carnot to take the portfolio of the Interior, and the leading liberal publicist, Benjamin Constant, to frame a Constitution. To point a contrast with the Bourbons, a national plebiscite was taken, and in a magnificent ceremony held in the Champ de Mars, where the Imperial splendour flashed forth for the last time, the Emperor swore before all the people to observe the Constitution.

Nevertheless there was an air of restraint, of gloomy acquiescence, about the capital. "Every one was gloomy," says de Broglie, "listless, uncomplaining, without hope, but not without anxiety." The nation wanted peace above everything, and they feared that it was neither in Napoleon's nature nor in his power to bring it about. And the Emperor himself knew while he held out hopes of pacific negotiations with the Allies that his late enemies would never accept the rupture of the treaties, and that only by war and victory could he reestablish himself on the French throne. "Europe and you, sire, will never come to terms," Metternich had replied to Napoleon in 1813. "When you have made peace it has been nothing more than a truce. To you success and failure are equally strong motives for war." It was a profound commentary on the situation in 1813; still more was it applicable to the state of affairs in 1815.

The Allies, having outlawed Napoleon as "the enemy and destroyer of the peace of the world," pledged themselves to put and keep their armies in the field until "Bonaparte should have been rendered absolutely incapable of stirring up further trouble." They virtually renewed the Treaty of Chaumont of the year before, which had bound them to a vigorous prosecution of the war and to a joint peacemaking. Even Marie-Louise placed herself and her son under the protection of the Allies. On the other hand Murat, King of Naples, who had been intriguing against the Powers to whom he had deserted, called upon Italy to accept Napoleon as king. He was Napoleon's only ally, and, in the event, a useless one.

And so yet another war was to break out under the star of Napoleon. The campaign was fought in Belgium, but from the very beginning Napoleon was hopelessly outnumbered. France, disenchanted and embittered, responded without enthusiasm to **War.** his appeal for men. He dared not re-enact the hated conscription, and with all the National Guards, sailors, militiamen, and customs officials that he could call up he could barely put into the field more than 120,000 men, not including those told off to suppress a Royalist rising in La Vendée. It was therefore clearly to his advantage to strike first, for when the Allies assembled their combined forces they could put 800,000 men into the field. On June 12 Napoleon left Paris, to return only nine days later, humiliated and defeated for ever.

The Allied forces in Belgium consisted of two armies, a mixed Anglo-Dutch-Belgian-German force under Wellington and the Prussian troops under Blücher. They numbered twice as many men as Napoleon had at his disposal, and were strung loosely along a line of a hundred miles from Ghent to Liége. The Prussians were on the left with their headquarters at Liége, the British on the right, centring mainly at Brussels. Briefly Napoleon's plan was that frequently adopted before, of dividing the enemy and then falling upon the separate parts. On June 15 the French crossed the Sambre and took Charleroi, thus coming into contact with the Prussian right. But the loss of valuable time, which was noticeable more than once during the campaign, and was perhaps due to Napoleon's ill-health, enabled Blücher to concentrate troops against the French at Ligny. Nevertheless Napoleon was able to drive them to a retreat on the 16th, in what was to prove his last triumph, although a con- **Ligny.** fusion of orders prevented the arrival of a contingent which would have given to the Emperor an overwhelming victory. On the same day Marshal Ney with another detachment held Welling- **Quatre-** ton's reinforcements in check at Quatre-Bras. **Bras.**

On the 17th Napoleon turned north-west to confront Wellington, under the impression that Blücher had retreated too far east to be able to come to the rescue of the British general. On Sunday the 18th the two armies met in battle a little to the south of Waterloo. At the beginning the two forces were not unevenly matched, but again Napoleon lost valuable time, and the fight did not begin till midday, thus enabling the Prussian reinforcements to come up before the issue was decided. The Allied troops and the 24,000 British—"the thin red line"—stood firm against the artillery and cavalry charges, and when,

a little too late, the Imperial Guard was brought into action it fell back
Waterloo.   mangled and repulsed by the British batteries. Toward
four o'clock in the afternoon the arrival of Blücher's troops
began to affect the progress of the battle and to convert the repulse

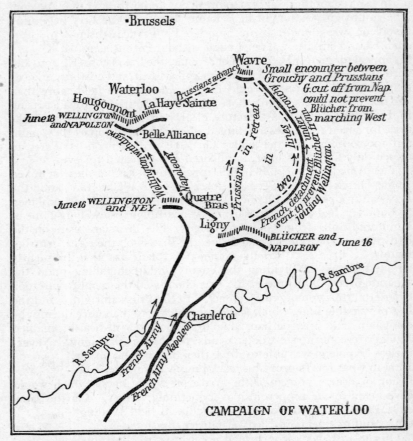

CAMPAIGN OF WATERLOO

into a rout, which, carried on late into the night by a relentless pursuit,
destroyed the last army of the French Emperor.

It was Napoleon's sixtieth and final battle. After vainly trying to
rally the fugitives he returned to Paris. But he had no longer the
The second   strength to combat the insistent demands for his abdica-
abdication   tion, and on June 22 he signed his renunciation. As the
(June 1815).   Prussians were approaching the French capital he withdrew
to the coast with some vague intention of retiring to America and taking

up literature. Then on a sudden impulse, or perhaps because the seas were infested with British cruisers, he entrusted himself "of his own free will"—"not as a prisoner of war," but as a "private person" —to Admiral Maitland of the *Bellerophon*. To the Regent he sent an appeal. "I come like Themistocles to throw myself upon the hospitality of the British people. I place myself under the protection of your laws." But England was insensible, or could not afford to yield, to the classical allusion and to the appeal to her generosity and hospitality. In Plymouth harbour Napoleon learnt his sentence—exile at St Helena, with three officers, a St Helena. physician, and twelve servants. Napoleon's star had set for ever.

There on the wind-swept, rocky island in the South Atlantic, after nearly six years of durance, Napoleon died on May 5, 1821.

CHAPTER V

EUROPE FROM 1815 TO 1850

I. The Concert of Europe (1815–25)

In violent contrast with the two decades which preceded it, the period from 1815 to 1850 was one of little dynamic achievement, and outside the important spheres of mechanical, industrial, and literary progress there was no great difference between the Europe of 1815 and that of 1850. Belgium had broken away from Holland, Greece from Tur-

Period of little political achievement. key; there were some changes in the wearers of crowns; France was calling herself a republic instead of a monarchy; there was more bitterness in the hearts of disappointed democrats, and more antagonism in the policies of trium-

phant autocrats, a change of emphasis here and there, but the great constructive political work of the nineteenth century lay still in the future.

In the political world the period seemed to have been a failure. Outside the Eastern Question, which must be considered apart, two

Two constructive ideas defeated. successive constructive ideas were put forward, that of the Concert of Europe, which emanated from the kings, and that of liberal nationalism, which was the product of the peoples. Both for different reasons failed to achieve suc-

cess in practical politics. Nevertheless the period was not one of stagnation. It was a time of restless struggle between opposing

Reaction and preparation. forces, neither of which completely triumphed. On the one side there was a reaction against the principles and im-pulses of the French Revolution, on the other a real pre-

paration for the democratic and nationalist achievements of later years.

For the French Revolution had propounded a problem which had not been solved by the defeat of Napoleon. It had, like all conflicts, asked a question, and the answers to it were to make history between the years 1815 and 1850 and in some aspect or other for the rest of the century. The question was, in different forms, applied alike to art and religion; in politics it was, briefly: What recognition in the government of states was to be given to the will of the peoples who compose them? It was the underlying issue in almost all the important struggles of the nineteenth century, the unifications of Italy and Germany, the development of Russia, the rise and fall of the Second French Empire, the socialist and feminist movements of modern times. It formed the main content of the history of Europe between 1815 and 1850, the tenor of the struggles between what was variously called legitimacy, conservatism, autocracy, on the one hand, and liberalism, democracy, nationalism, and revolution on the other.

The foundations of the European states system of the nineteenth century were laid at Vienna, by the monarchs and plenipotentiaries who assembled there by agreement after the defeat of Napoleon to dispose of the lands which had been surrendered and to resettle a disturbed Continent. It was a motley collection *The Congress* of diplomats and hangers-on, ambassadors and adven- *of Vienna* turers, princes and pretenders, priests and professors, *(1814–15).* soldiers and statesmen, agents of all the Powers of Europe except the Porte, and representatives of most interests, seeking amid intrigue and the gaiety and trifling which seemed so serious a part of the Congress's activities to serve a cause, avenge a grievance, or secure a profit. Ardent Catholics were there, and French marshals anxious about their pay, and Hanseatic Jews building their power on the financial necessities of the impoverished Austrian Emperor; "Turn-vater" Jahn, the German nationalist, and Czartoryski, the mainstay of Polish independence. Science was represented only *Per-* in the curiosity of Charles Augustus of Weimar, but *sonalities.* journalism could claim the notable publisher, Cotta, whose wide political and literary interests had already done so much to revive the fortunes of his house.

Francis I [1] of Austria played the host, "an unpretending figure in a shabby blue coat," a dull egoist, with the sinister flavour that pervaded some of the Habsburgs. His perspicacity was well content to spend £800,000 on the entertainment of the Congress, though his unpaid veterans begged in the streets, and his prying curiosity delighted in the reports of his indefatigable spies, in the reading of intercepted letters and the discovery of the scandalous diversions of his princely guests.

His Foreign Minister, Metternich, presided over the Congress and soon became its guiding spirit. For it was natural that the four great Powers, Austria, Russia, Prussia, and England, should arrogate to themselves the chief direction in the resettlement of Europe, though in the later sessions of the Congress Talleyrand's diplomacy secured a measure of influence for France. Since, however, Great Britain was not in full accord with the other three Powers, and her representatives, Castlereagh and Wellington, were not adequately

---

[1] He was Francis II, Holy Roman Emperor, until 1804. From that date he became Francis I, Hereditary Emperor of Austria.

supported by the British Parliament, and since Frederick William III, a modest follower and admirer of the Tsar, allowed the policy of Prussia to be largely determined by that of Russia, it fell to Metternich, the Austrian plenipotentiary, and Alexander, the Tsar of Russia, to play the chief *rôles* at Vienna.

Metternich, who from the year 1809 guided the policy of Austria for nearly forty years, was to become the most important figure **Metternich** in Europe during the next two decades. His personal **(1778-1859).** charm and social gifts, his diplomatic experience and powers, his astute insight into men, his suavity and his *flair* for the niceties of intrigue, the ease and versatility with which he handled intricate questions, gave him an ascendency at the Congress and later a "moral dictatorship" over Central Europe. He "could swim like a fish in the sparkling whirlpool" of Vienna. "No one knew so well as he how to carry through a political intrigue between dinner and a masked ball," or to envelop a difficult situation in a golden mist of fine phrases.

He has been attacked as merely an intriguer, as an opportunist, as "polished dust." Alexander I roundly called him a liar, while liberals and democrats then and since have charged him with obscurantism and reactionariness, with an unstatesmanlike obtuseness toward the needs of the age and an unpardonable hostility to the desires of the people.

Metternich was, however, an Austrian minister, and it was Austrian interests that determined his policy. He realized that the Austrian Empire consisted of an incoherent congeries of states and dominions irregularly accumulated by hereditary bequest or marriage dowry, as the fruit of war or diplomacy, in the interests of the Balance of Power or as a bulwark of Christendom against Turkey. It was held together by no consistent principles save common obedience to a single lord, and Metternich saw that its equilibrium would be as seriously disturbed by popular or nationalist agitation as by French or Russian aggression. Behind his opportunism therefore, and behind his obscurantism, there lay a logical, defensible principle, the preservation of the Austrian Empire. "At the crisis of Austria's fortunes, during the final struggle with imperial France, when every one was wavering, despairing, and trying to find a way out of a sorry tangle, it was he who had given to Austrian policy the vigorous and certain direction which enabled him afterward to boast himself the conqueror of Napoleon."[1] So with as vivid an apprehension of danger he set himself equally to suppress the disruptive nationalist and democratic movements of Germany and Italy, to counter the independent aspirations of the Balkans, and to check the Tsar, who

[1] Professor Alison Phillips, *Modern Europe, 1815-99.*

coquetted mischievously with nationalist democracy in his Jacobin moods and leaned dangerously toward exploiting Balkan independence in his imperialistic ones. But his policy does not bear the impress of great statesmanship; it was too negative, piecemeal, and opportunist, and too little animated by constructive ideals. For Metternich was at heart out of sympathy with his age; "I have come into the world," he said, "either too early or too late. Earlier I should have enjoyed the age; later I should have helped to reconstruct it. To-day I have to give my life to propping up mouldering institutions." In such a spirit of cynicism he stood on the threshold of a period of unparalleled material and mental expansion. "For a tired and timid generation he was a necessary man; and it was his misfortune that he survived his usefulness and failed to recognize that, while he himself was growing old and feeble, the world was renewing its youth." [1]

But the Europe which has passed judgment on him enjoyed for forty years the peace which it was largely his merit to have secured, and the Austria which abandoned his policy lies now disrupted and shorn of her largest provinces.

The most illustrious as well as the most enigmatical figure at the Congress was that of the Tsar Alexander I. The part that he had played in the defeat of Napoleon gave him an authority   Alexander I in Western affairs never before exercised by a Russian   (1800–25; monarch. For the first time in history Russia was assum-   b. 1777). ing the leadership of Europe, and Austria and England in particular, among contemporary states, regarded with serious apprehension the growth of a power which they both feared and exaggerated.

But Alexander had neither the diplomatic astuteness nor the cynical persistence of Metternich, and there was as little Napoleonic about his character as there was in his appearance, in his huge frame and round face, his irresolute mouth and dreamy eyes. To his contemporaries as to posterity he was a riddle, to Napoleon "a shifty Byzantine," the "Talma [2] of the North," to Metternich "a madman to be humoured." Even in death he remained a mystery, and controversy still flourishes over the personality of a certain hermit, Theodor Kuzmich, who died in Siberia in 1864 and was alleged to be the Emperor Alexander.

By nature Alexander was unstable, impressionable, well intentioned, but infirm of purpose, a susceptible, imaginative egoist, an unpractical, inconsistent idealist. He "erected incoherency into a system," guided by erratic impulses which were the ill-assorted fruits of the contradictory influences to which his receptive temperament

---

[1] Professor Alison Phillips, *Modern Europe.*
[2] François Joseph Talma, a contemporary French actor.

K

had been subjected. His contemporaries saw him variously and intermittently incited by liberalism and despotism, mysticism and imperialism, and thought him unreliable and dangerous, and often a deceiver and hypocrite to boot.

From his Swiss tutor, La Harpe, he imbibed the theories of Rousseau and the sentiments of French democracy. From his Russian governor he acquired a taste for militarism and military display which consorted with his autocratic traditions and instincts, his vanity and personal ambition. The murder of his father in a conspiracy to which, without foreseeing the end, he had been privy bred in his sensitive mind a horror and remorse which developed later into a settled gloom and made him easily susceptible to the religious and pietistic influences of the age.

In his liberal moods he granted a constitution to Finland, planned the regeneration of Poland, emancipated the serfs of some of the Northern Russian provinces, supported the abolition of slavery, and put forward proposals for a League of Nations. His imperialism led him to ambitious schemes for the territorial aggrandizement of Russia, to the conquest of Finland, to an alliance with Napoleon for the partition of Turkey and the subjugation of Asia. He became easily a prey to disillusionment, and then arbitrary and despotic actions betrayed his instincts, and fear of revolution and religious zeal confounded his liberalism.

In the middle and last years of Alexander's life the religious and visionary influences became dominant. As the defeat of his armies had been to him the manifestation of the wrath of God, so the turning of the French and the disasters of the retreat from Moscow were as clear a call to a heaven-sent mission. He conceived the idea, fostered by pietists and interested courtiers, that he was the divinely appointed instrument for the defeat of Napoleon, the "man from the North," "from the rising of the sun," spoken of by Isaiah, who should be summoned to the routing of Antichrist.

In the year 1815 Alexander may be said to have attained his apogee. He was the conqueror of conquerors, the liberator of Europe, the soldier of God whose sword had been blessed by the peoples and sanctified by the Lord.

The Congress of Vienna was heralded by lofty sentiment and high-sounding phrases in accord with the spirit of Alexander and the exalted mood of the moment, and much criticism has been directed toward the cynical commentary afforded by its achievements upon its protestations. The words of Gentz, secretary to the Congress, have been often repeated. "The fine phrases," he wrote, "about 'the reconstruction of the social order,' 'the regeneration of the political system of Europe,' 'an

The work of the Congress. Criticism.

enduring peace founded on a just redistribution of forces,' etc., were intended only to tranquillize the peoples and give to the solemn reunion an air of dignity and grandeur; the real object of the Congress was to divide among the conquerors the spoils of the conquered." It is an end which has inspired other congresses before and since.

The real charge that may be brought against the monarchs of Vienna is that they ignored the challenge of the French Revolution; that they failed to see that the new forces of democracy and nationality were becoming determining political factors. They accepted as the guiding principle of national demarcation the criterion of the Balance of Power, not the measure of popular sentiment. When they talked of securing the "rights, freedom, and independence of all nations" they did not mean to draw political frontiers round every group of articulate nationalists; they were bent on preventing another European cataclysm, upon imposing checks to potential tyrants. They thought in terms of traditional diplomacy, of dynasties and states, not in those of popular sympathies and national self-expression. Thus they set themselves against the forces of the age, and have been condemned by a century which has concerned itself with the undoing of their work. It is, however, given to few congresses to legislate for a century, while that of Vienna can at least claim to have inaugurated forty years of peace and of great activity, and in the name of international tranquillity history may even yet justify its work against the attacks of an age which brought about a world war in the interests of national self-expression.

Three chief principles moulded the Vienna settlement: that of rewards to the victors and retribution to the defeated, that of restoring where it was possible pre-revolutionary conditions, and that of providing guarantees for the future peace of Europe.

Thus Russia, Prussia, Austria, Great Britain, and in some measure Sweden were recompensed for the efforts they had put forth in the defeat of Napoleon. Russia received Central Poland as a constitutional kingdom allied in personal union to her crown, and the ratification of Finland and some small conquests from Turkey; Prussia was given Western Pomerania (taken from Sweden), part of Saxony, and valuable Rhenish provinces; to Austria was restored most of what she had lost, save Belgium and some scattered lands in South Germany, which she renounced in exchange for Venetia; Great Britain, whose commercial, naval, and colonial triumph had emerged from the wars in which she had been engaged, acquired Malta, Heligoland, a protectorate over the Ionian islands, the Cape of Good Hope, and other imperial advantages. She also induced the Powers to issue a declaration against the slave-trade.

Territorial arrangements.

Sweden was granted Norway (taken from Denmark) in exchange for Finland and Western Pomerania, which she had ceded to Russia and Prussia respectively.   Saxony was allowed to keep her royal title, but with Denmark she paid in territorial losses the penalty of having supported the unvictorious side.   The Grand Duchy of Warsaw and the kingdom of Westphalia were abolished.   Switzerland was restored to much of her previous cantonal disunion.   The return of the Pope to Italy and of the Bourbons to Naples, Spain, and France was sanctioned.   Proposals for the dismemberment of the country which

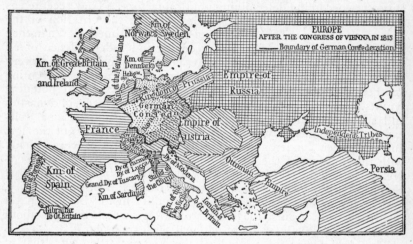

was prime author of the disturbance of Europe were defeated. France was permitted to retain her monarchical frontiers, as she was also guaranteed some of her revolutionary constitutional gains. Against future French aggression—for France in 1815, like Germany in 1918, was still feared, although she had been defeated—bulwarks were created by the transference of the former small Rhenish principalities to Prussia, by the union on the north-east frontier of Holland and Belgium into one kingdom, and by the strengthening of the kingdom of Piedmont-Sardinia in the south-east.

In some respects the arrangements of Vienna embodied the profound changes in political relationships and values which had taken place during the previous twenty years.   They marked the aggrandizement of Russia and her intrusion into Western affairs; they acknowledged the disappearance of the Holy Roman Empire, the withdrawal of Sweden into a comparative Scandinavian isolation and the abandonment of her trans-Baltic ambitions.   The simplification in the number of German states was a step in the direction of the later union; the concentration of Austria in Central Europe a stage on the way to her exclusion from Germany; while the newly strengthened kingdoms of Prussia and Sardinia formed the nuclei of two of the proudest achievements of the nineteenth century.

If the Congress of Vienna failed to satisfy the aspirations of Poland, if it ignored the population of Belgium and yoked Norway to an uncongenial partner, whom she endured nevertheless for ninety years, if it restored disunion to Italy and gave no permanent settlement to Germany, yet it showed both moderation and political wisdom, and it provided a real foundation on which later Europe was to build; and it preserved forty years of international stability.

The Vienna treaties were entrusted to the collective guarantee of the Powers, but the experience of the last few years had aroused a desire for greater international security and for some machinery for mutual protection. It was in response to this desire that the autocrats who were the masters of Europe attempted one of **The Concert** the most interesting political experiments of the century. **of Europe.** They tried to give practical shape to the idea of the Concert of Europe.

There was nothing new in the conception of a European federation in the interests of European peace. It was a commonplace of Revolutionary talk if not of Revolutionary practice; it entered into the politics of Napoleon and into the vocabulary of many monarchs and diplomatists of the day.

Two conflicting schemes were put forward which are often confused with each other. The first was that of the Holy Alliance, which seems to have been the result of the colloquies of the Tsar Alex- **The Holy** ander with the religious prophetess the Baroness von **Alliance.** Krüdener. It was signed in the first instance by the monarchs of Russia, Prussia, and Austria, and was proclaimed on September 26, 1815, at a great review of Allied troops held on the Champ des Vertus, near Paris.

The Holy Alliance was not a treaty; it was a solemn declaration initiated by Alexander and affirmed by the sovereigns of Europe with varying degrees of seriousness. They bound themselves "in the name of the most Holy and Indissoluble Trinity" to take for their political guidance "the sublime truths of Holy Religion." Like brothers "united in bonds of a true and indissoluble fraternity," and like members of one great Christian nation, they were to lend each other aid; "the sole principle of force shall be that of mutual service." Like fathers of families, they were to lead their subjects, "to protect religion, justice, and peace"; thus confessing that "the world has in reality no other Sovereign than Him to Whom alone all power really belongs, because in Him alone are found all the treasures of love, science, and infinite wisdom—that is to say, God our divine Saviour, the Word of the Most High, the Word of Life."

All European potentates except the Pope and the Sultan were invited to sign the document, and all finally did so except the Prince Regent of England, who covered Great Britain's refusal to commit herself to so vague a protestation by a letter expressing his general sympathy with the "sacred maxims" and explaining that all such declarations would need the counter-signature of a responsible minister.

In its intention the Holy Alliance was neither insincere nor anti-liberal; in fact, Alexander subsequently stated that he considered every member was bound by it to grant a Constitution to his subjects. But as political machinery it was useless, and as a diplomatic instrument a failure. Hardly anyone except Alexander regarded it seriously. To Castlereagh it was "a piece of sublime mysticism and nonsense" which, if it meant anything at all, might involve its members in dangerous and unforeseen commitments. To Metternich it was a "loud-sounding nothing" which might, however, possibly serve to harness the Jacobin Tsar to the more conventional diplomacy of the other European monarchs. Alexander was suspected of an ambition to make himself autocrat of Europe, and the omission of the Porte was held to be ominous—though Turkey could hardly have been invited to adhere to so essentially Christian a compact. Vainly from time to time the Tsar sought to give a "body" to "its transparent soul." But although the name of the Holy Alliance has become popularly attached to the European system between 1815 and 1825, neither its spirit nor its basic conceptions were really applied to contemporary politics. It survived only, in fact, to confuse but not conceal, like a misty veil, the self-interest common to diplomatic relations; a short-lived figment of Alexander's imagination; a memory or an ideal to inspire occasional action of subsequent Russian sovereigns, and to bear in later years a riper fruit in the great international peace movement which began with the Hague Conference of 1899.

Instead of Alexander's vision of a brotherhood of sovereigns inspired by Christian ideals there was substituted what was virtually a dictatorship of the Great Powers, guided largely by the diplomacy of Metternich. In November 1815 a Quadruple Alliance was signed by Russia, Prussia, Austria, and Great Britain for the maintenance of the treaties with France and for the consolidation "of the intimate relations now uniting the Four Sovereigns for the welfare of the world." They agreed to hold periodical meetings of the four signatory powers, "either under the immediate auspices of the sovereigns, or through their respective ministers," meetings "devoted to the grand interests they

The
Quadruple
(Quintuple)
Alliance.

have in common, and to the discussion of measures which shall be judged to be most salutary for the repose and prosperity of the nations and for the maintenance of the Peace of Europe."

The alliance was followed by a real attempt in congress and conference to bring about a practical international co-operation, and for a decade the idea of the Concert of Europe informed with diminishing vitality the tangled and self-interested diplomacy of the period.

The first congress was held in 1818 in the ancient Carolingian capital of Aix-la-Chapelle, where Napoleon had adumbrated his own scheme for the welfare of Europe, and where now the popular homage accorded to the Austrian Emperor marked that supremacy which was about to be assumed by his country and his ministers. (1) The Congress of Aix-la-Chapelle (1818).

On the chief question which came up for consideration—the position of France—compromise and agreement were reached. It was decided to withdraw the Allied army of occupation from French soil and to admit her representatives to the Concert of Europe. Her admission reopened, however, the question of the basis of union, and once again Alexander tried vainly to galvanize his Holy Alliance into life. But both England and Austria were against him, France was to be admitted simply on terms of treaty alliance with the four Powers, who—so strong was still the attitude of mistrust—renewed their own Quadruple Alliance as a protection against another half-anticipated crisis in French politics. At the same time, as a concession to Alexander, a new and grandiose statement was issued of the aims of the now enlarged Pentarchical Union. It set itself to a "strict observance of the rights of peoples," to give an example of "justice, concord, and moderation," to protect the "arts of peace," to "increase the prosperity of states," and "to awaken those sentiments of religion and morality which had been so much weakened by the misfortunes of the times"; while its sphere was to be extended by admitting to its deliberations lesser Powers whose affairs were under discussion.

Inspired by these ideals, the five Powers advanced to fresh triumphs of co-operation. They called King Bernadotte of Sweden to account for ignoring treaty rights with regard to Norway and Denmark; they ordered the ruler of Monaco to see to the better government of his principality; they disposed of the ambition of the elector of Hesse to take the title of king, and they gave a verdict in a Baden succession question which deprived Bavaria of the fat hope of the Rhenish Palatinate. Europe was profoundly impressed, and Bernadotte entered a protest on behalf of the lesser states against the tyranny of the Great Powers.

Before the Congress was dissolved, however, signs had already

appeared of the divergent interests and mutual jealousies which were
to paralyse action and break up the Concert of Europe. First was
the question of the rebellious South American colonies of Spain.
Between England and these as yet unrecognized states an informal
but important trade had grown up, and Castlereagh would agree to
no proposal either to bring them back to Spanish allegiance, or even
to mediate between them and the mother country, unless British
commercial interests were safeguarded. Joint action was similarly
checked against the troublesome Barbary pirates from North Africa,
who infested the southern coasts of Europe and carried their depredations as far as the mouth of the Elbe. Austria had even been compelled to put her sea-borne trade under the protection of the Ottoman
flag. England, however, resolutely refused to admit Russian ships
into the Mediterranean to put down the pirates.

Therefore the other Powers refused to give to Great Britain authority to search the seas for slave-traders who still carried on their
traffic in spite of prohibition. They thought it but another insidious
device of perfidious Albion to gain a commercial advantage.

Nevertheless the Congress separated with complacent tributes to
its unanimity; and at no stage in the subsequent history of the
Quintuple Alliance were the agreement of the Powers and the concerted action of Europe to reach so high a point. "I have never
seen a prettier little congress," wrote Metternich, for whom it had
been no less a triumph. Had he not already practically established
his position as pivot of the European system, and begun that
eminently desirable conversion of the Russian Tsar to his own anti-
Jacobin principles? Armed with the authority and prestige of the
Congress, he turned to the suppression of revolution in the German
Confederation, but, except that the repressive Carlsbad Decrees called
forth a disclaimer from Castlereagh against what he held to be an
unjustifiable interference in the affairs of sovereign states, his activities there lie more properly in the history of Germany than in that
of the European pentarchy. In Castlereagh's protest, however, was
the germ of the destruction of the Concert of Europe.

The second congress of the Powers, held significantly in Austrian
territory, first at Troppau in 1820, and then by adjournment at
(2) The   Laibach in 1821, revealed already the fatal anomalies of
Congresses   the European situation and vital differences of views and
of Troppau   interests between the Allied states.
and Laibach
(1820,   The core of the situation lay in the revolutions which
1821).   broke out in the early months of 1820 in Spain, Portugal,
and Naples. Within six months the democrats and malcontents of
these three states had risen against their 'legitimate' rulers and
forced them one after the other—Ferdinand VII of Spain, John VI

of Portugal, and Ferdinand I of Naples—to accept what had come to be regarded by the democrats of Southern Europe as the palladium of popular liberty—namely, the famous Spanish constitution of 1812.

These events were not without their reaction upon the five Powers of the Alliance. There was not one of them who did not condemn the revolutions as such, but there was by no means agreement as to the action to be taken. The Tsar, on the news of the Spanish revolt, called for a European congress to suppress that 'Jacobinism' in which he had come to see the chief enemy of Christendom, and he generously offered to dispatch 15,000 Russians through Austria and the South of France to the help of the Bourbon Ferdinand. Neither France nor Austria, however, wished to see such a demonstration of Russian power; Metternich therefore belittled the revolution, deprecated the need for European intervention, and so postponed the calling of a congress.

Then occurred the revolution in Naples, which wore an entirely different complexion. In the disturbance of the Bourbon kingdom of Naples Metternich saw a threat to Austrian supremacy in the Italian peninsula, and a menace to her empire. Thus although there was no need for intervention in Spain there had arisen an urgent need for intervention in Italy, and since neither Russia nor France would allow the isolated interference of Austria the Congress of Troppau was called practically for the purpose of sanctioning the suppression of the Italian revolution. It was opened, however, with a demand for the recognition of certain general principles, to which neither France nor England could adhere. Constitutions to be satisfactory must be granted by the king; a member of the Alliance which had undergone through revolution a change of government "imperilling the well-being of other states" was to be excluded from membership, and "in cases of immediate danger" the other states of the Alliance were to be empowered "to bring her back, if necessary, by force." These principles, embodied in the Troppau Protocol, and signed by the three Eastern Powers, were entirely foreign to British policy; they justified an intervention in the internal affairs of sovereign nations to which England herself would not have submitted and which she did not wish to see extended to Europe. For although she would have made no objection to Austrian intervention in Italy, which she recognized as coming within the sphere of purely Austrian politics, she feared a general application of the principle all over Europe, from Spain to Poland, from the Balkans perhaps to Ireland. Castlereagh therefore strongly demurred, and although there was as yet no actual breach of the Alliance there was a considerable widening of the rift within it.

At Laibach, where the adjourned Congress met in the following year, it was decided that Austria was to be entrusted with the task of restoring Ferdinand of Naples to his throne as an absolute monarch, and after a few weeks of what can only be called military burlesque the Austrians entered Naples and the revolution of Southern Italy came to an inglorious end. A further suppression of liberalism in Piedmont gave Italy into the hands of Austria.

The Congress had in the meantime arranged to reassemble at Verona, where the rupture already visible at Troppau and Laibach was to reduce the Concert of Europe to nothing more than a diplomatic fiction. In the interval an insurrection which broke out in Greece introduced further modifications into the relations of the Powers. Alexander, who considered the Balkan Question a dependent issue of Russian politics, was as anxious to take isolated action in Turkey as Metternich had been in Italy, while Metternich was as much determined to prevent him. In the desire to maintain the integrity of Turkey against Russian aggression Austria was supported by Great Britain, and in one of the greatest of his diplomatic triumphs Metternich succeeded not only in checking Russian action, but in staving off a discussion of the Greek Question at Verona.

To that congress it is probable that no British representative would have been sent but for the pressure of George IV and the possibility of a consideration of the Greek Question. The main issue turned upon the Spanish revolution. The Bourbon Ferdinand VII had appealed for help to the Bourbon Louis XVIII, and France, now at the height of an ultra-Royalist reaction, was inclined to play in Spain the *rôle* of intervener which Austria had played in Italy and Russia desired to play in Turkey. England, however, was opposed to any intervention in Spain, still more now that Canning had succeeded to the Foreign Office on Castlereagh's tragic death, and that the support of the Spanish royal cause seemed likely to bear the character of a revival of the Bourbon family compact. The other Powers were divided between the dangers of an isolated intervention by France and those of admitting Russian troops to Western Europe, but when they decided to send a joint note to Madrid calling the Spanish Government to order England, declaring that she would hold no common language with them, withdrew from the discussion.

The Alliance was thus formally sundered, and with the Spanish manifesto the Congress separated. The fate of Spain was left to depend upon the attitude of the French Government, and in April 1823 95,000 French troops crossed the Bidassoa, and within six months restored absolutism to Madrid. Their success reopened the question of the relationship of the Spanish-American colonies, but to any attempt to extend the dictatorship of the Powers to the New World

(3) The Congress of Verona (1822).

both the United States and England were resolutely opposed. In December 1823 President Monroe of the United States set forth the famous Monroe Doctrine—proclaiming the principle of non-intervention for the New World—and the independence of the Spanish colonies was recognized by the United States and by England. It was Canning's reply to the French invasion of Spain. "I have called a new world into existence to redress the balance of the old."

One more feeble tribute to the idea of European co-operation was paid in 1825, when the Tsar summoned two conferences at St Petersburg to consider the Eastern Question. The discussions were fruitless; to the second Great Britain sent no representative, and even Alexander I announced, on what was, in fact, the eve of his death, that Russia would henceforth act in the Eastern Question as befitted her own dignity and interests without entering into further explanation with her allies.

With the growth of public and treaty law the chief Powers of Europe came to have a common interest in such matters as the preservation of the neutrality of Belgium and Luxemburg and the Near Eastern Question. But such common obligations—ignored at the dictates of national policy—differed from the conceptions of the Holy Alliance, as they differ from those of the League of Nations.

The only attempt made by Europe before the twentieth century to bring about a real international co-operation in the guidance of public affairs had failed, and the nations returned to their individual diplomacy on the principles of the Balance of Power. It had gone to pieces on many rocks, chiefly on Great Britain's withdrawal and on the mutual jealousies of the Powers. But the British assertion of the principle of non-intervention was more than a claim for national isolation and national liberty; it was a stand against the autocracy of Europe and a protest against the dictatorship and system of Metternich. For the attempted Concert of Europe was based upon no league of democratic nations; it was an alliance of monarchs, three at least of whom were autocrats, and an acceptance of the principle of intervention might easily have resulted in the establishment of an intolerable despotism. It is doubtful whether England ever held herself committed to the ideal of a common European policy; the Quadruple Alliance was to her the renewal of the Treaty of Chaumont directed against a known enemy, limited in its scope, and defensive in its bearing. In its subsequent history it had, in Castlereagh's phrase, "moved away from Great Britain."

The Concert of Europe broke also, however, on the divergent interests of the Powers. No federation can endure without a modicum of common interest, and neither in political or commercial ambition nor in constitutional outlook did such exist. It has been seen how a common hostility to revolution, which, under Metternich's guidance, alone held together any group of the Powers, rapidly reduced the Holy Alliance for the preservation of peace into a *clique* of the "three gentlemen of Verona" for the preservation of autocracy; but even within the minor group political considerations cut athwart constitutional interests, and tended to stultify action.

The experiment was partly a tribute to a positive ideal of international peace which has proved of more than ephemeral value; but it was largely a by-product of the Napoleonic wars, a transient impulse arising from a unique historical and psychological experience. It was the fruit of the common uprising against the common enemy, a fading spark from the glowing inspiration of what had been, for a short time, a single-minded Europe.

II. The Democratic and Nationalist Aspirations of Europe (1815–50)

It has already been pointed out that in the realm of politics the period 1815 to 1850 was one rather of aspiration than of achievement. The honours of the age fell not to the statesmen, but to the poets, musicians, and scholars, to the men of science and letters; and posterity, which lingers fondly on the names of Beethoven, Goethe, and Heine, of Wordsworth, Shelley, Byron, and the English Romanticists, of Châteaubriand, Victor Hugo, and Balzac, of Hegel, Mill, and Comte, of Faraday, Corot, and Chopin, cannot recall half a dozen contemporary politicians. The shape of life was altered less by the negotiations of diplomats than by the introduction of railways, and society moulded not by the modicum of constructive political development, but by the growth of industry and the march of scientific research, by the artistic stimulus and the widespread religious movements, by the new interest in philanthropy and education.

A period of great constructive work in art, science, and industry, but in politics one of aspiration rather than achievement.

Although there was a political counterpart to all this human activity the period was one of little constructive work, of much disappointment, but withal of real preparation. Men dreamed dreams of political freedom and saw visions of national union and independence, but they awoke from their dreams to a world of repressive autocrats and invincible inertia, and found too often that their visions were bounded by prison walls or the frontiers of exile. Their revolutions failed and their armies were beaten, and reaction seemed to prosper. In most cases it was not until a later age that their efforts received their reward.

Most of the struggles of the age centred in the fact that the French Revolution had transferred the domain of politics from royal Courts and antechambers to the newspapers and the streets, and that the monarchs of Europe and their chancellors were unable or unwilling to recognize the development. They sought to preserve the former character of *la haute politique*, as a game for kings and decorous diplomats, and many of them would have been not unwilling to ameliorate the conditions of their peoples as long as they themselves were regarded as the fountains of power; for enlightened despotism had been the latest fashion for kings until the French Revolution ruled kings out of fashion altogether. Thus it followed that when the sovereigns of Europe sought to silence the voice of the people and suppress their demands it was not only because they often held their demands to be unreasonable, but also because they would not admit the conception on which they were based, that politics and the governance of states were a proper and legitimate subject for popular consideration.

The aspirations of the peoples were mainly twofold, democratic and nationalist. In countries where national unity and independence had been already achieved, as in England, France, Spain, Sweden, and Russia, the struggles of the peoples were **Democratic.** directed predominantly toward such familiar adjuncts of democracy as majority government, a representative Parliament, manhood suffrage, religious toleration, and a free Press, mingled in some cases with one or two agrarian or industrial measures.

In Germany and Italy, however, where a people racially one was politically divided; in Belgium, Norway, Ireland, Poland, and the Christian Balkan states, where a nation was linked with or subjected to an alien and unsympathetic state, popular **Nationalist.** aspiration, although often democratic in addition, turned primarily toward union or independence.

The history of the United Kingdom, which lies properly outside the scope of this book, marched with certain reservations side by side with that of the Continent. There were democratic United agitations in Britain, and nationalist agitations in Ireland; Kingdom to there was a similar alternation of reaction and revolt, and an some extent echo of the European revolutions of 1848 was heard on both an exception. sides of the Irish Sea. In certain respects, however, Great Britain stands apart from the other states of Europe. Her grievances were less acute and her disturbances less violent. The Commons of England had attained to the stature of self-government while the peoples of the Continent were in the cradle of autocracy, and were already possessed of a treasury of rights and privileges; nor could the sharpest reaction wholly eradicate that tradition of popular concession and piecemeal reform which has been both her foible and her safeguard. The Six Acts [1] of 1819 may bear some resemblance to the Carlsbad Decrees,

[1] Restricting the liberty of the Press and of public meeting.

but they were passed under the auspices of the party which reformed the criminal law, improved the condition of prisons, removed the political disabilities of Catholics and hampering laws of trade, and later championed the cause of the artisans. The country which imprisoned O'Connell gave sanctuary to most of the nationalist exiles of Europe.

Steady general development

The worst ills which England suffered were economic, consequent upon the introduction of machinery and the unemployment and high prices of the "hungry forties"; in spite of these the period was marked by a measured financial, social, and political development to which, except for the half-dozen years immediately following the conclusion of peace with France, there was no important check, while the Whig ministry of Grey stood out from the barrenness of its contemporaries for its real constructive work. On the series of statutes initiated in the thirties—the Reform Act of '32, the Factory and Education Acts of '33, the Poor Law of '34, the Municipal Corporations Act of '35—modern England is based. The introduction of a new reforming spirit into the Government of India, coupled with the Canada Act of 1840, showed that England was not dead to her imperial responsibilities, while the abolition of slavery at the cost to herself of twenty million pounds set an example to the world.

and intense constructive political activity (1830-35).

It was hardly to be expected that the history of France after the violent alternations of the last twenty-five years—from monarchy to regicide, Terror to Empire, victory to defeat, and Bonaparte to Bourbon—should be free from oscillation. There was the heritage of the Revolution to be reconciled with the restoration of royalism, the lilies with the tricolour, the natural desire of the returned exiles for restitution with the irrevocable march of time and the growth of new vested interests.

France.

Louis XVIII, the uninspired but not vindictive brother of Louis XVI, had returned to France with a constitutional charter granting an elective chamber, personal equality, freedom of religion and the Press, and certain other *desiderata* of liberalism. Like Charles II of England, he had no wish to go on his travels again, and was disposed to pursue a moderate and conciliatory policy. He was, however, unable to control the ultra-Royalist forces which pressed upon the ministry and the country. Immediately after the Hundred Days a popular outburst in the South of France against the Republicans and Bonapartists recalled, in the White Terror, the worst excesses of the French Revolution, while a Royalist Chamber of Deputies demanded the proscription of the 'traitors' of the Hundred Days, even putting to death the indomitable Ney. The

Louis XVIII (1815-24).

reaction was strengthened by the unfortunate murder in 1820 of the Duc de Berri, son of the Comte d'Artois, although the Bourbon line was saved from extinction by the birth of a posthumous heir.[1] Louvel, the assassin, a Bonapartist soldier, swore that he had no accomplices, but his act was made to recoil upon the Liberal party, and the King allowed the country to drift upon the tide of a clerical and anti-Liberal reaction, headed by the *émigré* party which had "learnt nothing and forgotten nothing" during its exile.

An opposition began to form itself; the secret revolutionary society of the Carbonari, which was spreading through Italy, Spain, and Germany, opposed itself to the aristocratic clerical organization known as the Congregation; there were insurrections in the army and a protest from the Académie Française, and the Napoleonic legend was beginning to hallow the name of the dead Emperor. But Louis XVIII died peacefully in his bed; there was even a faint stirring of patriotic pride in the lilies when the Duc d'Angoulême successfully invaded Spain. It was the Comte d'Artois, raised to the throne in 1824 as Charles X, who drove the opposition to rebellion. **Charles X (1824–30).** "There is no such thing as political experience," wrote Wellington. "With the warning of James II before him Charles X is setting up a Government by priests, through priests, for priests." A Government based on the pretensions of divine right, conducted in the interests of *émigrés* and Jesuits, carried on by the repression of criticism and free election, and at the expense of popular liberty and equality, provoked a furious discontent which not even the French participation in the battle of Navarino and the conquest of Algiers could assuage. In July 1830, as an answer to the appointment of the reactionary Polignac ministry and to the issue of four repressive ordinances, the people of Paris rose in revolt. For three days the mob held the narrow streets of the capital barricaded with impromptu defences;[2] several regiments of royal troops deserted, **The July Revolution (1830).** others withdrew, and Charles X in his *château* of Rambouillet found his belated attempts to compromise rejected and the elder line of the Bourbon dynasty once again turned off the throne of France.

A few days later Louis-Philippe, son of that Philippe Égalité who had tampered with the first Revolution, was set up as King of the French, and Charles X, "continuously weeping," embarked at Cherbourg for England. "Égalité Fils," says Carlyle, speaking of him as a young man at Valmy, "Equality Junior, a light, **Louis-Philippe (1830–48).**

---

[1] See genealogical table, p. 601.
[2] The new ' omnibus ' which had driven into history two years earlier, where all might ride without distinction of class and rank, introduced into Paris by M. Baudry, was found useful for this purpose.

gallant field officer, distinguished himself by intrepidity—it is the same intrepid individual who now as Louis-Philippe, without the equality, struggled under sad circumstances to be called King of the French for a season." After a career of strange vicissitudes and many wanderings he made a brave beginning as a citizen-king, draping a tricolour scarf over the frock coat of the *bourgeois*, shaking hands prodigiously with sundry deputations, sending his sons to the public schools, or enrolling them as privates in the National Guard. But an intrigue of Talleyrand, a theatrical gesture of the aged La Fayette, the limited support of a group of Orléanists, and even the acquiescence of the Great Powers, formed an inadequate basis on which to found a stable dynasty. The July days had awakened the Revolutionary tradition without satisfying the national aspirations. The Orléanist monarchy reposed on no real alliance with any important section of the state, and preserved its existence for eighteen years mainly through the disorganization of the forces arrayed against it.

The Legitimists could not transfer their loyalty to a monarchy shorn of divine right and based ostensibly on the will of the people, nor the Catholics defend a Government which had forced a breach between the throne and the altar. The Republicans showed increasing hostility to what gradually became a thinly disguised attempt at personal rule, for although there had been a change of head there had been little change of heart. The growing socialist or communist party, infuriated by economic grievances which there was no attempt to redress, inspired by socialistic literature, and supplied by Louis Blanc with a formula and a programme, grew more intent upon the social revolution against the narrow *bourgeois* plutocracy which kept itself in power by a corrupt alliance with the throne. The Bonapartists and the Chauvinists, stirred by heroic memories and the reviving cult of the great Emperor, titillated by the quixotic exploits of his nephew, Louis Napoleon, betrayed growing boredom with a foreign policy which, all the more because of tentative essays into the adventurous, seemed a docile and uninspired betrayal of a great tradition. "La France s'ennuie," wrote Lamartine ominously.

Thus every sentiment in the state was disappointed, and, in spite of an increase of wealth and of great material prosperity among the middle class which gave an outward appearance of success, the reign of Louis-Philippe was filled with incessant agitation. There was the Legitimist insurrection of 1832, when the Duchesse de Berri tried to stir up Provence and La Vendée on behalf of her son "Henri V"; there were the dashing exploits of Louis Napoleon at Strasburg and Boulogne in 1836 and 1840; there were constant attempts on the lives of the King and the royal family; there were plots and riots in Paris; and, most serious of all, there was the batch of proletarian insurrections in many towns of France, notably those at Lyons in 1831 and 1834.

It was a franchise question which precipitated the crisis by which in February 1848 the Orléanist monarchy was overthrown and Louis-Philippe driven into exile. The Revolution of 1848 was a composite movement, showing clearly the various hostile elements which had been gathering against the Government. It progressed through four main stages. The cry of the first two days, February 22 and 23, was "À bas Guizot!" epitomizing the impatient boredom of the nation with the ministers of Louis-Philippe and their slogan "Enrichissez-vous," with a Government which, in de Tocqueville's words, "had come to resemble a limited company in industry which undertakes all its operations with a view to the profit to be exhausted from them by shareholders." So far it was a "revolution of contempt." It was followed by the genuine Republican movement that had been baulked in 1830, and looked back to 1792, which drove Louis-Philippe from the throne, abolished monarchy, and set up a provisional Government. But its triumph was quickly challenged by a third party, appearing for the first time as an organized political force—the socialist artisans of the towns, especially of Paris, the product largely of the Industrial Revolution and of a disappointment in the fruits of constitutional and political methods. Through the summer months of June and July the conflict continued between the tricolour of republicanism and the red flag of socialism. In the end socialism was defeated largely—as the Communards of 1870 were to remember—because the peasants came in from the countryside to defend with the middle class the heritage which they both had received from the Revolution of 1789. *[The Revolution of 1848.]*

Nevertheless there was a fourth stage to the revolution, and in the end it was the Bonapartists, acting nominally for and on behalf of the Republicans, who were to carry off the final honours. When Louis Napoleon Bonaparte, nephew of the great Emperor, was put forward for the presidency—an office set up by the new constitution drawn up by the Republicans in November—he was elected by an overwhelming majority, many of the peasants half believing that they were voting for the Little Corporal himself. After ten months' struggle France had given herself a second Republic and a second Bonaparte. *[The Second French Republic and Louis Napoleon.]*

For a keenly interested spectator with a great name and a great ambition had been watching since the days of the July Revolution of 1830 the fluctuations of French politics. Louis Napoleon Bonaparte, born in 1808 of that inauspicious marriage between Hortense Beauharnais and Louis Bonaparte, at the time of his son's birth King of Holland, was perfectly equipped for that romantic *rôle* of pretender

L

which he was to play with such success. "A royal birth, a princely heritage, an imperial name; a king for his father, queens for his nursing mothers, a cardinal to christen him, emperor and empress to stand his sponsors; early exile, puerile persecution, youthful wanderings in search of a home; headstrong resolution, reckless invasions, miraculous escapes, transportation, imprisonments, flights in disguise, these for circumstances; and for central figure a dreamer, an adventurer, a conspirator, a suspect in his teens, a rebel in arms while still a beardless boy, thrice the leader of forlorn hopes whence no ordinary man had once escaped with his life—if we have not here the stock-in-trade of a pretender, we confess we should despair of any further quest of him." [1]

At the age of seven he had seen the Napoleonic eagles presented to the troops during the Hundred Days; on the eve of Waterloo he had been embraced by his uncle with the—perhaps legendary—words, "Who knows but that the future of my race may not lie with this boy?"—he who, grown to manhood, was to retrieve the Imperial crown which had been lost there. He had seen the Allied monarchs who had visited his mother at the Château de Saint-Leu—the Tsar Alexander and Frederick William III, King of Prussia, with his two sons, one of whom was to become first Emperor of Germany after the war of 1870, in which Louis Napoleon was himself to forfeit the crown he had twenty years before restored to the Bonaparte family. He had wandered with his mother in exile, and learnt from her a veneration for the Emperor. He had visited old Letizia Bonaparte at Rome.

In 1831 he made his *début* in politics as a member of a Carbonari insurrection against the Pope, thus early showing that interest in Italian affairs which later became a principle of his Imperial foreign policy. In 1832 there died a young man of twenty-one, known variously as the King of Rome, the Duke of Reichstadt, and Napoleon II, and Louis Napoleon began to consider himself henceforward the representative of the Bonapartist claims. From his exile in England he watched the legend of the dead Emperor growing like a tender sentiment in the heart of France. He saw the mists of history and tradition coloured by the sunset glow that came from across the Atlantic. He read the literature which began to pour from the St Helena companions, and the fresh interpretation of history which issued from the Emperor's creative reminiscences. He saw May 5—the date of the death—become a day of national mourning, and shops and homes fill with Napoleonic portraits and souvenirs as the apotheosis of the martyred Emperor proceeded. He saw the image of a Prometheus chained to a far Atlantic rock transformed to a Christ crucified. He heard the thundered eloquence of Victor Hugo, and beheld Thiers

[1] Dr F. A. Simpson, *The Rise of Louis Napoleon*, Preface.

turn from a history of the Revolution to that of the Consulate and the Empire. He watched the homeopathic attempts of the Orléanist dynasty to divert to its own ends the new force which might so easily undermine its throne. The Little Corporal came back to the Vendôme column, the Arc de Triomphe was finished and dedicated, and by a supreme resolve the ashes of the dead Emperor were brought from St Helena in accordance with his will and placed under the dome of the Invalides. " Je désire que mes cendres reposent sur les bords de la Seine, au milieu de ce peuple que j'ai tant aimé." And France said that there were two kings in Paris, one at the Tuileries, the other at the Invalides.

Louis Napoleon had already made one attempt in 1836 to win his throne, by stirring up the garrison of Strasburg to revolt. The affair had ended in his transportation to America, from which he had almost immediately returned to England. The second exploit was in 1840. He would himself receive the ashes of the Emperor as they came to Paris. It was a miserable fiasco at Boulogne, leading to Louis Napoleon's capture, but as he entered into the fortress of Ham the people of Paris were shouting "Vive l'Empereur!" as the Imperial ashes passed into the Invalides. It was a cry that he remembered.

After six years' imprisonment, or, as he afterward called it, "study in the University of Ham," he escaped in disguise to England. On the news of the Revolution in 1848 he hastily repaired to Paris, and as hastily departed. France was not yet ready for him, and while Republicans and socialists fought out the issue during the spring months he entertained himself with London gaieties, and enrolled among the special constables enlisted to put down the Chartist trouble. In June he was elected to the new National Assembly by four constituencies, but he wisely refrained from accepting the election. In September the honour was repeated by five more districts, and on September 26 he modestly took his seat. Three months later he became President; four years later he was Emperor of the French.

Thus France had called the heir of the Bonapartes to herself again, and he had followed faithfully in the Napoleonic tradition. But it was no easy task to wear the mantle of the great Emperor, and he who made so successful a pretender was to renounce in defeat the throne that he had won.

It is possible to give only the merest abridgment of the long story of confusion and ineffective struggle which confounded for nearly a century the history and prosperity of the kingdoms of Spain and Portugal on the other side of the Pyrenees, which Spain and Portugal. precluded them from taking any but an incidental part in European affairs, and which lost to them their fairest treasures. In both states there were three problems, constitutional, dynastic, and colonial, and to some extent they were interconnected.

In Spain the constitutional question dated from the national uprising against the French, which had been an example to Europe and an inspiration to herself. A constitution had been drawn up based largely on the French model of 1791, reproducing the separation of the legislature and the executive and the non-re-election of members of Parliament, and, except for the establishment of the Roman Catholic Church, ignoring characteristically native institutions. In spite of its imperfections—which were hardly demonstrated, as it was only put into practice for very brief spells—it became not only the admiration of Southern Europe, but the Magna Charta of popular liberty and the inspiration of constitutional effort for more than half a century.

Ferdinand VII reluctantly accepted the constitution upon his return in 1813, but, trading on his popularity and his native cunning, he rapidly infringed it. He revived the Inquisition and restored the wealth of the monasteries, persecuted the liberals, and embarked upon a course of reaction which led in 1820 to a revolution, originating, like most Spanish movements of the nineteenth century, with the army. The constitutionalists enjoyed a short success, but in 1823 they were defeated by French intervention, and Ferdinand, in spite of French cautions and counsels of moderation, returned to his absolutism. There followed a veritable reign of terror.

In the meantime Spain had lost what in this age of commercial development might have gone far toward restoring her to the front rank of Powers—an empire that was also a continent. Although the greatness of the sixteenth century had fallen from her, and her imperial vitality had faded, she still held, in her withered hand, the extensive possessions of the New World. Mistress of all Central and South America except Brazil and the small district of Guiana, she had seen the French Empire perish and the British Empire ruptured. But a long course of misrule and of economic oppression, the stimulus of the example of the United States, the infection of French ideas, and the deliberate provocation of Britain, who for half a century had been Spain's customary enemy, had induced in the colonies a discontent which not even a grant of representation in the Cortes of 1810 could dissipate. The Napoleonic humiliation fired the fuse, and rebellions broke out from Mexico to Patagonia, which the mismanaged and ineffectual efforts of the mother country could not defeat. The recognition awarded by the United States and Great Britain to the independence of the former Spanish colonies was but the technical appreciation of an accomplished fact.

Detached and abandoned, the mother country became immersed in the obscurity of her futile struggles. On the death of Ferdinand VII in 1833 a civil war of succession broke out between the supporters of Don Carlos, the late King's brother, and the party of Isabella, his three-year-old daughter. Don Carlos based his claim on the Salic Law, which had come into Spain with the **The Carlist** Bourbons at the beginning of the eighteenth century; he **wars.** rallied round him the Church and the Absolutists, and he found useful soldiers among the Basques, whose tenacious provincialism he exploited. The advocates of Isabella were provided with a Pragmatic Sanction repealing the Salic Law, and a determined woman, Christina, the Queen-mother. They strengthened their position by leaning toward the side of the Constitutionalists, which brought them also in 1834 the alliance of France and Great Britain. After seven years of guerrilla warfare the Carlists laid down their arms and Don Carlos retired from Spain. It was, however, an inglorious victory, which brought little profit to liberalism. The Constitutionalists were divided; the Queen-mother, who, after a short retirement, returned again, apparently to enrich herself at the public expense, was dominating and self-seeking; the Queen, Isabella, both self-willed and weak; the husband, the Duke of Cadiz, whom an inauspicious marriage brought to her side in 1846 after a flutter among the Courts of Europe, was an unloved consort and a narrow-minded intriguer—"an absolute and an Absolutist fool," according to Palmerston. **Isabella II** The reign of Isabella II was a miserable record of con- **(1843–68).** fusion, intrigue, and scandal; the royal Court was given over to an irregular despotism and to the rule of favourites against which the country vainly struggled. A military insurrection in 1854 which secured a short-lived triumph was followed in 1868 by a revolution in which the Queen's deposition was demanded, and on September 30 the train from San Sebastian bore her into exile. "I thought," she said, "that I had struck deeper root in this land."

In some respects the history of Portugal resembled that of Spain. Upon the French invasion of 1807 the royal family retired to Brazil and the mother country became almost a dependency of its colony. The prevailing voice in Portuguese affairs was that **Portugal.** of Wellington or Beresford until 1820, when, after the example of Spain, a revolution broke out which set up what was practically the Spanish constitution of 1812. The King, John VI, returned to Portugal, and soon afterward restored absolutism. In the **Revolution.** meantime, in 1822, his son, the ambitious Dom Pedro, declared himself Emperor of Brazil, which, like the Spanish American colonies, broke away from the mother country. Upon the death of John VI

in 1826 a situation arose not unlike that which occurred a little later in Spain. Dom Pedro, although he was emperor of an independent
Loss of Brazil. Brazil, sought to retain his claims on Portugal on behalf of his seven-year-old daughter, Donna Maria da Gloria. These were disputed by his brother, Dom Miguel, and, as in Spain, the uncle supported the Absolutists, the niece the Constitutionalists. Dom Miguel made himself king, however, until in 1834 Dom Pedro returned from Brazil, and with some British and French help placed his daughter on the throne. The Carlist wars in Spain had just broken out, and a quadruple alliance was concluded between the two constitutional parties of Spain and Portugal and the two constitutional kingdoms of France and England. It was a set-off to the alliance of the three autocratic Powers of Russia, Prussia, and Austria, and a definite assertion of the diplomatic rearrangement of Europe.

The reign of Donna Maria was, however, turbulent and unsettled.
Donna Maria (1834–53). Portugal was disturbed by the troubles of her neighbour, disorganized by the rapid constitutional transition from mediævalism to modernism, crippled by a heavy national debt, and burdened by acute social and economic distress.

The history of Italy [1] during the years 1815–50 was one of disunion, foreign domination, and apparently fruitless struggle. The Napo-
Italy. leonic creations were swept away; the faithful stepson, Eugène Beauharnais, retired to Germany as Prince of Leuchtenberg; the ambitious, self-seeking brother-in-law, Murat, having failed by twice turning his coat to further his fortunes and preserve his kingdom, was shot by the command of Ferdinand King of Naples for attempting to raise an insurrection. Italy
Division and absolutism restored. was restored to her former dynasties and to that division which had been her lot since the days of Rome. Politically speaking, there was no Italy; there were the kingdom of Piedmont-Sardinia, the Austrian provinces of Venetia and Lombardy, the independent duchies of Tuscany, Parma, Lucca, and Modena, the Papal States, the kingdom of Naples and Sicily.

The restorations of 1815 were followed generally by reactionary or demoralizing administrations. In the kingdom of the Two Sicilies the Bourbon Ferdinand I retained, it is true, some of the laws, institutions, and officials of the Murat *régime*, but he restored the hated police system, the Press censorship, and the authority of the clergy; he persecuted liberal opinion, gave a natural preference to Royalists, and offended the anti-Neapolitan sentiment of Sicily by abolishing its autonomous constitution and turning it into a bureaucratic province of Naples.

[1] See map at p. 217.

In the Papal States, which ran diagonally across Italy, the Pope was temporal as well as spiritual ruler, and a unique system of theocracy prevailed, for not only was the head a priest, but the important officials were all ecclesiastics. Antiquated Pontifical statutes superseded the French laws ; the Inquisition, the Index, and all the paraphernalia of mediæval Church government were restored, and a corrupt and inefficient administration, coupled, in spite of a ferocious police system, with brigandage and social anarchy, rapidly fostered a general discontent.

Of the north-central duchies Modena endured an extreme tyranny ; in Tuscany there was a mild but enervating Government; in Parma, where Napoleon's wife Marie-Louise reigned as Duchess, many French codes were retained.

In the Austrian provinces the Government was efficient, but rigidly centralized, and the subject Italians were increasingly irritated by the reference of every question to Vienna and by the deliberate attempt to 'Austrianize' their political life.

In the kingdom of Piedmont and Sardinia the house of Savoy under Victor Emmanuel I was popular, but although the French system of taxation was preserved because it yielded larger revenues the government was conducted on the general principle of returning to the conditions which existed before the French domination. Feudalism and an antiquated legislation, the power of the clergy and the privileges of the aristocracy, were restored, and former officials, though in their dotage, were reappointed. Discontent increased, while Genoa smarted under the additional humiliation of recent subjection to Piedmont.

Excessive provincialism pervaded Italy, and next to provincialism, and partly because of it, the most striking feature of her condition was the domination of Austria. Austria governed directly only Lombardy and Venetia, but princes of her house ruled in Parma, Modena, and Tuscany; her garrisons were in Piacenza, Ferrara, and Comacchio; Ferdinand of Naples had bound himself not to introduce a form of government unacceptable to her, while Metternich counted upon securing the election of an Austrophil Pope. It soon became evident that the petty principalities could preserve their existence only by leaning on Austria, who was the real mistress of Italy. In Piedmont alone was there a native prince and a ruler who strove to be independent.

Excessive provincialism and Austrian domination.

To the mass of the people the restorations of 1815 were undoubtedly popular as a relief from the constant drain of men and money for the wars of France, but the Napoleonic *régime* had infused a new life into the devitalized Italy, and given an impulse to union which had been strengthened on many a battlefield. As the restored princes proceeded with policies of reaction the democratic and nationalist ideas began to work among the people like a leaven. Patriots were roused to **Discontent.** a sense of their country's humiliation, and democrats inspired to resist oppression as Italians, not as Sicilians or Neapolitans, or Venetians or Piedmontese. Secret societies began to spread over Italy, especially the Carbonari, which had been formed in Naples during the *régime* of Murat. Beneath mystic rites and symbolic language drawn partly from Christianity, partly from the processes of charcoal-burning, it concealed and fostered a determined political purpose, the expulsion of the foreigner and the achievement of constitutional freedom. All classes joined it—nobles, military officers, peasants, priests, but especially the *bourgeoisie* and the gentry, among whom liberal and patriotic ideas had taken deepest root. It spread beyond Italy, and within the peninsula the black, red, and blue of the Carbonari became the flag of revolution, until it was superseded in 1831 by the red, green, and white tricolour.

Under the impetus of the secret societies a revolutionary movement began in 1820 which was not exhausted for thirty years. Into the **Revolutions, 1820–21.** incidents of the successive revolutions it is not possible to enter. The first revolt, set in motion by the Spanish revolution of 1820, broke out in Naples, achieved a brief success, and then fell a victim to Austrian intervention.[1] Before its suppression was complete Piedmont was in rebellion and Lombardy was stirring. But Austria again moved her troops, revolution buried its head, and save for some unimportant agitations in the Papal States Italy was quiet for a few years, with the suppressed smouldering of discontent.

In 1830 the July Revolution in Paris raised echoes beyond the Alps. In Romagna and the Marches, in Parma and Modena, insurrec-**1831.** tions broke out against the Pope, against Marie-Louise and the tyrant Francis. Austria intervened; the dispossessed rulers were restored and liberalism cowed. The enterprise failed before the might of Austria, because democratic efforts were as yet spasmodic and disunited, because the people were not ripe for revolution, because unity, without which success was nearly impossible, was only the cry of a few leaders and not the creed of the masses. Nevertheless there were also signs of hopeful augury. If the democratic-nationalist movement was weak so was the hold of the reactionary dynasties. It had been shown that only by foreign intervention could they preserve their thrones. Foreign intervention was an undoubted ill, but it might also prove a means of salvation. For Austria's success was arousing the jealousy of the Powers; France already had shown that she would dispute the supremacy of her rival in Italian affairs. Two foreign armies in Italy might mean a restoration of the devas-

[1] See also *supra*, p. 154.

tating wars of the sixteenth century; on the other hand, out of the quarrels of her masters might not some profit accrue to the victim—a new, awakened Italy, alive to her own needs? For the Italy of the nineteenth century was far removed from that of the sixteenth century, and where the scheming counsels of Machiavelli had failed the passionate pleadings of Mazzini might, and did, succeed.

For within a prison cell of Savona, amid the 'infinities' of the sky and the sea, drawing a mingled inspiration from a scanty library of his own choice, consisting of a Tacitus, a Byron, and a Bible, an ardent young patriot, a Carbonaro, Giuseppe Mazzini, had seen a vision of a regenerated Italy and heard a call to leadership. Thence ensued the Society of "Young Italy," which, with its more definite aims and a more inspired direction, soon superseded the Carbonari as the nucleus of nationalist revolution. "Place youth at the head of the insurgent multitude; you know not the secret of the power hidden in those youthful hearts." From Piedmont there spread all over Italy societies of young men, bound by oath, dedicated to the achievement of a national republic, fed by the eloquence of their exiled founder—for most of Mazzini's life was spent in exile in France or England—fortified by appeals to the martyrs of the holy Italian cause, to "the memory of our greatness and the sense of our degradation," to "the blush which rises to the brow of an Italian when he stands before the citizens of other lands, knowing he has no citizenship, no country, no national flag." God, the People, and Italy were the cries of the society; education, literary propaganda, and, if necessary, insurrection its methods; the conversion of an idea into a popular cause its achievement.

Mazzini and the Society of Young Italy.

Besides the inflammable revolutionary sentiment of "Young Italy" there was a more moderate growth of patriotic opinion, which did not a little to prepare the way for Italian unity by a more restrained advocacy of economic development and popular education, whose political conceptions centred more in the idea of a federation under a Papal presidency, or on a liberal monarchical basis. Outside Italy, moreover, another useful propagandist work was being done by the Italian exiles in the cultivation of that favourable public opinion of Europe, and especially of England, which played no inconsiderable part in the final achievement.

Moderate opinion.

A new hope dawned for Italy with the election of 1846 of Pope Pius IX to the Papal chair. He inaugurated his pontificate with a general amnesty which was the beginning of his immense if short-lived popularity. He further granted some moderate administrative reforms, admitted the laity to certain offices in the Papal States, permitted political newspapers, and there was talk of railways.[1]

---

[1] " Chemins de fer, chemins d'enfer," had been the attitude of his predecessor.

Elated liberals pressed for further concessions, and the novel
shout of "Viva Pio Nono!" was heard proceeding from democratic
lips. Austria grew anxious. Metternich comforted himself with the reflection that a liberal Pope was a natural impossibility, but decided, nevertheless, that a little sabre-
rattling would introduce a useful cautionary note into
Italian politics. Austrian troops occupied Ferrara, to the indignation
alike of democrats, of the Pope, and of the reforming Charles Albert,
who had become King of Sardinia in 1831, while the occupation called
forth a protest from Great Britain.

A new stage. Reform initiated by the Pope.

The Pope's reforming example had in the meantime been followed
by Tuscany and Piedmont, but by no other states, and democratic
excitement, mingled largely with a strong anti-Austrian feeling,
surged through the country during the year 1847. The next year
revolution, which washed like a flood over Europe, broke also upon
Italy.

The political situation opened at the beginning of the year 1848
with three different problems. In the kingdom of Naples and Sicily
no reforms had yet been granted, while popular agitation
was increasing; in the Papal States, in Tuscany and Piedmont, the democratic party, not content with the moderate reforms
already conceded, were demanding a 'constitution' and the transference of real political power to the people; in Lombardy and
Venetia the issue, though also democratic, was mainly nationalist;
the yoke of Austria had become intolerable, but the chances of successful revolt seemed slight.

1848–49.

Thus the movements of 1848–49 had a double orientation, democratic and nationalist, and two revolutions at opposite ends of the
peninsula set them going.

On January 12 a revolution broke out in Palermo which demanded
reform, Sicilian autonomy, and the constitution of 1812. After a
futile attempt at repression Ferdinand II was forced to grant their
demands. The demonstration of Neapolitan weakness naturally inflamed the democrats of Naples, whereupon Ferdinand, to escape the
threatened revolution, granted a constitution to his mainland as well
as his island kingdom. The effect upon the rest of Italy was in-
stantaneous,[1] and popular demonstrations in favour of a 'constitution' occurred in Piedmont, Tuscany, and the Papal States; in March
1848 constitutions and Parliamentary governments were granted in
all these principalities, save that in the Papal States Pius IX forbade
Parliamentary discussion of religious questions.

---

[1] As Ferdinand had anticipated. An element of malice in him sought revenge
upon the reforming princes whose 'evil' example had led to risings in Sicily and
Naples.

EUROPE FROM 1815 TO 1850

Thus the result of the first three months of 1848 was the establis‑
ment of what might be called constitutional monarchical governmei
throughout practically all Italy except the Austrian dominions.

Then came the second or nationalist *motif.* In March the news
came to Italy of a revolution in Vienna and the flight of Metternich.
Revolution immediately broke out in Milan, the viceroy fled, and after
a five days' sanguinary struggle the Austrian troops under Radetzky
withdrew. A similar though less violent result followed in Venice,
where a republic was proclaimed. The rulers of Modena and Parma
fled, and there seemed a general collapse of Austrian authority. From
moderates and extremists alike there arose a demand for war, **The War of**
a war to terminate the Austrian domination; but in such a **Independ-**
war Piedmont alone could take the lead. The young Count **ence.**
Cavour, editor of the *Risorgimento,* joined in the appeal. "The sup‑
reme hour of the Sardinian monarchy has sounded. . . . There is
only one path open to the Government, the nation, the King—imme‑
diate war." Charles Albert heard, and understood that he was called
to fulfil the historical mission of his house. On March 23, 1848, he
declared war against Austria, and the struggle for Italian freedom had
advanced to a new stage, from popular insurrection to national war,
led by an Italian prince with contingents from all Italy, for Leopold
of Tuscany enthusiastically embraced the cause, while the Pope
and Ferdinand of Naples were forced by their own subjects to lend
support. But the impulse to unanimity was short-lived. The Pope,
alarmed by the protests of Catholic Austria, declared that his troops
were destined merely for the protection of his own dominions;
Ferdinand recalled his army to put down an insurrection which had
broken out in Naples. As a political set-off to the withdrawal of Papal
and Neapolitan support, popular votes in Lombardy and Venetia, in
Parma, Modena, and Reggio, were recorded in favour of union with
Piedmont; but in the face of the double military defection Charles
Albert failed to maintain his stand against Austria, and by the defeat
of Custozza in July was forced to a capitulation. Lombardy and
Venetia returned to the Austrian yoke.

The chief effect of the Sardinian defeat was to discredit the moderate
monarchical party, and to transfer the direction of the national move‑
ment, especially in Tuscany and Rome, to the more extreme repub‑
lican party headed by Mazzini, who had returned to Italy. Charles
Albert had shown himself weak, Pius IX vacillating; "the war of the
princes was finished, that of the peoples begun."

After a period of turbulence which entirely alienated the waning
sympathy of the Pope a republic was declared in Rome, **The Roman**
of which Mazzini took the lead; the temporal dominions **Republic.**
of the Papacy were abolished, and the Pope fled for refuge to Gaeta

on Neapolitan soil, and appealed to the Powers. There he was joined by Leopold of Tuscany, driven from his duchy by a similar republican movement at Florence. The two republics resolved to unite in the election of a Constituent Assembly which should draw up a form of government for all Italy.

The fate of Italy hung, however, upon Piedmont and its king, who, yielding to the pressure of the popular demand, had resolved to make one more bid for Italian independence. On March 12, 1849, he denounced the armistice with Austria, on the 20th he crossed the frontier, on the 23rd he was defeated and his army routed at Novara. The next day he abdicated rather than sign a humiliating convention, and two days later his son Victor Emmanuel II came to terms with the Austrian general Radetzky.

The battle of Novara was the beginning of the reaction. Italian resistance was at an end, and one by one the absolutist dynasties were refastened upon Italy. In May Sicily was reconquered by Ferdinand, "King Bomba," a soubriquet which dated from his bombardment of Messina, and Leopold was restored to Tuscany. Rome, after a brilliant defence by Garibaldi, fell not to Austrian, but to French troops—for Louis Napoleon, newly elected President of the French Republic, desired to make a counter-demonstration against the power of Austria in Italy, even at the expense of the suppression of a sister republic. Pius IX was restored, to embark upon a course of reaction. In August Venice fell to the Austrians.

Thus throughout Italy Austria and absolutism triumphed, save in Rome, where France stole the honours of restoration, and in Piedmont, where Victor Emmanuel remained loyal to the constitution of his father. A few more exiles made their way through England to America, and Strauss senior in Vienna composed the Radetzky March to celebrate the defeat of revolution.

Failure.

But though the nationalist and democratic struggles seemed to have ended in failure something had been gained. Although the Pope had dropped out as a possible leader of a united Italy Sardinia had come as markedly to the front. For the first time the people had fought for the cause, and in the name of Italian nationalism Neapolitans had shed blood for Venice, Lombards for Rome, and Piedmontese for all Italy. The efforts of the "terrible year" were not all fruitless if they made Italy conscious of herself and gave to the national cause "a dynasty to represent it and a people to defend it."

In Germany, as in Italy, the historical record of the years 1815–50 was one of Austrian domination based upon native division and weakness, of democratic and nationalist aspirations ending in apparent failure.

The Germany of the nineteenth century was founded upon the settlements of 1815, and was, only slightly less than Italy, a mere geographical expression. It consisted of thirty-nine sove- *Germany.* reign states (considerably reduced, it is true, from the three hundred independent principalities which formed the Holy Roman Empire) bound together in a loose confederation. There were the two large states of Austria and Prussia, President and Vice- The Con-President respectively, a group of middle-sized kingdoms, federation. Bavaria, Hanover, Saxony, Würtemberg, a number of smaller principalities, and four free cities. Holstein belonged to Denmark, Luxemburg to the King of the Netherlands, Hanover was attached to the English Crown, thus giving to the Confederation something of an international character. It possessed a central representative Diet which sat at Frankfurt, and which as an organ of government was useless. Although nominally endowed with wide powers for the regulation of the common interests of the German states, any effective or united action was paralysed by the deliberate purpose of the President, by the lack of executive power, by the jealous particularism of the lesser states, and by the rivalry of Prussia and Austria, while a unanimous vote was declared essential to any change in "fundamental laws, organic institutions, individual rights, or in matters of religion" —a formula wide enough to cover every question of importance. A confederation without either army [1] or real machinery of government provided only a sentimental bond, and the Diet, under Austrian guidance, sank into "little more than a court of chancery for considering the outstanding claims of private individuals against the old Empire."

It soon became obvious that Austria intended to treat the Diet of the German Confederation as a mere department of her Foreign Office. Prussia alone could have withstood her, but, Austrian occupied with her own internal development and scared control. by the fear of revolution, she allowed her external policy for nearly half a century to be dominated by Austria. "Prussian policy was made in Vienna," wrote Bismarck, and there was hardly a diplomatic issue between 1815 and 1850 in which Prussia did not in the end adopt a policy sympathetic if not subservient to Austria.

Thus Metternich was able to pursue his own reactionary policy with little hindrance. He wanted neither a strong Germany nor a liberal one. He succeeded in the first aim by gaining over Prussia, fostering the particularism of the smaller states, and nullifying the action of the Diet. In the second too he won his way. Article XIII of the Act of Confederation, which declared that "there The consti-should be Assemblies in all states of the Confederation," tutions. had seemed to guarantee the political freedom of the German states.

[1] There was a small Federal navy, which was sold by auction to Prussia in 1852.

Charles Augustus of Weimar, the patron of Goethe and friend of liberalism, had set up a constitution, to Metternich's disgust; some of the South German states, in sympathy with France, had also granted political privileges analogous to those of Louis XVIII's charter, and Frederick William III had promised a constitution to Prussia. This promise he would probably have kept but for the use Metternich was able to make of a bombastic liberal students' festival held at the Wartburg in October 1817, and of the murder in March 1819 of the reactionary play-writer, Kotzebue, who was known to be an agent of the Russian Tsar. Metternich seized the opportunity to preach sermons to both Alexander and Frederick William on the revolutionary danger of liberalism; the Prussian consti-

The Carlsbad Decrees (1819).

tution was dropped, and before the year was out the Carlsbad Decrees, passed first by an assembly of the more important German princes and then forced through the Diet, laid Germany under the heel of reaction.

The students' societies (*Bürschenschaften*) and gymnastic establishments, which were centres of liberal revolutionary agitation, were dissolved. A heavy censorship of the Press was established, and 'curators,' who were practically Government spies, were placed in the universities to watch the proceedings of professors and students alike.

Thus Metternich could afford to ignore the sullen opposition of the small liberal states. Prussia turned away from the constitutional issue, and only a few spasmodic revolts—a burlesque Darmstadt revolution in 1820, which forced the King to set up the Spanish constitution of 1812, which the Darmstadters had just read about, a few echoes of 1830 in Brunswick, Hesse, Hanover, and Saxony, some student demonstrations and a Hanoverian crisis in 1837 [1]—disturbed the political quietude which, under Metternich's system, descended upon Germany until 1848.

But the attentive listener might have heard "the hum of mighty workings." Two quite different developments were taking place during these years, which were to upset all Metternich's calculations and in the end reverse the relative positions of the Central European Powers.

The first began with a small tariff agreement in 1819 between

---

[1] On the accession of Queen Victoria to the English throne in 1837 Hanover, where the Salic Law was in operation, passed to the Queen's uncle, the Duke of Cumberland, the "best-hated man" in England. The separation was in almost every way satisfactory to England ; the connexion had often caused in English sovereigns an irritating division of interests. The first thing Cumberland did in his new kingdom was to abrogate the constitution and to dismiss and exile seven of the most distinguished professors from Göttingen University, including Gervinus, Ewald, Grimm, and Dahlmann.

Prussia and Schwarzburg-Sondershausen, so insignificant in its origin that it had at first the support of Metternich. The irregular frontier line of Prussia's dominion with the numerous enclaves of foreign territory and the existence of multiple and com- *The Prussian* plicated customs duties led to a revision of the Prussian *Zollverein (1819).* tariff system. A union on practically a free-trade basis was formed, first with the thirteen foreign enclaves, then with neighbouring states, until, having broken down opposition and rival systems, Prussia found herself by 1850 at the head of what was a powerful economic union of very nearly all Germany, excluding Austria. The political value of this grouping of German material and economic interests round Prussia was immense. It was a direct preparation for the Empire of 1870.

Secondly, in Germany as in Italy, while political development had been checked by Metternich, nationalism had made considerable headway in the realm of ideas. It became part of every *Pan-* liberal man's outlook, tinged with the romanticism which *Germanism.* coloured the intellectual revival of the time. A great literary outburst had followed the French wars, and poets, philosophers, and historians extolled the German idea. Fichte gave his *Addresses to the German People*; Hegel, his successor in the chair of philosophy at Berlin, exalted the conception of the state and the historical *rôle* of the Teutonic race; Stein, the eminent Prussian statesman, founded the *Monumenta Germaniæ Historica* for the study of German history; Dahlmann, Böhmer, Häusser, Giesebrecht, began their great work in the examination of historical records and the literary re-creation of Germany's historical greatness. There was a renaissance of German universities at Berlin, Breslau, Bonn, Munich, Leipzig, and elsewhere. Students went about singing Arndt's poem:

> Was ist der Deutschen Vaterland ?
> Ist's Preussenland, ist's Schwabenland ? [1]

with its answer:

> So weit die deutsche Zunge klingt,
> Und Gott im Himmel Lieder singt. [2]

Soldiers broke into the stirring refrain of *Deutschland, Deutschland über Alles*, and hearths and barracks and students' halls resounded with the melodies of *Die Wacht am Rhein*. It was the men of letters, the poets, and the professors who made Pan-Germanism articulate, who preserved Germany from the provincialism which threatened to engulf her.

In 1848 the nationalist and democratic ideas broke out again into

[1] " What is the Fatherland of the Germans ? Is it Prussia ? Is it Swabia ? "
[2] " As far as the German tongue resounds, singing praises to God in heaven."

revolution—it was the year of revolutions. "When France catches cold Europe sneezes," was an epigram of Metternich's, and the storm which raged in France and Italy and Hungary swept also over Germany. In Prussia and Austria, in Bavaria, Saxony, Hanover, Baden, and Schleswig-Holstein, the people rose in revolt. Excitement spread from the Rhine to the Danube, thrones tottered, and one monarch after another turned his thoughts to Charles I of England and Louis XVI of France. Several rulers hastened to grant constitutional reforms; the King of Bavaria, half the tool of Metternich, the other half the puppet of the dancer Lola Montez, abdicated; the King of Prussia almost followed his example; the Kings of Saxony and Hanover made concessions.

The year of revolutions in Germany.

In Prussia Frederick William IV, the imaginative and romantic successor of Frederick William III, a man "whose rich fantasy lacked wings when it entered on the domain of practical politics," wavered from one mood to another according to whether fear of the revolutionaries or susceptibility to a will stronger than his own prevailed. He was a man of real though timid conscience; it is true that he had declared that he would never allow "a blotted parchment to come between Almighty God in heaven and this land, to rule us with paragraphs and to replace the ancient sacred bond of loyalty," but he had both liberal and nationalist leanings. He disliked revolution, but he thought it incumbent upon him to fulfil in some measure at any rate the constitutional promises that had been made to Prussia in the days of hope after the War of Liberation; and he looked back with reverence and desire upon the Golden Age of German history, upon the glorious majesty of the once vital Holy Roman Empire. With such weak places in his defence Frederick William IV could not remain wholly impervious to the idealism of 1848.

Prussia.

He yielded in the first month of the revolution (March), and he granted a constitution; he headed a procession through the streets of Berlin, wearing over his uniform a red, gold, and black sash, the colours of the Holy Roman Empire; he issued a proclamation solemnly assuming the leadership of Germany. "I have assumed to-day the old German colours, and have placed my people under the revered banner of the German Empire. Prussia's interests shall henceforth be those of Germany." He wrote a letter to the indignant Tsar extolling the "glorious German Revolution." The mood passed; reaction against the revolution began to triumph in Vienna and in the other states of Germany; Frederick William began to fall under its influence and that of a new, vigorous defender of the Prussian Crown and enemy of revolution, who came forward in Berlin at this time, Otto von Bismarck; the King began to move away from the nationalism and democracy of 1848. The revolution in Berlin was suppressed, the constitution was revised in a monarchical direction; a reactionary ministry was appointed.

Frederick William's change of tone had another significance.

The most interesting, important, and in a sense disheartening manifestation of the nationalist revolutionary movement of 1848 was the Frankfurt Parliament. It was the first national Parliament of the German-speaking peoples of Central Europe; it met in St Paul's Church in the old imperial city and existing Federal capital; it consisted of representatives, elected by manhood suffrage, of all the states of the German Confederation, including Austria; its task was to draw up a constitution for a united Germany.

The Frankfurt Parliament (1848–49).

It was the flower of the revolutionary democratic nationalism of 1848; an unparalleled spontaneity had given it birth; a magnificent opportunity lay before it. But multiple problems complicated the task of the deputies. Austria was hostile to any revision of the German Federal constitution, and speed was essential, for the movement could only be carried to success on the flowing tide of the first enthusiasm. But the lawyers and professors who composed the Assembly had never had such a good opportunity of airing their theories, of discussing 'fundamental rights,' and of defining the boundaries of the new Germany. It was almost a year therefore before they had drawn up their scheme of union; by that time the tide had begun to ebb. Austria had put down revolution in Vienna and defeated nationalism in Italy; Frederick William, embarrassed by his own earlier impulses, was surrendering himself to the forces of reaction. When therefore he was offered by the Frankfurt Parliament the crown of a new German Empire he refused it "because of its Parliamentary or even revolutionary basis," and the last hope of the nationalists perished. It had come too late. The source of German nationalism was now contaminated in the King of Prussia's eyes. He was afraid of Austria and his fellow-princes. With the rejection of the Frankfurt crown the union of Germany on a democratic monarchical basis passed out of practical politics; the Empire, when it came, rested not on the spontaneous democracy of the people, but on the military might of Prussia.

Nevertheless Frederick William did not wholly or immediately abandon the cause of German unity. After the failure of the Frankfurt Parliament he timorously put forward a scheme of his own. He persuaded the four kingdoms of Hanover, Saxony, Würtemberg, and Bavaria to form a union with Prussia and the petty states of Germany, and a German Parliament was summoned at Erfurt. The details of the plan are unnecessary, for it met with a speedy defeat. Austria, now triumphant, with the arms of Russia behind her, declared against it. The kingdoms broke away, and

The Union of Erfurt.

Prussia, finding herself isolated, unprepared to take the alternative of war with Austria, gave in. The old Federal constitution was restored unaltered, and in the Convention of Olmütz in 1850 Prussia bowed her head before Austria and Russia in complete and humiliating surrender. Nationalism and Prussia had found the bitter depths of defeat.

No other state of Europe was faced with so many conflicting problems as Austria-Hungary, vanguard of East and West. It hung upon **Austria-** the Danube like a political hinge, on which swung the **Hungary.** fate of the Balkans and of Poland, of Italy and of Germany. It was composed of two kingdoms and of no less than twelve races —Germans, Magyars, Czechs, Slovaks, Poles, Ruthenes, Croats, Serbs, Slovenes, Italians, Rumanians, and Jews. The nationalism which in Italy and Germany was a centripetal force working toward union could only be a disintegrating factor in the Habsburg dominions, and as the nineteenth century advanced the Empire of Austria-Hungary became **Nationalist** a cluster of nationalities simmering with race consciousness. **problems.** Metternich, fully aware of its inharmonious composition, saw that it was manifestly impossible to conduct the policy of the state in any accordance with nationalist principles. It was only by working across and not with the currents of race consciousness, by setting them as far as possible to neutralize each other, that the Empire could be preserved. Thus Croat and Hungarian regiments and officials were sent to Italy, Italians to Galicia, Poles to Austria, Austrians to Hungary. A rigid attempt was made to keep liberal and nationalist influences out of the Empire, while in the interests of the Habsburg monarchy liberal and nationalist movements were to be suppressed in Germany and Italy, the integrity of Turkey maintained against the Greeks, the Tsar to be turned from Jacobinism, and Frederick William induced to abandon the Prussian constitution.

In the Austrian dominions stability was to rest on what Karl Marx called "a Chinese principle of immobility," and a protective wall of tariffs and of censors was set up. A general stagnation began to choke the country. Agriculture was depressed by burdensome feudal privileges as in France of the *ancien régime*; trade languished and food prices were high, though the introduction of machinery seemed to keep alive a spirit of restlessness; national credit was exhausted by repeated issues of paper money; the only books that were read were those that were forbidden; the vitality of the Empire achieved its only glory in the music of Vienna.

On the succession to the throne of the epileptic Ferdinand I in 1835 the weakness of the Austrian *régime* was increased by divided counsels **and a regency.** But Metternich's system was so far successful that

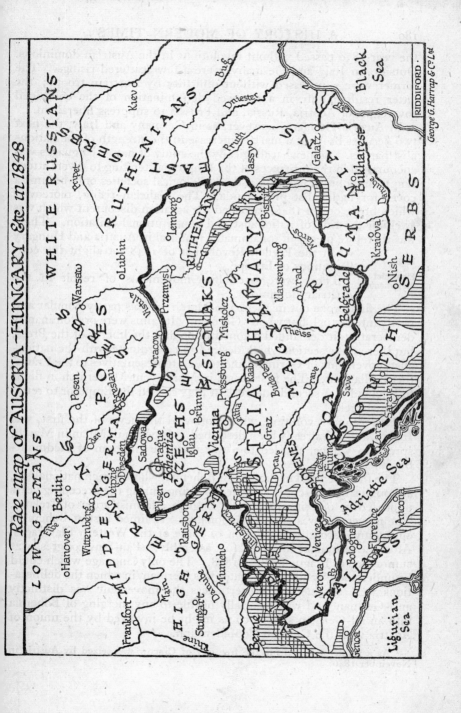

Race-map of AUSTRIA-HUNGARY etc. in 1848

George G. Harrap & Co. Ltd.

RIDIFORD·

autonomy - self gov't

the year 1830 passed without revolutions in the Austrian dominions. Outside, in Italy and Germany, were a few scattered risings. The former were suppressed without difficulty by Austrian troops; the latter resulted only in a renewed determination of the combined sovereigns of Austria, Russia, and Prussia to suppress liberalism.

In Austria-Hungary, however, as in Germany and Italy, the next two decades brought a marked increase in the strength of the nationalist parties. Somewhat illogically the study of native languages was encouraged in the provinces of the Empire, as tending to divert attention from political issues, but the philological societies only became a cover for nationalist propaganda. The Galician rising, moreover, which broke out in 1846,[1] revealed the agrarian discontent which was swelling the tide of nationalist and constitutional agitation. There was therefore plenty of inflammable material in Austria and Hungary

1848. when the French Revolution of 1848 set alight the conflagrations of Europe.

Five chief movements. There were five chief movements of revolt in the Austrian dominions.

constitutional N.B.
revolution
reaction

1. The first broke out in Vienna in March; it was partly popular and partly intellectual, but wholly German. Its aims were predominantly democratic; it demanded a constitution and the liberty of the Press, but there was a section which desired to co-ordinate with the nationalist movements of Germany and to send representatives to the Frankfurt Parliament. The first spasm in March sent Metternich in flight to England. A second outbreak in May caused the Emperor to retire to Innsbrück.

The second revolution, which followed the news of the first, was Italian, and has already been described. It began in Milan in March, spread to Venice, and led to a war with the kingdom of Piedmont-Sardinia.

3. The third centred in Prague, in Bohemia, where Czech nationalism, although small in scope, had been growing during the preceding years under cover of criticism of the English administration of Ireland. The movement was entirely nationalist. It aimed first at Bohemian autonomy, secondly at a union of some of the Western Slav races. After the fashion of the Frankfurt assembly, a Pan-Slav congress was summoned at Prague in June 1848. The only language which could be understood by all the delegates was German, in which the deliberations were conducted. Nevertheless the movement was distinctly anti-German, and was especially hostile to any merging of Bohemia into an all-German state such as might be involved by the union of Austria with the German Confederation.

[1] As a result of this rising the free city of Cracow was seized by Austria in November 1846.

The fourth movement was Hungarian or Magyar, with its headquarters at Budapest. Like the Italian revolt, it was both nationalist and constitutional, and it also led to war with Austria. The Hungarians had a long tradition of self-government, and on the outbreak of the Viennese revolt the nationalist party led by Kossuth, in some respects the Mazzini of Hungarian nationalism, demanded a separate Parliamentary government, which the Austrian Emperor was forced to concede. Hungary thereupon passed the famous 'March laws' abolishing feudalism, serfdom, and aristocratic privilege.

There was, however, another side to the Hungarian movement. It was intensely nationalist, but Hungarian nationalism meant not only the separation of Hungary from Austria, but the establishment of a Magyar ascendency over all the races within the Hungarian borders. Thus to the Croats, the Rumanians, the Slovenes, and the Serbs were denied the independence and consideration which Hungary herself demanded from Austria. "I cannot find Croatia on the map," said Kossuth.

This led to the fifth revolutionary movement, which was anti-Hungarian rather than anti-Austrian in its bias, and had its origin in that literary fomenting of 'Illyrism,' carried on by Louis Gaj, one of the greatest of political journalists. Its headquarters were in Illyria, at Agram, and its object was to unite the Croats, Slovenes, and Serbs in a general resistance to the Magyarization which was proceeding from Hungary. It was the first step toward the union of the Southern Slavs which has to-day resulted in the formation of the state of Yugo-Slavia.

There were thus five centres of disaffection, at Vienna, Milan, Prague, Budapest, and Agram. There was no collaboration between the movements, and some of them were mutually hostile. They seemed to have only one end in common, the disintegration of the Austro-Hungarian Empire. But it was saved from imminent dissolution by the very factor which constituted its weakness—the multiplicity and diversity of the component races.

The Bohemian revolution was the first to surrender, in June, after barely a fortnight's duration, to the troops of the Imperial general Windischgrätz. In July Charles Albert was defeated at Custozza, and in September the Croatian statesman and **Failure** soldier, Jellachich, led the Croats, whose national movement Austria had decided to encourage, to the invasion of Hungary. The Vienna revolution had in the meantime fallen to pieces of its own disorganization, and in October Windischgrätz reduced Vienna.

The Hungarian problem still remained, and in December the Emperor Ferdinand abdicated in favour of his young nephew Francis Joseph, who thus entered on a reign which, lasting until 1916, saw his

double kingdom almost to the end of its journey. Hungary refused
to accept the change of ruler, and declared itself independent. "The
house of Habsburg-Lorraine, perjured in the sight of God and man,
has forfeited the Hungarian throne," exclaimed Kossuth. War broke
out, but after a resistance of some months the Magyar armies were
forced to surrender in August 1849 to the Russian troops which had
come to the assistance of Francis Joseph. The Hungarian constitution was abolished, and the country quelled by harsh reprisals.
Kossuth was outlawed, and went into exile first in Turkish territory
and later for a time in England, where his eloquence had no inconsiderable effect in turning British liberal sympathies against Russia at
the time of the Crimean War.

Thus one by one the movements collapsed. The Austro-Hungarian Empire, marvellously preserved from dissolution, lay quiet
and for the next ten years. Trade and commerce and agri-
reaction. culture were improved, but nationalist and constitutional
aspirations were smothered in a policy of absolutism, centralization,
and Germanization.

Thus Austria was the pivot on which the revolutions in Italy, Germany, and Hungary turned. They seemed to have ended only in the
restoration of her power and the triumph of reaction, except in Piedmont, Prussia, Bavaria, and Hanover, where some constitutional
successes were recorded.

"The future of Europe," said Napoleon, "depends upon the
ultimate destiny of Poland." Certainly the dismemberment of
Poland. Poland, which was completed in the east while the French
Revolution was absorbing attention in the west, was to
alter fundamentally the European balance of power. Poland was dismembered and destroyed in three stages—in 1772, 1793, and 1795.[1]

The idea of Polish partition was not new, but the initial move to
action came from Frederick the Great of Prussia. By a political
manœuvre he hoped to achieve several ends at one and the same time
—extricate himself from an awkward situation that was arising out
of the Russo-Turkish War of 1768, enrich his kingdom by the
appropriation of territories that would join Brandenburg and East
Prussia, satisfy Russia's ambitions, bribe Austria, and deflect France.
He succeeded, and in 1772 Prussia, Russia, and, reluctantly, Austria
appropriated Poland's border provinces. The opportunity and excuse were found in the administrative weakness of Poland's elective
monarchy and in her internal disunion.

The partition shocked Europe, but no Power attempted to defend

[1] See map at p. 194. After 124 years of dismemberment independent Poland was
restored in 1919, only to suffer a fourth partition by Germany and Russia in 1939.

Poland. Still less could Poland obtain help twenty years later when Catherine II of Russia seized the chance of the French war in the west to appropriate more Polish territory. Nor was Poland any stronger internally, in spite of an effort in 1791 to set up a reformed constitution. In 1793 Prussia and Russia therefore came to terms over a second partition of Poland, and two years later the remnants of Polish independence were destroyed in a third partition at the hands of Prussia, Russia, and Austria.

But though her territory had been appropriated and her independence destroyed, the national consciousness of Poland lived on to be a vital factor in European politics until the present day. It was exploited by Napoleon and subsequent enemies of the partitioning Powers. It was the inspiration of repeated Polish attempts to recover independence during the nineteenth century, all of which failed. The Tsar Alexander I had granted a constitution to his "Congress Kingdom," and had himself opened the first Diet in March 1818. But his surrender to Metternich's influence, his growing fear of revolution, and some resistance offered to his measures by the Poles themselves led him, not, indeed, to suspend the constitution, as he at one time contemplated, but to evade it in some of its more important principles, while Russian officials, aware of their master's change of mood, governed with diminishing regard for Polish liberties. The Poles, hankering after the restoration of greater Poland, and at no time entirely satisfied with their constitution, grew increasingly resentful of its infringement, and directed their hostility largely against the Grand Duke Constantine, the Tsar's brother, who ruled with the powers, if not the title, of viceroy. The death of Alexander in 1825 substituted a confirmed autocrat for a renegade liberal, and the accession of Nicholas I was the signal for the rapid growth of secret agitation and conspiratorial societies. The Polish army, the Grand Duke's hobby, was particularly infected, and on the news of the French revolution of July 1830 a military insurrection broke out in Warsaw in November. The projected assassination of the Grand Duke failed; he escaped with his life, but, execrated by Poles and abused by Russians as the cause of the Polish troubles, he wandered about from place to place until he died of the cholera plague which swept across Europe in 1831.

In the meantime, on January 25, the Polish revolutionaries had declared the throne of Poland vacant; it was a declaration of war against Russia, and on the 5th of February 200,000 Russians crossed the Polish frontier.

The Poles fought with heroism, but showed the disunion and lack of discipline which had always been their undoing. Only the help of a foreign Power could have saved them, and none was given.

Although Metternich coquetted with the idea of an independent Poland the attitude of the other Powers and the fear of revolutionary infection in his own dominions deterred him from action.

On February 25 the Poles were beaten in the bloody battle of Grochow, and the outbreak of cholera hastened the surrender which military defeat had practically made certain.[1] In September the Polish resistance was unconditionally broken, and in February 1832 the Organic Statute was issued by the Emperor Nicholas, abolishing the consitution of Alexander I and incorporating Poland in the Russian Empire, though with a separate Government. The Organic Statute was followed by harsh disciplinary measures. An amnesty conspicuous more for its exceptions than its inclusions was granted; soldiers who had taken part in the insurrection were drafted into remote Russian regiments; the male children of rebels were carried off to Russia and brought up in Russian military schools. Polish universities and schools were abolished; even the national pictures were removed from the museums of Warsaw to Moscow and St Petersburg. The Organic Statute, which was not wholly illiberal, remained a dead letter, and all effective government was conducted from the Russian capital. Spasmodic risings in 1833 provided further excuse for its neglect, and after a rising in 1846 it was revoked by an imperial ukase.

Echoes of the prevailing nationalist and democratic aspirations were heard in Scandinavia, and even as far afield as the Danish colony Denmark.   of Iceland, which demanded from Denmark free trade and home rule, receiving the one in 1854 and the other during the seventies.

The loss of Norway to Sweden was bitterly resented in Denmark, and, together with the agricultural depression which followed the fall in the price of corn at the end of the Napoleonic wars, caused for some years considerable economic distress. It was followed after a decade, however, by a recovery and advance toward prosperity.

The two other most noteworthy Danish movements during the first half of the century were nationalist and democratic. The nationalist movement was a double one; in the southern provinces of Schleswig and Holstein, where there was a large German population, there was an articulate German agitation for separation from Denmark. This produced a natural Danish counter-movement in Jutland for the suppression of the German movement and for the closer incorporation of the provinces with Denmark. The Schleswig-Holstein Question became, however, of European importance, and will be reserved for a later chapter.[2]

[1] "So this is an end of the Poles," wrote Lord Palmerston. "I am heartily sorry for them, but their case has become for some time hopeless."
[2] See Chapter VI, section III, pp. 243 et seq.

The constitutional movement in Denmark was formed on much the same pattern as in other countries. It was encouraged by the French Revolution of 1830, and the establishment in 1831 by the Danish King Frederick VI of provincial Consultative Assemblies merely stimulated its ardour without satisfying its demands. It continued to agitate for a free constitution, and in 1848, the year of revolutions, a revolt was only averted by a royal promise of a constitution—a promise which Frederick VI, dying in the same year, left his successor to fulfil.

A constitution was, indeed, granted, but as it did not wholly meet the wishes of the democrats it occasioned constant demands for revision. It is this same constitution which by an attempt to apply it to the duchies of Schleswig and Holstein became entangled in the Schleswig-Holstein Question.

Sweden, which received Norway from Denmark (in exchange for Finland, which Russia wanted), had to contend with serious nationalist opposition from its new partner. The Norwegians refused for a time to accept the proposed union; they drew   **Sweden and Norway.** up a constitution for themselves at Eidsvold, chose a Danish prince as their king, and prepared to defend them both with arms. There was an indecisive conflict for a few years, yielding no complete success to either side, but since the elected Danish prince refused to continue the struggle, and resigned his Norwegian crown, Norway was forced to give in. She accepted the Swedish union, but strictly on the understanding that it was brought about "not by force of arms, but by the free conviction" of the Norwegian people, and that the Eidsvold constitution should be retained. Sweden, nevertheless, tended to treat Norway as a subject state; there were in consequence perpetual disagreements between the two countries, leading finally to separation in 1905.

The nationalist agitation of Norway was coupled further with a democratic discontent with the more aristocratic features of the Swedish Government. But Sweden too had her constitutional agitation. During the reign of Charles XIV—the French marshal Bernadotte, who was adopted by King and people during the life of the infirm and childless Charles XIII as heir to the Swedish crown—the democratic movement made little headway. Charles XIV gave his attention chiefly to the material prosperity of his adopted kingdom. His son, however, Oscar I, was liberally minded and proposed several reforms which were rejected by the privileged Riksdag, or National Assembly, in which the aristocratic classes had the real power. The discontent of the popular party grew, and there were riots in the streets of Stockholm in March 1848. It was not, however, until 1866, in the reign of Charles XV, that a new constitution was granted.

Against the general record of liberal or nationalist defeat which was the story of most of Europe outside England during these years must be set three successes among the smallest countries of Europe, in Greece, Belgium, and Switzerland.

While Europe had been engaged in a Brobdingnagian effort in the West to throw off Napoleon, the peasant people of Serbia had been

Serbia.

struggling for independence against Turkey. It was the first national rising of the Balkans, led by a pig-dealer, Kara George, a wild, fighting barbarian of strange broodings, immense strength, and fierce activity, who in his passionate hatred of the Turks had killed his own father rather than let him fall into their hands, and in a terrible love of justice had hanged his brother for deeds of violence. The issue between Serbia and Turkey was remote from the interests of a preoccupied Europe; the Serbs fought on alone, hampered, after the predisposition of Balkan races, by their own feuds. In 1817 Kara George was assassinated by a rival party; nevertheless Serbia under Milosh Obrenovič was granted by Turkey a small measure of autonomy, and ten years later was placed under Russian protection.

About the same time a powerful national movement had been growing in Greece. In many ways the Greeks had been treated with

Greece.

toleration and favour among the subject races of the Porte. They had been given high administrative posts in the Turkish Foreign Office and in the government of dependencies; they had largely manned and partly commanded the Turkish navy, and no impediment had been offered to their commercial prosperity. They had enjoyed, especially on the coasts and in the islands of the Ægean, a practical autonomy, subject only to the payment of tribute; and had been allowed a religious toleration that might have been envied by the Catholics of Ireland or the Protestants of Austria. Their racial unity had been preserved beneath an active and common religious life. Their Hellenic consciousness was awakened by a literary revival at the end of the eighteenth century which recalled the glories of the classical tradition. Their political aspirations, stimulated by the influence of French ideas, were fostered, as in France and Italy, by the secret society, and the *Philike Hetairia*, or Society of Friends, was formed for the dissemination of nationalist doctrines, to secure the expulsion of the Turks and the revival of the Greek Empire.

There were hopes of Russian support. Was not Alexander's chief minister, Capo d'Istria,[1] a Greek, and a member of the *Philike Hetairia*? The Serbian revolt stimulated daring. A quarrel be-

[1] After leaving the Russian service Count Capo d'Istria was elected in 1827 to the Presidency of the Greek Republic. He held office until his assassination in 1831.

tween the Porte and an ambitious vassal, Ali Pasha, "the Lion of Janina," provided in 1821 an opportunity. There was a preliminary flash in the pan in Moldavia, where Prince Hypsilanti, relying on Russian support, ill-advisedly raised the standard of Greek independence among a Rumanian population who felt no enthusiasm whatever for the cause. Russia disowned him; Turkey rapidly defeated him; he passed into exile, and that episode of the Greek war of independence ended ingloriously. *War of Greek Independence (1821-29).*

It was in the Morea and among the islands of the Ægean that the real insurrection took place. Much may be forgiven to a people with a great name and a Christian faith fighting to throw off an infidel yoke; nevertheless the Greek struggle was a chequered mingling of treachery with heroism, of brutality with valour, corruption with patriotism, avarice and irresolution with a heroic resistance and a noble loyalty. From the first the Greeks set an evil example which was only too faithfully followed by the Turks. The war was one of mutual extermination. The Greeks massacred the Moslems in the Morea; the Turks put the men of Thessaly and Macedonia to the sword, sold the women into slavery, and hanged the Greek Patriarch of Constantinople and three archbishops on an Easter Day.

The Greeks managed to hold their own until in 1824 Turkey called in the help of her vassal, Mehemet Ali of Egypt, and his resolute son Ibrahim Pasha, who was to earn the title of "Black Hell." [1] With the help of the latter Turkish authority was reestablished "by harrying, devastating, and slaughtering in all directions." Missolonghi fell in 1826, Athens in 1827, and the Greek cause was on the point of collapse. *Defeat.*

In the meantime the insurrection had raised a thorny international problem, complicated by Metternich's dread of supporting revolution against established authority, and by British and Austrian jealousy of Russia. In 1822 the Tsar Alexander had made a move toward intervention which, as far as its effects on the Greek struggle were concerned, had been rendered futile by the combined diplomacy of Metternich and Castlereagh. The Powers continued resolutely neutral, except that Great Britain recognized the Greeks as belligerents in order to secure compensation for commercial loss.

Before 1827, however, it was evident that outside intervention could not be much longer delayed. Nicholas I, a man with a will of his own, had succeeded the wavering Alexander; the more liberal Canning had taken Castlereagh's place at the British Foreign Office. Russia would not see the triumph of Turkey nor England the destruction of Hellenism, for whose sake Byron had already given his life, and many volunteers money and *Foreign intervention.*

---

[1] The title was won on the occasion of the suppression of a mutiny of janissaries.

service. In France also sympathy for the race to whose progenitors Western culture owed so much was growing. But Metternich never wavered from the position that the Greeks were rebels who must be left to their fate, and Prussia followed the policy of Austria.

In 1827 Russia, France, and Great Britain dispatched a joint Note to the Porte demanding an armistice, and offering the mediation of the Powers, and the French and British squadrons in the Mediterranean were given watching orders. Although neither England nor France had declared war on Turkey these ships were drawn into a battle with Ibrahim Pasha's Turco-Egyptian fleet, which on October 20 was destroyed, with all its treasure on board, in the Bay of Navarino. Europe was amazed, England embarrassed, Turkey indignant; the incident profoundly modified the diplomatic situation. Canning was dead; Wellington, who had succeeded him as Prime Minister, hastened to apologize for the "untoward event," and to withdraw from direct intervention in the Greek Question. Although French troops occupied the Morea, the situation which Canning had striven to avert had come to pass, and the position in the Balkans lay virtually in the hands of Russia. A short Turco-Russian war brought the Porte to terms, and the Peace of Adrianople in 1829, besides giving commercial and territorial advantages to Russia, recognized the independence of Greece, which was the next year placed under the guarantee of the Powers. In 1833 Prince Otto of Bavaria accepted the sovereignty of the new state.

Navarino (October 1827).

The Russo-Turkish War (1828–29).

Peace of Adrianople.

The emancipation of Serbia and Greece was the beginning of the emergence of the Christian states of the Balkans from Turkish dominance, which was to excite acute national ambition and make many political complications for Europe up to the present day.

The emancipation of Belgium, from the sixteenth century successively under Spanish, Austrian, French, and Dutch dominion, began with the revolt of 1830.

In 1815 Belgium, the Austrian Netherlands of the eighteenth century, had been united with Holland in the Kingdom of the Netherlands, largely in order to strengthen the north-eastern boundary against France. The treaty-makers of Vienna had congratulated themselves upon a masterpiece of political construction, but they had unfortunately ignored—as in the contemporaneous union of Norway and Sweden—the traditional and living differences between the two peoples. They had ignored the sensitive nationalism of a country which for more than three hundred years, while its northern neighbour had been a free and independent state, had been living in subjection to one or another foreign Power. The union wore,

Belgium.

to Belgium, too much the guise of compensation to Holland for her colonial and mercantile losses, and the common Government, under a Dutch king and a majority of Dutch officials, was calculated too much in the interests of Protestant, commercial Holland, and too little in those of Catholic, agricultural, and industrial Belgium. It protested—in the interest of nationalism as much as of euphony—against the substitution of Dutch for French as the official language; it felt aggrieved that its three and a half millions of inhabitants received exactly the same representation in the joint Parliament as the two million Hollanders. The Belgian clericals objected strongly to the proclamation of freedom of worship, and complained of a Government bias toward Protestantism; the liberals thought the King had too much power. The marked industrial prosperity, the development of Belgian mineral wealth, the growth of iron, woollen, and cotton manufactures, and the advantages presented by the Dutch overseas markets were entirely ignored. A liberal-Catholic agitation was directed toward an independent Belgian Government, and even toward complete separation from Holland. The example was provided by the Paris Revolution of July 1830.

On August 25, the anniversary of the King's accession, an excited Brussels crowd, stimulated by a revolutionary opera called *La Muette*, burst out of the theatre crying, "Imitons les Parisiens!" and fell to destroying the public buildings. The infection spread to other towns of Belgium. A half-hearted, hesitating, and dilatory resistance offered by the Dutch Government allowed the movement to fall into the hands of the extremists, and at the beginning of October the independence of Belgium was proclaimed by a provisional assembly which had been summoned at Brussels. The situation rapidly produced international as well as national complications, for Louis-Philippe, the new King of the French, showed every intention of turning the revolt to the profit of France. This Palmerston was determined to prevent—"not a cabbage garden nor a vineyard" should go to France—and it was largely owing to his vigorous diplomacy that the negotiations which led to the recognition of Belgian independence were conducted without war. Leopold of Saxe-Coburg, uncle of Queen Victoria, was placed upon the throne, and in 1839 an international treaty guaranteeing the neutrality of Belgium was signed by the sovereigns of Europe. It was the famous "scrap of paper."

In Switzerland different issues were at stake. The Swiss Confederation, like the Austro-Hungarian Empire, was not a racial unity. It was a number of small states or cantons, differing in race, language, creed, and political conditions, bound together *Switzerland.* by a loose Federal tie. The short-lived Helvetic Republic, formed in

1798 under the inspiration of the French Revolution, and largely under the direction of the French Government, had given them a brief and tumultuous experience of political unity. It had been replaced, in Napoleon's Act of Mediation, by a Federal constitution more in accordance with native tradition. In 1815 the loose Confederation of pre-Revolutionary times had been restored and placed, like the German Confederation, under the guarantee of the Powers. But some definite gains accrued from the last twenty years. Many political irregularities had disappeared, certain subject lands had been emancipated and confirmed as free states, and the experience of union and of governmental machinery remained as a common memory. The history of the thirty years after the Congress of Vienna, in Switzerland as in Germany, was concerned with two main movements, one toward democratic reforms within the states, and the other toward a revision of the "Federal Pact" in the interests of closer unity. The political question was complicated in Switzerland by a religious and Jesuit reaction which was sweeping through the Catholic provinces. In **The Sonderbund war (1847).** 1847 the conflict between Catholicism and its liberal and radical opponents came to a head in the war of the "Sonderbund." The Sonderbund was a separate league of seven Catholic states, pledged to resist anti-Catholic reforms and the infringement of cantonal rights, which, in their eyes, was involved. In many respects the Swiss war of the Sonderbund was analogous to that civil war which fourteen years later broke out in America. The League of Catholic Cantons, like the Southern Confederacy, took their stand upon state rights, and both wars were in essence a struggle between the centripetal and centrifugal forces which federalism represents.

The Sonderbund League was defeated and dissolved, the Jesuits **Forces of union triumph.** expelled, and in 1848, while the Powers of Europe were occupied with their own revolutions, a revision of the Federal Government was carried through.

Switzerland, like the United States, was in many respects eminently adapted for that peculiar form of composite government known as a federation. There was among the Swiss cantons no powerful leader which, like Austria or Prussia in the German Confederation, or even Piedmont among the Italian states, might be capable of welding into a whole the half-discordant parts. The issue in Switzerland never lay between separate independent groups and a single state; it lay between separate independent groups and a federated state. The defeat of particularism in 1848 meant, therefore, the triumph of the forces working toward union, and was, in fact, a justification of the political value, in special circumstances, of federalism.

CHAPTER VI

EUROPE FROM 1850 TO 1871

I. THE CRIMEAN WAR (1853–56)

FOR a generation Europe had rested from war. Napoleon had receded into a nursery bogy, save in France, where he had become a national excuse for political discontent and a platform for an ambitious but second-rate plagiarist. The half-blind gropings of the people, here and there illumined by the light of leadership or the vision of destiny, obscured mostly by the comprehensive triumph of authority, were of the nature and dimensions of revolution rather than of war. The great International Exhibition of 1851, held in London under the patronage of Prince Albert of England, seemed the epiphany of that new age of international peace and commerce which was held to have come upon the world. It was to inaugurate, on the contrary, the most eventful and disturbed twenty years between the battle of Waterloo and the murder of the Archduke Franz Ferdinand at Serajevo. The two decades from 1850 to 1870, in significance as in time the central years of the century from 1815 to 1914, covering the formation of the German Empire, the Italian kingdom and the dual monarchy of Austria-Hungary, the rise and fall of another Napoleon, the advance of Russia across Asia, the marvellous awakening of Japan, the Civil War of America and the Canadian Federation—the decades which saw these developments saw all over the world the dawn of a new era. The Balance of Power was shifted; the age of Metternich became the age of Bismarck; the Europe of 1815, which was substantially that of 1850, was transformed into the Europe of 1914, which, except in the Balkans, was that of 1871.

An era of achievement and construction.

It was the Crimean War which disturbed the states system established at Vienna—that apparently insignificant conflict between Russia on the one side and England, France, and Turkey on the other, which has seemed to many critics so trivial in its occasion, so inglorious in its character, so vain in its issues; "a war to give a few wretched monks the key of a Grotto," [1] "the only perfectly useless modern war that has been waged." [2] On the other hand "Had it not been for the Crimean War," wrote Lord Cromer, "and

---

[1] Thiers.   [2] Sir Robert Morier.

the policy subsequently adopted by Lord Beaconsfield's Government, the independence of the Balkan states would never have been achieved, and the Russians would now be in possession of Constantinople."

Whatever its political value, the Crimean War was a chapter in the Eastern Question, and the prelude to the most important political development of the nineteenth century.

The Eastern Question, which in ever-shifting phases has been present in some form or other throughout Western history, became The Eastern by the end of the nineteenth century "that intractable and Question. interwoven tangle of conflicting interests, rival peoples, and antagonistic faiths" described by Lord Morley. At the beginning of the century it presented itself to politicians in a less involved form, and certain main threads may be clearly distinguished.

In the South-east of Europe lay an alien body which had never been absorbed into the general polity of European nations. An Asiatic Power holding the northern shores of Africa had flung its Turkey. empire across the Bosporus, and for four centuries had imposed upon the commonly quiescent but not wholly lifeless remains of fallen Christian kingdoms the military superstructure of Turkish dominion. Although from time to time European nations had made terms for their own peace and advantage with the enemy of Chris-A decaying tendom, insuperable differences of race, creed, social Power. customs, and political aptitude had denied to the Porte an equal place among Christian states. But the problems of Turkish advance, which from the fifteenth century to the end of the seventeenth had confronted Europe, were now superseded by those of Turkish decay; and the essential factor of the Eastern Question of modern times was that Turkey was a declining Power. In the eighteenth century it was evident; in the nineteenth it was marked. From the date of her second repulse before Vienna, in 1683, by John Sobieski, King of Poland,[1] she had never won more than a temporary military success. It was, however, wholly a fighting genius which had built up her power, and on it alone her empire rested. She had never been able to weld together into a political whole the disparate dominions she had amassed. Corruption, administrative inefficiency, and incapacity had lent no support to her arms, and when these were defeated her strength began to fail.

A moribund state, however, was no unfamiliar political phenomenon; before Turkey there was Poland, before that Spain, and in both cases stronger powers had fallen upon the dying body, and sooner or later international bargains had been made over the spoil. The

[1] " That other fool who saved Vienna," as Nicholas I was afterward to call him, in bitterness at Austria's ingratitude for 1849.

eighteenth century had seen the partition of the Spanish and Polish territories; and there seemed no reason why the European dominions of the Porte should not provide a third territorial feast. It was not out of consideration for Greek nationalism or Serbian memories, for Europe of the eighteenth century felt no tender regard for the national rights or political potentialities of the subject races, and Turkish schemes of partition were a common diversion of European partition diplomats throughout the eighteenth century, from delayed Alberoni to Czartoryski. Nevertheless by the beginning of the nineteenth century, except on the shores of the Black Sea, no serious inroad had been made upon her territories for a century, and she still held dominion up to the Danube and tributary lands beyond the Dniester.

Two factors delayed the dismemberment of European Turkey, the one military, the other geographical. In the first place the by military Porte never sank during the eighteenth century to the and geo- military decrepitude of Poland or Spain. She could still graphical offer considerable resistance to both Russia and Austria, factors. and as late as 1788 her armies defeated the Habsburg forces.

Secondly Turkey, like Poland, to a smaller extent, was by her geographical position remote from the centre of political gravity, which lay considerably farther west. Had she, like Spain with her rich Italian possessions, lain more within the orbit of Western interests she would most probably have suffered a speedier political demise. As it was, Europe was not primarily concerned with her. France, perhaps alone of Western countries, had fully grasped the commercial opportunities of the Ottoman Empire. Even Austria-Hungary, the European state to whose safety the Ottoman Empire had been a real menace, kept her face turned to the West, and once the fear of Ottoman aggression was removed only looked at her south-eastern border over her shoulder. She was more concerned in Western than in Eastern issues, in her rivalry with France and Prussia, in the defence of the Netherlands and the extension of her power in Germany. She was more covetous of Bavaria than of the Balkans, and as late as the end of the eighteenth century Joseph II of Austria furthered the schemes of the Tsarina Catherine II, his natural rival in Turkish questions, in order to advance the Western interests of the Habsburgs.

The situation of the Porte was, however, fundamentally changed by the advent to power, in the eighteenth century, which saw her own decline, of Russia. Russia too looked westward, strove Turkey and for position among Western Powers, and for the first time Russia. in her history Turkey, like Poland and Sweden, lay in the western path of advance of a European state. Sweden, Poland, and Turkey

N

were alike natural enemies of Russia's Western ambitions, and with all three Russia was consistently at war during the eighteenth century. She secured her window in the Baltic at Sweden's expense, and added

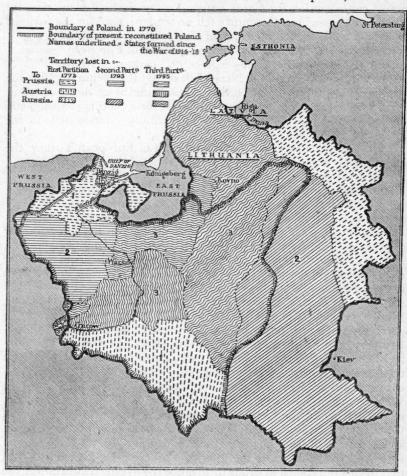

THE PARTITIONING AND RECONSTITUTION OF POLAND

This map does not take account of the dismemberment of Poland in 1939 by Germany and Russia.

Finland in 1815 to guard it. In the three partitions of 1772, 1793, and 1795 she divided with Prussia and Austria the territories of the weakened Poland. In Turkey Russia had special interests. Not only was she bent upon the control of the Black Sea and the Straits, that she might command a passage to the Mediterranean, but she looked upon herself as the historical successor of that Byzantine

Empire which had once shared with Rome the rule of the civilized
world. Her Tsar was patron of the Greek Church, to which most
of the Christian subjects of the Porte belonged. It was
his political mission to place the Cross upon St Sophia, to *Russia's ambitions in the Balkans.*
restore a degraded capital to its former dignity; Con-
stantinople should grow great again as Tsargrad, and the
Byzantine Emperors, protectors of the Orthodox Church, heads of the
Eastern European world, should find a historical reincarnation in the
Tsar of All the Russias, who had inherited their blood and their policy.

The ambitions of Russia at the expense of Turkey were a constant
factor in the Eastern Question from the days of Peter the Great to the
war of 1914, but the means by which she hoped to achieve her ends
varied. They alternated between the expulsion and dismemberment
of Turkey on the one hand, and on the other the maintenance of an
enfeebled state over which she might assume a lordship.

During the last half of the eighteenth century, especially during
the reign of Catherine II, Russia made considerable progress in her
ambitions. The foundations of her success were laid in *The Treaty of Kujuk-Kainardji (1774).*
the Treaty of Kujuk-Kainardji, which in 1774 ended a six
years' war with Turkey. All later treaties, it has been
said, are but commentaries upon its text. Territorially she
acquired a firm grip on the north shore of the Black Sea and the
control of the mouths of the Don and the Dnieper, and she pushed
Turkey back to the frontier of the Bug; commercially she gained
trading rights in Turkish waters, in the Black Sea and the Danube.
She was conceded a permanent diplomatic footing in Constantinople,
and the right of placing consuls and vice-consuls where she wished.
Religiously she was granted an ambiguous protectorate over the
Greek Christians of the Ottoman Empire, and a "public Church of
Greek ritual" was to be set up. Certain terms regarding the govern-
ment of the principalities north of the Danube—Wallachia and
Moldavia—gave her a vague but acknowledged right of interference
in the internal affairs of the Porte.

It was a magnificent leap toward egress to the Mediterranean,
toward territorial dominion and religious and political control. A
few years later Catherine took another step. In alliance with Austria
she made war against Turkey in 1788, and it has already been pointed
out how she manœuvred to engage the Western Powers in war
against Revolutionary France that she might have a free hand for
her own schemes. Some form of partition, probably with Austria,
was undoubtedly in her mind, but events halted upon her hopes.
Austria was forced to withdraw from the Turkish campaign in 1791
by military defeat, internal disaffection in her own dominions, the
turn in French affairs, and by the Triple Alliance between Prussia,

Holland, and Great Britain. The next year Russia was also compelled by the war with Sweden and stirrings in Poland to make peace

Peace of Jassy (1792). at Jassy, but she had nevertheless secured the Crimea
and advanced her frontier to the Dniester. "I came to
Russia a poor girl," said Catherine II. "Russia has
dowered me richly, but I have paid her back with Azov, the
Crimea, and the Ukraine."

For the next few years Russia was occupied with the dismemberment of Poland, and participation in the Second and Third Coalitions
against France, until in 1807 the alliance with Napoleon stimulated
the ambitions for which it set her free. Alexander turned to war
with the Porte in the certain hope of French aid, and the partition
of Turkey flashed again into practical politics. Napoleon, however,
had no serious intention of furthering Alexander's ambitions in the
Balkans, and once again the failure of an ally and the development of

Peace of Bukarest (1812). other European events cut short Russian enterprise. On
the eve of the Moscow campaign, in 1812, Alexander made
the Peace of Bukarest with the Porte, by which he received
Bessarabia, and so advanced Russian territory to the river Pruth.

Thus in 1815 the Russian Empire had reached by varying stages
the borders of the Principalities; but with the nineteenth century
new factors arose to complicate what had appeared a relatively simple
issue between Russia and Turkey.

Napoleon, in many ways a great educator, had turned men's
thoughts to the East, and Europe had begun to realize that her

New factors in the nineteenth century. interests in the Turkish Empire were vital. From the sixteenth century France had maintained a traditional friend-
ship and a commercial understanding with the Porte, which
had been confirmed in the capitulations of 1740. In gratitude for a diplomatic check which the French Foreign Minister,
Villeneuve, had administered to Russia and Austria, who were brow-
beating Turkey, the Porte had guaranteed to France trading privileges
in the Ottoman dominions and conceded special rights to the Latin
monks in the Holy Land, to French pilgrims to the Holy Places, and
to Roman Catholics throughout the Empire. The capitulations of
1740 must be compared with the Treaty of Kujuk-Kainardji of 1774,
and during the negotiations preceding the Crimean War the former
was quoted with as much emphasis by France as the latter by Russia.

Napoleon, however, introduced a new note into French Eastern
policy. He had definitely contemplated the partition of Turkey, to
the advantage of France, not Russia, and he had deliberately acquired
the Ionian islands as a stepping-stone to such a measure. It was
the *motif* of Imperial dominion *à la Russe*, and more than once France
of the nineteenth century was to return to it.

Austria and Great Britain emerged from the Napoleonic wars with an enhanced fear of Russia, who in 1815 stood out as the real menace to the Balance of Power. "In fifty years Europe will be either Cossack or republican," Napoleon had said. Europe was inclined to agree, and after the Congress of Vienna it seemed more likely to be the former than the latter. Metternich, anxious to preserve the stability of the existing Habsburg dominions rather than to add to them, was driven to counter Russia's Balkan ambitions with the political doctrines of "legitimate dynasties" and Turkish integrity.

(1) Change in the attitude of European Powers.

The acceptance in 1815 of a protectorate over the Ionian islands by Great Britain signalized the latter's increased attention to the affairs of the Near East, although in the days of the younger Pitt she had already begun to see her Eastern interests jeopardized by Russian aggrandizement. The Triple Alliance of 1788 was the first step toward the policy pursued by Castlereagh, Canning, Palmerston, and, later, Disraeli. Its cardinal principle was to check the advance of Russia; its second aim, subservient to the first, to preserve the Ottoman Empire.

With the conversion of Europe to a sense of the Russian danger the Eastern Question entered upon a new stage. The days were past when the Western Powers might have looked on at the disruption of the Turkish Empire at the hands of Russia, seeking only their own compensation from the dismembered dominions. At the time, however, that the Porte under the external protection of the Powers and the internal reorganization of reforming sultans in Selim III (1789–1807) and Mahmud II (1808–39) might have entered upon a new lease of life, there arose from within her own house new antagonists in the Christian Balkan nations and powerful rebellious vassals.[1] Thus Europe was confronted with a fresh aspect of the problem. Would the check to the old enemy mean the triumph of the new? If she held up her hand to Russia, was it in the interests of the Ottoman Empire, or in those of Christian states and ambitious pashas? And in any case which would best serve the policies of the Powers? It is round this triangular situation in some form or other that the Eastern Question revolves during the nineteenth century.

(2) Rise of the Christian nations.

For the first half of the century, until after the Crimean War, the part played in the Eastern Question by the Christian states was confined to the struggles of Serbia and Greece and some more obscure

---

[1] Further trouble at the beginning of the century arose from the special troops of the Porte, known as the janissaries, who were mutinous and hostile to reform. In 1826, during the Greek war, they were massacred after a mutiny by order of the Sultan, and the regiments entirely abolished.

efforts in Montenegro. It has already been shown that, what with Great Britain's doctrine of non-intervention and Metternich's dread of insurrection, their common jealousy of Russia and respect for the integrity of Turkey, the Greeks were left for six years to their own unaided efforts,[1] while Canning tried to induce the Porte to come to terms with the insurrectionaries. It will be remembered, too, how Great Britain and France were driven partly by the protests of their subjects against so ruthless a suppression of a people with so great a heritage, and partly by the fear of isolated action on the part of Russia, to a common intervention with the Tsar in 1827; and how after the battle of Navarino Canning's policy was reversed by Wellington, and Russia given a free hand. The Peace of Adrianople, which ushered an independent Greece into the world under Russian patronage, placed Serbia and the Principalities under what was practically Russian protection, and confirmed to the Tsar increased territorial, commercial, and political rights. An attempt was made to remove some of the laurels from the brow of Nicholas by placing the Greek kingdom under the joint guarantee of Great Britain, France, and Russia, and by giving a common backing to a Greek loan. But the Treaty of Adrianople remained, nevertheless, a signal victory for Russian policy. Within four years, in 1833, she gained a still greater triumph.

Treaty of Adrianople (1829).

The Greek Question had been illuminating; it had demonstrated the common interest of the Powers in the Near East and the practical possibility of a resuscitation of the Christian states; it had given to Russia, during a temporary surrender of British vigilance, a further opportunity of fishing in Balkan waters to her own profit, and it had revealed the innate weakness of the Porte, who on the one hand had called in Mehemet Ali to her aid, and on the other had surrendered to a foreign Power.

The weakness of Turkey was readily appreciated by the Sultan's vassal, Mehemet Ali, whose ambition opened the next episode in the Eastern Question, lasting intermittently for a decade, from 1831 to 1841.

Mehemet Ali, an Albanian, like Ali Pasha, had been a small tobacco-trader to whom Napoleon's Egyptian expedition had brought a great opportunity. Out of the confusion he had made himself Pasha of Egypt, and his title had been confirmed by the Sultan. He had driven back the English in 1807; he had suppressed the Mamelukes and the Wahabis; he had conquered the Sudan and Arabia. He was, however, no mere conqueror. Napoleon's invasion had left a heritage of Western ideas which Mehemet Ali adopted, and through French agents, though he himself, it is said,

Mehemet Ali (1831–41).

[1] See Chapter V, section II, pp. 186–188.

could not read or write, he reorganized the army, science, trade, and education of his kingdom on the most progressive lines of a modern European state.

To such a man the pashalic of Crete was a ludicrous reward for the services which he and his son had rendered to the Sultan in the Greek War of Independence, and he determined upon the acquisition of Syria. Upon a pretext in 1831 Ibrahim invaded Palestine. He captured Acre and Damascus, defeated the Turkish army, advanced into Asia Minor, and was on the point of threatening Constantinople. In 1832 the Sultan appealed to the Powers, but, partly owing to the preoccupation of England and France with the affair of Belgian independence, Russia alone was willing and ready to give help. Her pressing offers of assistance caused the Porte no little embarrassment, but finally and reluctantly the Sultan accepted, for "a drowning man will clutch at a serpent." Russian ships therefore anchored in the Bosporus, and Russian troops began to pour into the Turkish dominions. It was a spectacle which increasingly alarmed the Western Powers, and since Russia would not withdraw until Ibrahim had recrossed the Taurus mountains, and Ibrahim would not retire until his father had received satisfaction, Great Britain, France, and Austria put pressure upon the Porte to cede Syria to Mehemet Ali. Turkey was forced to give way, and in April 1833 the claims of Mehemet Ali were conceded.

But Russia also demanded her price, and in July the Treaty of Unkiar Skelessi was signed, which marks the zenith of Russian influence at Constantinople. Turkey was virtually placed under a Russian military protectorate; a free passage through the Straits was guaranteed to Russian warships, and in time of war the Dardanelles were to be closed to every other Power. In England and France the news of the treaty excited the liveliest apprehension, but although the incident passed off without war Palmerston, the British Foreign Minister, was determined not only to watch Russia unceasingly, but to tear up the treaty at the first opportunity.

Treaty of Unkiar Skelessi (1833).

In 1839 the Sultan Mahmud II, who had made a commercial alliance with England and reorganized his army with the aid of a young Prussian officer, von Moltke, of whom Europe was to hear more, sent a force against Mehemet Ali, upon whom he had been desiring to avenge himself since 1833. The Sultan's troops, with their "Russian tunics, French drill-books, Belgian muskets, Turkish caps, Hungarian saddles, and English sabres," were defeated by Ibrahim; at the same time the fleet deserted to Mehemet Ali, and the old Sultan died, leaving as his successor Abdul-Mejid, a boy of sixteen. At this point the Powers intervened. Neither England

nor Russia wished to see the triumph of Mehemet Ali, whose ambition had grown with his success.   France, on the other hand, vainly
attempting under Louis-Philippe to mitigate the national boredom
by Napoleonic gestures, began to see visions of French control in the
Mediterranean.   She had recently conquered Algeria; she was
united with the Bourbons in Spain; the alliance of Mehemet Ali,
that "Napoleon of Egypt," who had so flatteringly adopted French
ideas, might give her a paramount influence in the Levant, and, by
enabling her to cut a canal through the isthmus of Suez, open a route
to India and the East, which would neutralize the advantages secured
to England by the possession of the Cape.   Secret French support
was therefore given to Mehemet Ali, and Palmerston began to foresee
a French dominance in Egypt as dangerous as the Russian supremacy
at Constantinople.   Either was equally undesirable; he set himself
to maintain the integrity of Turkey and to prevent the isolated interference of any single Power.   "All that we hear every day of the week
about the decay of the Turkish Empire and its being a dead body or
a sapless trunk and so forth is pure and unadulterated nonsense.
. . . If we can procure ten years of peace under the joint protection of the five Powers, and if those years are profitably employed in
reorganizing the internal system of the Empire, there is no reason
whatever why Turkey should not again become a respectable Power."

Before the designs of France Russia drew closer to England,
offering to renounce the Treaty of Unkiar Skelessi in return for co-
operation in the Eastern Question.   She had no desire to see a
vigorous Albanian supplant a weak Osmanli at Constantinople, and
to break up the unity of the Western Powers would give her a sweet
diplomatic triumph.   In 1840 a convention was signed "for the
pacification of the Levant" between Great Britain, Russia,
The
Convention   Austria, and Prussia.   Mehemet Ali was to receive the
of London   hereditary pashalic of Egypt, and the Straits were to be
(1840).   closed to the ships of all nations in time of war.   This
Quadruple Alliance was on the one hand a rebuff to France; on the
other it was a check to Russia.   It was a bold piece of diplomacy
characteristic of Palmerston.   As he anticipated, although France
might talk furiously of the slight that had been put upon her, she
would not dare to go to war.   In the East the troops of the signatory
Powers forced the terms of the Convention of London upon the
Sultan and his vassal.   The Porte recovered Syria, Crete, and Arabia;
Mehemet Ali was confirmed in the hereditary pashalic of Egypt
under the suzerainty of the Sultan.   The next year France, accepting
her defeat, was admitted to the alliance of the Powers.

The Egyptian Question was settled, and the Powers had committed
themselves to the policy of Turkish integrity; Mehemet Ali retired

from European politics, and Turkey, saved from a powerful dependent, from the reawakened ambitions of France and the dangerous hostility of Russia, turned to internal reforms and the discord they provoked; the Treaty of Unkiar Skelessi was wiped out; Russia and France had both learnt that England would not admit a protectorate of the one over Turkey or of the other over Egypt. It had been the will of Great Britain that had prevailed; no one had triumphed—not Mehemet Ali, nor Abdul-Mejid, not Louis-Philippe, nor Nicholas I—save Palmerston, the self-confident English statesman, with a keen eye for foreign potentates and British interests, a bland temerity, and a reputation for good luck. In 1841 Palmerston went out of office with the Melbourne ministry.

For ten years the Eastern Question remained quiescent. The Anglo-Russian *rapprochement* of 1840 lost much of its nervousness when Palmerston retired. The Tsar Nicholas visited England in 1844, complimented the Queen, praised her children, showed himself "full of politeness," talked to the ministers about a joint solution of the Eastern problem, and returned to Russia with the impression that in no circumstances would England make war as long as the pacific Aberdeen was in the Government. In 1846 the Corn Laws were repealed, and Peel's ministry fell, and Palmerston went back to the Foreign Office for five years. A little later political conflagrations flared up over Europe; by the light of one of them a short, thick-set man with a long, heavy face, dreamy, calculating eyes, and a Napoleonic nose took the oath of allegiance to the Second French Republic.

"There was repose in the empire of the Sultan, and even the rival churches of Jerusalem were suffering each other to rest, when the French President, in cold blood and under no new motive The for action, took up the forgotten cause of the Latin Church Crimean in Jerusalem, and began to apply it as a wedge for sundering War. the peace of the world." Thus wrote Kinglake, the contemporary English historian of the Crimean War, who, it was hinted in London Society, had his own reasons for bearing a grudge to Louis Napoleon.[1] That the French President raised the storm cannot be denied. Nevertheless the *rôle* of mere international villain which Kinglake has ascribed to him in his brilliant romance was utterly alien to Louis Napoleon's inconsistent nature, to his tortuous methods, his double contradictory policies. He never pursued clearly a simple issue, but mingled impulsiveness with hesitation, and complicated undoubted personal ambitions by spasmodic attempts to justify them before a confused but evident political conscience. After two humiliating failures in 1836 and 1840 he had achieved not yet a crown, but the

[1] They were both, it was suggested, suitors for Miss Howard.

highest place in the French State. He had returned to France as the exponent of the Napoleonic idea. "I represent before you a principle, a cause, a defeat. The principle is the sovereignty of the people, the cause that of the Empire, the defeat Waterloo. You have recognized the principle, you have served the cause, you wish to avenge the defeat." The words were spoken in 1840 in the proper Napoleonic spirit; in 1850 they were even more pertinent, as Louis Napoleon, encircled with the halo of popular sovereignty, set out in the footsteps of his master toward empire and glory.

To a faithful meditator on the career of the great Napoleon the course was not without direction. Had not the master exchanged the republican toga for the imperial robes? *Coups d'état* could be repeated, and the principle of popular sovereignty turned again to Bonapartist ends. Louis Napoleon proceeded cautiously; he had a four years' term of office from 1848 in which to mature his plans. He shuffled his ministries and put his agents into power, men like Morny, Saint-Arnaud, Fleury, and Persigny, whose fortunes were bound up with his own; he fed the nation with Napoleonic sentiments, toured the provinces, spoke of a revision of the constitution, even allowed himself from time to time to be hailed as Emperor

Louis
Napoleon
makes
himself
Emperor
Napoleon
III.
by the troops. So with his finger on the popular pulse he awaited his opportunity. It was provided by the Electoral Chambers, who on May 31, 1850, in fear of socialist disturbance, had passed a law disqualifying some three million voters. Louis Napoleon saw his chance, and, posing as the champion of an enlarged suffrage, proposed the next year a revision of the law of May 31. In either case he stood to gain; the Chambers saw the trap and threw out the proposed revision; whereupon Napoleon prepared his *coup d'état*. The soldiery were won over, the director of the State printing-office

The
coup d'état
(December
2-4, 1851).
suborned. On December 1, 1851, the usual Presidential Assembly was held at the Élysée, and soon after the guests had departed the plot was put into execution. In the dead of night seventy-eight deputies were carried off to prison from their homes, while compositors, with the *gendarmerie* at their elbows, printed meaningless words which, when pasted together, formed a proclamation dissolving the Assembly as a hot-bed of plots, proposing a new constitution, placing Paris under martial law, and the Republic under the protection of the President. In the meantime Morny at the Home Office telegraphed to the provinces to inform them with what joy Paris had received the change of Government.

The next day there was some resistance; more deputies were carried off to prison; and two days later the troops shot down the populace in the *boulevards*. But Louis Napoleon had triumphed. A plebiscite endorsed the *coup d'état* and extended the period of his presidency. The President moved significantly from the Élysée to the Tuileries, and on January 14, 1852, issued a new constitution, which was a thinly veiled despotism. On December 2, 1852, a year after the *coup d'état*, and forty-eight years to the day after the establishment of the First Empire, a second plebiscite made him Emperor. He took the title of Napoleon III, "by the grace of God and by the will of the people, Emperor of the French."

Thus the domestic part of Louis Napoleon's programme was accomplished; there remained the achievement of international glory. Like his prototype, Napoleon III turned to the East. In the dominions of the Porte were the Holy Places of Palestine, tended by monks of the Roman and Greek Churches. By the capitulations of 1740 the Roman monks had long been regarded as under French protection, and had been given special privileges, but during the atheistical days of the Revolution the interest of France in the everlasting quarrels of the Roman and Greek Churches had lapsed, and the Greek monks had encroached upon the rights of their Latin rivals. The cause of the Catholic monks, like the defence of the Pope in 1849, would appeal to the clericals of France, on whose support Louis Napoleon rested. It would awaken traditions as old as the Crusades; and if a contest with the Greek monks should lead to conflict with their protector, the Russian Tsar, what better defence could there be of the Napoleonic tradition than a war which should avenge Moscow, as well as the diplomatic defeat of 1840? The Napoleonic name should echo again from one end of Europe to the other; and Nicholas Romanov be forced to acknowledge the title and the might of the Bonaparte whom he had scorned to take as his *bon frère*.[1]

Thus during 1852 Napoleon pressed the claims of the Latin monks which he had taken up in 1850. "Stated in bare terms," writes Kinglake, "the question was whether for the purpose of passing through the building into their grotto, the Latin monks should have the key of the chief door of the Church of Bethlehem and also one of the keys of each of the two doors of the sacred manger, and whether they should be at liberty to place in the sanctuary of the Nativity a silver star adorned with the arms of France." Napoleon demanded a full restoration of the rights of the Latin monks, and after some delay the Porte conceded them. Nicholas immediately supported the Greek monks, and insisted upon the withdrawal of the concession. The Porte, driven between the two Powers, attempted a compromise which, stated in ambiguous language, did not satisfy Russia. In

---

[1] Nicholas refused to address Napoleon III after the usual courtesy among monarchs as *mon frère*, and used the phrase *mon ami*.

truth neither France nor Russia wanted a compromise, and Russia startled Europe in March 1853 by sending to Constantinople a special envoy, the overbearing and haughty soldier, Prince Menschikoff, the **Russia claims a protectorate** highest grandee in the Russian Empire, to obtain satisfaction with regard to the Holy Places, and to demand a virtual acknowledgment from the Sultan of the Tsar's protectorate over all the orthodox subjects of the Porte. The claim was based upon the Treaty of Kujuk-Kainardji, but it immediately shifted the issue to a new plane. The Eastern Question was reopened. **and returns to the policy of partition.** The controversy with France had awakened the ambitions of Russia. In a series of conversations with the British ambassador at St Petersburg, Sir Hamilton Seymour, Nicholas I showed that he had abandoned the policy of maintaining the integrity of Turkey, which, with the other Powers, he had supported since 1830, and that he had developed again the idea of dismemberment held by his eighteenth-century predecessor. "Turkey," he said, "is in a critical state . . . the country seems to be falling to pieces . . . we have on our hands a sick man—a very sick man; it will be, I tell you frankly, a great mis- **The "sick man" of Europe.** fortune if, one of these days, he should slip away from us before all necessary arrangements have been made." The interests of Russia and England, Nicholas insisted, were identical, and he proposed a general scheme of partition by which Russia might hold Constantinople "*en dépositaire*, not *en propriétaire*," and England might receive in compensation Egypt and Crete. "If the Turkish Empire falls it falls to rise no more; and I put it to you, therefore, whether it is not better to provide beforehand for a contingency than to incur the chaos, confusion, and certainty of a European war." The Tsar's proposals were reported to England, and "courteously but very firmly declined." "She would admit neither the accuracy of the prognosis" nor "the propriety of the treatment."[1]

In the meantime the British ambassador at Constantinople, the able but by no means conciliatory Lord Stratford de Redcliffe, began to dominate the situation in the Turkish capital. He was convinced of Russia's dangerous ambitions, and that no real peace could exist in the Near East until they had been unmistakably repudiated. With consummate skill he disentangled the claims regarding the Holy Places from those concerning a Russian protectorate, persuaded the Porte to concede to Russia the first, where the Russian position was strong, and to withhold the second, where it was weak. Consequently in May 1853 Menschikoff and the staff of the Russian Embassy quitted Constantinople. The Porte published a justification of its position to the Powers and began apprehensively to take measures of

[1] *Cf.* J. A. R. Marriott, *The Eastern Question*, Chapter X.

self-defence. On July 21 a Russian force crossed the Pruth and occupied the Principalities, not as an act of war, but as a "material guarantee" for the concession of her just demands.

And so the situation remained until the end of October, while the Powers grew busy with conferences at Vienna, where Count Buol, who had inherited Metternich's policy without his ability, still believed that crises could be tided over with prudent diplomacy. The outcome was the Vienna Note—an attempt of the four Powers, England, France, Austria, and Prussia, to solve the problem with a formula. Turkey and Russia, to whom the joint note was dispatched, were to accept the " letter and spirit of the Treaties of Kainardji and Adrianople relative to the protection of the Christian religion." It was believed that the formula covered the issue, but it merely evaded it, for Russia read "protection by the Tsar," and Turkey "protection by the Sublime Porte." Nevertheless ambiguity might have served the interests of peace but for the agency of Lord Stratford de Redcliffe, who urged the Porte to insist upon a narrower definition, in Turkey's favour, of the term 'protection.' "No man ever took upon himself a larger amount of responsibility than Lord Stratford when he virtually overruled the decision of the four Powers, including his own Government, and acquiesced in—not to say caused—the rejection of the Vienna Note by the Porte after it had been accepted by Russia." [1] Lord Stratford considered it essential to force from Russia a specific renunciation of her claims, and this she refused to give.

When diplomacy broke down it was obvious that the question would be submitted to the arbitrament of war. As Lord Aberdeen remarked, with the prospect of English and French support Turkey had never had such a favourable opportunity of driving back Russia, and "may never have again." On October 23, 1853, the Porte, having called upon Russia to evacuate the Principalities, declared war. Her troops took the offensive on the Danube, and the Russian Black Sea fleet retaliated by the entire destruction of the Turkish fleet in the Bay of Sinope, on November 30.

> Turkey declares war upon Russia (October 1853).

It was not to be expected that the war would long remain confined to Turkey and Russia. "The Turks," wrote Lord Aberdeen, "with all their barbarism, are cunning enough to see clearly the advantages of their situation. Step by step they have drawn us into a position in which we are more or less committed to their support." Both France and Great Britain believed that the integrity of the Turkish Empire was at stake, and British and French ships had already passed the Dardanelles. In France a war would be popular and useful to a somewhat unsteady throne. In England there was a surprising unanimity

[1] *The Edinburgh Review*, quoted by J. A. R. Marriott, *The Eastern Question*, p. 263.

arrayed against Russia. Palmerston at the Foreign Office was all for vigorous measures, so was *The Times*. Liberal opinion was ready to

Followed by France and England (March 1854).

draw the sword for the sake of oppressed Poles and Hungarians, and imperialists remembered Russian intrigues in Afghanistan and saw the security of British India threatened. For Great Britain, in an age when faith came easily, implicitly believed in the Russian menace. But Lord Aberdeen, the Prime Minister, held back, while popular feeling waxed white hot at the "massacre of Sinope," and denounced with irrational fervour the so-called Russian treachery. In spite of Lord Aberdeen England was drifting into war, while France, reluctant to move without her, waited uneasily. On January 4, 1854, the combined fleets entered the Black Sea. On February 27 a joint ultimatum was dispatched to Russia, demanding the evacuation of the Principalities. At the end of March both countries declared war.

As late as the end of January Nicholas had persuaded himself that England would not actually go to war. Still more he miscalculated

Austria.

the attitude of Austria, upon whose support he had counted —for had he not saved the Austro-Hungarian Empire from disruption in 1849, and supported Francis Joseph in the diplomatic contest with Prussia at Olmütz in 1850 ? But Nicholas learnt in bitterness that gratitude did not weigh against political considerations. Austrian politicians viewed the Russian occupation of the Danubian Principalities as a menace to the Habsburg interests, and with a cynical remark that Austrian thanklessness would astonish Europe they adopted a suspicious and threatening attitude before which Russia was forced to give way. On two occasions they delivered ultimata which Russia had no choice but to accept, unless she would bring another enemy into the field against her, and although Austria never actually went to war her attitude of hostile neutrality was of vital significance to Russia's defeat. The Austrian ingratitude was not quickly forgotten, and in 1866 it bore bitter fruit.

What Austria lost Prussia gained. In Court circles at Berlin there was a demand for war against Russia which Bismarck, who was rising

Prussia.

to diplomatic but not yet to ministerial importance, resisted with all his might. "We have no real cause for war with Russia, and no possible interest in the Eastern Question. Why without provocation should we attack our hitherto friend and perpetual neighbour either out of fear of France or for the *beaux yeux* of England or Austria?" This was the tenor of his arguments, which so far triumphed as to keep Prussia out of the Crimean War. A promise of assistance, "if necessary," was indeed given by Frederick William IV to Austria, but it was never called upon. Prussia's actual neutrality counted as friendly to Russia. It was the beginning of an understanding between the two neighbours which secured to Prussia the Tsar's invaluable support ten years later in her struggle with Austria.

One other state must be mentioned which in 1855 entered the Crimean War, though it had no interest in the Eastern Question. For the sake of the French alliance the kingdom **Sardinia.** of Piedmont-Sardinia sent 15,000 troops to fight the Russians that Victor Emmanuel might reign in Rome.

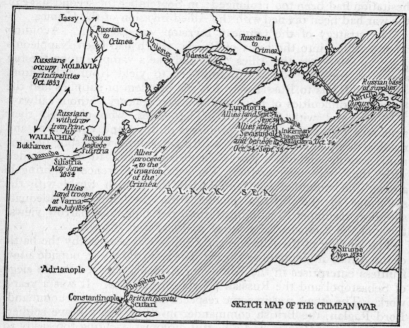

SKETCH MAP OF THE CRIMEAN WAR

The war falls into two unequal parts. The first was short, lasting only from March to July 1854. The Russian troops who were already in occupation of the Principalities crossed the Danube on March 23 and besieged Silistria. On May 29 **The war.** the French and British fleets stationed off the Turkish **First stage** shores of the Black Sea landed troops at Varna. Five **(March–July** days later Austria delivered her first ultimatum to Russia, **1854).** demanding the evacuation of her Principalities. Nicholas, held up by the unexpected Turkish defence of Silistria, with French and British troops approaching to its aid, yielded, raised the siege, recrossed the Danube, and slowly withdrew his forces from the Principalities. As he retired, Austrian troops advanced, occupied the Principalities, and remained there for the duration of the war. Thus by the end of

July Russia's first offensive had failed, and encouraged by her weakness the Allied statesmen put forward four demands, known as the "Four Points," on which Russia was to give them satisfaction. They concerned her claim to the protection of the Greek Church, her naval rights on the Black Sea, her commercial privileges on the Danube, and her vague power of intercession in the Principalities. Russia hesitated, and finally in November conceded the Allied demands. But the hesitation had been too prolonged; in September the second stage of the war had been opened with the Allied invasion of the Crimea.

The strategy of the Crimean invasion was excellent. Avoiding an expedition into the heart of Russia, which had been Napoleon's **Second stage (September 1854– September 1855).** undoing, the Allies "fastened like a vampire upon the big toe" of Russia, forcing her to yield from exhaustion. Thus to Russia were left the problem of supplies and the difficulties of transport in a vast country without railways and with few roads. The Allies, who obtained their resources by sea, found the problems of food and equipment and medical service hard enough; to Russia, whose very soil, become mud, was in Nicholas's words "a fifth element" to be contended with, they were insuperable. The work of Florence Nightingale among the wounded has familiarized the British world with the sufferings of the British soldiers from the climate, inadequate supplies, incompetent administration, red tape, and narrow views; those of the Russians were worse, and less well known.

The landing of the Allies in the Crimea was secured by the battle of the Alma,[1] in September 1854. The rest of the war, outside a few fruitless enterprises in the Baltic and Armenia, centred in the siege of Sebastopol and the Russian efforts to relieve it. It was a year's work. The attack was in some respects unfortunate in its command. Lord Raglan, the British commander-in-chief, was a brave soldier, a courteous gentleman, and a tactful diplomat, yielding too easily to the counsels of others. He was a veteran of the Peninsular War, with the valuable experience gained from serving with Wellington marred by the rigidity of forty years of subsequent staff work. He was sharply criticized in the British Press, and died from disappointment and dysentery in the midsummer of 1855. The first French general, Saint-Arnaud, a "stage" Frenchman, by Kinglake's description, was suffering from a mortal disease, and died in September, before Sebastopol was invested. He was succeeded by Canrobert, a man of excessive caution and moral timidity, who resigned his post in May 1855 to Pélissier, who was the first vigorous commander the French had possessed.

[1] One of many Tartar words, showing how incomplete was the Russianization of the Crimea. Alma = apple.

The defence was admirably conducted almost to the point of success by Todleben on the land side and from the sea by Admiral Kornilov, "the only man of genius whom the war threw up on either side." [1] The relieving force was less efficiently directed by Menschikoff. Two attempts to raise the siege were made within three weeks of the first Allied bombardment. They were beaten off in the battles, famed in British story, of Bala- clava and Inkermann, and the Allies settled down to a long and bitter siege through the Crimean winter. Florence Nightingale achieved her great medical organization at Scutari, and a young Russian volunteer, Leo Tolstoy, told stories to his comrades before the camp-fires. In the spring and early summer both Allied and Russian efforts were renewed. An attempt in June to storm the outworks of the Malakoff and the Redan was repulsed by Todleben. A descent of the Russian covering force in August was on the other hand driven back at the river Tchernaya, where the Sardinian army contributed not a little to the Allied victory. In early September the attack upon the Malakoff was renewed, and with success, and the next day, September 9, the Russians blew up the magazines of Sebastopol and surrendered the fortress.

Balaclava (October 25).

Inkermann (November 5).

Other than military factors had, however, fundamentally modified the situation during 1855. Palmerston had succeeded Aberdeen as Prime Minister, Pélissier had taken over the French command, and Sardinia had sent a contingent of troops to the Allies. On the other hand Austria was playing a double game, and Napoleon III was wavering in the British alliance. Most important of all was the death of the Tsar Nicholas I in February 1855. "General February," in whom, with "General January," he had placed so great a confidence, had "turned traitor," and struck a fatal blow.

"You must make peace and set free the serfs. . . . As for me, I cannot change." In these words to his son was concentrated the tragedy of Nicholas's life. He was a man of an age that had passed; a sincere Christian, a chivalrous king among brother monarchs, a devoted lover of Russia and things Russian, a patron of the Russian language and Russian literature. Baptized with the blood of the Dekabrists,[2] who in 1825 had inaugurated his reign with an insurrection, he acquired a hatred of democracy and revolution which he indulged with all the staunchness of his limited mind and the mysticism which was part of his nature, as of that of his brother, Alexander I. The "Don Quixote of autocracy," the "doctrinaire of

[1] Professor C. R. Beazley, *Nineteenth-century Europe and Britain.*
[2] Russian insurrectionaries with a large following in the army, who revolted in the month of December (Dekabre) 1825.

O

absolute power," he regarded himself as a divinely commissioned champion of law and order. But for all his pedantic autocracy, and for all his love of military display, there was neither honest administration in his state nor efficiency in his army. Toward the end of his life he began helplessly to realize the new and unfriendly spirit of an age which he could neither appreciate nor retard. He could not change; he could not build railways nor forgive injuries, neither accept defeat nor make terms with democracy. In profound depression, he courted the death that came upon him by a reckless disregard of precautions for his health.

The death of Nicholas was not immediately followed by peace, but it was impossible for Alexander II to resist for long the political and military pressure that was put upon him. The Russian capture in November of the Armenian fortress of Kars paved the way to a slightly less humiliating surrender; a second Austrian ultimatum proposing terms was accepted, and in March 1856 the Peace of Paris was concluded.

There were three main groups of clauses. The first neutralized the Black Sea, opened it to the merchant-ships of all nations (but "interdicted the flag of war"), forbade the building of either Russian or Turkish arsenals on its shores, and extended the navigation of the Danube equally to all countries. The second achieved the renunciation of the Russian protectorate over the orthodox subjects of the Porte. The third removed the Russian frontier from the Danube by demanding the cession of Southern Bessarabia.

The Peace of Paris (March 1856).

Finally the Sublime Porte was formally admitted to "participate in the public law and concert of Europe." The Powers engaged themselves collectively to guarantee the "independence and territorial integrity of the Ottoman Empire," and the Sultan, "in his constant solicitude for the welfare of his subjects," promised—vainly, as it proved—a better and more equitable government. The liberties of Serbia were guaranteed.

No event can be without results, nor is it wise to compare them with the hypothetical effects of a different course of action. The Crimean War checked and humiliated Russia, and gave a new lease of life to Turkey under the joint protection of the Powers. Napoleon III gained a great advertisement, England a heavy National Debt, Austria an enemy for a generation.

Its indirect results were greater. "Out of the mud of the Crimea" a new Italy was made, and, less obviously, a new Germany. A new impetus was given to Russian reorganization and a new direction to Russian expansion, whose tide, dammed in Europe, flowed into Asia. A fresh movement was set on foot toward Balkan reconstruction.

Europe was saddled with new responsibilities, forced into new paths, and the edifice built at Vienna was shaken to its foundations.

II. The Unification of Italy (1850–70)

The first fruit of the Crimean War was the union of Italy.   In 1849 the national cause had been everywhere defeated.   The Sardinian war with Austria had ended disastrously at Novara.   Charles Albert had resigned his throne, and after a few months in a Portuguese monastery had died before the end of the year; Garibaldi *Apparent* had stood on the Piazza of St Peter's offering, like a god, *shipwreck* "thirst, forced marches, battles, and death" to those who *of the* followed him, and with four thousand volunteers had set *national* out on the retreat from Rome; Mazzini, after four months *cause* *in 1849.* of brief authority—all that he ever enjoyed—had returned to a London lodging-house and to the Carlyles at Chelsea, with "a greyish beard," writes Mrs Carlyle, "altogether a new feature . . . 'no *efflorescence* of Republicanism,' he begged me to believe, 'but *necessitated* in the first instance.' . . . For the rest he looks much as he did—and is the same affectionate, simple-hearted, high-souled creature—but immensely more agreeable—talks now as one who had the habit of being listened to."   Pius IX, restored to Rome by the grace of God and the arms of Louis Napoleon, began to prepare his anathemas against democracy and liberalism, while French regiments guarded his capital.   The Venetian Republic after an obstinate resistance had also been forced to surrender, and Daniele Manin had struggled wearily to Paris, where he was giving Italian lessons to keep himself alive.

But in the north Victor Emmanuel II sat upon the throne of Piedmont-Sardinia as the *re galantuomo*, who, though not yet fully acclimatized to a political atmosphere—he preferred a hunter's life in his native Alps—had proved a brave soldier, a sincere patriot, and an honest king, as later he was to reveal himself a judicious statesman; and from Turin, out of the Parliament—itself a pledge that the preceding struggle had not been wholly in vain—there came *The* echoing through Italy in the spring of 1850 a promise and *nationalist* a prophecy which sent the hopes of patriots fluttering *hopes* *turned to* toward Piedmont and turned the footsteps of exiles toward *Piedmont.* its capital.   "Piedmont, gathering to itself all the living forces of Italy, will soon be in a position to lead our mother country to the high destinies to which she is called."   The words were *Cavour.* spoken by a quiet, stout, short-sighted little man, Camillo Benso, Count Cavour, whose good-natured, unworldly, and untidy appearance gave little indication of a master-diplomat of the age.   In

1852, exactly a decade before Bismarck, with whom he can alone be coupled, entered upon his great work, Cavour became Prime Minister of Sardinia, and began to conduct her policy with a vigour and self-confidence that evoked from Thiers the remark, "Do the Piedmontese fancy that it was they who won the battle of Novara?"

A keen constitutionalist of an English type—his enemies called him sarcastically "Milord Cavour"—he set himself to maintain and develop Parliamentary government in Piedmont; he built railways, promoted trade, and expanded commerce, stabilized finance, reorganized the army, abolished antiquated inequalities, and reduced the clerical power. But his internal measures, which alone would have given him rank as an able minister of modern enlightenment, were eclipsed by his Italian and foreign policy.

No cause was more blessed in leaders of devoted patriotism and of excellent though dissimilar parts than that of the Italian Risorgimento. But Mazzini, its fervent though unpractical apostle, and Garibaldi, its soldier and knight-errant, might have been martyrs of a barren hope without Cavour, the real creator of Italian unity. With an unswerving devotion as great as that of Mazzini and Garibaldi, he yet held markedly different views as to how union could be achieved or what form it should take. A liberal monarchist, and a servant of Victor Emmanuel, he had no more sympathy with the republican ends and insurrectionary methods of Mazzini—though he came to use them—than with the designs of the so-called Neo-Guelphs for an Italian federation under Papal presidency. Unlike Garibaldi, who was a child in such matters, he knew the political necessity and the political value of renunciation. His was the master-brain which mobilized the inspiration of Mazzini into a diplomatic force, which beat the sword of Garibaldi into a national weapon, and turned what might have been the political quixotries of ill-guided enthusiasts into instruments of State.

Cavour's whole policy was dominated by an inflexible ambition to effect the emancipation of Italy from Austria and her union under His Italian the house of Savoy; it was based upon the fundamental policy. assumption that only by European support and foreign alliance could his great end be achieved. The multiple problems of Austrian rule, princely interests, and Papal power could not be solved by popular revolts, nor by the unsupported efforts of a comparatively minor state, the kingdom of Sardinia, but only by international co-operation, by European diplomacy and war. Italian unity must be lifted out of the enervating obscurity of Austrian domestic politics, in which since 1815 it had been stifled; it must become a European question, on which the Powers should fight, as for Turkish integrity or the Balance of Power.

Thus Cavour's double aim was to bring his cause before the political consciousness of Europe and to secure a foreign alliance.

He began by educating the liberal sympathies of the Western peoples with a vigorous and judicious literary propaganda, all the more powerful that Austria relapsed into a defensive taciturnity. He turned the band of exiles at Turin into "a brilliant army of scribes," which he set, with articles and foreign correspondence in *Literary* the *Morning Post*, *The Times*, *Le Matin*, and *L'Indépen-* *propaganda.* *dence Belge*, to the winning of the battle of Italian freedom in the field of journalism. The British Government was friendly, and a firm ally in Sir James Hudson was sent as ambassador to Turin. In France, in spite of the clerical party and the complications of the French occupation of Rome, the Emperor was known to favour a cause in which as a young man he had fought himself and lost a brother, and to which, in spite of his public policy, he gave secret diplomatic encouragement

When the Crimean War broke out, therefore, Cavour saw an opportunity which he grasped in one of the boldest moves in the history of diplomacy. He joined the Anglo-French alliance not as a *The* subsidiary, but as an equal—proudly refusing a subsidy *Crimean* that England offered; he dispatched 15,000 picked soldiers *War* under La Marmora, who distinguished themselves at the Tchernaya; and he received in return, in the face of considerable opposition, which he fought down, a seat at the Peace Conference of Paris, side by side with the plenipotentiaries of England and Russia, France and Austria. "You have too much tact to take part in affairs which do not concern you," remarked Walewski,[1] the Austrophil French minister of foreign affairs. Nevertheless the whole part had been played that Europe might learn that the affairs which concerned Italy concerned her too. Sardinia had no interest in the Eastern Question; Cavour's policy was one of simple adventure, pursued defiantly and skilfully, that Sardinia might rank as a European state, that the Italian Question might be forced before the diplomatic attention *and the* of the Powers, and that at least one of them should dispose *French* herself to support it. It was a gamble upon the political *alliance.* conscience of Napoleon III, and upon the sense of moral obligation of England and France; a gamble without reserve, guarantee, or condition, for all that Cavour carried away from the Peace Congress for his consolation was the memory of a sympathetic speech by Lord Clarendon, and an ominous remark from the French Emperor—"I have a presentiment that the actual peace will not be long."

In reality Cavour had achieved his aim; Italian independence had become a European question; and Napoleon III considered himself committed to its support.

[1] The son of Napoleon and the Polish Countess Walewska.

For two years nothing ensued, and then Cavour's schemes were nearly wrecked by the rashness of a Mazzinian republican, Orsini, who, on January 14, 1858, tried to assassinate Napoleon III on his way to the opera. It was a repetition of the episode of 1800, and, like the first Napoleon, the third miraculously escaped death, though men round him were killed. There was a period of restraint between the Courts of Paris and Turin, and then the Emperor turned his resentment against England, where the plot had been hatched and the bombs manufactured. Toward Italy he began to direct a reawakened compassion. "So long as Italy is not independent the tranquillity of Europe, no less than that of your Majesty, is a mere chimera. . . . Deliver my country, and the blessings of twenty-five million citizens will follow you in posterity." So wrote Orsini from prison. The letter was read in Court by his advocate, Jules Favre; the people no less than the Emperor were stirred. Orsini died with the cry of "Vive l'Italie" upon his lips, and from his scaffold there came a new impulse toward Italian freedom.

In May 1858 a Dr Conneau, a friend who had helped Louis Napoleon to escape in 1846, arrived at Turin and remarked to Cavour that the Emperor was about to spend a month at Plombières, a spa in the Vosges, "quite close," said Dr Conneau, "to the Sardinian frontier." It was characteristic of the diplomacy of the Second Empire, and without further invitation Cavour decided to take a holiday in Switzerland, whence he leisurely proceeded to Plombières. There the French Emperor and the Sardinian minister, having met with no other ostensible purpose than to drink the waters, planned between them a war with Austria and a reorganized Italy.

The Pact of Plombières (June–July 1858).

Napoleon, however, was concerned with Italian independence and not with Italian unity; he would make war on Austria, but he would not countenance the formation of a united Italian state. Austria was to be excluded from Lombardy and Venetia; so much was clear, and the Sardinian kingdom was to extend from the Alps to the Adriatic. As to the rest of Italy, there was to be a central principality carved out of the duchies for his cousin Prince Jerome Bonaparte—"Plon-Plon," [1] as he was more familiarly called in Paris. The Papal States were to be maintained, and the kingdom of the Two Sicilies left to itself.

For reward France was to receive in actual territory Nice and Savoy.

[1] Supposed to be derived from *Plomb plomb* or *Craint plomb* ("Fear lead"), acquired during the Crimean War. Prince Jerome, or Napoleon (he assumed the name of Jerome on the death of his brother, in 1847), was the son of the great Napoleon's brother Jerome, and was considered to bear a striking resemblance to his uncle. He regarded himself as the exponent of the Napoleonic traditions in their democratic aspect, and supported the liberal party during the Second Empire.

The two royal houses of France and Piedmont were to be allied by the marriage of Prince Jerome Bonaparte to Clothilde, daughter of Victor Emmanuel, and for the rest Napoleon undoubtedly hoped to acquire a powerful influence over a grateful and divided Italy.

The fourfold division of Italy was no part of Cavour's ultimate ambition for his country, but he was forced to accept an immediate limitation of his schemes for the sake of the French support against Austria. Victor Emmanuel was also dissatisfied with the nuptial arrangements, but was finally persuaded to sacrifice a daughter to a *parvenu* prince for the weal of Italy.

It had been part of the Pact of Plombières that war against Austria should be planned as soon as possible; Napoleon was to send 200,000 men, Cavour 100,000. "Not only shall we make war at the first opportunity, but we will seek a pretext." On January 1, 1859, therefore, at a New Year's *levée* at the Tuileries, the taciturn Emperor pointedly remarked to the Austrian ambassador, "I regret that our relations with your Government are not as good as formerly." Its significance was fully appreciated. A few days later Victor Emmanuel opened the Sardinian Parliament with the words, "We are not insensible to the cry of pain which arises to us from so many parts of Italy." This was followed by the issue of a huge loan, and the publication in Paris of a semi-official pamphlet, *L'Empereur Napoléon III et l'Italie*; and on January 13 Prince Jerome started for Turin to claim his bride. The intentions of both states were transparent, but a 'pretext' had still to be found.

The diplomacy of the next few months is by no means clear. Napoleon III and Cavour were both looking for a *casus belli*, but Napoleon was beginning to waver, to look apprehensively toward Prussia, while Cavour grew more desirous of war, more provocative, and more desperately impatient; and Victor Emmanuel threatened to resign if Napoleon did not keep to the resolution. Austria was stiff, but astonishingly patient, England was working hard for peace, and for settlement by mediation or conference. On March 9 Cavour ordered the mobilization of the Sardinian forces, but by the end of the month it seemed that the war would after all be averted, and the issue transferred to a European congress. With a heavy heart Cavour agreed to the demobilization of Sardinia, when suddenly and unaccountably Austria dispatched to Turin an ultimatum, demanding instant demobilization or war. The hope that Cavour had almost abandoned was realized, and Austria stood forth before Europe as the aggressor. "The die is cast, and we have made history," he cried exultantly. Napoleon's qualms were satisfied, and on April 29 France also declared war.

The Franco-Sardinian war against Austria (May–July 1859).

Austria had taken the initiative in offering battle, but her armies did not get into touch with the enemy until May 7, by which date French troops were pouring into Italy. On May 20 the Franco-Sardinian forces defeated the Austrians at Montebello, on May 30 at Palestro, on June 4 at Magenta, and on June 7, within a month of the first encounter, they entered Milan. On Midsummer Day they won the brilliant victory of Solferino, and drove the enemy back into the famous quadrilateral of forts, Mantua, Peschiera, Verona,

Napoleon's desertion.

The armistice of Villafranca (July 11).

and Legnano. Austria had been forced to evacuate Lombardy; her expulsion from Venetia seemed imminent, when Napoleon III called a halt, and on July 11, at a personal meeting with the Austrian Emperor Francis Joseph, in a house at Villafranca, arranged terms of truce which were embodied later in a general peace.

The action was dictated partly by the losses of the French army and Napoleon's temperamental irresolution, partly by the fear of Prussia, who, armed to the teeth, was threatening to come to the help of Austria, but chiefly by the unexpected revelation of Sardinian strength and Italian patriotism. "With each advance of the Allied arms Napoleon's vision of an Italian federation under the patronage of France faded, and the dream of a united Italy assumed more shape and substance; and he had not made war in order to create upon his flank a vigorous and united military power which might in after days resent her debt to France." [1]

To Piedmont and to the nationalists throughout Italy Napoleon's move bore only one appearance—it was a desertion and a betrayal, in the fact of its existence, in the manner in which it had been done, and in the nature of its result. To halt in the middle of victory was a betrayal of Italian hopes; to make an independent truce—and not even through the usual avenues of negotiation—was a desertion of the Allied cause; to sanction a continuance of Austrian rule in Venetia was a breach of the Franco-Sardinian pact, by which the kingdom of Piedmont was to reach *jusqu'à l'Adriatique*. By

The Treaty of Zurich (November 1859).

the Treaty of Zurich, which confirmed the armistice of Villafranca, Piedmont was to receive Lombardy, except the fortresses of Mantua and Peschiera; Austria was to retain Venetia, which was to form part of an Italian federation under Papal presidency; a further clause concerned the rulers of the central duchies, who had been forced to flee by revolutions in their own states; they were to be restored "by their own subjects."

Cavour urged Victor Emmanuel not to accept the infamous treaty, but his counsel was unheeded, and in utter despair at the failure of his hopes, and with violent, uncontrolled reproaches against his

[1] Professor Alison Phillips, *Modern Europe, 1815-1899.*

FRANCE

Strassburg

GERMANY ·Stuttgart

CZECHO - SLOVAKIA

Munich Rhine

Danube Vienna

L.Constance

AUSTRIA Buda.Pest

·Berne HUNGARY

SWITZERLAND Drave Danube

SAVOY ceded to France AUSTRIAN-1866 Caporetto

PIEDMONT LOMBARDY Udine

Magenta·1859 VENETIA Gorz

Milan·1859 Trieste

Novara· Custozza Verona

Turin· Solferino Villafranca Venice Fiume

PARMA Gulf of YUGO - SLAVIA

Parma 1860 MODENA Venice

Genoa 1860 Modena Pola DALMATIA

Bologna ROMAGNA

San Remo PAPAL San Marino Serajevo

Nice LIGURIAN Florence STATES

SEA Pisa Ancona ADRIATIC

C.Corso Leghorn TUSCANY 1861

Elba 1860 Perugia SEA

CORSICA UMBRIA

Ajaccio 1861 Aquila

Strait of Bonifacio ABRUZZI

Rome MOLISE

Gaeta CAMPAGNA APULIA

THE Bari

Naples BASILICATA Brindisi

SARDINIA KINGDOM OF Gulf of

TYRRHENIAN Taranto

Cagliari NAPLES

1861

C.Teulada AND CALABRIA

Messina

SICILY Palermo C.Spartivento

Marsala 1861 Str.of Messina

Dates indicate year of annexation Syracuse

to Kingdom of Italy

·····Present frontier of Italy Pantellaria L. C.Passero

THE UNIFICATION OF ITALY, 1848–70

king, he retired into private life. With his resignation he abandoned
for ever the policy of "working out the salvation of Italy through
foreign alliances." Nevertheless the war had not been wholly a
failure. The initial and therefore the most significant rupture in
the Vienna treaties which bound Italy to Austria had been made,
and, what was more, sanctioned by the Powers. The recognition
by Europe of the cession of Lombardy was a tacit acknowledgment
of Italy's moral claim upon Venetia. Moreover the kingdom of
Piedmont-Sardinia had been publicly accepted in a new rôle; it had
become the admitted nucleus of a kingdom of Italy.

There was to be a further result. The impetus given to the Italian
The central Question by the war with Austria was to reach further than
states. the cession of Lombardy, and Piedmont was to receive some
compensation for the withholding of Venetia.

Upon the outbreak of war and the evacuation of Lombardy by
Austria there had broken out in Central Italy, as Cavour had anticipated, revolutions prepared by the National Society.[1] In Tuscany,
Modena, and Parma the rulers were driven from their dominions,
Papal legates were expelled from Bologna and the Romagna, provisional Governments were set up, and votes were everywhere recorded
in favour of annexation to Sardinia. Although Victor Emmanuel
had not definitely accepted the proposals of the central states, he had
already given them his approval when the armistice of Villafranca,
which enjoined the restoration of Papal and ducal authority in Central
Italy, entirely cut across the situation. Victor Emmanuel had reserved to himself a certain liberty by adding to his signature the
qualifying phrase "as far as concerns myself," but he could no longer
encourage the annexationist movements in Central Italy without a
breach of the treaty terms.

In the meantime the central states were raising large volunteer
forces, officered to a considerable extent by Piedmontese volunteers;
they formed a military league for mutual defence, and it became increasingly evident that the clause of the Treaty of Zurich enjoining a
restoration of former rulers "by their own subjects" would remain a
dead letter. Sardinia was sympathetic to the annexationist movements; the issue depended, therefore, upon the foreign Powers. Eng-

[1] The National Society was an organization formed in 1857 for the promotion of
an Italian Union under the house of Piedmont, in contrast with the republican aims
of the Mazzinians. Its motto was "Unity, Independence, and Victor Emmanuel."
It marked the rise of a new unionist party, and the reconciliation of many of the
democrats with the Sardinian monarchy. Many of Mazzini's followers, including
Garibaldi, joined it, although Mazzini himself held aloof. Cavour gave it much
secret support, and soon came almost to direct its policy through its secretary, La
Farina. "Make your national society," he had said to La Farina, "and we shall
not have long to wait for our opportunity . . . but if I am questioned in Parliament
or by diplomats, I shall deny you, like Peter, and say 'I know him not.'"

land and her Whig ministers Russell and Palmerston were openly sympathetic to Italian aspirations, and brought forward the doctrine of non-intervention to defend their doing nothing. Austria was naturally hostile to any enlargement of the kingdom of Sardinia or reduction of Papal power. The Catholic influences were also against it, and Russia and Prussia were coldly disapproving of any infringement of the Treaty of Zurich. France formed the pivot of the situation. Napoleon III gyrated between two contradictory ideas; on the one hand there was the Treaty of Zurich, on the other the manifest intention of the central states, his own professed sympathy with national movements, and a promise given to Victor Emmanuel that he would not permit foreign intervention in favour of the exiled rulers. At length he saw a way out; he returned to the proposed cession of Nice and Savoy to France, which in view of the incomplete fulfilment of the Pact of Plombières he had not claimed after Villafranca. Suppose a plebiscite were held in all the territories concerned, in Nice and Savoy, in the central duchies, and in the Papal States? The result was a foregone conclusion; Nice and Savoy, on a notoriously engineered vote, showed a desire for transference to France; the central duchies and the Romagna for annexation to Piedmont. The arrangement was, in fact, another bargain between Napoleon and Cavour, who had returned to office in January 1860, having in reality largely guided the policy of his state from his country retirement. Napoleon was to receive Savoy and Nice in return for permitting the annexation of the central states to Sardinia.

In April 1860 Victor Emmanuel became king of a North-Central Italy, stretching from the Alps to the Papal States, with the omission of Venetia. The mountain cradle of the royal house of Savoy on the other side of the Alps passed to France, with the birthplace of Garibaldi. In England there was intense feeling against any increase of French territory. "Louis Napoleon—that scandal to royalty—what can I say of him? Hypocrite and footpad combined. He came to carry out an 'idea,' and he prigs the silver spoons. 'Take care of your pockets,' ought to be the cry whenever he appears, either personally or by deputy." [1] So wrote Sir James Hudson to Lady John Russell, repeating current abuse perhaps rather than voicing his own opinion, for he saw the political necessity of the surrender. As for the great Nizzard Garibaldi, he never forgave Cavour, who had made him a foreigner. "This man, you know, has sold my fatherland. Poor Nizza! [2] Well, all the same I deal with him as a good friend and ask him to give me a thousand firearms, so that we can go and get ourselves cut to pieces in Sicily. It seems to me not to be asking much, eh?" [3]

---

[1] Quoted by G. M. Trevelyan, *Garibaldi and the Thousand.*   [2] Nice.
[3] Quoted by G. M. Trevelyan, *op. cit.*

Cavour had convinced himself of the necessity for surrendering Nice and Savoy; he calculated also upon its political advantages. "Now we are accomplices," he remarked, rubbing his hands, to the French agent. Cavour had other schemes on foot, schemes to which Garibaldi's letter, quoted above, referred; and it was no unwise thing to have tied beforehand the hands of Napoleon III with some of the spoils of Italian freedom.

The first advance toward Italian unity had been made; to Cavour it was a mere stepping-stone, and within a year, to the amazement of Europe, he had added to the Italian kingdom the whole of Naples and Sicily and the Papal dominions except the patrimony of St Peter. "They have stopped me from making Italy by diplomacy from the north; I will make it by revolution from the south." From princes and foreign alliances Cavour turned to Mazzini and Garibaldi and the insurrectionary instinct of the people; he heard the cry echoed from Charles Albert in 1848—"Italia fara da se." With the utmost diplomatic caution and ingenuity he embarked upon one of the most amazing enterprises in the history of the Italian union. "The public law of Europe scarcely received lip service; and diplomacy did not even have the compliment paid her of being asked to draw a decent veil over naked acts of piracy." [1]

Cavour modifies his policy.

The kingdom of Naples and Sicily, already branded in Gladstone's vivid phrase as "the negation of God erected into a system of government," was seething with discontent; from 1821 to 1860 its history was contained in the annals of its police. In 1859, at the beginning of the critical war with Austria, Ferdinand II, King Bomba of 1848, died, leaving as his successor a foolish son, Francis II, whose helpless indecision between conflicting councils rendered impossible any effective attitude toward the urgent problems of foreign war and internal progress. Naples took no part in the war, and discontent, stimulated by events in the north and the movements in the duchies, grew ripe for revolution; while after the armistice of Villafranca, which discredited the French and Muratist tradition, it turned more distinctly toward union and the Piedmontese connexion—a serious measure to an ancient state to whom union meant the merging, and therefore the loss, of identity.

The kingdom of Naples and Sicily.

In Sicily the dissatisfaction was magnified, as was common, by a strong racial feeling and a national indignation against the rule of a foreign Neapolitan dynasty. Abortive revolutions had already broken out, and the National Society, whose secretary, La Farina, was himself a Sicilian, determined as a desperate reply to the armistice of Villafranca to raise in the island another insurrection. Mazzini encouraged it, and Francesco Crispi, one of his principal agents, later

[1] R. B. Mowat, *A History of European Diplomacy, 1815-1914.*

to be a famed minister of Italy, organized it, but its success depended upon two men, Garibaldi and Cavour.

Like a Norse god, with his giant strength and golden shining hair, his simple, romantic nature, his magnetic power and adventurous sword, the heroic figure of Garibaldi appears and reappears Garibaldi in Italian history, the strangest personality of the nine- (1807-82). teenth century. He was born, the son of a skipper, at Nice, then an Italian town, in the year 1807, when Giuseppe Mazzini, a doctor's son farther along the coast at Genoa, was two years old. He did not take kindly to the ambitious education which his father tried beyond his means to give him, and only acquired "just enough book-learning to feed his naturally freedom-loving, romantic, and poetical disposition, but not enough to chasten it, or to train his mind to wide understanding and deep reflection." [1] Ten years in the coasting trade gave him a varied experience of the Mediterranean, many adventures— three times he was captured by pirates—and an intimate contact with Italian patriots and exiles, who inspired him with that love and zeal for Italian freedom which filled the rest of his life. "He believed in Italy as the Saints believed in God." He was introduced to Mazzini and joined the Young Italy Society. "When I was a youth and had only aspirations toward good I sought for one able to act as the guide and counsellor of my youthful years. I sought such a guide as one who is athirst seeks the water-spring. I found this man. He alone watched when all around slept; he alone kept and fed the sacred flame." In 1833 he joined in one of Mazzini's many conspiracies, in which his part was to enter the Sardinian navy and win over the sailors to the plot. The conspiracy failed; Garibaldi was prosecuted and forced to flee, and the first time that he saw his name in print was in a public notice of the Sardinian Government condemning him to death.

From 1836 to 1848 Garibaldi disappeared from the Old World. For the twelve years he lived a wild, roving life in South America, leading the local wars, participating in adventures worthy of the purest romance, carrying off a wife whose companionship is a subject for saga, who "looked upon battles as a pleasure and the hardships of camp life as a pastime," and, finally, acquiring an experience of guerrilla warfare that was of infinite use to Italy in 1860.

In 1847 an unfamiliar portent—a reforming Pope—appeared in the Italian firmament, and Garibaldi offered his services to the Papacy, but returned in 1848 to place them at the disposal of Charles Albert of Sardinia, who had declared war against Austria. After the defeat of Custozza Garibaldi was called by Mazzini to defend the Roman Republic against the French troops. An heroic defence was followed by an heroic retreat after the city had fallen, with a devoted wife and

[1] G. M. Trevelyan, *Garibaldi's Defence of the Roman Republic*.

devoted followers.   Most of the Legionaries were shot down by the
Austrians; near Comacchio his wife died.   Garibaldi himself escaped
across to Tuscany, thence to Piedmont, and so to America.

In 1854 Garibaldi was back again in Italy with a little wealth,
which he spent in buying the small island of Caprera, near Sardinia,
and in building there a house, where he lived with the simplicity of a
crofter and the status of a king.   There, neither in nor out of the way
of Italy, he filled his soul with "the breath of liberty, the utter release
from crowds and Courts and officials and the whole scheme of modern
life, to which he was always in mind and heart a stranger; and this
liberty would have sufficed him to the end of his days as he gazed over
the unbroken surface of the sea, had he not in his mind's eye seen
beyond the eastern horizon those still enslaved shores." [1]

In 1856 Garibaldi had his first interview with Cavour, and the next
year he announced his conversion to the cause of the Sardinian
monarchy.   It was in a sense the most important action of Garibaldi's
life.   It did more than anything else to heal the breach between the
republicans and the monarchists and to turn into one current forces
which separately might have destroyed each other and defeated their
common aim of unity.   At heart Garibaldi remained a republican,
though he loyally and under great stress served Victor Emmanuel to
the end.   Fortunately there existed between the King and the soldier
a real sympathy and understanding which served Italy in good stead
when the relations between Cavour and Garibaldi were strained to
breaking-point.

Thus, largely owing to the influence of Garibaldi's decision, many
patriots accepted in 1859 an alliance with the Frenchman Louis
Napoleon, whom in 1849 they had held in detestation as the greatest
enemy of their cause.   Garibaldi himself, whose name had brought
many volunteers to serve with the great leader, was given a Sardinian
regiment, which he commanded with a success only cut short by the
armistice of Villafranca.

As early as the autumn of 1859 the conspirators in Sicily began to
appeal to Garibaldi for help in the coming insurrection.   His presence
alone would give success to the enterprise.   After some
hesitation he accepted, on condition that the revolt took
place in the name of Italy and Victor Emmanuel, and that
it was started by the Sicilians themselves.

The
revolution
in Sicily.

Cavour also was approached.   To encourage a raid upon the shores
of a neighbouring state was an act outside the public law, one which
might not only provoke a quarrel with the kingdom of Naples, but
bring upon Piedmont the censure and intervention of the Powers.
On the other hand, Cavour was not blind to the political potentialities

[1] G. M. Trevelyan, *Garibaldi and the Thousand.*

of a rising conducted in the name of Victor Emmanuel, as his teeming imagination played with fresh schemes for achieving his life's ambition. He too had undergone something of a conversion since Villafranca; insurrections, properly controlled, might have their uses. There was the problem, too, of the Garibaldini, the men who had fought with their chief in 1859; they were restless, like their leader, and spoiling for fresh encounters.

In short Cavour, though outwardly preserving an attitude of strict neutrality, determined to give secret encouragement to the revolution. While the negotiations were proceeding for the cession of the central states, however, he would allow nothing to be done that might jeopardize the interests of Sardinia and union.

On April 4, 1860, the revolution broke out near Messina, and after a brief gleam of success was crushed by Swiss and German mercenaries in the pay of the King of Naples. But Garibaldi heard only of its initial success, and, abandoning with some reluctance an expedition to Nice to burn the ballot-boxes, in order that the proposed cession to France might be prevented, he renewed his promise to the Sicilians and appealed to Cavour and the King for authorization and help.

April 1860.

The actual rising threw Cavour into a "conflict of calculations." It was impossible that he should give open and official encouragement, but the expedition had now become not only a political venture, but a popular cry. Garibaldi's name was upon every one's lips, and to have forbidden him to proceed would have been to forfeit a considerable amount of loyalty to the Sardinian throne. Hesitatingly and cautiously, therefore, Cavour pursued his double game, disclaiming the while to the ambassadors of the Powers all knowledge of the affair. The preparations were allowed to go on; Garibaldi collected his volunteers, only Victor Emmanuel stipulated that officers of the Sardinian army should not be allowed to enlist. Arms were collected from the arsenals of the National Society; the Sardinian Government maintained its blindness. The harbour authorities of Genoa connived at the embarkation of the expedition, and Admiral Persano of the Sardinian navy was secretly instructed "to keep between Garibaldi's ships and the Neapolitan fleet."

Cavour's attitude.

On May 11 Garibaldi appeared off Massala, on the west of the island of Sicily, and disembarked his troops under what was practically the protection of a small British naval squadron. This semi-diplomatic intervention saved the expedition, and was part of Britain's contribution to the cause of the Italian patriots. "We had once a great filibuster who landed in England in 1688," declared Lord John Russell in the House of Commons a few days later.

From Massala Garibaldi advanced across to the capital, Palermo.

He possessed hardly more than a thousand men, of whom one in twenty—there were as yet not enough to go round—wore the red shirt which after the taking of Palermo became the famous dress of the band. There were 20,000 Neapolitan troops opposed to them. On May 15 the first engagement occurred at the hill of Calatafimi; it was a hard-won fight which nearly ended disastrously, but at the end of the day the Neapolitans were seen streaming in flight across the plateau of the hill and down the other side. A fortnight later, after a series of bold and brilliant measures, Garibaldi entered Palermo and proclaimed himself dictator of Sicily, and by the end of July, after another fiercely contested battle at Milazzo, the whole island except the fortress of Messina and one or two minor ports was in his hands. The Thousand were a picked band of men, but Garibaldi's name had worked miracles. As much as the Neapolitans were disheartened, the revolutionaries were encouraged and rallied to his side. The cowardice and incompetence of the Neapolitan general did the rest.

Garibaldi's brilliant success presented to Cavour and Piedmont an urgent and embarrassing problem of extreme complexity. It was certain that the adventurous general would cross to the mainland, and probable that he would advance farther into the Papal States, even to the Eternal City itself. Moreover, with every victory Garibaldi grew more independent, more impatient and distrustful of Cavour and his cautious, diplomatic methods and political considerations, and more sympathetic to Crispi and the extreme republicans among his followers. Mazzini was himself in Italy, and additional volunteer expeditions were being equipped with the deliberate intention of invading the Papal dominions. It was as important to Cavour's far-reaching schemes that whatever success Garibaldi should achieve should be won for the Italian kingdom as that the intervention of the Powers, especially of France and Austria, should not be brought about by an ill-timed attack upon Rome. So far the diplomatic situation was more favourable than Cavour had dared to expect. England was enthusiastically friendly. The French Government was growing uneasy, but Napoleon III was still on the whole sympathetic, and in any case reluctant to move without England. Austria could not act without the other Powers, and was in addition deterred by the fear of a Hungarian rising, for the Italians were in close touch with the Hungarian patriots. The blusterings of Russia Cavour could afford to ignore. The King of Naples had already appealed in a panic to the Powers, but none of them was able or willing to help him.[1]

Garibaldi's brilliant success.

Garibaldi and Cavour.

[1] Trevelyan, in *Garibaldi and the Making of Italy*, quotes a letter of June 7 from Odo Il, the British representative at Rome, to his uncle, Lord John Russell : " The

Cavour, therefore, having failed to persuade Garibaldi to consent to the immediate annexation of Sicily, determined to play his own game against the general.   He resolved to create both in Sicily and Naples a public opinion strong enough to force the dictator's hand, and before Garibaldi had crossed the Strait Cavour's agents were intriguing in the kingdom of Naples, spreading disaffection and stirring up the revolutionary fervour of the country in favour of the monarchical union.   Admiral Persano was even set to win over the Neapolitan fleet.[1]   It was political conduct for which there was no defence except the urgency of the situation and Cavour's entire personal disinterestedness.   "If we had done for ourselves the things which we are doing for Italy we should be great rascals," he remarked.   In the meantime Piedmont carried on futile negotiations with the Neapolitan Court, which had at length pocketed its pride and appealed to the northern kingdom for help—an appeal which it was not difficult to refuse, for Naples had given no support to Piedmont against Austria the year before.

In the second week in August Garibaldi, with a much enlarged force, crossed the Strait and landed in Calabria.   Napoleon III had proposed that an Anglo-French squadron should blockade the Strait of Messina and so keep Garibaldi in Sicily, but Great Britain had rejected it by an appeal to the doctrine of non-intervention; thus for the second time Garibaldi's advance was due to British support. *Garibaldi crosses to the mainland.*

The Bourbonists hardly put up the merest defence. The Neapolitan kingdom, crumbling with its own rottenness, fell at a touch.   On August 31 Garibaldi captured Reggio and began to advance toward Naples.   The troops fell back to the Volturno, and Garibaldi's progress became a simple triumphal march; the people received him with adoration as "a second Christ."   On September 6 the King sailed for Gaeta, and the next day Garibaldi entered the capital by train from Salerno, alone, ahead of his army, having altogether abandoned any pretence of leading a hostile force.   The only obstruction he suffered was from the excited Neapolitan mob which crowded about his train.   As he left the station for the centre of the city his carriage passed under the muzzles of the loaded cannon of the Carmine. *The fall of the Neapolitan kingdom.*

other day the young King of Naples was seized with such a panic that he telegraphed five times in twenty-four hours for the Pope's blessing.   Cardinal Antonelli, through whom the application had to be made, telegraphed the three last blessings without reference to his Holiness, saying that he had been duly authorized to do so.   The convents are awfully scandalized at this proceeding."

[1] On one occasion the Admiral disguised himself and mixed with the men of the royal dockyard, and so damaged the machinery of some ships that King Francis II, when he came to flee, had to take a passage on a Spanish steamer, and not on a ship of his own navy.

P

The soldiers were seen looking at the carriage and its occupants, whom they could have blasted to pieces by moving a finger. Garibaldi stood up, folded his arms, and looked them straight in the face. Some of them saluted, and no one fired a shot. It is true that they were only acting in accordance with the pacific order of the King, but it is a matter of deep congratulation that no one in that unscrupulous and undisciplined force was tempted loyally to disobey.[1]

Garibaldi proclaimed himself dictator of the kingdom; appointed Bertani, a Mazzinian, as Secretary of State, but as a proof of his loyalty he consigned the Neapolitan fleet to the Sardinian Admiral Persano. But both the French and the Neapolitan Governments were growing alarmed; Garibaldi, inspired with victory, and encouraged by the extremists about him, made no secret of his plans; after Naples, Venice and Rome. That such an advance would inevitably involve war with Austria and France seemed to him unimportant. He was blind to all compromise and deaf to the appeals of Cavour and Victor Emmanuel that he should not ruin his achievements by unwise action. He poured contempt on their "hypocritical but terrible pretext of necessity; the necessity of being cowards; the necessity of grovelling in the mud before an image of transitory power," of which the onrush of a "free people," "determined at any cost to acquire a real existence," would scatter the fragments "in the dust-heap whence they came."

The revolutionary infection was also spreading to the Papal States, and the Papal troops were preparing to put down the insurrection. If the revolts succeeded there would be no holding back Garibaldi from Rome; if on the other hand they were suppressed the Papal troops might then threaten the newly annexed Papal territory of the Romagna.

Cavour therefore determined upon a bold stroke; "Italy must be saved from foreigners, evil principles, and madmen." He resolved

Cavour forestalls Garibaldi

to anticipate Garibaldi, to invade the Papal States with the royal troops of Piedmont, and to defend Rome from Garibaldi. It was an ironical position. Agents were dispatched to sound Napoleon III and to find what view he would take of a Piedmontese occupation of Umbria and the Marches. "Do it quickly," was said to be the reply of the Emperor, who was in the

and invades the Papal States.

habit of detaching himself from his own Foreign Office. Cavour asked nothing more, and, seizing an excuse in a hostile movement on the part of the Pope, he ordered the invasion of the Papal States on September 11. On the 18th the Pontifical army was crushed at Castelfidardo; on the 29th Ancona fell, and Umbria and the Marches were in the power of Piedmont.

[1] G. M. Trevelyan, *Garibaldi and the Making of Italy*.

It was a race between Garibaldi and the royal troops. "If we do not reach the Volturno before Garibaldi reaches La Cattolica," declared Cavour, "the monarchy is lost, and Italy will remain in the prison-house of the revolution." Garibaldi was unexpectedly delayed by the resistance of the Neapolitan town of Capua, and Cavour won.

Immediately after the occupation of the Papal States plebiscites were held in Sicily and Naples; they showed an overwhelming desire for annexation to Sardinia. Thus Cavour's hands were strengthened, while Garibaldi had learnt that without the assistance of royal troops he could not hope to reduce the fortresses of Gaeta and Capua, which still held out.

On October 18 King Victor Emmanuel, whose strong, soldierly character had ever appealed to Garibaldi, crossed the Neapolitan frontier at the head of his army. On the 27th Garibaldi, outwitted by the diplomacy of Cavour, but loyal to the King, surrendered his power and his army to Victor Emmanuel. The united forces turned against the remnant of the Neapolitan defence; Capua fell in November, Gaeta, after a longer siege, not until February.

In the meantime on November 9, at an imposing ceremony in the throne-room of the Palace of Naples, Victor Emmanuel was invested with the kingship of Sicily and Naples; Garibaldi formally resigned his dictatorship and called upon the people loyally to lay aside their differences, and to accept the *re galantuomo*, "the symbol of our regeneration and of the prosperity of our country."

The next day, with a bag of seed-corn for his farm as his only spoil, Garibaldi returned to his island of Caprera. There, in the sweetness of his contact with nature, he lost some of the bitter melancholy which had filled his heart during the last months on the mainland. There in his island empire he found a richer consolation than the world of politics and vice-regal entanglements would have given him, had Victor Emmanuel granted his wish and made him viceroy of the southern half of his kingdom. Many times during the twenty years that remained of his life he reappeared in national and international affairs, in the war with Austria in 1866, in the defeat of Mentana in 1867, as a volunteer in the French service in 1870, as a Roman deputy; but it is not unfitting that memory should recall the knight-errant of Italian freedom, who turned history into an epic and politics into romance, as he tilled the scanty soil and nursed his vineyards, as he "called the cows by name from their pasturage among the wild and odorous brushwood," and sought his straying goats among the crags of Caprera.

With the annexation of Naples and Sicily went that of the Papal States, except Rome and its immediate neighbourhood, for Cavour knew that if the "Patrimony of St Peter" were still left to the Pope France would not intervene. On February 18, 1861, the first Italian Parliament was held at Turin, and in March, less than two years after Villafranca, Victor Emmanuel was proclaimed King of Italy—an Italy which, save for Venice and Rome, had for the first time since the fall of the Roman Empire achieved that unity which nature seemed to have marked so clearly as its destiny.

The annexation of Naples, Sicily, Umbria, and the Marches.

That Venice and Rome would in time be added to the new kingdom Cavour was convinced, but he did not live to see the final completion of Italian unity. On June 6, 1861, he died, worn out with the intense strain of the last three years' "race for victory."

Death of Cavour.

Italy as a nation is the legacy, the life-work of Cavour. . . . Others have been devoted to the cause of national liberation, he knew how to bring it into the sphere of possibilities; he kept it pure of any factious spirit; he led it away from barren utopias; kept it clear of reckless conspiracies; steered straight between revolution and reaction; and gave it an organized force, a flag, a Government and foreign allies.[1]

There still remained Venetia and Rome; the one in the hands of Austria, the other, the treasured possession of the Church, protected by France, and the centre of the Catholic world. That Italian patriots should seek to add them both to the new kingdom was inevitable; it was no less obvious that they could not long be held, stray fragments of alien Powers, against the determined will of the whole peninsula.

Their fate was bound up with the general international situation, and it is rather upon Prussia than upon Italy that the rest of the story of Italian unity hangs. Prussia, like Italy, had her quarrel with Austria, and when in 1866 she decided to make war upon the Habsburg empire Italy joined with her in alliance, of which the reward was to be the acquisition of Venetia. In the short war of 1866 the Italian armies were, in fact, defeated, but Prussia's success in the north achieved what Italy's failure in the south might have lost, and after a military farce had been staged to soothe the pride of the Italians Venetia was handed over to the kingdom of Italy. The small piece of Austrian territory consisting of the Italian-speaking Tyrol she could not win; it was not granted to her until the break-up of the Austro-Hungarian Empire after the Great War, when she received also over 200,000 German-speaking subjects.[2]

Italy and Prussia.

Venetia, 1866.

Like Italy, Prussia had her quarrel with France, and it was again the Prussian victory of 1870 that gave Italy her national historical capital. In 1867 Garibaldi had made an unsuccessful attempt to seize

[1] Quoted by W. Alison Phillips, *Modern Europe*, p. 389.
[2] By an arrangement between Germany and Italy in 1939 most of them have been transferred to the German Reich.

Rome, which had been defeated by the Franco-Papal forces at Mentana. The Garibaldini, fighting until their last cartridges were exhausted, were mown down by the new French *chassepot* rifles. "The *chassepots* have done marvels," wrote the commanding officer; among other things they had shot away the last link that bound Italy to France. On September 2, 1870, news arrived that the French Empire had fallen in the defeat inflicted by the Prussians at Sedan. The French regiments had been recalled at the outbreak of war. On September 11 Italian troops entered Papal territory and occupied Rome. A plebiscite was held, which gave an overwhelming majority for union, and in July 1872 King Victor Emmanuel made a solemn entry into the new capital. Rome had at last been reached. The temporal power of the Papacy, which arose with a Frankish king of the eighth century, had fallen at last with a French emperor of the nineteenth, and the long conflicts which came out of it had ended in the triumph of a monarch whose ancestors were obscure Alpine counts when Gregory VII thundered his excommunications from the Vatican against the most powerful ruler in Europe.

Even as a purely spiritual prince, the Pope was a serious problem to the new kingdom. In May 1871 the Italian Parliament passed the Law of Guarantees, embodying Cavour's ideal of a "free Church in a free state." The Pope was accorded the personal inviolability of a sovereign, royal honours, an armed guard, and a civil list of over three million lire. He was allowed the unfettered exercise of his spiritual functions, free communication with the Catholic world, and diplomatic immunities were granted to representatives to his Court. The Italian kingdom also surrendered to the Pope the powers it had previously exercised over Italian clergy, including that of nominating to bishoprics.

Pius IX refused to accept either the loss of the temporal possessions of the Church or the Law of Guarantees. From the position of *non possumus* he never departed, and after 1870 he shut himself in the Vatican, a voluntary prisoner, finding consolation in the glorious plenitude of the Infallibility that had just been made an Article of Faith, and seeking a mild revenge in that psychological device to depress the enemy that is common to many defeated persons—the prophecy of speedy downfall that is begotten of the wish : "But again I tell you, you shall not long enjoy the fruits of your violence."

The Pontificate of Pius IX was one of the most remarkable as well as the longest—he alone reached the traditional years of St Peter—in the history of the Church. Its thirty-two years' duration and the loss of the temporal possessions of the Papacy would in themselves have distinguished it; but it saw a revival of Papal authority, a missionary advance, and a dogmatic development that recalled the most vital phases of mediæval ecclesiasticism.   In all parts of the world Roman Catholicism made a marked and in some cases a sudden progress, in America and the Ottoman Empire, in Africa and Madagascar, in India and the Far East, and, what was perhaps more spectacular, in the Protestant countries of Holland and England.   In both some of the romanticism and reawakened religious interest which marked the beginning of the nineteenth century turned into Roman Catholic channels.[1]   After a lapse of centuries the ecclesiastical hierarchy was restored, and Roman Catholic archbishops reigned again at Utrecht and Westminster.

The renewed vitality of the Church was shown no less in its inner history than in the extension of its sway.   In the realm of thought the Victorian era was one of transition and change.   The theories of the French Revolution were leavening the world of politics; the revelations of science were shaking those of religion.   A new renaissance had opened upon the world, a renaissance not so much of learning and art, although they too had their place, as of science and thought.   The age of science had dawned, and, as in the fifteenth and sixteenth centuries, ecclesiasticism gave way before secularism, the Church before the State.   But as the Renaissance of the fifteenth century was followed by the Reformation of the sixteenth, so the new mental activity of the Victorians was followed by its sequel of religious conflict.   The parallel may be pursued farther.   In both cases there was a counter-reformation.

The Papacy of the nineteenth century met the advancing tide as the Papacy of the sixteenth century had received it, not with concession, but with definition.   It tightened its dogma, strengthened its hierarchy, and reared up a still higher wall of pontifical authority. The meagre rationalism of a generation should be astonished by the faith and majesty of an eternal Church.

In 1864 the "reforming Pope" of 1846 published the famous encyclical *Quanta Cura*, to which was attached the *Syllabus Errorum*, or list of ninety "errors and perverse doctrines."   Rationalism, science, democracy, the liberty of the Press, secular education, and the encroaching power of the State were alike laid under condemnation.   "The pontiff neither can be nor ought to be reconciled with progress, liberalism, or modern civilization."   It was a declaration of war upon the spirit of the age that alarmed and amazed the Protestant world.

A still bolder appeal was made to the absolutist traditions of the Holy See.   The dogmatic and the conciliar precedents of the six-

[1] In England the two most famous converts to Roman Catholicism were the saintly Newman and that typical ecclesiastical statesman Manning.   Both of them were made cardinals.

teenth century were revived. Three gatherings were held among the bishops of the Church: in 1854, to define the doctrine of the Immaculate Conception; in 1862, for the canonization of Japanese martyrs; and in 1867, for the eighteenth centenary of the traditional death of St Peter. The great event of the pontificate of Pio Nono came, however, two years later. In 1869 the 400 bells of Rome and the cannon of St Angelo announced the opening of a great Œcumenical Council of the Church, the twentieth in its history, the first since the Council of Trent. The long-disputed subject of Papal Infallibility was laid before it. Many of the 750 Fathers thought its definition inopportune; Gladstone was alarmed. But the Pope was eager and confident. Had not the authentic miracles of Lourdes given divine sanction to the doctrine of the Immaculate Conception, promulgated a few years before? The Pope had, moreover, an able ally in the English convert Manning, *Il Diavolo del Concilio*. After a long discussion and much intrigue the Fathers gave their verdict.

As the voting began a thunderstorm broke over Rome. Through the whole morning each man stepped forward to the flash of lightning and the roar of thunder. The scene in St Peter's seemed to have its counterpart in heaven, and both sides claimed it as a portent. In Europe the dogma of Papal Infallibility and the Ultramontane triumph were received with some opposition, especially among the Old Catholics, as they called themselves, of Germany. But Pius himself had no doubt as to the validity of his stupendous claim. "Before I was Pope I *believed* in Papal Infallibility. Now I *feel* it."

III. The Unification of Germany (1850–71)

(a)

Superficially the unification of Germany bears some resemblance to that of Italy. In both cases one state stronger than the others led the way under the guidance of its ministers and the protection of its armies. In 1852 Cavour became chief minister of Sardinia, and by 1861 the green, white, and red tricolour charged with the white cross of Piedmont floated over all Italy except Venice and Rome. In 1862 Bismarck became chief adviser to King William, and by 1871 the Prussian eagle soared over a united German Empire. In the details of the respective problems of Italy and Germany, however, and in the methods and results of their solution there are wide differences.

The unification of Germany bears some resemblances to that of Italy.

In 1850 Germany, like Italy, seemed to have only failure to look upon. One or two State constitutions, testimonies to monarchical grace rather than expressions of the popular will, were the only apparent fruits of the 'year of revolutions.' The nationalist effort of the Frankfurt Parliament had failed; the scheme for a less complete union put forward diffidently by Prussia had come to nothing; democrats and nationalists had been defeated or rebuffed; Prussia had been scolded and humiliated for her temporary weakness in yielding to the spirit of change; the Federal Diet had been restored under Habsburg patronage; the policy of the *status quo*, which was the embodiment of Austrian statesmanship, had prevailed; Austria had triumphed, and behind Austria was an armed and reactionary Russia.

Germany in 1850.

The years from 1848 to 1850 had, however, served to bring out more clearly the problems and factors in the German Question. They had at least revealed the futility of many hopes and pointed the way to one solution. The reformation of Germany through the Federal Diet and its union through Austrian agency had been proved dreams, to be abandoned as fantastic. The paradox had been shown to be truth, that the path of nationalism lay through provincialism, that only in the strength of one state could all the states of Germany be united, that Germany could only find herself in Prussia.

For to Prussia had men turned in 1848, and for all her failure she stood out as the only possible leader of German unity. Austria had tradition and great prestige, but in spite of Metternich's long supremacy she was fundamentally weak and prevalently non-Germanic. She was internationalist in an age of nationalism, static by conviction in the midst of dynamic aspirations; she had turned her back upon a new Germany, and restored that instrument of nullity, the Federal Diet.

Prussia, on the other hand, since her humiliation by Napoleon had grown stronger in everything except self-confidence. The work of Stein and Scharnhorst, though a little out of date by 1850, had set her internal economy upon a new civil and military basis. The War of Liberation had covered her name with glory and linked it with national victory. Her gains of 1815 had brought her into closer contact with the southern states, and laid upon her shoulders the defence of Germany, from which Austria seemed to have retreated. The lands of Prussian Posen marched with those of Russia; the possession of Westphalia committed her to the watch on the Rhine, to the national guardianship of Germany against the hereditary Gallic enemy—had not Arndt written *Wo jeder Franzmann heisset Feind,*[1] and proposed a defensive attitude toward France as one of the qualifications for German patriotism? The Zollverein, moreover, had already given to Prussia an economic headship of Germany, and bound the smaller states to her with the strong cement of material welfare.

[1] "Where every Frank is called an enemy."

In short, Prussia's interests were bound up with the strength of Germany, Austria's with its weakness. Nevertheless in 1848–50 Prussia had failed. Her policy had been vacillating and timorous, and in the end treacherous to the cause of national unity. She had failed through fear and timidity, because her king was without conviction, her advisers without perspicacity and confidence, because had she resisted she must have fought not Austria alone, but Austria and Russia together.

It is easy in the light of subsequent history to see the "German mission" of Prussia, and her clear destiny to lead and unite Germany. To statesmen of the day it was only a dawning vision encompassed by mists and fogs, the mist of long deference to and alliance with Austria, the fog of multifarious counter-schemes, of princely interests and popular wishes.

It was not until the advent of that great political partnership between king and minister, between William I and Bismarck, that the necessary clear vision and resolution were introduced into the counsels of Prussia.

The character of the monarchy altered with the change of sovereign in 1858. In that year the imaginative mind of Frederick William IV became permanently unhinged, and Prince William, whose hostility to the revolutionaries of 1848 was commemorated in the title of "Prince Cartridge," became Regent, and, in 1861, on his brother's death, King of Prussia. The new ruler had neither the imagination nor the mental alertness of his predecessor, but he had exactly the qualities of firmness and general evenness of mind which his brother lacked. He was a man who "put things through." [1] He was primarily a Prussian soldier, brave, honest, pious, and practical. He believed in the Prussian monarchy as the strongest centripetal force in a state of ill-defined boundaries and weak natural defences; and next to the Prussian monarchy he had faith in the unity of Germany through the instrumentality of Prussia. His national sentiments were not, like those of his brother, "hindered in their practical realization by a garnish of mediævalism and by a dislike of clear and firm decisions." [2] He had a soldierly love for direct methods, practical issues, and staunch resolves. "Whoever aspired to rule over Germany must seize it for himself." He was a Prussian to the core, sensitive to the humiliation of his kingdom and confident in its destiny, and not unwilling, if necessary, to avenge the one and prove the other.

All his life he remained an enemy of liberalism, although he allowed

Margin notes: Prince William. Regent (1858). King of Prussia (1861).

[1] See von Sybel's description in *The Founding of the German Empire.*
[2] Bismarck.

himself to be influenced by counsels of expediency and was sensible of the fact that a wise Government must adapt itself to changing conditions. He was in no respect a doctrinaire. As he was "conscientious in deliberation and fearless in danger," so he showed that rare combination of firmness and flexibility in policy which marked the statesman. "He had a natural gift of perceiving what was attainable, and an unembarrassed clearness of view, which was shown above all in his almost unerring judgment of men." [1] He had the skill or the luck to select good servants of State, and the wisdom and strength to support those to whom he had given his confidence. Through sore trials and in spite of many differences of opinion he gave to Bismarck, from the time when he appointed him to office, a growing trust and a steadfast friendship matched only by the loyal devotion with which the minister served his king.

Otto von Bismarck-Schönhausen, whose life from 1815 to 1898 practically covered the nineteenth century, was the greatest man the age produced, greatest in the political manifestations of his powers and in the influence which his achievements have exercised in the history of the world. To the Prussian state, which in 1850 had not a port that was not land-locked by Sweden or Denmark, he gave an empire and colonies; to Germans who, in Treitschke's words, "sailed the sea like pirates without a national flag" he gave an ensign which came to be as politically respected as that of England or France; he transposed the political capital of Europe from Vienna or Paris to Berlin; he created the German Empire, which, until the advent of present-day America, was the most remarkable phenomenon of modern times.

Bismarck (1815–98).

Bismarck came from the landed squirearchy of the Altmark of Brandenburg, the very kernel of the kingdom of Prussia, from an old family which, he proudly claimed, had been there before the Hohenzollerns. Its Junker record was long and creditable, but distinctly parochial, and the Federal Chancellor was the first of the Bismarcks to distinguish himself in public affairs. Soon after the birth of the third son, Otto, the family moved to its Kniephof estates in Prussian Pomerania. There the future Chancellor forged that link with the soil which was never broken during his long political career, and acquired the country tastes, the love of hunting, shooting, riding, and swimming, which remained his chief recreations. Three years of university life at Göttingen and Berlin gained him a reputation for duelling, beer-drinking, and the riotous escapades of undergraduate life rather than for intellectual aptitudes or mental powers. A short experience of the civil service on its judicial side gave him an impression of the "petty and tedious business" of quill-driving, of "pigtail

[1] Von Sybel, *op. cit.*

and periwig," that choked his ambitions, and he renounced without regret any career that lay before him in that direction to undertake in 1839 the management of the family estates at Kniephof, and later at Schönhausen. Like Cavour, he devoted himself to agrarian pursuits. "I have made up my mind to live and die in the country, after attaining successes in agriculture—perhaps in war also, if war should come." Good returns from his estate and a lieutenancy in the Landwehr comprised the sum of his ambitions.

For eight years he was the landed proprietor, managing his estates, travelling abroad, taking an active part in local politics, and reading widely. Gossip attributed to him wild actions, hard drinking, and atheistical views. He once described himself as 'republican' by nature—that is, naturally impatient of restraint—and in his student days he had been inclined to support republicanism in politics, until its excesses and general association with "Utopian theories and defective breeding" had repelled him, leaving him with a mild liberalism imbibed from his mother. A great change, however, was wrought in him during these years by the influence of a neighbouring group of friends, known as the 'Trieglaff' circle, who were in touch with important members of the conservative party in Berlin. Gradually he sloughed off both his liberalism and his atheism; he reverted to a staunch Lutheran orthodoxy, which he never afterward abandoned, and absorbed a strong political conservatism which became the keynote of his Prussian policy.

In the year 1847 Bismarck married a wife and made his *début* in Prussian politics, introducing himself to as much domestic happiness in the one relation as public fame in the other. He entered history as a member of the United Prussian Diet, summoned by the King in 1847 in a measured concession to democracy that alarmed Metternich and the Tsar on the one hand as much as its shortcomings disappointed the liberals on the other. It was the beginning of a vivid spell of Prussian history, from 1847 to 1851, covering a constitutional crisis, revolution, the rejection of the imperial crown offered by the Frankfurt Parliament, the formation and defeat of the Erfurt Union. The young squire from Pomerania played an active and vigorous part, making a name for himself as an independent and trenchant speaker, as a fearless, even reckless, opponent of democracy, as a champion of the ultra-conservatives, as, in his own words, a "royalist Hotspur." His politics undoubtedly displayed at that time a crudity much of which the later Prussian Minister and Federal Chancellor left behind him; but they reveal a forcefulness and a temperamental attitude that were permanent.

To Bismarck the history of the four years was primarily a conflict with democracy, either in its revolutionary or in its less extreme liberal

forms, and the dominant theme of his speeches was the shameful‐
ness of any union between the Prussian monarchy and the hydra‐
headed monster. "I fear the whimpering sentimentality
of our century, which discovers a martyr in every fanatical
rebel." Any truckling to revolution was criminal and dis‐
graceful pusillanimity. By the same standard he measured and con‐
demned the German and national policy of Prussia during these years.
He was opposed to the acceptance of the Frankfurt crown and rejoiced
in the failure of the Erfurt programme for the same reason—that the
Prussian monarchy would be delivered bound to democracy or con‐
stitutionalism, "drowned in the putrid yeast of South German
anarchy"; that ancestral Prussianism would be dissolved in a "mon‐
grel German unity." His expressions were as forcible as his views.
"The Frankfurt crown may be very brilliant, but the gold which gives
reality to the brilliance must first be won by melting down the Prussian
crown, and I have no confidence that the recasting will fit the form of
our Prussian constitution." "We all desire the Prussian eagle to
spread its guardian and governing wings from the Memel to the
Donnersberg, but free we will see him, not fettered to a new Parlia‐
ment at Regensburg, not sheltering under the feathers of the levelling
vulture from Frankfurt." And again, "Prussian honour does not
consist in Prussia's playing the Don Quixote all over Germany for
the benefit of sickly demagogues who consider their constitution in
danger."

The Erfurt Union, based upon an incompatible alliance between
Prussia and liberalism, was a step in the wrong direction. It would
have sacrificed the real interests of the Hohenzollern kingdom and
the historical heritage of Frederick the Great for what Bismarck held
to be "Gallican Jacobinism," and a myth to boot. It would have
involved a war which was not justified by any profit to be gained, a
war in which Prussia was ill-prepared to meet not only Austria, but
Russia, while France, "eager for booty," watched upon the frontier
for an opportunity for attack. "The sound basis of a great power,"
declared Bismarck, in memorable words, "which differentiates it
essentially from the petty state, is political egoism, not romanticism,
and it is unworthy of a great state to fight for what does not concern
its interest. . . . It is easy," he continues, "for a statesman to blow
a blast with the wind of popularity on the trumpet of war, warming
himself the while at his own fireside . . . but woe to the statesman
who in these days does not look around him for a reason for war
which will hold water when the war is over."

Bismarck was at all times a good hater; yet his hatred of democracy
was the obverse of a very positive ideal—an unlimited faith and pride
in Prussia and Prussianism, which was partly the monarchy and

*Bismarck
from 1847
to 1851.*

partly the army, and partly the conservative interests of the landed agricultural classes, and something more than them all, an ancestral spirit refined by the fires of history, the supreme product of the German race. "Prussians we are, and Prussians we will remain. I know that I express in these words the creed of the majority of my countrymen, and I hope to God we shall remain Prussians long after this piece of paper [the constitution] has been forgotten like a withered autumn leaf." It was an ideal that Bismarck never lost, and when the political union of the German people was achieved it was, as he intended, Germany that was merged in Prussia, not Prussia in Germany. That is the chief difference between the unifications of Italy and Germany; Sardinia moved to Rome, Germany to Berlin.

By 1851 Bismarck had revealed himself as a man of undoubted power with a capacity for leadership. He had attracted the notice of the King, and his friends hoped to see him appointed to office. But Frederick William, although pleased by Bismarck's loyalty to the Crown, was embarrassed by an attitude so uncompromising; "a red reactionary, smacking of blood, only to be used when the bayonet governs unrestricted," he is said to have written against Bismarck's name. He believed that Bismarck's education was still incomplete, and appointed him, instead of minister of the Crown at Berlin, Prussian plenipotentiary to the Federal Diet at Frankfurt—honour enough for a man of no diplomatic experience.

There is no doubt that the King was right, whether fear or fore-sight dictated the appointment. The experience and education of the next eleven years turned the Junker politician into a statesman. He was always a learner and something of an opportunist, **At** but in the development of his personality, in the moulding **Frankfurt.** of his ambitions, in the crystallization of his principles of statecraft, in the acquisition of essential knowledge of German and European politics, it was the real formative period of his political life. Eight years at Frankfurt, three at St Petersburg, a few months in Paris, a little deputizing in Vienna, a visit to England, the acquaintance of every statesman of importance except Cavour—no better political education could have been devised for one who was to lead Germany to union by defeating Austria, conciliating Russia, and checkmating France.

In the Federal capital Bismarck acquired a larger view of the German Question, a more just appreciation of its problems, a new conception of the part he might himself play in solving them. He learnt—what the history of Germany from the days of the Great Elector to his own time had revealed—that Austria and Prussia were set as rivals in Germany, that the Habsburg had no real intention of accepting the Hohenzollern as an equal, that the union of Germany under Prussian leadership could only be achieved at the price of war with Austria. Bismarck had gone to Frankfurt still holding what was the orthodox conservative view in Berlin, that Austria and Prussia were natural allies, that they should work in double harness for the security of Germany against revolution, and that problems of leadership and rivalry could somehow be adjusted. But at the Federal Diet Bismarck slowly surrendered to the conviction, which he afterward strove to explain to his king and to Prussia, that the issue between Prussia and Austria which had been gathering for two hundred years was real and vital, and could not be diverted by "leagues of conservative interests," that the logic of history provided a more powerful argument than democracy.

Bismarck learnt at Frankfurt that the fundamental problem of the German Question was the adjustment of the relations between Austria and Prussia; a secondary one was the attitude of the smaller German states. There he found—and it was to become a vital element of his subsequent policy—that the smaller princely interests of Germany regarded Prussia with innate antagonism, in spite of the fact that many of them owed to her their preservation in the years of revolution. Bent upon preserving their particular individualities, they leaned naturally upon the Power whose policy was a defence of the *status quo*, and looked apprehensively and suspiciously toward the kingdom which had already once declared itself the champion of German nationality, and which might adopt under vigorous direction a progressive policy of union in which they might be submerged.

The eight years at Frankfurt were a time of disillusionment as well as of elucidation, and Bismarck learnt political cynicism as well as political wisdom. He found the uses of intrigue and dissimulation, and discovered the secrets of a diplomacy without inspiration and the venality of a human nature without faith. "The marked contempt of later years for the sincerity of public opinion, for newspapers, for journalists, who could always be bought, for all the dark magic of an official Press bureau, for diplomatic *reconnaissances* by the circulation of lies, for lashing up public sentiment by dictated paragraphs inserted in avowedly independent journals—all this can be traced to his Frankfurt period." [1] By 1860 Bismarck had become a less pleasant character than in 1850; his autocratic personality had been coarsened, his health temporarily impaired, and his temper permanently soured by nervous and physical illness, and much of his honest *joie de vivre* had faded.

From the Frankfurt days Bismarck set himself to assert the equality and independence of Prussia, and in small affairs and large to thwart

[1] C. Grant Robertson, *Bismarck* ("Makers of the Nineteenth Century" series).

Austria's efforts to degrade her to a secondary position. He did not neglect the significant detail. The assumptions of Austrian superiority could be challenged by the lighting of a cigar, and the Habsburg empire defied by the removing of a coat.[1]

So also in matters of State policy he proposed vigorous and independent measures that were sometimes too bold to be adopted by the Prussian King. He succeeded in excluding Austria from the Zollverein, which she was anxious, having at last realized its significance, to enter or destroy; and he was largely instrumental in preventing Prussia from adopting a pro-Austrian policy during the Crimean War. In the crisis of 1859 Bismarck desired a firm alliance with Sardinia against the common Habsburg enemy, but Prince William, who was by that time Regent of Prussia, would make no terms with liberal France or Italy, and offered his support to Austria.

In the same year Bismarck was transferred to St Petersburg. There too he did fruitful work. He had not forgotten that Austria had won in 1849 and 1850 largely because the Tsar Nicholas had **At St** given her his support. In any future conflict Bismarck **Petersburg.** was determined to have the Romanovs upon the side of the Hohenzollerns. The Crimean War had broken the Austro-Russian alliance of a generation, and had paved the way for a Prusso-Russian *rapprochement*. The personal freindship with the Tsar Alexander II which Bismarck cultivated while he was ambassador to the Russian Court strengthened the *entente* and afforded a basis for the deliberate pro-Russian policy which he pursued as minister of Prussia.

A few months in Paris enabled him to take the measure of Napoleon III and his ministers, and to sow seeds that he hoped would bear political fruit in his own good time. His appointment there was, however, avowedly temporary, and in **In Paris.** September 1862 he became Minister-President to the Prussian Crown.

The eleven years between 1851 and 1862, which had been of such significance in Bismarck's life and the history of Europe, were comparatively unimportant to Prussia until the Regency of 1858 began to show that the spirit of Frederick the Great had returned again to the Hohenzollern dynasty. The reign of Frederick William IV dragged on through a weary absolutism to a pathetic close; **New vigour** the disillusioned radicals of 1849 turned disconsolately **in Prussian** from political Jacobinism to seek a new salvation in **policy.** economic socialism. The star of Rousseau paled before that of Karl Marx. With the advent of the new regent, however, a new

[1] Hitherto the President of the Diet—*i.e.*, the Austrian representative—had alone smoked at committee-meetings. On another occasion Thurn, the Austrian, received Bismarck in his shirt-sleeves. " Yes, it is very hot," remarked Bismarck, taking off his coat.

fillip was given to foreign and domestic politics. In 1859 Prussia armed and became the arbiter of Europe. France stopped short in her victory lest Prussian troops should cross the Rhine; Austria accepted defeat rather than the humiliation of being rescued from it by her northern rival. The armistice of Villafranca, which brought a blush of anger or shame to Frenchman, Austrian, and Italian, was a triumph for Prussia alone. "It was no longer safe," remarked Bismarck, "to count upon her timidity."

At home the feeble Manteuffel ministry, engineer of the Olmütz surrender, was dismissed, and, partly owing to the influence of the Princess Regent Augusta, a group of moderate liberals took its place; democrats began to lift up their hearts and take courage again in the hope of a liberalized Prussia which should unite Germany on a constitutional basis. They held a Pan-German congress at Eisenach and drew up a programme.

It soon appeared, however, that the Regent had little love for liberalism, and was by no means inclined to conform to Eisenach principles. Prince William was a soldier, and like Bismarck he put his trust in the "God of Battles." He too believed that the strength and the spirit of Prussia were contained in her army. The bayonet alone could close the road to Olmütz, and only military power enable her to grasp the sovereignty of Germany, which lay within her reach. The Regent resolved, therefore, to strengthen the army, which had not been revised since the War of Liberation, and no longer corresponded to Prussia's increased population. He appointed von Moltke Chief of Staff, and von Roon Minister of War, a thoroughgoing conservative, introduced "like a Greek horse into a liberal Troy," a man who was "determined like George II to keep the army free from the interference of the scoundrels in the House of Commons."

In the autumn of 1859 the new army bills were laid before the Prussian Parliament, proposing to raise thirty-nine new regiments of **The army question and the constitutional crisis.** infantry and ten of cavalry. They were rejected, and a bitter conflict opened between the Crown and the Parliament. The Regent persisted, strengthened by the acquisition of the title of king on the death of his brother on January 2, 1861. He ignored the constitution, enrolled the regiments, and had their standards consecrated. The opposition grew more violent with the royal persistence. One Assembly was replaced by another even more hostile; the liberal ministry resigned, a conservative one followed its example; the whole military policy of the Government was attacked; a reduction rather than an increase in its forces was threatened; the army estimates were thrown out of the Budget; popular excitement outside the House reflected the antagonism within.   The situation seemed to be rapidly developing toward one end—the abdication of the Prussian King in favour of his son, the Crown Prince Frederick, who was known to have liberal inclinations.

It was Roon who persuaded King William to adopt first the alternative of calling in Bismarck.   It was something in the nature of a desperate remedy, for the King had not wholly given his confidence to this man of large visions, independent views, immense power, and bold decisions.   The Queen, moreover, was against him.   But urgent necessity was the master of the hour.   Roon had telegraphed to Bismarck in France "Periculum in mora.   Dépêchez-vous"; and Bismarck, who had been impatiently awaiting the summons, was at **Bismarck** hand in Berlin, the only man with the will or the capacity **Minister-** to stand with the King against the Parliament, even to the **President** end—"the thought of perishing with him seemed a natural **(September** **1862).** and congenial conclusion to my life."   On September 23, 1862, King William committed himself and Prussia into the hands of the boldest, most resolute, and skilful statesman of the age, and a new era began in the history of Europe.

The appointment of Bismarck—"a bully and an absolutist"— merely lashed the opposition to greater rage; but Bismarck was unmoved.   He speedily proclaimed his political philosophy in words which have become part of the vocabulary of the Western world— "Germany is looking not to Prussia's liberalism, but to her power. . . . The great questions of the day will not be decided by speeches and majority resolutions (that was the blunder of 1848 and 1849), but by blood and iron."   There was the same contempt "for moral conquests" as in 1848, the same appeal to the "God of Battles, Who would cast the iron dice of history."   Phrases and epigrams are dangerous political instruments; the opposition could not understand them, and turned them against their author.   The breach between the Parliament and the Crown and its minister became complete.   The latter no longer attended the sittings of the "House of Phrases."   The personal feeling against Bismarck grew so violent that he was advised to transfer his property to his brother.   "Men spat," said Bismarck, "on the place where I trod in the streets," and many hoped "to see me picking oakum for the benefit of the state."   One of his strongest opponents he challenged to a duel, which was, however, refused.   For four years he stood with his back to the wall, fighting with a Parliament and a people, resting for authority solely on the royal support, often reluctantly given; trusting for sympathy, but not always for understanding, to Roon, his only friend; carrying on government without a Budget, leaving his vindication to the future and to his German policy.

"We give Herr Bismarck one year," said the opposition.   Actually

Q

he held power for twenty-eight years. Within nine years he had fought three wars, ousted Austria from the German Confederation, made peace with the liberals, and united Germany under the Prussian monarchy. He dissolved the Prussian Question in the German, and healed the domestic breach with the balm of national triumph. Bismarck had no clear cut-and-dried programme of political action when he entered office, and there is often enigma and contradiction in his policy as in his character. Pride, independence, boldness, resoluteness, and combativeness can be counted on, for they were of his temperament; long views were as native to him as a large appetite, and his ambitions and intellectual powers were on the same grand scale as his physical frame. But he was an artist in politics, selecting and moulding his material to his designs; an opportunist, "of means, not of ends," grasping his chances with acute vision and a nice calculation, utilizing them without scruple as they suited his purpose.

He fully apprehended his difficulties, and knew that he was bound by conditions as they arose. Nevertheless he had a clear conception of the ends he desired and that he had set himself to achieve, and there seems to be no doubt that he had come to office determined to make a bid for the leadership of Germany and to force an issue with Austria. He had said as much on a visit to England just before he became Minister-President. "As soon as it [the army] was strong enough, I should take the first opportunity of settling accounts with Austria, dissolving the Germanic Confederation . . . and establishing a united Germany under Prussia's leadership." The others thought it was bluff; only Disraeli entered a caveat. "Take care of that man, he means what he says."

The first question of international importance which arose was the second Polish rebellion of 1863. The Poles won the sympathy of half Europe; France and Napoleon III were friendly to the countrymen of Chopin, and the Prussian liberals were enthusiastic in their cause. Again Bismarck opposed them; there were Poles in Prussia who might easily be infected by a successful Polish revolution. "Would an independent Poland," asked Bismarck, "leave her neighbour Prussia in possession of Danzig and Thorn?" "The inclination to make sacrifices to foreign nationalities at the expense of the fatherland is a political disease peculiar to Germany."

The Polish Question, 1863.

There was, however, still a stronger consideration. Bismarck wanted the support of Russia in the far greater conflict with Austria which was in front of him. The Polish rising gave him the opportunity to lose or secure it. To the indignation of the Prussian liberals, he concluded a convention with Alexander II by which he agreed to take strong action against any Poles who should take refuge in Prussian

territory, or seek to recruit there, or in any way use it as a base of
operations. Revolutionary committees in Warsaw, and as far afield
as Barcelona, sentenced him to death, Prussian liberals committed him
to national execration; nevertheless he had bought the friendship of
Russia.

Strong in that knowledge, he took his next step. The policy of
Austria had in several respects been forced to a revision by the war of
1859. The Emperor now proposed a scheme for the reform
of the German Confederation, and summoned a Diet of the   The
Princes at Frankfurt. Francis Joseph in person invited the   Congress of
Prussian monarch to attend, and when he hesitated the   Princes
King of Saxony brought a renewed invitation from the Diet. "Thirty   (1863).
reigning princes—and a king for their courier." William I found it
hard to resist so tempting a bait. Bismarck, however, fearing that the
King might be trapped into concessions, and seeing in the Frankfurt
scheme only a device for riveting the Habsburg presidency more firmly
upon Germany, opposed with all his might the King's attendance.
The contest between the two men was typical of many, and illustrative
of the inner difficulties with which Bismarck had to contend. The
Queen was, of course, against him, and it was a threat of resignation
that forced his will upon the King, then as later. "Literally in the
sweat of my brow I persuaded him to refuse the proposal. . . . When
I had succeeded in making him commit himself to a definite refusal I
was so utterly exhausted I could hardly stand. When I left the room
I was staggering, and was in such a nervous and excited condition that
as I shut the door from the outside I actually broke off the handle."
The King burst into tears at having to refuse; Bismarck smashed some
glass to relieve his feelings; but the minister won his point.

But Prussia's rejection of the Congress of Princes—except for two
minor principalities, she was the only absent state—ruined the
attempt to reform the Confederation. "At a word from Prussia the
Austrian plan and all others of the same kind went, unhoused,
unanointed, and unannealed, into the limbo reserved for the acro-
batics of pseudo-statesmanship." [1] It was the last effort of Austria
to retain and consolidate the leadership of Germany. Before the
end of the year she was involved in the Schleswig-Holstein imbroglio,
which led straight to her downfall.

The affair of the Danish duchies revealed Bismarck; it displayed
for the first time his statesmanship in its completeness,
that combination of power and unscrupulousness, of   The
fixed aim hidden behind an apparent opportunism, that   Schleswig-
mixture of foresight with a bold and deft use of good luck, Holstein
that constituted his policy. In itself the question is loaded with   Question.

[1] C. Grant Robertson, *Bismarck*, p. 147.

a mass of historical and legal detail, which has made it one of the most complicated controversies of modern times. Three people only, remarked Palmerston, were fully acquainted with the truth: the Prince Consort of England, who was dead, a German professor, who was in a lunatic asylum, and himself—and he had forgotten it. But the main features can be simplified.

The relationship between Denmark and the two duchies of Schleswig and Holstein lying at her base was ancient, irregular, and incomplete. It was as old as the tenth century, and each duchy was joined separately to Denmark, though they were bound closely to each other, a royal decree of the fifteenth century having granted that they should not be disposed of separately.

The connexion with Denmark was not with the Danish state, but with the Danish Crown; the duchies were principalities of the Danish royal family, and related to Denmark as some of the Habsburg dominions were to Austria, or Poland to Russia for a few years

The irregular traditional connexion of the duchies with Denmark. after 1815, or even, in some respects, Scotland to England between 1603 and 1707. The parallels are not exact, but will serve as illustrations. Thus the duchies retained their own estates and law of succession; the King of Denmark only became Duke of Schleswig and of Holstein after he had been accepted as such in their own provincial estates, and it was not until Danish statutes had been submitted and passed by the same bodies that they became operative in the duchies. Further, while Schleswig had been a fief of Denmark, Holstein, the southern duchy, had been a fief of the Holy Roman Empire while it was in existence, and was after 1815 a member of the German Confederation. For the anomalous and traditional position had been confirmed in the resettlement of Europe that was made at Vienna after the Napoleonic wars. Thus Frederick VII, who was King of Denmark from 1848 to 1863, was also Duke of Schleswig and Duke of Holstein, in which last capacity he sat in the German Diet. It is this connexion with the German Confederation which explains and to some extent justifies the special interest taken by the Federal Diet in the duchies.

The position was in many ways unsatisfactory, but it had endured; many attempts had been made to incorporate the duchies in the

Disintegrating factors.
(1) Nationalism. Danish kingdom, but they had been successfully resisted. At the beginning of the nineteenth century, however, certain disturbing elements had begun to undermine the stability of the traditional bond; the fundamental disintegrating factor was the growing nationalism of the time, while the accidental and coincident failure of the male line of succession to the Danish kingdom provided an opportunity for dis-

Salic Law.

ruption to those who desired it. For Holstein was predominantly German in race, while Schleswig was predominantly Danish, except for a small disputed belt in the south. When the national self-consciousness awoke, therefore, German sentiment began to extend covetous arms to Holstein, and Danish to Schleswig, while each showed a disposition to include the neighbouring duchy in its embrace if it could do so. Clamant Teutonism raised the banner of 'unredeemed Germany'; clamant Danism that of 'unredeemed Denmark.' It is not necessary to enter into the variations of the schemes proposed; briefly the Danes desired the closer incorporation of the duchies with the kingdom of Denmark, while the Germans demanded their identification with Germany, as a separate state of the existing Confederation, and as an integral part of the new union when it should be formed. In the meantime the succession question was being driven like a wedge between the duchies and the Danish kingdom, and while one candidate was proposed for the latter, another was put forward in the former. The situation was not unlike that between England and Scotland on the eve of union.

(2) The succession question.

In January 1848 Frederick VII, the last of the Oldenburg line, succeeded to the throne of Denmark, and, yielding to the importunity of the Danish party, issued a constitution for the whole realm, including the duchies. The action immediately provoked a rising, the first of three which, stimulated by the revolutionary fervour of the time, encouraged by German sympathy, and supported by German arms, convulsed the duchies between the years 1848 and 1851. The Danes might have been easily ousted from the duchies, especially when Prussia took up the revolutionary cause; but the moral support of the Powers of Great Britain, Russia, Sweden, and even Austria was on the Danish side; Prussia was compelled to withdraw—another of the defeats that was inflicted upon her at that time—and the question of the duchies was submitted to a congress of the Powers at London.

Risings in the duchies, 1848–51.

A treaty was drawn up which recognized the *status quo—i.e.*, the possession of the duchies by Denmark—although it forbade their absolute incorporation into the Danish kingdom and extracted a promise of consideration for the German inhabitants. It proclaimed the "unity and integrity" of the Danish state and guaranteed the succession, both to the kingdom and to the duchies, to Christian of Glücksburg. The rival claimant, the Duke of Augustenburg, renounced his claims—or was held to have done so—and sold his Danish estates to the Crown. Both Prussia and Austria were parties to the agreement. The Federal Diet was not, and, not having been consulted, refused to recognize the treaty;

The Treaty of London (1852).

nevertheless, despairing of ever acquiring the duchies, which had been thus confirmed to Denmark by the Powers, it sold the Federal fleet, largely created with a view to operations against Denmark, by auction, and most of it was bought by Prussia.

The Danes began, however, to take advantage of their victory, to ignore the promised consideration to the German subjects, and to pursue a deliberate policy of forcible 'Danizing.' A powerful section of Danish opinion known as the "Eider-Dane" party demanded the extension of the Danish kingdom to the river Eider, which meant the complete incorporation of Schleswig.

The 'Danizing' of the duchies.

In 1855 a new constitution was issued for the whole kingdom and imposed upon the duchies; by it the revenues of the two provinces were to be swept into the common exchequer, and their Estates subordinated to the Danish majority at Copenhagen. Holstein protested and appealed to the Prussian Diet, and upon the representations of the latter Frederick VII agreed to leave Holstein out of the new constitutional arrangement. The King was powerless, however, before the chauvinistic Danish forces in his own kingdom, and in March 1863 he went back upon his agreement, decreed the absolute incorporation of Schleswig with Denmark, and bound Holstein with closer ties. He had thus committed a double offence in the eyes of the Holsteiners and their sympathizers in Germany and Schleswig; he had tightened the Danish connexion with the duchies, and at the same time he had severed the close historical and legal relationship between Schleswig and Holstein. He was supported, however, by an overwhelming radical majority in his own country, and when the German Diet entered a protest the Danes ignored it. At that moment, in November 1863, Frederick VII died and Christian IX, the candidate of the Convention of London, ascended the throne. Christian, in the difficult position of having to choose between opposition in Germany and the duchies and revolution in Denmark, decided to prefer the former, and confirmed the acts of his predecessor.

The constitution of 1855 and 1863.

Christian IX confirms the constitution.

Immediately the duchies and Germany broke out into violent protest; and Frederick, the son of the Duke of Augustenburg, who had renounced his claim in 1852, appeared in the duchies, offered himself as their ruler, and put himself at the head of the resistance to Denmark. His claim was supported with enthusiasm in the duchies and in Germany; the Diet ordered "Federal execution," and in December 1863 Federal troops, mainly Saxons and Hanoverians, occupied Holstein. The Danish forces withdrew, Danish sovereignty was abolished in the duchy, and the Duke of Augustenburg proclaimed himself Duke Frederick VIII of Schleswig-Holstein.

The German Diet intervenes on behalf of Augustenburg (December 1863).

Thus the Schleswig-Holstein Question was again before Germany, and there seemed every prospect that *Germania irredenta* The intervention of Prussia and Austria in alliance. would be added to the German states system. But a new and unknown factor had arisen; the Prussia of 1850 had vanished, and in its place was a new Power in new hands. Already the great Prussian statesman had begun to tower above his contemporaries.

With extreme caution and circumspection, with one eye on his own king and one on the Powers, Bismarck entered the Schleswig-Holstein maze. "My method in foreign policy to-day is like my method in old times, when I used to go snipe-shooting, and when I would not put my weight on a fresh tussock until I had tried it carefully with my foot."

William I of Prussia had to be converted to Bismarck's policy, the Powers to be outwitted or bullied; for Prussia had, after all, been a signatory to the Treaty of London, which had confirmed the duchies to Denmark and the succession to Christian. But if Bis- Bismarck's ambitions. marck did not wish the duchies to be retained by Denmark neither did he desire the formation of a new German state under the Duke of Augustenburg, "who would probably vote against Prussia in the Diet." His ambitions were bolder still. "From the first I kept annexation steadily before my eyes, without losing sight of the other gradations." It is true that Prussia had no rights in the duchies, as King William remarked, but "had the great Elector," argued Bismarck, "had King Frederick any more rights in Prussia and Silesia?" The King was silent, the Crown Prince lifted his hands to heaven, as if doubting Bismarck's sanity. Nevertheless Bismarck steadily proceeded, several times seeming to lose the game before he had won it.

It happened that there existed just then an unprecedented understanding—unprecedented since Bismarck's will had prevailed—between Prussia and Austria. It was due a little, perhaps, to some personal sympathy between Bismarck and the new imperial minister, Count Rechberg, and a great deal to the Austrian fear of a new move in Italy on the part of Napoleon III, who had recently declared in a speech from the throne that the treaties of 1815 no longer existed and that he intended to invite the European Powers to a congress which "should act as a supreme tribunal concerning all questions at issue." The declaration caused something of a panic among the Foreign Offices of Europe, and drove Austria to the side of Prussia.

Bismarck made good use of the Austro-Prussian *rapprochement*. If he had attacked Denmark alone he would have had Austria in the rear and Europe in the front. Instead he persuaded Count Rechberg— threatening otherwise to undertake alone the liberation of the duchies, the most popular cause in Germany at the time—to a secret agreement, to the effect that Prussia and Austria should undertake to settle the matter of the duchies without the interference of the Diet or the other German states.   This alliance with Austria was Bismarck's first triumph.

With Austria on his side Bismarck could afford to ignore the Germanic Confederation.   A pretence was made of appealing to the Diet with a motion that it should occupy Schleswig "as a pledge for the observance by Denmark of the compacts of 1852." This would have meant the recognition of the rights of Christian IX and the rejection of Augustenburg.   The Diet naturally refused, whereupon Austria and Prussia announced that they would act as independent Powers.   A joint ultimatum was dispatched to Copenhagen, demanding the repeal of the November constitution (as the constitution of 1863 was called) within forty-eight hours.

Independent action on the part of Austria and Prussia

That was Bismarck's second move—intervention with Austria in the name of the treaties of 1852.   There was, however, always the chance that Denmark might have refused to fight, in which case Bismarck would have lost the game.   Two considera- tions chiefly caused Denmark to reject the ultimatum: first, the shortness of the time allowed for consideration and the impossibility of calling the Rigstaad, which alone could make the repeal of the constitution legal; secondly, the hope, which Bismarck secretly fostered, of British support.   Had not the Prince of Wales just married a Danish princess, and the Prime Minister, Palmerston, declared that "if any violent attempt were made to over- throw the rights and interfere with the independence [of Denmark] those who made the attempt would find that it would not be Denmark alone with which they would have to contend."

in the name of the treaties of 1852.

When it came to action Palmerston's words proved to be only the "senseless and spiritless menaces" that Disraeli called them.   Neither the British Cabinet nor the British Court, nor any Conti- nental Power, was willing to support Palmerston in a war with Austria and Prussia on behalf of Denmark.   Thus, lured by a false belief, the Danish kingdom went to its doom, entering alone into war with the German Powers.

War with Denmark, February– April 1864.

At the end of January the combined forces of Prussia and Austria passed through Holstein, while the Saxon and Hanoverian troops of the Confederation looked sullenly on.   On February 1 they passed the Eider and entered Schleswig.   Within a fortnight the Danes had been driven from the duchy, and after some hesitation on the part of Austria the German armies passed into Denmark proper.   The lines of the Düppel to the east were strongly held; it was not until after a month's siege that they were stormed on April 18.   The question was rapidly passing, however, from the military to the diplomatic sphere. England and Sweden were loud in their sympathy with the Danes; Napoleon III was in a characteristic mood of indecision; Russia was advising caution; the German Confederation was resentful; Austria, looking anxiously toward Magyar disaffection and Italian intrigues, desired peace. A conference of the Powers was called by Lord John Russell in London, where the arrangements of 1850–52 had been made, and a truce was declared between Denmark and her two German enemies, while the subject of the duchies was under discussion.

The conference sat until June, and then, having found no way out of the labyrinthine problems into which it had plunged, broke up without a decision. It had served, however, to advance Bismarck's ambitions. With marvellous astuteness, and with luck on his side, he had played off one programme against another. He had prevented Austria from supporting the 1852 arrangements and the retention of the duchies by Denmark by pleading the excessive unpopularity of such a course in Germany. He had forestalled her adoption of the Augustenburg claims by taking them up himself. He had evaded any commitment in that direction, however, by demanding such an extensive military, naval, and economic control over Schleswig-Holstein in return for his advocacy of their separation from Denmark that Augustenburg had rejected his offer of assistance. He had thus gained a quasi-moral justification for turning his back upon Augustenburg; he further secured a quasi-legal defence in the fact that the conference turned down Augustenburg's claims in favour of the non-separation of the duchies from Denmark. Bismarck was obviously manœuvring for the Prussian acquisition of at least Holstein. Had not Napoleon III already pointed out the value of the duchies to Prussian sea-power—a consideration to which Bismarck was by no means blind? Thus, as Lord Clarendon declared to the Prussian ambassadors, "you came into the conference as masters of the situation, and as masters . . . you leave it."

The London conference (April–June 1864).

At the end of June, after the dissolution of the conference, Prussia and Austria renewed the war against Denmark, committed now to the separation of the duchies from the Danish kingdom and to the joint disposition of them afterward. The Augustenburg claims, having been drawn as a red herring across the trail, had been abandoned as a serious political programme—at any rate by Bismarck, for Austria was again to bring them forward. The Schleswig-Holstein Question had entered upon its third phase.

War renewed with Denmark for the separation of the duchies, June–August 1864.

The new campaign was quickly decided. The Danish mainland

was overrun; the island of Alsen invaded, Copenhagen threatened. No foreign country moved a soldier in support. In despair the Danes surrendered, and on August 1 preliminaries of peace were signed, and confirmed in October by the Treaty of Vienna. Denmark gave up all her rights in the two duchies to Austria and Prussia conjointly, and agreed to recognize any dispositions that they should make of them. By the loss of the duchies—and of Norway, fifty years earlier—Denmark was reduced to a political insignificance from which she has not yet recovered, and Great Britain was shamed before Europe and her own people. "If Mr Cobden [1] had been Foreign Secretary," said Lord Robert Cecil, afterward Marquis of Salisbury, "I believe this country would occupy a position proud and noble compared to that she occupies at this moment. She would at least have been entitled to the credit of holding out no hopes which she did not intend to fulfil, of entering into no engagements from which she was ready to recede." [2]

The Federal troops were withdrawn from Holstein, on Bismarck's insistence, and Prusso-Austrian contingents took their place. The fate of the duchies had still to be settled. The essential difficulty of the situation lay in the fact that Prussia coveted territory in that part of Germany, whereas Austria did not; but all the same she could not allow Prussia to expand without corresponding compensations to herself. "We are standing in front of the duchies," said Bismarck to the Austrian ambassador, "like two guests before whom an admirable banquet is spread, but one of them, who has no appetite, sternly forbids the other, who is hungry, to fall to." After long discussion and much proposing and counter-proposing, with the gulf between the two Powers growing wider all the time, it was agreed to divide the spoil. The territories were to be held in joint sovereignty, but Austria was for the present to occupy and administer Holstein (the southern duchy—*i.e.*, the nearer to Prussia) and Prussia Schleswig, while the Duchy of Lauenburg, a small appendage too insignificant to quarrel seriously about, was sold to Prussia for two and a half million talers. The terms embodied in the Convention of Gastein were highly favourable to Prussia, for in addition to the unimpaired possession of Schleswig she was given numerous rights in Holstein—practical control of the port of Kiel, the right of cutting a canal, the inclusion of the southern duchy in the Prussian Zollverein; moreover, it was obvious that Austria could not permanently retain so isolated an outpost of her empire as Holstein. Thus the fourth stage had been reached in the process of transferring the Elbe duchies from Denmark to Prussia, and the end was in sight. "That

[1] An avowed pacifist.
[2] Quoted by Professor C. R. Beazley, *Nineteenth-century Europe and Britain.*

was the last time I ever played quinze," [1] said Bismarck. "I played so recklessly that every one was astonished. Count Blome [2] had said that the best way to understand people's character was to play quinze with them, and I thought I would show him mine! I lost several hundred talers . . . but I succeeded in fooling him, for he believed me to be more venturesome than I am, and gave way."

The first of the three wars which Bismarck waged in the course of making the German Empire had ended in the extension of the Prussian state, and the promise of a good deal more. The first act had been played in the great political drama which Bismarck was staging, revealing something of the turmoil of German politics, something of the aggressiveness of the new German nationality, and something—for much was still unsuspected—of the force of the new German power. For the first time the world had seen the foreign policy of Bismarck in action, and it stood amazed before the daring, unscrupulousness, and diplomatic skill of the Prussian Minister. He had driven Austria, a generation ago the leader of Europe, where he would have her go; the force of his will he had impressed upon Europe and upon his own king. Step by step he had led William of Prussia, half reluctant, half blindfolded, along his own path. The King had not held back, save only from war with Austria, and on the next occasion when his will should run counter to Bismarck's he would not be able to do so much. Bismarck had entered into possession of his king, so that the royal master had even come to think of his servant's policy as his own; and the minister's gratification was not unmingled with amusement at the royal delusion, as he received the King's embrace, donned the new decoration of the Black Eagle, and entered the ranks of the nobility as Count Bismarck.

(b)

The Schleswig-Holstein war was a mere stepping-stone; Bismarck had not lost sight of his aim of driving Austria from Germany that Prussia might grasp the leadership. At one time during the negotiations between the Treaties of Vienna and of Gastein it had seemed as if war might break out between Austria and Prussia, and Bismarck's blood had flowed faster at the thought that the opportunity he sought had at last come. William I would have no "fratricidal" war, however, and bade his minister patch up the rent. But the Convention of Gastein had not averted the coming conflict. It had merely postponed it for ten months. "We have papered over the cracks," said Bismarck, and threw himself with energy into preparing for the coming fissure.

"We have papered over the cracks."

[1] A card game.   [2] The Austrian agent.

The Gastein arrangements with regard to the duchies contained many germs of discord, out of which Bismarck deliberately set himself to produce a war that would yield the final conclusion to the problems of Germany. War alone would serve his purpose—of driving Austria out of Germany and forcing from her a recognition of Prussian supremacy, of justifying territorial annexations in Germany, "without which Prussia's mastery of the new German organization would be incomplete," and of enabling the Prussian monarchy to dictate its will to the malcontents of its own state.

Austria provided Bismarck with an excuse in her administration of Holstein. There was no finality about the Convention of Gastein, and Austria, regarding her presence in the southern duchy as merely transitional, began to lean to a Federal and Augustenburg policy. She allowed agitation in the Press and from the platform on the Duke's behalf, even to a large mass meeting at Altona in January 1866, at which the Prussian Government was denounced. Bismarck protested, and even William I was aroused; he who eighteen months before had stated that Prussia had no right in the duchies now declared that they were "worth fighting for." "I want peace, but am resolved to make war [on behalf of the duchies] if needs must, for I regard the war as a just one, now that I have prayed to God to show me the right path." "The King had developed a taste for conquest," remarked Bismarck, concealing in the phrase a profound psychological revolution which he had himself worked in his master's mind.

On March 16 Austria announced her intention of referring the whole question of the Elbe duchies to the Federal Diet. It was a definite bid for German popularity, a direct violation of the Convention of Gastein and of the secret policy underlying the whole Danish episode. It destroyed the possibility of any Prusso-Austrian agreement, and war was now only a matter of time. In the interval Bismarck hastened to complete his preparations, to manœuvre foreign Powers and convert his king to full agreement.

Austria violates the Convention of Gastein.

With regard to Russia, Bismarck had played his moves in the political game of chess long before, in the St Petersburg days, in the Crimean War, and in the Polish rising, and he now counted on the close understanding which he had established with the Tsar to bear its fruit. It was on France and Italy that his mind and diplomacy were chiefly concentrated. The neutrality of the one was an essential, the armed alliance of the other an obvious resource.

Back in the Frankfurt and Paris days Bismarck had held himself toward the French Emperor with an absence of prejudice which had been far from popular with the two successive Prussian kings and with conventional conservative circles in Berlin. He had refused to prejudge him as the enemy of legitimacy, or to condemn him *a priori* as a liberal, a *parvenu*, an abetter of revolution. To Bismarck, with some such contingency always in sight as had at last arisen in Germany, the French Emperor was potentially an important factor in a delicate and highly critical political situation, to be studied and approached dispassionately as such. *Bismarck seeks the neutrality of France.* Besides, Bismarck had always had his own opinion as to the Emperor's character, which had not coincided with the picture that was common in Europe of a potent, malevolent, ambitious, and able designer. Ten years before he had aroused the somewhat suspicious and irritated amusement of the King of Prussia's dinner-table by his unconventional description of the ogre of the day. "It is my impression," remarked Bismarck, "that the Emperor Napoleon is a discreet and amiable man, but not so clever as the world esteems him. The world places to his account everything that happens, and if it rains in Eastern Asia at an unseasonable moment chooses to attribute it to some malevolent machination of the Emperor. . . . I believe he is happy when he is able to enjoy anything good at his ease; his understanding is overrated at the expense of his heart; he is at bottom good-natured, and has an unusual measure of gratitude for every service rendered him." An amusing man, this Junker Bismarck, thought his hearers, quite original, but of course not to be taken seriously. Napoleon, on his side, seemed to have a friendly feeling for the Prussian Minister. "A really great man," he called him a little later, "free from affectation and full of *esprit*."

Even before Gastein, Bismarck had approached the French Emperor, and although the relations between France and Prussia had been temporarily clouded by the convention between the two German states, a friendly understanding was renewed at Biarritz, where Bismarck met Napoleon in October 1865.

The Biarritz interview was almost as important to Prussia as the one at Plombières, seven years earlier, had been to Sardinia, but much of what passed there is a matter of conjecture. The whole procedure was informal—confidential talk in the Villa Eugénie, conversations on the terrace with the Biscayan rollers breaking on the shore beneath them. There were no witnesses—save the dog Nero, who followed at their heels—and the records that have been given to us are meagre and partisan. *The Biarritz interview (October 1865).*

It may be generally concluded, however,[1] that Napoleon promised the neutrality of France in the event of a Prusso-Austrian war; that he agreed to the annexation of the Elbe duchies by Prussia in case of victory, and approved of the cession of Austrian Venetia to Italy in the case of a Prusso-Italian alliance; that he made no protest against

---

[1] *Cf.* Professor C. R. Beazley, *Nineteenth-century Europe and Britain.*

the reform of the German Confederation, and the reconstruction of a new state, at any rate of North Germany, under Prussian leadership. It is certain that the question was raised of compensation to France for her neutrality, and that Bismarck accepted the possibility of "une petite rectification des frontières," so long as it was not at the expense of Prussia or Germany. He seems to have freely offered what did not belong to him, and suggested that France should seek adjustment in "French-speaking territories," such as South-eastern Belgium.

Bismarck's aim was clear enough—to secure French neutrality without any awkward bills of exchange which might be presented for payment. Napoleon's policy is more difficult to interpret. As the two men walked together—the one large and powerful, vigorous, ambitious, alert, with his great work still ahead of him, the other bent and sallow, prematurely aged, with weary, dull eyes looking out upon disillusionment, physically ill, with the shadows already falling on his reign—it is not difficult to imagine which of the two would impose his will upon the other. He who could bend William of Prussia could no doubt hypnotize Napoleon III. What more lay concealed in the interview must be interpreted according to men's estimate of the "great Imperial Sphinx," as Disraeli called Bismarck. Undoubtedly something was due to real sympathy with Bismarck's nationalist aims, and still more with the prospect of adding Venetia to the new Italian kingdom. "Le spectre de Venise erre dans les salles des Tuileries," and at its beckoning Napoleon followed.

There was something, too, of the subtle calculation which loomed large in the eyes of Napoleon's ministers. If Prussia should win and reconstruct Northern Germany the southern states and Austria would naturally lean more to the French side. But, in fact, Napoleon and France made one serious miscalculation; they did not believe that Prussia would be successful. To them a Prusso-Austrian conflict could end only in Prussia's defeat, after a longer or shorter struggle; it would weaken Germany, enable France to intervene, restore her preponderance at least over the lesser states, justify her in tearing up the treaties of 1815, and so give her an opportunity of pushing her frontiers again to the Rhine. Such, at any rate, was the attitude of the French Foreign Minister, Drouyn de Lhuys.

There were yet, however, many moods to be countered in Napoleon III before Prussia went to war. From France Bismarck moved to Italy, a more difficult problem at the time. A commercial treaty was readily arranged between the two kingdoms, but it was by no means

The alliance of Italy. easy to bring about an offensive alliance. Such an arrangement would have obvious advantages—a joint attack on Austria from Prussia in the north and Italy in the south would ensure her certain defeat, while Italy had every chance of winning

Venetia if Austria and Prussia went to war. But both countries were full of distrust, each believing that the other would only use the alliance as a lever to force concessions out of Austria. At last, on April 8, 1866, a secret treaty was signed, by which, "if April 8, Prussia within three months should take up arms for the 1866. reform of the Federal system of Germany, Italy would immediately attack Austria." It was an arrangement of "mutual insurance and suspicion," the time limit indicating Italy's distrust.

Bismarck had therefore twelve weeks in which to mature a war against Austria. But now the King of Prussia was an obstacle. He had been sufficiently roused to a warlike mood at the Prussian Council meeting of February 28 by the news of the Austrian patronage in Holstein of the Augustenburg claims, and on March 3 he had at Bismarck's instigation written personally to Napoleon III, that "man of sin" with whom he had scorned to have any contact a little earlier, suggesting a definite understanding between France and Prussia—a letter which Bismarck supplemented with secret negotiations through the great Jewish banker Rothschild. The Emperor had replied with a promise of benevolent neutrality toward the formation of a North German union under Prussian leadership, stipulating that in the event of the enlargement of Prussia he would later put in a claim for compensation.

Now, however, that the conflict with Austria approached William of Prussia began to draw back from the thought of a fratricidal war. All the influences of his family were exerted to prevent it, his wife, the Queen Augusta, his son, the Crown Prince, and his English daughter-in-law, who did not scruple to write to her mother, Queen Victoria. The conservatives, traditional royal allies, were horrified at the prospect of a war against a sacred German Power, with the alliance and support of liberal Italy and Bonapartist France. The King Bismarck broke down before the royal defection, and both of Prussia he and Roon seriously considered resignation. "I believe weakens, in the war," cried Bismarck, "without knowing whether I shall see it, but I often feel overcome by exhaustion."

In spite of every opposition, of royal discouragement, of the imprecations of his former friends, the Gerlachs and their conservative circle, Bismarck persisted, striving to bring about this war which no one wanted but himself. At last his pleading and arguments began to prevail with the King. An Austrian move gave him an excuse to point to treachery, to recall Olmütz, to stir but is won the King's blood with appeals to his religious faith, his over by soldierly instincts, his Prussian pride. "I am content to Bismarck. leave it to Almighty God to guide your Majesty's heart for the welfare of the Fatherland, and I am more inclined to pray than to

advise," and then, proceeding to give advice, "but I cannot hide my
conviction that if we keep the peace now the danger of war will recur,
perhaps in a few months, and under less favourable conditions. . . .
One who, like your Majesty's most faithful servant, has for sixteen
years been intimately acquainted with Austrian policy, cannot doubt
that in Vienna hostility to Prussia has become the chief, I might
almost say the only motive of State policy."

Bismarck knew how to play upon his king, and William at last
agreed to war; but he was still fearful of defeat. "If a Prussian
whispers Olmütz in my ear I shall abdicate." But Bismarck and
Moltke and Roon were confident of the strength of the Prussian
army. At the beginning of May the King ordered a mobilization
of the Prussian troops. The Queen Augusta protested, and left
Berlin. "I know," said the King, "that they are all against me.
Every one of them! But I shall myself draw the sword at the head
of my army, and would rather perish than that Prussia should give
way this time."

In the meantime Bismarck had changed the ground of dispute to
the question of the reform of the Federation, for he would not go
to war with Austria for the duchies alone. At the end of
March he had raised the subject in response to Austria's
announcement of her intention of submitting the disposition of the duchies to the Federal Diet, and on April
9, the morrow of the Prusso-Italian alliance, he had
handed in his schemes of reform at Frankfurt. The
Prussian Bismarck had begun to turn into a German. Had the
conservative Junker begun to turn into a liberal, or only into a statesman? Among the reform proposals was the astounding suggestion
that the reconstructed Germany should possess a German national
Parliament elected by universal manhood suffrage. Germany and
Prussia were stupefied by the revolution in Bismarck's policy, and
conservatives and liberals hardly knew which of them was mocked
the more. They could not as yet believe that it was other than a
mere political subterfuge.

As events began to march toward war Federal reform played a
large part in Bismarck's programme and preparations. It had been
used as an argument to convince France, to convince Italy, to convince the Prussian King, and had been definitely embodied in the
Prusso-Italian alliance, and he had made it perfectly clear to the lesser
states that the reconstruction of Germany would follow Prussia's
victory in the war. At the end of April Austria mobilized her
Southern army in view of suspicious stirrings in Italy, of new Garibaldian activities. La Marmora replied with the mobilization of the
Italian army. The declaration of war was, however, still to be delayed.

Marginal note: Bismarck makes Federal reform the chief ground of dispute.

Austria made a desperate effort—a month too late—to buy off the Florentine Government from the Prussian alliance. She would surrender Venetia, and France and Italy would no doubt let her take compensation from Prussian Silesia. Everything hung for a moment on La Marmora's loyalty and faith in Prussia. Bismarck's fears rose. But the Italian Prime Minister and general-in-chief decided that Prussia meant to play honestly; he refused the offer, and kept to his compact, although it meant a war with the possibility of failure to secure what he could have had definitely in peace. *War delayed by Austria*

After that Napoleon's ever-shifting policy postponed the issue for a few weeks longer. A section of French opinion was violently hostile to what it held to be the sacrifice of French interests for the sake of the aggrandizement of Prussia and Italy. *and France.* "Never," cried Thiers in the French Chamber, "never must Germany succeed in reaching political unity. Prussia's aim manifestly lies in the line of creating German unity by means of a victorious war against Austria. To make this war impossible is the duty of every French patriot." Napoleon had listened, and had been partially convinced. He had therefore supported Austria in her proposal to surrender Venetia, and when that failed he had made a fresh move to Prussia for 'compensation'; and when that failed also he had proposed his favourite panacea for the ills of Europe, a congress. Russia and Britain approved, and Bismarck, like Cavour eight years before, had no choice but to accept. *A congress proposed.*

With a heavy heart he realized it would mean the ruin of his plans. Again the incomprehensible political ineptitude that dogged the policy of Austria played into his hands, as it had before into those of Cavour. She conditioned her acceptance with such impossible stipulations that it amounted to a refusal, and the congress was abandoned. When the telegram arrived with the news Bismarck leapt to his feet. "It is war!" he cried. "Long live the King!" The tide had turned at last in his favour. A few days before a Tübingen student, half English by descent, had attempted to assassinate the enemy of the people. One of the bullets passed through his clothes, and slipped along outside a silk under-vest. The next day, for the first time in his life, Bismarck was cheered by the crowd in the Wilhelmstrasse. The courage of the man of iron was growing impressive; Prussia was beginning to respond to the beating of the drums; and Bismarck himself, after what seemed to him a miraculous escape, "felt himself," remarked a daily companion, "to be God's chosen instrument, though he did not express the thought in words."

If that shot had gone home there could hardly have been an Austro-Prussian war.

R

The last diplomatic formalities were concluded in the early part of June. On the 1st Austria summoned the Estates of Holstein, and, realizing her threat of March 16, formally invited the Federal Diet to adjudicate on the question of the Elbe duchies. To this Prussia replied by declaring the Convention of Gastein at an end, and by invading Holstein on June 7. Austria therefore protested before the Federal Diet, and demanded the mobilization of the Federal forces against the disturber of the peace. On the same day, June 14, Prussia laid her own scheme before the Diet for the reform of the Confederation, demanding that reconstruction should precede the discussion of the question of the duchies. Of the two rival motions the Austrian one was accepted by a majority of nine to six. Prussia therefore declared the Confederation at an end, withdrew her representative from the Diet, and dispatched ultimata to the lesser states.

The lesser states join Austria. All of them, except Weimar and a few of the petty principalities of the North surrounded by Prussian territory, joined the Austrian side. On June 16 the Prussians crossed the Saxon frontier, and on June 20 Italy declared war upon Austria, a little more than a fortnight before the end of the time limit fixed in the Prusso-Italian treaty.

The two sides. The fate of Germany now lay with the men of arms. Superficially the odds seemed unequal, and it is hardly to be wondered at that Europe and Germany should almost universally have counted upon the success of Austria. The Prussian army chiefs were confident, but, said Bismarck, "we must not forget that Almighty God is very capricious. . . . Perhaps Prussia will be beaten. . . . If so, I shall not come back. I shall fall in the last onslaught. A man can die but once, and if one is conquered it is better to die." He uneasily opened his Bible in search of an oracle, and by chance lighting upon the passage in Psalm ix, verses 3 and 5, was greatly comforted.

On the one side was Prussia, a small state of eighteen millions with weak frontiers, broken by enemy territory, with no allies, as King William expressed it, save "the Duke of Mecklenburg and Mazzini." On the other was Austria, with more than twice the population of Prussia and the adhesion of the important lesser states of Germany. Prussia, with an unexampled call upon her resources, could put only 350,000 men in the field—a marvellous feat, nevertheless, for her size —against the reputed " 800,000 good troops " of the Austrians.

Austria was, however, considerably weaker than she appeared. The South German states were lukewarm, and the confusion and poverty of their military organizations gave them good excuses for a weak defence against Prussia and a speedy retirement from the war. Saxony alone defended herself with vigour. The alliance of Italy also, although it brought little real military strength to Prussia, at least compelled Austria to divide her forces at the beginning of the war.

It was, however, in command, equipment, and general efficiency that the advantage lay with Prussia. Moltke had said that the Prussian army was ready, and he was as good as his word. Plans were prepared, and equipment up to date; the new breech-loading needle-gun, which had already been tried in the Danish war, gave an accuracy and rapidity of fire hitherto unmatched. In big matters and small, in all departments and all grades, the Prussian army had been raised by Roon and Moltke to a maximum point of efficiency. Its rapidity of movement in the field completely dazzled and outwitted the cautious and leisurely Austrians. For the 'only possible' general whom the Habsburgs could send to confront Moltke was Count Benedek, distinguished by nobility of character, but not by military genius, commissioned to a field and an army that he did not know, that an archduke might win victories in Italy, accepting his appointment reluctantly and deprecatingly, while deploring that Austria "did not possess a better general."

The Austro-Prussian War lasted seven weeks, the decisive fighting ten days. Italy's share may be speedily dismissed. On Midsummer's Day, June 24, she suffered a disastrous defeat on the historic Custozza, after which she took no further part **The war.** of importance in the war. Thus Austria was able to recall her forces from Italy to Germany, but so rapid had been Prussia's success that they arrived too late to change the course of victory.

Prussia put four armies into the field. The first and largest was to invade Bohemia from Prussian Silesia to the east. It was under the command of the Crown Prince Frederick, who, in spite of his strong liberal opposition to the policy of his royal father and of Bismarck, was now to take a prominent place in the war. The second and third armies were also to invade Bohemia—on which the main Prussian attack was thus concentrated—but through Saxony, an ally of Austria. A fourth covering force was to operate against the smaller states of North and Central Germany. With incredible swiftness the Prussians struck, and on the third day of the war they occupied three capitals, Hanover, Cassel, and Dresden. At the end of a week the two Prussian armies had forced their way through Saxony into Bohemia; three days later, on June 28, the Hanoverian armies surrendered, and the Austrian coalition began to crumble. On July 1 Benedek telegraphed to the Austrian Emperor, "Sire, you must make peace at any price. A catastrophe for the army is unavoidable." His advice was, however, rejected, and the two armies disposed themselves for what was to be the decisive and final struggle.

The central battle of the campaign took place between Sadowa
and Königgrätz, in Eastern Bohemia, on July 2. Somewhat recklessly King William, whose military appetite had been
whetted by events, insisted upon opening the attack while
the Crown Prince's army was still ten miles away. Bismarck, watching from a huge chestnut-tree not far away, bitterly
reflected that the international and national advantages for which
he had manœuvred so long and so successfully seemed likely to be
thrown away "by these infernal generals." The Crown Prince
arrived, however, in time, stormed the heights of Chlum, which
formed the central defence of the Austrian army, and won not only
the battle but the campaign for Prussia. The Habsburg forces,
hopelessly exposed and broken, fell back upon Königgrätz, and took
refuge in the fortress on the other side of the Elbe. "Now, your
Excellency," remarked an *aide-de-camp* to Bismarck, "you are a great
man. If the Crown Prince had come too late you would have been
the greatest of rascals." At which Bismarck burst out laughing.

*Sadowa, or
Königgrätz
(July 2).*

Twenty-four thousand prisoners lay in the hands of the Prussians,
and the Austrians, materially shattered, were morally defeated. In
eight days the Hohenzollern forces were in Prague, two
days later they were at Brünn, between Benedek and
Vienna. During the same time the Bavarians had been
defeated in the valley of the Main, and Frankfurt and
Darmstadt, then Würtzburg and Nuremberg, had fallen to Prussia.

*Prussia's
triumph
in other
fields.*

The Austro-Prussian War, which had been Bismarck's in its inception, was no less his in its conclusion, for in the face of the wishes
of the King and the military party, with Vienna almost in
sight and the humiliation of Austria imminent, in spite of
every consideration to the contrary, Bismarck decided that
the time had come to make peace. The next fortnight became the
most critical period of the whole struggle, not in a military sense,
but in that wider sphere of statesmanship whose province it is to
translate the victories of arms into wise and lasting political attain-
ments. Never did Bismarck show himself a more skilful diplomatist
or a greater statesman.

*Bismarck's
arguments
for peace.*

Many considerations influenced his decision. The Prussians had
achieved a memorable victory over a great Power by a swift and
brilliant initial offensive. Their prestige was heightened by the very
suddenness of their triumph. But their enemies, although defeated,
were not broken. They had appealed to France, and she had
listened; there was an uneasy stirring in Russia, and although
England was too much immersed in franchise questions to take the
initiative she might easily follow the lead of the other Powers. There
were murmurs of a congress. The Italian alliance had from a

military point of view proved a disappointment. Prussia herself could advance no farther for a fortnight until her artillery arrived; cholera was breaking out in the army. It was easily conceivable that a continuation of the war or the formation of a European coalition would rob Prussia of her victory or whittle it away to impotence.

Peace on moderate terms—for to Austria Bismarck was determined to offer generous terms—would be both a supreme act of statesmanship and of enlightened self-interest. "If we are not excessive in our demands," he wrote to his wife, "if we avoid believing that we have achieved the conquest of the world, we shall secure a peace which will have been worth the trouble. But we are just as easily exhilarated as we are depressed, and it is my thankless task to water the fermenting wine and to remind people that we do not live alone in Europe, where there are three other Powers which hate and envy us."

The day after Königgrätz Bismarck had already remarked, "Now is the time to restore the old friendship with Austria." In the middle of victory he was able to envisage a future alliance with his present enemy, and to resolve neither to humiliate nor wound her beyond reconciliation. "My chief concern was to avoid anything which would impair our future relationships with Austria." The entry into Vienna demanded by the military party would have been an unforgivable insult to Austria. The annexation of "anciently held dominions" which would not have amalgamated with Prussian lands would have involved future wars for their defence—as the Seven Years War followed the Silesian wars. Prussia, moreover, had no need of them; she could seek and find her enlargement north of the river Main. "We are not a court of assize to administer retributive justice," he urged to the King, now entirely carried away by his soldierly instincts, and by this time seeing only a righteous Prussian crusade against an aggressive Austria whom God had delivered for chastisement into the hands of the Hohenzollern. "Austria's rivalry of Prussia is no more culpable than Prussia's rivalry of Austria. Our business is to establish German national unity under the leadership of the King of Prussia." In short, Bismarck considered that the essential objects of the war had already been won—the reconstruction of Germany under a dominant Prussia, and the exclusion of Austria from any part in it.

They were sound, statesmanlike arguments, justified by the success which followed their adoption, justified still more by the political tragedy which followed their abandonment after the Franco-German War.

There was, however, still another and perhaps more powerful inducement to peace in the attitude of France. The battle of

Königgrätz had overturned Napoleon's assumptions as much as it had falsified the too wise prognostications of English journalism.

Negotiations with Napoleon III.
The day after the battle Francis Joseph had telegraphed to the French Emperor offering to surrender Venetia to France on behalf of Italy if the latter country would retire from the war. Napoleon thereupon resolved to adopt the *rôle* of mediator. Bismarck was furious. "Louis Napoleon shall pay for this," he remarked, when Benedetti, the French envoy, having made his way through the Prussian lines, appeared suddenly at Bismarck's bedside with a proposal for an armistice. It is not easy to thread one's way surely through the complicated negotiations which filled the interval between the battle of Königgrätz and the Peace of Prague; to reconcile the conversations at Nickolsburg between Bismarck and Benedetti with those at Paris between Napoleon and the Prussian ambassador, von Goltz; to see clearly amid the skilful duplicity and prevarication of the Prussian Minister and the indecision and vacillation of a weary Emperor striving vainly to adapt himself to the bellicose clamour of his own people. Italy further clouded the issues by refusing, in a fit of self-mortifying pride, to accept the Venetia she had gone to war to obtain unless a sop was offered to her wounded military honour.

Napoleon himself seems to have been neither unduly alarmed at the aggrandizement of Prussia nor hostile to the satisfaction of German nationalist aspirations. What he had approved of in Italy and Rumania he would not deny to Germany. He would not oppose a small extension of Prussian territory nor a reconstruction of Germany that was confined to the states north of the Main.

Behind Napoleon, however, there was France—Thiers, eloquent in the Chamber of Deputies, and Drouyn de Lhuys, Minister for Foreign Affairs, both exponents of an infuriated and assaulted Gallicanism. Prussia's alarming growth must be paid for; German unification must be checked; France must be given guarantees and compensation. Thus Napoleon the mediator turned bargainer with a man immeasurably his superior in conviction and diplomatic skill. It was a simple matter to demand compensation, and Bismarck could not easily refuse it; the whole problem was what should be given. "If only Germany had a Savoy!" murmured Napoleon. The French Emperor did not know, in fact, what he wanted; he was not in sympathy with his ministers, nor did he wholly resist them. He was physically ill, prostrated by pain, tossed by conflicting impulses. He must do something—a principle on which most mistakes are made. He therefore flitted from one proposal to another, from Belgium to Luxemburg, from Luxemburg to Mainz.

He failed utterly to take advantage of France's opportunities or of

Germany's need; he succeeded only in irritating Prussia and gaining nothing for France. He was hopelessly outwitted in diplomacy. He committed the serious mistake of accepting Bismarck's proposals without any guarantee for the acceptance of his own terms. Such "matters of detail" as compensation could be deferred until after the preliminaries of peace had been signed. It was then too late. Bismarck was not the man to pay for something which he had already obtained without payment.

When therefore in August (after the truce of Nickolsburg and before the Peace of Prague) the Emperor raised the question of the left bank of the Rhine—Mainz and part of the Bavarian Palatinate, some Prussian territory and a little Hesse-Darmstadt—Bismarck was obdurate. He secured a statement of the proposed claims, which he locked up in his drawer for future use, and refused to yield an inch. "Is it Mainz or war?" he asked. The French envoy nodded. "Very well, you shall have war," replied Bismarck. He had been afraid of war at first, but now he thought France could be defied with impunity. His calculation was just. Napoleon could not go to war; the army was unprepared—the new *chassepot* was just being introduced—and its resources were strained by the Mexican expedition. "De loin c'est quelque chose, et de près ce n'est rien"; in such words Bismarck had described the Second Empire two or three years before.

Thus while Bismarck was using the French proposals to win over the southern states of Germany to an alliance with Prussia Napoleon was left helpless and apologetic, explaining to Prussia that his minister had exceeded his instructions, explaining to his own humiliated and resentful people many things, that "political thought should rise above the narrow prejudices of the age," that there could be no real Balance of Power save in the satisfied wishes of the nations of Europe, that there should be no danger to France in a united Germany; and, moreover, that French diplomacy had in reality weakened Germany by dividing it into three parts, and by laying the foundation of a South German League, which should look to France as its protector. But French sentiment was unimpressed. "The Peace of Westphalia condemned Germany to impotence for many years. . . . We can understand Germany seeking to raise herself from such a position, but that a French sovereign should look on and let her do so is incomprehensible."

At one stage of the proceedings, however, Bismarck's own king presented as great a difficulty as the French Emperor. When the Prussian statesman had drawn up terms acceptable to Austria and to France William angrily and obstinately refused to agree to them. He had strengthened the *The resistance of the King.*

"taste for conquest" that he had acquired during the Schleswig-Holstein war; he demanded greater concessions, the abdication of the sovereigns of the hostile states, the continuation of the Prussian advance to Vienna itself, and his attitude was encouraged by the jealousy of the military chiefs. Bismarck has himself related how he fought to persuade the King to accept his proposals.

> The resistance which I was obliged to offer to the King's views . . . excited him to such a degree that a prolongation of the discussion became impossible; and, under the impression that my opinion had been rejected, I left the room with the idea of begging the King to allow me, in my capacity as officer, to join my regiment. On returning to my room I was in the mood that the thought occurred to me whether it would not be better to fall out of the open window, which was four storeys high; and I did not look round when I heard the door open.

There entered the Crown Prince. "I felt his hand on my shoulder," continued Bismarck,

> while he said, "You know that I was against this war. You considered it necessary, and the responsibility for it lies on you. If you are now persuaded that our end is attained, and peace must now be concluded, I am ready to support you, and defend your opinion with my father." He then repaired to the King, and came back after a short half-hour in the same calm, friendly mood, but with the words, "It has been a very difficult business, but my father has consented."

The next day the King pencilled a note on the margin of Bismarck's proposals. "Inasmuch as my Minister-President has left me in the lurch in the face of the enemy . . . and as [my son] has associated himself with the Minister-President's opinion, I find myself reluctantly compelled, after such brilliant victories on the part of the army, to bite the sour apple, and accept so disgraceful a peace."

Thus with watchful and anxious eyes upon Napoleon III and William I, upon Austria and Italy, upon foreign Powers and the small German states, upon the anti-Teutonism of France and the no less vociferous anti-Gallicanism of his own Prussians, upon the restive nationalism of Hungary and Bohemia, Bismarck at last brought the war to an end and the negotiations to a conclusion. The terms were embodied in the truce of Nickolsburg on July 26 and confirmed in the Treaty of Prague on August 23, 1866.

Austria was to surrender Venetia to Italy, to pay Prussia an indemnity for war expenses equivalent to £3,000,000, to consent to the dissolution of the old Confederation, and to the formation of a North German Union, in which she should have no part. Prussia was to annex, in actual territory, the duchies of Schleswig-Holstein, the kingdom of Hanover, the Electorate of Hesse-Nassau, the old Imperial city of Frankfurt,

The Peace of Prague (August 23, 1866).

and a few smaller additions, comprising in all about three and a quarter million inhabitants and 28,000 English square miles. She was also to form in alliance with the kingdom of Saxony (whose independence was preserved mainly as a concession to Napoleon III)[1] and the other states north of the river Main a new state or empire, which was known as the *Norddeutsche Bund*, or the North German Confederation.

The southern states, Bavaria, Würtemberg, and Baden, were excluded from the North German Confederation, in deference to French objections; they were to retain their separate and independent sovereignties, but they were to be free to form a union among themselves and conclude alliances with the northern group if they chose.

The war of 1866 had thus brought the new Italian kingdom almost to its natural completion—almost, for there were still two districts to which Italians considered themselves by right and by the bonds of race entitled. One was Rome with its immediate neighbourhood, as inevitable a metropolis for Italy as any country was ever provided with. Rome, a capital of the world, the centre of the Catholic Church, was still more clearly the capital and centre of the Italian peninsula. The cession of Venice made the fall of Rome practically unpreventible. "The world is tumbling about our ears," said Cardinal Antonelli. The Roman world was shaken by the defeat of Austria, and the repercussions from the blow at Sadowa sent the most Catholic and Imperial throne of France rocking to its downfall. When the French Empire fell then fell Rome.

The results of the Austro-Prussian War.

The other district was that small area known as the Trentino, beyond the northern Venetian frontier. The cession of Venetia was in the bond between Prussia and Italy, and Venetia Italy should have. But she had done little in the war to deserve a gratuitous gift, and Bismarck was resolved that she should have no more than the stipulated pound of flesh. The province of Venetia was defined with a sparing hand. It was not to include the wedge of Italians in Austrian territory—which, it is true, had not formed part of the political state of Venice—nor the eastern Adriatic provinces of Istria and Dalmatia, which had. From these omissions came the acute Italian problems of recent times.

Prussia had enlarged her kingdom and given herself "the frontiers of a sound state" by the annexation of most of that "corridor" of alien and possibly hostile principalities which had separated the two chief portions of her territory. She had completed that linking up

---

[1] The renunciation of Saxony—a prize thus twice lost to Prussia—was bitterly deplored by King William.

of scattered pieces of her soil which had long marked her historical development. One annexation, that of Hanover, might have caused her a serious international complication but for the accident of Queen Victoria's accession to the English throne in 1837, which had severed the direct connexion between Great Britain and her Continental brother.

Further, the war and its victorious conclusion had justified Bismarck's policy at home—or had seemed to do so. The army for which the Crown and its ministers had struggled had covered the Fatherland with glory and its enemies, domestic and foreign, with shame. The Minister-President, the 'best-hated' man in Prussia, had become its idol, and from the Brandenburger gate the people showered roses upon him whose would-be assassin they had decked with laurels a few months before. He had been vindicated by success, and the liberals were confounded by the man who had served them so faithfully in their own despite. He astonished his friends as much as he converted his enemies. Instead of pressing his new popularity and taking his revenge for past wounds, he graciously asked, after another tussle with the King and the die-hards, for an indemnity for his previous defiance of the constitution. It was overwhelmingly voted, of course, but was it not unnecessary and an admission of culpableness? But Bismarck confused all principles, as he dissolved all parties. A few radicals and ultras remained intransigent, but the main stream of political activity was swept by successful Bismarckism into a new party, with the name of the "National Liberals," whose dominant policy for the next twelve years was not Prussian liberalism, or German nationalism, but, in one word, Bismarck.

It was, however, in his German policy that the war had brought to Bismarck his greatest triumph. In the North German Confederation Prussia had advanced more than half-way toward the unification of Germany under her own leadership. Her dominance was asserted by the new annexations; it was marked in the new constitution [1]—a forecast of that of the Empire of 1871. The new Federal presidency was vested in the Prussian Crown; the Prussian Minister became the Federal Chancellor, the Prussian army, economic system, and postal service became Federal pillars.

Prussianism was strengthened by what seemed at first sight an anti-Prussian measure, the promised Federal Parliament elected by manhood suffrage, the hope of the revolutionaries of 1848. When

---

[1] This constitution was one of Bismarck's most brilliant feats. After two months' serious illness on the island of Rügen, in the Baltic, during which he could only gaze at the blue sky and the green fields and flick the pages of a picture-book like a child, he returned to Berlin and dictated the whole of the constitution of the North German Confederation at a single sitting.

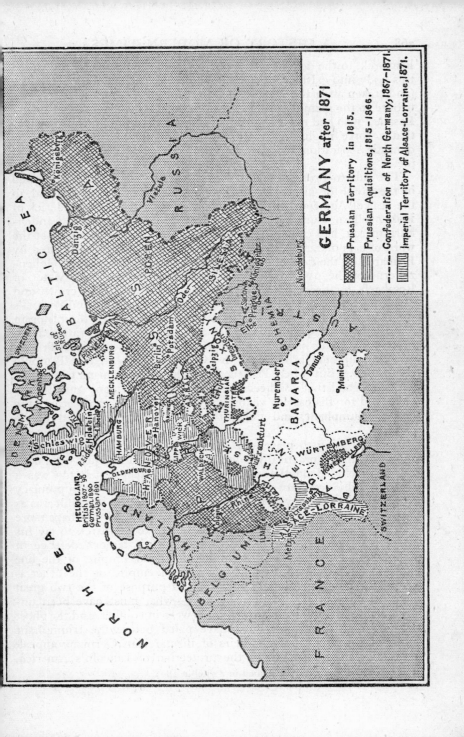

GERMANY after 1871

Prussian Territory in 1815.

Prussian Aquisitions, 1815-1866.

Confederation of North Germany, 1867-1871.

Imperial Territory of Alsace-Lorraine, 1871.

Bismarck, to the delight of the liberals, stood by his word and called this body into existence it was not only as a concession to democracy (and, taken with the rest of the constitution, a small one), or as a tribute to the memory of that great German socialist Jew, Ferdinand Lasalle,[1] who had made so great an impression upon him; it was also that a force might be created strong enough to break down the dynastic separation and particularism which was Prussia's strongest foe.

The Austro-Prussian duel was over. The long contest, conceived in the womb of history when the Habsburg Emperor Sigismund, in the year of Agincourt, had appointed his trusted friend Frederick of Hohenzollern, Burgrave of Nuremberg, to keep the sandy Brandenburg march, had come to fulfilment to the sound of trumpets at the word of a Pomeranian Junker. The word *finis* had been written by Bismarck on the field of Sadowa, with a hand guided by the Hohenzollerns of the past, by his master, Frederick the Great, victor of Rossbach, by Frederick William I, who in 1701 took a crown and defied an Emperor, by the Great Elector, who learnt to find Prussia's profit in Austria's confusion. The great thesis which the historian Treitschke was spending his life and art in demonstrating from professorial chairs seemed to have been proved in action, that Prussia was the supreme product of the German race and the Teutonic civilization. But when Prussia triumphed Prussianism triumphed with her—and that has been the price which Germany and Europe have paid for Bismarck's victories. The nation militant became the nation triumphant, and militant nationalism was justified of its children.

It is tempting to place side by side with the Teutonic struggle another conflict, practically contemporary, which had just been concluded on the other side of the Atlantic. It too was a division between people of one race, a bid for supremacy bound up with the defence of an idea, and its result was as important to the development of the world—perhaps more so. Although it would be unjust to Bismarck to lay his "blood and iron " speech alongside Lincoln's famous defence of popular government, yet the militarist federal Empire of the one must stand beside the democratic federal empire of the other as respective manifestations of the will and purpose of the two great political visionaries. Fifty years later—what must have been unpredictable in 1866—the two empires were in conflict, and the ghost of the great Chancellor must have paled before the triumphant spirit of Lincoln to see the heirs of Bismarckian Germany appeal, in surrender and defeat, to the protection of Lincoln's America,

The results compared with those of the American Civil War.

1 Killed in a duel in 1864.

claiming the privilege of its principles and the charity of its remoteness.

It was not unnatural that Austria, excluded now from Italy and Germany, should turn to the readjustment of her relationship with Hungary. The Franco-Sardinian war of 1859 had already put an end to the "black ten years" which had followed the defeat of the revolution in 1849 and had introduced a period of experiment which culminated after the Austro-Prussian War in the *Ausgleich* or compromise of 1867. On this foundation the Dual Monarchy rested until the Habsburg Empire fell to pieces at the end of the Great War. On the Magyar side the achievement of 1867 was largely the work of the great Hungarian statesman Francis Deák, the Cavour of Hungary, who, like the Italian statesman, leading his country away from extremists, defeated the efforts of the Kossuth nationalists to destroy all connexion with Austria save that of the Crown. He too, gambling, like Cavour, for his reward, kept Hungary out of the Bismarckian intrigues against Austria in 1866. His price was the new partnership of 1867.

The compromise between Austria and Hungary (1867).

The severance of the Austrian connexion with Germany facilitated a working relationship between Austria and Hungary. It has always been one of the chief grievances of the non-Germanic peoples that Vienna looked beyond the Imperial borders to Germany. In their opinion the Habsburgs' place was in the home, and to Hungary especially it was an advantage that outside interests should be curtailed. "Hungary is far better without Austria's German connexions, in which she has no interest," remarked one of the Magyar leaders. Austria's defeat was Hungary's victory; what the former lost in prestige the latter gained. Thus the two were brought nearer to equality.

For the compromise of 1867 was an arrangement between Austria and Hungary, and Austria and Hungary alone, on an egalitarian basis. Although some autonomy was granted to the Poles and the Croats the remaining eight races had no share or profit in it. They remained dependent groups as before, kept under by a league of the two dominant races, German and Magyar, and attempts at 'federation' which aimed at including some of the smaller races in the political partnership were frustrated by the triumph of dualism.

The Empire was divided into two parts, separated by the little river Leitha, the lands of the Austrian Crown to the west, the reconstituted kingdom of Hungary, called the lands of the Hungarian Crown, to the east. The Habsburg sovereign reigned as emperor of the first half and as constitutional king of the second, wearer of the apostolic crown of St Stephen. Each part conducted its own separate government, with a separate Parliament for each. For certain common purposes, for foreign affairs, finances, and the army, joint ministries were to be formed. Disputed points between the two halves of the Empire as well as the Budget for the common ministries were to be arranged by two delegations, consisting of sixty members elected by the Hungarian Diet and sixty by the Austrian Reichsrat, who were to meet every year, alternately at Vienna and Budapest. They were to debate separately and communicate their decision in writing, and if they could arrive at no decisions they were to meet and vote—in silence, to avoid the prickly language question.

On the whole, the arrangement may be said to have worked as long as it lasted, and as far as it referred to Austria-Hungary. It was from the subject races that were kept under by it that the chief discontent of the following years arose.

(c)

It has been seen that the Austro-Prussian War of 1866 was the essential and critical one of the triad in which Prussia was engaged, and it was as the result of that war that the vital foundations of her subsequent power were laid. The third war, to the misfortune of the world, was important enough to the future; to the story of German unity it was something of the nature of a sequel. Prussia and Germany went to the altar in 1866; in 1870 they enlarged their house.

Perhaps the two most urgent aspects of the political situation in Germany immediately after the Austro-Prussian War were the estrangement between Prussia and France and the incompleteness of any union of Germanic states which left out the southern belt of Bavaria, Baden, Würtemberg, and Hesse-Darmstadt. It was the next achievement of Bismarck's statesmanship to bring these two

The Franco-German War. aspects together, to use the estrangement with France to bring the remaining four states into the Prussian system and complete the unification of Germany. "A war with France lay in the logic of history," wrote Bismarck; the logic was also to be pressed into the service of German unity.

Fundamentally the cause of the Franco-Prussian conflict was the deep rivalry between the two countries which had revealed itself in

Underlying cause 1866. The startling growth of Prussian power and the unexpected demonstration of her strength had given to Europe, and more especially to France, an unmistakable challenge. Prussia's victory was a menace to French international prestige, possibly to her national security. "It was felt," says the historian M. de la Gorce, "that in the ground of old Europe something had been broken. Like the Athenians after Philip of Macedon's conquest of Elatea, they had no dead to keep, yet they divined by instinct the loss of their pre-eminence; without having fought, they were oppressed by the sensation of defeat." [1] "It was France," cried Thiers, "who was defeated at Sadowa."

Germany, on the other hand, resented the sense of grievance felt by France; she denied its justification and challenged its equity. There were bitter memories left by the first Napoleon; there was the long historical grudge demanding satisfaction against the Gallic neighbour who had kept Germany weak and divided for her own aggrandizement. France had long enough withheld from Germany her national right to development, and asserted outrageous and intolerable claims to interference. By what authority did she call her still to account?

By such arguments were the tempers of the two peoples lashed to passion and prepared for war. Into the equity of the case it is not necessary to enter. "As long as little Europe suffers from the infatuation of leadership and hegemony, of great Powers and alliances, no nation will be allowed by the others to achieve unity, and thereby acquire enhanced power, except at the cost of war." [2] An occasion of dispute speedily arrived, within less than a year of Königgrätz. Napoleon, egged on by his own ministers, was still bent upon what Bismarck called "a policy of *Pourboires*." When the Mainz proposal was rejected in August 1866 [3] Napoleon turned to the idea of Belgium, [4] and another dangerous document in the French ambassador's handwriting was added to Bismarck's collection—the outline of a suggested treaty between France and Prussia, by which the Hohenzollern monarch should undertake to support the French Emperor if the latter should "be led by circumstances to make his troops enter Belgium, or conquer it." Bismarck held Napoleon in play for a time, but the negotiations went no farther.

French compensation.

The French Emperor thereupon made a further—and last—bid for compensation. This time it was Luxemburg, a little Grand Duchy which had been conferred by exchange upon the King of Holland in 1815 and retained by him after the separation of Belgium. The country had been a member of the German Confederation until 1866 and of the Prussian Zollverein; the city had been declared a Federal fortress by the Congress of Vienna, and had been garrisoned—as there was no Federal standing army—by Prussian troops. As a possession of the house of Orange it could not be included in the

---

[1] Quoted from M. de la Gorce's *Histoire du Second Empire*, vol. xii, by Professor R. B. Mowat, in *A History of European Diplomacy*, p. 205.
[2] Emil Ludwig, *Bismarck*, p. 348.
[3] See p. 263.
[4] According to the French Ambassador (M. Benedetti), it was Bismarck who suggested the idea at Nickolsburg.

new North German *Bund*, and a question had arisen as to the removal of the Prussian troops. It possessed a strong French-speaking element and seemed to Napoleon a sound acquisition. The King of Holland, who was in debt, declared himself willing to sell the Grand Duchy on condition that France undertook to secure the consent of the King of Prussia. Bismarck does not seem to have been at first hostile to the scheme. "As far as Luxemburg is concerned, I will not ask whether the majority is on the side of France, but will simply say 'Take it.'" It seemed a cheap way of satisfying France. As soon, however, as the project became known in Germany it aroused so violent a demonstration of German national hostility that Bismarck was forced to convey to Benedetti and the King of Holland that his Government would be unable to agree to the transfer. The Franco-German rivalry immediately flashed forth. "A land that is essentially German must not fall into the clutches of our hereditary enemies," cried the Germans. "The unification of Germany must go no farther," cried Thiers from the rostrum of the French Parliament. Bismarck published the secret treaties of alliance between Prussia and the South German states, which had been signed the year before. The King of Holland now naturally refused to sell Luxemburg without the consent of the Powers. "Bismarck," said Napoleon, "has tried to dupe me." "He has tried," added the French Foreign Minister, "to lure us into a position without retreat, and to outrage us before Europe." The situation seemed ripe for war; the German war staff wanted it in the belief that France was not ready. But Napoleon again postponed it. Bismarck too can hardly have desired it, or he would not have let pass so favourable an opportunity, nor have suffered in consequence what was regarded in many circles as a diplomatic defeat.

For the French Foreign Minister, then M. Moustier, determined to cover France's retreat with honour, put forward the demand that
The Treaty of London (May 1867). Prussia should evacuate the fortress of Luxemburg. Again the possibility of war lay behind a refusal. But the Powers were working for peace, and Prussia, finding herself isolated in Europe, agreed to Russia's suggestion of a European congress. The Luxemburg Question was therefore laid before the Powers,
The neutrality of Luxemburg guaranteed. who after a four days' session agreed that the Grand Duchy should be declared a neutral state and placed under an international guarantee, that the fortress should be dismantled and the Prussian troops withdrawn. In Paris it was called a French triumph, in Berlin a German victory.

The crisis had passed without war, but for the next three years the international atmosphere was heavy with the threatening storm. On both sides there were warnings and rumours, Benedetti reporting to

France, even Mazzini offering his help to Berlin; there were rumours of alliances, of military preparations. Napoleon turned to Italy, but how could Italy ally with France when French troops garrisoned Rome? There was an exchange of royal visits between Paris and Vienna, but Count Beust, the Austrian statesman, was cautious. With Hungary unwilling and Russia unfriendly it would be safer to wait until after the first French victories. As for Russia, the Bismarckian alliance still held good; the grudge against Austria was still green. A Russo-Prussian understanding would protect Bismarck from Austria, and it proved invaluable to him for that reason in the war crisis; but Alexander II wanted something for Russia from it too, the undoing of the Crimean War.

Without allies abroad or real preparations at home—in spite of the incessant pleadings of Marshal Niel and the untiring activities of the French commander at Strasburg, General Duirôt—France drifted on a general tide of ineffectiveness to the coming disaster.

In the spring of 1870 the political sky seemed clear. Disarmament proposals were in the air; Napoleon III reduced his contingent of conscripts for that year by 10,000 men (a fact duly noted by Moltke), and M. Ollivier and Lord Granville (like Pitt in 1792) asserted that the prognostications for European peace had never been more assured. Suddenly in the hot weather of July the storm broke over Europe. It was an unexpected affair at the last, coming up quickly from the south-west. In 1868 there had been a Spanish insurrection which had driven the sovereign, Queen Isabella, into exile. For nearly two years the Spanish Government looked round for a suitable monarch, finally offering the crown to Prince Leopold of Hohen- *The Hohen-* zollern-Sigmaringen, a South German and Roman Catholic *zollern can-* branch of the Prussian house. His elder brother, Prince *didature.* Charles, had in 1866 been selected to fill the empty throne of Rumania, and had ruled with great success. Prince Leopold was also a grandson of the Murats, and therefore a connexion of the Bonapartes, which seemed to make him acceptable both to France and Prussia.

In March 1870 an important meeting was held in Berlin to discuss the matter; it was partly a family deliberation and partly an informal council of State. Bismarck was present, and pressed for the accept-ance of the offer, but Prince Leopold, after much hesitation, declined. The rejection was conveyed to Spain, and the matter—to Bismarck's disappointment—seemed at an end. At the beginning of June 1870, however, the Prussian Minister suggested to Marshal Prim, the Spanish Minister of War, that the offer should be renewed. A special ambassador was dispatched from Spain to Sigmaringen, and on July 3 Europe was startled by the news that Prince Leopold had

s

accepted the Spanish throne.[1] The French Government had already expressed its disapproval of the candidature; at the news of Prince Leopold's acceptance the Parisian newspapers broke out into violent denunciation of the German menace to the Balance of Power and the safety of France. The French Foreign Minister, the Duc de Gramont, took his cue from the popular mood. On July 6, after a ministerial council at which the Emperor had presided, he declared in the Chamber that unless the candidature were withdrawn "we shall know how to fulfil our duty without hesitation and without weakness." It was a deliberate challenge flung in the face of Germany.

France then set herself to secure the withdrawal of the candidature in an offensive, irritating, and menacing manner, which soon made her appear the aggressor in the war which followed. From the Foreign Office in Berlin Count Benedetti could secure no satisfaction; Bismarck was away on holiday, and his subordinates denied that the affair had any official connexion whatever with Prussia. It was a family affair of the Hohenzollerns, and nothing more. Benedetti therefore turned to the King, who was drinking the waters at Ems, a German spa eleven miles east of Coblenz. On the way he was met by a French *attaché* with definite instructions "to obtain from the King a revocation of the acceptance of the Prince of Hohenzollern. . . . Otherwise it is war."

William I, while protesting that he could not or would not force his relative to a revocation, and pointing with dignity to Gramont's hostile speech on the 6th, was, however, friendly, reasonable, and entirely favourable to a peaceful solution. He was expecting, he said, news from Sigmaringen, and would see the ambassador again. In the meantime from the Quai d'Orsay came urgent messages to Benedetti to demand a definite and speedy renunciation. On July 10 the King of Prussia actually telegraphed to Sigmaringen advising the withdrawal of the candidature, and two days later news was wired to Madrid and to Paris that it had been withdrawn. France had been given her answer. "We have peace now," said M. Ollivier, the head of the liberal ministry, "nor shall we let it escape from us." The Emperor, who was ill, also believed that the danger of war had passed. They were both wrong. Gramont and the French military party wanted war as much as Bismarck and his army chiefs. Benedetti was therefore instructed to demand further from the King "guarantees" that the Hohenzollern candidature should never be renewed, while the ambassador to Paris from the North German *Bund*, Baron Werther, was persuaded to forward to the Prussian King a draft letter of apology. The pride of a nation and a monarch could not

[1] Whether there was any promise of Prussian support behind this acceptance is not known.

have been more insulted. On July 13 occurred the fateful interview on the promenade at Ems between Benedetti and the King. Benedetti pressed for pledges; William I, who had not yet heard of the withdrawal of the candidature, was surprised. Benedetti continued to be insistent, whereupon the King, after a firm but not discourteous refusal, put an end to the interview; the next day he sent an *aide-de-camp* to inform the French ambassador that he had received confirmation of the news from Sigmaringen, and that he now considered the incident closed.

It is probable that war would in any case have followed upon this refusal of pledges, for at a council meeting held subsequently at Saint-Cloud it was decided to stand by the request. But the next impulse came from Bismarck. The Prussian Minister had now become convinced that "war was a necessity which one could not avoid with honour." On the 12th he had received news of the withdrawal of the candidature, which had reduced him to a profound depression and to a disposition to resign from office.

On the 13th he invited Moltke and Roon to dinner with him to discuss the future. It was a melancholy party. Bismarck announced his intention of resigning; the two soldiers complained of their professional inability to do so. During the evening a telegram came in from Ems, with an account of the King's interview of the morning with Benedetti. Bismarck read it aloud, and the dejection of his two guests was "so great that they turned away from food and drink." Then the Minister saw his chance, put a few questions to Moltke as to the state of the army, and made up his mind to publish the telegram in a shortened form to the Press. "If I do this," he explained, "it will have the effect of a red rag upon the Gallic bull." Roon and Moltke were delighted. They fell to eating and drinking again. "Our God of old lives still, and will not let us perish in disgrace!" cried Roon. Moltke smote his breast and said, "If I may but live to lead our armies in such a war then the devil may come directly afterward and fetch away the 'old carcass.'" The telegram was not altered in word, merely abridged, but the difference between its longer and shorter forms was that between "a parley" and "a flourish in answer to a challenge." [1]

The Ems telegram (July 13).

---

[1] The Ems telegram and its modification is famous enough for its text to be given. The original form of the telegram dispatched by Abeken, his Majesty's secretary, ran as follows:

"His Majesty writes to me: 'Count Benedetti spoke to me on the promenade, in order to demand from me finally, in a very importunate manner, that I should authorize him to telegraph at once that I had bound myself for all future time never again to give my consent if the Hohenzollerns should renew their candidature. *I refused at last somewhat sternly, as it is neither right nor possible to undertake engagements of this kind à tout jamais. Naturally I told him that I had as yet received no news, and as he was earlier informed about Paris and Madrid than myself he could*

The effect of the publication of the telegram was as Bismarck had anticipated. It was July 14, the day of national *fête*; the populace was already excited; the Chamber no less so. No Government could have resisted the national demand. Three Cabinet councils were held, the Emperor making a feeble effort to avert the war. "Sire," cried Gramont, "if you mention a congress again I shall throw my resignation at your feet." At last war was decided upon, and announced the next day with rejoicing. "Guarantees we cannot bring you, but we bring you war," cried Gramont. "We accept a great responsibility with a clear conscience and a light heart—*le cœur léger*," added Ollivier, who was to spend forty years arguing away the phrase.

In France and Germany alike the decision was hailed with enthusiasm. Any hopes which the French Government may have entertained that the war would divide the enemy were quickly falsified. In non-Prussian as in Prussian territory the war was equally approved as a righteous and just defence against a tyrannical and aggressive France, the obstructer of German unity. Even Bavaria, which had long nourished ambitions of her own to lead Southern Germany, and had often leaned to a French alliance with some such end in view, determined to fall into line under the Prussian leader against the Power that wanted the left bank of the Rhine and part of the Palatinate. Everywhere the songs of the War of Liberation were revived, and a German nation consolidated and united "in a fit of universal wrath" marched joyfully to war to the strains of *Die Wacht am Rhein*.

While the Prussians shouted "Nach Paris!" outside the Schloss, the Parisians cheered to the cry "À Berlin!" The *Marseillaise* was sung again by permission in the theatres after forty years, and Marshal Le Bœuf proclaimed that "the soldiers of Jena are ready . . . to the last gaiter-button." When the troops marched out of quarters, however, they were found to be unprovided "with the most necessary articles." They often had "no artillery or baggage, ambulance or magazines." Recruits trailed vaguely after their units; a brigadier in Belfort could

French unpreparedness

clearly see that my Government once more had no hand in the matter.' His Majesty has since received a letter from the Prince. His Majesty *having told Count Benedetti that he was awaiting news from the Prince,* has decided *with reference to the above demand, upon the representation of Count Eulenburg and myself,* not to receive Count Benedetti again, *but only to* (and) let him be informed through an aide-de-camp that his Majesty *had now received from the Prince confirmation of the news which Benedetti had already received from Paris, and* had nothing further to say to the ambassador. *His Majesty leaves it to your Excellency whether Benedetti's fresh demand and its rejection should not be at once communicated both to our ambassadors and to the Press.*"

The words in italics were these omitted by Bismarck in the revised version. It was not until 1892 that the German Government published the original form of the telegram.

not find his command. Their officers were insufficient, the railway accommodation inadequate, the intelligence service poor. The staff was better provided with maps of the Germany they were supposed to invade (in order to strike across to an Austria which was supposed to be in alliance with them) than of the French borders which, as it turned out, they had to defend.

Diplomatically too France was isolated. Bismarck had published in *The Times* the draft treaty drawn up by Benedetti for the proposed French conquest of Belgium. Gladstone's Government, at no time in favour of a vigorous foreign policy, was alarmed by the apparent French unscrupulousness. One by one the countries of Europe declared their neutrality. Austria hesitated, but Russia put pressure upon her from the east, and banished the prospect of a Franco-Austrian alliance. Italy too, conscious of a feeling of strain toward Prussia since 1866, wavered; she only needed assurances as to Rome. But Napoleon, faithful to the end to the Roman policy, would not give them, and Victor Emmanuel joined the list of neutrals. "What an escape!" he exclaimed after Sedan.

Within a fortnight the German mobilization was complete, and on August 2 King William arrived at Mainz to take command of the army.

The German forces, consisting of 450,000 men, were divided into three armies, the first toward the north under Steinmetz, the hot-blooded "waster of men," for all his seventy-four years; the second under King William's nephew, Frederick Charles, the "Red Prince," who had already distinguished himself in the Danish and Austrian campaigns; the third, consisting mainly of South Germans, under the Crown Prince. These three armies were to invade France at different points of a line drawn from neutral Luxemburg to the Rhine, along the frontiers of Lorraine and North Alsace.

The French armies were stretched awkwardly upon the same frontier, with the Emperor, as became a Bonaparte, in command at Metz, to the north-west, with MacMahon to the south-east to lead the advance across the Rhine.

It was the Germans, however, who opened the campaign, with a swift offensive. On August 4 the Crown Prince stormed Weissenburg, the scene of early exploits in the French Revolution, and entered Alsace. The next day there was some skirmishing between the French and the first and second German armies round Saarbrücken. The Prince Imperial received his *baptême de feu*; the Germans crossed the Saar. On the 6th there was a battle at Spicheren, which forced the French advance divisions back toward Metz and opened Lorraine to the Germans.

The same day news came from the south. The Crown Prince had decisively defeated the French at Wörth. A detachment of Germans marched south to invest Strasburg, and as Mac-Mahon's broken divisions streamed into Champagne with the Crown Prince's troops upon their flank France began to reflect bitterly that Alsace was lost. There was a crisis in Paris upon the successive defeats, the Ollivier ministry resigned, and the Empress Eugénie [1] remarked that it was now all over with the dynasty, and all that remained was to look after the country; the Emperor transferred his command to a general whose reputation had—exceptionally —survived the Mexican fiasco, the burly Bazaine, and withdrew to Châlons to join MacMahon's army.

Wörth.

Disaster followed disaster. Bazaine's army was hammered back into Metz by a series of blows of which the battle of Gravelotte on August 18 was the most important, and a whole French army was locked in the Lorraine fortress with insufficient supplies. Paris clamoured that MacMahon should advance to Bazaine's relief. He began therefore to march north, intending to approach Metz by a *détour*; with him was the Emperor. "Louis, fais bien ton devoir!" Eugénie had cried in the railway station at parting. Now there were murmurs as to his safety. But the sick man knew his duty. "Je suis décidé à ne pas séparer mon sort de celui de l'armée." He painted his white face and waxed his greying hair, and continued with the army.

Gravelotte (August 18).

Before the brilliant manœuvring of Moltke MacMahon's scheme hopelessly miscarried. An engagement at Beaumont closed the road to Metz and drove him north toward the Belgian frontier. MacMahon's army was soon in worse straits than Bazaine's. On September 1 it was enclosed in the hollow of Sedan in the valley of the Meuse. On all sides it was raked by the German fire, and escape was impossible.

Sedan (September 1).

Toward evening a courier arrived at the German camp with a note for the Prussian King. It contained a single sheet of Imperial note-paper and a brief message:

MONSIEUR MON FRÈRE,

N'ayant pas pu mourir au milieu de mes troupes, il ne me reste qu'à remettre mon epée entre les mains de votre Majesté.

Je suis de votre Majesté le bon Frère,

NAPOLÉON

SEDAN, *le 1 sept.* 1870

---

[1] The Emperor's Spanish wife, whose calmness and courage supported him in his fall as much as her beauty and charm had adorned his Court at its height. She long survived both her husband, Napoleon III, and her son, the Prince Imperial, who was tragically killed in his early manhood, and after many years of retirement, mainly spent in England, she died in 1920 at the great age of ninety-four.

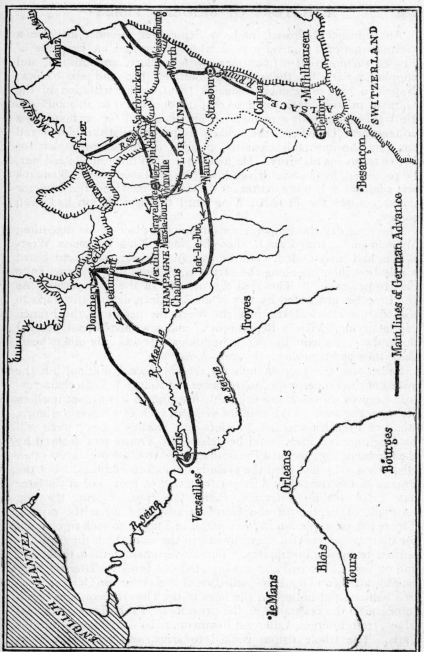

THE FRANCO-GERMAN WAR

Main lines of German Advance

An armistice followed, and on September 2—since become a German national anniversary—a whole army and an Emperor of France surrendered—83,000 men, with artillery, ammunition, and supplies. Early in the morning, between five and six o'clock, Napoleon had summoned Bismarck (who to the irritation of the German military staff would accompany the army) to an interview. He went alone, with a revolver in his belt; and for an hour, in a cottage near Donchery, the broken Emperor, in white gloves and smoking the inevitable cigarette, pleaded in the morning mist for better terms for his army. He had not desired this unhallowed war, he protested, but he was driven into it by public opinion. Bismarck was adamant. It was a matter for the military men; no, the Emperor could not see the Prussian King until the capitulation had been signed.

The next day the Emperor set out for the place of his detention, Wilhelmshohe, near Cassel, where his uncle, King Jerome of Westphalia, had once resided. On the way, in a Belgian station, he heard a newsboy shouting along the platform, "Chute de l'Empire; fuite de l'Impératrice!" Thus fell the dynasty of the Bonapartes. As the Empress proceeded by way of an American dentist's in Paris to the Marine Hotel at Hastings she heard the people of the French capital crying "Vive la République!" and saw them already tearing down the eagles from the public buildings. It was only ninety years since they had torn down the *fleur-de-lis*.

Sedan was the greatest military *débâcle* since Waterloo, but the sword of the Emperor was not the sword of France. With characteristic heroism the new Government, insecure as it was, set itself to carry on the war. "We will not yield an inch of French soil nor a stone of French fortresses." Metz and Bazaine's army were still holding out, and Paris could be defended. France was decoyed by the legend of 1792, when a Prussian invasion and the overthrow of an effete monarchy had been the prelude to glorious victories. But the Prussia of 1870 was very different from that of 1792, and at the later date there was no distracting Polish Question. During the first fortnight of September the Germans advanced upon the capital. Thiers left on a mission to the capitals of Europe to seek foreign aid for the new provisional Government in the war which they had inherited from the Bonapartes. The Government retired to Tours, and on September 19 Paris was invested. A few days later the fiery republican, Léon Gambetta, sailed from Paris over the German lines in a balloon, put himself at the head of the Government, and began to organize the resistance of the provinces. From Tours, from Le Mans, from Bourges, Lille, and Besançon, relief forces set out toward Paris. The whole nation flocked to arms, and volunteers from abroad came to the help of France—Garibaldi and his sons, and a young soldier who was to make a name in greater story, Lieutenant Kitchener. But Gambetta's efforts, like Thiers', were largely unsuccessful. There was a brief gleam of success in the region of Orléans, then failure. On September 27 Strasburg fell; on October 27 Metz and 180,000 men surrendered. There was talk of treason; Bazaine was summoned for trial, and escaped to Spain. At the beginning of the next year, on January 18, Bourbaki's brave army, which had gone to the relief of Belfort, was driven back into Switzerland, and so put out of action. On that day also the King of Prussia was crowned German Emperor.

In the Hall of Mirrors, in the palace of Louis-Quatorze at Versailles, King William stood with the princes of Germany around him, while Bismarck read the Imperial proclamation. The *The King* Prussian Minister looked "pale but calm, elevated, as it *of Prussia* were, by some internal force which caused all eyes to turn *crowned German* on the great figure with the indomitable face, where the *Emperor.* will seemed to be master and lord of all." Then the Grand Duke of Baden raised the cheer "Long live the Emperor William!" The bands burst forth with the national anthem, and the huzzas reached the ears of besieged and besiegers round the Paris walls, eight miles away. Then the new Emperor embraced his son, and, ignoring Bismarck, who was out of favour,[1] shook hands with his generals and walked out of the hall to the strains of the Great Frederick's *Hohenfriedeberg March.* One hundred and seventy years before, to the day, the first King of Prussia had been crowned at Königsberg.

On January 28, ten days later, Paris surrendered, on the edge of famine,[2] after a four months' siege and four weeks' bombardment. Then followed the vain struggles of Thiers, agent of the provisional Government, to secure a reduction in the terms of peace. "I still see him [Thiers]," wrote Jules Favre of an inter- *Interviews* view between Thiers and Bismarck, "pale and agitated, *between Bismarck* now sitting, now springing to his feet; I hear his voice *and Thiers.* broken by grief, his words cut short, his tones suppliant and proud. I know nothing grander than the sublime passion of this noble heart bursting out in petitions, menaces, prayers, now caressing, now terrible, growing by degrees more angry in the face of the cruel refusal."

But Bismarck, looking like a giant in his white cuirassier's uniform,

---

[1] During these days Bismarck stood alone ; he was in open conflict with Moltke and the military party, in disagreement with the Crown Prince, and out of temper with the other German princes. He had lost the favour of his own king over the question of the new title. William had no desire to lose his Prussian title in a German one, but if he must do so he preferred the territorial rank of Emperor of Germany, rather than the title of German Emperor.

[2] Elephants from the Jardin des Plantes were used for food, as well as cats and rats.

was obdurate. The principles of 1866 were not to be adopted in 1871. No potential alliance between Germany and France was to be safeguarded. Bismarck had made the war of 1870 primarily in the interests of German unity, which would be served by a common interest in a conquered possession. "Out of the *Reichsland* should grow the *Reich*." He had made it also in the memory of the past. The victory of Germany over Napoleon III and the provisional Government was a victory also over Louis XIV and Henri II, and from these two kings, who in the seventeenth and sixteenth centuries had robbed her of Alsace and Lorraine, she would obtain belated satisfaction in their recovery. The call from the whole nation was forcing Bismarck's hand. Aggressive Teutonism should be indulged, and this time the military men who wanted a strong defensive frontier for Germany should have their own way—or practically so. Besides, one never knew by what political vagary France would next be dominated. "We have no guarantees of permanence either from you or from any Government that may come after you."

"Well, let it be as you will," cried Thiers; "these negotiations are a pretence. We appear to deliberate, we have only to pass under your yoke. We ask for a city absolutely French, you refuse it to us; it is to avow that you have resolved to wage against us a war of extremity. Do it! Ravish our provinces, burn our homes, cut the throats of our unoffending inhabitants—in a word, complete your work. We will fight to the last breath; we shall succumb at last, but we will not be dishonoured."

It was a vain gesture of helpless defiance. Actually Thiers achieved a slight reduction in the terms of peace. Forty million francs was knocked off the indemnity, and France was to retain the fortress of Belfort, which had held out so heroically, on condition that the Germans had the satisfaction of a military entry into Paris.

The preliminaries of peace, signed at Versailles on February 26, were confirmed in the Peace of Frankfurt on May 10. France agreed to surrender Alsace-Lorraine, including Metz and Strasburg, but excluding Belfort and its territory. The ceded lands covered rather more than 5000 English square miles, and contained 1,600,000 inhabitants and useful iron deposits. She also agreed to a war indemnity of five milliards of francs (£200,000,000),[1] to be paid over a period of three years, during which period German troops were to remain in occupation on French soil.

The Peace of Frankfurt (May 1871).

The Franco-German War made Germany mistress of Europe and Bismarck master of Germany. The political unification under Prussian leadership for which Bismarck had waged

Results of the war.

---

[1] It was reckoned on the basis per head per population of the indemnity demanded by Napoleon of Prussia in 1807.

three wars, for which revolutionaries of 1848, thinkers and writers, poets, philosophers and historians, had all in their different ways prayed or worked, was at last complete. Germany took her place among the nations.

As a pledge of the new union there was Alsace-Lorraine, "Reichsland," neither Prussian nor Bavarian, but Imperial territory. There was also the unhealed wound in the side of France, from which it had been torn. Alsace, seized by Louis XIV at the end of the seventeenth century, might be said to be racially German. Much of Lorraine and the town of Metz were mostly French, however, having been added to the French kingdom by Henri II at the time of the Protestant wars in Germany. "I do not like so many Frenchmen in our house," said Bismarck, who would probably, but for the pressure of the army chiefs, have drawn the line of demarcation east of Metz. Ethically the Alsace-Lorraine Question depends upon the rights accorded to victors in war, upon the respect due to the principle of nationality, upon the circumstances and the length of time in which historical situations can be reversed without wrong. Politically there is no doubt that the annexation of the provinces left in France a demand for vengeance which was not satisfied, and a sense of injury which was not relieved, until more than forty years later a greater war restored the ceded lands to the tricolour.

"Je ne vois plus de l'Europe!" exclaimed Count Beust. As at the releasing of a spring, political forces all over Europe had been set in motion. The troops of Victor Emmanuel had marched into Rome on the news of Sedan, and the Pope was holding aloof in the Vatican. On the surrender of Metz there was a fine gesture from St Petersburg, when Gortschakoff tore up the Black Sea clauses of the Treaty of Paris and cancelled half the results of the Crimean War. There was an empire in Germany that was not Austrian; there was a republic in France. William of Prussia was the greatest sovereign of his day, and Napoleon III an exile in a Kentish village.

The end of Bonapartism had come—not suddenly, for the disasters of the Franco-German War in which the Second Empire fell to the ground were only the culmination of a general Imperial enfeeblement which had set in from 1860. The tragedy of Napoleon III was that he lived on after his reconstructive aims were achieved. The apex of his life had been reached by 1860. He had by then restored the Bonapartist dynasty and persuaded Europe that the Second Empire had a Napoleonic flavour. Men were still sufficiently startled into thinking him a statesman whom up to 1851 they had accounted only an idiot.[1] The illogicalities of his

The end of Bonapartism.

---

[1] Napoleon III, said a relative, deceived Europe twice, once when he succeeded in passing off as an idiot, and next when he succeeded in passing off as a statesman.

position and the inconsistencies of his policy had not yet proved themselves in the ineffectiveness of his Government. For Napoleon III was in a false position. He could not play the part to which he had called himself. He had established a despotism by despotic methods, yet he was no despot. He had invoked the spirit of Bonapartism, and he did not know what to do with it when it responded. He had tried to found a Napoleonic Empire on a good deal of hero-worship and a multiplicity of interests.

He was neither ungenerous nor unenlightened, and "his mind was as full of schemes as a warren is full of rabbits." At home he promoted the welfare of his people, improved housing, gave medical, legal, professional, and financial facilities to the poorer classes; he encouraged agriculture, industry, education, and art, opened up harbours, developed canals, roads, and railways; he patronized the town-planning schemes of M. Haussmann in Paris, and drew the eyes and feet of the world to the French capital by international exhibitions. Nevertheless he never succeeded in attaching to himself any strong party in the state. The socialists and republicans were against him, so were the monarchists. His policy of enlightened despotism failed to convince, for the enlightenment was overlooked in the despotism which dispensed it; nor were the liberals conciliated when the autocratic empire of 1860 was turned by progressive infusions of Parliamentarianism into the liberal empire of 1870. His concessions had the appearance of following rather than leading public opinion, of indicating weakness rather than regeneration. Industry prospered, but the commercial classes were antagonistic to his free trade policy with England and the other European states; and the Church, for whose goodwill he staked his crown, denounced his Italian achievements and called him a traitor.

He sought rather to dazzle than to govern France, by a brilliant Court, by international exhibitions, by far-flung enterprises, by the Suez Canal,[1] by expeditions to China and Syria, by a prospective empire in Mexico, by an active foreign policy. Inconsistently he tried to crown military glory with an empire which he had proclaimed should be synonymous with peace—"L'Empire, c'est la paix."

His foreign policy, after a striking beginning, also turned to failure. Success was essential to his hold over France after 1860, and success evaded him. He could not outmanœuvre an enemy, nor hold firm an ally. Neither the Danish nor the Polish nor the Austrian Question brought him credit. The attempt to found a Latin Catholic empire in Mexico, on which he wasted good years of the sixties while Prussia

[1] The architect of the Suez Canal, M. de Lesseps, was a cousin of Napoleon's wife, the Empress Eugénie.

was growing strong, ended in disastrous failure. French troops were defeated; the Austrian archduke Maximilian, whom Napoleon had persuaded to play the *rôle* of emperor, was put to death, and the enterprise finally abandoned at the bidding of the United States. The Imperial resources were strained, and the Imperial prestige destroyed beyond recovery.[1]

The strong Anglo-French alliance of the Crimean War had dwindled away by the time of the Schleswig-Holstein affair. The *rapprochement* with Russia which the French Emperor cultivated after the Congress of Paris he destroyed by his sympathy with the Polish rising of 1863. When Bismarck performed a service he secured a friend; Napoleon gave great gifts to Italy, but forfeited her gratitude; the annexation of Savoy wiped out Magenta, and the support of the Papacy lost him the alliance of his *protégé*, the Italian kingdom. So in 1866 he alienated Prussia without winning Austria to his side.

Nevertheless his policy was not as self-seeking as that of many a European state of the time. His formula for international peace, a European congress, was a reversion to the abandoned ideal of the Concert of Europe, and in a sense an anticipation of the co-operative aims of to-day. His professed sympathy with nationalist aspirations was sincere in spite of its tendency to be directed to France's profit and to be accompanied by a *note d'aubergiste* (innkeeper's bill). But he puzzled rather than guided Europe, and in the end was neither understood nor trusted.

His policy both at home and abroad was inconsistent and unreliable, tending to piecemeal devices to stave off the immediate problem. "I never form distant plans; I am governed by the exigencies of the moment." His ambitions, his interests, and his principles conflicted, and "Napoleon le Petit" had not the genius of "Napoleon le Grand" to harmonize them within a dominating personality. A curious sense of fatalism and a vein of diffidence stultified his powers, prevented synthetic thought and effective action. "Il ne faut pas brusquer." Things would come to him as the Empire had come, in his destiny. In the last years illness further weakened his grip. Such men are not well served, and *où trouver l'homme* was one of his constant problems. So the Bonapartist

[1] The Mexican enterprise of Napoleon III is comparable to the Louisiana Purchase and the San Domingo exploit of the first Napoleon. Each man's Central American venture ended disastrously. Upon the failure of Mexico to pay its foreign debts, France, England, and Spain determined upon a combined intervention. But "while England was proposing to assure herself an advantageous compensation for her wasted loans in Mexico by administering the customs, while Spain was dreaming of re-establishing one of her own princes there, Napoleon III was seeking to satisfy both the Catholics and the liberals at the same time, by the establishment of a great Catholic and Latin empire in Mexico."

dynasty, which in the memory of France had stood above all things for efficiency and power, came to be associated with corruption, incompetence, and defeat, and in 1870 France drifted alone to disaster, for the man at the helm "lived by the light of a star" that had paled.

IV. RUSSIA, 1855–81

The Crimean War was in a general sense the watershed of European history; the statement may be with particular force applied to Russia. The Russian defeat discredited wholly the system of Nicholas I and set on foot a movement toward democracy which in one form or another has been the principal theme of her internal history from that day to this.

The thirty years' reign of Nicholas was spent in the defence of autocracy. Abroad the Russian armies were lent for its support; at home all kinds of measures were adopted to exclude or suppress liberal ideas. A "stringent intellectual quarantine" was maintained upon the western frontiers; foreign literature of a political or philosophical nature was excluded; Russian subjects were prevented from travelling abroad; the native Press was censored, and writers who did not show themselves "well intentioned" were silenced; the humblest as well as the most powerful servant of the Emperor was rigidly protected from criticism, even to the actors in the Court Theatre. The universities were circumscribed in their personnel and their curricula, the number of military schools was increased, and the police, the "Third Section of the Tsar's Private Chancellery," were given arbitrary powers of "arresting, imprisoning, deporting, and making away with" anyone whom the chief of the department selected.

The rule of Nicholas I (1825–55).

Russian literature was encouraged, that the interests of the people might be diverted from politics, and nationalism emphasized as a defence against the influences of international liberalism. The whole nation was treated as an army, to be drilled in habits and thoughts.

Then came the disasters of the Crimean War; the armies of the great Russian autocrat were defeated by those of the liberal West; the Treasury was found to be empty through the dishonesty and incompetence of the bureaucracy before whom the people had bent their backs. The military idol to whom so much had been sacrificed had led them only to defeat. The system of Nicholas was condemned by the same standard by which the system of Bismarck was approved ten years later in Prussia. Russian autocracy was shamed by failure, and Russian discontent, smouldering before the war, flared into open protest. Liberal propaganda was circulated by hand in manuscript literature; satire, and philippic, and pasquinade, and appeal were drawn into its service, against the Government.[1] Russian society was stirred by as violent a movement and as naïve an optimism as was France on the eve of the French Revolution.

The way to reform was prepared by the death of Nicholas I in the beginning of 1855, and by the accession of the "Tsar Liberator" Alexander II. He was a man of kindly and humane instincts, with none of his father's love of soldiering. His education had given him little chance of developing political opinions other than those which were popular at Court, nor up to the time of his accession had he shown any strong individual

Alexander II (1855–81).

[1] Sir Donald Mackenzie Wallace, in his history of Russia, quotes an example of this kind of literature which, though unprinted, was widely circulated :

" ' God has placed me over Russia,' said the Tsar to us, ' and you must bow down before me, for my throne is His altar. Trouble not yourselves with public affairs, for I think for you and watch over you every hour. My watchful eye detects internal evils and the machinations of foreign enemies ; and I have no need of counsel, for God inspires me with wisdom. Be proud, therefore, of being my slaves, O Russians, and regard my will as your law.'

" We listened to these words with deep reverence, and gave a tacit consent ; and what was the result ? Under mountains of official papers real interests were forgotten. The letter of the law was observed, but negligence and crime were allowed to go unpunished. While grovelling in the dust before ministers and directors of departments, the officials stole unblushingly ; and theft became so common that he who stole the most was the most respected. . . . The offices were filled up with little attention to the merits of the candidates. A stable-boy became Press Censor ! an Imperial fool became admiral ! ! . . .

" And what did we Russians do all this time ?

" We Russians slept ! With groans the peasant paid his yearly dues ; with groans the proprietor mortgaged the second half of his estate ; groaning, we all paid our heavy tribute to the officials. Occasionally, with a grave shaking of the head, we remarked in a whisper that it was a shame and a disgrace—that there was no justice in the courts—that millions were squandered on Imperial tours, kiosks, and pavilions—that everything was wrong ; and then, with an easy conscience, we sat down to our rubber, praised the acting of Rachel, criticized the singing of Frezzolini, bowed low to venal magnates, and squabbled with each other for advancement in the very service which we so severely condemned. If we did not obtain the place we wished we retired to our ancestral estates, where we talked of the crops, fattened in indolence and gluttony, and lived a genuine animal life. If anyone, amidst the general lethargy, suddenly called upon us to rise and fight for the truth and for Russia, how ridiculous did he appear ! How cleverly the Pharasaical official ridiculed him, and how quickly the friends of yesterday showed him the cold shoulder ! Under the anathema of public opinion, in some distant Siberian mine he recognized what a heinous sin it was to disturb the heavy sleep of apathetic slaves. . . .

" But amidst all this we had at least one consolation, one thing to be proud of—the might of Russia in the assembly of kings. ' What need we care,' we said, ' for the reproaches of foreign nations ? We are stronger than those who reproach us.' . . . Then British statesmen, in company with the crowned conspirator of France, and with treacherous Austria, raised Western Europe against us, but we laughed scornfully at the coming storm. ' Let the nations rave,' we said ; ' we have no cause to be afraid. The Tsar doubtless foresaw all, and has long since made the necessary preparations.' Boldly we went forth to fight, and confidently awaited the moment of the struggle.

" And lo ! after all our boasting we were taken by surprise, and caught unawares, as by a robber in the dark. . . . One courier brought the order to advance ;

bias or independence of judgment. He was, however, a great lover of Russia, deeply sensitive to her humiliations, and conscious of his own responsibility. He was not a doctrinaire or theorist, and the liberal sentimentalizings of his uncle, Alexander I, were anathema to him. The reforms upon which, to the general surprise, he embarked at the beginning of his reign were not the emanations of democratic conviction so much as concessions to practical need. Russia had lost her high place in the world, and only by a profound transformation of her whole economy could she recover it. He committed himself to no policy, announced no lofty programme of social amelioration. He felt the new spirit of the age, and he responded to the dictates of a generous humanity, but he guided the course of reform with moderation; he carefully guarded the royal prerogatives, and obstinately refused to go farther than he wished.

He began by releasing the Dekabrist exiles—those that were left of them—who thirty years before had been banished to Siberia for **The first ten years of reform.** participation in the army insurrection which had inaugurated the reign and soured the political temper of his father, Nicholas I. He then turned to the development of Russia's natural resources, to the encouragement of industry and commerce, to the planning, for both military and economic reasons, of a railway system, for want of which the empire had suffered so disastrously in the Crimean War. But the most urgent reform was the suppression of that social evil which dishonoured Russia before Europe, compromised her security, and retarded her economic development—serfdom.

There were nearly forty-five million serfs in Russia, forming about half her population. Twenty-three million belonged to the Crown, the rest to private lords, the Church, and other institutions. Those on the royal domain were far better off than those in private hands.

another brought the order to retreat ; and the army wandered about without definite aim or purpose. With loss and shame we retreated from the forts of Silistria, and the pride of Russia was humbled before the Habsburg eagle. . . .

" Awake, O Russia ! Devoured by foreign enemies, crushed by slavery, shamefully oppressed by stupid authorities and spies, awaken from your long sleep of ignorance and apathy ! You have been long enough held in bondage by the successors of the Mongol Khan. Stand forward calmly before the throne of the despot, and demand from him an account of the national disaster. Say to him boldly that his throne is not the altar of God, and that God did not condemn us to be slaves. Russia entrusted to you, O Tsar, the supreme power, and you were as a God upon earth. And what have you done ? . . . You buried Truth, rolled a great stone to the door of the sepulchre, placed a strong guard over it, and said in the pride of your heart : For her there is no resurrection ! But the third day has dawned, and Truth has arisen from the dead.

" Stand forth, O Tsar, before the judgment-seat of history and of God ! . . . Bow down before your brethren and humble yourself in the dust ! Crave pardon and ask advice ! Throw yourself into the arms of the people ! There is now no other salvation ! "

The former suffered from heavy taxation, from forced labour, from extortion and oppressive fiscal dues; their movements were restricted, as was their right to acquire or dispose of property. But they were grouped together in village communities known as *mirs*, and enjoyed a certain measure of self-government through elected councils and village elders. The condi- The emancipa- tion of the serfs (1861). tion of the serfs of private landlords and of those in domestic service varied with the character and views of their owners. They had no power of redress against any abuse that was chosen to be practised upon them, and instances of cruelty and intolerable op- pression have been multiplied. The Russian law of serfage em- powered a proprietor "to impose upon his serfs every kind of labour, to exact money dues and personal services from them." He could sell them as he chose, transport them to Siberia, or threaten them with the 'shaving of the head'—*i.e.*, hand them over as recruits to the army.

They perished by hundreds in the factories established . . . to aug- ment the incomes of the great landed proprietors. They were sub- jected to inhuman punishments, imprisoned in underground cellars, kept in chains, or flogged to death with the knout. . . . A whole series of such crimes were brought to light . . . on the properties of the highest dignitaries of the State—men who enjoyed in St Petersburg the reputa- tion of statesmen and even of philanthropists.[1]

These serfs were far more unfortunate than those of France before 1789; they were, in fact, veritable slaves, and it is no defence of the system that there might commonly be found in Russia before 1861, as in America before 1865, serfs and slaves who were fortunate in their conditions, contented in their lot, and happier than many a free man in other times and countries.

Russia suffered the common consequences of the system in the moral degeneration of the serf-holding classes, economic stagnation, and the constant fear of insurrection. From the days of Peter III, when, in 1762, the nobles had been released from the obligation to military service, the peasant serfs had not ceased to demand emanci- pation. Serfage was to them a corollary of compulsory military service among the nobility, and the abolition of the latter implied the abolition of the former. Numerous revolts during the reign of Nicholas I emphasized the social insecurity of unredeemed serfage. Nicholas himself had contemplated the manumission of the serfs, but he had only advanced as far as burying the question in commis- sions of inquiry. On the conclusion of the Peace of Paris, however, Alexander resuscitated the problem and made definite proposals to

[1] *The Cambridge Modern History*, vol. x, Chapter XIII.

T

his nobility. "You know that the present system of serf ownership cannot remain as it is; it is better that we should abolish it from above, than wait until it begins to abolish itself from below. . . . Gentlemen, I beg you to examine how this reform can be made."

Nevertheless the nobility, though it accorded generous homage to the theoretical doctrines of human equality, dallied with the practical problem of setting free its own serfs, and the Imperial Government was again forced to take the initiative. At the end of 1857 the nobles of the Lithuanian provinces of the Russian Empire petitioned for a revision—in their favour—of the relations between the nobles and the serfs. Alexander I, however, pretending to believe that the Lithuanian nobles desired the emancipation of their serfs, invited the other provinces of Russia to emulate the generous and patriotic example of Lithuania. The royal tact was rewarded, and committees authorized by the Tsar were formed "for the ameliorating of the conditions of the peasants." An examination of the question revealed an entanglement of conflicting interests and confused problems, and it was not until 1861 that the Imperial ukase was finally issued which abolished serfdom and set free nearly 35,000,000 people. Four years later, in another hemisphere, the Imperial edict was matched by a Presidential decree, and in philanthropic intention and political power "Abe" Lincoln, the backwoodsman, President of the Republic of the United States of America, is linked for all time in the history of civilization with Alexander the Romanov, autocrat and Holy Tsar of All the Russias.

The edict of emancipation of Alexander II—a measure not only of profound moral, but also of the greatest economic, importance—was based on four main principles.

The first was embodied in the concession of full civil rights. The serf became a free peasant, absolved from bondage to his master.

To the other three principles a special economic interest is attached. The serf was to be given not only freedom, but land, and the noble was to lose not only his labourer, but some of his property. It was realized that one of the dangers of emancipation would be to form a very large class—half the population—of landless proletarians, who would be thrown with no means of livelihood upon the country, who would cheapen labour, easily fall victims to capitalist exploitation, and create a greater number of social and economic problems than had been removed by liberation. The same problem confronted emancipation in the British Colonies in 1833, and in America in 1865. In Russia it was hoped to avoid the threatened evil by transferring land—i.e., part of the estates of the nobles—to the peasants. The amount was to be fixed in each case by magistrates, called Arbiters of the Peace, who were to decide between the nobles and the peasants.

The arbiters were in most cases local proprietors, but the division is generally conceded to have been done with astonishing impartiality. The third principle enjoined, however, that the land was not to be bestowed upon the peasant in personal ownership,[1] but in communal ownership upon the village group, or *mir*, to which he was attached. The *mir* held the land, and the *mir* was collectively responsible for certain yearly payments which were to be given to the lord in compensation.

Lastly the Government was to help the village groups to redeem the annual dues to the former owner of the soil by lending them sums of money equal to the capitalized value of the land. On these amounts the Government was to receive 6 per cent. interest for a period of forty-nine years.

By these arrangements the peasant was provided with a means of subsistence, and Russia protected from the evil of numbers of penurious peasants. The collective ownership of the *mir* was substituted for the private ownership of the lord, and the responsibility for the collection of redemption dues was placed upon the entire peasant body.

So sweeping a measure did not pass without considerable criticism. The Tsar recorded the generosity of the nobles—and with justice—but they raised vigorous protest "against the invasion of the sacred rights of property," and the dangerous stimulus that would be given to the covetousness of the peasants; the safety and prosperity of the countryside, they alleged, would be threatened, and authority transferred from the educated classes to the ignorant and irresponsible *moujik*.

The practical effects of the emancipation on the land-owning classes varied in different parts of the country, but it generally resulted in an enforced economy and in a more scientific administration of their estates. "Formerly we kept no accounts, and drank champagne," said one of the nobles. "Now we keep accounts, and content ourselves with beer." [2]

To the peasants it brought deep disappointment. On the surface the edict was revolutionary; in practice it effected little economic improvement in their condition. They found themselves burdened with new taxes—often in excess of the normal rent of their land—which were a heavy drain on their resources, and were "What, then, is this liberty?" held to be a grave injustice. They had come to regard the land they occupied as their own, and saw no reason why they should now pay compensation to the lords for it. The authority of the *mir* was as irritating as that of the lords. As for

[1] Except in the west of Russia.
[2] Quoted by Sir Donald Mackenzie Wallace, *Russia*.

the compulsory labour on the lord's estate, they claimed that they were entitled to relief from that from the day when the lord was released from military service. "What, then, is this liberty?" the peasants demanded, and their answer was in effect that it was an illusion.

The emancipation of the serfs, the greatest of Alexander's reforms, was speedily followed by others, and for the first time in the history of Russia public opinion was allowed to influence public affairs. The disabilities were removed from the universities and from foreign travel; the Press censorship was considerably modified, the army and navy reorganized, the annual publication of the Russian Budget begun, and, more especially, important changes were introduced into the judicial administration and into local government.

The judicial system was full of abuses, and it was rotten to the core with wholesale venality and corruption; litigation was hedged Judicial about with formalities and encompassed by secret pro-reforms. cesses. An entirely new judicial structure was set up, modelled on French and English lines. The administrative and judicial functions were separated, the independence of the magistrates promoted, oral procedure and trial by jury established. A new penal code was introduced, and civil and criminal cases simplified. Justices of the Peace, chosen by popular election, were instituted to deal with minor affairs; more important suits were reserved for regular tribunals composed of trained judges appointed by the Crown. New measures required new men, however, and these Russia did not possess. For a time the working of the reformed system was hampered by the absence of a personnel trained by and for the new conditions. Habits of corruption were difficult to eradicate; the magistrates were often incapable, the juries ignorant and extravagant; but corruption was reduced, and a sense of justice was gradually fostered throughout the nation and the judicial services.

The Crimean War had shown up the inefficiency of the administration, and radical changes were introduced in the Moscow provinces, Adminis- in the direction of decentralization and local autonomy. trative New councils, or zemstvo,[1] were set up, representing all reforms. classes of the community, the nobles, the peasants, and the bourgeois, or commercial sections. The councils were of two kinds, the district council, elected by a popular suffrage, and the provincial council, elected by the district council. The new local bodies were entrusted with the duties of electing the Justices of the Peace, of repairing roads and bridges, of supervising sanitation and primary education, and of taking measures against famine. Their power was restricted by the right of veto over their decisions pos-

[1] Etymologically the word means 'land councils.'

sessed by the governor of the province, and by their lack of adequate financial resources.

By these wide reforms, especially of serfage and of the judicial and local administrations, Alexander II performed as great a service as Peter the Great in bringing Russia into line with Western nations. A new spirit began to pervade Russia, a new literature of economics, philosophy, and politics sprang up, a marked impulse was given to education, and the Press swarmed with Utopias. The concession of local autonomy was to be merely a preface to the grant of complete political self-government. Russia was to imitate the nations of the West.

Then followed bitter disappointment. From 1866 the direction of Alexander's reign began to change. There were a few subsequent edicts affecting local government and the army, but the Disillusionspirit of reform had withered. Progress was checked, and ment. the first ten years of rapid movement were followed by stagnation and then reaction. The change was due partly to the general and profound disillusionment which followed the new measures; the peasants still felt themselves oppressed, the new law-courts were not working well, the administration was still corrupt and discontent great. It was also largely caused by the second Polish insurrection of 1863.

To the Polish as to the Russian subjects of the Tsar the concessions of Alexander had brought a new dawn. The vigorous repressive system of Nicholas I was relaxed, and the political exiles The Polish were allowed to return. The Polish Council of State was insurrection re-established, together with the Commission for the Regu- of 1863. lation of Religious Affairs and Education, which had been abolished in 1839. A considerable measure of self-government was granted; the Polish and Russian administrations were made separate; the civil and military departments differentiated, and the former put into the hands of Poles. A system of local government by means of elected councils was set up as in Russia; Polish education was encouraged, the University of Warsaw restored, and the use of the Polish language was authorized in schools. In short, a real attempt was made to conciliate the nationalist aspirations of the subject Poles, and to turn the country into a self-governing province of the Russian Empire.

The conciliating efforts failed utterly. The declaration of religious equality, welcome to the Jews, was held by the Roman Catholics to be a device for furthering the hated cause of the Orthodox Church. The political concessions were held to be signs of weakness, and, encouraged by the emancipation of the Russian serfs, the extremists increased their agitations and raised their claims. They demanded not only the complete independence of a new Polish republic, but also the reconstitution of the old "Great Poland" as it existed before the first partition of 1772. This would have meant the cession—besides West Prussia, Prussian Posen, and Austrian Galicia—of Western Russia as far as Kiev and Smolensk, territory which had been in Russian hands for more than a century, and which was, moreover, ethnographically Russian, having been won previously by Poland in conquest. As King Leopold of Belgium wrote to his niece, Queen Victoria, to whom he was in the habit of giving advice, "It is impossible for Alexander or the Russian nation to give up these provinces." The Pan-Slavist sentiment of Russia was roused to intense indignation, and Alexander felt himself bound to check such extravagant Polish propaganda. The Poles replied with intrigue, conspiracy, and violence that raised the country to a ferment of unrest. The extremists were set upon producing a revolution, and every step of Alexander's, conciliatory or repressive, was used only to add fuel to the conflagration that was being prepared.

In the spring of 1863 the spark was added to the powder. In characteristically Russian fashion the Tsar tried to put an end to the revolutionary agitation which had already aimed at the life of one of his viceroys by enrolling a number of political suspects in Russian regiments scattered throughout the Empire. The threatened men fled to the forests and raised the banner of insurrection.

The extremists, or 'Reds,' rose at once, the 'Whites,' or moderates, hesitated, but being assured that only after a national rising had already broken out would Napoleon III give any help they finally joined the revolutionaries.

The second Polish insurrection, of 1863, was not a war between organized armies, as in 1830. It was a sporadic conflagration, breaking out in one place while it was being suppressed in another, a war not of regular tactics and of pitched battles, but of raids and surprises, of ambuscades and skirmishes, characterized by frightful brutality on both sides. It showed heat and force, but without systematic organization it would have little chance of success against the Russian armies. The Poles were themselves divided. The nobles, gentry, townsfolk, and priesthood rose with zeal, but the peasants were too full of grievances against their own lords to join with them with enthusiasm.

Failure.

Only foreign support could have made the rebellion of the Poles a success, and upon this they confidently counted. But Prussia, the nearest and therefore the most important foreign country, where Bismarck had his own reasons for desiring to cultivate Russian friendship, turned sternly against them. "It is a matter of life and death to us also," said Bismarck, and posted cordons of Prussian troops along the Polish frontier. It was to France, indeed, that

Poland looked with most hope. Had not Napoleon given help to Rumania and Italy? Was not Napoleon's minister and adviser in Polish affairs the Pole Count Walewski, whose mother, if rumour could be credited, had already done so much to further Poland's cause?

Napoleon interested himself in the Polish cause, and a spate of diplomatic notes flooded the chancelleries of Europe. He was ready with his proposal of a European congress, but England, to whom the cession of Nice and Savoy was still a recent grievance, who had come to suspect Napoleon of a desire to fish in troubled waters merely for his own advantage, gave a curt refusal to serve the purposes of France. Austria was put out of court by Napoleon's raising the Venetian Question at the same time as the Polish; thus "the sorry results of weeks of negotiations was the presentation, first to Prussia and finally to Russia, of colourless protests which those Powers could afford to treat with contempt." As in 1830, the Poles were left to their fate.

The struggle on the Polish side passed into the hands of a self-constituted body, the secret national Government at Warsaw, who kept the insurrection alive by the assassination and the terrorization of their own people. Vainly the Tsar promised an amnesty and the preservation and continuation of reforms. The rebellious Poles dared not give in their submission.

Though the end was by this means postponed the result could not be uncertain, and by March 1864 the insurrection was suppressed.

For a whole year terror had reigned in Poland—the terror of war, the terror of the secret Government, and the terror of the Russian repression, and as the outcome there was nothing but the revelation, to the best of those who had taken part in the insurrection, of the tragic folly of their actions. " The insurrection of 1863," wrote Stanislaus Kozmian, " helped the greatest enemy of Poland and the Polish cause to success. On the ruins of the Polish Revolution rose the work of Bismarck and the system of Russification in the Empire of the Tsars." [1]

On the terms of the resettlement that followed Poland was governed until the war of 1914. The policy varied in detail with the will of the viceroy or governor, and with internal affairs in Russia, but its main lines were generally followed.

First Poland was deprived of all autonomy. The Polish kingdom was incorporated in the Russian Empire as the "Ten Governments of the Vistula."

Secondly, the Polish nobility being entirely discredited, an appeal was made to a new class—to the Polish peasants who were their enemies. A vast scheme of agrarian reform was undertaken in

[1] Professor W. Alison Phillips, *Poland*, Chapter X (" Home University Library").

pursuance of this principle. All the peasants, whatever the tenure by which they held their land, were turned into freeholders, retaining at the same time their right of access to the forests and pastures of the lords. The landlords received compensation, but were compelled to take it in 4 per cent. Treasury bonds, which would give them, it was hoped, an interest in maintaining the credit of the Government. The result of these decrees was to create a body of 1,340,000 peasant proprietors. "We hold Poland by its rights of Common," boasted a Russian statesman.

Further laws were passed establishing a new local administration which would segregate the peasants from the rest of the community. The peasants were grouped into communes with an elected assembly and mayor to each commune, taken wholly from the peasant class. The larger landowners and clergy were excluded. To the assembly was given the regulation of all the affairs of the village community and the conduct of its relations with the Russian Government. "The intention was to keep the happy peasant pure and undefiled by contact with the elements most hostile to Russia; the effect was to deliver him body and soul to the petty tyranny of the local representatives of Russian majesty." [1]

The third principle on which the settlement of Poland was based —although its application varied considerably during the years following the insurrection—was that of 'Russification.' This was a deliberate attempt to remove or repress every stimulus to Polish nationalism, and to effect a complete organic incorporation of Poland with Russia. The Roman Catholic Church, which was the backbone of Polish nationalism, was deprived of its privileges; the ecclesiastical lands were confiscated and the monasteries suppressed. The Russian language was authorized as the sole medium of public communication, in schools, universities, and the State. Poles were in time replaced by Russians in the courts of justice and other official posts. All who had taken part in the political troubles were banished, and all motions toward independent political activity were suppressed. On the other hand a great effort was made for a time to keep those who refrained from politics well amused. The social life of Warsaw was encouraged in every way; large sums were spent by the Government on the opera and the theatres, and the Polish capital rapidly developed into a cosmopolitan city of pleasure, the Paris of Eastern Europe.

As the liberal movement at the beginning of the reign of Alexander II had strengthened the aspirations of Poland, so the Polish insurrection confirmed the reaction in Russia. Russian society fell from a mood of extreme exaltation to one of extreme depression, and a

[1] Professor W. Alison Phillips, *Russia*, Chapter X ("Home University Library").

violent division of opinion formed itself among the educated classes. On one side were the conservatives and reactionaries, who thought that the reforming phase had already gone too far, whose creed consisted of three articles—Holy Russia, the Orthodox Church, and the Imperial autocracy.   On the other were the nihilists.

It was Turgeniev, in his novel *Fathers and Sons*, who in 1862 baptized the movement which was beginning to manifest itself in Russian universities with the name of nihilism.   The nihilist, in the character of Bazarov, is represented as "one **Nihilism.** who does not bow down before any authority, who does not take any principle on faith, whatever reverences that principle may be entwined in."   He is convinced that "there is no single institution in our present mode of life, in family or in social life, which does not call for complete and unqualified destruction."   "The autocracy of the Tsar, the authority of the State, the sanctity and truth of the Church, the obligations of society," were called in question as much as the merits of family life, the justification of private property, or the binding character of legal contracts.   The gods of a *bourgeois* civilization were hauled down from their pedestals, its private and public codes of morality and respectability, the subjection of its women, the capitalist exploitation of industry, its sycophantic art.   A shoemaker had made a greater contribution to the world than Shakespeare or Goethe, for shoes were more needed than poetry.   The nihilist set himself to be a stern realist and a rigid utilitarian, to remove from the eyes of the world, if not by persuasion then by shock or force, the blinkers of cant, sentiment, prejudice, authority, tradition, and convention.   Turgeniev calls nihilism the "spirit of absolute negation, and of barren criticism."   The description partakes of the exaggeration of caricature, for although nihilism was primarily destructive there was a positive side to the movement.[1]   The ground was to be cleared that society might be built anew from a *tabula rasa*. It is true that the prophets of the new creed were not very clear as to the shape that the future social erection should take; some were inclined to trust to the natural forces of evolution; others supplied formulæ based on the latest scientific, biological, or philosophical theories.   Religion was to be replaced by the exact sciences, family life by free love, private property by collectivism, and a centralized administration by a federation of independent communes.   A complete transformation was at any rate to be effected from below, not from above.

There was about these ideas a strong socialist bias, and many nihilists were in close touch with the revolutionary and anarchist socialism of Bakunin and his followers in Western countries, especially

[1] As illustrated in Tchernishevski's book *What is to be done?* written in prison.

in France. It would, however, be no fairer to identify them all with socialism [1] than with enthusiasm for the natural sciences with which they were equally strongly associated. For a marked impulse toward scientific education and a distaste for the humanities dominated the universities at this time, and was encouraged by the Government until its political tendencies were revealed.

Nihilism was essentially the creed and the mood of the intelligentsia; some of its catchwords became later the property of the proletariat, but they were coined in the universities. It began as an academic movement of reckless youth and impatient reformers; it developed into a revolutionary anarchism of a terrorist type.

The tightening of the Press censorship drove the nihilists to a tremendous effort to spread their propaganda by direct intercourse among the working people of town and country. Ardent young enthusiasts of both sexes went among the people, as doctors, nurses, teachers, or disguised as artisans or labourers. Many sought peacefully to rouse the poorer classes from a lethargic acceptance of abuses. Many, on the other hand, tried to stir them to revolution, urging them to get rid of the selfish landed proprietors and district officials, who, they alleged, were keeping from them the land bestowed upon them by the Tsar.

A rigorous Government repression of the agitation—between 1863 and 1874 nearly 150,000 persons were deported to Siberia [2]—turned it into more dangerous channels. It entered upon the stage of political terrorism by assassination and outrage. "The propagandist movement was a sublime test of the power of words. By a natural reaction the opposite course was now to be tried, that of Acts. . . . The cry of 'Let us act' became as general as 'Among the people' had been a few years before." [3] First hostile demonstrations and street insurrections were tried, under the inspiration of the Paris Commune, but after repeated failure recourse was had to conspiracy and assassination, directed against officials of the Government, 'spies,' the police, and the Tsar himself. The Prefect of St Petersburg was shot by a woman under pretext of presenting a petition; the chief of the police and Prince Kropotkin, Governor of the Province of Kharkof, were two more of the victims, and many attempts were made on the life of the Tsar.

The Government was in consequence driven to increased repression. Harsh sentences were passed for trifling offences, the old rigorous restrictions placed on the universities, the Press more strictly censored, police powers increased. Juries were abolished

[1] Although the term is vague enough to cover wide divergences of opinion.
[2] E. Lipson, *Europe in the Nineteenth Century*.
[3] Stepniak, *Underground Russia*. Quoted by Lipson, *op. cit.*

in certain cases, the law-courts and local councils were rigidly controlled, the abuses of the old *régime* reappeared. But Government repression was greeted with increasing nihilist violence.

At length the Tsar was persuaded to adopt a policy of conciliation, but on the day when he announced the summoning of a 'representative body' to prepare new reforms the revolutionary bombs found their mark. On March 13, 1881, he was fatally wounded in a street in St Petersburg on his way to the Winter Palace. His assassination put an end to the movement of conciliation.

In foreign affairs the reign of Alexander II was marked by a great Russian advance in Central Asia and a period of retirement in Europe. Foreign affairs.

Russia sought in the East toward China and <u>Persia</u> and <u>Afghanistan</u> compensation for the check she had suffered in the Crimean War, and great successes fell to her arms and her diplomacy. By the Treaty of Aigun with China she received in 1858 the peaceful cession of a great part of the basin of the river Amur and the port of Vladivostok, which provided her with a terminus for the subsequent trans-Siberian railway and a base for the Russian fleet on the Pacific Ocean.[1] A rapid extension of power in Central Asia brought her to the frontiers of <u>Persia and Afghanistan</u>, and magnified the fear of <u>England for the safety of India</u>. Most of the newly annexed territory was formally incorporated in the Russian Empire, while the petty rulers were allowed to retain some semblance of their sovereignty on condition of becoming obsequious vassals of the Tsar.

In the south, in the Caucasus district, the expansion which had begun earlier was also continued.

In Europe the foreign policy of Russia was stated by Prince Gortschakoff in the words, "Elle ne boude pas, elle se recueille." [2] The policy of intervention which Nicholas I had practised so generously was abandoned, and Russia, withdrawing from foreign complications, devoted her attention to internal reorganization. An incipient Franco-Russian *entente* was destroyed by Napoleon's attitude in the Polish rising of 1863, and Russia turned more definitely to the Prussian alliance which Bismarck offered her.

A strong Prusso-Russian understanding was achieved which lasted for fifteen years, until 1878. To Prussia it brought immeasurable gains. It secured her right flank in 1864, her left flank in 1866, and her rear in 1870. The German Empire was founded upon it. To Russia too it brought its advantages; in the humiliation of Austria by Prussia Russia found her revenge for the treachery of 1854–56, while it seemed for a time as if, strong in the support of Prussia, she

[1] See Chapter XI.
[2] "She is not sulking, she is recuperating."

was about to make another bid for the revival of her power in the Balkan peninsula.

On the Prussian success in 1870 she repudiated the clauses of the Treaty of Paris which had restricted her on the Black Sea. She refortified Sebastopol, and began to reconstitute her naval power. Seven years later, in 1877, she was at war again with Turkey, but in the hour of need Germany deserted her, less crudely than, but as certainly as, Austria in 1854. Russia carried away from the Russo-Turkish War of 1877–78 some measure of success; she recovered Bessarabia and gained the Caucasian fortress of Kars, which she had twice captured; she effected a revision in more than one respect of the Treaty of Paris, but at the command of Europe she had been forced to halt, and at its bidding to lay down some of the harvest that she had hoped to reap.[1]

[1] See Chapter VII.

CHAPTER VII

THE NEAR EASTERN QUESTION, 1856–1914

"This damned Eastern Question is like the gout," remarked a Russian statesman. "Sometimes it takes you in the leg, sometimes it nips your hand. One is lucky if it does not fly to the stomach." A mere comparison of the map of the Balkans in 1856 and 1914 respectively will reveal the multiplication and complexity of the new interests that were defined there during the intervening half-century, while the startling and disastrous consequences of the Serajevo murder in 1914 need no emphasis as an indication of the prominence which the Eastern Question has assumed in European affairs.

Complexity and importance of the Eastern Question.

It has already been pointed out that the fundamental problem lay in the disappearance of Turkey in Europe, with its corollary—what was to take her place. Neither the optimism of a Palmerston, nor the ostensible protection of the European concert, nor the arms of France and Britain, could make the Porte either strong enough to hold her own against her numerous enemies or liberal enough to win the respect of Christian democracies. The Crimean War gave her such a chance as she had not had for a century, such as was not given to declining Poland, but she could not take it. The Congress of Berlin gave her another reprieve twenty years later, and again she profited nothing by it. The Turkish Empire in Europe was doomed, and though Europe and especially England long refused to believe it, they were finally forced to accept the facts. The official Eastern policy of Europe, set always against the incoming tide, was reduced often, therefore, to a succession of barren expedients, to a perpetually grudging recognition of *faits accomplis*. It showed before the War neither statesmanship nor vision, and condemned itself in futility.

In 1856 the Turkish Empire stretched still to the Danube. Some inroads had been made upon it. There was a people among the Black Mountains of Montenegro who amid impregnable fastnesses had resolutely maintained its independence. There was Greece, an independent kingdom under the protection of the Powers since 1833, and there was Serbia, practically independent, although still nominally in subservience to Turkey and actually garrisoned by her troops. With these exceptions over

The Ottoman Empire in 1856

all the peninsula south of the Great River the flag of the Crescent still waved; and beyond, over the two principalities of Moldavia and Wallachia, Russian protectorship had just been excluded and Turkish suzerainty asserted.

In 1914 the Porte possessed only her capital and a foothold in Thrace. The history of the intervening fifty odd years is concerned chiefly with four main problems. First there were the efforts of the Balkan peoples to throw off the overlordship of Turkey, and win, with or without foreign help, by negotiation or by war, recognition of their independent status from Turkey and—what was almost harder—from Europe.

and in 1914.

Four main problems.

Secondly there were the internal struggles within each new state, to put its own house in order and solve domestic problems of government, finance, and economics.

Thirdly there were the ambitions which the newly established Christian states soon began to develop toward an increase of territory, either at the expense of Turkey or, just as often, at the expense of each other. There was much reversion to historical pasts and much idealism as to historical futures; there was talk that might have come straight from the Courts of Europe, of expansion, and the Balance of Power, and imperialism.

Lastly there was the diverse ambition of the Great Powers of Europe, and none of them was wholly free from it, to turn to their own advantage the autumnal weakness of the Ottoman Empire or the germinal immaturity of the new nations. Especially there were the ambitions of Russia and Austria-Hungary and of the German Empire.

The first disturbance in the Eastern Question after the Crimean War came from the two provinces Moldavia and Wallachia, north of the Danube. These two principalities had been given promises at the Congress of Paris that "they should enjoy an independent and national administration, with full liberty of worship, legislation, and commerce," that they should have an armed force, and should settle in their own National Convention their "future definitive organization."

On these promises the principalities built hopes of practically determining their own future, and their common desire was to procure their formal as well as virtual independence of the Porte and, chiefly, their union with each other.

The Powers opposed this wish—not France, for there had long been a link of sympathy between the Rumanians, who occupied the principalities and held themselves to be the outposts of the Latin race and culture, and the supreme exponent of Latin civilization in the West. Moreover, Napoleon III constantly favoured the aspirations of other nations than his own to have the type of Government they desired. He won over the Tsar Alexander II to his side.

The Porte, however, was naturally reluctant to accept a union of the principalities which would strengthen their move toward independence. Austria, ever nervous of racial stirrings in her own empire, was afraid of giving any recognition to nationalist principles which would react upon her own Rumans. England finally joined the opposition, on the ground that having just waged war to support the integrity of Turkey it would now be illogical to further measures which would threaten it.

At this point the elections were held in Moldavia and Wallachia, and yielded a result favourable to Turkey. France thereupon demanded a fresh election, declaring that the returns had been notoriously manipulated. England replied with a denunciation of France's unwarrantable interference; feeling ran high on both sides, and for a time the Eastern Question seemed about to produce another European war, with a rearrangement of sides. Neither England nor Russia, however, really wanted to fight again so soon, and Napoleon was conciliatory. He pointed out to England and Austria that the union of the principalities would provide a far more effective barrier against Russia—still the bogy of the East—than their separation, and that therefore it was really in Turkey's interests that it should take place.

The revised elections had in the meantime resulted in a declaration in favour of the "union of the principalities in a single neutral and autonomous state, subject to the suzerainty of the Sultan and under the hereditary and constitutional government of a foreign prince."

Still, however, the Powers would not admit the union. From May to August 1858 they met in conference, and finally decided that the two principalities must remain politically separate, that each should have its own Parliament and its own prince, but that common affairs should be entrusted to a joint commission.

It was the device which nine years later was used to solve the Austro-Hungarian problem. To the principalities, however, it was clumsy and irritating, and they determined to defy and evade it. In the beginning of 1859 National Assemblies were held in the two capitals, Jassy and Bukarest, to choose a prince. They both unanimously elected the same man, a native nobleman, Colonel Alexander Couza.

This flagrant defiance of the Powers caused considerable excitement among the chancelleries of Europe, but eventually it was agreed to recognize the *fait accompli*, and on December 23, 1861, the union of the principalities was formally proclaimed. The name of

Rumania was adopted by the new state, and Bukarest, not without heart-burnings at Jassy, was chosen as the capital.

From 1859 to 1866 Prince Couza battled with the numerous problems of the new state, and contended with the rivalry of the other noble families of Rumania. He encouraged educa-

Prince Couza (1859–66). tion, founded universities in Jassy and Bukarest, established primary, secondary, and technical schools; he secularized the property of the monasteries, turned the monks adrift, and converted their homes into hospitals and gaols. He tackled the feudal question; abolished the compulsory labour dues, handed over one-third of the seignorial land to the peasants, giving the lords compensation from the State funds. But the peasants of Rumania were as dissatisfied as those of Russia after the emancipation of the serfs. On all sides Prince Couza's measures had created enemies, and in February 1866 he was deposed during a revolution at Bukarest.

The crown of Rumania, declined by Prince Philip of Flanders, son of the King of the Belgians, was then offered to Prince Carol, or Charles, of Hohenzollern-Sigmaringen, the brother of the Prince Leopold who, four years later, was to provide a stalking-horse for Franco-German hostility. The story is told by his wife, the famous Carmen Sylva,[1] that Prince Carol had never heard of Rumania when the offer reached him, but on looking at a map he found that a straight line drawn from London to Bombay passed through the new state. "That is a country with a future," he exclaimed, and accepted the crown. Bismarck in any case was in favour of it, "if only for the sake of a piquant adventure." Further, it would provide a Hohenzollern outpost on Austria's flank.

The Powers of Europe, of course, voted against the candidature, but were finally forced to accept it. The long reign of Prince, after-

Prince (King 1881) Carol (1886–1914). ward King, Charles of Rumania lasted, in spite of many impulses to abdication, until October 1914, a few months after the outbreak of the Great War. He turned his principality from a mediæval into a modern state; he gave her a constitution based on the Belgian model; "alone among the Balkan states may Rumania be said to possess a monarchy that is genuinely constitutional in the English sense."[2] He achieved the independence of the Roman Church from the Greek Patriarchate at Constantinople; and in 1881 he turned his principality into a kingdom. He developed her railways, industry, and agriculture. Her exports and imports rapidly increased.

[1] Princess Elizabeth, daughter of Prince Herman of Neuwied, adopted the pseudonym of Carmen Sylva for her numerous writings.
[2] Sir J. A. R. Marriott, *The Eastern Question*, p. 304.

In foreign policy it was natural that Prince Charles should lean toward Germany, and after the formation of the Prusso-Austrian alliance toward the Central European system. It was, in fact, commonly stated that Rumania's policy was dictated by Berlin or Vienna. It was not wholly true, however, for, as in the Second Balkan War of 1913, some concession had to be made to popular demands, which were nearly always opposed to the Governmental policy. As early as 1870 the people were on the side of France, the Prince on the side of Germany. Later the strong pan-nationalist sentiments which dominated Rumania, and the consequent desire to bring the Rumanians of Austria-Hungary into the Danubian state, prevented any real understanding between the kingdom of Rumania and the Dual Monarchy. In spite of the royal *rapprochement* the two countries were sentimentally antagonistic. As long as King Charles was on the throne no outbreak occurred between the kingdom and the empire. After his death in October 1914, however, Rumania turned from the neutrality she had adopted, and in 1916 she joined the camp of Austria's enemies.

After the formation of the united principality of Rumania there was no outward disturbance in the European dominions of the Porte for more than ten years, for the Straits Question, reopened Turkish by Russia in 1870, was quickly settled. During the oppression. interval the Powers saw the promises which the Porte had given to the world in 1856, of better government toward its Christian subjects, fade into emptiness. It saw the gathering of forces fermented by Turkey herself to her own destruction. On paper every subject, without distinction of race, creed, or class, was granted personal liberty, equality before the law, complete religious freedom, eligibility for civil and military offices, equity of taxation, security of property, and equal representation in communal and provincial councils and in the Supreme Court of Justice. But in practice the concessions remained a dead letter. The Sultan Abdul-Aziz, who succeeded to the throne in 1861, though well intentioned was too weak to keep his own officials in order. He did something to secularize and modernize his empire and to attend to the admonitions of the Powers; he developed means of communication and made advances in public education; but it was all to no purpose. The Ottoman Empire was, and always has been until the present day, a theocracy, and although Turkey has herself finally shown that it is not impossible to secularize a theocracy she has also proved by repeated failure how difficult it is to do so, or to reform law that rests upon religious sanction.

Justice and honour and property were at the mercy of local officials, and as the Sultan himself plunged deeper into personal extravagance,

U

as his demands for money increased, so the rapacity and extortion of his subordinates grew too.   The evidence of Turkish misgovernment and oppression was abundant.

But the despised and conquered races of the Balkans were no longer in a mood to endure.   Montenegrin, Serbian, and Greek struggles had all borne fruit in increasing the restlessness, impatience, and aspirations of the subject Christian states. Pan-Slavist agents of Russia were also undoubtedly at work, stirring up racial consciousness and national hostility.   " Ever since the Crimean War missionaries of the new gospel of Pan-Slavism—mostly Russians—had been engaged in an unceasing propaganda among the peoples of their own faith and their own blood." [1] A great Pan-Slavist congress had been held in Moscow in 1867 under the disguise of a scientific meeting.   A central Pan-Slavist committee had been formed, with headquarters at Moscow and a sub-committee at Bukarest; books and pamphlets were circulated in the Balkans, young Slavs flocked to Russian universities, just as the Rumanian youths flocked to Paris.   Every Russian consul in the peninsula and the Russian ambassador at Constantinople were enthusiastic in the cause, and Serbia, Bosnia, Montenegro, and Bulgaria were honeycombed with secret societies.

Resistance of the Christians.

Pan-Slavism.

It was from these districts that the next movement in the Eastern Question was to come.   Suddenly in the seventies the Ottoman Empire in Europe began to crack in all directions from the heat of the smouldering fires within, and before the decade was out the doctrine of 'Turkish integrity' had become a diplomatic delusion.

The leadership of the South Slav agitation seemed about to be assumed by Serbia, thus forestalling her destiny by fifty years. Prince Milosh Obrenovič III had gone far toward realizing an elaborate combination between Serbia, Bosnia, and the Herzegovina.   He had entered into relations with the nationalist leaders of Croatia, with a patriotic society in Bulgaria, and even with Greece.   His assassination, however, in 1868 threw back the development of Serbian ambitions by half a century.   It postponed it until other factors had arisen in antagonism, until Bulgarian rivalry and Austro-Hungarian interests and the might of a vigorous German Empire stood between Serbia and a Yugo-Slav union, bringing her, and Europe with her, into war for its achievement.

It was not Serbia, then, but Bosnia and the Herzegovina who gave the signal for the outbreak of the movements of 1875 and 1876.   The grievances of these districts were as much social and economic as national.   Oppressive feudal systems were in force; the peasants were exposed to the double exactions

Bosnia and the Herzegovina.

[1] Sir J. A. R. Marriott, *The Eastern Question*, pp. 319–320.

of Ottoman officials and of native landowners who, to save their property, had turned Mohammedan, and were "more Turkish than the Turks."

In July 1875 the peasants of the Herzegovina refused to pay taxes or to perform the customary labour services, and when a Turkish force was sent against them they defeated it. Sympathizers flocked to their cause from the neighbouring districts of Serbia, Montenegro, and Dalmatia. At the same time Turkey went bankrupt. The Powers of Europe were seriously disturbed by the double event. They saw the Eastern Question opening again, and the Secretaries of State once more grew busy with the framing of Notes. Propositions were made to the Herzegovina and to the Porte; the Herzegovina was obstinate and the Porte politely elusive. The Porte was quite willing to promise almost as much as Europe liked, a more equitable government to the Christian subjects, and reform in this and the other matter, but it would give to Europe no satisfactory guarantee of the fulfilment of these promises. The murder of the French and German consuls in Salonica did not facilitate an amicable agreement, but since Great Britain refused to join with the other Powers in putting pressure upon the Porte the Sultan felt that he could almost ignore the protests of Europe. *(Insurrection in the Herzegovina, 1875.)*

In the meantime the Balkan insurrection had spread. Bosnia joined the revolt in May, and in June Serbia and Montenegro declared war upon the Porte. The infection was spreading eastward; it reached Bulgaria, the district south of the Danube, once a mighty kingdom, but now a subject province of the Porte. To this point hardly anything had been heard of Bulgarian aspirations, except that in 1870 the Bulgars—like the Serbs and Rumanians—had managed to secure the independence of their Church from the Greek Patriarchate of Constantinople—a bad sign, from Turkey's point of view, of the trend of affairs. Then they looked across to their neighbours at the other side of the peninsula, and suddenly, in May 1876, their name leapt into immortality. Like the peasants of the Herzegovina, the Bulgars defied the order of some Turkish officials, and emphasized their defiance by murdering over a hundred of them.

The Porte, enraged at the growth of insubordination and afraid of an attack upon its right flank while it was engaged in war with the other peoples, determined upon an effective revenge. A force of 18,000 regulars was marched into Bulgaria, and hordes of irregulars, Bashi-Bazouks and Circassians, were let loose upon the Bulgarian villagers. Of the atrocities which followed it is impossible to give an accurate account. An agent dispatched by the British Government estimated the number *(The Bulgarian atrocities (1876).)*

of murdered Christians at 12,000; others have put the figure as high as 30,000.

At the news the Christian world was roused to intense anger. Mr Gladstone came out of his retirement to stir the British nation to action. "Let the Turks," he demanded, "now carry away their abuses in the only possible manner—namely, by carrying off themselves. Their Zaptiehs and their Mudirs, their Bimbashis and their Yuzbashis, their Kaimakams and their Pashas,[1] one and all, bag and baggage, shall, I hope, clear out from the province they have desolated and profaned." The doctrine of Turkish integrity was rent by one flash of emotion. But the ardent Christian Mr Gladstone was not then Prime Minister of England, and Mr Disraeli, the Jew, who was, had other views.[2] He had a very lively sense of England's Oriental responsibilities and of her Indian Empire. Two years before he had bought up the Khedive's shares in the Suez Canal. In 1876 he had persuaded a Prince of Wales to undertake a tour in India for the first time in the history of that country, and on January 1, 1877, at the most brilliant ceremony ever held there under British patronage, Queen Victoria was proclaimed Empress of India. India, in fact, loomed much larger in Mr Disraeli's eyes than Bulgaria, and the enemy of India was not Turkey, but Russia, with her agents in Afghanistan and her empire steadily advancing in that direction.

On April 24, 1877, Russia declared war on the Porte. That there should be an Eastern problem in which Russia was not involved was unthinkable. The Serbian armies consisted largely of Russian volunteers, and were officered by Russian generals, while a war with Turkey offered the chance of recovering the part of Bessarabia which had been lost to the Tsar in 1856. All through the autumn and winter of 1876 Russia had restrained her growing impatience while the Powers carried on the solemn farce of discussion with each other and negotiations with the Turks. Absolute agreement among themselves was as difficult to achieve as effective guarantees from the Porte, and on the conclusion of the Convention of Reichstadt with Austria in January 1877 Russia resolved upon war. By this convention Austria-Hungary undertook to preserve neutrality in case of war between Russia and Turkey, in return for which the Dual Monarchy was to secure preponderant influence over Bosnia and the Herzegovina.

The Russo-Turkish War (1877-78).

[1] All these are the names of Turkish officials.
[2] To Disraeli Gladstone's pro-Christian fervour was a malign embarrassment of British policy at a critical time. "Posterity will do justice," he wrote to Lord Derby, "to that unprincipled maniac Gladstone—extraordinary mixture of envy, vindictiveness, hypocrisy, and superstition, and with one commanding characteristic—whether Prime Minister, or Leader of the Opposition, whether preaching, praying, speechifying, or scribbling—never a gentleman."

The next essential to Russia besides the neutrality of Austria was the co-operation of Rumania, for she could only advance to Constantinople by land. Another treaty, however, gave her a free passage through the Rumanian principality, and at the end of June Russian troops crossed the Danube and began their advance toward the Turkish capital. Montenegro reopened hostilities against the Porte, and Serbia also at the end of the year. At Plevna, however, the Russians suffered an unexpected check, and for five months, in alliance with Rumanian forces which now joined them, they were held up by the siege of the town. After a gallant defence Plevna fell to Todleben, the hero of Sebastopol, in December 1877, and the Russian troops proceeded toward Constantinople. On January 5 they reached Sofia, and on the 20th they entered Adrianople, 160 miles from the Turkish capital.

In the Caucasus they had been equally successful. The great fortress of Kars had fallen in November. The Porte, unable to offer further resistance to the victorious Russians, made the Treaty of San Stefano in March 1878.

By this treaty Montenegro and Serbia were to be recognized as independent states, and each was to receive an accession of territory. Turkish reforms were to be immediately introduced into Bosnia and the Herzegovina, and to be executed under the joint control of Russia and Austria. The fortresses on the Danube were to be razed; reforms were to be granted to the Armenians. *The Treaty of San Stefano (March 1878).* Russia was to acquire Batum, Kars, and other territory in Asia, and in Europe Bessarabia and part of the Dobrudja, while Rumania was to receive certain other Turkish territories in exchange for the retrocession of the strip of Bessarabia [1] to Russia. The independence of Rumania was to be recognized. The most striking feature of the treaty, however, was the new Bulgarian creation. An autonomous state was to be erected, tributary to Turkey, but with a Christian Government and a national militia. It was to extend from the Danube to the Ægean, to stretch nearly as far south as Midia, on the Black Sea, and to include in the west the Monastir territory of Macedonia. The Turkish Empire in Europe was practically annihilated.

It was a magnificent triumph for Russia. It wiped out the Treaty of Paris and promised her once again the dominance of the Balkans, and for that reason Europe, and especially England, was determined that she should not enjoy her triumph.

Outside Bulgaria and Russia no one was satisfied with the Treaty of San Stefano. Rumania, excluded from the negotiations, was conscious of base neglect and Russian ingratitude. Serbia,

[1] Which she had lost in 1856.

Montenegro, and Greece resented the elevation of greater Bulgaria, and Greece even went to the length of invading Thessaly. Austria jealously saw her interests threatened and the Convention of Reichstadt disregarded, and though to Germany the Balkans were "not worth the bones of a Pomeranian Grenadier," Bismarck was anxious to support Austria. It was, however, to England that the Russian triumph in the Balkans caused the gravest disquietude. As early as June 1877, before the Russians crossed the Danube, England had secured an engagement from the Tsar not to occupy Constantinople or the Straits, and to respect British interests in Egypt and the Suez Canal. In January 1878 Lord Derby, the British Foreign Secretary, reminded the Tsar of his promise, and warned him that any treaty concluded between Russia and Turkey which might affect the engagement of 1856 and 1871 "would not be valid without the assent of the Powers which were parties to those treaties." For in order to check Russia England was determined to secure the recognition of the Eastern Question as a matter of general European concern. Upon the conclusion of the Treaty of San Stefano Disraeli's fears were still more excited. "It abolishes the dominion of the Ottoman Empire in Europe. . . . All the European dominions of the Ottoman Porte are . . . put under the administration of Russia. . . . The effect of the stipulations will be to make the Black Sea as much a Russian lake as the Caspian." Austria, also determined upon a revision of the treaty, proposed a European congress, and to this Disraeli agreed on the firm condition that "all questions dealt with in the treaty of peace between Russia and Turkey should be considered as subjects to be discussed in the congress." Russia demurred, England insisted, and for six weeks the threat of war hung over Europe. On April 17, as Russia still held out, Disraeli announced that he had ordered 17,000 Indians to embark for Malta. It was possibly only a sensational gesture, but it was effective.[1] The Russian armies were depleted, Russian finances strained; but she might even so have resisted to the length of war had the old Russo-Germanic alliance stood firm. But once again Russia was the victim of the self-interest of her allies. Bismarck was, indeed, anxious "to keep open the wire between Berlin and St Petersburg," but he was still more anxious to consolidate the understanding with Austria and set up that Central European Germanic bulwark against the rest of Europe. If St Petersburg quarrelled with Vienna it was now to Vienna that Bismarck would turn. Moreover, in a late scare of

[1] Neither the Cabinet nor the country was unanimous for war. The war party came to be known as Jingoes, from a popular music-hall song of the period, sung by "the Great MacDermott," "We don't want to fight, but, by Jingo, if we do," etc.

war between France and Germany Russia had not shown that whole-hearted support of Germany which Bismarck could have desired.

With Austria and the new German Empire against her, therefore, Russia could not afford to go to war with England, and she reluctantly agreed to a European congress to revise the terms of the Treaty of San Stefano. As a tribute to the new Power which had arisen in Europe, the congress was held at Berlin, under the presidency of the "honest broker" Bismarck. But the dominating personality was that of Disraeli, Lord Beaconsfield. "The old Jew, that is the man," said Bismarck. The revised treaty was signed on July 13.

The Congress of Berlin (July 1878).

Russia's gains were reduced to the strip of Bessarabia, Batum and Kars, in the Caucasus, and part of Armenia. The independence of Rumania was recognized by the Porte, and she received part of the Dobrudja, in poor exchange, as she viewed it, for Bessarabia. Bosnia and the Herzegovina were handed over to the administration of Austria, who was also to garrison the Sanjak of Novibazar, between Serbia and Montenegro. England was to occupy and administer the island of Cyprus as long as Russia retained Kars and Batum. France sought for authority to occupy Tunis in the future. The new Italy marked her accession to the rank of a European Power by putting forward claims upon Albania and Tripoli. The new Germany asked for nothing, and gained the gratitude of the Sultan, which turned out to be as good an investment as any. The Balkan states were no less forward in their demands. Serbia and Montenegro received most of the districts conceded at San Stefano, as well as the recognition of their independence. Greece asked for Crete, Thessaly, Epirus, and a part of Macedonia, but received nothing at the moment. It was to Bulgaria that the revised treaty made the greatest difference. The Bulgaria that was defined by the Treaty of Berlin was reduced to a population of two millions between the Danube and the Balkan mountains, and to a little more than one-third of the area mapped out at San Stefano. It was to be formed into an independent state tributary to Turkey. South of Bulgaria there was to be a smaller district known as Eastern Rumelia,[1] which was to be restored to the Porte, but was to be given a Christian Government approved by the Powers. The Macedonian territories were allotted again to Turkey. Bulgaria was thus entirely cut off from the Ægean.

Disraeli's policy at the Congress of Berlin was bold, and to a point effective, but out of it arose most of the causes of the Balkan wars of 1912 and 1913 and of the Great War of 1914. "There is again a

[1] But the two together did not equal the territory of Bulgaria as defined by the Treaty of San Stefano.

Turkey in Europe," he remarked, and he counted it one of his proudest achievements that he had saved the Ottoman Empire from disintegration. The Porte, it is true, recovered two and a half millions of people and 30,000 square miles that she had lost at San Stefano, but her empire, reduced by more than half its area and nearly half its population, was mutilated beyond revival. All that Disraeli had done was to prolong the process and multiply the pains of extinction. The restoration of Macedonia cost the Balkan war of 1912, and the curtailment of Bulgaria the war of 1913.

A check had also been administered to Russia, and victory snatched from her hands. For a time, especially after an ungrateful Bulgaria had embittered the humiliation that she had suffered at Berlin, she retired from an active policy in the Balkans to active empire-making in Asia. Thirty years later she returned again with ambitions renewed, and in 1914 she set out to recover—and it is part of the endless irony of history that Great Britain was her ally in arms— far more than she had lost in 1878.

Moreover, in holding back one foreign Power from the Balkans Disraeli had merely let loose another. The introduction of Austria-Hungary, with the German Empire behind her, into the very heart of the peninsula, pointing with threatening finger toward the Ægean, frowning menacingly upon the ambitions of Serbia and their fulfilment in Yugo-Slavia, created a new Balkan problem. From the Austria of 1878 to the Austria of 1914, and so to the Great War, there is a continuous development.

It is also, perhaps, no matter for surprise that the Porte should be left with the bitter reflection that the self-styled friends who had forced themselves upon her to save her had turned into robbers in her extremity. The proclamation of Serbian, Montenegrin, and Bulgarian independence was a natural and inevitable measure ; the annexation of Cyprus and the extension of Austrian control over Bosnia and the Herzegovina were less natural moves on the part of Powers who professed the doctrine of Turkish integrity. Disraeli's famous boast of having brought to England "Peace with honour" seemed to need translation into "Peace together with the island of Cyprus and a check, in British interests, to the ambitions of Russia."

That the settlement of Berlin actually lasted without serious disturbance for a generation is a tribute as much to the impotence and mutual rivalries of the Powers and to the ineffectiveness of the Concert of Europe as to the enduring nature of its terms, but no human architect could have reared out of the discordant elements of the Eastern Question an edifice that could have finally withstood the buffetings of Balkan storms.

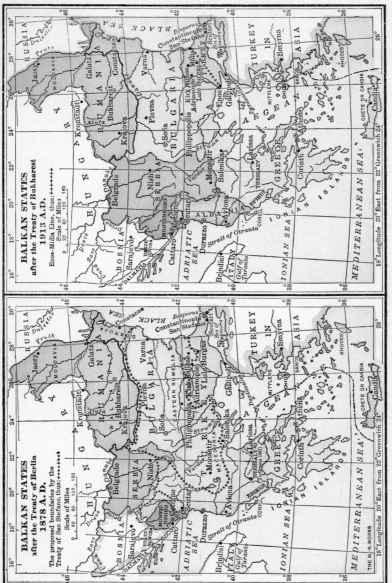

BALKAN STATES
after the Treaty of Bukharest
1913 A.D.

Enos-Midia Line, thus:+++++++
Scale of Miles
20 40 80 120 150

18° Longitude 20° East from 22° Greenwich 24°

BALKAN STATES
after the Treaty of Berlin
1878 A.D.

The proposed boundaries by the
Treaty of San Stefano, thus:++++++
Scale of Miles
40 80 120 150

18° Longitude 20° East from 22° Greenwich 24°

THE M. N. WORKS

From "World History," by Hutton Webster (D. C. Heath and Co.)

There were now five independent principalities carved out of the one-time Turkish Empire—Rumania, north of the Danube, Bulgaria and Serbia south of it, diamond-shaped Montenegro among the mountains to the west, touching the coast at the southern point, and Greece on both sides of the Gulf of Corinth.   Eastern Rumelia was in an anomalous, semi-independent condition, and Bosnia and the Herzegovina were under Austrian administration.

For the next twenty years it was on the whole Bulgaria which contributed most to keep the Eastern Question alive, although other excitements were provided by Egypt and Armenia, **Bulgaria.** and rather less distracting sideshows by Greece, Crete, and Serbia.

Bulgarian politics during this period centred in four main questions —the constitution, the Prince, union with Rumelia, and finally Russia. The constitutional question was approached first. A brand-new Parliamentary constitution was constructed of parts which came ready-made out of the democratic factories of the West, together with an utterly inconsistent autocratic executive. It was imposed upon a people without experience or constitutional tradition, and was, in short, unworkable.

The Prince, Alexander of Battenberg, proved to be a better choice than the constitution, though the difficulties with which he had to contend overcame him in the end.   He was a nephew of the **Prince** Tsar Alexander II, and his nominee; he was also a scion **Alexander** of the house of Darmstadt, and an officer in the Prussian **berg (1879–** army, and he became later a connexion by marriage of the **1886).** British royal family.   He reigned for seven years, from 1879 to 1886, and there is irrefutable evidence of his good character and ability. "He was described as a wise statesman, a brave soldier, and a remarkable man in every respect," but he was hampered by the jealousy of the Sobranje, the Bulgarian Parliament, and by the high-handed arrogance of Russia, to whom he refused to be subservient, especially after the accession of Alexander III in 1881.   In the end he was forced to abdicate.   He retired into private life, and on the failure of Queen Victoria to secure for him the hand of her granddaughter, the Princess Victoria, he married an opera-singer, and died in 1893. He was succeeded by Prince Ferdinand of Saxe-Coburg-Gotha, who lived to bring Bulgaria into the Great War of 1914 on the side of Central Europe.

The question of union with Eastern Rumelia was for a time the most acute.   The separation between Bulgaria and Eastern Rumelia effected at the Congress of Berlin was an arbitrary and artificial one, and corresponded to no racial divisions.   Bulgaria had learnt the new political creed of ethnology more quickly than, but as thoroughly as, many of the other Balkan and European states, and the agitation for union, fostered by athletic clubs and other corporate societies, increased in each province with every year of separation. It was largely directed by a man who has won one of the greatest of Bulgarian names, Stephan Stambolov, an innkeeper's son, an ex-nihilist, President of the Sobranje, and from 1886 to 1894 practically dictator of Bulgaria.

At length the provinces determined to take the matter into their own hands. In September 1885 the Turkish governor at Philip-

The Union of the Bulgarias (1885-86).

popolis, in Eastern Rumelia, was shown out of the province, and Prince Alexander, offered the alternative of assuming the double crown or abdicating, declared himself Prince of the United Bulgaria. As in the case of Rumania twenty-seven years before, the Powers felt that they must do something about such a flagrant defiance of a European treaty. Moreover, the question was made more urgent by a sudden and capricious declaration of war against Bulgaria by Serbia, who declared that the Bulgarian aggrandizement threatened the 'Balance of Power' in the Balkans.

A brief war ensued. The Serbians were decisively defeated, and their state was invaded by the young Bulgarian army, which marched

The Serbo-Bulgarian War (1885).

upon Pirot, and the Porte was edified by the prospect of Serbian humiliation, possibly annihilation, at the hands of her sister state, Bulgaria. At this point, however, Austria called a halt, threatening Bulgaria with war unless she ceased hostilities. A peace was signed at Bukarest; it restored the *status quo*, and Serbia was saved. In the meantime the question of the Bulgarian union had been laid before a conference of the Powers. A complete reversal of attitude, however, had taken place in Europe from the days of the Berlin Congress. The Powers who had then been most instrumental in effecting a division between Bulgaria and Eastern Rumelia were now inclined to support the union, while Russia, on the other hand, was now opposed to the formation of the greater Bulgaria which had been her own creation by the abortive Treaty of San Stefano—a mutual reversal of positions on the part of these Governments.

There was, however, something to account for the modification of Europe's policy in the unexpected fact that Bulgaria, instead of

Europe's change of policy.

turning into the cat's paw of Russia, which had been anticipated at Berlin, had shown herself obstinately independent and even hostile to her imperial patron. England and Austria, therefore, still adhering to the main object of checkmating Russia, had come to the conclusion that it would best be achieved not so much by maintaining an effete Turkey as by strengthening an independent Bulgaria.

A Bulgaria friendly to the Porte, and jealous of foreign influence, would be a far surer bulwark against foreign aggression than two Bulgarias severed in administration, but united in considering the Porte as the only obstacle to their national development.[1]

A dynastic connexion, arising from the marriage of Princess Beatrice to Prince Alexander's brother, Prince Henry of Battenberg, strengthened the diplomatic argument, and England took the lead in pressing upon the Porte the recognition of the union of Bulgaria and Eastern Rumelia. It resulted in the formal recognition in 1886 by the Sultan Abdul-Hamid of United Bulgaria. To this Russia replied in a dramatic fashion.

In 1878 Bulgaria, however much reduced by the Congress, had come into political existence as Russia's *protégé*. The Russian army was in occupation, a Russian nominee was placed upon the throne, and a Russian diplomacy proposed to take full guidance of the infant state. For the first few years Bulgaria was ruled practically as a Russian satrapy; Russian officers were appointed to the chief Bulgarian ministries, and the Bulgarian ministers took their orders from the Tsar. Prince Alexander's position became unbearable.

In Bulgaria the Russian dominance was bitterly resented, and soon wiped out any disposition to gratitude in the infant state. "Bulgaria for the Bulgarians" became the cry of the national party, headed by Stambolov, and Prince Alexander determined to put himself at the head of the anti-Russian movement. The result was to give dire offence to the Tsar, who withdrew his officers from the Bulgarian army just at the outbreak of the Serbo-Bulgarian War. A state almost of open war soon existed between Sofia and St Petersburg. "Russia hates me because she fears me," wrote Prince Alexander, "but I rejoice in this hatred, which I reciprocate with all my heart." Alexander III thereupon resolved that he would on no account support the union of the two Bulgarias unless Prince Alexander was replaced by a Russian nominee.

When, therefore, in 1886 the Powers and the Porte sanctioned not only the union of the Bulgarias, but the appointment of Prince Alexander as ruler of both, Russia's wrath overflowed. On the night of August 21 some Bulgarian officers, acting under Russian orders, entered the palace at Sofia, forced the Prince, at the point of the revolver, to sign an abdication, and hustled him out of the country. "Words fail me to express my feelings," wrote Queen Victoria to him. "Your parents could hardly be more anxious. My indignation against your barbarian, Asiatic, tyrannical cousin is so great that I cannot trust myself to write about it." A provisional Government, however, hastily set up at Sofia under Stambolov, recalled the Prince

[1] Lord Salisbury (December 1885), quoted by Sir J. A. R. Marriott, *op. cit.*

to Bulgaria, and he set out again for his own capital. At Rustchuk he seems to have been bullied or overpersuaded by the Russian consul, and to have resolved to give up the unequal struggle. He telegraphed to the Tsar an abject surrender. "Russia gave me my crown, and I am ready to return it into the hands of her sovereign." The message produced as much consternation and indignation in Bulgaria as King John's surrender of his kingdom to Innocent III caused in England. The Tsar pressed his advantage by refusing to sanction Alexander's restoration; but in any case the Prince had sealed his own doom. On reaching Sofia he resigned his crown, protesting that one man could not stand alone against Europe, and wishing his successor better fortune. He then left the country which, in spite of immense difficulties, he had served with devotion.

Prince Ferdinand of Saxe-Coburg-Gotha, who was chosen to succeed him, reigned until 1918. He was young and ambitious, but for the first seven years he took a passive rather than an active part in the government of Bulgaria, while the real power was wielded by Stambolov. In 1894 Stambolov resigned, or was dismissed, and the next year he was assassinated.

Ferdinand of Saxe-Coburg-Gotha, Prince (King 1908) of Bulgaria (1887–1918).

Prince Ferdinand was then at last ruler of the state, and his first step was to bring about a reconciliation between Russia and Bulgaria. It was facilitated by the death of Tsar Alexander III in 1894 and the succession of the milder Nicholas II. It was sealed by the baptism in 1896 of the young heir, Boris, into the Orthodox Faith, and by a State visit two years later of the Prince and Princess of Bulgaria to Peterhof.

Under Prince Ferdinand Bulgaria advanced to a rapid prosperity until the disastrous war of 1913–14.

From 1896 to 1898 it was the Armenian question that was in the forefront of the Eastern stage. There is nothing which illustrates more completely the futility and powerlessness of the European concert. In 1878 the Powers, and Great Britain in particular, had shown an awakened interest in the Christian Armenian subjects of the Ottoman Empire, lying in that ill-defined geographical area between the Caspian and the Black Seas. In the Treaty of Berlin, as well as in the Cyprus convention between Great Britain and the Porte, promises had been extracted from the Sultan of better government. But the attention of Europe proved a curse rather than a blessing.

The Armenian massacres (1894–96).

It stimulated the hopes of the Armenians and drove the Sultan to drastic retaliation. The promises of the Porte remained as usual a dead letter, but though Great Britain protested from time to time, Abdul-Hamid soon perceived that the Powers were too divided for any effective action to be taken. He resolved therefore to teach his Christian subjects a lesson. He saw the growth of revolutionary agitation among the Armenians and the prospect of another independent Christian state rising out of the Turkish Empire. He saw Armenia turning into another Bulgaria unless the movement toward autonomy was checked. "The only way to get rid of the Armenian Question," grimly observed a Turkish statesman, "is to get rid of the Armenians." An excuse was provided in the resistance of some Armenians in 1893 to the Turkish authorities, and in 1894 the process of retribution began. Regular and irregular soldiers of the Porte were let loose among the villages of Armenia and incited to massacre. The scenes that followed are indescribable. Through 1894 and 1895 the stamping out of the Armenians went on, and at the end of the year over 50,000 had fallen victims to murder and outrage.

In August 1896 the scene was shifted to Constantinople, where the Armenians living in the Turkish capital, frenzied by the appeals of their brothers and despairing of help from the Powers, rose in revolt and attacked the Turkish bank in Galata. In consequence, within the next twenty-four hours 6000 Armenians were done to death in the streets of the capital.

What of the Powers of Europe who had so often proclaimed their collective responsibility in the Eastern Question? The impotence of Russia looked the other way. The Armenians had shown nihilist tendencies, and as they were Gregorian the Powers and not Orthodox Christians there was no appeal of a common faith. Russia, not yet recovered from the chagrin of her Bulgarian failure, had no mind to raise up another ungrateful Bulgaria in Armenia. She was turning her thoughts toward the Pacific. Besides, Armenia was England's hobby, and as Disraeli had thwarted Russia in Bulgaria in 1878 so Russia would now thwart Salisbury in Armenia in 1896. In fact, the Tsar expressed his opinion that England was responsible for the whole movement, adding that although he was very fond of England and the English he mistrusted their policy.

The new Germany, no longer under the guidance of Bismarck, was now embarked upon the policy of courting Turkey's friendship, and far from putting pressure upon the Sultan the Kaiser William II took the opportunity of Abdul-Hamid's birthday to send him a signed photograph of himself and the Imperial family as a mark of affection. Austria-Hungary fell into line with Germany. France, still estranged from England over the Egyptian Question,[1] refused to take part in any concerted action.

England therefore protested and threatened in vain. The Sultan could afford to ignore her. Her people and her ministers were

[1] See Chapter X.

roused to burning indignation against Abdul-Hamid, "the Great Assassin," [1] "immortally, beyond all mortals damned," [2] but Lord Salisbury dared not allow the tragedy to provoke the still greater catastrophe of a European war.

Thus the Armenians fell victims to the general interests of European policy and the greater jealousies of the Powers, but Lord Salisbury, together with most of his countrymen, came to a significant conclusion, that in supporting Turkey hitherto England had "put her money on the wrong horse."

Greece and Crete.
The Armenians had barely finished counting their dead, and the diplomatic agitation aroused by the whole affair had not subsided, when the Eastern Question appeared before Europe in another form and from another quarter, from Greece and Crete.

King Otto of Greece (1833–62).
In 1833 the Powers had placed the new Greek kingdom under a young German prince, Otto of Bavaria. He was seventeen years old, of indifferent abilities, hampered by entire ignorance of his new kingdom and by his religion, which was Roman, while that of his subjects was Greek Catholic. A bigger man than he might have failed before the almost impossible task that confronted the first ruler of Greece, and the twenty-nine years of his reign constitute a miserable tale of administrative inefficiency, political quarrels, constitutional misrule, social disorder, brigandage and insurrection, financial bankruptcy and futile and repressive Government devices. A Parliamentary constitution, at first withheld, was granted only to be burlesqued. Local self-government, passionately demanded, was denied. At length, in 1862, a military revolt drove King Otto out of his own capital and forced him to abdicate. The

King George I (1863– 1913).
crown of Greece was hawked round the Courts of Europe, and after being rejected by Prince Alfred, son of Queen Victoria, and by Lord Stanley,[3] was finally accepted by Prince George of Denmark, who as George I, King of the Hellenes, reigned from 1863 to 1913.

It is, however, to the external aspirations of Greece rather than to her internal development that attention must in this context be given.

The Eastern ambitions of Greece.
From the time of the definition of her boundaries by the European Powers in 1832 Greece had suffered from a sense of grievance because many undoubted Greeks had been excluded from the new kingdom. There were Greeks in the Ionian islands, there were Greeks in Crete, and there was a particularly large number of Greeks in Thessaly and Epirus and Macedonia, outside her northern frontier. The fundamental direction of Greek

---

[1] Gladstone.   [2] Sir William Watson.
[3] Mr Gladstone's name was also mentioned, to his own great amusement.

foreign policy had been toward the acquisition of these parts of unredeemed Greece.

It was upon Thessaly and Epirus that she concentrated her earliest
and most urgent attention. These districts belonged to the Porte,
and it was from the Porte that she must win them. Her national
policy therefore was to try to take advantage of every important
embarrassment that befell Turkey to invade Thessaly and Epirus
and snatch the prize from a broken enemy.

She reckoned, however, without the Powers, who did not wish
their higher European interests to be complicated by irrelevant Greek
ambitions. When therefore during the Crimean War Greek
soldiers raided Thessaly the Powers called them back and forced
upon King Otto a highly distasteful neutrality. Nor was Greece
rewarded for her obedience in the Congress of Paris.

In the Russo-Turkish War of 1877-78 the same play was acted
again. Greece raided Thessaly, the Powers forced her to withdraw,
and again she received nothing at the ensuing congress. "Greece is
a country with a future, and can wait," remarked Lord Beaconsfield.

Two years later, however, in 1880, Mr Gladstone, a Philhellene
and an enemy of Turkey, became Prime Minister of England, and
proceeded to put pressure on the Porte to yield the coveted territories
to the Greek kingdom. In 1881 the unwilling Sultan therefore conceded about one-third of Epirus and the greater part of Thessaly.
Greek aspirations were, however, by no means satisfied.

Nearly twenty years earlier Mr Gladstone had been instrumental
in conferring upon the Greeks the seven Ionian islands, held under
a British protectorate since 1815. The islanders were themselves
discontented and demanded union with Greece. After an attempt
to fob them off with constitutional reform as a substitute, the English
Government of Lord Palmerston finally decided to make them over
to Greece. The gift, gratefully received, was presented simultane-
ously with the new sovereign, Prince George of Denmark.

There remained the question of Crete, "the Greek island *par
excellence*." The rule of the Turks in Crete showed most of the
qualities that marked the Ottoman Empire in the Balkans,
and the Cretans were as oppressed and discontented and   Crete.
rebellious as the other Christian subjects of the Porte. It is not
possible to give details of the fourteen Cretan insurrections which
took place between 1830 and 1910. In addition, however, to the
desire to throw off Turkish sovereignty they were nearly all devoted
to the object of union with Greece, an object with which the mainland
kingdom fully sympathized. Practically nothing was achieved by
any of the revolts before 1896 and 1897 save empty promises of
reform from the Porte. In those years the nationalist sentiment,

which had been growing in intensity in both island and mainland ever since the Bulgarian union of 1886, culminated in another Cretan revolt. The revolutionaries in Crete—of whom one of the leaders was a certain young man Eleutherios Venizelos—proclaimed the union with Greece, and Greece, carried away by her own fervour, sent an expedition to the help of Crete, and raided Thessaly. Turkey thereupon declared war in 1897. The war lasted for thirty days.

The Græco-Turkish War (1897). Greece was wholly unprepared for the conflict she had provoked. The Turkish army, newly refurbished with German help, was overwhelmingly successful, and the Powers, unwilling to see the outbreak of a general Balkan conflagration, insisted upon peace. It was thus a disastrous venture for Greece. She was compelled to cede to Turkey a strategic advantage on the Thessalian frontier and to pay a heavy indemnity, which strained her resources to the utmost; and she did not win Crete.

Over this island the Powers had assumed responsibility, but as in the Armenian Question international jealousies complicated and delayed settlement. Germany and Austria, unwilling to agree to any arrangement not acceptable to the Porte, withdrew from the deliberations. The other Powers finally decided that Crete should be autonomous under Turkish suzerainty, an arrangement which did not please Turkey, or Crete, or Greece. The island was placed under a commission of the four Powers—Great Britain, Russia, Italy, and France—and Prince George, son of King George of Greece, was appointed ruler. The Turkish troops were withdrawn, but a Turkish flag still waved over the island,[1] side by side with the Cretan. To Greece and Crete the situation was held to be merely an irritating preparation for union, and on the outbreak of the Turkish revolution of 1908 and the declaration of Bulgarian independence another attempt was made to bring about the desired consummation. Again the Powers intervened in the interests of the Porte; they withdrew their own troops from the island, but it was not until after the Balkan war of 1912, fifteen years after the revolution of 1896–97, that they permitted the union with Greece at last to take place.

From the eighties, and still more from the early nineties, a new factor began to appear in Turkish and Balkan politics, of the deepest importance to the destiny of the world—the new German Empire.

German influence in the Ottoman Empire. For very nearly a century England had held toward Turkey a special position of friend and patron. But from the time of the Congress of Berlin that relationship had been increasingly strained, by the British acquisition of Cyprus, by the Greek convention of 1881, by the occupation of Egypt in 1882,

---

[1] Venizelos suggested that there should be set up a tin flag, whose rusting would symbolize the decay of Turkish power.

and still more by the massacres in Armenia. The growing estrangement between Great Britain and Turkey left "a vacancy in the Ottoman Empire," and that vacancy was filled by Germany. Bismarck had regarded the Eastern Question as on the whole of minor importance, yet in certain ways he had turned the German Empire toward Constantinople. It was, however, after his fall that the pro-Turkish attitude was adopted with excessive emphasis by the young Emperor William II. His first ceremonial visit was paid in 1889 to the Sultan Abdul-Hamid at Constantinople. In 1898 the visit was repeated, and a pilgrimage, arranged by Messrs Thomas Cook and Son, was made through the Holy Land. At Damascus the German Emperor proclaimed, in words which resounded through Europe, that "his Majesty the Sultan Abdul-Hamid, and the three hundred million Mohammedans who reverence him as Caliph, may rest assured that at all times the German Emperor will be their friend."

As early as 1881 the reorganization of the Turkish army, which proved so effective in the Græco-Turkish war, had been undertaken by Baron von der Goltz and other German officers.[1] Behind German soldiers came traders and financiers. German commercial travellers penetrated to every corner of the Ottoman Empire, assisted by consular agents and diplomatic influence. A branch of the Deutsche Bank of Berlin was established in Constantinople. The most startling, however, and—as far as the other Powers of Europe were concerned—the most menacing demonstration of German ambitions and policy was seen in His Most Exalted Majesty's Bagdad railway. This bold and enterprising scheme became the keystone of the German system in the East, and was in consequence one of the most serious of international problems from the opening of the twentieth century. It was a grandiose conception, typical of the aspirations of the new German Empire—and of the new German Emperor. Based on concessions granted in 1899 by Turkey to the German Company of Anatolian Railways, a railway system was to be constructed right through the heart of the Ottoman Empire in Asia from the Bosporus to Bagdad and thence to Basra, seventy miles from the head of the Persian Gulf. Its strategic and political importance was fully realized by all the Powers in Europe. A link in a longer chain of communications which reached to Berlin, it opened the way to the commercial penetration and political dominion of Germany in the East. It pointed to the fulfilment of a dream which seems to have begun to haunt German consciousness from this time, that in the event of any dissolution of the Ottoman Empire Asia Minor might fall to Germany.[2] The German Empire,

The Berlin to Bagdad railway.

---

[1] In 1841 Moltke had been sent on a military mission to Constantinople.
[2] See Professor C. Andler, *Pan-Germanism*.

x

having come late to political maturity, coveted the rank of World Power enjoyed by Great Britain, and France, and Russia. She hoped to find it in the East, in the decaying Turkish Empire. As the opening up of the sea-routes of the sixteenth century had diverted trade and power to the Western nations who commanded them so the development of the new land-route eastward would once again turn the tide of empire to that nation which should develop it. The German railway-train to Bagdad should be the harbinger of distant and extensive empire as surely as the sailing-ships of Columbus or of Cabot.

If this vision of empire was not fully apprehended by the other Powers it was realized that the Bagdad railway carried Germany through the dominions of the Porte to the gates of India, that it gave her strategic military control over the Turkish Empire, that it necessitated the adherence of the Balkans to the Kaiser in time of war, and that it menaced the security of French power in Syria and of the British Empire in the East. It was natural that France and Great Britain should regard its construction with apprehension and seek to secure a share in its direction. In the Great War of 1914 these fears were fully realized; Turkey, as she was bound to do, enlisted in the German camp, and the railway, though it was—and is —not yet completed, was of serious importance in the Dardanelles and the Eastern campaigns. After the War, as part of the price of Germany's defeat, the Bagdad railway passed out of German hands into Turkish, British, and French, and with it Germany's visions of Eastern dominion faded, at any rate temporarily.[1]

The new German influence in Turkey at the beginning of the twentieth century was part of a vast political combination which the German Empire was building up and consolidating. It began with the formation of the alliance between Germany and Austria in the seventies; it was enlarged in 1882 by the inclusion of Italy. Ten years later it was extended to Turkey, while a Hohenzollern on the throne of Rumania, another Hohenzollern in the Court of Athens,[2] and even, on occasion, the Saxe-Coburg in Bulgaria proved valuable outworks of the German system.

Its importance has been only too tragically proved. Europe saw forming in her midst a vast and strong coalition stretching from the Baltic to the Gulf of Persia, and centring in an indefatigable and ambitious Germany. The Triple Entente of France, Russia, and Great Britain was the reply to it.

To the Balkans more was involved than the influence of the

[1] When the railway is completed it will be possible to travel by through train from Europe to Basra.
[2] The Kaiser's sister, Princess Sophia, married Constantine, Crown Prince of Greece (king 1913, abdicated 1917).

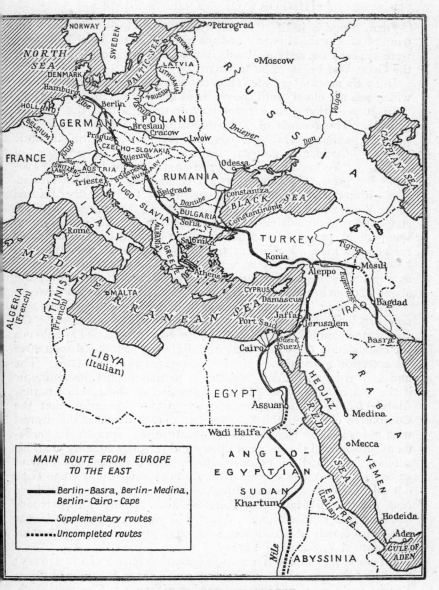

THE BERLIN TO BAGDAD RAILWAY

German Empire itself, for the triumph of Germany meant the triumph of Austria-Hungary, and the interests of the Dual Monarchy were opposed not only to Russia, but to Serbia. So the shadow of the Great War began to be apparent.

In 1908 a new and crowded chapter opened in the Eastern Question, which was not closed until the whole of Europe was in flames.

In July of that year a revolution occurred within the Turkish Empire. The records of Turkish history are full of palace conspiracies and uprisings, but this was after the authentic Occidental pattern. It was organized by a group of "Young Turks" called the Committee of Union and Progress. For many years a reforming party had been in existence within the Ottoman Empire, consisting of Turks mostly educated in the West, who were desirous of rejuvenating the decaying Turkish state, and of reorganizing it along Western lines. Their inspiration was twofold, partly democratic—they put forward familiar demands for a constitution, a Parliament, freedom of speech and worship—and largely nationalist. They were bent upon Turkey's taking her place as a great empire among the progressive nations of the world, and above all upon her freeing herself from the tutelage of foreign Powers.[1]

The "Young Turk" propaganda had been spread by means of secret societies, and had made particular headway in the army. On July 23 the Committee of Union and Progress proclaimed at Salonica the constitution of 1876, which Abdul-Hamid had issued soon after his accession to the throne and had abrogated two years later. The 2nd and 3rd Army Corps threatened to march on Constantinople if the Sultan refused to endorse the action of the revolutionaries. Abdul-Hamid, however, immediately yielded, declaring that the Committee of Union and Progress had only anticipated the dearest wish of his heart. He reissued the constitution, summoned a Parliament, proclaimed the personal liberty and religious equality of all his subjects, abolished the Press censorship, and dismissed his army of 40,000 spies. A few months later Abdul-Hamid prepared to wipe out all his concessions and bring about a counter-revolution by a *coup d'état*. In May 1909, therefore, the "Young Turk" troops marched into Constantinople, declared Abdul-Hamid deposed, sent him into closely guarded seclusion, and proclaimed his brother, Mohammed V, Sultan of Turkey.

An era of reform and liberal rule seemed to have set in in Turkey; the new Government received the warmest congratulations of Great Britain, and for a time Germany was out of favour at Constantinople. The hopes roused by the "Young Turk" revolution, however, proved

The "Young Turk" revolution of 1908-9.

[1] The Anglo-Russian Entente of 1907 also modified the situation and made it clear that Turkey would no longer be able to trust for survival, as she had done for a century, to the quarrels and rivalries of the two Great Powers.

illusory. A reaction set in; a vigorous nationalism became the keynote of the policy of the new party, and the Porte embarked upon a rigid policy of Turkification, of national and religious persecution, which was more irritating and oppressive than ever.

The outbreak of the revolution, however, had set all the problems which had accumulated round the Eastern Question in motion again, and precipitated a series of events which led in six years to the Great War.

In October 1908 Prince Ferdinand of Bulgaria, taking advantage of the difficulties at Constantinople, and afraid that a rejuvenated Turkey might strengthen her hold upon the Bulgarian state, resolved to defy the Treaty of Berlin, to throw off the sovereignty of the Porte, and to turn his principality into a kingdom. In the church of the Forty Martyrs in the ancient capital of Tirnova he assumed the historic title of Tsar of Bulgaria. *Bulgaria proclaimed an independent kingdom.* The Sultan was furious, and appealed to the Powers, but finally consented to take a money compensation. This Bulgaria refused to pay, and war seemed imminent. It was averted, however, by Russia, who arranged to lend to Bulgaria most of the required indemnity, and in April 1909 the Turkish Parliament recognized the independence of the Bulgarian kingdom.

Two days after Prince Ferdinand's proclamation, on October 7, Austria announced her annexation of Bosnia and the Herzegovina, which she had occupied as a mandatory of the Congress of Berlin. "When the Eastern Question is solved," prophesied Mazzini, "Europe will be confronted with an Austrian problem." From her expulsion from Germany *Austria annexes Bosnia and the Herzegovina.* in 1866 Austria had turned with increasing purpose to the southeast, realizing that her interests there were more vital to her than the control of the Straits to Russia, or the Suez Canal to Great Britain. For they were both economic and racial, and consequently affected the whole integrity of her empire.

Economically it was essential that she should have a secure outlet to the sea. Her Adriatic coastline was short, and her position there precarious. It was threatened not only by Italy, who desired to gain the former dominions of the Venetian Empire, but also by an ambitious Serbia, anxious to acquire, *Austro-Serbian rivalry.* both for ethnological and economic reasons, the Dalmatian fringe of the Adriatic. The annexation of Bosnia and the Herzegovina doubly strengthened the Dual Monarchy; it gave a hinterland to the Dalmatian coast, linking it up with Hungary, and so fortifying the Austrian position on the Adriatic; further, it brought her several miles nearer the Ægean, which, if ever she were cut off from the Adriatic, would become her only maritime outlet.

In so far as the annexation advanced Austria's purposes, however, it retarded those of Serbia. The small principality [1] had been one of the first to achieve emancipation from Turkey, and although much of the nineteenth century had been occupied with dynastic quarrels between the rival houses of Obrenović and Kara Georgević, with internal organization and measures to buttress her independence, she had never lost sight of the historic greatness that had once been hers. To restore the mediæval kingdom of Serbia had been to her people a constant ambition, fortified, as the nineteenth century developed into the twentieth, by economic considerations and racial aspirations. To her as to Austria it was economically vital that she should go down to the Adriatic. Moreover, she had come to look upon herself with growing conviction as the champion and liberator of the South Slavs,[2] not only in the Turkish territory of Macedonia, but in Bosnia and the Herzegovina, and of the Croats and Slovenes in Dalmatia. Her ambitions grew side by side with the discontent of the Slavs under Magyar dominion. The one fostered the other, and the Habsburg empire soon saw itself seriously threatened with disruption in the interests of Serbian nationalism. From the fall of the decadent Obrenović dynasty in 1903 with the murder of King Alexander of Serbia and his wife Queen Draga,[3] the rivalry of the two countries grew acute. Austria tried to cripple the ambitious Balkan state with restricting tariffs, which led to the so-called 'pig war' of 1905-6. Antagonism merely bred fresh antagonism, and the relations between the two became a network of hostile intrigue.

When, therefore, the "Young Turk" revolution of 1908 introduced a new factor into the Eastern Question and confounded diplomatic calculation Austria determined to act quickly, lest the new *régime* at Constantinople should thwart her later. She therefore annexed Bosnia and the Herzegovina, which she had hitherto merely administered. To Serbia it was a serious blow, to Europe a menacing disturbance of the Balance of Power, and an international crisis was precipitated. But behind the Dual Monarchy was the German Empire "in shining armour," strong and ready to defy Europe. On the other side Russia, weakened by her conflict with Japan, was unprepared for a fresh war. For the sake of peace France, Russia, and Great Britain swallowed their humiliation, accepted the annexation, and tore up the twenty-fifth article of the Treaty of Berlin,

[1] Kingdom in 1882.

[2] The Slav races are commonly divided into three groups—the Eastern in Russia, the North-western, consisting mainly of the Poles and Czechs, and the Southern, or Yugo-Slavs (*yug*, a Slavonic word, meaning 'south'), formed by the Serbs, Croats, and Slovenes.

[3] The assassination is sometimes said to have been instigated by Austria. If so it was not in her interest.

while Serbia, sullen and defiant, had perforce to retire.   As a sop to Turkey Austria withdrew her garrisons from the Sanjak of Novibazar, and paid the Porte an indemnity.

The crisis passed without war, but in a triumphant Austria-Hungary and a Germany intoxicated with success—for it was her victory—in an alarmed Europe, in an irritated Russia and an incensed Serbia, was all the fuel heaped up for a future conflagration.

The next blow came from an unexpected quarter.   The new kingdom of Italy had joined the ranks of empire-seekers, and she, like Germany, had staked out her claim in the Ottoman Empire.   The Tripoli war between Italy and Turkey (1911-12). It was to the north shore of Africa that she looked, and since France had appropriated Algeria and Tunisia, and England was in possession of Egypt, the Turkish vilayet or dependency of Tripoli was alone left for her enterprise.   As early as 1878 Italy had indicated to Europe the direction of her desires, and it had gradually come to be recognized by the Powers that in the event of any liquidation of the Turkish Empire Tripoli should go to Italy.   For some years she had been clearing the path of empire by commercial and economic penetration.   Then came the "Young Turk" revolution, followed by a determined attempt to drive out European influence from the Turkish dominions.   About the same time Germany began to show a suspicious zeal for scientific research in Tripoli.   Was this the prelude to awakened German ambitions in Tripoli, or was it part of the bid which Germany was making for the renewed favour of the Turkish Empire?   Germany was, it is true, an ally of Italy, but the German-Italian alliance was beginning to show signs of strain.   In any case Italy began to see before her the prospect of being entirely ousted from Tripoli unless she struck at once.   On September 25, 1911, therefore, she suddenly declared war on Turkey and occupied the coast towns of Tripoli, Bengazi, and Disna.   In the following spring the Italian navy attacked the Porte at several points, bombarded the entrance to the Dardanelles, and occupied Rhodes and the Dodecanese Archipelago.   Turkey, hoping to be relieved by an international complication, obstinately refused to make concessions.   The war dragged on through 1912, until the sudden appearance of a new danger forced the Porte to terms, and by the Peace of Lausanne in October 1912 Tripoli was ceded to Italy.

The new danger arose from the Balkans.   An unprecedented phenomenon had arisen.   A union of the Christian states, long discussed and long delayed by mutual rivalries, had at last been formed, and, largely owing to the statesmanship of the The Balkan League. great Cretan, Venizelos, who had become minister of Greece, a league had been formed between Greece, Serbia, Montenegro, and Bulgaria.

Since the beginning of the nineteenth century the serious condition of the Christians in Macedonia had engaged the attention of the Powers of Europe and of the Balkan states. It had been the subject of many Notes on the part of the European Powers, and of many empty promises of reform on the part of Turkey. The condition of the Macedonian Christians had, however, grown no better, and in 1903 the Powers had placed the whole matter in the hands of Austria and Russia, who had by an agreement at Mürzsteg in that year established a form of joint control over Macedonia as a guarantee for the execution of Turkish reforms. Subsequently an international finance committee was formed to watch over the collection of taxes. The arrangement was unsatisfactory all round. The Austro-Russian condominium went to pieces on Austria's ambitions in the Balkans, and in return for a railway concession from Turkey the Habsburg Government practically abandoned the reforms in Macedonia. Turkey, on the other hand, saw Macedonia gradually passing from her into the hands of the Powers, and it was largely to save this last remnant of her empire that the "Young Turkish" revolution broke out. On the triumph of the "Young Turks," therefore, an attempt was made to rivet the rule of the Ottomans more firmly on Macedonia, and the lot of the Christians grew worse. The existing Balkan states, seeing the helplessness of the Powers, determined to take the matter into their own hands and to demand the execution of reforms in Macedonia. The Balkan League was formed for this purpose,[1] and when Turkey refused to concede to their demands war was declared by the four allied states in the beginning of October 1912. In vain the Powers issued a warning that no territorial modifications would be allowed in the peninsula. The Balkan states were determined to defy them; they had never had so good an opportunity of attacking their ancient enemy; they were embarked upon a Holy Crusade which promised them also territorial aggrandizement.

The first phase of the war lasted for three months. On four sides the Turkish Empire was assaulted. The Bulgarians crossed into Thrace and won the battle of Kirk-Kilisseh; they followed it up with a week's hard fighting known as the battle of Lule Burgas, invested Adrianople, and drove the Turks back upon their own capital.

The First Balkan War, (1) October–December 1912.

The Serbians marched into Novibazar, defeated the Turks at the battle of Kumonov, and so wiped out the historic defeat of Kossovo.[2] They captured the ancient Serbian capital of Uskub, advanced to Monastir and into Albania, and in November seized the Adriatic

---

[1] It was alleged by Germany that Russian ambition lay behind the Balkan League.
[2] Famous in Balkan history and legend as the battle (1389) in which the power of Serbia was destroyed by the Turks.

port of Durazzo. The Montenegrins also invaded Albania. The Greeks invaded Thessaly and walked into Salonica, which fell to them on November 8. At sea, for Greece alone had any pretensions to sea-power, they blockaded the Turkish ports and captured numerous Ægean islands. At the beginning of December, however, the Powers imposed an armistice, and a conference of belligerents was called to London. Turkey had been overwhelmingly defeated by four small Balkan states whose combined populations numbered ten millions. She did not hold a foot of ground in Europe outside the four cities of Constantinople, Adrianople, Janina, and Albanian Scutari. The problem of Turkish disintegration was again before Europe.

That Turkey must surrender a large part of her European dominions was evident; that she should surrender all of it neither she nor the Powers of Europe would recognize. As far as the negotiations between Turkey and the Balkans were concerned the difficulties centred in two main problems—whether Rumania should have compensation in the Dobrudja for her neutrality, and whether Turkey should retain the four cities she still held. By January 1913 the former question was settled in Rumania's favour; with regard to the latter, it was decided that Turkey should surrender Adrianople and retain the other three.

The proposed surrender of Adrianople, however, roused the furious indignation of the "Young Turks." The terms were denounced, the armistice terminated, and at the be- (2) February ginning of February war was renewed between the Porte -May 1913. and the Balkan League. The resumption of war merely heaped up disaster upon Turkey. In March Adrianople fell to Bulgaria and Serbia, the Greeks achieved a brilliant capture of Janina, and after persistent efforts Scutari, in Albania, was won by the Montenegrins and Serbs. The question of Scutari, however, was part of the whole Austrian problem, and Montenegro and Serbia were quickly robbed of their triumph by the Powers, who forced them to surrender the town to an international commission.

The Balkan victories again forced Turkey to terms, and in May 1913 peace was made at London. Turkey lost everything except a small portion of Thrace which covered Constantinople. All her territory outside a line drawn between Midia, on the Black Sea, and Enos, on the Ægean, and running south of Adrianople, was to be ceded to the Balkan allies, who were to settle its disposition. Albania was set up as an autonomous state under the Prince of Wied. Crete was at last allowed to unite with Greece. These terms were not reached without extreme difficulty, and more than once it seemed as if the peace of Europe would be broken. The approach of Bulgaria toward Constantinople had threatened to raise what was to Russia a question of the direst significance. But the fate of Constantinople was postponed for another war by the conclusion of the armistice and the final retention of the Turkish capital by the Porte. It was the question of Albania that caused the sharpest division, for it reopened the Austrian question of 1908. Serbia's own wish was to divide the province with Montenegro, and so secure the Adriatic outlet which she seemed never likely to acquire in Dalmatia. To this Austria was resolutely opposed.

Great Britain, France, and Russia, on the other hand, were inclined to support the claims of Serbia, and between December and March there was an imminent danger of war between Austria and Russia, both of whom went as far as to mobilize their troops. Russia secured a promise of aid from France,[1] and behind Austria-Hungary was Germany. To Germany the success of the Balkan League had come as a disagreeable surprise. She had barely succeeded in regaining her influence at Constantinople, shaken by the "Young Turk" revolution of 1908. Now a new obstacle, in the Balkan League, appeared between Berlin and Constantinople. The solidarity of the Christian states must be broken down. If Serbia were cut off from her ambitions in Albania and toward the Adriatic she would turn for expansion toward the Ægean, and so come into conflict with Greece and Bulgaria. Discord would be introduced among the Balkan allies, and in a divided camp Germany would once again win a dominant place.

Germany was therefore fully in sympathy with Austria-Hungary, and Austria-Hungary was undoubtedly spoiling for a war. Whether it was because Germany was not yet fully prepared for a conflict or for some other reason, she urged caution and moderation upon her Habsburg ally. In addition, Sir Edward Grey, president of the conference, exerted all his powers to keep the peace. For the second time, therefore, in the interests of peace Austria triumphed, and the European war which was threatening to break out over the Eastern Question was averted. It was, however, only postponed for fifteen months.

In the Balkans the quarrels of the Powers were being reproduced with fervour, and the Balkan League was rapidly breaking up over **The Second Balkan War (June–August 1913).** the division of the spoils. Macedonia was a microcosm of the Balkan problem. It was a 'no man's land,' or an 'all men's land,' where every interest was represented. To Greece the existence of a large number of Greeks and the 'cultural' and spiritual affinities between the Macedonians and the Hellenes constituted strong claims to ownership. It had, moreover,

[1] She could also count at least upon the friendly neutrality of Great Britain.

once been part of the Hellenic empire of the past, and was essential to any revival of it in the future.

Serbia based her claim partly on the presence of Slavs in Macedonia, but chiefly on the need for compensation for the Albanian disappointment.

Bulgaria protested that the bulk of the Macedonian population was formed by Bulgars, and that as long as the Straits were held by an alien Power it was essential that she should have an outlet to the Ægean. She had not forgotten that at the Treaty of San Stefano she had once been awarded the greater part of Macedonia, and it had been her constant ambition ever since to recover the Greater Bulgaria which had then been framed.

The rival claims of the Balkan states, aggravated by Central European intrigues, were irreconcilable, and at the end of June 1913 war broke out between Bulgaria on the one side and Serbia, Montenegro, Greece, and Rumania on the other. The war lasted for a month. Bulgaria, surrounded by enemies on all sides, was hopelessly outranged and severely defeated. Turkey seized the opportunity to try to recover part of what she had lost; she also declared war on Bulgaria and recaptured Adrianople. At the instance of Austria, who had no wish to see Bulgaria further humiliated by a triumphant Serbia and Greece, peace was made at Bukarest in August 1913. On all sides Bulgaria was forced to make concessions. To Rumania in the north she surrendered Silistria and a large part of the Dobrudja; to Greece, Serbia, and Montenegro she abandoned considerable sections of the Macedonia which she had claimed; to Turkey she gave up Adrianople and part of Thrace, so that the Porte gained as much again as had been left to her by the Treaty of London. Territorially the final results of the two Balkan wars were the practical extinction of the Turkish Empire in Europe and the enlargement of the Christian kingdoms. Turkey retained Constantinople, Adrianople, the two straits of the Bosporus and the Dardanelles, and the territory between them. Rumania added 286,000 subjects to her population, which was, and is, the largest in the Balkans, and gained 2687 square miles of territory at the expense of Bulgaria. Bulgaria's gains consisted of 125,000 inhabitants and 9000 square miles in Macedonia. She reached to the Ægean, it is true, but her acquisitions were less than half of what she had claimed. Montenegro nearly doubled her small principality by the addition of the western half of Novibazar. Serbia and Greece were the greatest gainers. Serbia increased her population from three millions to four and a half, and her territory from 18,000 to 33,000 square miles. Greece won Crete and other Ægean islands and extensive gains in Macedonia, including Salonica and the northern coast of the Ægean as far as the island of Thasos. She increased her population by nearly two millions, and her area by more than 15,000 square miles.

There were other results. Bulgaria nursed a deep resentment—which she was to indulge, to her own disaster, in the Great War—against the Balkan neighbours who had robbed her of the fruits of her victories over the Turks. Russia appeared again in the *rôle* of protector of the Balkan states, no longer against the Porte, but against Austria. Germany took in hand the reorganization of the Turkish army. Above all the bitter rivalry between Austria and Serbia came again to an issue, in which again Austria triumphed and Serbia was worsted. The smaller kingdom sought revenge and an outlet to her exasperation in desperate intrigues among the South Slav subjects of the Dual Monarchy, in an attempt to detach the Bosnians and Herzegovinians, Croats and Slovenes, from their allegiance. The larger empire, equally determined to put an end to Serbian ambitions, and apparently convinced that a severe military defeat was necessary to teach her Balkan rival a lesson, began to look for a *casus belli*. On so modern a period considerable further elucidation is needed. As far as is known, in 1913 Austria-Hungary informed the Italian Foreign Office that she intended to make war against Serbia, and that she expected Italy's support under the terms of the Triple Alliance.

On June 23, 1914, the Austrian Archduke Franz Ferdinand was assassinated by a Serbian anarchist in the Bosnian town of Serajevo. The opportunity had at last come to settle accounts. The fuse that fired the bomb fired also the Great War.

CHAPTER VIII

THE AGE OF ARMED PEACE (1871–1914)

I. INTERNAL AFFAIRS IN THE CHIEF COUNTRIES OF EUROPE

THERE was peace in Europe for four decades; in the west from the Treaty of Frankfurt in 1871 to the Great War of 1914, and in the east from the Congress of Berlin in 1878 to the Balkan war of 1912.[1] As after the Revolutionary and Napoleonic wars, a long period of consolidation and conservation followed one of intense movement and great constructive activity. In both cases Europe was striving to adapt herself to new forces and new phenomena; in the first case to French republicanism, in the second to Imperial Germanism, each the vital and essential product of the preceding activity. Both periods were also years of great political preparation, but of no marked political reconstruction; of considerable cultural achievement, and of rapid economic development.

A period of international peace.

The age preceding the war of 1914 was distinguished on the whole by three chief tendencies, common to the greater part of Europe.

Three chief features.

The first was its industrialism, which transformed the nations of the West and penetrated into the hinterland of Poland and Russia. With ever-increasing skill and confidence mankind turned to its uses the resources of the economic revolution which had been consummated during the century. With growing acceleration the pace of industrial and scientific progress advanced. Each new invention outreached the one before it. Hand labour had long given way to mechanical labour; mechanical labour itself became the subject of successive revolutions. The age of steam passed into the age of electricity, the age of coal into the age of oil. The train from the forties, the bicycle from the eighties, the motor-car with the beginning of the new century, superseded the horse as the agent of transport. Successful experiments with the aid of petrol fuel began to be made in aeronautics; the marvels of the telegraph began to yield to those of wireless telegraphy, while similar advances were made in medicine, chemistry, and other sciences.

(1) Industrialism.

Simple processes and small units tended to be merged in the

---

[1] The Russo-Japanese War of 1905, although concerned with a European Power, may be held to be outside the range of European wars.

growing complexity of industrial organization. The improvement of the means and rate of transport minimized distance and extended time; it facilitated the linking up of all parts of the world, the opening up of unexplored regions, the development of foreign markets and world-trade. It encouraged the centralization and consolidation of nations, and brought them into closer touch with each other. The internationalization of finance followed the internationalization of trade and industry. Vast systems of credit spread like a web over the world. The people of all nations became economically and financially dependent upon each other, their incomes came from foreign investments, the food on their tables was drawn from all parts of the earth.

Within the nations new forces arose out of industrialism; new classes reared their heads to claim rights and powers. Women and the working classes presented new demands and a new attitude to life.

A chain of advocates, from the learned Dutch Labadist of the seventeenth century, Anna von Schürman, and the better-known wife of Godwin, Mary Wollstonecraft, and the Revolu-

A revolution in the position of women.

tionaries of the late eighteenth century, to John Stuart Mill and others in the middle of the nineteenth, has pleaded for political and professional freedom for women. The greater social security, the wider opportunities of education and economic independence, which came with the extension of industrialism toward the end of the nineteenth century, were the causes— as they were also the objects—of a renewed and more general woman's movement at the end of the nineteenth century and the beginning of the twentieth. Much was achieved before the War. New schools and colleges offered unprecedented facilities for education; one by one the barriers that closed the professions to women were broken down by the efforts of pioneers; public examinations were thrown open to them; commerce was invaded; married women were allowed to hold property in their own title; other disabilities were removed; and after the War a full or approximate political equality has been accorded to women in most modernized countries of the world.[1] In professional and economic opportunities, in political and legal status, and in social independence a revolution has been accomplished in the life of the average woman.

As great a revolution has been produced in the position of the artisan, and the great working-class movement in all its

(2) The movement of, or on behalf of, the working classes.

aspects is the second dominant feature of the period under review.

The Industrial Revolution did not create privileged— and by implication unprivileged—orders, nor did it introduce poverty or class distinctions. It did, however, open up new

[1] They have not yet received the vote in France, and have recently suffered a marked recession of status in Nazi Germany and Fascist Italy.

avenues to privilege and power, as well as new causes of poverty, while the great increase of population which attended the Industrial Revolution magnified the scale upon which these features were produced. It created, in fact, the capitalist employer and the factory hand—on the one side a class of men acquiring wealth, privilege, and power through the organizing and hiring of the labour of other men, and on the other a body of wage-earners, giving their labour on hire, forced into a practical economic dependence by the necessities of subsistence, and by the lack of capital, ambition, enterprise, or organizing skill on their own account. Moreover, at the beginning of that revolution in industry which followed the introduction of machinery certain obvious and intolerable evils were insinuated into the factory system and the life of the working classes by the haste, inexperience, ignorance, callousness, selfishness, and hardships accompanying any transitional period. Men, women, and children were employed for meagre payments and excessive hours, under insanitary and deleterious conditions, until the worker, with ruined health, brokenly fighting the starvation and oppression that continually threatened him, seemed the veritable 'wage-slave' described by his most ardent champions. There were other burdens, the constant fear and the periodic recurrence of unemployment, deliberately fostered, declared the enemies of the capitalist system, by the employers themselves that they might have a reserve of cheap labour on which to draw. There was the æsthetic and intellectual depression of factory organization, of over-specialization of labour, and the deadening confinement of a worker to a single repetitive process.[1] He was allowed to have neither interest in the completed article nor profit in its merchandizing. There were many workers, of course, who, of greater energy or ability than their fellows, rose to the ranks of the capitalist and employing class; the greater number who could not do so formed the ranks of an often discontented proletariat.

Such briefly were the circumstances and considerations which led to a demand throughout the industrial world for the amelioration of the conditions of the working classes. The impulse has expressed itself in three ways.

It has led first to the trade union movement, which is in essence a spontaneous form of defence adopted by the working man to protect himself against the dependence and oppression to which he **(a) Trade** was exposed. He speedily realized the ancient principle **Unionism.** that combined action is more effective than isolated effort, and collective bargaining than individual negotiation. The suggestion to organize was contained in the economic grouping of the workers

[1] See, for example, Adam Smith's famous description of a pin factory in *The Wealth of Nations*, Book IV.

already at hand. Combinations of workmen employed in the same occupations—as also of employers, who as readily grasped the fact that union served their interests—were in existence before the end of the eighteenth century, but largely on account of the violence to which they gave rise they were condemned in England by statute until 1824 as illegal and criminal associations. From 1825 they were given a measure of toleration, but it was not until Gladstone's law of 1871 that they were legalized. In France they were dissolved by the Revolutionary Act of 1791, which closed all guilds or corporations affecting the regulation of trade or industry. During the last years of the Second Empire they began to be tolerated, but they were not legalized until Waldeck-Rousseau's measure of 1884. In Germany also, although an Act passed by Bismarck in 1878 prohibited trade unions, the law was evaded, and industrial organizations grew up there as in other countries. All over Europe trade unions multiplied and prospered. Agricultural unions were formed on the model of the industrial bodies, but later, owing to the more scattered nature of agrarian occupations and the greater difficulty of organization. There is to-day hardly an industry, occupation, or even profession without its union. There is, of course, no legal compulsion upon a worker to join the union of his trade; he is usually inclined to do so, and in any case it is in practice very difficult for him to remain outside. All kinds of pressure—often beyond the bounds of equity or liberty—are brought to bear upon all workers in a trade to induce them to join the union and accept its regulations of hours and wages. For it is obvious that much of the effectiveness of combination will be vitiated if a large number of workers in an industry refuse to co-operate. Large funds invested in Government stocks, raised by contribution from the members, are now at the disposal of the unions for benefit purposes, for political action through Parliament and local governing bodies, and for financing strikes. For Labour's greatest weapon is the strike, either of a single union or of several unions in sympathy.[1] The employer's corresponding weapon is the lock-out.

The unions were organized primarily to fight the employer; but the practical monopoly which they have acquired, together with the necessity of uniform action and regulation among the members, has enabled them to exercise over the worker a power which is sometimes felt to amount to tyranny. His rate of work and pay is rigidly super-

[1] A general strike—i.e., a simultaneous laying down of tools by all employed workers—long advocated, was attempted in Sweden in 1909, in Italy in 1914, in Great Britain in 1926, and elsewhere. The strike usually defeated its own ends by stirring up against the unions a violent public opinion, infuriated by the general dislocation and by the attempt to make war upon the community. The Communists, with a view to securing possession to the workers, advocate the 'stay-in strike,' by which the workers lay down tools but remain inside the factory.

vised, independent enterprise, such as working faster or longer, is sternly discouraged; and although the trade unions are ostensibly democratic bodies the will of the majority is often seriously obstructed. On the other hand the unions have secured immense benefits for the workers; they have achieved successive reductions in the hours of work and increases in the rate of pay, until in most industries the workers have attained a standard of living undreamt of by their fathers.

Other factors have, of course, entered into this result, in particular various national, municipal, and private enterprises which are to be regarded as the expression of another impulse toward (b) Reforms improving the lot of the people of the working classes. from above. This may be summarized as reform, or attempted reform, from above, from the State, the municipality, or the employer, induced partly by the agitation of the working men and partly by spontaneous philanthropy. The welfare of the poor man and the working classes has been the direct or indirect object of the host of Factory Acts— more than forty in England during the nineteenth century—regulating hours and age of employment, enjoining safe and sanitary conditions of work, appointing factory inspection, fixing minimum rates; of the housing, sanitation, and public-health laws, of the establishment of extensive free education and medical benefits; of the progressive democratization of local and central government, of the Workmen's Compensation Act, and of national insurance schemes for sickness and unemployment, of old age pensions, and of many municipal undertakings. It has been, among other things, the consideration of enlightened and philanthropic employers, who have set up model factories, instituted profit-sharing systems of wages, furthered housing schemes, encouraged the study of industrial psychology, and promoted the general contentment and welfare of their work-people.

There still remains the third expression of the working-class movement, socialism. To a certain number of people the achievements and reforms sketched above are only partial (c) Social- remedies, or no remedies at all, of fundamental industrial ism. evils, or they are Greek gifts, securing the betrayal of the working classes. Men and women of such a way of thinking have turned to socialism. The term is vague, and is used to cover everything from a philanthropic attitude to an anarchistic impulse, from a mood of revolt in the 'have-nots' of the world, and a tendency to Utopianism, to an economic formula.[1] "There are as many varieties of socialism," it has been said, "as there are socialists." The title may be more strictly applied, however, to three main tenets, upon which socialists

---

[1] There are said to be more than 260 contemporary definitions of socialism.

Y

A HISTORY OF MODERN TIMES

are generally agreed. First, it is an indictment, on account of the evils of modern industrial civilization, of private capitalism, sometimes only as an economic system, sometimes as a social structure. Secondly, it is a championing of the wage-earning class—in some cases this is held to cover the professional classes, in others it is not—as against the employer, the capitalist, the financier, and those who derive an income from invested capital. Thirdly, it includes the advocacy in some form or degree of the communal ownership of land, capital, property, and enterprises of public benefit—in short, of the means of production.

The chief varieties of socialism centre in two main questions—first, what form of 'community' is to own the means of production and whether any admixture of private enterprise is to be accepted; secondly, when and by what means shall this transference from private to communal ownership be made? Most socialists are agreed upon the abolition or partial abolition of private property, but they are disagreed as to what form of public ownership shall supersede it. The moderate socialist, the British Labour Party, sections of French and German socialists, advocate what is known as 'collectivism,' the ownership by the State of the means of production. Syndicalists, on the other hand, who are strong in France and Italy, and are allied to the I.W.W.[1] in America, aim at ownership by 'organized labour' along the lines of an industry or craft.[2] Under collectivism the railways would be owned and managed by the State; under syndicalism they would be owned and run by the railway workers. Another manifestation has appeared in 'anarchist communism,' though its force is now largely spent, which pressed for free ownership of the means of production by everbody, without explaining clearly how it was to be done. Bakunin and Kropotkin, chief exponents of these views, would have abolished wage systems entirely, as well as the obligation to work. "There is to be no compulsion, no law, no Government exercising force; there will still be acts of the community, but these are to spring from universal consent, not from any enforced submission of even the smallest minority." [3] All things were to be shared equally among the whole population.

There are similar divisions as to the methods of achievement. The moderates would obtain their ends by Parliamentary machinery and constitutional means, with the help of occasional strikes. The syndicalists press for a class war, conducted by industrial rather than

[1] Industrial Workers of the World.
[2] There is to-day a growing tendency for socialists to group themselves into two classes, Communists on the one hand and non-Communists on the other.
[3] See Bertrand Russell, *Roads to Freedom*, pp. 65 and 39.

political methods, by the strike, boycott, label,[1] and sabotage.   The Russian communists and their friends, on the other hand, preach the necessity of immediate revolution to overthrow the capitalist state.

Two other distinctions should be noticed.   While the moderates are usually nationalist in their sympathies, and confine their programme predominantly to economic matters, the extremists tend to advocate world-wide revolution and to include in their hostility such *bourgeois* or capitalist institutions as the Church, marriage, and so on.

The most important figure in modern socialism is Karl Marx. There were socialists before him, in England such men as Thomas Hodgskin (1787–1869), William Thompson (1785–1833), and, above all, Robert Owen (1771–1858); in France Fourier (1772–1837), Saint-Simon (1760–1825), and Proudhon (1809–65).   The years 1793 and 1848 had, moreover, witnessed the "proletariat in action," and seen direct socialist experiments in France.   None of the socialists who preceded Marx, however, had founded a strong or stable political party; to him, in collaboration with Engels, is due both the formulation of a body of socialist doctrine and the foundation of an international socialist movement.

Karl Marx was born in 1818 at Trier, in Rhenish Prussia.   His father, a Jewish convert to Christianity, was a legal official in the Prussian service; and his home was one of enlightenment   **Karl Marx** and easy means.   Marx studied at the universities of Bonn   **(1818–83).** and Berlin, concentrating chiefly on history, philosophy, jurisprudence, and political economy, and falling under the influence, like most of the youth of his day, of the philosopher Hegel.   It was from him that he imbibed the conception of history as a developing idea and an irresistible process that cannot be deflected.   Marx rapidly became one of the keenest sympathizers of the revolutionary and democratic agitations of Young Germany, and in 1842 he began to edit a Radical newspaper, which was suppressed in the following year by the Prussian Government.   Marx thereafter moved to Paris, where he came into contact with the French socialists, and where he also met Friedrich Engels (1820–95), who became his lifelong friend and co-worker.   Engels, the son of a wealthy German cotton-spinner, had lived for some time, for business purposes, in Manchester, where he had become acquainted with the doctrines of English socialists.   In 1845 Marx was expelled from Paris, and with his wife, who followed him through all the vicissitudes of his life, and with Engels, he went to live in Brussels, where he carried on his activities.   He was by this time becoming well known as a socialist, and in 1847 he was asked to

---

[1] To show that work is done under trade union conditions.

draw up a manifesto for the German Communist League in Paris. Thus was published the famous *Communist Manifesto* of 1848, "the birth cry of modern socialism." During the German revolutions of that year Marx paid a brief visit to Cologne, and edited a Socialist paper, which was suppressed upon the failure of the revolutions. He then took refuge in London, chiefly in the British Museum, where he spent most of his remaining years in preparing his *magnum opus*, *Das Kapital*.[1] *Das Kapital* is a stiff economic work, but it has become, like Rousseau's *Le Contrat Social*, the Bible of a new faith, and the herald of a revolution in ideas and even in politics. There is an interesting similarity of interval, on the one hand of twenty-three years between the publication of the last volume of *Das Kapital* and the outbreak of the Russian Revolution, which undoubtedly owed something to its inspiration; and on the other of twenty-seven years between the appearance of *Le Contrat Social* and the French Revolution.

Marxian Communism is primarily the offspring of German Hegelianism and French socialism. Its fundamental article is that of historical materialism. Marx followed Hegel in the interpretation of historical development on the basis of an irresistible, irreversible "dialectical" process, but whereas Hegel found in this development the manifestation of the "Universal Spirit," Marx saw only economic forces. To Marxian socialists the economic impulse provides the mainspring of human aspirations, and shapes consciously or unconsciously human actions, judgments, institutions, and society. Religion, art, systems of philosophy, are "ideological veils," emanations of, or escapes from, primary economic factors, and the crises and transitions of history are economic in their real significance.

Further, again accepting the Hegelian doctrine that the historical process is dialectical (*i.e.*, the product of continual tension between "opposites"), Marx saw the development of history through continuous conflict, or tension, between "opposing" economic classes. History was to Marx a perpetual class warfare, and the historical progression from ancient to mediæval, from mediæval to modern, was the record of the destruction of oppressor, and the liberation of oppressed, economic classes. The next historical development must also consist in a conflict of economic classes, and to Marx the time seemed ripe for the final [2] war between capitalists and the proletariat.

The immediate programme, then, was to bring about the class war, to educate the proletariat in class-consciousness and the recognition

---

[1] The first and most important volume appeared in 1867; the other two volumes were published posthumously, in 1885 and 1894.

[2] By a curious argument the historical processes were to come to an end in the attainment of the millennium, of the universal triumph of humanity implicit in the victory of the proletariat.

of their capitalist enemy, to enlighten them as to their destiny, to prepare them for their

> inevitable triumph and that of their disciples, to incite to revolution. The Communists disdain to conceal their views and aims. They openly disclose that their ends can be attained only by the forcible overthrow of all existing social conditions. Let the ruling classes tremble at a Communistic revolution.

This declamation from the Communist manifesto of 1848 has formed part of the consistent challenge of Marxian Communism ever since.

On the more technical economic side Marx developed the thesis, derived from Ricardo and the classical English economists, of the "labour theory of value"—that the economic value of a commodity consists in 'human labour crystallized," being directly derived from the labour that has gone to its construction.

Many attacks have been directed upon the Marxian exposition of the labour theory of value and upon the materialistic conception of history. Modern criticism, however, is tending to concentrate upon the secular Messianism and Chiliasm [1] of the Marxian revelation, upon the extraordinary assumption that the wheels of history will stop at the fulfilment of the proletarian revolution, and, above all, upon the weakness of the Marxian application of "dialectical opposites." Marx's whole case rests mainly upon the assumption that capitalism and proletarianism are true "opposites," whose tension will produce the next synthetic historical development. But history is showing that modern industrial development, with its growing complexity and variety, is producing out of Capital and Labour not ever-diverging opposites, but ever-coalescing groups, whose differences and "tension" are being reduced by State regulation, trade union action, philanthropic interest, a rising common standard of living, and the growth of a wage-earning class with capitalistic investments. Thus an interdependent labour-capitalist society is emerging, a complex economic and financial organization of wage-earner, shareholder, manager, and employer. That is the reason, though he did not recognize it, why even Marx doubted the success of a Proletarian Revolution in England, where a highly industrialized civilization has developed on continuous lines through moderate economic and political regulation. In spite of recurring economic agitation, the modern proletariat in such a society is not revolutionary according to the Marxian prescription, and it is interesting to note that the only country where revolutionary Marxism has obtained any considerable success is the highly rural, industrially undeveloped state of Russia.

[1] Messianism is the expectation of the millennium in this world, Chiliasm the hope of heaven upon earth. For these aspects see *Unto Cæsar*, by F. A. Voigt.

Marx's socialism was international. "The Communists are further reproached with desiring to abolish countries and nationality. The working men have no country. We cannot take from them what they have not got." The proletariat is united in bonds of self-interest throughout the world. To promote this consciousness and this end Marx formed in 1864 the "International Working Men's Association," which has become known to history as the First International. It consisted of delegates from most of the countries of Europe; its rules and programme were drawn up by Marx, and The Inter- congresses were held in different European towns. It nationals. seems to have been involved in fostering the Paris Commune of 1870.[1] From about 1868 the Marxian socialists were joined by a strong current, coming mainly from the Latin countries, of anarchists, headed by Bakunin. Marx and Bakunin soon fell, however, to bitter quarrelling, and to mutual accusations of various offences. The quarrel was fomented by national antipathies, which came to a head in the Franco-German War, Bakunin leaning toward France, and Marx naturally to Germany.[2] In 1872 Marx succeeded in suppressing the Bakunin faction and in expelling it from the Association. With that expulsion, however, the First International lost vitality, and it died of inanition after a congress at Geneva in 1874.

Two attempts have been made to revive the International organization of socialism. In 1889, after Marx's death, what is called the Second International was founded. The earlier meetings were devoted to the discussion of the tactics and methods of the affiliated parties; the later, with the shadow of an imminent European conflict upon them, to the questions of war and peace. It was agreed to press counsels of peace upon the different nations, but it was also made clear that should war actually break out each socialist party would take sides with its own Government. This, with few exceptions, is what actually happened, and with the Great War the Second International collapsed like a pricked bubble.

The Third International was formed in 1919. It was organized by the Russian Communists, with headquarters in Moscow, and is definitely revolutionary in character, approximating thereby more nearly to the First than to the Second International. "Its chief purpose is to accelerate the development of events toward world revolution."

Rigid, and more especially revolutionary, Marxism never made great headway in England, whose socialism, like its other institutions, tends to evolve itself in a gradual, practical, and piecemeal fashion. In France also a strong opposition to Marxism comes from the

---

[1] This is also disputed.   [2] Though he did not approve of annexations.

syndicalists, who are at one in preaching the class war, but argue
that the strong central organization by which the proletariat would
establish its 'dictatorship' would merely substitute one tyranny for
another.   In Germany the Marxian revelation was for a time faithfully accepted by the Social Democratic party, founded in 1862
by Ferdinand Lasalle, a man whose charm, culture, and incisive
independence impressed even Bismarck.   At the beginning of the
twentieth century, however, a new movement appeared, known as
'revisionism,' which was in effect a breaking away from Marxian
socialism.   Its leader was Bernstein, whose object "as is common in
Broad Church writers, consists largely in showing that the Founders
did not hold their doctrines so rigidly as their followers have done."[1]
He pointed out that Marx's prophecies had not been fulfilled, and
that his doctrine needed revision.   He emphasized the need for
piecemeal reform, for evolution rather than revolution; he pleaded
for co-operation with other progressive bodies in the state; he
defended the spirit of nationalism rather at the expense of internationalism, and he even went so far as to uphold colonization and
empire-making (that most condemned of *bourgeois* and capitalist
vices) on the grounds that Europeans have a right to tropical territory, owing to their higher civilization.   In other words, revisionists
have fallen into the trap of capitalist nationalism.

In Russia both political and economic conditions favoured violent
opposition to the Government, and revolutionary Marxism there
gained the greatest foothold.   In 1917 a revolution that was partly
political and largely economic broke out; the class war was actually
precipitated, and a definite attempt was made to establish the "dictatorship of the proletariat."

Industrialism and the working-class movement are two of the most
prominent features of the forty years preceding the War.   A third is
the militant nationalism of the age.

In certain respects the age was more international than any which
had preceded it since the birth of nations.   Commerce and trade
tended of themselves to expand beyond political frontiers; (3) Militant
the woman's movement and socialism were common to nationalism.
the Western world; there were improved facilities for travel,
for the spread of the knowledge of other countries, for the communication of ideas; no English musician considered himself worthy
of his art who had not been trained in Germany, and every painter
made a pilgrimage to France.   There was hardly a field of human
endeavour, from religion to seismography, from medicine to yacht-
racing, that had not its international conferences.   There was
co-operation between the Governments on matters of patent and

[1] Bertrand Russell, *Roads to Freedom*, p. 45.

copyright. The growing interdependence of the world was more than ever marked in politics; a development in the Balkans, in China or Africa, and all the chancelleries of Europe were set in motion. There were European conferences on the Eastern Question, on the Moroccan crisis, on the setting up of the Congo Free State. Luxemburg and Belgium were under the protection of the Powers; an international expedition was sent to China. There was an attempt to arrive at an international agreement on the laws of war; the Declaration of Paris in 1856 laid down certain rules for maritime warfare, the Geneva Convention of 1864 neutralized the medical—or, as it came to be called, the Red Cross—service in time of war. There was the endeavour, tragically premature, to promote international arbitration, which, initiated by the Tsar Nicholas II in 1898,[1] found expression in the two Hague Conferences of 1899 and 1907. To the first conference twenty-six out of fifty-nine independent nations sent delegates, and in the second forty-four sovereign states were represented. The efforts of the conferences, especially those directed toward disarmament, broke down, however, before fundamental national rivalries.[2]

For in the light of the Great War of 1914 the internationalism of the preceding decades, however valuable, appears superficial. Underneath was the deep pulsing of national consciousness, able, at the trumpet's blast, to scatter the solidarity of Europe to the winds. There was the unsatisfied national spirit of the Balkan states, of Poland, of the races of Austria-Hungary; there were the quasi-nationalist ambitions of Russia toward Constantinople; there was the exuberant nationalism of the new Germany, restless in its energy, straining at any stabilization which imposed barriers or checks upon its ' drive ' to expansion; there was the partly discontented, partly assertive, nationalism of Italy; there was the outraged nationalism of France, demanding revenge and the reclamation of its lost provinces. All these were storm-centres of Europe, the more so that the atmosphere was charged with the self-consciousness which was

[1] The following extract is from the rescript of the Tsar of Russia convening the first Hague Conference : " 'The preservation of peace has been put forward as the object of international policy. In its name the great states have concluded between themselves powerful alliances; the better to guarantee peace, they have developed their military forces in proportions hitherto unprecedented, and still continue to increase them without shrinking from any sacrifice. All these efforts, nevertheless, have not yet been able to bring about the beneficent results of the desired pacification. . . . In proportion as the armaments of each Power increase do they less and less fulfil the objects which the Governments have set before themselves. Economic crises, due in great part to the system of armaments à outrance and the continual danger which lies in the accumulation of war material, are transforming the armed peace of our days into a crushing burden, which the peoples have more and more difficulty in bearing. It appears evident, then, that if this state of things continues it will inevitably lead to the very cataclysm which it is desired to avert, and the horrors of which make every thinking being shudder in anticipation."

[2] There was a further definition of the laws of war, at the second conference.

the inevitable outgrowth of the emphatic articulateness of the age. There is no greater testimony to the exaltation of the national idea than the part it played in the formulation of the aims of war and the terms of peace from 1914 to 1918.   Before the War it revealed itself, among other ways, in the commercial and military policies of the nations.   Commercialism in itself, as has already been pointed out, tends to break down national delimitations,[1] but in its organization it can and did become a potent source of national rivalry.   In all parts of the world nation competed with nation for the monopoly of markets and in the pursuit of wealth.   At home one state after another adopted high protective tariffs to foster its own industries, to exclude the manufactures of other countries.

A more serious demonstration of the national rivalry was seen in the military competition which turned Europe into a congress of vast armed camps.   At the beginning of the new century nations stood face to face, armed as never before, to the extent of all the resources of a scientific age and of a democratic Treasury, for only a democracy can afford such preparations.

Modern militarism has received two great impulses during the last century.   The first came undoubtedly from the military necessities of the French Revolution, endorsed by the deliberate policy of the Directory and the ambitions of Napoleon.   To that extent militarism must be held to be a product of French democracy, for conscription, introduced first in France, was only adopted in the German states in imitation and in self-defence.

The second impulse came from Prussia.   The might of Prussia and the unity of Germany, as historically achieved, were built upon the Prussian army, upon the practice of conscripted military service and on the principles of scientific warfare.   The sudden—or so it seemed—appearance of Prussia as a powerful military state, her swift, decisive victories over Austria and France, awakened Europe to a realization of a startling fact.   A new force had appeared, scientific militarism created by Prussia—militarism based on detailed preparations conducted with absolute and characteristic thoroughness in the education of each unit, in the study of principles, and in the modernization of equipment.   Some appreciation of this lies behind the dictum that "it was the schoolmaster that won at Sedan."

The immediate consequence of France's defeat in 1870 was to lead to the drastic reorganization of the French army on the basis of compulsory military service.   Then ensued an intense competitive struggle between France and Germany, each watchful, suspicious, and

[1] An interesting illustration of this is that machinery made at Sheffield, England, was used in the Krupp works, the great German armament factory at Essen, for the construction of guns which ultimately were used against England in the War.

afraid of the other, each striving to keep level with and outdo the other in military strength, in the size of the standing army and the quality of its training. In 1885 the French army at its peace strength was 500,000 men, that of Germany, with a slightly larger population, 427,000 men. Twenty years later the French forces had risen to 545,000 and those of Germany to 505,000. Germany possessed, however, not one, but two frontiers to defend. France and Russia were firm allies, and there was a suspicious military development in Russia. Once again Germany set herself to gigantic exertions, and in the spring of 1913 passed a new Army Act which would bring her forces by a stupendous heave to more than 800,000 men.[1]

France followed suit; another Army Act, a peace force to match that of Germany, and the raising of the term of compulsory service to three years, so that in fifteen days she could mobilize an effective force of nearly four million men. It was a stupendous, ruinous effort. France and Germany were almost literally nations in arms.

There was hardly a country which was not affected by this drastic race of armaments, and every major Power of Europe except Great Britain adopted compulsory military service.[2] Britain's island position enabled her to hold aloof to some extent from the military competition, and in 1914 the total strength of the British Army, in all theatres of action, amounted to about 250,000 men.[3] From 1909, however, she became involved in a naval rivalry no less acute, though less greedy of man-power. Great Britain's navy was greater not only than that of any single other country, but than the combined strength of the two next largest navies put together, and it was her ambition to preserve this 'two-power' standard of superiority. Germany had no ambitions toward naval power until the accession of the Emperor William II, but with the new century formidable naval programmes began to be prepared and carried out; naval estimates were increased, battleships and the new type of Dreadnought [4] were built, until Great Britain awoke to the realization not only that her 'two-power standard' superiority was threatened, but that at the existing rate of progress Germany would in five years' time have more capital ships than England. The British Navy estimates went up with a leap, the building of new Dreadnoughts was planned, and Great Britain also entered the race for armaments. Mr Winston Churchill, First Lord

[1] As a basis of comparison it is worthy of note that Germany's post-War army is limited by the terms of the Peace of Versailles to 100,000 men, raised by voluntary enlistment.
[2] In the Great War, of course, Great Britain and even the United States of America adopted it.
[3] Including troops in India and the Colonies, but excluding reserves and Territorials.
[4] First constructed in Great Britain in 1906.

of the Admiralty from 1911 to 1914, explained in 1911 that it was
necessary for the British Navy to be superior to any foreign navy and
to any probable combination which might be formed against her.
This meant in practice a policy of developing in Dreadnought-build-
ing a 60 per cent. superiority over the German navy. From time
to time Great Britain proposed a cessation of shipbuilding, or a

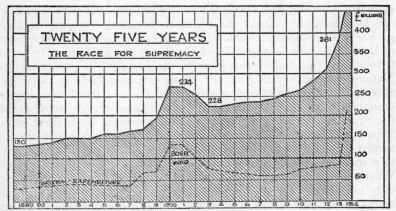

TWENTY FIVE YEARS

THE RACE FOR SUPREMACY

The top curve of this graph indicates the total armament expenditure of Great Britain, France,
Austria-Hungary, Russia, and Italy.

From " Organizing Peace," by permission of the League of Nations Union

'naval holiday,' but Germany had no mind to crystallize her 60 per
cent. inferiority.[1] Thus every nation while protesting its love of
peace continued to prepare for war, justifying defensive measures on
the ground of hostile preparations made by its neighbours.

These three tendencies of modern history before the War—industrialism, the working-class movement in all its phases, and
national militarism—have been emphasized by way of preface to a
brief account of the individual history of the chief nations.

In many ways Germany was accounted a dominant state of
Europe from 1871 to the Great War. William I had been proclaimed German Emperor in the halls of defeated France. Germany,
The Imperial title was an historical reversion and a 1871–1914.
memorial of Germany's mediæval grandeur, but constitutionally it
was something of a misnomer as applied to a federation.[2] There is
an inherent contradiction between the conceptions of empire[3] and

[1] By the Anglo-German Naval Treaty of 1935 a 35 per cent. ratio was accepted
by Germany.   [2] For the general principles of federation see Ch. XII, sect. I.
[3] The word is, of course, now used so commonly, vaguely, and widely that it
is perhaps foolhardy to challenge any application of it.

the conceptions of federation, and it is significant that the German Imperial Federation has not lasted fifty years.[1] Germany was until 1933, like the United States of America, Canada, Switzerland, and (since 1900) Australia, a federal state, bearing resemblance to most of them in some feature. It was an incomplete union formed of twenty-six states, each of which retained full sovereignty in local matters while surrendering it in others. Each state preserved its own Government, legislature, executive, and law-courts. In addition there was a central or federal Government, consisting of a two-housed legislature, an executive, and a supreme court of law. The two Imperial legislative houses embodied, as in other federations, the double character of the State. The Reichstag, or National House, represented the whole empire according to the respective populations of each principality; it was elected by universal manhood suffrage. The Bundesrat, or Federal House, represented the principalities as separate units, not, however, as in the United States of America, on a basis of equality, but according to a quota [2] agreed upon between the Governments. Thus Prussia sent seventeen members, Bavaria, the next largest state, only six; Saxony and Würtemberg four each, while each of seventeen smaller states held only one seat. The Federal executive was vested in the Prussian king as *Deutscher Kaiser*, and in the almost more important Federal Chancellor—an office made, as the Kaiser William II expressed it, to fit "the big cuirassier boots" of Bismarck. His counter-signature was required for the validity of the Imperial decrees, and he "thereby assumes responsibility for them." The phrase meant very little, however, beyond the fact that Bismarck had framed the constitution of the empire "so as to fit in with his extraordinary preponderance as a statesman." [3] There was no such feature as responsible government in the German Imperial constitution until the revision of 1918. The Federal Chancellor was appointed by the Emperor, by whom alone he could be dismissed. An adverse vote in the Reichstag had no power to overthrow him.

The Imperial constitution.

It was natural that the German Empire should show, as an example of federalism, wide differences from the United States of America. It was composed of states of intense independence, with long separate histories, some of them with proud records. Any union between them must be based upon the political situation as it was, with its accumulated historical heritage of centuries, its irreducible irregularities and inequalities, its large states and small states.

---

[1] The monarchical character of the Federation was destroyed in the revolution of 1918. Germany became, for fifteen years, a Federal Republic and a Federation of Republics; then Hitler substituted what is for all practical purposes a unitary state.

[2] In this respect the German Federation resembles the federal dominion of Canada.   [3] *Cf. My Memoirs, 1878–1918,* by ex-Kaiser William II.

The two most marked features of the German Federation were, first, its prevailing monarchical character, and, second, the primacy of Prussia. The first principle revealed itself directly and indirectly. Alone of all federations, the German Federal state was a monarchy and a collection of monarchies, with the exception of the three free cities of Hamburg, Bremen, and Lübeck. The preamble to the constitution declared "that his Majesty the King of Prussia, his Majesty the King of Bavaria, his Royal Highness the Grand Duke of Baden, etc., conclude an eternal alliance." The Federal constitution, like the constitutions of the separate states, was granted from above rather than formulated from below. It was ratified by the State legislatures, but it had already been agreed upon by the Governments.

The monarchical principle was also shown in the nature of the union, which granted to the Federal and Imperial Government extensive legislative powers, but a comparatively small executive authority.[1] Thus it was the legislatures of the separate states that were curtailed by union, not the executive Governments. The executive of the states was in practically every case exercised by the prince and the ministers appointed by him. The State legislatures, like the Federal Reichstag, possessed a controlling or criticizing rather than a ruling power. There was representative but not responsible government. The union, therefore, emphasized through-

---

[1] The executive authority of the German Federation was limited, except for foreign affairs, the navy, and to some extent the army and postal service, to supervision and regulation, as in Switzerland. The customs duties were collected by State officials, who were inspected by Federal inspectors and must act in accordance with Federal laws. Even the coining of money was entrusted to State mints, which were provided with the necessary amount of metal. The states also retained their own law-courts. There was only one Federal law-court—the Reichsgericht—with 100 judges, located at Leipzig, not Berlin. The military organization of the Empire was peculiar ; it was neither wholly Federal nor left entirely to the states. It was in harmony, however, with the general principle of the German Federation —legislative centralization and administrative decentralization. Very elaborate arrangements were made in the constitution concerning the army, for it was characteristic of Bismarck to devote himself to practical details of this nature rather than to theoretical generalizations. Universal obligation to military service was declared throughout the Empire, and every recruit upon enlistment took a joint oath to his territorial sovereign and to the Emperor. But there was no Imperial army in time of peace. There were four armies belonging to Prussia, Saxony, Bavaria, and Würtemberg respectively. A certain uniformity of organization on the Prussian model was demanded, and the armies were inspected by the Emperor and were under his command, their composition, disposal, and regulation were determined by Imperial laws, and the expense of maintaining the army was borne by the Federation. The Emperor also appointed all officers commanding troops of more than one contingent, and the appointment of generals was subject to his approval, but the subordinate officers were left to the choice of each state. In all other respects the management of the troops was left entirely to the control of each state. In time of war, however, the armies were placed under the direct authority of the Emperor.

The navy was on quite a different footing. Prussia alone possessed a navy of any importance in 1871, which she had bought by auction in 1852 from the

out the power of the State executives—*i.e.*, of the princes. It entrusted to them the carrying out of Federal laws and the appointment of representatives to the Bundesrat. Moreover, the endowment of the Bundesrat, which was in practice the organ of the princes, with extensive functions, gave it a predominant voice over the Reichstag, and repeated the monarchical *motif* in the Federal constitution.

The preponderant part played in the Federation by Prussia was the inevitable concomitant of her size and population, of her more important historical *rôle* and her military record. She possessed two-thirds of the total territory of the Empire and three-fifths of its total population. She held 235 seats in the Reichstag, and commanded twenty [1] votes in the Bundesrat, which gave her an absolute veto on all amendments to the constitution.[2] Her king was hereditary Emperor, commander-in-chief of the army and navy, and director of foreign affairs. He appointed the Federal or Imperial Chancellor, who has been in practice, though not of necessity, the Minister-President of Prussia.[3] Her military organization and codes, even to the cut of her soldiers' uniforms, served as model for those of other states. By separate treaty rights with several of the smaller states she acquired additional administrative powers in postal and military matters; she was chairman of all the standing committees of the Bundesrat except that on foreign affairs, and her capital was the seat of the Federal Government. The German Empire was, in short, a Prussian hegemony.

Bismarck, created a prince of the empire that was of his own building, became the first Federal and Imperial Chancellor, and until 1890 the great man was the real ruler of Germany. Bismarck will always be remembered chiefly for the great constructive achievements of the first ten years of his official career, and in a sense his great life-work was over

Bismarck Imperial Chancellor (1871–90).

Confederation, and this she transferred to the Empire. The merchant vessels of all other states were likewise federalized. The navy was therefore under the supreme command of the Emperor, who was charged with its constitution and organization and the appointment of its officers, and in whose name the seamen were sworn in. The harbours of Kiel and Jade were Imperial harbours. The conditions of the commercial marine were in the same way Imperial and Federal affairs. The navy belonged therefore to the Federal Empire and not to the states, but the army was not directly an Imperial force, but was chiefly controlled and managed by the four states, although subject to Imperial laws and in time of war at the disposal of the Federation.

[1] Seventeen in her own right, two belonging to Brunswick, of which a Prussian prince was regent, and one which she acquired by purchase from the Prince of Waldeck.

[2] Fourteen negative votes were necessary to cause the rejection of an amendment.

[3] There have been two exceptions. In 1873 Roon held the Minister-Presidency for nine months while Bismarck was Imperial Chancellor, and in 1892 Count von Caprivi resigned the Minister-Presidency, but retained the Chancellorship for two more years.

by that time. Germany was made; in his own words, she was a "satiated" power. But though less dramatic, it is no less remarkable that Bismarck should have held the reins for another twenty years. With a policy devoted no longer to war and bold constructive enterprises, but to peace, conservation, and development, through the period of inevitable reaction which follows the achievement of any long-desired aim, in spite of opposition, attack, and calumny that came from every direction, from socialists, liberals, and conservatives, from the Court, the Press, and the people, Bismarck kept his place, a figure of power and passion and nerves, the autocrat of Germany. The Emperor held him there, to whom he had become indispensable, whom he controlled and bullied as he chose; the Emperor and his own instinct for power, an instinct which he indulged imperiously, tyrannically, and often capriciously.

In foreign affairs he remained as ever the supreme artist, statesman, and diplomatist. He was "the only man who could juggle with five balls of which at least two were always in the air," said the old Emperor—Austria, France, Russia, England, and Italy. He juggled with them all, keeping the irreconcilable France diplomatically isolated; forming the strong *Mittel-Europa* alliance with Austria, thereby securing from her the ratification of his work in Germany; bringing Italy, Austria's old enemy, into the Austro-Germanic combination; insuring himself against attack on his eastern frontier from Russia; striving to keep Great Britain from continental *ententes*.

In home affairs Bismarck was less the artist and more the dictator. There he despised his adversary and fell consequently into errors of judgment. His chief aim was to consolidate and strengthen the Empire and to crush its enemies. He extended the scope of the Federation and enlarged the functions of the Imperial Government; an Imperial bank was founded, Imperial codes of law formulated, the State railways were put under the supervision of an Imperial board, new Imperial coins were issued.

He adopted a policy of discouragement and 'Germanization' toward the 'submerged nationalities' which were included in the German Empire, the three and a half million Poles on the eastern frontier, the 150,000 Danes of North Schleswig, and the nearly two million Frenchmen of Alsace-Lorraine. Every attempt was made, both by Bismarck and his successors, to assimilate these foreigners in the German system, but though they profited considerably by the economic, educational, and scientific advantages offered them they remained to the Great War aliens in sentiment. In fact, the 'Germanizing' efforts seem merely to have fostered their own national self-consciousness.

It was, however, in the Catholics and the socialists, the 'Black' and the 'Red' internationals, that Bismarck saw the greatest enemies of the Empire. Both of them were organized in powerful political parties, and each was the antithesis of what the German Empire represented. With both of them Bismarck threw himself into close combat in a vigorous endeavour to expel them from the German system, and by both of them he was defeated.

The Kulturkampf (1871–78).

Bismarck's enmity toward the Roman Catholic Church dated at least from 1866. Were not the Roman Catholics avowed supporters of Austria, and confirmed opponents of the Protestant dynasty of Prussia? Had not the Pope openly prayed for a Habsburg victory? The Roman Catholic Church was as fundamentally hostile to the new German Empire as the Popes of history had been to the old German Emperors. If France had been victorious in 1870, asked Bismarck, what would have happened to the Catholic provinces of the Rhine? The Pope had far too much power in Germany, and too much authority over the laity. The Catholic party was an antinational body, looking outside the state for its authority, embarrassing domestic politics by its consistent and deliberate opposition to Bismarck's measures, and foreign policy by its upholding of the temporal power of the Papacy, and so putting difficulties in the way of an alliance between Germany and the Italian kingdom. It was a veritable *imperium in imperio*, and with the new doctrine of Papal infallibility no sovereign was ruler in his own state if Catholics were among his subjects. "It is the Infallibility of the Pope," said Bismarck, "which threatens the state. He arrogates to himself whatever secular rights he pleases . . . declares our laws null and void, levies taxes. . . . In a word, no one in Prussia is so powerful as this foreigner." Bismarck tried to emphasize the political nature of the conflict. "The struggle is purely political," he said, "and not one between a Protestant dynasty and the Catholic Church; it is not one between faith and unbelief, it is only the reappearance of the conflict—older than the advent of the Redeemer of the world, as old as the human race itself, the same contest for power as Agamemnon waged with his seers at Aulis, and which cost him his daughter, while preventing the Greeks from setting sail for Troy; the conflict that raged all through the Middle Ages between the Pope and the Kaisers."

But all the elements antagonistic to the Church were drawn into the struggle; the 'Old Catholics,' who, under the historian and theologian Dr Döllinger, contested the new Papal claim to Infallibility; the liberals, whose outlook and tenets had been denounced in the Papal syllabus of 1864; Virchow, the atheist scientist.

In 1871 there were sixty-three members of the Centre or Catholic party in the Reichstag, a disciplined, organized body of opponents under the small but powerful Windthorst, the skilful Parliamentarian and tactical debater, a man burning with spiritual fire. Bismarck determined to break the party. In the south the contest between the friends and enemies of Infallibility was going on; the Old Catholics were being threatened with excommunication, with expulsion from the universities. Bismarck accepted these measures as a challenge, and threw himself into the conflict.

An Imperial law in 1871 expelled Jesuits from Germany, and made it a penal offence for priests to discuss State affairs in the pulpit. The famous May Laws of 1873, passed by the Prussian Landtag, carried the attack considerably further. They enjoined compulsory civil marriage, ordered all candidates for the priesthood to attend Government schools and universities and to pass Government examinations, forbade public excommunications, authorized appeals against ecclesiastical sentences and strict supervision of Catholic institutions, and proclaimed the authority of the State in the appointment and dismissal of priests. Two years later all religious Orders were dissolved.

The Pope declared the laws null and void, and forbade Roman Catholics to obey them. Bismarck replied with renewed defiance. "We shall not go to Canossa,[1] either in body or in spirit." For five years the Kulturkampf, as it was named by Virchow, continued, but when the more diplomatic Leo XIII assumed the Papacy Bismarck was willing enough to compromise. The struggle had brought him little satisfaction, and had multiplied the sources of annoyance. Leo XIII was skilful in discovering grounds of agreement without abandoning any theoretical claim. Bismarck on his part allowed the harshest of the anti-Catholic laws to lapse. Diplomatic relations were restored between the Papacy and the Empire, and in 1887 something like an *entente* was established between them, so that the Pope, to the general astonishment, forbade the Centre and Catholic party to vote against the new Imperial Army Bill.

With Bismarck's capitulation the Old Catholics dwindled to an insignificant group of schismatics, and the hope that Bismarck seems to have held that out of them might have come a German national Church was doomed to disappointment. Their position was too negative and their basis too narrow to build on them so broad a structure.

Bismarck had decided to abandon the struggle with the Catholics partly because by a change of economic policy he was losing the support of the liberals. On the eve of the Franco-German War

[1] A reference to the historic incident of 1077 in the quarrel between Pope Gregory VII and the Emperor Henry IV. The latter presented himself before the Pope in the Italian town of Canossa, and made an abject submission.

Z

it had seemed as if Europe was about to be united in a common commercial system. England, France, and Germany were virtually free-trade countries. But toward the end of the seventies Bismarck began to abandon these economic principles; in 1879 he imposed a tariff upon foreign corn and foreign commodities, which benefited the German agricultural classes, but alienated the industrial interests, and served to strengthen the Social Democrats.

The Catholic struggle was mainly abandoned, however, that Bismarck might enter upon the conflict with the socialists. The Social Democrats were the best-organized political party in Germany. They were anti-monarchical, anti-militarist, and, like the Catholics, "men without a country." They were therefore enemies of the Empire.

Two attempts on the life of the Emperor in 1878 provided the excuse for forcing through the Reichstag a number of exceptional laws, prohibiting all associations, meetings, or publications which sought to subvert the existing system of society and government, and granting extensive powers to the police. **War against the socialists.** The socialist leaders were arrested, socialist publications were suppressed, their editors were imprisoned, and their funds confiscated;[1] owners of assembly halls were forbidden to rent them for socialist meetings. Rigorous persecution failed in its object, however, as on so many other occasions. Socialist discontent was merely driven underground. Trade unions were declared illegal, but working men's associations were formed, as in England of the early nineteenth century, under other guises. Secret societies sprang up, and meetings which could not be held in Germany were held outside in Switzerland. Bismarck was defeated by the socialists as he had been by the Catholics. The Social Democrats captured more seats at elections, and in 1890 the exceptional laws were not renewed.

Bismarck also tried to wean the working man from the socialist party by an experiment in State socialism, as it has been called, by proving that the Imperial Government was alive to its responsibilities toward the artisan class, and would take steps to ensure its welfare. The Imperial laws of insurance were passed in 1883, 1884, and 1889 respectively, against sickness, accident, and old age. They were subsequently unified in 1911 into a comprehensive social insurance of about two thousand articles and formed the most enterprising scheme for ameliorating the lot of the working man hitherto adopted by any Government. It became a model for the legislation of England and France, but in so far as it was devised to break the Social Democratic party in Germany it failed.

---

[1] During the twenty-seven years in which the Acts remained in force 1400 publications were suppressed, 900 persons deported, and 1500 condemned to prison.

In March 1888 the long alliance between sovereign and Minister which, formed for heroic ends, had been preserved in spite of irritations and disagreements for more than twenty-five years, through the most heroic period of modern German history, came to an end. The old Emperor died after a short illness at the age of ninety-one. "He was a gentleman expressed in terms of a king," wrote Bismarck, "a nobleman in the primary sense of the word, who never felt himself dispensed from the principle *noblesse oblige* by any temptations of the power which belonged to him."

The ninety-nine days' reign of his son and successor Frederick was a tragedy of disappointed hopes and of physical illness, culminating in the Emperor's death in June 1888. What influence his liberal and constitutional ideas and his English sympathies might have had on the development of Germany cannot be estimated, for he must go down to history "wearing the halo of the untried idealist." With the accession of his son, the Kaiser William II, Germany received a new master, and opened a new page of her history. *(The Emperor Frederick III (March 9–June 15, 1888).)*

For the young man of twenty-nine, ambitious and adventurous, self-willed, restless, impressionable, and imaginative, with an overpowering consciousness of the divine mission of the Hohenzollerns and something of the mental instability of his great-uncle, Frederick William IV, was bent upon ruling in his own kingdom. His impatience and inexperience would not tolerate the absolute power which Bismarck had accumulated in his hands, nor his pride endure the implied insult in the phrase which was not uncommon at the time, that the Bismarcks were the major-domos of the house of Hohenzollern. The Foreign Office under Bismarck's son, Count Herbert, was a mere tool in the Minister's hands; the Kaiser found himself powerless in his own Cabinet meetings. Sharp differences between the new Emperor and the old Minister quickly showed themselves; all the interests antagonistic to Bismarck collected themselves in force round the sovereign. The whole relationship between Minister and King was incompatible and contradictory. Bismarck held his position in reality solely by virtue of the King's support; but he claimed a right of control and supervision over the political actions of the King as if William were a constitutional sovereign and Bismarck a Minister responsible to an all-powerful Parliament. The servant was usurping the master's place. The crisis came in March 1890. The Emperor began to talk of 'commands,' a word which Bismarck had not heard on the lips of his old master. He insisted that his will should be carried out, if not by Bismarck, then by another. "Then I am to understand, your Majesty," said Bismarck, *(The Emperor William II (1888–1918).)* *(" Dropping the Pilot " (March 1890).)*

speaking in English, "that I am in your way." "Yes," was the answer. Bismarck returned home to compose with care his formal resignation. How many times before had he not threatened to resign, often merely to prove his power? The Emperor tried to cover his dismissal with honours and titles, and princes and people vied with each other in expressions of appreciation and affection. But Bismarck had received an affront that he could not forgive; after taking a hasty farewell of the Emperor, of the royal princes, and of his friends and colleagues he drove to Charlottenburg, placed a rose on the tomb of his old master, and went into retirement. He took with him a rancour to which he gave bitter public expression in a manner that was seriously embarrassing to the Government. The quarrel between the Emperor and the Minister was never healed, though it was patched up by a superficial reconciliation on Bismarck's eightieth birthday. In lonely misanthropy the old man lived on until 1898.

The pilot who had so long guided the ship of State, who knew better than any man the shoals and rocks on which she might founder, had been dropped. The old Emperor, Roon, and Moltke were dead. There were new times and new men; four men succeeded in turn to Bismarck's office. First von Caprivi, "a novice and a nonentity," a "cipher Chancellor," an ex-army man who had also been head of the Admiralty, but had resigned his post on learning (according to the Kaiser's version) that he knew less of naval matters than the Emperor himself; then, after four years, the aged Prince Hohenlohe, whose appointment was meant to conciliate Bismarck; on his death in 1900 came Prince von Bülow, a man of adventurous policy, in keeping with the Kaiser's own views; and in 1909 Bethmann-Hollweg, fourth successor to Bismarck. Over them all rose the dominating will and personality of the Kaiser.

There was the new navy and great industrial and scientific development; there was the penetration of the Near East and the ambitious *Weltpolitik*. There was the growing shadow of the Great War and at home the unceasing demand for electoral reform and ministerial responsibility; and as, every five years, the electoral returns came in there was the gathering force in the country of Social Democracy, which in 1912 captured 110 seats in the Reichstag, and became the strongest single political party in the House.

In the 'terrible year' from 1870 to 1871 France was faced with a disastrous foreign war, an internal dynastic and political crisis, and a social revolution that resulted in a sharp and bitter civil war.

France, 1870–1914.

On September 4, when the news of the disaster of Sedan and the surrender of the Emperor was known, a republic was proclaimed in

France, and a provisional Government, termed the "Government of National Defence," assumed the direction of the war and of French destinies. On February 12, on the morrow of the fall of Paris, a National Assembly met at Bordeaux to ratify the treaty terms with Germany, and to give to France permanent political institutions. To Bismarck's conditions of surrender there was no alternative save war, and France ardently desired peace. Not for four years was the form of government to be defined.

The Prussians entered Paris on March 1, and retired on the 3rd, though German regiments were to remain in occupation of France until the indemnity had been paid. On the 18th began the rising of the 'Commune.' The Commune was an extraordinary compound of explosive elements, of pride and hunger and politics, of republicanism, socialism, and anarchy. At bottom there was Paris, which ten times in a century had forced or tried to force its will upon the rest of France; which, in a siege unexampled in history, had borne the brunt of war-suffering; Paris, "strangled in its pride," striking desperately like a wounded animal blind with pain. *The Commune (March-May 1871).*

Step by step it had descended into the black pit of fury. It had waited during the siege with growing tension for the Government help which never came; it had seen its walls battered by the bombardment in which, until it took place, it had resolutely refused to believe; it had seen the German army enter in triumph, while a Monarchist assembly at Bordeaux voted away its political honour to Monarchist Versailles, denied it a moratorium to relieve its financial embarrassments, and dissolved the National Guard, which had defended the capital and was dependent on its thirty cents a day for subsistence. The four months' girding to heroism and action had ended in the relaxation of humiliation and defeat, and a sense of grievance against a Government "which withheld help during the siege and gratitude afterwards."

There were other factors: reckless discontent, resulting from commercial and financial disintegration ; fear of a Monarchist restoration, opposition to the excessive centralization that was the heritage of the Napoleonic *régime*; socialism, revolutionary nihilism.

An attempt of the Government to remove the guns from the capital precipitated the conflict. The soldiers, surrounded by the mob, were speedily disarmed, and the insurgents, the city in their hands, declared the Acts of the Versailles Parliament [1] null and void, proclaimed the Commune, ran up the red flag, restored the Revolutionary calendar, attempted to establish national workshops, and

---

[1] It had been decided that the National Assembly should sit at Versailles instead of at Paris.

issued manifestos to the provinces urging them to set up other communes on the Paris model. France was to become a land of federated communes, a network of local units, with complete self-government, where the proletariat, triumphing over the *bourgeoisie*, and freed from the peasantry, which was in alliance with the *bourgeois* enemy,[1] would set up at last the social commonwealth. The dawn of a new era was announced, and "the end of the old political and clerical world, of militarism, bureaucracy, exploitation, stock-jobbery, and special privilege, to which the proletariat owe their servitude and the Fatherland its misfortunes." Elections were held in Paris, which, since only the radicals went to the poll, confirmed these measures.

To Thiers there was only one course open, that of the forcible reduction of the rebels, and while the Germans in their camp looked on a new siege of Paris was begun in April, a siege of Frenchmen by Frenchmen. Since the Communards were not recognized as belligerents, those taken in arms were summarily shot, whereupon in revenge the rebels seized the chief men of Paris as hostages. The capital was a fortified city with defensive walls, ramparts, and bastions, and for six weeks it held out. But as one point after another was taken by the Government troops, as the movement drifted nearer to collapse, so it grew more violent, until it culminated in the terrible scenes of the last bloody week. The Communards' hostages, including the Archbishop of Paris, were put to death, buildings were destroyed by fire, the Vendôme monument razed to the ground, as the soldiers forced the Communards from street to street, shooting them down "till the Seine flowed red with blood," and taking hundreds prisoner. The last struggle was fought among the tombs of Père la Chaise.

The Government took a terrible revenge. About 17,000 Communards had perished, 45,000 were arrested, most of them to be condemned to imprisonment, or to exile or death, and many fled. The "brutal dictatorship" of Paris was ended; democracy was "bled for a generation"; socialism did not dare to raise its head until the end of the century; between Capital and Labour flowed the blood and the memories of the Commune.

After the suppression of the Commune the Government turned to the work of national reconstruction. The first task was to pay
The indemnity. off as quickly as possible the heavy war indemnity. With astonishing rapidity the money was subscribed. An appeal for three thousand million francs brought in forty-two thousand. Bismarck had hoped that France would be crippled for a

---

[1] As in 1848, the Commune of 1870 was partly a revolt of the artisans of the towns against the privileges which had accrued to the peasants and the middle classes of the towns in the revolutions of 1789, 1830, and 1848.

generation, but in two years the whole sum was paid and the German troops withdrawn from France.   There were also railroads, bridges, public and private buildings to be restored, and fortresses to be erected, but France met the strain with marvellous ease; the commercial progress of the Second Empire had been real.   Nor did it seem to have been seriously disturbed; commerce and industry boomed again as before the war, and the international exhibition of 1878, though lacking the splendour, rivalled the prosperity of that of 1867.

A vital part of reconstruction was the reorganization of the army. The war of 1870 had disclosed its fundamental inefficiency and un-preparedness.   Before the deliberate and scientific mili- Reorganiza-tarism of Prussia France was defenceless.   By the Army tion of the Law of 1872 the French army was reorganized on the army. Prussian model; compulsory service was established, with a heavy five years' term with the colours, and a subsequent period with the reserve.   The law was readily accepted by the people, and was the prelude to a military revival which caused Bismarck serious alarm.

The form of the constitution still awaited definition, but in this matter it was not easy to secure agreement.   The National Assembly itself was monarchical, elected on the question of peace The form or war, for the Monarchists were held to be more favour- of Govern-able to peace than the Republicans.   There was, however, ment. a strong feeling in the country in favour of a republic considered only as a constitutional question; in the end this feeling was to prevail, owing to the divisions among the Monarchists, who appeared to hold the country at their mercy.   The establishment of the republic, in spite of the initial monarchical majority, and its defence against the attacks, flagrant or subtle, which have been levelled against it, provide the chief interest in the internal history of France after her recovery from the war of 1870.

There were three monarchical parties in the Assembly—a small Imperial group of thirty odd, supporting the son of Napoleon III, a hundred Legitimists in favour of the Comte de Chambord,[1] the grandson of Charles X, of the elder Bourbon line, and three hundred Orléanists, whose candidate was the Comte de Paris,[1] grandson of Louis-Philippe.

Thiers, appointed in 1871 "chief of the executive Government," was himself an Orléanist, but in view of the cleavages in the Monar-chical party he was willing to accept a republic as the form Thiers of government "which divides us least"—a republic, (1798–1877). but a conservative one, he held to be the best solution of the constitutional difficulty.   His countenancing a republic, however,

[1] See genealogical table, p. 601.

annoyed the Monarchists, who by an adverse vote caused him to resign office in 1873. Thiers was seventy-three years old when he was called to the 'Presidency' of France. "Since early manhood his name had been a household word in French politics, and his huge spectacles and elfish body a fortune to the caricaturist." He was a man of brilliant parts, which showed better in power than in opposition—journalist, historian, politician; he had taken part in the overthrow of Charles X in 1830; he had been a Minister of Louis-Philippe; he had helped to form the Napoleonic legend, and he had voted for Louis Napoleon as President of the Second Republic. After a period of retirement he returned to politics in 1863, and embarked on a general criticism of the Imperial Government, of the disastrous Mexican expedition, of the apathy of the Emperor's foreign policy after Sadowa. He contributed to the fall of the Second Empire, and must be held to have fostered the war spirit which led to 1870. To the war itself he was, however, opposed, and for a time he was the most unpopular man in the country. After the disaster of Sedan, which only justified his judgment, France turned to him in her defeat, and his public life ended in a blaze of patriotic service. He toured the chancelleries of Europe, he was commissioned to negotiate the terms of peace with Bismarck—a thankless task which did not destroy his popularity—he suppressed the Commune, and put France on her feet again.

Thiers's fall was followed by an attempt to reconcile the divisions of the Monarchists, and bring about a fusion of their aims. The **Monarchist efforts.** two parties agreed to combine in accepting the childless Comte de Chambord as Henry V, King of France, on condition that he should appoint as his successor the rival claimant, the Comte de Paris. A restoration of the royalist line seemed an imminent possibility, but the Monarchist forces were broken not by hostile republicanism, but by the uncompromising Bourbonism of the Comte de Chambord. True son of his house, having learnt nothing and forgotten nothing, he would accept no less than a return to the days of his grandfather, Charles X, to the lilies and the white flag of unsullied royalism. The negotiations failed on the symbolical question of the national colours. Never would Henry V replace "the white flag of Henry IV" with the tricolour, which had been the standard of two revolutions.

The attitude of the Comte de Chambord proved the real hopelessness of the monarchical cause. France would never abandon what had become to her a symbol of imperishable memories and indisputable benefits. The efforts of the royalists were thus checked at the moment when their aims were nearest to realization, and the Republicans were given an opportunity of which they took full advantage. Marshal MacMahon, a royalist and a tool of the royalists, was in the Presidential chair, and the Monarchists had succeeded in passing an Act to prolong his power to seven years; but Thiers's fall was provoking a Republican reaction, the *The Republican victory, 1875.* fiery Gambetta was preaching a republic throughout the countryside, and the rising tide of republicanism was carrying the by-elections to the Chamber. The country could continue no longer without an organized Government, and in 1875 an 'omnibus' constitution was drawn up. It was of the Parliamentary kind, with a responsible Cabinet, a Senate, and a Chamber of Deputies, the latter elected by universal suffrage. So much was a minimum, whether under monarchy or republic. It was on another point that the fateful issue was determined. By a majority of one vote it was decided that the head of the State should be called "President of the Republic." Thus in 1875 France declared herself a republic, not boldly and defiantly, as in 1792 and 1848, but timorously, insinuatingly, almost apologetically, with one eye all the time upon the monarchy. The constitution was short, provisional, 'neutral,' a constitution *d'attente monarchique*; *The constitution.* there was no doctrine, no theory of fundamental rights; but of the nine constitutions which France had framed for herself since 1789 it endured the longest, lasting, with one or two modifications in 1884, to the present day.

The new elections gave the Republicans a majority in the Lower Chamber, but they did not feel themselves assured until they had captured the Senate and put Jules Grévy, a firm Republican, into the Presidency in 1879. Their victory was now com- *Republicanism reasserted.* plete, and it was the greater that it was the answer of the country to an attempt of the royalists, working through MacMahon, to effect in 1877 a *coup d'état* against the Republicans. The attempt failed, and in 1879 MacMahon resigned, but it is noticeable that the Republicans long felt suspicion of the Presidential office, and until 1913 it may be said that they chose their Presidents rather for their negative than their positive qualities.

By the date of Gambetta's death in 1882 the republic to which he devoted his efforts may be said to have been firmly established, able to withstand the assaults to be directed against it.

The next crisis was to come from the Boulangist movement at the end of the eighties. The strength of the Republicans had fluctuated all through the decade; in 1883 and 1884 they had been *The Boulangist movement.* strong enough to enact that the Republican form of government should never be subject to revision, and that members of families who had reigned in France should be ineligible for the Presidency. In the elections of 1885, however, the Monarchists carried nearly half the votes, while the Republicans were further weakened by a split in their own ranks between the 'opportunists,' who followed the tradition of Gambetta, and the radicals, led by the "brilliant gladiator" Clemenceau. They managed to secure the election of Grévy again to the Presidency, and the next year they nervously exiled the leading members of the royal families from France; but they were conscious of weakness, emphasized by the fact that owing to the absence of a clearly defined two-party system ministries rose to office and fell again mainly according to the unreliable and fluctuating combinations of groups who had probably no inherent sympathy with each other. In France, as in Germany, Parliamentary majorities were uncertain quantities. A Presidential crisis arising out of a political scandal connected with the sale of honours further embarrassed the Republicans, and it was at this point that Boulanger and his followers appeared most formidable.

Boulanger, described by Gambetta as one of the four best officers in France, had been made Minister of War in 1886. He was an unscrupulous, attractive man, with lively ambitions. He ingratiated himself with the soldiers by increasing their comforts, and set himself to win popularity in the country. He preached chauvinistic doctrines, fostered the *revanche* spirit, and worked up a facile clamour for the restoration of Alsace-Lorraine. He soon collected a formidable band of followers throughout the country, who had no bond of unity whatever save 'Boulanger' and opposition to the Government. There were Monarchists, clericals, Bonapartists, and socialists, as well as chauvinists of all colours. His aim seems to have been the overthrow of the Parliamentary *régime* and the institution of a Boulangist dictatorship. On the fall of the Government in 1888 he was dispatched to the provinces to command an army corps, but at the end of 1888 he returned to Paris without leave, and, on being deprived of his commission, was elected to the Chamber by several departments, including, in January 1889, that of the Seine and Paris. Had he struck immediately he might have brought about a successful *coup d'état*, but he let his opportunity go by. The Republicans rallied against the threatened danger; Boulanger's arrest was ordered, whereupon he fled from the country. In his absence he was tried and condemned for treason, and a few months later the would-be Napoleon committed suicide in Brussels.

Once again the Republic had triumphed. The Monarchists made as much capital as they could out of the Panama scandals in which the Government was involved,[1] but they lost heavily at the

---

[1] In 1888 the Panama Company went bankrupt, involving many people in heavy financial loss. Upon inquiry it was found that certain Government officials and members of Parliament were corruptly associated with it.

polls. The growth of trade and commerce, the development of popular education, the conquest of a great overseas empire, second only to that of Britain, in Africa and Madagascar, all served to consolidate the Republic, and in 1893 the Pope himself, Leo XIII, ordered the Catholics to rally to the Republican Government.

M. Clemenceau and the radicals were regularly overturning Governments, but the greatest excitement of the next years came from the famous Dreyfus case. The story began in 1894, when Captain Alfred Dreyfus, an Alsatian Jew attached to the General Staff, was arrested on a charge of high treason, for betraying military secrets. He was tried in secret and found guilty, and after a public degradation in the courtyard of the military school in Paris, in which the stripes were torn from his uniform and his sword broken, he was transported to a life imprisonment on Devil's Island, an unhealthy French possession off Guiana. He protested his innocence, but the verdict was generally approved in France, according as it did with a strong anti-Semitic feeling which had arisen out of the Panama scandals, in which Jews had been concerned.

The second episode occurred in 1896, when the case had been almost entirely forgotten. A few people had entertained the suspicion that Dreyfus's condemnation had perhaps been an error, and a certain Colonel Picquart, a young officer appointed chief of the Intelligence Bureau, having found and examined the document on which Dreyfus's conviction had been largely based, came to the conclusion that it was a forgery, and demanded a retrial. He moreover asserted that the forged document was the work of a Major Esterhazy, a well-known but dissolute army officer. The Government and the army now made the mistake of trying to hush up the case, and upon Picquart's renewed agitation for a revision he was deprived of his post, transferred to a military station in Tunis, and replaced by Colonel Henry.

The case immediately assumed immense proportions; it became the pivot of a social, political, and constitutional conflict. The whole nation took sides, and the unfortunate officer languishing on Devil's Island was almost forgotten in the great issues that were raised. Those who believed Dreyfus to be innocent were called enemies of law and order, property, patriotism, and religion. The army, the Church, and the Monarchists leagued themselves to defend the country by upholding Dreyfus's guilt against an imaginary "syndicate of Jews, Freemasons, Protestants, England and the Triple Alliance, socialists and anarchists, enemies of the Faith, enemies of the flag, enemies of society."[1] It became a struggle

_____
[1] J. Salwyn Schapiro, *Modern and Contemporary European History*.

between conservatism and progress, between absolutism and revolution, a battle of dogmatism against criticism, of the Church against the scientific spirit, of authority against liberty.

The anti-Dreyfusards carried off the first honours. Major Esterhazy, tried on the charges preferred against him by Picquart, was acquitted, and completely exonerated. He was awarded a popular ovation, and Picquart was seized and imprisoned. Next Émile Zola, whose stirring indictment entitled *J'accuse* had thrown the anti-Dreyfusards into confusion, was arrested on a charge of defamation, and sentenced to a year's imprisonment. He escaped by fleeing from the country, but the Zola case merely exaggerated the excitement of the Dreyfus case. Further, the Government refused a revision of the trial, and declared the affair closed.

From 1899, however, the tide began to turn. First Colonel Henry, who had replaced Picquart at the Intelligence Bureau, confessed that he had forged one of the documents concerned, and committed suicide. This was followed by another confession of forgery from Major Esterhazy, who fled from the country. The anti-Dreyfusards tried to defend themselves by arguing that the guilt of Henry and Esterhazy did not prove the innocence of Dreyfus, but it became clear to the Government that an inquiry must be held into all the circumstances. The new ministry of Waldeck-Rousseau ordered a retrial; the prisoner was brought back from Devil's Island before a manifestly biased military court at Rennes. He was again found guilty, but "under extenuating circumstances," and the sentence of imprisonment was reduced to ten years. The President of the Republic then exercised his right of pardon, thus relieving Dreyfus of his punishment, but the verdict satisfied no one, and the Dreyfusards were bent upon securing an assertion of his innocence. The anti-Dreyfusards were equally incensed by the pardon, and the President was publicly insulted in the street. At last in 1906 another revision of the trial took place; Dreyfus was completely exonerated; by way of amend he was promoted to a higher rank in the army, and in the courtyard where he had been publicly degraded he was subsequently awarded the decoration of the Legion of Honour. Colonel Picquart was made a general, and later Minister of War. Zola, who had died in the interval, was reburied with great pomp in the Panthéon, and the officers concerned in the conspiracy were dismissed from the army. There was, in fact, a general distribution of rewards to the innocent and punishments to the guilty.

The vindication of Dreyfus meant the defeat of forces which were in themselves antagonistic to the Republic. It meant also the triumph of the civil authority over the military, and the invasion by the Republic of that last stronghold of monarchism, the army.

Another quarrel was reopened by the Dreyfus agitation, that of the Republic with the Church. The initial hostility between the Church and the Republic had been to some extent mitigated by Leo XIII's tactful recognition of the French Government. This had not removed, however, a fundamental antipathy between the clericals and the Republicans, and after the opening of the Dreyfus agitation the radical Left began to press for an attack upon the ecclesiastical position in France, and particularly for the separation of the Church and State. A beginning was made with the Law of Associations passed in 1901 by the Waldeck-Rousseau Ministry, which, under cover of forcing all associations to seek Government authorization, dissolved a large number of religious and, especially, teaching orders. Their property and convents were forfeited. In 1904 another law forbade all teaching whatever by religious orders, and ordered the closing or 'secularization' of their schools. The quarrel was exacerbated by the unwise action of Pius X, the successor of Leo XIII, who in 1904 indignantly protested against the French President's visit to the King of Italy as "a grave offence to a sovereign pontiff." This naturally strengthened the anti-clerical party, and the next year they succeeded in passing a law for the separation of Church and State and repealing the Concordat of Napoleon.

The Church separated from the State (1905).

With the decline of the Republic's contest with the Monarchists on the one hand and the clericals on the other social and socialist questions began to play a larger part in internal politics. Legislation on behalf of the working class came into force later in France than in Germany and in England. In 1884 trade unions were legalized, and in 1898 a Workmen's Compensation Act was passed; it was not until 1906 and 1910 respectively that a Ten Hours' Factory Act and an Old Age Pensions Law were put on the Statute Book. Many of the industrial measures of the new century were due to the influence of M. Millerand, the socialist member of the Waldeck-Rousseau Cabinet. M. Millerand's acceptance of office in 1900 raised to an acute pitch the prolonged controversy which divided the ranks of the socialists themselves. One section was for making terms with the radicals and other advanced political bodies. To the compromisers belonged Millerand, Viviani, and Briand, who all held portfolios in *bourgeois* Cabinets. The other section, on the contrary, strongly deprecated any sacrifice of principle to political expediency. In this group of intransigents was contained the growing syndicalist party, which condemned all forms of constitutional agitation, and pinned its faith to direct economic action by strikes and sabotage. From 1906 to 1910 French industry was regularly disturbed by annual eruptions. In 1910 a great railway

Social and socialist questions.

strike seemed to be the prelude to a social revolution, but it was defeated by a socialist Premier himself, M. Briand, who took the unusual step of calling up the reserves, thus mobilizing most of the strikers as soldiers. They were then given as a military duty the task of protecting the trains, and so forced to break the strike they had themselves engineered.

If the history of Russia during the nineteenth and twentieth centuries were portrayed graphically it would consist of a series of peaks and valleys, corresponding to successive moods of exultation and depression, of progression and reaction; and the highest peaks would be found to synchronize with four great wars in which Russia was involved. For her history swings from the Napoleonic wars to the Crimean War, from the Crimean to the Russo-Japanese War, from that again to the Great War. The first brought her an unprecedented European renown and, under Alexander I, a reforming impulse. The second gave her the emancipation of the serfs and other important measures; the third introduced the first Parliament; the last overthrew Tsardom and set up the Union of Soviet Socialist Republics. Between each two has been an intervening mood of reaction and national depression.

Russia, 1881–1914.

It has been pointed out in another chapter how the reforming movement engendered by the Crimean War petered out through the reign of Alexander II, how the country gave itself over to disillusionment, and the reformers in despair destroyed their own cause when they assassinated their Tsar in 1881. In consequence Russia was for twenty-five years to go through the valley of reaction.

Alexander II was succeeded by his son Alexander III, a 'bullock' type of man, physically powerful, with a stern will, narrow mind, elementary notions, and the outlook of a peasant. It is said that he momentarily considered carrying out the decree establishing representative institutions issued by his father on the day of his death, but he quickly abandoned the idea, and surrendered himself and the country to the reactionary Pobyedonosteff, the Procurator of the Holy Synod, or civil head of the Orthodox Church. Under his guidance a course of repression was adopted toward all those elements which failed to conform to the creed of "One Tsar, one Church, one Russia," which were alien to the ideal of a holy, orthodox, autocratic, and nationalist State. The policy of reaction was exalted to a philosophy, and the special characteristics of Russia, divinely preserved from the Parliamentarianism, democracy, and liberalism of the West, were magnified into a dedication to regenerate the world. Reformists, evangelicals, socialists, nihilists, Jews, the Germans of the

Reaction under Alexander III (1881–1894) and Nicholas II (1894–1917).

Baltic, Finns, and Poles constituted alike deflections and defilements of the supreme Russian destiny.

Participators, proved or suspected, in the conspiracy of 1880 were executed or banished to the prisons of Siberia. Other nihilists and revolutionaries were exiled or similarly imprisoned. The Press and the universities were muzzled, the power of the *zemstvos* curtailed, martial law declared, and agitation driven into a subterranean ferment.

A policy of 'Russification' was adopted toward the subject races. Russian was made the official language, the Finnish postal, monetary, and fiscal systems were made to conform to those of Russia, the University of Dorpat was converted from a German to a Russian institution. 'Russification' of subject races.

The Protestant Stundists [1] of the south, an evangelical, God-fearing sect proselytized from German sources, were stamped out at the instigation of the Holy Orthodox Church.

But of all the races and sects the Jews suffered most. They were confined within certain towns, excluded from local government, partly debarred from education, forbidden to engage in agriculture or to hold property outside the specific area to which they were limited. They were subjected to popular attack, to outbreaks of pillaging and plundering known as pogroms. In scores of places the mob broke into their quarters, fired their homes, beat and sometimes killed the inmates, for the rabble had learnt that such raids would not be unpopular with a Government which was continually denouncing Jews as revolutionaries, as enemies of the Faith and Crown. The result of this anti-Jewish policy was three-fold: first, to create in the large towns extensive ghettos of exacerbated and impoverished Jews; secondly, to set on foot an important emigration movement—between 1880 and 1900 over a million and a half Jews emigrated from Russia, mainly to America; thirdly, it stimulated the nationalist or Zionist [2] movement among the Jews, who began to look to Palestine with the longing of outcasts for a lost home. The Jews.

No classes regretted the death of Alexander III in 1894, save perhaps the peasants and the anti-alcoholic groups of the state, in whose behalf alone he adopted sympathetic measures.

The hopes of the reformers had centred in the heir, Nicholas II, but to their disappointment he announced that he intended to

---

[1] These peasants had taken a German name because the founder of their sect had been converted at the *Stunden*, or hour-long services, of German Lutherans long settled in the South of Russia.

[2] The Zionist movement has engaged the somewhat spasmodic interest of statesmen of different countries. It suffers, however, from being confined mainly to the persecuted or impoverished among the Jews.

"preserve the principles of autocracy as firmly and unwaveringly as my late father of imperishable memory." Pobyedonosteff was kept in power. The liberties of the Finns were more restricted than before, war was declared against the intellectuals, from whom the revolutionaries were largely recruited; an army of spies was employed to give information; the attacks on the Jews grew more violent. In one direction alone, in that of industry, under Count Witte, progress was made. He attracted foreign capital to the country, extended transport facilities, improved the national credit, and considerably developed the economic possibilities of Russia.

Nicholas II.

But revolutionary agitation was increasing throughout the country, springing up under every disguise, taking cover under societies founded for no apparent political purpose. Certain agricultural committees set up by Count Witte began to demand freedom of the Press and representative government. In 1903, therefore, Count Witte was dismissed after eleven years' service; he was succeeded as Minister of the Interior by the reactionary Plehve. In July 1904, however, Plehve was murdered. The Russo-Japanese War had broken out. The country was stirred by stories of peculation and incompetence; it began to be aroused by news of defeat as it had been once before at the time of the Crimean War. But while the people and the *zemstvos* put forward demands for reforms, for freedom of conscience, of the Press, of association and education, for personal liberty and representative government, the Tsar continued, though in hesitation and with some modifications, along the path of repression and censorship. A fever of agitation began to seize the masses; the militant section among the reformers began to grow stronger and the terrorist activities of the revolutionaries to increase. There was rising one of the periodic flood tides of Russian emotionalism.

The Russo-Japanese War.

On a day in January 1905 a bullet narrowly missed the Tsar. Three days later occurred the events of "Bloody Sunday." A gigantic procession of strikers, headed by a priest known as Father Gapon, proceeded to the Winter Palace in St Petersburg to petition the "Little Father" for the redress of grievances. As they approached they were shot down by armed troops. Immediately there broke out a rising throughout the country. The peasants attacked the houses of the lords, assassinated the police officers; the Tsar's uncle, the Grand Duke Serge, was murdered.

The revolution of 1905.

The more moderate of the Tsar's advisers recommended concessions, and reforms were promulgated concerning the Press, the Jews, and the subject nationalities. In August the Tsar issued a decree summoning a consultative Duma, or Parliament, and in

October he dismissed Pobyedonosteff and the more reactionary of his Ministers, recalled Count Witte, and published a manifesto promising wide and sweeping reforms. The Russian mood rose to exultation, only to fall when little more than a year was out to one of depression.

In December 1905 another great uprising of a desperate character took place in Moscow; about five thousand people were killed before it was suppressed by the troops. It unfortunately helped to bring about a counter-revolutionary movement in the Government. The liberal Witte had already been dismissed, and the Tsar's ministers began to divide into two camps, one favouring concession, the other repression. Thus the Government spoke with two voices.

The revolutionaries were also divided. They did not form an organized political party, but were broken up into groups. There were the moderates, or Octobrists, who took their stand upon the October manifesto of the Tsar; there was the more advanced group known as the Cadets, who advocated the establishment of responsible as well as representative government, and pressed for the bestowal of land upon the peasants by the forced sale of some of the larger estates. There were also socialist sections. Between the counter-revolution which set in in the Government and the divisions in the ranks of the revolutionaries the cause of reform fell to the ground. The first Duma was opened with great ceremony on May 6, 1906, by Nicholas II, but it soon became a scene of wrangling between the Government and its critics. The Duma had no real power, and when it tried to control the executive it was accused of exceeding its bounds, and was dissolved on July 21, 1906. In bitter disappointment about half the deputies withdrew to Viborg, in Finland, and issued the manifesto which takes its name from that place, exhorting the people not to pay taxes or render military service to a Government which had violated its pledges. But the people were not behind their deputies; the only result was to stiffen the Government and to lead to the prosecution of the signatories.

In March 1907 a second Duma was elected, but, proving even more stormy than its predecessor, it was dissolved before it had sat for four months.

A third Duma was then summoned on a revised electoral law, and a considerably reduced franchise. Proving amenable to the Government, it was allowed to live out its five years, and in 1912 was followed by a fourth Duma, even more docile.

For from 1907 reaction had set in, autocracy was in the saddle, and the exultation of the reformers had given place to a listless depression. Socialists were tried behind closed doors and sent to Siberia. Conspirators were constantly being found and executed. Organizers of *pogroms* were officially pardoned. There were in reply recurring murders of officials and police, but on the whole the country seemed quiescent, and the revolutionary movement abated.

The history of Italy from her unification until the end of the century is one of swift decline from the epic grandeur to which she had attained during the forties, the fifties, and the sixties.
Italy, 1871–1914. It is a story of disappointment and discontent, of poverty, intrigue, and disorganization. The tide of high purpose had receded. An outward unity had, indeed, been achieved, but, the work of a comparatively small class, it had been won in advance of the general spiritual conversion of the mass of the people.

In reality Italian unity was obtained too suddenly by a people for centuries divided and heterogeneous. Liberty, preserved as a torch in the little country of Piedmont, was rather given as a gift than won by the efforts of the people; and nationality, affirmed as self-determination and self-government by an *élite*, did not find an equal echo in the popular consciousness.[1]

The national problems, therefore, although in part those common to all states of the day, consisted mainly in the attempt to infuse into the somewhat artificial framework of united Italy a real spiritual and political unity.

One of the central difficulties of the new kingdom lay in the relations between the State and the Church. Pius IX, shutting himself up in the Vatican, refused to accept the Law of Guarantees,[2]
The Papacy. and issued the encyclical *Non expedit*, forbidding Catholics to vote at the elections to Parliament, or to enter the service of the Italian Crown. In 1878 Pius IX died, and the scenes at his funeral attested the ill-will that was borne toward him by many of the people. His successor, Leo XIII, although considerably more of a diplomat, pursued officially the policy of his predecessor, maintaining the isolation of the Vatican and the hostile attitude to the Crown. Nevertheless toward the end of the century the strain between Church and State began perceptibly to grow less. Conversations took place between secular and ecclesiastical authorities, and with the menace of socialism there was a tendency for conservatives and clericals to drift together. Catholics began to return to politics; in 1905 the encyclical *Non expedit* was partially removed by Pius X, and in 1919 it was repealed by Pope Benedict XV. During the lifetime of Benedict the Roman Question remained still unsolved, but when Pius XI on his accession in 1922 gave the long-withheld blessing of "Orb and Urb" to the royal Italian troops it seemed as if, after the

---

[1] Luigi Sturzo, *Italy and Fascismo*, p. 13.   [2] See Chapter VI, p. 229.

lapse of half a century, time was bringing about the reconciliation that negotiation had failed to effect.

The new kingdom was confronted with internal problems of great variety. Underlying all was the prevalent regional spirit of the recently united state, a spirit that persists to the present day, and distinguishes even the national literature. There was also an extreme disparity between the political levels
Social and economic problems.
of such provinces as Piedmont in the north, which for some time had enjoyed an organized administration and a moderate constitutional Government, and Sicily and Naples in the south, the home of *banditti* and secret societies, with little experience in self-government and no civic sense. The Government turned therefore to the introduction of uniform conditions throughout the peninsula, or, as it was called by its critics, to the Piedmontization of Italy. It reorganized and centralized the administrative and judicial systems, and formed local government units on the French geometrical and bureaucratic pattern, in entire neglect of existing historical divisions. It nationalized the railways and established compulsory military service. It set itself to the suppression of brigandage and the extermination of secret societies like the Mafia of Sicily and the Camorra of Naples. In 1897 the Government of Depretis tried to reduce the high percentage of illiterates by a Compulsory Education Act, which, however, it was too poor to enforce. For poverty was one of the sorest afflictions that beset the new state. Ill-management and corruption in high places, a crippling National Debt, the burden of the army, the cost of public improvements, and the general impoverishment of the southern half of the kingdom defeated for many years all attempts to bring about financial order. Taxation was heavy, but fell upon the poorest classes, and the Government was perpetually on the verge of bankruptcy.

Politically, socially, and economically the country was ill-conditioned and suffering. Politics, even under the able Parliamentary tactician Crispi, the old Garibaldian, was a tale of intrigue, corruption, and scandal. Bureaucratic centralization dried up the springs of local energy, and conducted all vitality to a Government which was a centre of jobbery. The Catholic and religious forces were alienated, the people, illiterate, often unenfranchised, were hostile or apathetic. Economically the agricultural South was undeveloped, and in the industrial North the conditions of the working classes occasioned constant agitation. The rapid increase in population magnified the poverty of the people and intensified the economic problems, until a large emigration, especially to North and South America, began slowly to drain off the surplus and to ease the situation. In 1893–94 serious labour revolts took place in Sicily, and in

1898 an insurrection of working men broke out in Milan which led to street-fighting after the manner of the Paris revolutions. The Government suppressed the riots of Milan, as those of Sicily, with great harshness, and aroused considerable opposition by anti-socialist legislation. An expression of the general disaffection was seen in 1900 in the murder by an anarchist of King Humbert, successor to Victor Emmanuel II.

With the accession of Victor Emmanuel III, young, sympathetic, and democratically minded, and with the turn of the century the fortunes of Italy began to mend. The emigrants, both by their departure and by the money which they often sent back to their own people, relieved the general impoverishment of the masses. The vine culture of the South and the industry of the North began to grow more profitable; the Merchant Marine expanded, and foreign capital helped to develop Italy's economic possibilities. The estrangement of Catholics was to some extent mitigated. Giolitti, who from 1903 became the leading figure in Italian politics, adopted a conciliatory attitude toward the working classes; an amended Social Insurance Act was passed, and in 1904 a new Education Act. In 1905 the Budget for the first time showed a surplus, and in 1912 a Franchise Act established practically manhood suffrage. Nevertheless the socialist party grew in Italy as it was growing in other Western countries; under the influence of France it turned to syndicalism rather than Marxism; and strikes and acts of sabotage were frequent. In 1914 a general strike held up the industrial life of the country for forty-eight hours. At the end of that time the men returned quietly to work, the general strike having failed then, as on other occasions, because of its very comprehensiveness and its complete dislocation of ordinary life.

The foreign policy of Italy was concerned with three main questions. First, whether the cry of the "prisoner of the Vatican" would awaken in France or Austria any determination to inter-
Foreign affairs.
vene in Italian affairs on behalf of Rome. Secondly, how to get from Austria the parts of 'unredeemed Italy,' the Trentino, Trieste, and bordering districts, for the acquisition of which the Italian 'Irredentists' carried on an unceasing propaganda. The ambitions of this party even went as far afield as Dalmatia and Albania. Thirdly, there was the imperial or colonizing idea which was awakening in the new kingdom, to revive the glories and empire of classical Rome, and to turn the Mediterranean into an 'Italian lake.'

The three currents, often flowing different ways, produced for some time a state of uncertainty in Italian politics. Thus while one section of Italian thought feared France, and, viewing the recovery of the unredeemed lands as hopeless, leaned to Austria and Germany, another saw in the democratic and anti-clerical tendencies of France the best guarantee for security in the Roman question. In the meantime the Government timorously refused the offers made to it by Great Britain to occupy Tunis (in 1876) and Tripoli (in 1878).

Italy was therefore all the more annoyed when in 1881 France occupied Tunis and she found that her chance of it had gone for ever. The immediate consequence was to drive Italy into the arms of Austria and Germany, and in 1882 the Triple Alliance was formed, under promise from Bismarck that the Roman Question should not be raised. As the Roman nightmare began to fade, however, the Italian kingdom began to feel that it had sacrificed the substance of the Tyrolese lands for the shadow of the Roman fear, and as Italy failed to secure any pronounced benefits from the Triple Alliance she began cautiously to turn to a policy of limited *ententes* with England and later with France. Italy thus

became a pawn in the various vicissitudes of the European political game, useful now to this Power, now to that, in a subtle contest of skill in which she seemed to derive benefits, but which earned her only pricks and disappointments. This was due partly to the inherent difficulties of her position, and partly to the lack of continuity in her foreign policy, so that time and again there slipped from the hands of her ministers those very cards which they had guarded with jealous care. In this way Italy received no help from her allies and gave none.[1]

Under Crispi's influence the colonial question came more prominently to the front. When the French went into Tunis in 1881 and the British into Egypt in 1882 Italy began to seek The colonial compensation in the Red Sea and Somaliland. The idea. latter district, not a very profitable area, was acquired by conventions with local sultans. The former was the centre of the Eritrean enterprise, an experiment in empire-making of an aggressive character. An advance into the interior was made from the Red Sea port of Massowah, which brought Italy into conflict with the rulers of Abyssinia and other native princes. After some exhilarating successes an Italian army was overwhelmingly defeated in 1896 at Adowa by a native force five times as large. The disaster brought about the fall of Crispi, the mainspring of the colonial activity, and considerably reduced the borders of Eritrea and the Red Sea land; it also induced a mood of national depression in which for a time aggressive imperialism was abandoned.

With the new century, however, with the advance of France in Morocco and the growing interest of Germany in the Mediterranean,

[1] Luigi Sturzo, *Italy and Fascismo*, p. 28.

Italy's African ambitions revived, and, taking advantage of the "Young Turk" revolution, she declared war upon Turkey in 1911, and conquered Tripoli and Cyrenaica, which were formed into the Italian colony of Lybia.

The problem of the Italian-speaking districts in Austrian hands was for a long time shelved by Italy's participation in the Triple Alliance. From the beginning of the new century, however, with the reconciliation between Italy and France, with the forward policy of Austria and Germany in the Balkans, the attachment of the Italian kingdom to the Central Powers grew increasingly weaker. The appeal of the Irredentist claims grew correspondingly stronger. On the outbreak of the war of 1914 Italy, distracted by serious internal troubles, declared herself neutral, but she did not fail to apprehend that the opportunity had arrived for her to secure from either side the Austrian lands as the price of adherence. After some vacillation between neutrality and intervention, and some negotiation with both the Western and the Central Powers, Italy finally entered the war on the side of the Entente in May 1915, under the guarantee of the Treaty of London that in case of the victory of the Allies she should receive the Trentino as far as the Brenner, Venezia-Giulia, a part of Dalmatia with Zara, Sebenico and the islands—that is, all the 'unredeemed' Italian territory save Fiume and a few small districts in Southern Dalmatia.

II. INTERNATIONAL RELATIONS AND EVENTS LEADING TO THE GREAT WAR

We live in the shadow of the greatest war in history, the consummation of forty years of peace. War is the product of a multiplicity of psychological and historical factors, and no satisfactory formula has yet been found for it. The nations of the nineteenth century, whether autocratic or democratic, believed that war was an effective political weapon. War had propagated French political freedom; war had checked the tyranny of a Napoleon; by that means Italy and Germany had found union, the United States justified federation; by the same path the West had entered into the wealth of the East. The age had reason to believe that war was an effective device. Some nations believed it more than others. The Prussians looked back upon their history and their defenceless sandy frontiers, and having noted, with their capacity for scientific tabulation, that war had brought them protection, prestige, and dominion they exalted it, with their capacity for faith, into a national creed and a principle of life. To a Frenchman, glowing to the martial memory of the Grand Monarque or the Petit Caporal, burning with the military disgrace of 1870, war was an instinctive resource. Other illustrations might be given to show that, in spite of pacifistic ventures, men believed in war as a means of national satisfaction. They had relegated it, for the most part, to the category of ultimate resources, and a long step toward the peace of mankind had thereby been taken. But as long as war was—and is—held to be an effective political instrument wars will from time to time break out,[1] and the historian should perhaps more properly be asked not what caused the war of 1914, but what kept the peace for the preceding forty years. For there was no dearth of international controversy—international history is in outline a sequence of such conflicts—and there was plentiful occasion for serious rivalry and mutual hostility in so vast a problem, for example, as the partition of Africa.

From 1871 to 1890 Bismarck was the arbiter of European politics, and Bismarck as Chancellor of the new German Empire wanted peace. Germany, he declared, was a "satiated" country. **Bismarck, 1871–90.** War, which had brought her national unity and international pre-eminence, would, if risked again, bring her only an imperilling of the acquisitions she had gained. It would set the Powers in the field against her, and threaten the internal consolidation and cohesion that was necessary to the development of her political unity. All this Bismarck saw clearly, and for this reason he routed the war-mongers in his own camp, who, in 1875, seeing the unexpected rapid recuperation of France and her thirst for revenge, would have liked to fall upon her before she could become again a serious military menace.

Bismarck's influence was therefore, like that of Metternich after 1815, directed toward peace because his policy was concerned with the maintenance of the *status quo* in the interests of his own state. He who had before so fundamentally disturbed the Balance of Power that was established at Vienna had now become the preserver of a new Balance of Power that had been established at Königgrätz and Sedan. Bismarck was afraid of France, in whom he found an irreconcilable enemy who would not be persuaded nor intimidated into accepting the Peace of Frankfurt. The German Chancellor therefore employed his diplomatic skill and his political insight in the building up of alliances for the protection of Germany, and, conversely, in the prevention of counter-alliances against her. The enemy of Germany was France, and Bismarck's achievement was the diplomatic isolation of France. The linch-pin of his system was a strong alliance with

---

[1] This paragraph, written in 1928, is unhappily illustrated by the outbreak of another war in 1939. But while the events preceding it have shown the increasing use of force and the threat of force in international affairs, they have also shown the immense reluctance of Great Powers to engage in full conflict with well-matched opponents, and to unloose upon their peoples the annihilating destructiveness of modern warfare.

Austria, while to a homogeneous *Mittel-Europa* he succeeded in attaching Italy, and, less securely, Russia. He took pains also to cultivate the friendship of Great Britain;[1] and except for a few years of strain in the early eighties, over colonial matters, the two countries were on good terms down to the end of Bismarck's administration. For, once England had decided to accept Germany's colonial aspirations, there was little ground for rivalry between an island-empire which was pursuing a diplomatic isolation that kept it aloof from Continental entanglements and a European state that had not yet adopted a serious naval programme. There was no reason for war, declared Bismarck, between "a land rat and a water rat."

The Prusso-Russian alliance had been a cardinal principle of Bismarck's policy since his appointment as Minister-President of Prussia. The German Empire had been founded on it, and although Russia had not seen without envy Prussia's phenomenal success in 1870 she had taken her own profit from the alliance and attested its reality. Austria, however, a defeated enemy of recent standing, had to be wooed more carefully. From the morrow of Königgrätz Bismarck had envisaged a possible Prusso-Austrian alliance, and had therefore striven to give no cause of permanent alienation to the Habsburg empire. On the morrow of Sedan he began to approach its realization, and so far succeeded that in 1872 a Three Emperors'

The Drei- League, or Dreikaiserbund, was formed between the
kaiserbund rulers of Germany, Russia, and Austria-Hungary. It
(1872). was a personal alliance of sovereigns, nominally directed
against the "Red International" and the advance of socialism, but it was of deep political significance. It meant that Sadowa was forgiven, that Austria had accepted her expulsion from Germany and the dominance of Prussia therein.

The Triple Entente did not endure long, however, on the footing on which it was placed in 1872. In 1875 there was a scare of war between Germany and France, in which Russia showed herself

The weaken- an uncertain ally, and it is probably from that date
ing of the that Bismarck determined to cultivate more definitely the
Russo- friendship of Austria. When therefore in 1878 in con-
German sequence of the Russo-Turkish War Russian ambitions
alliance came into conflict with the interests of Austria and Great
(1875-78).
Britain Bismarck in spite of his alleged "honest brokerage" at the Congress of Berlin cast his influence against Russia. The Tsar was therefore compelled not only to make peace in the full tide of victory, but to submit his terms to the revision of a European congress, and to abandon all thought—if such had been his intention—of acquiring Constantinople. Bismarck's attitude may have averted a European

---

[1] In spite of his dislike of English liberalism and other attitudes.

war, but it lost Germany the friendship of Russia.[1] Bitterly incensed, Alexander II withdrew from the Dreikaiserbund.[2] **The Dual**
In compensation Bismarck secured the firm alliance of **Alliance**
Austria, who in 1879 concluded with Germany a treaty [3] **(1879).**
of reciprocal protection in case Russia should attack either Power.

Three years later by using as an excuse—and fomenting—the
Franco-Italian rivalry over Tunis Bismarck persuaded Italy to
forget her hereditary enmity towards Austria. A secret **and the**
Triple Alliance was concluded between Italy, Austria- **Triple**
Hungary, and Germany, explicitly defensive, in part **Alliance**
(1882).
against France, in part against Russia.[4]

Bismarck, however, was never a man of one line of argument. He
had consolidated the Triple Alliance, but he had no intention of
making Russia into an enemy who might drift toward an alliance
with France. Though "the public telegraph between Berlin and
St Petersburg might be broken," the "private wire" could be restored. Bismarck had therefore barely concluded the Dual Alliance
with Austria before he was turning again to Russia, and, for all
that Alexander II complained that the Chancellor's friendship
was *trop platonique*, he succeeded in checking the Franco-Russian
rapprochement, and in arresting Russia's alienation from Germany.

A temporary revival of the Three Emperors' League in 1881 broke
down in the Bulgarian crisis of 1885–86, which brought the danger
of war between Austria-Hungary and Russia near enough to imperil
Germany herself through the Dual Alliance of 1879. **German**
Bismarck thereupon concluded with Russia a secret **alliances**
"Reinsurance Treaty," by which each state guaranteed **(1884–90).**
the other her benevolent neutrality in case of attack.[5]

Thus before his fall Bismarck had built up for Germany a complicated protective system of alliance and counter-alliance. He
had secured Russian neutrality in case of an Austrian attack upon
Germany, Austrian neutrality in case of a Russian attack, Italian

[1] See also Chapter VII, p. 311.
[2] *Cf.* the statement of ex-Kaiser William II in *My Memoirs, 1878–1918*, p. 17.
[3] The terms were kept secret until 1887.
[4] Italy, who with her vulnerable sea-coast had no wish to alienate the chief sea
Power, expressly stipulated that it should contain no threat against Great Britain.
This treaty, concluded at first for five years, was in fact renewed at intervals up to
the Great War.
[5] The treaty was primarily designed to keep the peace between Russia and
Austria-Hungary, but it was kept secret from Austria-Hungary (though the
terms of the Dual Alliance were revealed to Russia), as well as from England,
to whom it would have given umbrage, for it promised support to Russia's
Near Eastern policy at the time when Bismarck's allies, Italy and Austria-Hungary,
were planning an agreement with England on the basis of an anti-Russian policy
there.

support against a French attack, and Austro-Italian assistance against a combined Russian and French attack. It was a complicated system of juggling that needed a Bismarck to work it. It is true that, besides temporarily isolating France, it succeeded in maintaining the *status quo* and preserving peace during Bismarck's tenure of office—more, perhaps, because it evinced his determination not to go to war than of its own innate coherence. For the German-Austro-Russian triangle contained implicit, if not explicit, contradictions, as Russia herself learned in the later stages of the Bulgarian crisis, and, in fact, even before Bismarck's retirement, she was beginning to drift away from Germany toward France. [But the Bismarckian system had other demerits. Its foundation—the alliance with Austria-Hungary and Italy—was weak. There was no place in it for Great Britain, whose friendship Bismarck had sacrificed more than once to Russian interests,[1] or for France. It is true that on his retirement Anglo-German relations were good; Great Britain was not then a member of an opposing camp. She was, in fact, a detached Power, but Bismarck's system of alliances had made detachment a highly dangerous condition.] So, also, though Bismarck had temporarily isolated France, he had neither conciliated nor disarmed her. He had, in fact, built up a combination against her that compelled her to look for allies.

Thus Bismarck left to his successor difficult and entangled problems of international relationships. Kaiser Wilhelm II showed no diplomatic skill in their handling, but Bismarck himself must bear considerable responsibility for raising or aggravating them.

Between Bismarck's fall in 1890 and the outbreak of war in 1914 four men successively held the Imperial Chancellorship, and from time to time the new German Emperor, William II, would throw responsibility for measures of foreign policy upon them. The Kaiser by his own confession, however, found it a "hard task for a ruler to think and act constitutionally," and although during von Bülow's term (1900–9) there was a harmony of *Weltpolitik* between sovereign and servant, the real initiator of German foreign policy and the real director of the great influence which the German Empire had come to possess in the councils of Europe was, from 1890 to 1914, the Emperor. William II was equipped with

1890–1914.

---

[1] The Mediterranean Agreement of 1887 between Great Britain, Italy, and Austria-Hungary might have been extended on more than one occasion to Germany had not Bismarck, from a desire to avoid alienating Russia, allowed his support of Russia's Near Eastern interests to stand in the way and even to antagonize Great Britain. Certainly on other occasions Bismarck made conciliatory approaches to offset this opposition, while he deliberately fostered Anglo-French rivalry in Egypt and the colonies to distract both Britain and France from European problems.

many qualities which go far to make a great ruler. He had a quick, receptive mind, versatile interests that ranged from naval technique to archæology, imagination and wide vision, a high sense of duty, and a capacity for hard work, but he lacked, nevertheless, some of the essentials of statesmanship. Egoism and self-consciousness clouded his judgment of men and peoples. He had none of the realism and reserve necessary to diplomacy; he often wounded unnecessarily and wooed unsuccessfully; he was a theorist, with none of Bismarck's power of cool, unsentimental analysis. He could not avoid enmities or disarm antipathies, and in the making of alliances he was a failure.

He set out from assumptions totally different from those held by the old Chancellor. Germany, to the new Kaiser, was not a "satiated" country, but a nation capable of infinite expansion. It was peopled by a vigorous Teutonic stock, which had proved itself, and would prove itself still more, the dominating race of the world.[1] Its destiny was not merely European, but world-wide.

From this arose the natural corollary that Germany should play a leading part not only in European but in world politics, that "without Germany and the German Empire no important step in international matters should be taken, even beyond the seas." "We stand under the sign of world-policy and world-traffic." It also followed that the German Empire should extend and develop her colonial enterprise not only as a sign of her world importance, but as an outlet for her expanding population and economic interests, and the Kaiser comments critically on Bismarck's intention to utilize the colonial possessions that Germany acquired during his administration "for purposes of political barter, rather than to make them useful to the Fatherland, or regard them as sources of raw materials." "I called the Prince's attention," he continues, "to the fact that merchants and capitalists were beginning energetically to develop the colonies."

From colonies the Kaiser argued to a navy. The new German colonists counted upon the protection of the Imperial Government. They could not, as Bismarck himself held, be defended by Germany in Europe. A navy was necessary to afford them adequate protection, otherwise Germany would be reduced to a state of inferiority to Great Britain, and exposed always to British attack.[2] Without a

---

[1] In the Kaiser's opinion, the English race, partly Teutonic, had shown some of this quality, but then unfortunately the English race with its large admixture of Latin elements had, according to him, become decadent. Lord Oxford in *The Genesis of the War* (pp. 49–50) relates that the Kaiser was much impressed by Houston Chamberlain's *The Foundations of the Nineteenth Century*. *Cf.* also the Kaiser's own remark (*My Memoirs, 1878–1918*, p. 181): "The Germanic idea in all its splendour was first revealed and preached to the astonished German people by Chamberlain in his book *The Foundations of the Nineteenth Century*."

[2] Bismarck himself had in earlier days used this argument as a reason for Germany's not acquiring colonial burdens.

navy the German Empire would be dependent upon England, who was always engaged "in the pursuit—constant, though concealed by all sorts of little cloaks—of world hegemony."

World politics, expansion, and the navy became the three dominant notes of the Kaiser's foreign policy, reiterated with increasing emphasis as the new century advanced. Thus the whole foundation of Bismarck's policy was undermined, and in consequence much of the superstructure fell to the ground. The policy of the German Empire was no longer one of saturation, of maintaining the *status quo* and the Balance of Power. "There is no Balance of Power in Europe except one—me and my twenty-five army corps,"[1] the Kaiser is said to have remarked. The national policy was to be a forward, dynamic one of expansion. In the wisest hands such a policy involved a serious disturbance of international relations; in the hands of a man without caution or wisdom, who committed himself dangerously to nationalist propaganda, and indulged rashly in a profusion of martial metaphors like "the mailed fist," "the shining armour," and "the well-sharpened sword," who supported his views with an army and a navy in a high state of preparation, such an attitude appeared at times like a menacing attempt to establish a militaristic hegemony of Europe.

With the "bankruptcy of German statecraft,"[2] which resulted from the Kaiser's handling of foreign affairs, Bismarck's elaborate system of alliances broke down. Within three years Russia had been alienated and driven to a *rapprochement* with France; within six years England had been antagonized; two years later Admiral Dewey, of the United States Navy, declared that the next war would be with Germany; by 1907 the Triple Entente was already in existence as a counter-coalition to the Triple Alliance, Japan had come to an understanding with Russia, and Italy had shown a considerable weakening in her adherence to the Triple Alliance. In exchange for all this the Kaiser had won one new ally, Turkey, and strengthened the cohesion of *Mittel-Europa* at the cost of seriously committing Germany to the Near Eastern interests of Austria-Hungary.

The break-down of Bismarck's system of alliances.

The Russian 'reinsurance' was allowed to lapse immediately after Bismarck's retirement, as being "too complicated," and containing a "threat against Austria which would unavoidably lead to very unpleasant consequences." "In my opinion," declares the Kaiser, "it had already lost its main value from the fact that the Russians no longer stood whole-heartedly behind it." The abandonment of the Russian treaty, an announcement that Germany intended to

---

[1] The Earl of Oxford, *The Genesis of the War.*
[2] *Cf.* Professor C. R. Beazley's *Nineteenth-century Europe and Britain*, p. 253.

surrender herself to an unqualified support of Austria, resulted directly in a *rapprochement* between France and Russia. Partnership with France constituted Russia's only escape from a dangerous isolation. The Triple Alliance had been renewed, and England, antagonistic to France in Africa and to Russia in Afghanistan, seemed more disposed to give her sympathy at that time to the Triple Alliance than to any counter-league. Alexander III, therefore, swallowed his dislike of French atheism and French republicanism and his distrust of ever-changing French politics, and turned to France. In 1891 the French fleet paid a ceremonial visit to Kronstadt, thus entering Russian waters for the first time since the Crimean War. It was received with great cordiality, and the emotion shown by the French fleet at the strains of the Russian national anthem was equalled only by the Tsar's gesture in listening bareheaded to the *Marseillaise*,[1] played by his own naval band. "When the fleet weighed anchor the *rapprochement* was made. It only remained to translate it into official language. The Tsar had committed himself." [2] The visit was followed by the somewhat prolonged negotiation of a treaty, by the issue of a Russian loan in France and an appeal to French investors.[3] In 1893 a Russian squadron visited Toulon, and the officers went up to Paris, where, according to a contemporary account, "men and women ran about beside their carriages, to kiss and touch their hands." It was not, however, until January 1895, after the death of Alexander III, that the Franco-Russian alliance was publicly proclaimed. The new political *liaison* aroused in Europe, and especially in Germany, serious alarm. A convention based only on a common hatred to Germany was held to have necessarily an aggressive purpose. Great Britain feared a more vigorous assertion of French claims in Egypt and a recrudescence of Russian ambitions in Turkey. The Kaiser, who had not believed that such an alliance would actually arise, looked apprehensively at Alsace-Lorraine, noted nervously that in case of war Germany would have to defend two frontiers, increased his army, and wrote protestingly to Nicholas II, who had in 1894 come to the Russian throne:

The Dual Alliance between France and Russia (1891 and 1895).

> I perfectly understand that you do not dream of attacking us, but you cannot wonder that the Powers get alarmed, seeing how the presence of your officers and high officials . . . in France fans the inflammable Frenchman into a white-heated passion. . . . If you are allied

---

[1] Its playing had hitherto been forbidden in public places.
[2] Freycinet, quoted by G. P. Gooch, *History of Modern Europe, 1878–1919*, p. 172.
[3] The house of Rothschild refused to accommodate the Russian Government as long as it persecuted its Jewish subjects.

for better or worse with the French, well then, keep those damned rascals in order and make them sit still.

A further letter explained that

it is not the friendship of France and Russia that makes me uneasy, but the danger to our principle of monarchism through the lifting up of the Republic on a pedestal. . . . Nicky, take my word, the curse of God has stricken that people [the French] for ever. We Christian kings and emperors have one holy duty imposed on us by heaven—to uphold the principle by the grace of God [*von Gottes Gnaden*].[1]

Nevertheless the Dual Alliance was maintained until Tsardom itself perished; and in 1896 the Tsar and Tsarina paid an official visit to France—the first time that a reigning sovereign had so complimented the Third Republic.

France, of course, was jubilant to see the end of her diplomatic isolation and the fulfilment of an alliance which was described as "the cry of nature, the revelation of geography, the bond of war, the balance of peace."[2] "We have nothing now to fear from anyone," it was officially declared; "we greet this dawn which rises on our destiny." A new chapter had opened in the history of France and of Europe.

It must be noted that the German Emperor tried from time to time during the next ten years to obviate the growth of an antagonism between the Dual and Triple Alliances, and to cultivate friendly relations with France and Russia, even to realize an obstinate dream of a great Continental *bloc* against Great Britain. He sought the friendship of the young Tsar Nicholas, he joined with France and Russia in ordering Japan out of the Liao-tung Peninsula in 1895, refused for Russia's sake the offer of a British alliance in 1899, and even tried to form a German-Russo-French alliance in 1905. He thus aroused in the minds of British statesmen, especially during the Boer War, lively apprehensions of a general Continental coalition against Great Britain and the British Imperialism which was execrated alike by France, Russia, and Germany. England was, however, saved from so critical a situation by the Kaiser's own mishandling of German foreign policy, by his refusal to co-operate entirely with the Dual Alliance, by a certain disingenuousness and vacillation which led him to abandon a policy which he had up to a point pursued. Thus after having raised expectations among the Boers, and incidentally infuriated England by a pronounced pro-Boer attitude, he executed a *volte-face* and submitted to the British Court military plans for the destruction of the "clowns." Having apparently encouraged France in a forward colonial policy he left her

---

[1] G. P. Gooch, *op. cit.*, p. 185.   [2] Professor C. R. Beazley, *op. cit.*, p. 228.

unsupported in the Fashoda incident [1] with England in 1898.
Having sacrificed British friendship from time to time to a pro-
Russian policy, and supported Russia in opposition to Japan, he gave
the Tsar no help in the war of 1904-5, and seemed rather to take
advantage of his defeat to push Austro-German interests in the
Balkans. Thus the Kaiser's efforts produced only an impression of
"cajolery" or even "betrayal." [2] With the adoption of a pronounced
pro-Turkish policy any hope of a reconciliation with Russia was at
an end, and from the Bosnian crisis of 1908 the paths of the Dual
and Triple Alliances began seriously to diverge.

It would seem as though the German Emperor, realizing as he
did the danger to which Germany was exposed from the potential
enmity of two neighbours, should have sought in compensation a
strong alliance with England, while in the Far East an understanding
with Japan would have imposed something of a check upon Russia.
Yet he not only allowed an attitude of rivalry to develop in the
Pacific between Germany and Japan, but he also sacrificed repeated
opportunities of an alliance with Great Britain, and in the end
definitely antagonized her.

Bismarck had been primarily a Continentalist; nevertheless the
German colonial empire was largely founded by him, in the Pacific,
in East and West Africa and the Cameroons. He allowed
Germany to enter into the competition for African lands,
and thereby considerably to accelerate the international
scramble for the Dark Continent. For a few years in the early
eighties Great Britain was inclined to regard with irritation the new
aspirant to colonial empire, but Bismarck's diplomacy succeeded not
only in allaying the friction that had already arisen, but in winning
from Great Britain a cordial welcome to her colonizing efforts. At a
conference at Berlin during the winter of 1884-85 the two Powers
arrived at an amicable agreement on the question of the partition of
Africa, and in the spring of 1885 Gladstone announced in the House
of Commons that "if Germany is to become a colonizing Power, all
I say is, 'God speed her!' She becomes our ally and partner in the
execution of the great purposes of Providence, for the advantage of
mankind."

The relations between England and Germany were never better
than during the late eighties and the early nineties, when William II
came to the throne and Bismarck fell from office. Visits
were exchanged between the Kaiser and his English
relatives, and the German Emperor never tired of expressing his goodwill for England. "I have always felt at
home in this lovely country. . . . I shall always, so far as it is in my

Relations with Great Britain.

The cession of Heligo-land to Germany (1890).

[1] See Chapter X, pp. 486-487.   [2] *Cf.* Professor C. R. Beazley, *op. cit.*, p. 255.

power, maintain the historic friendship between our nations." One of the fruits of this friendship was the cession to Germany in 1890 of Heligoland, in exchange for Zanzibar and Witu. The island had been an English possession since 1807, and in view of the projected Kiel Canal had become of late of more importance to Germany. Although Bismarck never attached to it the value placed upon it by the Kaiser, he had tried in 1884 to recover it for the German Empire, suggesting (it was during the years of strain) that it would strengthen the good relations between Great Britain and Germany. His request had, however, received the ironical reply that no doubt the cession of Gibraltar would strengthen the good relations between England and Spain. Nevertheless six years later the Salisbury Government surrendered it, a tribute really to the cordiality which Bismarck had by that time established in Anglo-German relations, although since it occurred just after Bismarck's retirement the Kaiser claimed it as the first triumph of his independent policy. There was much discussion on both sides as to the relative value of what had been won and lost. In England the Government view was expressed in Stanley's words that "a trouser button had been exchanged for a suit of clothes." In Germany the reception of the transaction was complicated by the criticism of the Bismarckian party, which was directed against the whole Government policy. The Kaiser, however, was delighted; "without a battle, without the shedding of a tear, this beautiful island has passed into my possession. . . . I drink to the illustrious lady to whom we are indebted for the transfer." To the Kaiser's naval policy the possession of Heligoland was indispensable, and no one then anticipated a war between England and Germany.

The Kaiser did not profit to the full by the advantages that were offered him during this phase of Anglo-German cordiality. In 1893 **The Kaiser rejects a British colonial offer.** Great Britain offered, with a view to checking France, and assuming that Germany would be a friendly neighbour, to recognize German 'influence' over all Central Africa between Lake Chad and the basin of the Upper Nile. France strongly protested, for such an extension of the German colonial empire would have cut into her ambitions to establish French dominion from the Mediterranean to the Congo. The Kaiser therefore rejected the offer. He threw it aside without stipulating, as Bismarck would have done, for an adequate compensation[1] in a more desirable quarter. Nor did he secure by his action an adequate return in French goodwill.

It was in connexion with the South African policy of Great Britain that the first revelation was given of Anglo-German antagonism.

[1] For the completion which he asked for, of the Cameroon territories to Lake Chad, was practically inevitable. *Cf*. Professor C. R. Beazley, *op. cit.*

The telegram of congratulation sent in the German Emperor's name to President Kruger in 1896, after the failure of the Jameson Raid, was resented in Britain as an unwarrantable impertinence. The Kaiser himself charged his ministers with responsibility for the telegram, and it is now admitted to have been sent against his wish; but the view gained ground in England that Germany was lending encouragement to the Boers, and for her own reasons. It was fostered by the violent anti-British feeling shown during the Boer War by the people of Germany, as of the Continent generally, and it was not wholly dissipated by the Kaiser's change of attitude, nor by his visit to England on the occasion of Queen Victoria's death in 1901.

Anglo-German relations strained by the British policy in South Africa.

It was not only with Germany, however, that Great Britain's relations were strained. On all sides England was in conflict, and never in modern times has she been more unpopular on the Continent than at the end of the last century. The scramble for concessions in China, the seizure of Kiao-chau by Germany and Port Arthur by Russia, had set her against those two Powers, the Fashoda incident had nearly brought her to war with France, and her South African policy was generally criticized as a demonstration of aggressive imperialism. When Nicholas II called his first Peace Conference at the Hague in 1899 there was a good chance of war between England and any one of the three chief Powers of Europe—or even all three together. For Great Britain was perilously isolated. But however good the opportunity seemed for a Franco-Russo-German coalition against Great Britain, Germany let it slip, partly, von Bülow has informed us, because she distrusted France ("Fashoda would not drive out the memory of Sedan"), and partly because the new German naval policy was not sufficiently advanced to give to Germany that power at sea without which, the ex-Chancellor has stated, no real victory could ever be obtained against Great Britain.

England's perilous isolation during the Boer War.

The scare was not without its effects on British policy. In the first place, it is from the time of the Boer War, Lord Oxford has declared, that the first feeling of national antagonism to Germany may be dated. Secondly, it showed up in high relief the dangers of the policy of isolation.

It was evidently held at the time that the feeling of antagonism to Germany might be overcome, and that in any case it was less than that toward Russia or France, for the first approach of England toward a Continental alliance was made to Germany. It was Mr Joseph Chamberlain's scheme, proposed by him at the risk of great unpopularity in the country, that a firm alliance between England, Germany, and

Proposed Anglo-German alliance (1899–1901).

possibly America should be contracted.   It was the German Emperor
who rejected it, seeing that it was directed against Russia, thereby
throwing aside again an opportunity for a real *rapprochement* with
England. England thereupon concluded the Anglo-Japanese Alliance,
as a set-off to Russia in the Far East. The era of British isolation
was closed.

With the development of the Bagdad railway Great Britain began
to look with growing apprehension at the German approach to India.

The menace of the Bagdad railway.
The prospective establishment of a German naval base in
the Persian Gulf at the terminus of the railway would
involve a menace to British interests there, and Lord
Lansdowne in 1903 plainly announced that Great Britain
"would resist it by all the means at her disposal."   Through British
pressure the local ruler was persuaded to defy his suzerain, the Sultan
of Turkey, and to refuse to permit the extension of the railway to the
Gulf.

It was, however, the Kaiser's new naval policy which not only set
Great Britain against Germany, but drove her into league with her

Germany's new naval policy.
own traditional enemy, France, with whom for twenty
years she had been at loggerheads in the colonies.   Hitherto England had reckoned only with the French and
Russian fleets. The new German navy law of 1900 showed that the
German Empire was about to put upon the seas a navy greater than
either, a factor that would seriously disturb England's naval pre-
eminence.   Great Britain was touched at her most sensitive point,
and from this time the naval question—naval competition, challenge,
and precaution—began to usurp in English politics that all-dominat-
ing position which it subsequently filled.   Great Britain realized
that she must compose some of her Continental quarrels, and, aided
by the personal tact and diplomacy of her sovereign, Edward VII, she
turned to her nearest neighbour, France, with whom she had had
some of the sharpest differences.   In 1904 an Anglo-French agreement was made.   The long-standing dispute over Egypt—a French

The Anglo-French Convention (1904).
grievance since 1882—was at last settled.   France agreed
to recognize the British position in Egypt, and to lend it
her support; in return Great Britain agreed to support the
paramount claims of France in Morocco.   A subsequent
Franco-Spanish treaty further adjusted French and Spanish interests
in the African state.

The Anglo-French *entente* was a revolution both in French and
English politics.   It was enthusiastically received on both sides of
the Channel, save by Lord Rosebery, who declared, "My mournful
and supreme conviction is that this agreement is much more likely
to lead to complication than to peace."   It marked the turning of

Great Britain away from Germany, although it had no menacing intention toward her, nor real military significance. It laid the foundation of a general Anglo-French co-operation in international affairs which has increased in strength up to the present day. It certainly determined the direction of British policy up to the Great War, and gave France a greater self-confidence; it caused Italy to consider again her position in the Triple Alliance; it removed from Great Britain the need of dependence upon German support in her Egyptian policy; it contributed to the adjustment of Anglo-Russian relations at the time when the Russo-Japanese War was putting strain upon them; it cleared the path for the conclusion in 1907 of the treaty with Russia which completed the Triple Entente.

The conclusion of the Anglo-Russian alliance in 1907, which constituted the second diplomatic revolution in British foreign politics within three years, followed chiefly in consequence of three events—the Russo-Japanese War, the Moroccan crisis of 1905–6, and the new German Navy Bill of 1906. *The Anglo-Russian Convention (1907) following on the Russo-Japanese War (1904–5).*

The defeat of Russia at the hands of Japan and the cession of Port Arthur put an end for the time to Russian expansion in the Far East,[1] and together with the revolution at home considerably modified the fear of Russian aggression.

The Moroccan affair produced the first of four international crises which preceded the outbreak of the European War; it also gave the first proof of the solidarity of the Anglo-French *entente*. It arose out of the Anglo-French treaty of 1904.

Morocco was an independent Mohammedan province which, partly because of its iron deposits, partly because of its position on the Atlantic coast in proximity to the Strait of Gibraltar, and partly because it seemed too weak to defend itself against European expansion, had aroused the interest of many European states—Spain, Great Britain, France, Germany, and Italy. France held herself particularly concerned, for Morocco abutted on her own fairly recent annexation of Algeria, and the border tribes were troublesome. The province had for some years been regarded as a potential field for European trade and 'penetration,' and even as a proper subject for international barter. In the Anglo-French treaty of 1904 Great Britain had promised to give diplomatic support to French interests in the province. France, fortified by the treaty, had therefore pushed more vigorously her policy of penetration. She had begun to interfere in the internal administration of Morocco; she had lent the Sultan a large sum of money on the security of the customs, and she had put forward a programme of 'reforms,' which she desired to see adopted in the *The Moroccan crisis (1905–6).*

[1] See Chapter XI, pp. 512, 513, 521–524.

province—the construction of roads and telegraphs, the institution of a national bank, the French policing of the ports, and other measures. In short, France was rapidly acquiring a hold over Morocco which, in the light of many incidents in colonial history, could only be interpreted as a prelude to annexation. This at any rate was the construction which the Kaiser chose to put upon the development of France's policy. France and Spain, he asserted, were about to close upon Morocco, to shut out the trade of other nations, and in particular to strangle the economic interests of Germany, whose treaty rights were invaded. In a dramatic but tactless manner the Kaiser intervened. At the end of March 1905 (it was noted that Russia, having just been defeated at the battle of Mukden, was for the time being put out of action) the German Emperor visited Tangier,[1] formally took the Sultan under his protection, and loudly proclaimed that he would champion the integrity of Morocco, the sovereignty of the Sultan, and the equality of commercial and economic interests. His intervention was in keeping with his general befriending of the Mohammedan world, and was calculated to please the Pan-German and colonial party at home and to break up the Anglo-French *entente*. Its immediate result was to stimulate the Sultan to reject France's programme of reforms, and to demand, under German instruction, a general European conference to settle the questions raised. France vigorously protested against the German intervention. Germany insisted upon the conference. France hesitated; the alternative seemed to be war. At length, partly owing to American mediation, France accepted the conference, and Delcassé, the Foreign Minister, who had negotiated the Anglo-French treaty and was prepared to push French policy to the extreme of war, resigned. The conference was to meet in January 1906 at Algeciras. Germany had won a diplomatic victory.

It is unnecessary to describe at length the conference of Algeciras. It was a drawn battle. "We are neither victors nor vanquished," said von Bülow, and the French Premier expressed much the same sentiment. France won, subject to a certain international control, her police mandate, her State bank, and certain other demands. Her position was more regularized, and she was left free to proceed with her pacific penetration. On the other hand the French annexation of Morocco was forbidden and the 'open door' theoretically established, and Germany had secured acceptance of the principle

---

[1] Apparently the visit was the result of von Bülow's advice. " I landed to oblige you, because my country demanded it, mounted a strange horse, although my left arm was crippled and hindered my riding, and risked the loss of my life. I rode among Spanish anarchists because you wanted it, and because your policy was to benefit by it."—The Kaiser to von Bülow, quoted by G. Lowes Dickinson, *The International Anarchy*, p. 126.

of international responsibility. "We not only bolted the door," claimed von Bülow, "against the attempts of France to compass the 'Tunification of Morocco,' but we also provided a bell that could be rung at any time should France show any similar tendencies again." In retrospect, however, the conference appears as a check to Germany. Diplomatically she received support from none of the Great Powers except Austria, "her splendid second on the duelling-ground." France, Russia, and Spain were against her, and Great Britain by the Morocco treaty of 1904; Italy too declared her Mediterranean interests to be the same as those of France, and voted against the other two partners of the Triple Alliance. The United States also, playing the *rôle* of mediator, which she seemed to have adopted in international affairs, supported the cause of France behind the scenes.

Germany's action, instead of destroying, had strengthened the Anglo-French *entente*; it had, moreover, brought Great Britain into more cordial relations with Russia. The international crisis had for the first time grouped England, France, Russia, and Italy on the same side, and divided the nations in much the same way as they were to be divided later, in the Great War.

The question was asked in 1905 and 1906 that has been asked continually since then. How far was England committed by the *entente* to support France with arms should the latter be engaged in war with Germany? Great Britain's position from 1906 to 1914 has now been clearly exposed to us: it was one which caused infinite doubt and vexation to France. For while on the one hand Sir Edward Grey repeatedly warned Germany that we could hardly remain neutral in a Franco-German war, he as persistently refused French, and later Russian, demands for a definite military alliance or pledge of support in war. He refused to commit England in advance to a hypothetical situation, for "to make an agreement which would tie the hands of the British Government, would be a challenge to Germany " [1] and would outrun the opinion of the country. The Government nevertheless recognized the vital interest to Great Britain of a strong and independent France and allowed Anglo-French military staff talks to take place. Further, a definite naval convention was made in July 1912 entrusting Anglo-French interests in the Mediterranean to the French Navy and in the Channel to the British Navy, and naval talks were opened with Russia in May 1914.

Again, however, while Britain moved toward France in this way, she also moved toward Germany. She tried to mitigate Anglo-German naval competition, even to bring about an alliance in 1912, and she made concessions on colonial matters.

---

[1] See memorandum of Sir Eyre Crowe, Under-Secretary for Foreign Affairs, in *British Documents on the Origin of the War*, vol. iii.

On August 3, 1914, Sir Edward Grey assured the House of Commons that England was not committed to go to war with France, and he and Lord Oxford subsequently maintained that the Government had reserved entire freedom to intervene in war or not. But, while the position may, perhaps, be defended juridically, it is now clear that British and French statesmen alike recognized England's moral obligation to support France in war.

The German Navy Amendment Law of 1906, which increased the German foreign service fleet by five large cruisers[1] and augmented the normal naval expenditure by one-third, was the third contributory factor in the Anglo-Russian *rapprochement*. There were a few vain efforts to improve Anglo-German relations, and then in the summer of 1907 Great Britain turned definitely to Russia.[2]

The German Navy Amendment Law (1906).

A convention was concluded in August defining in a spirit of friendly accommodation the hitherto conflicting interests of the two countries in Persia, Afghanistan, and Tibet. Concessions, surprising in view of former enmities, revealing the depth of the mutual fear of Germany, were made on both sides with little regard for the outraged feelings of Moors, Persians, Afghans, and Egyptians, who repudiated and denounced the convention.

The Anglo-Russian convention completed the *entente* of Great Britain with the Dual Alliance. It "put an end once and for all," says Lord Oxford, "to the Russian 'menace to India,' which had haunted the minds of British statesmen and diplomats—even of those who used the largest maps—for generations." To the composing of long-standing quarrels between England and France and England and Russia there can be no objection. On the question of how far Great Britain was wise to abandon her diplomatic isolation—which, it must be remembered, had brought her into great peril during the Boer War—opinion is seriously divided. Although no military alliance was involved, nor menace to Germany implied, in the Triple Entente, it can only be regarded as a defensive combination against the Central Powers. It gave greater security to France; it heartened her chauvinists; and it encouraged, perhaps, especially after 1911, when Great Britian showed her French sympathies so strongly, her *revanche* policy, for

The completion of the Triple Entente.

[1] The *Dreadnought* (launched February 1906), the outcome of the Russo-Japanese War, was the type and standard of battleship then beginning to be adopted by England and Germany.

[2] It is now known that the German Emperor had been trying for some time to persuade the Tsar to join in an alliance against England, in the hope of attracting France to it later, and at a meeting between the two Emperors at Bjoerkoe Sound in July 1905 Nicholas II actually signed an agreement drawn up and presented by the Kaiser. But it seems never to have been regarded as a practical commitment by the Russian Foreign Office, and "was allowed to remain buried in a pigeonhole among the Tsar's private papers."

the new generation looked to the recovery of Alsace-Lorraine as keenly as the old generation felt its loss. Although Russia could not with certainty count on British support, the understanding gave her greater security, and Russia, checked in Asia, was awaking again to her interests in the Balkans and her rivalry there with Austria. It strengthened Great Britain in her bitter naval competition with Germany.

To Germany it caused intense disquietude, and a scare which produced something of a hysteria among Pan-Germans, and Navy Leaguers, and Prussian generals. It was not so much that Germany feared Great Britain, although she began to hate her for her successful imperialism, for her "traditional policy of opposing whatever Continental Power was for the time being strongest"; it was that she feared the effect of Great Britain's support upon France in Alsace-Lorraine and Russia in the Balkans. "England was well aware," cries Bethmann-Hollweg, "that the eyes of France were steadfastly fixed upon Alsace-Lorraine, and could hear the deep notes of the *revanche motif* sounding, even through the harmonies of the Russo-French fraternization." Again, "the general tension throughout the world originated, indeed, in the certainty of English support enjoyed by a Franco-Russian policy through whose ultimate objects we were endangered."[1]

It was from this time that Germany began to bring forward against Great Britain, and particularly against King Edward VII, the repeated charge of "encirclement," of a deliberate policy of surrounding Germany with a combine of hostile nations—France, Russia, Great Britain, Japan by affiliation, Italy by seduction from the Triple Alliance (even the United States was asserted to be in the conspiracy) —in order, "by the moulding of a serried and supreme combination of states," to obstruct her in the free development of her growing powers. It is the most persistent defence of the Kaiser, and of Germany's apologists, for the Great War, the most easily recalled cry in the revived Anglo-German hostility of 1939.

From 1907 Europe was grouped, somewhat artificially, into two armed camps, watching each other with suspicion and distrust. The political situation was tragically full of menacing possibilities; there were the piling up of armaments by land and sea, and Germany's naval ambitions, which Great Britain would not accept; there was the French desire for the recovery of Alsace-Lorraine; there was the periodical emergence of embarrassing incidents like that of Morocco; there were "the continuous counter-activities of Austria and Russia in the Balkans, the restlessness of the Balkan states themselves," the "cloud of uncertainty that hung over the future of Turkey."

There were the chauvinists of all nations ready to light the fuel that was heaped up. "We were often conscious," remarks Lord

[1] Theobald von Bethmann-Hollweg, *Reflections on the World War*.

Oxford, speaking of the years that preceded the Great War, "that we were skating on the thinnest of ice, and that the peace of Europe was at the mercy of a chapter of unforeseen and unforeseeable accidents."

Such a chapter of accidents might have developed out of any one of the international crises which recurred with increasing and alarming frequency during the next seven years, to inflame the hostilities of the nations and disturb the dreams of peace-lovers.

From the "Young Turk" revolution of 1908,[1] with its attendant problems of the Austrian annexation of Bosnia and the Herzegovina, the Italian war for Tripoli, the Balkan League, and the new Balkan wars, the ferment of the Near East began to keep the general international situation of Europe in a constant state of excitement and alarm. It was chiefly the unpreparedness of Russia which allowed the Bosnian crisis of 1908 to pass without war, and the challenge to the peace of Europe and the sanctity of public law contained in Austria's annexation of the two provinces to remain unaccepted. Thus Austria, and still more Germany, "in shining armour" behind her, were allowed to score their victory.

The recrudescence of the Near Eastern ferment.

Before the next Near Eastern crisis had matured the Moroccan Question had again come to the forefront of international politics, in the Agadir crisis of 1911. In spite of the check which France had received at Algeciras she was bent upon the annexation of the Moroccan province; on the plea of serious internal disorder she had marched her troops into the province, and then refused to withdraw them. Germany therefore sent a warship, the *Panther*, to Agadir, a Moroccan port, ostensibly to defend German interests, but in reality as a warning to France. Again a highly critical situation arose, but Great Britain came out firmly on the side of France, and Germany decided not to force the question to the point of war. It may be that she was seeking to gain time, that "the war party in Germany had not yet gained complete ascendancy, and that, in the opinion of their experts, neither their military, their naval, nor their financial preparations had reached the stage of forwardness which would justify the invention of a *casus belli*."[2] Or it may be that Germany was incommoded by a financial crisis, or weakened by the outbreak of the Tripoli war, which embarrassed the relations between Austria and Italy. At any rate, Germany and France composed their differences pacifically.

The Agadir crisis (1911).

[1] See Chapter VII, pp. 324–325. It is not an accident that the Turkish Question should have been reopened the year following the Anglo-Russian *entente*. Turkey was aware that her best hope had lain hitherto in Anglo-Russian quarrels. With their composure she must defend herself.

[2] The Earl of Oxford, *The Genesis of the War*, p. 95.

Germany agreed to the establishment of a French protectorate in Morocco on condition that the 'open door' was maintained; in return France ceded to her a piece of the French Congo. The next year (1912) France formally declared Morocco a protectorate. The Agadir incident, a forecast of the crisis of 1914, was a defeat for Germany; instead of breaking up the Triple Entente it strengthened it, as the Tangier incident of 1905–6 strengthened the Dual Entente.

In September 1911 Italy declared war upon Turkey. In October 1912 the First Balkan War broke out, and from that date the straining attention of Europe was hardly diverted from the Near East until a Near Eastern Question itself became the fuse that set alight the World War. It has been pointed out in another context [1] how during 1912 and 1913 Balkan problems were successfully isolated, two Balkan wars 'localized,' and two international crises surmounted, leaving, however, a serious residue of ill-feeling, especially between Austria and Serbia and Austria and Russia. "I shall not see the World War," remarked Bismarck to Herr Ballin, [2] "but you will, and it will start in the Near East." A notable prophecy which was remarkably fulfilled.

In the meantime the growing estrangement of Anglo-German relations was causing serious anxiety to the statesmen of both nations, and both the new German Chancellor, Bethmann-Hollweg, and the English Liberal Government of Mr Asquith made efforts to improve them. In February 1912 Lord Haldane, British Minister for War, arrived in Germany to discuss a basis for an Anglo-German alliance. The attempted *rapprochement* broke down, partly on the naval question, and partly because Great Britain would give no pledge of neutrality toward Germany in case the latter should be engaged in war with any other country. The Kaiser expresses himself convinced that the whole affair was a mere "political manœuvre" on the part of Great Britain, with the object of shelving the new German Navy Bill. If so [3] it failed, for in June 1912 the new German Navy Bill became law. The Bill provided for an addition of three battleships and two armoured cruisers, and planned an annual construction of six submarines. Anglo-German naval competition grew more tense. Mr Churchill proposed in March 1913 a "naval holiday," which was rejected; in consequence the British naval estimates for the year 1914–15 went up by twenty million pounds.

On land too the race for armaments continued. The year 1913 saw the climax of preparation. Two new German laws in 1912 and 1913

---

[1] See Chapter VII, pp. 329 *et seq.*
[2] Director of the Hamburg Steamship Company.
[3] But there is no reason to think that the affair was not a sincere pacific effort on Great Britain's side.

raised the peace strength of the German army to 870,000 men. They were followed in July 1913 by fresh Russian and French army laws, the former extending the period of active service in Russia, the latter raising the term of military service in France from two to three years. The peace strength of the Russian army exceeded 1,200,000 men, that of France consisted of about 650,000.

In January 1913 M. Poincaré became French President. Germany believed him to have strong anti-German sentiments. "All his pronouncements breathed nationalism," writes Bethmann-Hollweg. During the first half of 1914 both French and English politics were disturbed by internal disputes, in France with the socialists, in Great Britain with the Irish Nationalists and the Suffragettes.

In the summer of 1914 a round of festivities celebrated the completion of the enlargement of the Kiel Canal to permit the passage **The Sera-** of Dreadnoughts. They were interrupted by the news **jevo murder** that on June 28, 1914, Franz Ferdinand, nephew and **and the** heir apparent of the old Emperor of Austria-Hungary, **crisis of** **1914.** had been shot with his wife in the Bosnian capital of Serajevo. The "chapter of accidents" that was to lead to the Great War had begun.

The Austrian Government after some investigation ascribed the crime to deliberate Serbian propaganda, carried on with the support of high Serbian authorities, and with the object of detaching the Slav subjects of the Dual Monarchy from their allegiance. Austria-Hungary, therefore, in conjunction with her ally Germany, seems to have decided that the hour of Serbia's reckoning was come, that the Dual Monarchy, to maintain its authority in the Balkans, must put an end once and for all to the anti-Austrian agitation of Serbia. The programme seems to have been that Austria should be given a free hand to punish Serbia, while Germany, "in shining armour" again, as in 1908, would keep off the other Powers of Europe.[1] The affair should be localized in a conflict between Austria-Hungary and Serbia.

---

[1] This explanation is supported by a dispatch from the Prussian Secretary of State to the German ambassador in England about July 18, quoted by G. Lowes Dickinson (*The International Anarchy*, pp. 413–414). The salient points are:

(1) Austria is losing her position as a Great Power ; the Balkan crisis of 1908 particularly weakened her ; it is necessary in Germany's as well as her own interest that this decay should be arrested.

(2) If she neglects this opportunity against Serbia she may in a few years be no longer able to act, and Russia will then establish an absolute hegemony in the Balkans.

(3) " Austria is now going to come to a reckoning with Serbia, and has told us so."

(4) Germany will give her a free hand and full support.

(5) " We must attempt to localize the conflict between Austria and Serbia. Whether we shall succeed in this depends first upon Russia, secondly

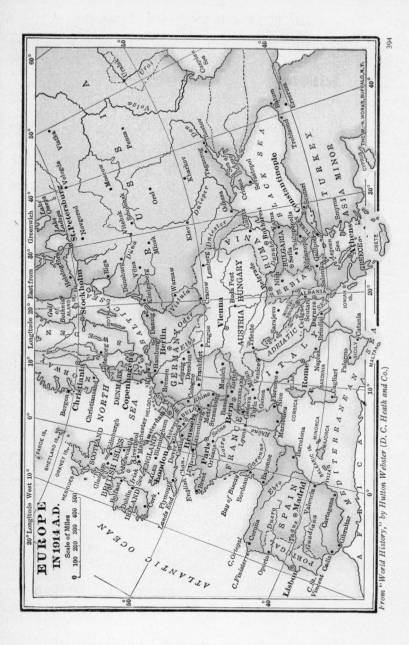

EUROPE IN 1914 A.D.

Scale of Miles
0 100 200 300 400 500

ATLANTIC OCEAN

NORWAY SWEDEN DENMARK

BRITISH ISLES SCOTLAND ENGLAND IRELAND WALES

NORTH SEA BALTIC SEA

GERMANY

FRANCE

SPAIN PORTUGAL

ITALY

AUSTRIA HUNGARY

SERBIA BULGARIA RUMANIA

TURKEY ASIA MINOR GREECE

RUSSIA U.S.S.R.

MEDITERRANEAN SEA

BLACK SEA

AFRICA

Berlin Paris London Vienna Rome Madrid Lisbon Constantinople Athens St. Petersburg Moscow Stockholm Copenhagen Brussels Bern

From "World History," by Hutton Webster (D. C. Heath and Co.)

While the Kaiser went off on a previously planned Norwegian cruise, so that the suspicions of Europe should not be aroused, Austria-Hungary, assured of Germany's support, dispatched on July 23 a stiff Note to Serbia. It complained of the "unfriendly propaganda" conducted by the latter against the Dual Monarchy, and demanded, among other things, that the Serbian Government should officially condemn all anti-Austrian propaganda, should suppress all publications and societies, and dismiss all officials and school teachers, engaged in it, that two Serbian officers named should be arrested for the crime of Serajevo and the help of Austrian officials accepted in the further investigation of it, as well as in the suppression of anti-Austrian propaganda. A reply was demanded in the remarkably short time of forty-eight hours.

The Austrian Note to Serbia (July 23).

On July 25 Serbia replied to the Austrian Note; she accepted some of its demands, but refused others on the ground that to grant them would involve a violation of her sovereignty. Her reply was considered unsatisfactory, and the Austro-Hungarian minister left Belgrade. On the 26th a part of the Austro-Hungarian army was mobilized, and on the 28th Austria-Hungary declared war on Serbia.

The Serbian reply (July 25).

Austria-Hungary declares war on Serbia.

The importance of the Austro-Serbian crisis was quickly realized all over Europe. Russia, seeing in the Austrian demands another attempt to extend the power of the Dual Monarchy in the Balkans, and consequently a menace to her own ambitions there, declared the cause of Serbia her own. "In no circumstances will Russia remain indifferent to Serbia's fate," telegraphed the Tsar to Serbia on July 27, and Austria-Hungary was warned that on the movement of Austrian troops against Serbia Russia would mobilize.

In the meantime, from July 24, Sir Edward Grey was doing his utmost to bring about mediation by the four Powers not directly concerned in Near Eastern issues—France, Germany, Italy, and Great Britain. But neither Austria nor Germany would accept his proposed conference of ambassadors, on the ground that the Serajevo murder was a "purely Austrian concern." For their object was, as has already been stated, to give Austria a free hand against Serbia.

Sir Edward Grey proposes mediation.

It was therefore with growing uneasiness that the Kaiser observed

upon the moderating influence of Russia's allies. The more determined Austria shows herself, the more energetically we support her, so much the more quiet Russia will remain."

(6) " On the whole Russia is not ready to strike at present. Nor will France and England be ready for war at the present time."

(7) If war should result between Austria and Russia Germany must in self-defence support Austria.

the determination of Russia to intervene on Serbia's side, and on July 28, 29, and 30 he telegraphed appeals to the Tsar, who was his friend, begging him not to let loose the European war which would follow upon Russian mobilization. Russia, however, was convinced that Germany was the real obstacle to the negotiations which she was trying to carry on with Austria, and when on July 29 the latter began the bombardment of Belgrade Russia decided to mobilize all her forces both on the Austrian and the German fronts. The attempt to localize the war had failed.

Russia mobilizes.

Meanwhile in Germany a war party was forming itself, in some antagonism to the Foreign Office, and the General Staff of the army was beginning to use the argument, which it was to repeat three days later against France, that the most important striking factor in a war was speed.

On the 31st, therefore, Germany, treating the Russian mobilization as a declaration of war, dispatched an ultimatum to Russia demanding that military preparations should cease within twelve hours under threat of German mobilization. On the same day she asked France to define her attitude in case of a Russo-German war, giving her a longer time limit.

From Russia no reply was received, and on the urgent advice of the war party Germany declared war on Russia on August 1. France, who on July 30 had informed Sir Edward Grey that in case of a Russo-German war she would stand by the Franco-Russian alliance, answered in effect that she would consult her own interests. It was held in Germany that there was no chance of France's remaining neutral, as her forces were being mobilized, and on August 3 Germany declared war on France.

Germany declares war on Russia (August 1), and on France (August 3).

On the same day Italy announced her neutrality, as the other members of the alliance were not engaged in a defensive war. England had up to this point hesitated, for her interests were not directly involved in the Serbian Question, and she had already declined to "announce her solidarity" with Russia and France. Sir Edward Grey's peace efforts had failed.

Italy neutral.

Great Britain.

Certain significant incidents, however, had taken place. On the 26th orders were given that the British fleet, which was concentrated at Portland after the naval manœuvres, should not disperse. Three days later Sir Edward Grey felt bound to warn the German ambassador in London, Prince Lichnowsky, that Great Britain would not necessarily stand aside in all circumstances. On that day (July 29) Germany made her famous "bid for British neutrality," offering if England would remain neutral to guarantee the territorial integrity of France after any war that should take place between Germany

and that country.   But since the German Chancellor refused to give
the same guarantee respecting French colonies Great Britain refused
the offer.   On Friday, July 31, Sir Edward Grey asked both France
and Germany whether they would respect the integrity of Belgium;
France gave an affirmative, Germany an evasive, answer.   The same
day the Stock Exchange was closed *sine die*, and on August 1 the Bank
rate was raised to 10 per cent. (from 4 per cent. on the 31st).   On
August 2 the British Foreign Minister promised according to the
Anglo-French naval convention to defend the French northern and
western coasts against hostile German naval attack.

The trend of events in England seemed to be toward participation
in what was rapidly becoming a vast European war, but the final
invincible reason which caused the whole British nation to lay aside
its own quarrels and enter with almost one will into the struggle was
supplied by Germany's own action.   On August 2 the Germans had
already invaded the neutral state of Luxemburg.   On August 4 the
King of the Belgians telegraphed to King George an appeal for help,
announcing that Germany had demanded passage for her troops
through Belgium, under promise to maintain, on condition of acceptance, the independence and integrity of the kingdom at the conclusion of peace, and under threat of war in case of refusal.   The
King of the Belgians also telegraphed that he had given a firm and
categorical refusal.   It has always been a cardinal principle of British
policy to preserve the independence of Belgium.   Sir Edward Grey
thereupon dispatched to the German Government an ultimatum
asking for assurance within twelve hours that Germany would respect
Belgian neutrality.   But German troops had already crossed the
frontier, and from midnight on August 4 Great Britain and Germany
were at war.   "If I am asked what we are fighting for," Great
said Mr Asquith in a speech in the House of Commons on Britain
August 6, "I can reply in two sentences.   In the first place, declares war
we are fighting to fulfil a solemn international obligation. (August 4).
. . . Secondly, we are fighting to vindicate the principle that small
nationalities are not to be crushed, in defiance of international good
faith, by the arbitrary will of a strong and overmastering Power."

Two days before, in the Reichstag, the German Chancellor, Bethmann-Hollweg, had announced the opening of war with France and
Russia.   " Gentlemen, I repeat the Kaiser's words : ' Germany enters
upon the war with a pure conscience.'   We are fighting for the fruit of
our peaceful labour, for the inheritance bequeathed to us by a great
past, and for our future. . . . The great hour of trial for our nation
has now struck. . . . Our army is in the field, our fleet is ready for
action—and behind them, the entire German nation."

CHAPTER IX

THE WORLD WAR OF 1914-18 AND AFTER

I. THE WAR

(a)

THE machines of war were set in motion. Sooner or later in all the great states of Europe; in their colonies, in Africa and Egypt, India and Asia, Australia and Canada, and, before the end came, in the Far East and the Far West, in China and Japan, in the United States and the South American republics; on land and sea, and under the sea; in the air; in industry, in finance; in the subtle and powerful sphere

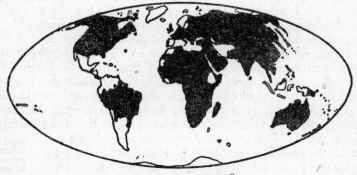

THE WORLD WAR, 1918
The countries marked black took part in the War.
From "Organizing Peace," by permission of the League of Nations Union

of modern propaganda; in every way that human ingenuity could devise men and women, soldiers and civilians, white, black, brown, and yellow races, bent their efforts to conquering, defending, and destroying on a hitherto unprecedented scale.

It was believed that a great state, with its intricate economic entanglements, could not long support a war under modern conditions; the Franco-German War had lasted little more than six months, the Austro-Prussian War six weeks. On the assumption of a comparatively speedy end most men and Governments made their preparations, only one by one to revise them as they learnt that

Europe was to be subjected to tests of strength and endurance, physical, spiritual, economic, such as civilization had hitherto never dreamt of.

Germany and Austria-Hungary (Italy declared neutrality) were confronted by Russia, France, Great Britain, Serbia, and Belgium. Germany (for she was the leading Power of the Dual Alliance) possessed the advantages of interior lines and a central position, of a better military equipment and organization, of an excellent strategic railway system, facilitating a speedy mobilization and disposal of troops.   She suffered from the disadvantages of a war on two fronts (or three, if the Serbo-Austro-Hungarian frontier be included) and of a comparatively weak ally in Austria-Hungary. The Entente Powers possessed a considerable superiority in numbers and resources—a superiority which markedly increased as the War advanced —and the command of the sea, on which the accessibility of those resources depended.   On the other hand, they were hampered by division, by unreadiness in certain quarters, and by the geographical aloofness of Russia, which from the end of 1914 was blocked by Turkey.

(1) The first five months (August–December 1914).

The German offensive in the west.

The advantages of the Entente Powers were such as would tell most effectively in a long campaign, those of the Central Powers in immediate and decisive action.   Germany's chief hope lay in a swift offensive.   Relying therefore upon the greater slowness of Russian mobilization, she resolved, while holding her eastern frontier with a minimum force, to make a rapid offensive in the west, to strike at the heart of France, and deal a "quick and shattering blow" that would bring the war to an end before the forces of her enemies were thoroughly in action.   She all but succeeded, and even her failure left her a dominating position on the western front for four years.

The road of 1870 and the eastern frontier of France were blocked by a strong line of forts from Belfort to Verdun.   Germany thereupon determined to make with the bulk of her army a wide sweep to the north by the comparatively undefended road of Belgium, against the weak French left wing, while some of her troops were to engage the French right wing in Lorraine.

As soon as war was declared Germany threw her troops into Belgium.   The shock in speed and mass was staggering.   Liége put up a gallant defence and threw back the German time-table by three days, but the new sixteen-inch siege howitzers were brought rapidly into action, and one by one its ring of forts was reduced. The cupola defences were smashed to pieces by a gun which could hurl a ton weight a distance of fifteen miles.   The new siege-gun had been a well-kept German secret; it was the first tactical surprise of

THE WORLD WAR

the War. The enemy Powers were astounded; their artillery was immediately placed in a position of inferiority, for they had underestimated the potentialities of the machine-gun and heavy howitzer.

THE WESTERN FRONT

The German invention effected in artillery operations a revolution comparable to that wrought in the naval sphere by the evolution of the Dreadnought eight years earlier.

After Liége the rest of South-eastern Belgium was rapidly conquered in a wide, circular sweep. On August 20 the Belgian capital surrendered without a blow; the Court and the army retired to Antwerp. British [1] and French forces arrived and made attacks in

---

[1] A highly trained British Expeditionary Force of six divisions and one cavalry division (about 70,000 men) under Sir John French began to land in France on August 8, but Earl Kitchener, Minister of War, had yet to raise a national army.

various places; they delayed but did not check the advance. Charleroi, Mons, and Namur fell, the principal fort of the last being razed in forty-eight hours. British and French troops tried to hold Louvain by the battle of Le Cateau. They failed, Louvain surrendered, and the English and French retired. By the end of August the Germans had invaded France and stormed Lille. Then, pouring into France like a great flood, they swept over Picardy and Champagne, ahead even of their own time-table, and consequently of their own supplies. As they approached Paris they began to concentrate their forces for a battle. The small British army of "Old Contemptibles," whom they had driven back at Le Cateau, they despised; the French left they hoped to roll up; by a bold manœuvre they wheeled in their own left before Paris, in an attempt to thrust themselves between the capital and the French army. The French forces hastily retreated beyond the Marne, and at the beginning of September the Germans were within fifteen miles of Paris. The Government withdrew to Bordeaux, and the reserves of all classes were called up; there was a wave of panic in France.

Then came the battle of the Marne and the great check. General Joffre, who had been carrying on a costly seesaw struggle in Alsace-Lorraine, which he had also been forced to abandon in defeat, now collected his forces along a line south of the river Marne. There he made the first real stand against the invaders. For four days the Germans tried in vain to batter down his defence; they were not quite strong enough, having sent two divisions from the west to the east. At length they fell back, methodically and of purpose, to the line of the Aisne, where they proceeded to dig themselves in, and to consolidate their position with the barbed wire and trench defences of modern warfare. The dash for Paris had failed; the "swift and shattering blow" had not shattered. Six weeks had been allotted for the defeat of France. Exactly at the end of that time the German offensive had been checked, and with it had been destroyed all real hope of a speedy end to the War.

The battle of the Marne (September 6-10).

During the middle weeks of September the French and British armies began to hammer upon the German defences of the Aisne. But it was to be shown throughout the War that it was far easier to hold a defensive than to carry an offensive. The German position, fortified by a superb technical skill and organization, proved impregnable. Frontal attacks were found to be useless. Therefore, while a stalemate situation grew up on the Aisne, there developed one of the strangest movements of the whole war. Each side began to extend its lines in an attempt to outflank the other, and the battle went rolling northward to the sea, a hundred

The race to the sea.

and fifty miles away, until it resolved itself into a rush for the Channel ports. The possession of these ports would give many advantages to the Germans, the command of the straits, the power to interfere with the transport of men and supplies, to check the economic blockade of Germany, even to bombard the south coast of England with long-range guns. To win them the German command undertook a second western offensive in the north. On October 9 Antwerp fell after a vigorous bombardment. Most of *The Belgian* Belgium that was yet unconquered was overrun; Ghent, *losses.* Bruges, Ostend, and Lille were taken. A terrible fight raged round Ypres. For sentimental and political reasons, it was important to hold the last corner of Belgium, and the Western Powers *The first* spent their men freely for its sake. The Germans retired *battle of* baffled; they failed also to reach Dunkirk and Calais; the *Ypres.* battle of the Yser checked the second German offensive as the battle of the Marne had checked the first. Their gains, however, were great enough: the rest of Belgium and an important industrial area of North France.

So during the winter of 1914-15 the two sides consolidated their positions along an extended front of four hundred miles, stretching from the Flanders flats to the edges of the Alps, settling down to a continuous, indecisive trench-warfare, with no other result than a daily list of casualties on both sides.

In the east during the same period it had also been proved that defensives were stronger than offensives, and a similar appearance of stalemate had been created. On August 7 the Russians *The Eastern* invaded East Prussia (which had been raided as early as the *Front.* 2nd) with half a million men. They overran much of the province, approached Königsberg and the Vistula, and the Western nations began to talk of the "Russian steam-roller" which should crush the Central Powers. The German army was compelled to ask *Failure of* for reinforcements from the west before it could turn upon *the Russian* the invaders. A subsidiary Russian force was outwitted, *offensive.* and the chief army disastrously defeated in a prolonged seven days' conflict, to which the name of the battle of Tannenberg was given, " in memory of 1410." [1]   A large part of the Russian army was *The battle of* totally destroyed; 80,000 prisoners and many guns were *Tannenberg* taken. The Russians were driven back, the conquest of *(August 26–* Prussia foiled, and Hindenburg and his younger chief *September* of staff, Ludendorff, became the heroes of Germany. On Sedan *1, 1914).* Day, September 2, with Paris fifteen miles from her western armies, and the Russians retreating from East Prussia, Germany

---

[1] There the Teutonic Order was defeated by the Poles and Lithuanians in a battle which checked the German advance eastward.

seemed to have cause indeed for a joyful anniversary. It was the
highest point of exaltation that the Central Powers ever reached.

But Germany's triumph at Tannenberg was dimmed by the weak-

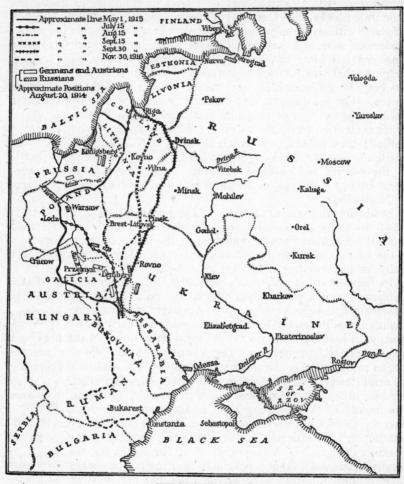

THE EASTERN FRONT

ness of her ally, Austria-Hungary. While the Russians had been
invading East Prussia the Austrians had assumed the offensive
against Russia. They had entered Poland in an attempt to seize
those parts of the Russian railway system which could be put to
strategical use against the Central Powers. Russia, making a bid

for Polish loyalty by a promise of autonomy, turned a million men against the invading Austrians. The latter were compelled to fall back; their advance was changed into a retreat; the successful Russians pushed on and invaded Austrian Galicia, and on September 3 Lemberg fell. While the battle of the Marne was taking place in the west the battle of the Galician front was swaying between the Russians and Austrians in the east. The Austrians were completely broken; the troops fell back, some through the Carpathians, some into Cracow or Przemysl. The Russians, under the Grand Duke Nicholas, continued to advance, hoping on the one hand to strike through Galicia into Silesia, the vital industrial mining province of Germany, and on the other to penetrate to the heart of Hungary. They were to succeed in neither hope. *Failure of the Austrian offensive.*

Hindenburg, after his success at Tannenberg, hoping to relieve the pressure on Austria-Hungary, assumed a counter-offensive against Russia and invaded Poland from the north, swinging his troops against Warsaw. Lodz, the Russian Manchester, fell, but the attempts on the Polish capital were parried, and by Christmas abandoned. Thus in the east too the position tended to be stabilized by the end of the year, over a huge front of two hundred miles, with the Germans in Poland, west of Warsaw, and the Russians in Galicia up to the foot of the Carpathians. *German offensive.*

In the meantime the Austrian invasion of Serbia had ended in failure. The Serbians, driven into the mountains, had made a magnificent rally, and forced back the Austrians to the Danube, out of Serbia. On Christmas Day 1914 King Peter kept the anniversary in his own capital of Belgrade. *Failure of the Austrian attack upon Serbia.*

The naval situation was of supreme importance. It was obvious that the brunt of any action on the part of the Central Powers in this sphere of warfare would fall upon Germany, for the Austro-Hungarian navy was too weak to make any serious contribution. It is evident, however, that in August 1914 the German fleet was unprepared for war; the programme of construction was not completed, and the naval plans were immature. The British fleet, which was considerably superior in numbers, blocked the path of communication between Germany and her colonies. The German naval command, surprised in a state of unreadiness, decided therefore to abandon all attempt to protect the German colonies or German ships which were in distant waters. It withdrew the High Seas Fleet hastily into the protection of its own waters and forts, until an opportunity should arise for a concentrated attack upon the British fleet. A strong defensive system of mines and submarines was developed to keep British ships at bay. *The War at sea.*

The British navy therefore, while guarding the British islands from invasion, convoying troops across the Channel, bringing home outlying garrisons to swell the forces in France, and protecting the commerce and shipping upon which the life and strength of the nation depended, devoted itself also to blockading the German navy and the German coasts. The Grand Fleet swept the waters of the North Sea from the base of Scapa Flow, in the Orkneys, ready for action should the German fleet emerge. Another section of the British fleet, consisting of rather older ships, guarded the approach to the Channel from the Harwich base; it controlled the trade routes and watched for contraband. In the meantime all over the world German commerce fell into British hands.

In the Mediterranean the French fleet was in command, according to the Anglo-French naval convention. Its main duty was to protect shipping against outlying German cruisers and to cover the transport of African troops to France.

With the High Seas Fleet locked up in German waters naval action between the two enemies was slight. It consisted chiefly in the incidents of blockade and of the seizing of contraband, in English raiding attacks upon Heligoland and the German coasts, in German retaliatory mining and bombing raids upon English seaport towns, and in the exploits of individual cruisers which had not been recalled or which escaped the blockade. Of these the two most famous were the *Emden* and the *Karlsrühe*, whose daring feats effected considerable damage before they were captured, the *Emden* alone being responsible for fourteen British ships.

In addition there was, when war broke out, a small squadron of five German ships, under Admiral von Spee, stationed in the Pacific. When Japan declared war upon Germany on August 23 the position of the German squadron became untenable, and von Spee resolved to bring it home. In an encounter off the coast of Chile he defeated a British squadron under Sir Christopher Craddock, who went down with his own flagship, but before the end of the year von Spee's ships were destroyed by Sir Doveton Sturdee in the small battle of the Falkland Islands.

Thus at the end of 1914 the naval position of the Western Powers was stronger than any calculation of chances on the outbreak of war had seemed to warrant. German commerce had been practically swept from the sea. The overseas trade of Great Britain was not as yet seriously interrupted, her transports had been landed, and her coasts were inviolate. The German High Seas Fleet was for the time reduced to a cipher. In short, Great Britain possessed an undisputed supremacy which, in spite of the great submarine challenge of 1917, she maintained for practical purposes throughout the War.

In the colonies British and French troops had fallen upon the German possessions. Togoland and the Cameroons were seized in the first year of the War. German South-west and East Africa put up a more stubborn defence, and their conquest was hampered [1] by a rebellion of Boer nationalists, stimulated by German propaganda. After several engagements the rising was suppressed, a termination which in itself was hardly more satisfactory to Great Britain than the fact that its suppression had been conducted by her two Boer enemies of fifteen years before, Generals Botha and Smuts. With the exception of this rebellion, of the abortive Sinn Fein rising in Ireland in 1916, and of discontent in the new protectorate of Egypt, the War bore eloquent testimony to the strength and union of the mighty commonwealth of nations, and the dissolution of the British Empire, foretold alike by enemies without and pessimists within, never entered the realm of practical politics. On all sides the self-governing dominions rallied round the mother country, giving help both locally and in Europe by contributions of men, money, and kind. More than a million men were contributed by Canada, Australia, and New Zealand alone, and their heroism in repeated engagements and in all theatres of war has become a tradition. India too remained cordially loyal, and of her own will gave nearly a million and a half men to the British cause.

On August 23 Japan declared war upon Germany, and it was the ambitious Eastern empire which fell heir to most of the German possessions in the Pacific, particularly to the port of Kiao-chau and to the German sphere of influence in Shantung.[2]

As an offset to the enmity of Japan, and to her colonial losses, Germany secured in November 1914 the support of Turkey, whose goodwill she had so long courted. Turkey's accession gave the Central Powers a strong though not yet continuous line from Central Europe to Asia Minor and Mesopotamia. It interfered with the communications between Russia and the Western Powers; it completely modified the situation in the Balkans; it seriously threatened the British position in Egypt and India. Its importance, as will be seen by the Gallipoli campaign, was not underestimated.

(b)

The year 1915 opened in hope for the Entente Powers, but it proved a year of delusion and disaster. On the western front [3] a prefatory

---

[1] German South-west Africa was conquered by South African troops by the end of 1915. Resistance in East Africa lingered on until 1918.
[2] See Chapter XI, pp. 512-513.
[3] See map on p. 401.

success at Neuve-Chapelle in March raised the optimism of the Western Allies to a high pitch, and encouraged the High Command **1915.** in the belief that a 'break through' could be made in the German lines.   The Germans, however, took the first initiative in a vigorous counter-attack with fire and poison-gas on the Ypres salient.   For four weeks the second battle of Ypres **The second** raged.   The British lost ground slightly, though not to **battle of** any serious extent, but they held the defence only at a **Ypres, April** heavy cost in man-power.   Thus the two counter-efforts **1915.** at Neuve-Chapelle and Ypres had introduced only a small modification, a local twisting in the long front.

In June the Allies launched their great offensive in Artois, in a long-planned attempt to break through the German line.   The attempt failed.   In September another attempt was made on a wider front in Champagne and Artois.   Again it failed, with a heavy loss of men; the German defence was impregnable.   "Hold the solid wall in the west and let the French and British dash themselves against it; strike down Russia in the east."   Such was the German plan for 1915, a plan which proved entirely successful.

In the east,[1] as in the west, the year opened with Entente successes. The Russians thrust back the Turkish advance through Armenia **The Eastern** upon the Transcaucasian provinces, and the Grand Duke **Front.** Nicholas, pursuing his advantage against Austria, took Przemysl, carried the heights of the Carpathians, and threatened Cracow by Easter.   Then quickly followed a complete reverse.

While the Grand Duke Nicholas had been fighting for the Carpathians Hindenburg had carried a successful drive against the Russians in the north from East Prussia.   In February he routed and destroyed a Russian army round the Masurian Lakes, taking 10,000 prisoners. He continued the pressure into Poland.   Warsaw fell on August 4, followed by Brest-Litovsk, Grodno, and Vilna.   The Germans were pushing on to Petrograd, and were held up only by the lines of Riga.

Before this campaign had come to a halt General Mackensen with German and Austrian forces had prepared a great offensive against the Grand Duke Nicholas in Galicia.   In May it was launched.   The Russian front was broken; at the battles of the Dunajec and the San rivers a Muscovite army was defeated and destroyed; the Russians fell back in disorganized retreat.   The Carpathians were abandoned; on June 3 Przemysl was retaken, then Lemberg.   The gains of the previous nine months were wholly lost, and when the Grand Duke stabilized his line again in September it ran two hundred miles east of Warsaw, from Riga to Dvinsk, through the edge of the Pinsk Marshes, with only the southern tip still in Eastern Galicia.   Galicia,

[1] See map on p. 404.

Poland, and the West Baltic provinces were lost, and Russia suffered a *débâcle* from which she was not to recover. To her monarchy it was a fatal blow. All authority was weakened. The defeat of Tsardom began to work like a leaven in internal Russian politics as it had worked in 1905.

From a military point of view Russia's fatal deficiency, which had never given her immense man-power a chance, had been lack of ammunition. She could have drawn upon fifteen million men of fighting age if only she could have armed them. On the outbreak of war she had been short of munitions, and carelessness, procrastination, and lack of organization had increased the initial shortage. In December 1914 her units at the front were already reduced to half-supplies, while her drafts in training had only one rifle to every three men. At the beginning of 1915 her reserve of ammunition was brought down to an average week's consumption, and it is said that during the retreat of the summer Russian soldiers fought hand-to-hand combats armed only with sticks.

It was primarily owing to Russia's fatal shortage in munitions of war that the Western Powers undertook the famous Gallipoli campaign—in strategical conception one of the boldest and most brilliant of the whole war. Its object was to force the passage of the Dardanelles, and so, by way of the Sea of Marmora and the Bosporus, open up a path to Russia. For Russia was isolated, the Baltic being closed by Germany, the Black Sea by Turkey. If communications could be estab-

The Dardanelles campaign (February–December 1915).

lished between the Western Powers and their Eastern ally munitions of war could be passed into the Muscovite empire on the one hand, and Russian wheat be brought from it on the other. A threat to the Turkish capital would serve also to divert large forces of Turks from the Russian front, and to strengthen the Allied position in Mesopotamia and Egypt. It would have, moreover (assuming it to be successful), a great effect upon the Balkan situation, and would probably bring over to the victorious side the wavering allegiance of the Balkan states. The Central Powers would have been taken in the rear, and an immovable wedge might have been inserted in the communications between Berlin and Constantinople.

It was a difficult and hazardous enterprise, conducted far from the home base, against what proved to be a position capable of impregnable defence.[1]

The attack was entrusted to the Allied fleets, and in the middle of February ships of the two nations attacked and silenced the forts at the entrance to the straits. But the Narrows were guarded [2] by well-planted mine-fields, swept by concealed guns from the Gallipoli

[1] See maps on pp. 410 and 411.   [2] Or believed to be.

peninsula. The fleet could not force them; three battleships, two
British and one French, were sunk by Turkish mines, and when the
heavy weather came operations were broken off.

It was then decided to send a military force under the direction of
Sir Ian Hamilton to support the next naval attack. But the troops
had to be concentrated, and it was not until May that a contingent of
British, French, some Indians, and the ever memorable Anzacs [1]

SKETCH MAP SHOWING
RELATIONSHIP OF THE
PENINSULA
TO THE MAINLAND

ENGLISH MILES

began their attack upon the peninsula at Cape Helles. A landing
was effected and secured, but the detachment was too small to force
the heights of Achi Baba. The Turkish position was strongly en-
trenched with all the fortifications which, with German aid, they had
prepared during the preceding months. They had throughout the
advantage of position; they were able always to command the invading force from a greater height.

Reinforcements were sent to help the attack, and another landing
was made in the neighbourhood of Suvla Bay. But the reinforcements came too late, and the story was the same. They won the

[1] Australian and New Zealand Army Corps.

beach, but could not secure the heights commanding it.   Several times both attempts came within an ace of success, and they were

GALLIPOLI AND THE DARDANELLES

pursued with the heroism which Mr Masefield has so worthily recorded.   The Turks were throughout too strong in man-power and defence, and heat, disease, and intolerable thirst wrought nearly as much harm among the Allied troops as the guns of the enemy. At the beginning of December the men were withdrawn, with the loss of scarcely a soldier, and the enterprise was abandoned. It had failed. It had cost the Western Powers several ships and a considerable number of lives. It had adversely affected the Mesopotamian campaign and the situation in the Balkans. It disheartened those who had been defeated. On the other hand, if it had succeeded it would have shortened the War—by how much cannot be estimated.

There were other blows to the cause of the Entente Powers besides the defeat of the offensive in the west, the shattering of Russia, and the failure of the Gallipoli campaign. If the Dardanelles expedition had been successful Bulgaria might have been prevented from joining the Central Powers; or, conversely, if she could have been persuaded to lend her support the Dardanelles expedition would no doubt have succeeded. Neither contingency took place, and in October Bulgaria entered the War on the side of Germany and Austria. She was to

Bulgaria enters the War (October 1915). have her revenge upon Serbia for the Treaty of Bukarest, two years earlier. Serbia might have saved herself by the surrender of certain portions of Macedonia which had been recognized as Bulgarian by the Balkan League. She refused to do so, and her doom was thereby sealed. The Austro-German army under Mackensen invaded Serbia from the north, while the Bulgars overran her from the east. By Christmas the two

Serbia overrun. armies had united, had swept the whole Serbian kingdom except for a corner, as in Belgium, had driven the army into Albania, and begun the conquest of Montenegro. Masses of fugitives fled over the mountains in the winter snows. An attempt of the Western Powers to create a diverson from Salonica [1] failed. Serbia and, by the beginning of 1916, Montenegro were in enemy hands, and Germany had established direct contact with Turkey.

The British expedition to Mesopotamia was also in a perilous position by the end of the year. It had been planned originally on a

Mesopotamia. modest scale, with the object of defending the Anglo-Persian oil-wells, of securing the head of the Persian Gulf, of providing the usual demonstration to impress native tribes on the borders of India, and as a reply to the Turkish threat upon the Suez Canal. The expeditionary force was a small one, consisting mainly of Indians. The campaign was entrusted for execution to the British Government in India, and was not designed to effect more than the occupation of Basra and its neighbourhood, but in a hand-to-mouth

---

[1] Greece was nominally neutral, but there were two rival parties. King Constantine and the royal party were pro-German ; the opposition party, under Venizelos, pro-Entente. The Salonica expedition was ostensibly justified on the ground that the King had committed a technical breach of neutrality.

way it developed into a considerably larger enterprise to the heart of Mesopotamia.

By the end of 1914 Basra had fallen to the British troops, which under the stimulus of success advanced farther up the Tigris and the Euphrates to Amara and An Nasiriya.   In view of Turkish reinforcements the British forces were increased, and it was decided to advance to Kut, and, as the scheme grew more ambitious and as the evident failure of the Gallipoli campaign needed a counter-demonstration, from Kut to Bagdad.   General Townshend therefore proceeded up the river, until in September he reached and seized Kut-al-Imara. Instead of being seventy miles from the sea he was three hundred and sixty miles from it, in a dangerous isolation, far within the enemy's territory, with no reserves, inadequate transport and communications, and a totally inefficient medical equipment.   Nevertheless he advanced to Bagdad in October, only to be beaten off by the Turks and driven back into Kut.   There in December he and his men were besieged by a Turkish army commanded by a German general.   It was decided to send forces to his relief, but they were too hastily dispatched and inadequately prepared, and when they had overcome the excessive difficulties of the approach they were beaten off with heavy losses.   In April 1916 General Townshend was forced to surrender Kut to the Turks.

On the sea the Germans had replied to the British blockade of the enemy coasts by proclaiming in February 1915 a blockade of the British islands, to be enforced by submarine warfare.   All Entente ships found within the 'war zone' would be torpedoed without warning, and neutral ships were warned that they entered the area at their own risk.   Quickly the effect began to be felt on British commerce, as the submarines took their toll of one ship after another.   Within the first six months nearly two hundred British merchant-ships were destroyed.   Many neutral ships also suffered.   On May 7 the *Lusitania*, a British passenger liner carrying among others citizens of the United States, was sunk off the coast of Ireland, with the loss of over a thousand persons.   From the British point of view, however, there was compensation in the fact that Germany thereby became increasingly embroiled with the United States. *(Loss of British shipping by submarine attack.)*

Against the general record of Allied disappointment must be set successes in the colonies, in Africa and the Pacific, and the entry of Italy into the War in May on the side of the Western Powers.   The new ally immediately dispatched troops against Austria to seize Trieste and the Trentino. *(Successes in the colonies. Italy enters the War (May 1915).)*

Although from a military point of view the year's balance lay undoubtedly with the Central Powers it became increasingly uncertain whether military success alone would ever achieve the final victory. After 1915 it appeared that the War must become one of exhaustion, in which every factor affecting national strength would be brought into play, in which the end would not come until the spirit of a whole nation was daunted by economic pressure, by psychological depression as much as by military defeat. If such a limit of exhaustion be postulated, the end, though it might be prolonged, could hardly be uncertain, for unless the Central Powers secured some powerful ally, like the United States, they were immeasurably outclassed by the resources of their enemies. Not only did they fail to secure an ally, but they turned America into a powerful enemy. After the adherence of Bulgaria in October 1915 no state joined the German side, while the Western Powers were constantly receiving new additions of strength, until, as the Kaiser points out, there were twenty-eight states arrayed in the field against Germany and her allies. Some of these made only a small, even negligible, contribution, and the defection of Russia and Rumania in 1917 and 1918 constituted an important set-off to the Entente gains, but in spite of superior organization, in spite of efforts that must ever be admired for their tenacity and heroism, the Central Powers could not in the end triumph against such a combination.

(c)

At the beginning of 1916, however, the end was yet far off; the support of many subsequent allies was still withheld, the loss of men and ships disheartening, the military situation confusing and depressing, and no such confidence of ultimate victory fortified the Western Powers. They only knew, like their enemies, that they must nerve themselves for greater efforts, that they must raise even more men [1] and more munitions. Neither side fully realized the price that was to be paid.

While the Allies [2] seem to have been contemplating a combined and encircling offensive upon the Central Powers on the part of Great Britain, France, Italy, and Russia, Germany fore- stalled them by a terrific offensive at the end of February upon the French salient of Verdun. [3] Having concentrated her artillery, she opened the offensive with a bombardment of the surrounding forts on a scale hitherto unimagined; a million shells are computed to have been

1916.

The German offensive on Verdun (February- June).

---

[1] England adopted compulsory service in June 1916.
[2] It is simplest to adopt the terms 'Allies' and 'Allied Powers' for the growing number of states ranged against the Central Powers.
[3] See map on p. 401.

discharged within the first twelve hours. Within the first five days the Germans had taken about eighty square miles of surrounding territory, and approached to within four miles of Verdun city. The question of its abandonment had to be faced by the French, but Joffre, Castelnau, and Pétain were alike resolute to defend it at all costs. "They shall not pass!" cried Pétain. For nearly seven months the battle lasted, each side putting forth its utmost efforts, each side paying heavily. It was a terrific moral as well as physical conflict. Still, though slowly, the Germans advanced, and by June 23 they were a mile nearer Verdun, and storming the last fort. Again there loomed the prospect of evacuation, and preparations were made down to the last detail. But the German success had come too late. At the beginning of July Verdun was saved by the great Anglo-French counter-offensive of the Somme, and in October and November the French were able to take the initiative and recover some of the forts that had been captured.

This attack, long prepared, had been planned on a gigantic scale, with forces and ammunition in proportion. For the first time the Allies were superior to the enemy in men, guns, and aircraft, and they sprang a tactical surprise in the tanks, which were used, somewhat prematurely, in September. The 'push' took place on a wide front between Arras and Montdidier. The phrase 'Somme fighting' has since become a byword. It was a "titanic grapple," as Ludendorff called it, lasting into November, with terrible casualties on both sides. By that time the Allies had advanced six miles and won about one hundred square miles of territory, a little more than the Germans had won at Verdun. Beyond that and the saving of Verdun they seemed to have gained little advantage with such a terrible expenditure of men and munitions. But many writers have seen in the Somme battle, taken in conjunction with the failure of the German offensive at Verdun, the turning-point of the War. Germany's losses on the Western and Eastern Fronts had been enormous, and no nation could long continue under such a strain. Her resources were depleted, the economic situation was nearly desperate under the continued British blockade, and the people were beginning to feel the intensity of the strain. In the summer the Kaiser had summoned Hindenburg and Ludendorff from the Eastern Front to take over the supreme command, but "the troops were getting exhausted," wrote Ludendorff. "Not only did our *morale* suffer, but there was a terrible wastage in killed and wounded. . . . If the war lasted our defeat seemed inevitable." And again, "the longer the war lasted, the more acutely we felt the overwhelming superiority of the enemy in numbers and raw material." In these words, and in the realization by Germany of her approaching

The Allied counter-offensive on the Somme.

exhaustion, must be summed up the result of the year's fighting on the Western Front. But she was to hold out for two years more.

While the Germans were pushing the attack upon Verdun the Habsburg armies under the Archduke Charles undertook another offensive against Italy, at the price of a dangerous weaken-

Italy. ing of their Russian front. Their object was to thrust through the Alps into Venetia toward Vicenza, and so turn the main Italian army. The attack opened on May 14, and seemed as likely to succeed at first as the German onslaught at Verdun. Within three weeks the Austrians had advanced to within eighteen miles of Vicenza. Then they were checked and forced to recoil, partly by an Italian rally, largely by a new Russian offensive on their eastern front, undertaken chiefly on the appeal of Italy.

After the *débâcle* of 1915 Russia's position had to some extent improved. The Allies had managed to convey to her a considerable quantity of munitions, a number of rifles had been brought

Russia. from America, and the home output had increased. In 1916 therefore she made a remarkable rally, and once again her allies began to hope that her enormous man-power would become a decisive factor in their victory. On June 4 the Russian armies under Brusilov began to advance. They swept again into Galicia, they recovered the Bukovina, they began once more to approach Lemberg.[1] They took thousands of prisoners; the Austrians retreated before them. It was as great a surprise to the Western Powers as to their enemies. Hurriedly Hindenburg, taking over the command of the Austrian as well as the German armies, dispatched help, and by the end of August the Russian forces were held. Tsardom had won its last victories, and Russia had made almost her utmost contribution to the Allied cause. The fever of revolution was rising in her veins.

Her summer victories had, however, done much to induce a new ally to join the growing coalition. In August Rumania entered the

Rumania. War. Her participation was to be brief and tragic. With rash impetuosity, and ignoring Bulgaria on her southern flank, she invaded Transylvania, clamouring that she came to deliver the three and a half millions of her kinsmen under Magyar rule. She forced the Carpathians, and that was the end of her triumph. Falkenhayn struck from Hungary and swept the Rumanians out of Transylvania; Mackensen crossed the Danube and invaded Rumania from Bulgaria. By December 6 Bukarest was taken, and by the end of the year Rumania was almost as completely subjugated as Serbia. The surface works of her valuable oil-wells were, however, destroyed lest they should fall into German hands.

Another ally had been added to the Western Powers in March by

[1] See map on p. 404.

the formal declaration of war between Portugal and Germany.
Portuguese sympathies had already been openly proclaimed,
and Portuguese troops had given help to the Allied cause **Portugal.**
in Africa. By July 1917 a Portuguese army of 40,000 was fighting
for the Allies on the Western Front.

Greece too was gradually drifting toward internal revolution on
the one side and an abandonment of neutrality on the other.
In November Venizelos went so far as to retire to Salonica **Greece.**
and announce the adherence of himself and his party to the French
and British side.

In the Tigris valley the British position was gradually being built
up, after the surrender of Kut, with reinforcements of men and
munitions for a fresh attack upon the Turks.

In the meantime the penetrating influence of sea-power was doing
its work, in furnishing munitions to Russia and to Italy, in carrying
troops into France, in keeping up British commerce in **Naval**
spite of heavy losses, in carrying on an ever more stringent **activities.**
blockade of the enemy coasts. All through the year the unceasing
conflict went on of blockade and submarine, of raiding attacks;
Germans and British redoubled their efforts in offence and defence.
The German naval authorities were beginning to persuade the Kaiser
to sanction unrestricted submarine warfare—that is, torpedoing at
sight—but as yet the Kaiser withheld his assent. The year of under-
sea and raiding struggle was broken by the battle of Jutland, the only
encounter during the whole war of the main fleets of the **The battle of**
two Powers. On May 31 a section of the German High **Jutland.**
Seas Fleet slipped out of Wilhelmshaven, in an attempt, apparently,
to cut off part of the British fleet and destroy or cripple it. Admirals
Beatty and Hood dashed out to try to force a general engagement,
which the German admiral, von Scheer, wished to avoid, for the
British were considerably superior in men and equipment. A
battle followed which in the number and size of the ships engaged
was the greatest naval encounter in history. Both sides lost heavily,
and each side claimed the victory. The British suffered more than
the Germans; the latter, under cover of a mist, withdrew, and
returned to Kiel harbour. But since the British Navy kept the
mastery of the sea and the Jutland experiment was not repeated the
advantage may be said to lie with Great Britain.

At the end of the year 1916 there was the first talk of peace negotiations. The German Chancellor, speaking through the Reichstag,
made a definite proposal that *pourparlers* should begin. It was summarily rejected by the Entente Powers. Woodrow Wilson, re-elected
President of the United States, called upon all the combatants to state
their aims, declaring that the objects of both sides were "virtually

2 D

the same." The Entente Powers were annoyed at the attempted American arbitration. Germany, while professing to welcome President Wilson's note, gave no specific statement of her aims. Both sides subsequently formulated their terms, but there was found to be nothing in common between them. There was no basis for negotiation, and the fight could only be continued.

(d)

Nevertheless the talk of peace was considered a promising sign, and the year 1917 dawned, like 1915, with premature hope. It was to bring, however, no end to the War, only further trials beyond common imagining.

1917.

The Central Powers were shaken, Austria-Hungary was weakening. The old Emperor Francis Joseph had died in 1916, and the subject races were agitating for more power. Germany had already called up all her men from fifteen to sixty-five in a supreme effort the year before. She was now to bring out her last weapon. On January 9 the decision to adopt "unrestricted submarine warfare" was taken. The navy staff promised that it would end the war in six months. Ludendorff thought twelve months, but in either case it was held that it would have a decisive effect before America, if she should be alienated, could bring her strength to bear on the Allied side. On February 1 the U-boats began to sink all ships at sight, and Allied ships disappeared at the rate of more than a hundred a fortnight. Neutral rights were annihilated. It was the sorest trial through which Great Britain had yet passed.

" Unrestricted submarine warfare."

Its result was, however, to bring into the war against Germany the last great remaining neutral country, the United States of America. President Wilson had shown extraordinary patience in spite of great provocation. There was, among other reasons, a large German population in America. There was also the century-old tradition that the United States took no part in European quarrels. In time of war conflicts between neutrals and belligerents often arise, and Great Britain has constantly been accused of exceeding her naval rights. In the early part of the War there was therefore some estrangement between Washington and London. President Wilson asserted that Great Britain was violating neutral rights, and he protested against the British blockade of Germany. Great Britain, on the other hand, alleged that goods were entering enemy countries under cover of neutral ships. It was the old quarrel. But Anglo-American disputes paled before the friction caused by the German submarine warfare. Germany early in 1915,

The United States of America.

in reply to the British blockade of German coasts, announced a 'war zone' round the British Isles, within which enemy ships would be sunk. International law, however, required that warning should be given and the lives of passengers and crews safeguarded. America protested against the establishment of the war zone, and gave warning to Germany that she would be called to account for any American ship sunk or life lost.

In spite of this, however, repeated incidents occurred during 1915. An American ship was sunk, American passengers in British ships were drowned, and in May the *Lusitania* was torpedoed. President Wilson dispatched a strong note denouncing the sinking of the ship as a violation of international law and of the rights of humanity, and demanding reparation. Germany, however, replied that she had given warning by an advertisement in the American newspapers, and that in any case the ship carried munitions of war. Still America was patient.

In 1916 there were further incidents. In March an English ship, carrying among others seventy-five American passengers, was torpedoed without warning in the Channel. President Wilson immediately protested. Germany denied responsibility, but yielding to the American demands promised that no merchant vessel should be sunk without warning unless she attempted to escape or offered resistance. Then in January 1917 came the announcement of unrestricted submarine warfare, that all ships, neutral or belligerent, found within the war zone would be sunk at sight. At last President Wilson was aroused. On February 3 he broke off diplomatic relations between America and Germany, but he still hesitated to declare war. It was not until April 2 that he gave his famous message to Congress, advising the United States to enter the war, "to make the world safe for democracy."

We shall fight for the things we have always carried nearest our hearts—for democracy, for the right of those who submit to authority to have a voice in their own Governments, for the rights and liberties of small nations, for the universal dominion of right by such a concert of free peoples as shall bring peace and safety to all nations, and make the world at last free. . . . The day has come when America is privileged to spend her blood and her might for the principles that gave her birth and happiness, and the peace which she has treasured.

Not long before the American people had been incensed by the discovery of a projected alliance between Germany and Mexico, in which the former promised to aid the latter in regaining Texas, New Mexico, and Arizona. Japan was also to be asked to join this alliance.

On April 6 the United States declared war on Germany, and by the

end of May American warships in the East Atlantic began to affect
the issue of the struggle against German submarines.   In all spheres
American preparations on a large scale went on.   In August the land
of liberty adopted compulsory military service—a step which few had
ever believed possible in the United States—and she declared herself
ready if necessary to raise ten million men.   Inevitably, however,
some time must pass before any large company of troops could be
equipped, trained, and transported, and it was not until the end of May
1918 that her contingents began to appear in the front fighting-line.
From that time her strength began increasingly to affect the situation,
and by the date of the Armistice there were over two million American
soldiers in Europe, mostly on the French front.   Morally the effect
of American intervention was hardly less valuable, and it was more
immediate.   During the summer a large number of the republics of
Central and South America followed the United States in declaring
war upon Germany; so did China, Greece, and Siam, until the whole
world seemed to be leagued against Teutonism.   In short, the entry
of the United States into the War, and the promise of increased resources that she brought, gave to the Allied cause the certainty of
ultimate victory.

It produced such a mood of exaltation in the Western peoples
as was hardly ever seen, and is only to be understood when it is
remembered that the American declaration of war followed immediately upon the Russian Revolution, which at its inception was held
to be a like testimony to political idealism.

Since the defeat of 1915 the anti-monarchical sentiment in Russia
had been rising.   There was an outcry against the shortage of munitions; there were the usual charges of treason and corrup-
Russia.   tion; there were rumours that the Tsar intended to make a
separate peace with Germany.   The War Minister was imprisoned.
There was talk of " dark influences " working against the people and in
the interests of Germany.   The monk Rasputin, who possessed a great
influence at Court, especially with the Empress, was murdered, and a
Grand Duke was among his murderers.   Patriotism began to combine
with liberalism.   There was a shortage of bread ; there was discontent
among the peasants and the working classes, in the Duma, among the
intelligentsia, even among the conservatives.   A coalition was formed
in the Duma for overthrowing the Tsar.

The Revolution was started, however, by a strike of the working
classes in Petrograd in February 1917.   The soldiers, instead of putting
down the movement, fraternized with the strikers.   The Duma thereupon declared a provisional Government, and in March the Tsar abdicated, and the Romanov dynasty, after three centuries, came to an end.
The provisional Government which was set up was essentially

moderate and liberal; it promulgated a number of reforms, granted autonomy to Poland, restored the constitution of Finland, repealed the anti-Jewish laws, decreed complete civil, political, and religious liberty, and declared its sympathy with the Western Allies and its intention to continue the War. Western democracy, which now proclaimed that it had long seen something incongruous in an alliance with an Eastern autocracy, rejoiced exceedingly.

But the revolutionary movement was not to be stayed. The suppressed ferment of two generations was breaking out, and a momentum to sedition had been given which was not to be checked by the provisional Government. Socialism began to break in upon feeble liberal defences. 'Soviets' were organized, committees of working men and soldiers, of which the most important was the Petrograd Council of Working Men's and Soldiers' Delegates. The army began to be disorganized, discipline was relaxed, officers were subjected to committees of the rank and file, the soldiers fraternized with the enemy. Liberals were turned out of the provisional Government, and socialists put in. Kerensky, a moderate socialist, but an original member of the provisional Government, tried to stem the tide by organizing a 'drive' against the Germans in Galicia. The Russians gained ten miles in July, but lost them almost immediately. The soldiers were deserting, mutinying, and killing their officers; the subject nationalities, the Finns and the Poles, announced their independence of the central Government. A counter-revolution was attempted under General Kornilov, but was dispersed. On September 2 the Germans took Riga.

In the meantime a struggle was proceeding between two factions of socialists, the moderates, or Mensheviks,[1] who believed in a gradual progress and constitutional methods, and the Bolsheviks,[1] or extremists, who proclaimed an immediate revolution and the class war. In November Kerensky and the moderates were overthrown in a second revolution, and Lenin[2] and Trotsky became the leaders of Russia. With socialism had come pacifism. The programme of the Bolsheviks was an immediate peace, the confiscation of landed estates, the calling of a convention, and the giving of power to the soviets. On December 15 an armistice was signed between Germany and the Bolshevik Government at Brest-Litovsk, and negotiations were set on foot for peace. Trotsky, the Russian agent, wanted the adoption of the formula "no annexations and no indemnities." Germany refused to accept this, and continued her advance on Petrograd. In

---

[1] The terms, meaning minority and majority, were used in a convention in London in 1903, when the moderates obtained twenty-five votes and the extremists, or Bolsheviks, twenty-six votes.

[2] Lenin had been living in exile in Switzerland, but was given a special permit by the Germans to return to Russia through Germany in a sealed train.

February 1918 the Ukraine, or Little Russia, broke away from the Petrograd Government, set up an independent rule, and made a separate peace with Germany. In March the Bolshevik Government was therefore compelled to accede to the German terms of peace. In any case, thinking in terms of world revolution, it was prepared to surrender. "There is no socialist who will not sacrifice his fatherland for the triumph of the Social Revolution." Russia renounced her sovereignty over Esthonia, Livonia, Courland, Lithuania, and Poland, whose fate was to be decided by the Central Powers, "in agreement with their inhabitants." The Ukraine was to be organized as an independent republic. Batum, Ardahan, and Kars, in the Caucasus, were permitted "self-determination in agreement with their neighbouring states, especially with Turkey." Finland and Georgia were declared independent. Russia was to pay heavy 'compensation' to the Germans for their losses, and certain economic arrangements were made, favourable to the German Empire. In all, Russia lost approximately half a million square miles of territory and sixty-six millions of people, representing 34 per cent. of her population, 32 per cent. of her agricultural land, 85 per cent. of her beet-sugar land, 54 per cent. of her industrial undertakings, 89 per cent. of her coal-mines, and all but a fragment of her Baltic coastline.

The margin note beside this paragraph reads: *The Treaty of Brest-Litovsk (March 1918).*

The Treaty of Brest-Litovsk was one of the most important events in the War. It enabled Russia to complete the work of revolution and 'liquidation' in the old *régime*. It gave Germany victory on the Eastern Front which, though immediately enabling her to send reinforcements to other fronts, proved in the end to confer entirely illusory benefits. For the expectation of economic supplies from Russia turned out to be vain, and she still found it necessary to guard her eastern boundaries with troops, while the spread of Communist propaganda through Germany by Russian agents seriously impaired her resources at home and hastened the internal revolution of November 1918.

On the other side, the treaty led to an inter-Allied expedition to Silesia to prevent German penetration into Asia, and this in its turn whetted Japan's appetite for adventure in the Asiatic continent. Finally, the object-lesson in German ruthlessness which the Treaty of Brest-Litovsk afforded reinforced the will to continue the war in America and the Allied countries and discredited a growing mood of pacificism there. So the War went on in the west.

The dissolution and defection of Russia and the unrestricted submarine warfare were not the only blows inflicted upon the Allies during the year 1917. It was in almost every respect, save for the intervention of America, a year of terrible ordeal.

TREATY OF BREST-LITOVSK 1918
SHOWING TERRITORY SURRENDERED BY RUSSIA

0   100   200   300
MILES

On the Western Front [1] General Joffre and his British colleague, Sir Douglas Haig, had planned an offensive on the Somme model, **The Western Front.** but the enterprise was thought to be too costly, and Joffre was superseded by Nivelle, who had his own scheme for breaking through the German lines.

In March the Germans themselves effected a strategical movement, with the object of shortening and straightening their line. They withdrew their men from certain forward sectors, laying waste as **The Hindenburg Line.** they went to embarrass the advance of the Allies, and took up their position upon the strong entrenchments known as the Hindenburg Line.

At Easter the British opened with an offensive in the neighbourhood of Arras. The battle lasted a month; there were heroic and **British offensive at Arras.** brilliant episodes, such as the storming of Vimy Ridge by the Canadians, but the net result of the month's stubborn warfare was no appreciable gain of territory, nor any effect upon the enemy.

In the middle of April Nivelle's attack began upon a fifty-mile front, from Soissons to near Reims. It was a complete failure; the Germans were well prepared, and the French losses were appalling. In the first ten days of action 100,000 men were killed or **Nivelle's offensive.** seriously wounded. Nivelle was replaced by Pétain and Foch, but the disaster had gravely affected the French spirit. There were serious mutinies in the army and a general feeling of disillusionment, and although by June the situation had partially recovered it became evident that France had done her utmost, and that the brunt of the defence in the west must fall upon Great Britain. Pétain, exercising his troops with economy, confined himself mainly to repelling a number of small counter-attacks made by the Germans through the autumn, and the result was to give him certain gains on the Meuse and the Aisne.

Great Britain was engaged for three months, from the end of July, in the deadly, monotonous slaughter of the third battle of Ypres, **The third battle of Ypres.** or the battle of Passchendaele. Strategically it achieved nothing; actually several miles of ground were gained, but the casualties were enormous, totalling nearly a quarter of a million men.

Toward the end of November another battle was opened round Cambrai, in which the British won an initial success by **The battle of Cambrai (November 1917).** means of a fleet of tanks, but their gains were lost in a brilliant rally and counter-attack on the part of Germany.

On the Italian front the position of the Allies was barely saved from total disaster. The collapse of Russia enabled Luden-

[1] See map at p. 401.

dorff to divert the greater number of his troops to other fields, and
the growing exhaustion of Austria-Hungary made it necessary to effect a bold measure to galvanize her again into
life.   He decided then upon a *coup* against Italy which
very nearly put her altogether out of action.   The most unlikely and
ill-prepared point in the Eastern Alps was chosen for the assault,
where "the difficulties of the ground seemed almost insurmountable
and the communications on the Austrian side were as bad as could
be."   On October 24 General von Below—for the operations were
under German command—broke through at Caporetto, and the invaders poured into Italy.   One Italian army was completely routed,
a second was in retreat.   It seemed as if Venice would fall before
Allied help could reach it.   In the second week of November, however, the Italians were able to establish a front north of Venice, along
a line from the Adriatic toward Lake Garda.   French and British
reinforcements arrived, and in spite of renewed efforts on the part
of the invading army the Allied line was able to hold its position.
The offensive, like so many of the German campaigns, had all but
succeeded, but the disaster, instead of breaking Italy, seemed rather
to inspire her to a greater unity.

In other fields success fell to the Allied arms.   In Mesopotamia
a fresh British advance under General Maude was made against
the Turks; in February Kut-al-Imara was recaptured, in March
Bagdad fell.

From Egypt another expedition advanced into Syria in the autumn,
and on December 9 Jerusalem fell.   In contrast with the Kaiser's
ceremonial entry into the Holy City nearly twenty years before,
General Allenby's action in dismounting from his horse and entering
the conquered town on foot was almost ostentatiously unostentatious.

On the sea too from the middle of the year, especially with the
appearance of American naval support, the losses in Allied shipping
began to decline.

On both sides there was a visible and growing war-weariness.
Raids by air, though of little strategical or tactical importance, were,
like the well-known torture of the continuous dripping of water,
wearing out the nerves of the civilian populations.   The labour
parties of all countries were pressing for peace.   Pope Benedict XV
had made a move in the same direction.   President Wilson was
beginning to bring forward his conception of a covenant of nations;
there were furtive, but, as it proved, premature, *pourparlers* for peace
between the chief belligerents.   On the side of the Central Powers
Turkey was being defeated, Austria-Hungary was beginning to
crumble.   Germany, on the other hand, though her reserves were
nearly exhausted and the blockade was telling fearfully, had made one

brilliant effort after another, and won success after success. From the military side, from the point of view of national endurance, of intellectual force and stamina, of technical proficiency, she was not less than superb. But from beginning to end she failed politically. She had failed in the invasion of Belgium, in the ruthlessness with which she had conducted the campaign, in her treatment of Russia and America.

From the Allied point of view much more cannot be said than that the Western Powers were holding on, stubbornly and tenaciously, waiting, like Wellington for Blücher, until the new forces could be brought into action. At the beginning of July an American advance guard landed in France, a small enough column, but an earnest and a symbol of the New World which was coming to redress the balance of the Old.

(e)

The new year, being still the fourth year of the War, brought the Peace of Brest-Litovsk in March, and the Treaty of Bukarest in May between the Central Powers and Rumania. Rumania and Russia had now both withdrawn from the War, but a million German soldiers were still employed in the east in holding the ceded territories.

1918.

Ludendorff therefore prepared for a supreme effort, or series of efforts, in the west. "Into that struggle Germany meant to throw not only her accumulated force to the last man, but her brain and fibre, exerted as never yet, her perfected experience, her pre-eminence in surprise, her inexhaustible powers of fresh contrivance." [1]

In March a new and tremendous offensive with massed artillery after the Verdun type was opened on the middle sector of the Franco-British front, toward Bapaume and Péronne, Saint-Quentin and Noyon. [2] It was an attempt to separate the main British army from the French and "crowd it up with its back to the sea." It was a staggering blow. The British centre was driven in and forced back behind the Somme; the left retreated beyond Arras; the French lost ground up to Montdidier. All the Allied gains of 1916 and 1917 were torn away. Amiens, the vital point of communication between the French and British, was in peril; the German guns were nine miles away.

Ludendorff's four offensives in the West.

Every available man was hurried to the front; thanks to Sir Douglas Haig's willingness to subordinate himself Foch was made general-

---

[1] J. L. Garvin, *These Eventful Years*.   [2] See map at p. 401.

issimo of the Allied forces, and unity of command was thus obtained. At length Anglo-French resistance stood fast. Amiens was saved. Germany had achieved a remarkable success, but in her primary aim of rolling back the British army and cutting it apart from the French she had failed.

In April therefore Ludendorff delivered another mighty attack farther north, where there was no depth of ground for the British to retreat. Again ground was wrested from the French, British, and Portuguese armies, but the two salients on which the Allied position hung, Béthune and Ypres, were held against terrible pressure. In March 83,000 Americans arrived in France; from May onward they began to land at the rate of nearly 200,000 a month.

In May a third offensive on the same terrific scale was launched in the south, between Soissons and Reims. The surprise was complete and the success alarming. The Aisne heights were broken, the Chemin-des-Dames stormed, a French and British corps completely annihilated. Soissons fell. In a few days the Germans reached the Marne, crossed it, and captured Château-Thierry, less than fifty miles from Paris. Reims held out, however. Foch rapidly moved his "reserve of manœuvre" to the threatened point, and again the Germans were held, though the Allies had lost heavily in men and ground. On May 28 the American advance guard came into contact with the enemy, and on June 2 five divisions were in the front line, but their first conflict only left the Germans with a " feeling of superiority."

In the middle of July Ludendorff hurled his fourth and last offensive on both sides of Reims. He gained a limited success, but he had shot his bolt. From now onward, with the Allied forces continually increasing, the tide began to turn, and the position of the two sides to be reversed. The Allied defensive began to turn into an offensive.

In July Foch took the initiative, and delivered his own counter-offensive. It was the last great manœuvre of the War. First slowly, then more quickly, the Allies began to advance. In three days they had driven the enemy beyond the Marne, then to the Hindenburg Line. The retreat widened and accele- **The last Allied offensive.** rated its pace. In September the Hindenburg lines were forced, the Americans under General Pershing made a memorable attack on the Saint-Mihiel salient, near Verdun, and the German *morale* began to break down. In October the defences were pierced, Saint-Quentin and Cambrai fell, and the whole Flemish coast was abandoned up to Zeebrugge. Lille and Laon were recaptured, and the industrial parts of France won back. By the end of the month the Germans had lost every inch of French territory. Their confidence and resolution had broken at last before the growing power of the enemy, finally before

America, who, they had believed, "would never fight, or if she declared war, would never be able to raise an army, or if she raised an army, would never be able to transport it to Europe."[1] An overweening self-confidence had led them into a fatal trap.

On all sides news arrived of disasters to the Germanic Powers and their allies. In June the failure of an Austrian offensive in Italy gave a decisive turn to the course of the War. "For the first time we had the foreboding of defeat," wrote Ludendorff in his diary. "We saw that victory which we had formerly felt certain to gather on the French front disappear in the mists of the Piave. With death in my heart I saw that our hopes were falling like dead leaves in autumn." The very river, the Piave, about which the lines were encamped rose in flood, carried away the bridges, and brought confusion upon the Austrians. Soon, beaten again at Vittorio Veneto at the end of October, they were in retreat over the mountains, and the Habsburg empire began to dissolve into its component parts. "At Vittorio Veneto Austria had not lost a battle: she had lost the war and herself, dragging Germany after her in her fall."[2]

In Palestine Allenby broke the Turkish front in Samaria, completed the conquest of the Holy Land, advanced into Syria proper, and captured Damascus. A naval attack secured Beirut.

From Salonica the Allied force under a French general dispersed the Bulgarian forces. At sea the submarine campaign began to be beaten down. Zeebrugge, a submarine 'nest,' was raided and closed in a famous expedition.

In September Bulgaria surrendered, and from the end of October the downfall of the enemy Powers came rapidly. On October 31 Turkey submitted unconditionally, on November 4 Austria-Hungary followed on the same terms. Germany was left alone. She could do no other than ask for terms. There was mutiny in her navy, socialism and revolution had broken out in the country. On November 9 the Kaiser abdicated. On November 11 an armistice was signed between the belligerent leaders, and from eleven o'clock on that memorable day firing ceased over the Western Front.

The end (November 11, 1918, Armistice Day).

In so brief an account of so great a war many things have been omitted, many merely touched on. It has not been possible to speak of the daily toll of death claimed by the mere routine of fighting, independently of the great offensives, of the heroism and endurance shown on all sides, of the humour that broke through the tragedy and the self-interest which darkened it, of invention and counter-invention, of the millions at home who never saw the front, working

[1] Professor C. R. Beazley, *Nineteenth-century Europe and Britain*, p. 317.
[2] Ludendorff.

on munitions or making chemicals or rolling bandages; of the revolutionary social effects, of the unprecedented financial situation, of newspaper forces, of the mental and moral shattering which the world received. The War struck at the very roots of life, and men and nations were proved in their utmost capabilities for good or evil.

Germany surrendered to the Allies on armistice conditions [1] which rendered her defenceless and incapable of renewing the War, and on the understanding that a final peace should be concluded "on the basis of the 'Fourteen Points' and President Wilson's subsequent discourses, notably that of September 27, 1918." [2]   At the beginning of 1919, therefore, plenipotentiaries of the Allied and victorious Powers met together, as after the Napoleonic wars, to discuss the final terms of peace. Thirty-two nations [3] were represented; neither Russia nor the enemy Powers were invited; there was to be no Talleyrand to sow dissensions among the victors. There was a host of technical experts, secretaries, and minor officials, the British delegation alone consisting of six hundred. For the more practical dispatch of business a Supreme Council of Ten was formed of representatives of the five nations with 'general' interests, the United States of America, France, Great Britain, Italy, and Japan, but the real control of the conference was in the hands of the "Big Four," of M. Clemenceau, from France, popularly known as "the Tiger," an inflammable patriot, apt to consider any notions which did not promote the interest of his own country as delusions, of President Wilson of America, of Mr Lloyd George of Great Britain, and Signor Orlando of Italy.[4] M. Clemenceau was elected President of the Conference.

The Conference of Paris (1919).

It is said that President Wilson deprecated any allusions to the Congress of Vienna lest the idealism which he strove to introduce into the Conference of Paris should be dispelled by such an example. Nevertheless a parallel holds good between the two great congresses, and had President Wilson kept it in his mind he might have better avoided the traps in which he and his idealism were ensnared. For not least may the comparison be maintained in the cynical contrast in each case between the professions of the peace-makers and the terms of peace. With little modification the words of Secretary Gentz

[1] Immediate evacuation of invaded territories and repatriation of inhabitants of Belgium, France, Alsace-Lorraine, and Luxemburg; surrender of specified war material and of submarines; internment of the High Seas Fleet, occupation by Allied garrisons of left bank of Rhine, certain forts, bridge-heads, etc.; delivery of a number of locomotives and motor-lorries; repatriation of prisoners of war, and other terms.

[2] The British blockade of Germany was to be continued. It was maintained until the signing of peace, at the end of June 1919.

[3] Counting the chief dominions of the British Empire separately.

[4] These four held constant informal and secret discussions.

might be applied to the Conference of Paris as to the Congress of Vienna.[1]

When the end of the War came there was no common understanding between the Allies as to the terms of peace. Each nation had its own ambitions and hopes; there were national programmes, but no single programme, for it had been considered inadvisable to promote discord between the Allied Powers and hamper their military efficiency by discussions which could have no practical value until the War was won. On two occasions, in December 1916 and January 1917, the Allies had declared their demands in general terms, and the secret treaties published by the Soviet Government revealed that certain members were bound by individual agreements. Thus Shantung had been promised to Japan, the "unredeemed lands" to Italy, Constantinople to Tsarist Russia; there was a Franco-Russian agreement relating to the restoration of Alsace-Lorraine and the neutralization of the left bank of the Rhine, and an Anglo-French treaty concerning certain spoils of Arabia. Rumanian intervention had been bought by the promise of territorial expansion.

The intervention of the United States, however, had brought prominently to the ears of both enemy and Allied peoples certain idealist principles of reconstruction, sponsored by President Wilson, the Tsar Alexander I of the day, and supported with varying degrees of seriousness by the statesmen of the Western nations of Europe. In repeated public pronouncements [2] the American President reiterated the importance of a just and lasting peace, founded upon an impartial respect for the wishes of the peoples affected by any readjustments, not upon the selfish interests of the victorious nations. "What we seek is a reign of law, based upon the consent of the governed and sustained by the organized opinion of mankind." On another occasion he declared, "The impartial justice meted out must involve no discrimination between those to whom we wish to be just, and those to whom we do not wish to be just." The President further drew up, in application of his views, a list of fourteen proposals, known as the "Fourteen Points," constituting in his opinion the essential conditions on which a lasting peace could be founded. They included the evacuation of all territories occupied by the Germans, the restoration of Alsace-Lorraine to France, the independence of Poland, the readjustment of the Balkan states, of Italy, and of Austria-Hungary on nationalist principles, "a free, open-minded, and absolutely impartial adjustment of colonial claims," the abolition of secret diplomacy and of economic barriers,

The "Fourteen Points."

---

[1] See Chapter V, section I, pp. 146–147.
[2] Notably the "Four Principles" speech, February 11, 1918; the "Four Ends" speech, July 4, 1918; the "Five Particulars" speech, September 7, 1918.

the establishment of the freedom of the seas, the reduction of armaments, and the setting up of the League of Nations. These principles were echoed by the statesmen of Allied countries, and formed what may be said to be the only programme in existence among the Allies. They were naturally seized upon by the defeated countries, and were accepted at the armistice by both sides,[1] as already stated, as the basis for the drawing up of the terms of peace.

At the Peace Conference two ideas were struggling for mastery; on the one side was the conception of an impartial and altruistic distribution of justice; on the other were the notions more familiar to peace conferences, of the Balance of Power, of security against a recurrence of danger from the defeated state, of territorial and economic compensation on the part of the victors. The result was the triumph of the latter notions, with some concession here and there, often in letter rather than in spirit, to the former. President Wilson, slow-tempered, with an imperfect knowledge of European conditions, and unprepared with practical propositions, was altogether outwitted by the more agile mind of Mr Lloyd George, the less idealistic minds of M. Clemenceau and Signor Orlando.[2]   In the end the Conference of Paris was guided by much the same considerations as the Congress of Vienna, the desire to safeguard the future peace of Europe and the natural determination that the victorious Powers and their Allies or dependents should gain by any transfer of territory which should be effected. The Conference of Paris based its guarantees for the future on the principle of nationality, the Congress of Vienna on that of Balance of Power; in both cases the principle was carried out at the expense of the defeated nations and in favour of the victorious ones. The peace treaties which emanated from Paris have their defenders and their apologists as well as their critics. The conflicting difficulties and the numberless complicated problems of the peace-makers must not be forgotten, nor their anxiety to preserve at least an outward appearance of harmony among themselves,[3] nor the bitterness

[1] They did not form part of the armistice terms between Italy and Austria. England also retained her independence with regard to the clause relating to the freedom of the seas. It was understood, too, that though there was no mention of an indemnity Germany would be asked for reparations for damage done to civilian populations.

[2] The story is told that M. Clemenceau in an attempt at auto-suggestion used to repeat to himself on rising in the morning the sentence " I believe in the League of Nations," while Signor Orlando is said to have answered a question as to his opinion of the League of Nations with the reply, " Yes, we believe in the League of Nations, but we want the question of Fiume settled first." See R. B. Mowat, *European Diplomacy, 1914–25.*

[3] Over the question of Fiume, which Italy desired, the Italian delegation left the Conference, but returned later. President Wilson on another occasion ordered his ship, the *George Washington,* to be in instant readiness for his departure. There was trouble with the Japanese delegation over the Shantung question, and the Chinese representatives refused to sign the peace.

of spirit bred in those lands occupied by the enemy. An islander, a Colonial, an American, have little understanding of the incessant play of fear in the mentality of a Continental. Europe had also seen in the treaties of Brest-Litovsk and Bukarest something of the lines on which Germany herself would have made peace had she been victorious.

The terms of peace were embodied in five main treaties, of Versailles,[1] with Germany, of Saint-Germain,[2] with Austria, of the Trianon,[3] with Hungary, of Neuilly,[4] with Bulgaria, and of Sèvres,[5] with Turkey. The treaties were not negotiated, but dictated by the victorious Powers.[6] The chief territorial rearrangements were as follows:

Germany was to lose Alsace-Lorraine to France, the three small Prussian districts of Moresnet, Eupen, and Malmédy to Belgium, the Baltic port of Memel to the Allies,[7] most of Posen and West Prussia to Poland, Upper Silesia and part of East Prussia [8] to Poland if a plebiscite of the inhabitants should so decide,[9] all her colonies and overseas possessions,[10] and all special rights in China,[11] Siam, Liberia, Morocco, Egypt, and Turkey. Danzig was made a 'free port' in Polish territory; the Saar valley, a German district [12] with a population of about half a million, was put under a nominally international commission for fifteen years, during which period France was to exploit the coal-mines for her benefit, as compensation for the destruction of her own mines in the north; at the end of fifteen years a plebiscite was to decide the ultimate fate of the district.

Territorial rearrangements.

Austria lost to Italy the Southern Tyrol (the Upper Adige and the Trentino), Trieste and Istria, and the islands of Cherso and Lussin; to Yugo-Slavia she lost Bosnia and the Herzegovina, the Dalmatian

---

[1] June 28, 1919.
[2] September 10, 1919.
[3] June 4, 1920.
[4] November 27, 1919.
[5] August 10, 1920. This treaty was never ratified by the Turkish Nationalists; it remained a dead letter, and was subsequently revised by the Treaty of Lausanne, July 9, 1923. It illustrates, however, the attitude of the treaty-makers of Paris toward the defeated countries.
[6] Except the Treaty of Lausanne; and the difference between this and the former Treaty of Sèvres illustrates partly the difference made by negotiation.
[7] After five years' dispute and some fighting this port was finally constituted an 'independent unit' within Lithuania. It was seized by Germany in 1939.
[8] Thus severing East Prussia from the old Brandenburg.
[9] East Prussia decided for Germany in July 1920, so did Upper Silesia in March 1921; France, however, supported Poland in resisting this decision, and the case was 'revised' by the League of Nations, which awarded the most valuable industrial territory to Poland.
[10] They were received by Great Britain, France, New Zealand, Australia, South Africa, and Belgium generally, to be administered on a system of mandate until they could attain to self-government.
[11] See Chapter XI, p. 529.
[12] A plebiscite in January 1935 showed an overwhelming majority in favour of reunion with Germany. The district was accordingly returned.

coast and islands; to Czechoslovakia,[1] Bohemia, Moravia, most of Austrian Silesia, and part of the Lower Austrian province; to Poland Galicia, and to Rumania the Bukovina. Austria was completely broken up, and reduced from 31,000,000 inhabitants to a small German area of 6,000,000 round Vienna on the Upper Danube. Lest, however, these 6,000,000 inhabitants of German race should, inspired also by the principle of nationality, seek to unite with their fellow-Germans in the northern republic—a consummation of which France was mightily afraid—a clause was inserted that Austrian 'independence' was to be preserved by the League of Nations. Only by a decision of the Council of the League—in which a unanimous vote is necessary—might the union of Austria and Germany be effected.[2]

Hungary, like Austria, was dismembered; from 21,000,000 her population was reduced to 8,000,000. She lost Transylvania to Rumania, Croatia to Yugo-Slavia, the Banat to Rumania and Yugo-Slavia, the Slovak provinces to Czechoslovakia.

Bulgaria lost all the Ægean coast to Greece, and some small but important strategical areas in the west to Yugo-Slavia. By the Treaty of Lausanne Turkey lost Syria, Palestine, Mesopotamia, and the shadowy overlordship which she had possessed in Egypt.[3] She kept Constantinople, in spite of previous Allied protestations, solely for the reason that there was no one to accept it now that Tsarist Russia had withdrawn from the field.

The following were the chief military and economic terms: The German army was to be reduced to 100,000 men and officers, and conscription was to be abolished;[4] a belt of territory thirty miles wide east of the Rhine was to be demilitarized, the size and number of guns and the number of battleships to be greatly reduced, the fortifications of Heligoland to be dismantled. The German High Seas Fleet, which had been interned at the Armistice, was to be surrendered to Great Britain.[5] Germany was also to surrender most of her merchant marine, and to deliver large quantities of coal to France, Belgium, and Italy. She was in addition

Military and economic terms.

[1] Partly or wholly appropriated by Nazi Germany in September 1938 and March 1939, under threat of force.

[2] An *Anschluss*, or union of Austria with Germany, was effected by Nazi Germany in March 1938 by a mixture of intrigue and threat of force.

[3] If the Treaty of Sèvres had come into force, she would have lost also Armenia, Smyrna, and Kurdistan.

[4] The fourth of President Wilson's "Fourteen Points" ran as follows: "Adequate guarantees given and *taken* that national armaments will be reduced to the lowest point consistent with domestic safety." Conscription was, however, retained in France and some of the smaller European countries. The French army in 1921 consisted of a total of 736,000 troops, of which 390,000 were home forces and 95,000 composed the armies of occupation.

[5] It was scuttled at Scapa Flow by order of the German admiral a few days before the peace was signed.

to pay 'reparations' [1] for damage done to civilian populations, which was extended to cover Government pensions paid to soldiers' families. As guarantee for the fulfilment of the treaty, the Allies were to occupy the left bank of the Rhine for fifteen years.

The Austrian army was likewise reduced to 30,000 and conscription was similarly abolished; war supplies and manufactures, military and naval aircraft, were reduced and limited. Similar restrictions were imposed upon Hungary and Bulgaria; the Hungarian army was reduced to 35,000, the Bulgarian army to 20,000. Bulgaria was also assessed for reparations and damages.

Certain political clauses affirmed the complete independence of **Political clauses.** Belgium, Poland, Czechoslovakia, and Yugo-Slavia; Germany was charged with war guilt, and a clause which remained a dead letter demanded the surrender of the ex-Kaiser and "other war criminals" for trial.

Finally the Covenant of the League of Nations was included in the Treaty of Versailles.

That the peace treaties were severe is admitted on all sides. They were passed when popular passions ran high, and in a democratic country a statesman who ignores popular passions is powerless. "We are well aware," declared the German delegates who went to Paris to receive the terms, "of the weight of hate that is here directed against us." Mr Lloyd George in a speech on another occasion put it differently:

> These terms are written in the blood of fallen heroes. . . . We must carry out the edict of Providence and see that the people who inflicted this [war] shall never be in a position to do so again. The Germans say they will not sign. Their newspapers say they will not sign. The politicians say the same. We say, "Gentlemen, you must sign. If you don't do so in Versailles you shall do so in Berlin." [2]

In short, the victors could dictate their own terms.

II. BETWEEN TWO WARS: 1919–39

In a titanic struggle, at an appalling price in men, money, and human effort,[3] the Central Powers had been defeated, and the nations,

---

[1] The amount was to be subsequently fixed by a commission. It proved to be the most difficult of all the problems confronting Allied statesmen. As many as eighteen conferences were held between 1920 and 1922 to discuss the matter. No solution was found until the Dawes Plan was adopted in 1924.

[2] Quoted in *The Times History of the War*, vol. xxi, p. 169.

[3] Estimates of the cost in men and money vary. France lost more men in winning back Alsace-Lorraine than the population of that province. To the British Empire the financial cost of the War is computed to be over £13,000,000,000. The number of men killed or permanently disabled in all countries is reckoned at nearly twenty millions.

victors and losers alike, turned with moral and physical forces seriously depleted, to bind up their wounds and meet the problems of internal and external adjustment that confronted them.

It is impossible in this short space to give more than a fragmentary sketch of the complex political, social, and economic problems that filled the twenty years between the Treaty of Versailles and the outbreak of a new major war between the Powers in 1939. They were years of disorder and confusion, of turmoil and strain, of discontent, agitation, and restless movement, whose direction is not

Map to illustrate the Treaties of St GERMAIN and the TRIANON

Statute Miles

Shaded portion indicates the former empire of AUSTRIA-HUNGARY

yet clear. An old world seems to have passed and a new age to have dawned whose shape is but dimly apprehended.

The twenty years fall into two rough divisions of a decade each, separated by the great world economic depression of 1929–31. The second decade is distinguished by the major problem of the rise of Nazi Germany; the first by a less clearly defined entanglement of political and economic problems arising more immediately out of the dislocation caused by the War and the territorial and economic conditions of the peace treaties. For peace did not come with the proclamation of peace. Many problems remained still unsolved; in other cases the treaty terms were defied. There were wars and quarrels; the states who had lost resented their losses; those who had gained had not gained enough. There were innumerable disputes, alike between nations which had been enemies and those which had been allies. The League of Nations, limping haltingly without the United States, Germany, and Russia, tried to thread its way between them. In the west of Europe there was the unappeased feud between France and Germany, drawing strength from the inability of Germany to pay the enormous reparations demanded of her, and from the incidents of the French occupation of the Ruhr in 1923.[1] There was tension in the relations between France and Great Britain owing partly to the same question of the Ruhr. There was a general disappointment in Western Europe and some bitterness, not concealed, arising from the refusal of the United States to ratify the Treaty of Versailles, to join the League of Nations, or to endorse the Anglo-American-French treaty by which President Wilson had hoped to satisfy France's cry for 'security.'

The east of Europe was in the throes of territorial redistribution and the economic adjustment accompanying it. Over eighty millions of people had been transferred in this quarter from one allegiance to another, and there was hardly a frontier which remained untouched. There was bitter contention between Germany and Poland over Upper Silesia, over Danzig and the Polish corridor through former Prussian territory which gave Poland command of the Vistula and an outlet to the sea. There were disputes and rivalries and confused fighting incidental to the establishment of the independent states of the Baltic, Finland, Esthonia, Latvia, and Lithuania. Finland contested with Sweden the sovereignty of the Aaland islands,[2] and with Russia the possession of Karelia. Lithuania warred with Poland over the town of Vilna, and seized Memel in 1923 in defiance of the Paris treaties. Russia, struggling with internal chaos and civil war, was combating attempts, supported by French and British arms, to effect a counter-revolution, striving to win back her outlying provinces, and to convert Asia and Europe to communism.

Austria, mortally injured by the Peace of Saint-Germain, was in a state of political and economic collapse, despairing of life save by the union with Germany that was denied her. Hungary, similarly mutilated, was looking resentfully toward her lost provinces, incorporated since the Treaty of the Trianon in Yugo-Slavia, Rumania, and Czechoslovakia. Rumania and Russia were quarrelling over Bessarabia.

[1] France claimed that she was entitled to occupy this important mining district on the right bank of the Rhine in consequence of Germany's 'default' of reparation payments. Her action called forth bitter protests, and strong local resistance was offered to the French troops. As a result of the Dawes Plan, which in 1924 put the reparations question on a new footing, France began to abandon first her economic and then her military control of the district. By August 1925 French troops were withdrawn.

[2] Awarded to Finland by the League of Nations in 1921.

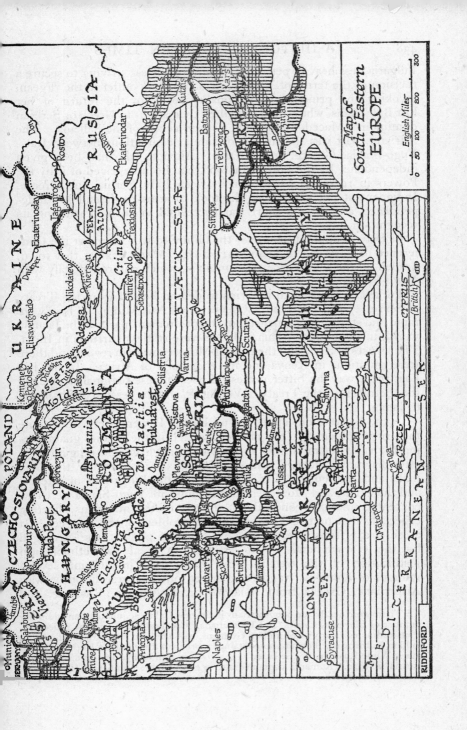

Map of
South-Eastern
EUROPE

English Miles
0 50 100 200 300

RIDDIFORD.

Bulgaria, less heavily penalized, was nevertheless striving to secure a revision of the terms of Neuilly, demanding an outlet to the Ægean, invoking the principle of nationality to claim the return of her lost Bulgarians, who would not adapt themselves to Greek or Serbian dominion. Macedonia was still a storm-centre of the Balkans. The Adriatic coast was the subject of similar contentions between Italy, Yugo-Slavia, Greece, and Albania. Albania, who had been given independence by the Powers in 1908, had been deprived of it by the Powers in 1919 and partitioned between Italy, Serbia, and Greece. Indignant at her extinction, she took to arms to defend her independence, and after a short war succeeded in 1920 in winning its recognition.

In Italy disappointment over the failure to win Fiume at the Conference of Paris led to unauthorized *coups d'état* against that town, headed by the soldier-poet D'Annunzio, which embroiled Italy with Yugo-Slavia.

Turkey too had taken up arms to defend herself from the Treaty of Sèvres, and had driven the Greeks out of Asia Minor. There were rapid and startling nationalist movements in many parts of the Islamic world, in Egypt and Arabia. There were restless stirrings in India. The Druses of Syria and the Rifis of Morocco were in revolt, and there were agitations in Kenya and in other parts of Africa. In the Far East there was the bitter protest of the Chinese nationalists against the 'betrayal' of the Treaty of Versailles, and the cession of Shantung to Japan.

In the 'succession' states set up by the Powers there were acute minority problems.[1] The clauses inserted in the treaties guaranteeing the rights of minorities to their own language and religion were often flagrantly violated, and the Hungarians of Rumania, the Germans and Ruthenians of Czechoslovakia, the Bulgarians of Greece, and the Croats and Montenegrins of composite Yugo-Slavia were discontented and unreconciled. Not least of the questions affecting especially that part of Europe was the problem of the refugees. It arose partly from a legalized "exchange of populations" arranged by the Governments in an attempt to create an ethnological justification of the treaties. But there were in addition several millions of homeless wanderers, driven out by persecution or war, Armenians, Greeks from Asia Minor, Bulgarians, Russians, and

---

[1] There were nearly 300,000 Austrians in the new Italian acquisitions and a similar number of Slovenes, Croats, and Dalmatians. Czechoslovakia and the ceded districts contained nearly three million Germans, half a million Hungarians, and half a million Ruthenians. Poland also contained more than three million Ruthenians and many White Russians. The latter were, however, gained by force of arms against Russia in 1920. Rumania contained also a considerable number of Hungarians, Germans, and Serbs.

Turks. There was the elementary problem of feeding and housing them, and the complicated political and economic questions that accompanied it.

There was the "menace of Bolshevism" to Europe and Asia, and nearly every state suffered political crises of a more or less serious nature. Kings were overthrown and princes exiled.

The economic difficulties were even greater than the political ones, and unprecedented industrial and financial troubles afflicted the world. There was the dislocation caused by the War in markets, industry, and production, and the hardly less great adjustment required by the peace. There was the economic collapse of Austria and Hungary, the defaulting of Russia, the desperate condition of Germany. Everywhere in Europe inflated paper currencies, enormous National Debts, and burdensome taxation were working ruin and dismay. Prices were high, and unemployment prevalent; industry was crippled. There was the question of inter-Allied debts, the almost insoluble problem of reparations. Revolutionary agitation went hand in hand with economic discontent; disputes between labour and capital multiplied, strikes were frequent. Everywhere there were grievances, dissatisfaction, and disillusionment.

Slowly, however, the post-War discontent began to subside, and apparent adjustments to the new conditions were made in more than one direction. Certain *faits accomplis* began to be accepted. Albania seemed to have secured her independence.[1] The Irish Free State had won dominion status; Italy was allowed to keep Fiume, Lithuania Memel, and Poland Vilna. The treaties of Dorpat,[2] Riga,[3] and Moscow[4] had defined the independence and boundaries of Finland, Esthonia, and Latvia, and the Russo-Polish frontier. Peace had been negotiated with Turkey,[5] who, like Albania, had proved by force of arms her title to consideration. Japan had promised to disgorge Shantung. Egypt had attained independence. The Ruhr had been evacuated by France, and what appeared a highly satisfactory treaty of security had been signed at Locarno in 1925 between Great Britain, France, Germany, and Italy, guaranteeing and stabilizing the existing Franco-German frontier. The old feud between France and Germany seemed at last to have been terminated by Germany's recognition of France's title to Alsace-Lorraine.

[1] Terminated by Italy April 1939.
[2] October 1920, between Russia and Finland; June 1921, between Russia and Esthonia.
[3] August 1920, between Russia and Latvia; March 1921, between Russia and Poland.
[4] July 1920, between Russia and Lithuania.
[5] At Lausanne in 1923.

The Dawes Plan [1] reduced the reparations problem to manageable proportions. Germany took her place in the League of Nations in 1926. There was an approach to internal political and economic stability; revolutionary movements began to subside, nationalism to be less clamant; Governments began to stay longer in office and to introduce internal order; dictatorships, though growing in number, seemed to be showing moderation and stability; the new national units began to consolidate themselves; famine and misery in Central Europe dwindled; trade and industry began to revive; the menace of Bolshevism appeared to fade; the Union of Soviet Socialist Republics received general recognition. The Powers began to examine seriously the possibilities of international agreement on Disarmament, and in 1928 the representatives of fifteen nations signed the Kellog-Briand Pact, solemnly renouncing recourse to war "as an instrument of national policy." [2]

The territorial frontiers which were based on the new treaties showed considerable variations on the pre-War map. In the north
The new four independent republics, Finland, Esthonia, Latvia,
map. and Lithuania, had been formed out of the Baltic provinces of the Tsarist empire, while Russia, describing herself as "a Socialist State of Workers and Peasants," consisted of a number (now eleven) of sovietized provinces—Russia proper, White Russia, the Ukraine, the Transcaucasian states of Georgia, Armenia, and Azerbaijan, and the republics of Turkoman, Uzbek, Tadzhik, Kazakh, and Kirghiz. The fragments of dismembered Poland had been reassembled from Russia, Germany, and Austria into a new whole state of twenty-seven million people. To the south lay the new composite republic of Czechoslovakia, formed out of Bohemia, Moravia, Slovakia, Silesia, and Ruthenia (most of them formerly Austrian provinces), and containing a mixed population of fourteen million Czechs, Slovaks, Germans, Magyars, Ruthenians, Poles, and Jews. Hungary was an independent but diminished state, and Austria, with six million inhabitants, had been reduced to the purely German

[1] The sum demanded from Germany in reparations was proved to be wholly beyond her ability to pay. In 1924 a plan was drawn up by a commission of which General Dawes, of the United States of America, was chairman, bringing the account more within her financial and economic capabilities, arranging for instalments to be paid on a sliding scale over a number of years, for the French evacuation of the Ruhr, for an international loan on internal securities, and certain other measures. Of the sums received from Germany France was to have 50 per cent., Great Britain and her colonies 24 per cent., Belgium 12 per cent., Italy $7\frac{1}{2}$ per cent., the United States $2\frac{1}{4}$ per cent., the rest to be divided among the other belligerent nations. Germany and Russia have mutually cancelled the reparation demands. It is estimated that owing to loan arrangements between the United States and her late allies the former country will in practice receive 65 per cent. of the sums payable annually by Germany under the Dawes scheme.

[2] M. Briand, French Foreign Minister, with French realism insisted upon including as a gloss upon the text "except in self-defence."

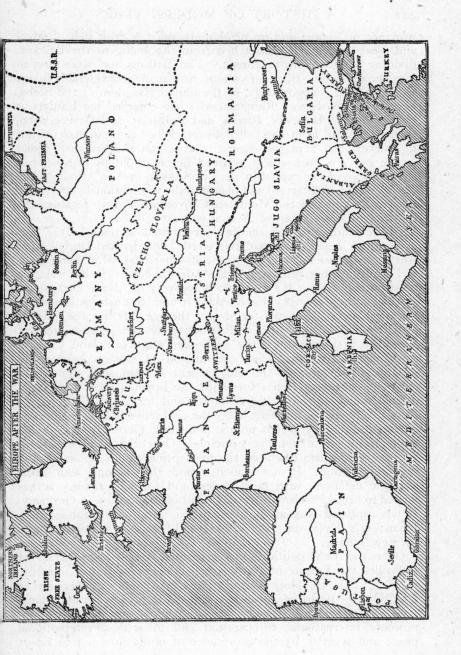

EUROPE AFTER THE WAR

province of Vienna and its neighbourhood. A great belt of small and weak buffer states stretched from the Baltic to the Balkans, dividing Germany from Russia. The Balkans too were broken into small states, three of whom had made considerable gains from the War—Yugo-Slavia, or the united Kingdom of the Serbs, Croats, and Slovenes; Rumania, who had enlarged her borders at the expense of Hungary, Russia, and Bulgaria; and Greece, who, though she had been compelled to forfeit her gains in Asia Minor to Turkey, had kept the Ægean coast which Bulgaria had ceded at the peace. Turkey still retained her foothold in Europe, but she had moved her capital in 1923 to Ankara, in Asia Minor. The Straits were demilitarized and placed under international supervision until 1936, when by the Montreux Convention Turkey regained the right to fortify and control them at will.

In the south, although she had not profited as much by the War as she had hoped, Italy had recovered "unredeemed lands" from Austria that took her frontier to the Brenner Pass, while her seizure of Fiume gave her command of the Adriatic head. In the west the most notable change lay in France's recovery of Alsace-Lorraine.

Most of these changes illustrated the triumphant nationalism which has been one of the chief features of the age. It was the guiding principle in the territorial redistribution of the peace-makers of Versailles, in the creation of the 'succession' states of Poland, Czechoslovakia, and Yugo-Slavia, in the mutilation of Germany, Austria, and Triumphant Hungary, in the enlargement of Rumania, Italy, and nationalism. France. It has furnished the impetus toward the self-establishment of the Baltic republics and the decentralization of Russia. There has not been, since the vital movement of the middle nineteenth century which unified Italy and Germany, so great a triumph of the nationalist principle. Over the greater part of Europe nationalism has been the mainspring alike of political and economic action. It has walled round the nations with great strategic defences, with tariff codes, and fortified zones. It has helped to breed Fascism in Italy and National Socialism in Germany. It has captured Russian Bolshevism; it is the dominant force in Japan; it is the power that has awakened China; it is the anchor of the new Turkey.

Over the new political and territorial system established at Versailles the League of Nations brooded hopefully but uneasily. Like the Holy Alliance, the League was an expression of The League the desire of a war-weary world to preserve international of Nations. peace and stability. Each member pledged itself "to promote international co-operation and to achieve international peace and security by the acceptance of obligations not to resort

to war." Its machinery was far more elaborate than that devised
by Metternich and Castlereagh in their periodical congresses of
statesmen. There was an Assembly consisting of three representatives of every member state, which met once a year at Geneva. A
smaller working Council, consisting of permanent delegates from
the Great Powers and temporary representatives of the smaller states,
met three times a year to transact the effective business of the League
and direct the expert committees. There was a permanent International Court of Justice for the arbitration of international disputes;
and side by side with the League, but not part of it, was the International Labour Office, containing worker and employer delegates
from member nations, whose work was to provide industrial arbitration and raise the level of labour conditions. No state made any
surrender of sovereignty or administrative power to the League,
which had no army or executive officials. League administrative
services, such as were exercised in relation to the ex-German and
Turkish colonies, were entrusted under a mandate to the officers of
particular member states.

The League of Nations, like the Holy Alliance, achieved some
initial success. By 1927 the International Court of Justice had
"handled twenty-six cases, delivered eleven judgments, and recorded
thirteen advisory opinions." Though seriously weakened by the
permanent abstention of the United States, the League admitted
Germany in 1926, and on the eve of 1933, when the first withdrawals
took place, it included all the Great Powers except the United States
and the U.S.S.R.,[1] as well as most of the little ones, who crowded into
its ranks. The League, like Metternich's early congresses, had
solved a number of minor problems and exercised authority in a
number of minor disputes (of which the sovereignty of Memel
and the Swedish-Finnish quarrel over the Aaland islands may be
mentioned as examples), though there is no reason to think that
these disputes could not also have been settled through the ordinary
diplomatic machinery. The League, however, like its nineteenth-
century predecessor, broke down when the major interests of Great
Powers were involved. Its attempt to check the aggressive careers
of Japan, Italy, Germany, and Russia has proved wholly ineffectual;
it has been helpless in the successive crises [2] that have disturbed the
last few years, unable to prevent the repeated defiance of international
law or to avert a new European war. It is true that resolutions

---

[1] Admitted 1934.
[2] Japan's invasion of Manchuria (1931); Italy's assault upon Abyssinia (1935);
the problems arising from the Spanish Civil War (1936–39), Germany's annexation
of Austria (1938), Czechoslovakia (1938–39), and Memel (1939), and her invasion
of Poland (1939); Italy's seizure of Albania (1939); Russia's domination of the
Baltic states and her invasion of Finland (1939).

were passed and that a limited and unsuccessful attempt was made in 1935 to employ the weapon of economic sanctions against Italy, who was condemned as the aggressor in the Abyssinian War, while in 1939 the rump of the League passed a resolution of expulsion against Russia for her invasion of Finland.

It was, however, easy to defy the League, and one by one the aggressor nations withdrew, first Japan (an original member) in March 1933, then Germany in the same year, after a short membership of seven years; then Italy, who gave the statutory two years' notice of resignation in 1937 and retired in 1939, expressing her satisfaction to be "out of it and for ever." When Germany and Japan withdrew, announcing thereby their intention of pursuing their ambitions without restraint, Russia, threatened by both, sought the protection of the League, and her representative was actually President of the Council in the year in which she was expelled.

By 1940, therefore, Great Britain and France alone of the Great Powers were left in the League, which then reverted to the original bias with which it had been fashioned. For President Wilson, in sponsoring the League in 1919, had insisted upon incorporating its Covenant in the peace treaty of Versailles. This secured the League's establishment, but gave it the appearance of an attempt on the part of the victorious nations of the Great War to preserve a political settlement that was favourable to them. "The victorious nations have taken what they want; now they set up a League to keep peace—that is, to guard their spoils," was the burden of Germany's complaint. Germany's initial prejudice against the League on this ground, however, might have been—and was for a time—overcome but for the fact that there was an inherent close connexion not only between the League and the Versailles system, but also between the League and the Anglo-French hegemony of Europe. The Versailles system might have been, and was being, modified in Germany's favour, but the recent history of Europe—and the reduction of the League to its present form of something resembling a flock of small states shepherded by France and Britain—shows very clearly that not only the Versailles system, but the security and protection of the small states of Europe against aggression, the preservation of international law and the European equilibrium, as well as the 'peace front,' rest fundamentally upon an Anglo-French hegemony. We have in this country, frightened by what may be mischarged against us as imperialism, long refused to recognize this fact, though it is the fundamental cause of our quarrel with Germany. It has, however, long been recognized abroad. Russia accepted it in seeking membership of the League in 1934, and Germany has acknowledged the British Empire's primary *rôle* in this task by selecting her as chief target in the war of 1939.

This is the explanation of the antagonism to the League of Nations of those Continental Powers who have aggressive ambitions of their own which could not be realized as long as Britain and France were strong and allied Powers. In seeking to undermine the League the aggressor nations strove to break down the 'peace front' and weaken Great Britain and France at the same time.

The League had also other drawbacks which impaired its chances of success. Its machinery, like its power, was also based in subtle as well as in obvious ways upon Anglo-French principles. As the congressional system of 1815–22 was closely associated with the autocratic principles favoured by Austria, Prussia, and Russia, so the League of Nations system was based on democratic practices and parliamentary traditions familiar enough to France and Great Britain, but wholly or partially alien to states which had only a short or no experience of real democratic government. Such states were unversed in the habits of parliamentary compromise and un-accustomed to the authority of a majority vote.

Finally, the League of Nations had no military and administrative power to enforce its will upon recalcitrant states. For this reason many people who deplore the failure of the League of Nations are now advocating a much closer union of states in which each member state would surrender sovereign power to a central authority. There is, however, little support to be found in the history of the League for the argument that closer co-operation could ever be established, or, once established, could be maintained against national self-will and self-interest.

The League has now come to be discredited on all sides—unjustly, for its "immensely beneficent secondary functions" have been over-looked. In the League an ideal was again incorporated in a political organization, and a real contribution to international co-operation was made. The tradition of the European concert has been immensely strengthened, and, in spite of failure, it is upon this tradition only that in the long run the reconstructors of the world can safely build. The International Court of Justice has acquired a high reputation; the work of the expert committees in matters of health, social hygiene, economic problems, and such acute international questions as that of the refugees has received recognition from all sides. A magnificent clearing-house for international projects, and a meeting-place for the statesmen, legislators, and thinkers of the world, exists in the Palais des Nations. When the second round of the Anglo-German duel is ended much may be built upon the foundations laid by the League if the will to co-operate exists among the victors.

External problems have been in many cases closely linked with, and complicated by, internal national problems. There is hardly **Internal** a state of importance that has not suffered serious internal **problems.** disturbances during these years, some experiencing one or more violent revolutions, others long periods of chronic disorder. A revolution of extreme violence had overthrown the Tsarist *régime* of Russia in 1917. On the defeat of the Central Powers revolutions broke out all over Germany and Austria, overturning the ancient Hohenzollern and Habsburg dynasties as well as the princes of the smaller German states. Serious Communist movements gained temporary successes there and in Hungary. In Italy the house of Savoy survived, though it was completely eclipsed by, the revolutionary Fascist triumph of 1922. The Balkan states were shaken by recurring agitations; the Greek monarchy, which, like the monarchies of Russia, Germany, and Austria, was made the scapegoat of national defeat, was overthrown in 1924 [1] after the disastrous Anatolian war with Turkey. In Turkey a spectacular Westernizing revolution, comparable to the Japanese revolution of 1867, abolished the Sultanate and the Caliphate, established a republican dictatorship, and introduced the Latin alphabet, the admission of women to public life, and other Western measures. In Spain chronic disorder found a temporary remedy in the dictatorship of Primo de Rivera (1923–30), but his fall in 1930, a prelude to the downfall of the monarchy in 1931, accentuated the divisions and conflicts of Spanish political life. Provincial nationalism, native and imported anarchy, Communist and Fascist intervention, prepared the bitter and brutal civil war of 1936–39 from which the Nationalist forces, under the "Caudillo," General Franco, emerged victorious. In China war and revolution went hand in hand. Civil war in Ireland, violence and agitation in India and Palestine, broke the peace of the British Empire, while serious strikes and Labour or Communist movements shook or threatened the stability of Governments in France and Britain.

It was by no means clear in what interest these revolutions were being formed and agitations conducted, what was the predominant influence behind them, or whether the immediate was also to be the ultimate beneficiary. Was it to secure nationalism or provincialism, democracy or despotism, secular materialism or freedom of thought, social welfare or predatory proletarianism, that empires were being shaken, thrones overturned, civil and international law defied, altars degraded, priests murdered, properties confiscated, order and

[1] In 1923 King Constantine was deposed in favour of George II. In 1924 a republic was declared, but George II was restored after a plebiscite in November 1935.

confidence and security shattered? The chief gain seems to have fallen to despotisms, some of unexampled ferocity, national or bureaucratic, party or personal, but it is not yet possible to place any interpretation within the proper perspective of history. But while no factor can be wholly isolated from the mass of political and economic influences at work during the period, two main ones may be selected for special though brief attention.

The forces of revolution have gathered and marched from two opposite directions, from the Left and the Right.

From the Left came all the influences which may be grouped under the heading of Communism, comprehensive in their bearing (for they aimed at the destruction of a whole civilization *Revolution-* and its reshaping on a new basis), revolutionary in their *ary Com-* intention, theoretical and emancipating in their objective, *munism.* instinctive, predatory, terroristic, and tyrannical in their operation.

From the Right have come, largely in reply to the challenge of Communism, a number of counter-revolutionary movements which, though they all have national integration as a common *Counter-* factor, cannot fairly be grouped under a single name. *revolutionary* They include the comparatively moderate movement *movements.* of Italian Fascism and the extreme manifestations of German National Socialism. They too are comprehensive, or 'totalitarian,' in their bearing, disciplinary and unifying in their intention, highly practical in their objective, opportunist, expedient, or piecemeal in their programme and policy, dynamic (so far) in their character, revolutionary, predominantly instinctive, often predatory, terroristic, and tyrannical in their operation. Though these two movements are professedly antagonistic to each other, and differ in their ostensible economic and political aims, they have adopted similar tactical methods, bear similar tyrannical characters, and have produced closely resembling totalitarian despotisms.

Revolutionary Communism, though finding its rationalization in the teachings of the German Jew Karl Marx, derived its impetus and character from the successful Bolshevik Revolution in Russia in 1917 and the following years. When Tsardom was overthrown in March 1917 a moderate democratic Government was installed which oscillated uncertainly between Marxism and constitutional democracy, between Utopianism and opportunism, between militarism and pacifism. After a vain attempt to conduct a war and a revolution at the same time Kerensky's moderates were overthrown in November 1917 by the Bolshevist party under Lenin and Trotsky, a party which, though in a minority, was, like the Jacobins of France, one of action and decision. Lenin quite definitely abandoned the War and devoted himself to the Revolution. He at once turned all the doctrines and theories of extreme socialism into legislative decrees.[1] He declared for peace with Germany on the idealistic basis of "no annexations and no indemnities." He offered freedom to all the subject peoples of Russia and renounced all the imperialistic ambitions of Tsardom. He gave the land to the peasants to be worked without payment, and the factories to the working men. He abolished money, disestablished the Church, and began to prepare for a world-revolution on the same lines.

The result was to effect the complete social and political and economic disorganization of Russia, to endanger the existence of the party and the integrity of the country.

Germany, taking advantage of Russia's military demoralization, but refusing to accept the principle of "no annexations and no indemnities," forced upon her the Treaty of Brest-Litovsk. The late allies of Russia, indignant at her defection and at her proselytizing attempts within their own borders, refused to recognize the new *régime*, and sent military expeditions to support counter-revolutions. Japan invaded Siberia; Russian provinces fell away. There were internal revolts from left and right; the soldiers murdered their officers and rushed home to secure their share of the land. No class was satisfied save the workmen; the peasants took advantage of the situation to seize the estates of the propertied classes, but they were not warm friends of the Bolshevists. Class made war on class, and refugees fled from the country; industry came to a standstill because capital disappeared, and the workmen could not organize and would not work. Famine fell upon the land because the peasants would not give of their surplus produce except in exchange for manufactured goods, which the dislocated industries of the towns could not produce. There was chaos, civil war, and bloody reprisals on all sides; thousands died of starvation or at the hands of their fellows.

Lenin, however, was a politician as well as a doctrinaire; with sound political instinct he set to work to avert the threatened catastrophe to Russia and to his party. He was successful, but only by establishing an absolute dictatorship, and by abandoning many of the principal articles of his creed. For five years Russia was distracted by civil and foreign war. One after another Lenin defeated the attempts at counter-revolution under Kerensky, Kornilov, Dennikin, and Wrangel; he forced foreign countries to abandon their intervention; he made peace with Poland and the Baltic republics; he imposed Soviet Governments upon the Ukraine, the Transcaucasian provinces, the Asiatic emirates, and Siberia, and won them back into a Russian federative system. He conducted a vigorous diplomatic campaign to bring Russia's Far Eastern neigh-

[1] 193 decrees were passed between November 8 and December 31, 1917.

bours within the orbit of Russian influence, and as the prospect of a Soviet revolution in Europe faded he made efforts to reverse the general outlawry against Russia, and to establish diplomatic and trading relations with the great nations of the world.   In 1924 Great Britain, under Mr Ramsay MacDonald, and France accorded official recognition [1] to the U.S.S.R., and other states followed suit in due course.

In Russia itself Lenin succeeded in keeping all power in the hands of the Communist party and in building up administrative and political machinery which has ensured its dominance to the present day.   Although the Soviet system consists of a hierarchy of councils, on a nominally elective basis (since 1936 with "universal suffrage and the secret ballot"), it is the Communist party which controls political activity at every stage, and, through the factory and agricultural 'cell,' supplies the motive power of economic life.   The Bolshevik *régime* was established, and appears to have been upheld, by a policy of terrorization—by the suppression of criticism, the conscription of labour, the repeated proclamation of martial law, the extensive use of spies, the seizure of hostages, by wholesale executions in the early years and repeated 'liquidations' and purges since.   The barbarous methods of the "All-Russian Extraordinary Commission for Combating Counter-revolution, Profiteering, and Sabotage," known more familiarly as the "Cheka" and its successor, the Ogpu, outrivalled those of the Tsarist police, recalled the short-lived Committee of Public Safety, and are only matched in modern times by the Gestapo of Nazi Germany.   During the years from 1918 to 1922 thirteen thousand *official* executions were reported by the Cheka, corruptors of public morals and dishonest or unsuccessful officials suffering, as in the days of Robespierre, side by side with political enemies.

Lenin was forced to abandon some of his original economic and social theories and to postpone the Utopian realization of the millennium.   The destruction of the Church and the family began to break down before the persistent religious and family sentiments of the Russian people.   Private enterprise and capitalism had to be allowed in some measure as concessions to the economic necessities of reconstruction and to the avaricious tenacity of the peasants. Russian peasants were the first to demand recognition of their title to the estates they had seized at the Revolution, and to the profit from them.   Lenin deplored the individualistic and capitalistic spirit which they showed, but he yielded in part to it.   He guaranteed the peasant's possessions, permitted them to sell their products, to

[1] Diplomatic relations between Russia and the United Kingdom were suspended in 1927 and resumed in 1929.

2 F

take their profits, to employ labour. Private enterprise was permitted, capital invited to return, foreign investors given leases of industrial concerns on terms of profit-sharing with the Russian State; discipline was introduced into the factories, strikes prohibited, capitalistic bribes of higher wages offered for better work or longer hours, and a new currency on the customary gold basis was introduced. But for all its modifications and inconsistent practices, and for all its ruthlessness, the Bolshevik Revolution under Lenin maintained a certain measure of faithfulness to its original inspiration. The programme of the world revolution, though it was bound to be regarded as a menace by other states, contained an element of genuine internationalism; though the oft-promised "withering away of the State" receded before intensified State action, and though tyranny and aggression are implicit in the Communist doctrine of class war and capitalist expropriation, the Bolshevik *régime* under Lenin did not clearly reveal that narrow national, self-interested aggressiveness that it has since acquired under Stalin.

Stalin, the Secretary-General of the Communist party, who in 1924, on Lenin's death, obtained the chief power in Russia, has been described as

> a man of narrow understanding and concentrated malignance, taciturn, a tedious orator, infinitely patient, experienced in slow but sure-maturing conspiracy, mendacious, cunning, calculating and more ruthless than Lenin and Trotsky put together.[1]

It is, however, difficult to distinguish in due proportion the characteristics of the Russian leader through the mists which invest the U.S.S.R. He has preserved a ruthless despotism by recurring exterminations, by 'purges' of potential or actual rivals or enemies, by the 'liquidation' of emergent *bourgeois*, capitalist, or individualistic elements, and by the exclusion of every foreign and liberalizing influence. He has carried forward the Bolshevik Revolution to a greater collectivization of agriculture and industry, to an intensive drive for production under the two Five-year Plans (1928–32, 1933–38), to an aggressive nationalist, bureaucratic tyranny. The State has assumed ogre proportions and totalitarian powers far exceeding anything in Tsardom. "The tyrannical character of the Socialist state and the semi-Oriental absolutism of the Russian Tsars over a subservient people are realized in an immensely concentrated form under the despotism of Stalin."[2]

It has in fact become increasingly clear that Russia has 'reverted to type,' that the Bolshevik *régime* is developing on traditional Russian lines, and that the Communist revolution must take its

[1] F. A. Voigt, *Unto Cæsar*.   [2] *Ibid.*

place with many other startling episodes in Russian history as a characteristic event.   The suddenness and violence of the national twist, the influence of German Marxism, the Utopian and theoretical ideals combined with practical brutality and inefficiency, the disregard of the individual and the State despotism, the feverish industrial drive and the servile labour conditions, the economic planning and the severe economic crises, the militarism and the nationalism, the mental isolation, the suppression of free thought, the rigid orthodoxy of the Hammer and Sickle instead of the Cross— all these are typical features of Russia's historical career.

Though no outside influences have been allowed to penetrate into Russia since the entry of Marxism, from Russia has come out, through the Comintern (Communist International), which has its headquarters in Moscow, Communist propaganda and active stimulus, support, and assistance for Communist revolutionary movements all over the world.   For a time Communism seemed to be making headway in China, in Germany, in Hungary, in Italy, in France.   It had its part in the Spanish war, and contributed to disorder, discontent, and disintegration among many other peoples, but it has made no permanent conquest outside Russia.   Occasionally, apparently to confuse rather than to clarify the issues, the Russian Foreign Office spoke with another voice.   Thus it made treaties of non-aggression with its neighbours, and when the rise of Japan and Germany constituted a threat to Russia wooed the Western democracies whom it professed to despise.   It made a pact with France, entered the League of Nations,[1] and when the German menace grew more acute entered into prolonged but close negotiations with the Western Powers for a common front against German aggression.   In August 1939, however, Russia executed a *volte face* and signed a treaty with Germany which must be regarded as the immediate factor in the precipitation of the new war.   It was followed by nearly two years of Russo-German economic and political co-operation, tempered by the natural suspicion inseparable from the records of the two countries.   Russia abetted Germany in the destruction and fourth partition of Poland, acquiesced in the defeat of France, in the overrunning of Norway, Denmark, Holland, Belgium, and the Balkan States, supplied Germany with economic resources, instructed foreign Communist centres to embarrass the war effort of Germany's 'capitalistic' enemies, and took her own profit from Poland, Finland, and the Baltic States.

In June 1941, however, Hitler suddenly terminated the association by a staggering invasion of Russia.

[1] And in the name of peace and disarmament supported the demilitarization of the Aaland islands.

Italian Fascism was in origin partly an answer to Communism, and wrested victory from it. It was, however, more than that. It
Fascism. was a primary impulse toward integration and order and strong government, spontaneously arising from chaos. It was also of the essence of nationalism both in its range and in many of its characteristics. Fascism began as an instinct, and only later developed a philosophy and a system of government. During the years following the War Italy was full of disorder and discontent arising from financial and economic hardship, and from disappointment over the peace terms. She was affected by the new American restrictions on emigration; there were agrarian riots, strikes and sabotage in the factories; there were Bolshevist demonstrations; the workmen seized the factories, the peasants the land. Italy seemed on the verge of a Communist revolution. The Parliamentary system had revealed inherent weaknesses that only long experience and a sound political tradition can avoid. The Governments of Nitti and Giolitti were powerless. In this situation of general lawlessness and confusion bands of volunteers, many of them ex-service men or young enthusiasts, took in hand the settling of Italy. They were organized by Benito Mussolini, himself once a socialist. They wore a uniform of a black shirt, adopted the *fasces* [1] as their sign, resorted to the direct method of the bludgeon or the more original castor-oil bottle for their enemies. While the constitutional Government looked helplessly on Italy became an irregular battle-ground between socialists and rioters on the one hand and Fascists on the other. But the Fascist movement, appealing by its vigour and enthusiasm, grew in numbers and power. In 1922 Mussolini with his Black Shirts marched upon Rome and seized the government. Had the King resisted civil war might have followed, but Victor Emmanuel decided to take the 'strong man' to his side, and from 1922 Mussolini has been the real ruler of Italy. The more demagogic elements have fallen away; Fascism has become the bulwark of monarchy; the Church has become its ally. The moral and political value of discipline, the exaltation of the State over class, the maintenance of private property, the encouragement of private enterprise in the service of the community, the protection of religion, the promotion of family life and a high birth-rate, and the control of the Mediterranean are its watchwords. But Mussolini is no doctrinaire, and during the years of his rule he has pressed no argument which has been unpalatable to his own people or other nations with sufficient fanaticism to precipitate a major catastrophe for his party or his country. He has therefore succeeded in maintaining his authority, in avoiding a war with any Great Power, and

[1] Bundles of rods, which were symbols of authority in ancient Rome.

in keeping the spoils of aggression that aroused considerable indignation abroad.

His services to Italy have received wide acknowledgment there. He has established civil and political order, put industry on its feet, increased production and the general prosperity of the country, completed and projected vast land-reclamation schemes, undertaken public works of many kinds, and introduced social welfare measures of great variety—at the price of an efficient and at times repressive autocracy, of a censorship of public opinion, and of the abolition of Parliamentary government and of economic freedom to strike or bargain. One of Mussolini's most successful achievements has been to make peace with the Vatican. The long quarrel between the house of Savoy and the Papacy which began in 1870 was healed in the Lateran Treaty of 1929; this definitely closed the 'Roman Question' and set free the 'Prisoner of the Vatican.' The Law of Guarantees was abrogated. The Papacy recognized the "Kingdom of Italy under the house of Savoy, with Rome as capital of the Italian state." The kingdom acknowledged the "absolute sovereignty of the Holy See over the city of the Vatican," a territory small in area, but sufficient to endow the Church with the status of independent sovereignty. Agreements were reached on matters of finance, religion, education, and marriage.

In 1939 Mussolini set up a new, though slowly matured, political system which is arousing considerable interest, and may prove to be Fascism's most conspicuous contribution to political science and institutions. It is based on what is called "Fascist syndicalism," represents the organization of the nation on an economic and not on a territorial basis, and embodies the principle of co-operation between workers and employers which is Fascism's fundamental reply to the Communistic doctrine of the class war. In place of the former Parliamentary Chamber, with its elected representatives of territorial constituencies, Mussolini has substituted a Chamber of Fascios and Corporations. This Chamber of 682 members consists, in one-third, of representatives of the Fascist party, mainly the provincial secretaries, while the remaining two-thirds are representatives of the twenty-two corporations into which the different economic activities of the nation are grouped. These representatives come from both the workers' and the employers' syndicates which compose the corporations.[1] They are chiefly officials, the chamber thus containing the key men of the Fascist party and of economic life. The delegates must be approved by the Government.

The functions of the Chamber are chiefly consultative or advisory

[1] Corporations representing (a) cereals, oil, wines, flowers and vegetables, fruit, sugar-beet, livestock and fisheries, timber, textile products; (b) metallurgy,

through its committees. The Government expressly retains legislative power. Essentially, the Fascist State is entrusted to the beneficent guardianship of the Government, but the Fascist constitution does not seem to have solved the fundamental problem which in the long run all constitutions must face—*Quis custodiet ipsos custodes?*

Though from the beginning the Fascist party was disposed to invoke the memories of ancient Rome, to talk of the Mare Nostrum and exalt the heroic virtues of war, it was not until the infectious aggressive thirties that Italian policy passed into an active and expansionist mood that alarmed Europe and threatened the peace. Her assault upon and conquest of Abyssinia in 1935 provoked the only attempt of the League to enforce economic sanctions and lost her British friendship—at any rate for a time. In compensation Italy won the friendship of Germany and of Japan, and in growing collaboration with these two ambitious Powers embarked on an assertive and perilous course. Together with Germany she intervened on General Franco's side in the Spanish war, in spite of a pretended non-intervention; she put forward menacing demands to France, and in 1939 she annexed Albania. In June 1940 she entered the second great war, joining Germany in the last phase of the rout of France. In November she invaded Greece, where her German ally rescued her from an ignominious defeat.

The National Socialist Revolution in Germany was at first regarded as an imitation of Italian Fascism from which, as from Russian Bolshevism, it borrowed certain features. It has developed, however, qualities of its own in response to particular German problems and to the German national temperament. It is National Socialism that has shaped the course and determined the character of the German revival, which has been the outstanding historical development of the decade of the thirties.

Germany's defeat and surrender in 1918, her loss of prestige, the humiliation of the treaty, of the war-guilt clause, of the military occupation, of the compulsory disarmament, of the
The Nazi Revolution. territorial cessions, and the burden of reparations sank deep into the national consciousness, producing in a war-strained and underfed people, with a tendency to hysteria and little capacity for realism, bitterness, revolution, and moral, political, and psychological collapse. Seeking a scapegoat for their suffering,

mechanics, chemical industries, clothing, paper and printing, building, water, gas, electricity, mining, glass and ceramics; (c) insurance and credit, arts and professions, sea and air transport, internal communications, public entertainment, hospitality. The corporations are charged with the welfare of their branch, with labour problems, problems of production, and technical improvement.

they overthrew their Governments and monarchies, and, after defeating in the Spartacist revolt a serious Communist movement,[1] they set up in 1919 a Parliamentary republican Government at Weimar. For a dozen years the Social Democrats of the Weimar Republic, uncertain of themselves, struggled to deal with the immense internal and external, moral, economic, and political tasks which lay before them. On the one hand was a people, disunited, discouraged, suffering, resentful, with no love and no experience of Parliamentary government, bewildered by the complications of a party system which fell rapidly into a confusion of twenty or thirty political groups, embittered by the economic suffering of the great inflation and the scandals in the industrial world that accompanied it, demoralized by violent experimentalism in every department of life, by cynical teachings and secular, materialist, irrational, and sensationalist philosophies, lacking the military and State discipline on which they were accustomed to depend, a prey to agitators and demagogues with their private armies, and longing for a leadership which would restore their self-respect and their pride, and provide them with a cause which would give them escape from their responsibilities and satisfaction to their emotions, good and evil.

On the other hand were the foreign Powers and the late enemies, demanding, with varying degrees and kinds of pressure, fulfilment of the treaty terms. An attempt on the part of Germany during the first four years (1919–23) to evade or refuse fulfilment, through protests, passive resistance, and inflation, merely made her position worse. It antagonized France, brought upon her the Franco-Belgian occupation of the Ruhr, and increased her own misery and humiliation. The terrible expedient of inflation brought a self-induced bankruptcy, ruined the middle class, and destroyed the most stable element in her national life.

Germany thereupon decided, under Stresemann's guidance, to revise her policy,[2] and for five years until his death in 1929 she on the whole co-operated with her late enemies and sought the favour of foreign Powers, especially of the United States of America. She accepted the Dawes Plan and foreign supervision of her finances. She signed the Locarno Treaty guaranteeing France's western frontier. Her reward was considerable. She began to gain the sympathy and confidence of other peoples. She received foreign capital (twice as much as she paid out in reparations), which she spent in putting her industry on its feet, in secret rearmament, and

---

[1] They took their name from Spartacus, the leader of a slave revolt in ancient Rome. Their leaders, Karl Liebknecht and Rosa Luxemburg, were arrested by the Government and assassinated by the mob.

[2] The publication of Stresemann's diaries now shows that it was also to be a temporary expedient.

in expensive social welfare schemes that the victorious Powers could not afford. The Versailles terms began to be modified; in 1926 the first of the three occupied Rhineland zones was evacuated, and Germany was admitted into the League of Nations with a permanent seat on the Council; in 1927 the inter-allied military-control commission which handicapped the expansion of armaments was withdrawn; in 1929 the second Rhineland zone was evacuated; and in 1930, after Germany had accepted the hated Young Plan, the third zone was evacuated and foreign supervision of German finance withdrawn.

The pace of treaty-revision was, however, too slow for the German people; the improvement in Germany's international position did not seem to relieve the internal suffering, or reduce the growing unemployment which the world economic depression of 1929–31 raised to an acute pitch. The Brüning Government floundered in a morass of insoluble economic problems; the Weimar Republic seemed to be paralysed, and some millions of young unemployed were ready to acclaim any vociferous demagogue who confidently offered them a remedy. Without Germany's national humiliation the remedy might have been Communist, but in face of the Treaty of Versailles it had to be nationalist.

It was in this way that Adolf Hitler, an Austrian, leader of the National Socialist party, with a private army of Brownshirts at his command, with great demagogic power, and a patchwork programme of violent nationalism, militarism, anti-Semitism, and socialism, manœuvred himself with a mixture of force and fraud, into power in January 1933.

It is not possible to trace the amazing career of the Führer and the Nazi party since they gained control of Germany. By terrorism and violence, by demagogic oratory, fanatical appeal, impressive showmanship, relentless propaganda, unscrupulous device, and promiscuous promises he has kept himself and his party in power since 1933, and established in Germany a *régime* which seems, like the Russian, to be stained with all the crimes in the black list of tyranny. Suppression of political self-government, of free speech and opinion, persecution of Communists, Jews, Liberals, pacifists, Catholics, Evangelicals, and others, have driven streams of German refugees to seek shelter and protection in other lands, and have alienated from Germany the sympathies of the greater part of the world. Predatory gangsterdom, internal and external confiscation and expropriation, while giving successive fillips to the Nazi *régime* and to Nazi finances, have shattered national and international security and confidence. It is not easy to see any consistent principle behind the party programmes, save the love of power, power over

Germany for the party and power over Europe for Germany. The approach to successive problems is predominantly tactical, according to the need or objective of the moment. Thus the party cries have varied. Anti-Communism, anti-Semitism, anti-feminism, anti-intellectualism, anti-liberalism, anti-pacifism, anti-internationalism (for it is a familiar Nazi device to unify through the emotions of fear and hatred, and to focus these emotions upon successive enemies), racial purity, fertility, and superiority, "blood and soil " "Aryanism," relief of unemployment, class-amalgamation, rearmament, militarism and might—these are some of the themes of Nazi propaganda.

The mass of the German people have accepted and followed the Führer—the old certainly with misgiving and doubt, the young with enthusiasm. They have followed him partly because they were susceptible to the most powerful and relentless propaganda ever imposed on a people, partly because they trusted his confident promises of a glorious future, partly through fear of his police, partly because they saw no alternative that did not mean revolution and great misery. They followed him partly because he did introduce a new unity and integrity into Germany, and an order and discipline that had been lacking in the Weimar Republic; his rearmament plans relieved unemployment; he restored their pride of place among the nations of Europe, through fear if not through respect; he broke the bonds of the Versailles treaty, and for a period he brought home a fresh piece of spoil every six months from his foreign ventures. Above all, they gave their heart to Hitler because, although an Austrian, he spoke for Germany and for their ingrained national pride and imperialism stridently, fanatically, giving them an orgiastic satisfaction, whereas the liberals, the socialists, and the democrats spoke for something that was certainly outside and might even be hostile to their nationalism. Therefore they condoned the brutality, crudity, vulgarity, and tyranny of the *régime*, accepted the concentration camps, the firing-squads, the Gestapo,[1] the burning of books, and the persecutions which were in any case not wholly out of accord with their own frenzied psycho-pathological emotions and supplied a sadistic whip to their masochistic abasement.

But when the Nazi Government proceeded to apply its unscrupulous and bullying practices to foreign affairs the matter became one of grave international importance. Successive *coups*, repeated breaches of the Treaty of Versailles, defiance of international law and foreign opinion, unilateral denunciation of inconvenient agreements, recurring acts of aggression, and a growing, menacing imperialism soon aroused Europe to the existence of a new peril in Nazi Germany.

[1] Geheime Staatspolizei (Secret Police).

With considerable patience Great Britain and France, the two Powers most concerned in the threatened destruction of the European equilibrium, refrained from hostile action while Germany left the League of Nations, reintroduced conscription, remilitarized the Rhineland, denounced the Locarno Treaty, intervened contrary to agreement in the Spanish war, built up a powerful army, annexed Austria, annexed the Sudetenland of Czechoslovakia, seized Memel, and even when she destroyed the independence of Czechoslovakia. In spite of increasing alarm, they let these actions pass, partly because they genuinely wished to help the recovery of Germany, partly because they hoped that the imperialist mood of the Nazi Revolution would spend itself, and above all because they wished to avoid war. But the pace of Nazi advance grew more rapid, their demands more outrageous, their pretentions more exorbitant, as each *fait accompli* seemed to be accepted by the Powers. At last, when Poland was threatened by Germany, the Western democracies resolved to make a stand against the German engulfment of Europe. Their intentions of supporting Poland in war, if she should resist the German threat, were clearly stated, but Hitler, counting on the startling effect of the unexpected Russo-German alliance (August 23, 1939) to frighten the two Powers into passivity, continued with his programme, and on September 1 the Germans invaded Poland.

On September 3 Great Britain and France, in fulfilment of their pledge to Poland, in defence of international order and decency, of freedom for weak nations, of security for themselves and their way of living, declared war on Germany. They were not able to save Poland from rapid destruction and conquest at the hands of the massed German troops. They have also had to watch the manifestations of Russian aggression, which the German treaty and the preoccupation of the Western Powers have brought forth. Night has again fallen on Europe, and none can yet see what may emerge from the darkness.

CHAPTER X

THE EXPANSION OF EUROPE, 1789–1920

ONE of the principal features of the nineteenth century has been the Europeanization of the world. From the fifteenth century the power and influence of Europe beyond her own borders have steadily grown as, in pursuit of wealth or trade or propaganda or liberty, Portuguese, Spaniards, Dutch, French, and British laid their hands upon non-European territory. But during the last century and a quarter the expansion of Europe has proceeded with unparalleled speed, and the whole world is either carved into the empires of European states, controlled by people of European extraction, or at least dominated by Europe's industrial and mechanical civilization. The western half of North America, all but the coastal fringes of Africa, and practically the whole of Australia have been explored and appropriated during this period by European or quasi-European [1] peoples. All through the nineteenth century, from the end of the Napoleonic wars to the outbreak of the Great War, Europeans have continued to migrate overseas in increasing numbers, strengthening the white populations where they already existed, and planting new settlements in all parts of the world. [2]

There were many reasons for this remarkable expansion of the last century. It followed directly from the needs and opportunities of the new industrial and political conditions, as it also fed them. The Europe of to-day could not exist without the rest of the world to draw upon, and the United States has owed much of its remarkable prosperity to the fact that it has had at its door the raw materials and the markets of a vast and untapped continent. Large-scale production and world-wide markets are complementary and necessary to each other, and the ramification of modern industry has created a Europe wholly or largely dependent upon outside sources for a variety of indispensable raw materials, such as rubber, oil, and metals. The rapid growth of industrial populations, the periodic recurrence of unemployment and economic distress, as well as the incidence of political

---

[1] In this context America's civilization counts as European.
[2] It is estimated that from 1816 to 1820 40,000 emigrants a year left the shores of Europe ; from 1900 to 1910 the average annual exodus had risen to more than one and a quarter millions.

agitation, have also driven many sufferers and malcontents of the Old World to look to the New for space, freedom, homes, and careers. The instinct of exploration and adventure was fostered especially by the discovery of gold and precious metals in California, South Africa, Alaska, and Australia.   Religious propaganda too played its part, as it has throughout the history of European expansion, and missionaries in China and Africa did much to open up fields to European influence. The increasing mobility of life favoured migration; improved means of transport and communication facilitated intercourse between all parts of the world.

In short, colonization and overseas settlement and enterprise grew easier as they grew more valuable; and as the Old World lost its self-sufficiency it became increasingly imperative for the states of Europe to acquire and develop colonial possessions and connexions, as outlets for overcrowded populations, as sources of raw material, as markets for trade, as assets in the world competition which became the keynote of international politics.

This fact is the more impressive because the nineteenth century opened in a mood of timidity and depression in colonial matters, **Crumbling** which seemed only too well justified by events.   On all **empires.** sides the empires which the European Powers had built up for themselves through the preceding centuries were falling to pieces. Between 1783 and 1825 there was not an empire which did not suffer serious loss, and with one exception all the great empires of the time, those of France, the Netherlands, Spain, and Portugal (the British Empire is the exception), fell into ruins.

France lost her St Lawrence and Mississippi territories during the Seven Years War, and saw her promising Indian enterprises frus-**France.** trated.   She was forced to surrender further stations during the Napoleonic wars, and by 1825 her overseas empire consisted of nothing but a few West Indian islands, a foothold in South America, and a station or two in India.

The Dutch, among the foremost travellers and traders of Europe, although too small a people for colonization, had at one time a footing **The** in every continent.   Their discoveries in Australia and **Netherlands.** New Zealand they had failed to develop; their holding of New Amsterdam in North America they had lost to the British. During the Napoleonic wars they were turned out of South Africa, out of Ceylon and part of Guiana, in South America, and by 1825 their empire was reduced practically to its present proportions, consisting of the group of islands in the Malay Archipelago known as the Dutch East Indies and one or two small West Indian possessions.[1]

The French and Dutch territories were lost in the course of war

[1] Dutch Guiana, or Surinam, is on the mainland of South America.

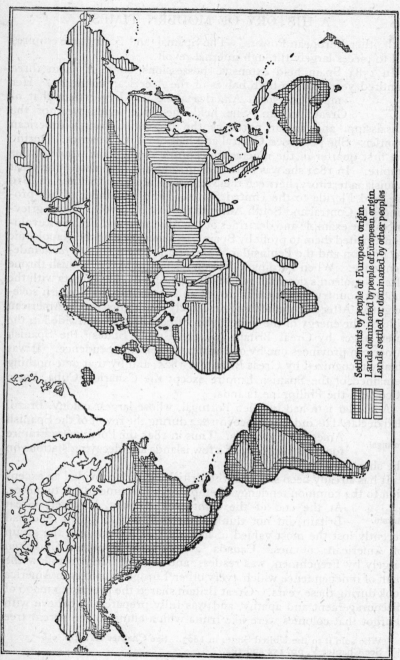

Settlements by people of European origin.

Lands dominated by people of European origin

Lands settled or dominated by other peoples

THE CONTROL AND SETTLEMENT OF THE WORLD BY EUROPEAN RACES

with other European Powers.   The Spanish and Portuguese empires fell to pieces largely through internal revolt.

In 1783 Spain held extensive possessions, some of them three hundred years old, in both halves of the American continent.   Her empire in North America alone was larger than that of Great Britain.   She held the wide lands west of the Mississippi and as far north as the present Canadian-American frontier.   She possessed Central and half of South America.   During the first quarter of the nineteenth century she lost the whole of this empire.   In 1801 she was forced to surrender to Napoleon [1] the great Louisiana territory, between the Mississippi and the Rockies; in 1819 she sold Florida to the United States.   The remainder of her provinces in Central and South America she lost by revolt.   Long grievances, the example and doctrines of the American and French Revolutions, incited them to profit by Spain's weakness during the Napoleonic occupation and the Peninsular Wars, and to establish a *de facto* independence.   When Ferdinand VII on his return to the Spanish throne after Napoleon's downfall refused to grant them equal rights with the mother country they rose in revolt and threw off the Spanish sovereignty.   After a sporadic struggle, largely maintained on the American side by the energy of the Venezuelan Simon Bolivar, and aided in the later stages by Great Britain and the United States,[2] the Spanish American provinces one by one achieved their independence.   It was finally recognized by Great Britain in 1825, and by that date nothing remained of the Spanish Empire except the Canaries, Cuba, Porto Rico, and the Philippine Islands.

A similar fate had befallen Portugal, whose largest colony, Brazil, had declared its independence in 1822 during the revolt of the Spanish American provinces.   Thus in 1825 the Portuguese Empire too consisted only of a few islands and decaying stations on the shores of Africa and India.

It has already been said that the British Empire provided an exception to the common tendency of empires at this time to fall to pieces.   At the end of the eighteenth century, however, Great Britain did not think of herself in that light.   She had recently lost the most valued of her overseas possessions, the group of American colonies.   Canada, a conquered province inhabited largely by Frenchmen, was restless, and seemed likely to follow the path of independence which every other European colony in America took during these years.   Great Britain shared the prevailing mood of discouragement and apathy, and was fully prepared to believe with Turgot that colonies were like fruits which clung to the parent tree

---

[1] Who sold it to the United States in 1803.   See Chapter XII, pp. 556–557.
[2] See Chapter V, pp. 152 and 164.

only until they were ripe.   The mercantile theory that colonies existed

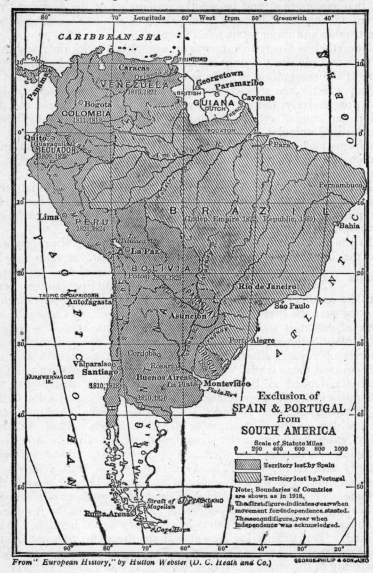

Exclusion of SPAIN & PORTUGAL from SOUTH AMERICA

Scale of Statute Miles
0   200   400   600   800   1000

Territory lost by Spain

Territory lost by Portugal

Note: Boundaries of Countries are shown as in 1918. The first figure indicates year when movement for independence started. The second figure, year when independence was acknowledged.

From "European History," by Hutton Webster (D. C. Heath and Co.)   GEORGE PHILIP & SON, LTD

for the economic advantage of the mother country was losing its appeal
before the practical demonstration of the American revolt that the

colonists themselves would not submit to imperial regulations based on that assumption, and before the onslaughts of the growing Free Trade movement at home. The making of empires hardly justified the trouble and money expended upon it.

Nevertheless Great Britain was an exception. Not only were the American Colonies the only colonial loss she suffered, but from the date of the recognition of their independence, with that disregard of theory which often characterized her actions, she continued steadily and progressively, though often unsystematically, to expand and develop her empire with an assiduity which made her, and kept her, the leading colonial Power. She found one reason or another to extend or make use of her overseas dominions, the need of a calling-station or a deportation ground, the protection of a vested interest, or the outcome of a war with another European Power.

During the years from 1783 to 1825, when, as has been illustrated, the Dutch, Spanish, and Portuguese empires were being broken up by conquest or internal revolution, the British Empire showed extensive development in four directions.

In the first place this period saw the first serious appropriation, and the first white settlement, of Australia. Whatever value may be accorded to the traditional acquaintance of the Chinese, of Marco Polo, of French, Portuguese, and Spanish travellers, with the southern continent, the Dutch discoverers of the seventeenth century were the first to give to the modern world any certain knowledge of Australia and New Zealand. But they too failed to pursue their investigations, and it was the Englishman Captain Cook who in a series of voyages during the seventies of the eighteenth century rediscovered these lands. He further explored the eastern coast of Australia, landed in Botany Bay, and hoisted the British flag on Australian soil. It happened that these discoveries coincided with the revolt of the American Colonies, which raised among other questions the problem of the disposition of British convicts. These had for many years been regularly transhipped to the British American Colonies, where they provided a supply of cheap labour for contractors and employers. The Government was thus relieved of responsibility, the agricultural and industrial enterprises of the Colonies were aided, and the convicts themselves given an opportunity of working their way to independence. But after 1776 the American Colonies were closed to British convicts, and a new scheme had to be devised. The British Parliament was on the point of establishing home penitentiaries when Captain Cook's explorations opened up a new possibility in the virgin Australian lands. It was decided to revert to the deportation system, and accordingly a fleet of nine transports and two men-of-war sailed for Australia in 1787. It arrived in Botany

Bay in January 1788, and immediately moved on to the more suitable Port Jackson. New South Wales (the name was then intended to cover the whole of Eastern Australia, including Tasmania, which was thought to be attached to the mainland) was claimed for the British Crown, and other penal settlements followed. But conditions in Australia were very different from those in America, and the new settlements hardly prospered. The convicts knew nothing about farming, were unwilling to embark on the necessary pioneer work, and failed to maintain themselves as "self-supporting citizens of a new society." They lived mainly on the rations which had to be sent out from the home country, while their presence helped to restrict, in spite of many Government bribes, the numbers of free immigrants who would have opened up the country and taken over the convicts as cheap labour, after the American system. It must be remembered, however, that these were years of prolonged warfare in Europe, when much enterprise and money that might have gone to Australia were used in the wars at home.

For some years, therefore, the situation remained stationary, expensive, and unpromising, consisting largely in the barren struggle for existence of the new settlements. Certain definite results of permanent value were, however, achieved. In the first place, Australia was appropriated for the British Empire; and certain ambitious schemes of Napoleon for developing French interests there came to nothing. Secondly, at the expense of the British Crown, and largely by the instigation of Governor Macquarie, valuable "preparatory works" were undertaken, which were of great importance to subsequent settlers. Magnificent roads and bridges were built, and schools and churches. Further, toward the end of the Napoleonic wars the situation began to improve. The finding of coal at Newcastle and the introduction of merino sheep helped to develop the occupational side. More free emigrants went out during the years of acute economic distress in England which followed the wars. Explorations were conducted, of the coast and inland parts. Tasmania had been circumnavigated in 1798, but for some years real knowledge of Australia was confined to about seventy miles north and south of Sydney, to a strip of land about fifty miles wide, lying between the Blue Mountains and the sea. In the second decade of the nineteenth century, however, the settlers themselves crossed the Blue Mountains, and expeditions sent out from home, notably under Lieutenant Oxley, explored as far as seven hundred miles north of Sydney, in search of further sites for penal settlements.

The Australian settlements at this time can hardly be considered as more than a variety of penal experiment. At the other end of the world another experiment of a different kind was about to   Canada. be made, of even more far-reaching importance to the British Empire.

2 G

There were two significant considerations about the British dominions in Canada: first, that the largest of them consisted of the French-populated province of Quebec, acquired by conquest in 1763; and secondly that they were situated next door to the newly independent republic, the United States of America. From the first arose the fact that Great Britain had to deal with a group of colonists of differing race, religion, and political outlook, who regarded her with antipathy, or at best indifference; and from the second it followed that Canada was easily accessible to American influence, to the propaganda and example of republican independence. In 1774, on the eve of the revolt of the American Colonies, the Government of Lord North had passed the Quebec Act, which had modified the military Government by which Quebec was ruled, granted to the French their own civil laws, and allowed to them their own Roman Catholic religion. This Act had no doubt done something to turn into mere apathy what might have been the open hostility of the French Canadians to the British Government during the American War of Independence. Moreover, after the war the Canadian situation was profoundly modified by the immigration of a considerable number of loyalists from the United States, to whom the British Government could not but offer grants of land in British territory. A large number of these "United Empire Loyalists," as they were called, settled in the maritime provinces; others formed a considerable English colony on the Upper St Lawrence—that is, within the French province of Quebec. Quarrels broke out between the French and English settlers, and in 1791 the British Government passed the Canada Act, separating the French settlement, which became Lower Canada, from the English one, which became Upper Canada, and granting to each colony a Parliamentary type of government consisting of two Houses and an appointed executive. The grant was made by Pitt's Government in a spirit of pessimism, as a half-anticipated prelude to a complete rupture between Canada and Great Britain. One of its consequences, however, was that many more emigrants from the United States, deterred previously by the military type of government in Quebec, passed north into British territory, until the number of United Empire Loyalists approached 80,000. There were other consequences, which must be described later. The grant of a representative House of Commons without a responsible executive proved, as it had proved before, to be the shadow without the substance of democracy, and had to be revised, but from this revision arose a revolution in the conception and government of empires.

In India a third development of the British Empire was taking place during this period, differing alike from that of Canada and that of Australia. There were neither the convict problems of the latter nor the constitutional problems of the former. There was a British trading company, nearly two hundred years old, the East India Company, which in the pursuance of its trade had India. acquired a considerable power in a country of ancient civilization and chaotic political conditions. There was also the British Government, asserting a distant, fitful, but increasing authority over a company whose agents did not show a sense of responsibility commensurate with the power they exercised. The British Government had taken to itself, by North's Regulating Act of 1773 and Pitt's India Act of 1784, the right to appoint the Governor-General and the chief political officers of the Company and to guide its political policy.

There was also a number of independent native princes, some, like Tippoo Sahib of Mysore and the Mahratta chiefs, ambitious, powerful, and hostile. Lastly there were the French, seeking at times when France and England were at war in Europe to reduce British influence and revive their own power. French and British alike used native troops and worked often through the agency of native princes, while the power for which both strove, and which Great Britain achieved, was often not that of direct territorial ownership, but indirect influence over dependent native rulers. Conditions in India were therefore irregular, unsystematic, and often confusing. It was, however, out of this very confusion that the British expansion at this time arose. It was no part of an imperial policy or of far-flung plans of empire-making on the part of the British Government. It was carried on not only without the acquiescence, but often against the will, of the home country. There was a clause in the India Act of 1784 forbidding further annexations, but in spite of repeated protests in Parliament one Governor after another found himself compelled to embark upon a forward policy. The British Government was concerned simply to maintain what was already held by Britain in India. It was the men on the spot who extended the British possessions and raised the British status, out of the exigencies of the local situation, or out of hostility to the ambitions of the European enemy, France.

Thus Warren Hastings (1772-85), who has been called "the greatest Englishman of the eighteenth century," [1] had preserved the British dominions in India during the American War of Independence against the combined onslaughts of the native princes and their French allies, of Hyder Ali in the south and the Mahratta Confederacy in Central and Northern India. He had established peace and order in Bengal and had reformed its administration, but his reward at home was a long-drawn-out impeachment.

[1] Ramsay Muir, *The Expansion of Europe.*

Lord Cornwallis (1786–92), whose appointment was meant to mark the abandonment of an ambitious policy in India, found himself compelled to follow in his predecessor's footsteps. He continued Warren Hastings' work of administrative reform in Bengal; like Warren Hastings, he was involved in war with the powerful ruler of Mysore, Tippoo Sahib, son of the old enemy, Hyder Ali. The result was victory and conquest for Great Britain.

It was, however, under Lord Wellesley (1798–1804) that the greatest advance at this time was made for the British Empire in India. Wellesley arrived to take up his governorship in one of the most critical years of British rule in India, in 1798, when Napoleon's Egyptian expedition was bringing the man of genius within threatening distance of the Anglo-Indian position, when French ambitions, allied with native hostility, had reached their most dangerous point for British safety. Wellesley, however, succeeded in routing the old enemy of Mysore, and, with the help of his brother, afterward the Duke of Wellington, in breaking the Mahratta Confederacy. He extended British sway in the south and north-east of India, annexed more territory to the British Crown, and achieved the final destruction of French ambitions, so that France gave no more trouble in that quarter for a century.

During the governorship of the Marquis of Hastings (1813–23), a convinced exponent of the forward policy and a firm believer in the advantages to India of British rule, the powerful Mahratta Confederacy was finally broken and British supremacy incontrovertibly established. Thus out of local disorder, out of the challenge given to England by French and native hostility, a large Anglo-Indian empire had been formed. To have ignored the challenge would have been to abandon the place that Britain had already won for herself in India, to turn back upon Clive's work and two centuries of patient effort and enterprise. To accept the challenge was to enter on the path of expansion. In 1785, on Warren Hastings' retirement, British control was confined to the province of Bengal, the Circar coastal strip, and the Madras and Bombay presidencies. Forty years later Great Britain ruled or controlled the whole valley of the Ganges except Oudh, extensive Mahratta lands in Central India, and practically the whole of the south. Lord Hastings' words may perhaps not inaptly be quoted.

> It is a proud phrase to use, but it is a true one, that we have bestowed blessings upon millions. . . . Multitudes of people have, even in this short interval, come from the hills and fastnesses in which they have sought refuge for years, and have reoccupied their ancient deserted villages. The ploughshare is again in every quarter turning up a soil which had for many seasons never been stirred, except by the troops of predatory cavalry.

Nevertheless the directors complained of the increase of British territory.

The fourth extension of the British Empire at this time consisted of conquests from France and her allies made during the Revolutionary and Napoleonic wars. The most notable gains were won from Holland, who surrendered the Cape of Good Hope,[1] Ceylon, and part of Guiana. The first, though valued at the time mainly as a strategic point on the route to India, has become the foundation of the British Empire in South Africa, the second an important annex to the British possessions in India, and the third the only British holding in South America. England also gained a number of scattered islands, useful mainly as calling-stations or fortresses, or as additions to the larger dominions. The most important were Trinidad, taken from Spain; Malta, from the Knights of St John; Seychelles, Mauritius, and others, from France.

Conquests during the French wars.

Thus in 1825 Great Britain was not only the largest colonial Power, but, if the Siberian empire of Russia be excepted, the only colonial Power of any importance. Her empire was extensive, scattered as far as the remote Antipodes, undeveloped, and, as it must of necessity be, transoceanic. It had been acquired largely by virtue of two great assets, in themselves connected, the command of the sea, which had enabled her to seize, hold, and develop foreign possessions, and secondly her island position, which had enabled her to participate, without becoming absorbed, in European questions.

From the discovery of the New World the European situation had largely dominated the colonial, and it continued to do so for the next fifty years. From the revolt of the Spanish colonies, or, indeed, from the end of the Napoleonic wars, to the Congress of Berlin, in 1878, Europe was concerned almost exclusively with European affairs. She was interested not in events in Canada, Australia, Africa, or India, but in the happenings in Paris, Berlin, or Vienna, in questions not of empire, but of liberalism and nationalism. Her outlook was essentially European. The policies of the Great Powers, the calculations of Metternich, Cavour, and Bismarck, hung upon the fate of revolutions in Italy or Spain or Greece or Poland, upon political crises in France or Germany or Austria, upon Austro-Sardinian or Austro-Prussian issues, upon Russia's intrigues in the Balkans or France's ambitions in the Mediterranean. It was the states which were least absorbed in the European questions of the day that showed the greatest imperial and colonial development —the United States of America, remote by distance and conviction;

1825–78.

[1] Great Britain in 1815 paid Holland £6,000,000 in compensation for the Cape of Good Hope, Ceylon, and Demerara. She also restored Java, which had been conquered during the war by that able and enterprising servant of the East India Company, Sir Stamford Raffles.

Russia, at the edge rather than the centre of the European world; France, who had her own reasons for diverting from time to time the attention of her subjects to distant fields; and, lastly, Great Britain.

In most of the chief European questions of the day Great Britain played only a subordinate part. She was involved in one war, in the Crimea, and she gave minor support to Greek and Italian independence, but the main stream of nationalist and democratic struggle, of war and revolution, passed her by. On the whole she stood aloof, a spectator watching her own interests rather than a participator in the battle of the day, pilot of her own destiny, mistress of the seas, free to attend to her own problems, to expand her trade and her empire. Of these problems internal affairs and trade certainly took precedence of empire-building. It was matters of Parliamentary and local government reform, of franchise and finance, of free trade and factory legislation, Ireland, religion, education, and philanthropy, that awakened the greatest interest both in the nation and the Government. Colonial questions, when they came up for consideration, wore often the appearance of an intrusion or an irrelevance, and among the statesmen of the front rank there is not one [1] who was imperially minded in the modern sense.

Time after time the British Government deprecated imperial expansion and the assumption of fresh colonial burdens; nevertheless, one after another, fresh responsibilities and burdens were assumed; unsystematically, at haphazard, and according to no clear, definite policy, the British Empire continued to grow.

In Canada the red shading which marked on the map the extent of British settlement gradually spread over the whole area of modern Canada, from its meagre dimensions round the St Lawrence River to the Pacific coast. Frontiers were defined and boundary questions settled with the United States. The great fur-trading company of the Hudson Bay extended its field of operations and absorbed its rival, the North-west Company of Montreal. Settlements starting from Selkirk's Highland colony of 1812 on the Red River were made on the central plains. Continuous emigration from the United Kingdom swelled the population; unceasing exploration led the tide of movement—in Canada as in the United States—westward to the Pacific. The discovery of gold in British Columbia accelerated the pace, and roads, canals, and railways contributed to the great expansion.

In Australia also it was through settlement and exploration that the British Empire was extended. Penal colonies continued to be made in New South Wales and Victoria until 1840, and in Van

Canada.

---

[1] Unless Lord Durham can be included in the first rank.

Diemen's Land, now called Tasmania, until 1853. British colonizing societies experimenting in emigration planted free settlements in what have since become Western and South Australia. The dis- Australia. covery of copper and gold brought more settlers, until six distinct colonies were formed, and the whole continent was annexed by Great Britain.

The British Government resisted for many years the pressure brought to bear upon it, especially by emigration societies in Great Britain, to annex New Zealand. It was not until it saw New itself about to be forestalled by France, and until it Zealand. realized that only by formal annexation could it exercise authority over the unruly British traders and settlers who had established themselves there, that it yielded. In 1840 the British flag was definitely hoisted in both islands; the Treaty of Waitangi was made, by which the Maori agreed to accept the sovereignty of Queen Victoria in return for a guarantee of their lands, forests, and fisheries. In spite of this the Maori strongly resented the increasing number of white immigrants who, attracted by the discovery of gold and the potentialities of sheep-farming and agriculture, poured into the islands. In the forty years immediately following the British annexation their numbers rose from two thousand to nearly half a million. Intermittent racial wars between the natives and the newcomers, provoked often by the reckless and piratical behaviour of the settlers, covered most of the period, until the resistance of the Maori was worn down.

In South Africa there was both an acute native problem, as in New Zealand, and a conflict of white races, as in Canada. On the one hand were Bushmen, Hottentots, Kafirs, Zulus, and kindred South races, pressing southward one upon another, disputing the Africa. land with the Europeans. On the other were the two white races spreading northward from the Cape—the Dutch Boer farmers, solitary, semi-nomadic, slave-holding, and of the seventeenth century in their treatment of the natives, and the British officials, soldiers, and settlers who had gone out from Great Britain under schemes of assisted emigration. Thus the two chief features of the early history of British South Africa were the frontier wars and the Great Trek. The frontier wars between the Kafirs and the Europeans could only end, in spite of the manifest reluctance of the British Government, in extending the British Empire over further native lands. The Great Trek, which during the years 1836-40 took over seven thousand Dutch out of British South Africa, northward into the lands of the Orange and Vaal rivers, hitherto unsettled by whites, also resulted in an extension of empire. The chief grievances of the Boers were that the British Government gave them inadequate protection against the Hottentots within and the Kafirs outside their borders, that it countenanced the dangerous intrigues of missionaries among the natives, and listened to their misrepresentations of Boer actions, and, above all, that the abolition of slavery had brought them economic ruin. They therefore resolved to secede, and moved northward into Natal and the region of the Orange River. The British Government was thus confronted with a new problem : with the possibility of hostile border states and of a dangerous maritime rival in Natal to Cape Colony. It adopted, however, a vacillating and irritating policy. For a time the Boers were allowed to be independent; then in 1842 the British Government claimed Natal, and in 1848 it annexed the Orange River Colony. Thereupon the Boers trekked again farther north into the Transvaal. Great Britain now partially reversed her previous policy. She recognized the independence of the Transvaal, and restored to the Boers the Orange River Colony—though not Natal—under the title of the Orange Free State. She was to reverse it yet again at the end of the seventies; until then the British rule in South Africa stretched from the Orange River in the west to the northern border of Natal in the east. The Boers, however, had carried white dominion to the Limpopo River, a thousand miles from the Cape.

The advance of British power in India was as remarkable during the fifty years that followed 1825 as during the half-century which preceded it. The British Indian possessions held at that time, and have always held, a special place among British colonies. They were valued for their wealth and their commercial opportunities, while since they were inhabited by native races not then permeated with French and American ideas of independence their connexion with the mother country was considered likely to be less fugitive than that of Canada. India, in short, was held to be worth keeping, but, since India could never be peopled or settled by whites, the British position, and that of any European Power in that country, could only be maintained by force of arms or by the will of the Indian peoples. Undoubtedly the latter was even then by no means a negligible factor, and there is more than one instance of a native state submitting itself to British protection and British rule. Great Britain showed also, as will be illustrated later, a real interest in, and a sense of responsibility for, the welfare of the subject Indians, but in the political, administrative, and social chaos which at that time constituted India the 'will of the people' became largely a meaningless term. The British empire of India had been won, and was largely held, by force of arms; England had gone to trade, and she had remained to conquer, although it is worth noting that, at any rate until the time of the Mutiny, the troops which maintained British power in India were largely native troops.

It was mainly by war and conquest that the great annexations of the nineteenth century were made.   French ambitions in India had been destroyed by Wellesley, but the advancing empire of Russia, approaching through Central Asia the north-west frontier of India, aroused acute fears in the minds of certain British statesmen and British Governors of India.   An attempt to forestall Russia in Afghanistan led to the Afghan wars (1837–43), which in their turn brought Great Britain into conflict with the border provinces of Sind and the Punjab. In 1843 and 1849 respectively these provinces were annexed, and wars (1824–26 and 1852) with the Burmese on the far east borders of India gave Great Britain a large part of Burma.   The policy adopted by Lord Dalhousie,[1] of annexing feudatory states on the lapse of a native heir, brought also to Great Britain Satara, Karauli, and Nagpur, while the chronic misrule of the native princes of Oudh was the reason for the annexation of that province in 1856.   "The British Government would be guilty in the sight of God and man," wrote Dalhousie, "if it were any longer to aid in sustaining by its countenance an administration fraught with suffering to millions."

Dalhousie's governorship was inspired by the same desire to promote the welfare of the governed as had previously led Lord William Bentinck [2] to abolish the barbarous customs of suttee [3] and thuggism.[4] Lord Dalhousie introduced the latest British ideas of reform, new roads, harbours, railways, telegraphs, and schools, just as if he had remained the President of the Board of Trade in England.   But his measures were the culmination of a long period of active annexation; they seriously offended native religious susceptibilities,[5] and seemed to be the preliminary to a wholesale substitution of British for Indian civilization.

The result of Dalhousie's administration and the previous ten years of British policy was the short, sharp crisis of the Indian Mutiny.   It began in May 1857, and was practically suppressed by the end of the year.   It remained throughout primarily a military mutiny of sepoys, and spread only to the peoples of Oudh, Delhi, and Rohilkhand.   The newly annexed Sikhs of the Punjab were quiet, and the trouble was confined to the Upper Ganges basin.

The Mutiny was followed by a complete change in the government of India.   The old Company, shorn gradually of many of its functions,

---

[1] Governor-General of India, 1848–56.
[2] Governor-General of India, 1828–35.
[3] The custom requiring the immolation of a widow on her husband's funeral pyre.
[4] The practice, of a semi-religious nature, of assassination by strangulation.
[5] Modern researches into the records of the Government of India seem to show that there was some foundation for the sepoys' charge that their cartridges were greased with cows' and pigs' fat.   See article on India in the *Encyclopædia Britannica*.

was abolished. Its army, the administration, and all its remaining functions were transferred to the British Crown, to a Secretary of State for India and a council. Twenty years of peaceful administration followed; a halt was called to the ambitious policy of annexation, but the internal development of India's resources was continued. On January 1, 1877, at a great durbar held at Delhi, the old Mogul capital, Queen Victoria was proclaimed Empress of India.

Thus in Canada, Australia, New Zealand, South Africa, and India the story of the British Empire during this period is that of remarkable and continuous expansion. The opening up of China, in which Great Britain also played a leading part, will be described in another chapter.[1]

There was, however, a second aspect of British Imperial development at this time, no less remarkable and perhaps more important **A new conception of empire.** than the territorial expansion which has already been traced. It is concerned with the great change which took place in the attitude of the mother country toward her colonies, and in the principles of imperial organization which began to be adopted. It is by no means possible, however, to trace always harmony and uniformity in the views and measures of the period. Just as the continually expressed reluctance to undertake new responsibilities was inconsistent with the continuous expansion of the Empire, so in other colonial matters one expedient was adopted which often conflicted with another, giving to the policy of the Government a character often vacillating and self-contradictory. Gradually, however, a new conception of empire shaped itself out of diverse elements, and a new Imperial policy began to be built up.

In the first place the adoption of Free Trade principles dealt the last blow to the old commercial system. By the middle of the nine- **Free Trade.** teenth century all the Navigation Acts which had proved so irksome to the American Colonies had been repealed; and trade between the mother country and her dominions was carried on on the same terms as between Great Britain and any foreign country.

Though the British Colonies lost in this way something of their value as sources of economic privilege they gained a new appreciation **Systematic colonization.** as outlets for the distressed industrial populations of the mother country. As has already been mentioned, numerous schemes of systematic colonization, largely associated with the name of Edward Gibbon Wakefield, were put into practice, and successful settlements made in Canada, South Africa, Australia, and New Zealand. The success of this type of regulated and assisted emigration depended, however, on the Crown control of the undeveloped lands, which were sold to emigrants at a low price. When

[1] See Chapter XI.

the disposal of the lands was put into the hands of the Colonies themselves systematic colonization was abandoned.

Thirdly, the new humanitarian and philanthropic spirit which
showed itself in home affairs entered also into the administration of
the Empire.   Its most marked result was the Abolition of   Humani-
Slavery Act of 1833, by which the British Government and   tarian spirit.
people paid £20,000,000 at a time of financial embarrassment that
slavery might be abolished throughout the British Empire.   The
measure was welcomed, however, neither by the planters of the
West Indies nor by the Dutch slave-owning farmers of South Africa,
and it did much to alienate the latter from British sovereignty.

The spirit of philanthropy showed itself also in the growth of
missionary enterprise to the non-Christian races of the Empire, in
the increased sense of responsibility and consideration for the interests
of the natives of India, and in the movement for the protection of the
backward peoples with whom Great Britain came into contact.

Lastly the changed attitude to the Colonies was marked by the
adoption of the principle of colonial self-government.   The Whig and
Liberal parties of the time held an almost fanatical belief in   Colonial self-
the virtues of self-government, which the rise of a political   government.
crisis in Canada led them first to apply to the Imperial dominions.

By Pitt's Canada Act of 1791 the English province of Upper Canada
was separated from the French province of Lower Canada, and representative, but not responsible, government was granted to   Canada.
each.   A type of government was set up similar to that
which existed in the American Colonies before the Revolution and
in England under the Stuarts.   The elected House of Commons
possessed no control over the nominated executive council, and, as
in both the parallel cases cited, constant friction arose between the
legislature and the executive, especially on financial matters arising
from the increased expenditure due to the Anglo-American war of
1812.   In French Lower Canada the situation was aggravated by the
racial question, for while the elected house was predominantly French,
the nominated executive was English.

The general disaffection rose at length to an acute political crisis,
and rebellion broke out in both provinces, headed by Papineau in
Lower Canada and by Mackenzie in Upper Canada.   For   Rebellion.
the second time the British Government was faced with
colonial rebellion.   The history of American Independence seemed
about to be repeated, and the conviction was strengthened that the
mother country would lose her colonies as soon as they were strong
enough to resist her.

The Whigs, who were in office under Lord Melbourne, determined
to send out, as "High Commissioner," one of the most advanced men

of their party, the son-in-law of Lord Grey, Lord Durham, known as
Lord   "Radical Jack." Lord Durham took with him two notable
Durham.   imperialists,[1] Charles Buller and the better-known author
of *A View of the Art of Colonization*, Edward Gibbon Wakefield.

Durham found that the rebellions were small affairs and easily
suppressed, but a high-handed ordinance for the deportation of some
of the rebels to the Bermudas brought upon him a virulent attack in
the British Parliament and led to his early resignation. Before Durham
returned, however, he had collected the material for his famous
report, which has become the text-book of modern imperialism, and
one of the greatest works in the literature of colonial government.

Lord Durham distinguished two main problems and proposed two
corresponding remedies. The first was constitutional: the provinces
must be granted full control of their own executive; they must be
given complete responsible self-government of the British type.[2] The
second was racial. "I expected to find a contest between a Government
and a people; I found two nations warring in the bosom of a
single state." To solve this difficulty Durham proposed the union
of the two provinces, in the hope that the French element would be
absorbed into the growing English population. Along the lines of
these proposals the Union of Canada Act was passed by the British
Self-govern- Parliament in July 1840. Five days later Lord Durham
ment (1840). died. "Canada will one day do justice to my memory,"
were his dying words. That day quickly came, for if he "marred a
career" he "made a nation."

The sequel to the Union of Canada Act of 1840 was the Dominion
of Canada Act of 1867. The principle of colonial self-government
which was granted in the earlier Act, and was stretched even to the
point, as was illustrated later, of allowing the Colonies to impose
tariff burdens on the mother country, was extended within ten years
to the other Canadian provinces of New Brunswick, Nova Scotia, and
Prince Edward Island. It created a revolution in Imperial organization, and laid the foundation of the Imperial structure of to-day.
Durham's second proposal of the union of the two Canadas was not
so successful. The Franco-English quarrels remained unreconciled,
and when in the early sixties a scheme was set on foot for a federation
of some of the provinces of Canada Ontario [3] and Quebec [4] resolved

---

[1] If so modern a title may be used.

[2] "The keynote of the Durham report is the memorable words, ' The Crown
must consent to carry on the Government by means of those in whom the representative members have confidence.' That sounds a truism now, but it was the
first recognition by a responsible statesman of the principle of self-government in
the Colonies " (Stuart J. Reid, *The Life and Letters of the First Earl of Durham,
1792–1840*, vol. ii, p. 314).

[3] Upper Canada.   [4] Lower Canada.

to loosen their connexion with each other and to enter the Dominion on the same federal terms as the other provinces.

The Dominion of Canada Act of 1867, passed by the home Parliament, but based on the representations of the Canadian provinces themselves, was an open expression of the new Canadian nationhood. It also established the first federation [1] within the British Empire, and the first to be set up since the United States of America. The general principles of federation have been explained elsewhere,[2] but although the Canadian federation was undoubtedly influenced by its American neighbour it shows also in some respects considerable differences. It is in the first place a 'tight' and not a loose federation, and much greater powers, including the residuary power, are allotted to the Canadian than to the American Federal Government. The framers of the Canadian constitution were conducting their deliberations at the time of the American Civil War, which seemed to them to illustrate the dangers of according great powers to the separate states. They therefore resolved to strengthen the central Government.

The Canadian federation.

As a corollary to this principle, the separate provinces of the Canadian federation—unlike the states of America, but like the states of the German Empire of 1871—have not equal representation in the Federal House. Ontario has twenty-four members, Nova Scotia ten, British Columbia three.

Since the Dominion of Canada was a member of the British Empire another factor—the British Parliament—was introduced into the complicated question of the division of sovereignty which is the essential feature of a federation. It was long debated whether a fourfold partition of power between the people, the state Governments, the Federal Government, and the British Crown could work successfully, but the actual results have confounded the pessimists. Actually the British Crown and Parliament reserved to themselves only a minimum of power, and even that they exercised with discretion—the right to appoint the Governor-General, to amend the constitution of the federation, but not those of the provinces, and to disallow Bills which directly conflicted with Imperial statutes or treaties. An appeal also lies from the Dominion courts to the Judicial Committee of the Privy Council.[3]

Canada, then, was the first of the British Colonies to receive full self-government and the first to work out for itself a federal type of constitution. Following the Act of 1840, the Imperial Government

---

[1] It was at first formed only of the four provinces of Ontario, Quebec, Nova Scotia, and New Brunswick. It has since been joined by Manitoba, British Columbia, Prince Edward Island, Saskatchewan, and Alberta. Newfoundland still remains outside.   [2] See Chapter XII, pp. 543–544.
[3] Modified by the Statute of Westminster (1931). See p. 490.

began to extend self-governing institutions to the other colonies.
The other Canadian provinces received them, as has already been
noted, and in 1852 the Australian colonies were empowered to elect
constituent assemblies to draw up a form of government for themselves. They also adopted institutions of the British type. In 1854
New Zealand was given similar institutions. The problem in South
Africa was complicated by the presence of the unfriendly Boer,
and self-government was not introduced until later into the South
African provinces, except Cape Colony, which received it in 1853.
It was also not thought suitable to introduce this type of government
into India,[1] into the tropical settlements, into the West Indian islands,
or into the military and coaling stations of the Empire.

In this brief review of the expansion and development of the
British Empire it will be seen that the greater part of the settlement,
colonization, and appropriation of the non-European
regions of the world fell to the British peoples. The
period has, in fact, been called the age of British monopoly.
Nevertheless three other empires of great importance were
being built up during these years of the nineteenth century.

*1825-78,
the age of
British
monopoly.*

In the Far West, on the other side of the Atlantic, the United
States of America was consolidating by war and by settlement a vast land empire, stretching from the Atlantic to
the Pacific.[2]

*The United
States of
America.*

In the East an even greater continuous land empire was adding
to its dominions. Reference is made elsewhere to the remarkable expansion of the Russian Empire by the acquisition
of Poland and Finland in the east and north, of the
Caucasian provinces in the south, of the Khanates of Central Asia
and Turkestan, the Amur province on the borders of China, and
half the island of Sakhalin. This expansion, most of it the product
of sixty years of warfare and treaty-making, undertaken largely during
the periods of 'reaction' in constitutional matters, was a by-product
of Russian nationalism. It was promoted by the Tsars largely in the
hope of diverting the attention of their subjects from the infectious
liberalism of the West, and from the humiliation of the defeat of the
Crimean War. Its chief result was by bringing Russia into contact
with Persia, Afghanistan, China, and Japan to throw her into the
full stream of some of the most important movements of modern
times. Her shadow hung over the Persian Gulf and the north-west
frontier of India, and she was placed in rivalry with Great Britain.
The fate of the Turkish Empire and its dependencies was of vital
importance to her, and Mohammedanism became a subject religion.
She entered from the north into that invasion of the Pacific which

Russia.

the other Powers were conducting from the south.   She became one
of the most important factors in the growing Pacific problem.   In
short, Russia's expansion, carrying her over the Caucasian Mountains,
the deserts of Central Asia, and the Amur River, turned her into a
world Power.

During the sixty years which followed Waterloo the foundations
were also laid of a new French Empire, which was in time **France.**
to rank next to the British and Russian empires.

Perhaps the most notable feature was the entry of France into that
region of North Africa which lies between the Mediterranean and
the Atlas Mountains.   The depredations of Algerian and North
African corsairs had been for centuries a curse to Europe, and many
countries had dispatched expeditions to put them down.   A series
of assaults upon the French flag, together with an insult offered in
1827 to the French consul by the Dey, led France reluctantly to send
a punitive expedition against Algiers.   The town fell to the French
in July 1830 about the time of the downfall of the Bourbon monarchy
in Paris.   Colonial acquisitions were not in harmony with liberal
principles, and were, moreover, half despised as mediocre gains after
the brilliant conquests of the Revolutionary and Napoleonic eras.
Nevertheless Algiers was not abandoned; on the contrary, after a
period of hesitation the systematic and regular conquest of the
regency of Algeria was undertaken by the Orléans monarchy.   It
was completed by 1847, and the province formally annexed in 1858.
The war with Algeria had already involved France in a victorious
campaign against its western neighbour, Morocco, but the formal
annexation of this province and of Tunis on the east were left for a
later date.

The foundation of the French empire of Northern Africa was laid,
and the great civilizing work begun which seems about to restore
to these districts the prosperity which they enjoyed under the Roman
Empire.   White immigrants of all races were encouraged to settle
in the colony.   French soldiers were induced to go there by gifts of
land.   Alsatians who disliked the transfer of Alsace and Lorraine to
Germany in 1871 were offered an asylum there.   Many Germans,
Italians, and a large colony of Spaniards have also settled in
Algeria.

It was not until toward the end of the reign of Louis-Philippe that
for reasons of State a real colonizing and imperialistic spirit was
fostered in France.   And what Louis-Philippe began Napoleon III
continued.   The expanding influence of France was seen in all
directions.   An important group of colonies began to be built from
the old French ports on the Senegal and the west coast of Africa.
An ambitious attempt was made under Louis-Philippe to penetrate

into Egypt through the patronage of Mehemet Ali.   Thirty years later French science and French money constructed the Suez Canal.[1] Farther afield Tahiti and the Marquesas Islands and New Caledonia, in the Pacific, were annexed by France, and New Zealand all but became a French colony.   The beginning of the French colony of Cochin-China was made with the conquest of Southern Annam in 1862.   A prominent part was taken by France in the opening up of China.   In another continent the ill-fated Mexican expedition was the product of another soaring ambition to revive the French colonial empire in America.

In the Pacific, in Indo-China, in Africa, the foundations were laid during this period of the great modern French Empire.   It consisted, however, mostly of tropical and sub-tropical lands, useless for white settlement; it was valued primarily for its commercial advantages.

During the forty years preceding the War a marked change occurred in the attitude of Europe to colonial questions.   Two new states, **1878–1914.**   Italy and Germany, had entered the comity of organized European nations.   The nationalist struggles which had largely absorbed the interest of the chief Continental Powers were over.   Europe began to take stock of the general situation.   There was a powerful American state in the West, stretching over half a continent, and a huge Russian Empire in the East, extending from Poland to China.   There was the British Empire spreading over the whole globe, with its huge dependencies of Canada and Australia, and its rich provinces of India.   Farther afield, the East was being invaded by the West, the isolation of China was being broken down, Japan was awakening to a new civilization.

It was clear that the scale of values had shifted, that little Europe could no longer retain a monopoly of power and importance.   The Far East and the Far West were claiming attention.   The great states were those who possessed world interests, and did not these involve world possessions?   There is no greater testimony to the new spirit of the age than the development during the years from 1870 to 1914 of the newcomers, Japan, Germany, and Italy.   Japan, an outsider and a spectator, concluded that imperialistic expansion was the sign of a progressive nation, and directed her course accordingly.   Germany, though Bismarck had called her in 1871 a "satiated" country, felt the successful vigour of her new nationhood driving her to extra-national enterprise and expansion.   Italy also,

---

[1] It was because Great Britain held it to be an example of insidious French enterprise in the East that she opposed it so strongly at one time.   The Canal, architected by De Lesseps, financed mainly from France, was formally opened by the Empress Eugénie in 1869.

desiring to put herself into line with the new imperialism, scrambled for a share of non-European territory.

The British Empire, with its untapped continents and inexhaustible economic resources, set a standard and at the same time gave a challenge to every ambitious state of Europe. Systems of protective tariffs began to be built up against Great Britain, and the desire for commercial monopoly became a great incentive to the acquisition of colonies. It is true that the British Empire was open to the commerce of other nations on Free Trade terms, but there was a natural feeling that French and German capital and enterprise which went into a British colony was so much gain for the British Empire and so much loss to France or Germany. The states of Europe saw the advantages of possessions which were under their own control, to provide markets and raw materials for their own trade, and outlets for their own capital. With the spirit of empire grew also the spirit of commercial monopoly.

There was another motive which began to actuate the Great Powers. Within recent memory the extraordinary sight has been seen of colonial native troops on guard over a great European nation. As transport improvements speeded up communication, and as the temper of the age grew more militaristic, so it slowly dawned upon the nations of Europe that colonies might have also a military value. Thousands of emigrants had during the nineteenth century left the states of Europe for America or the British Empire—so many citizens lost out of which good contingents might have been provided for their own countries.

In short, the gradual opening up of the world by European enterprise during the preceding centuries was bearing its fruit. Nationalism was not enough, and Europe could no longer be self-sufficing. A new era had dawned—

> an era of eager competition for the control of the still unoccupied regions
> of the world, in which the concerns of the remotest countries suddenly
> became matters of supreme moment to all European Powers and the
> peace of the world was endangered by questions arising in China or Siam,
> in Morocco or the Sudan or the islands of the Pacific.[1]

Great Britain began to turn her empire into a cult; France began to seek compensation from Africa and China for the Alsace-Lorraine she had lost to Germany. There was a rush for unappropriated or unprotected lands. Germany began to talk of *Weltpolitik*.

Two regions of the world were still open to European appropriation; one was Africa, the other was in the area of the South Pacific.

The partition of Africa is one of the most extraordinary facts

[1] Ramsay Muir, *The Expansion of Europe*, p. 135.

of the period.   It is no less extraordinary that this great continent
The partition should have been divided up without a European war.
of Africa.   The continent of Africa, although nearest to Europe, was
one of the least-known parts of the world, and the European peoples
had not touched more than the fringe of it.   In the north France held
Algeria, in the south Great Britain and the Dutch Boers had advanced as far as the Orange and Vaal rivers.   Portugal and France
and Great Britain also owned a few coastal stations in the east and
west.   Tunis and Tripoli were Turkish provinces, Morocco was a
decaying but independent state largely inhabited by Berbers and
Arabs.   Egypt was a tributary, but an independent and to some
extent Europeanized, province of Turkey.   The bulk of the "Dark
Continent," with its inhospitable tablelands and deserts, inhabited by
various negroid tribes, remained practically unknown to Europe until
modern times, and offered a fresh field for exploration.

It was the explorers and the missionaries, often indistinguish-
able, who began to open the eyes of Europe to the possibilities of
the interior of Africa.   Burton, Speke, Grant, Baker, Livingstone,
Stanley, and others explored the courses of the four great rivers, the
Nile, the Niger, the Congo, and the Zambezi.   Missionaries carried
on an active propaganda on the Guinea Coast and in South Africa.
The publication of Stanley's books [1] aroused intense interest just
about the time when Europe was learning to value colonial possessions.
The wealth, national resources, and potentialities of Africa began
to be realized.

Curiously it was Leopold II, King of the Belgians, and not one of
the Great Powers, who took the first action.   In 1876 he summoned
at Brussels an unofficial international conference of geographers to
consider steps for the exploration and civilization of Africa and for
the opening up of the interior to commerce and industry.   An international African Association was formed, with committees in various
countries.   But the international character which seemed about to
distinguish the new phase of African enterprise quickly disappeared.
The attention of the Association was turned by Stanley's voyages to
the Congo, and a fresh committee formed for its exploration.   This
work, financed largely by Leopold, soon became a purely Belgian
enterprise, and led after a few years to the establishment of a sovereign
state, the Congo Free State, under the rule, and, later, the personal
sovereignty, of King Leopold.

Leopold's interest had from the beginning aroused the ambitions
of other European states.   France and Portugal began to put forward
claims to the Congo; emissaries and agents of many nations of Europe

---

[1] The best known are *How I found Livingstone* (1872), *Through the Dark Continent*
(1878), and *In Darkest Africa* (1890).

swarmed into the interior making treaties with native chiefs, many of whom hardly understood what they were giving away, marking out spheres of influence, and appropriating territories. In 1884–85 a conference at Berlin recognized most of the arrangements made up to date. The work of dividing up Africa continued, at first with great speed, then more slowly; by 1914 the whole of it was parcelled out among the European Powers, with the exception of Abyssinia and Liberia.

The great basin of the Congo formed the personal state of the King of the Belgians until 1908, when the Belgian Government *The Belgian* took it over in response to the outcry raised against the ex- *Congo.* ploitation of the natives by the trading companies to whom most of the land had been leased.

South of the Belgian Congo Portugal, who had revived some of her old imperial ambitions, had expanded her decaying coastal stations into the large province of Angola. On the other side of *Portuguese* the African continent she had also formed the colony of *gains.* Mozambique, or Portuguese East Africa; she had, however, failed in her hope of making a belt of Portuguese territory right across Africa.

Italy, a late comer in the African scramble, secured Eritrea and Italian Somaliland, to which she added by war with Turkey in 1911–12 Tripoli and Cyrenaica. She failed in her attempt on Abyssinia at that time. In North Africa, to which her *Italy.* ambitions were naturally directed, she was checked by French expansion.

The interesting story of German enterprise in Africa cannot be told here. Though Bismarck was only a reluctant convert to the principle of overseas possessions Germany acquired *Germany.* the considerable territories of South-west [1] and South-east Africa, the Cameroons and Togoland.

Spain also entered the field, and acquired a province on the northwest coast, and in 1906 a sphere on the coast opposite Gibraltar. *Spain.*

The two largest gainers of territory were France and Great Britain. To her possessions on the north coast France added Tunis in 1882 and, practically, Morocco in 1912. Southward from these she extended her sway over the whole of the Sahara region, linking up with holdings on the Senegal and the Ivory *France.* Coast, and on the Congo. She thus formed a consolidated empire in North Africa. In 1896 she acquired the island of Madagascar off the east coast of Africa.

Great Britain secured the lion's share. The dream of some of

—————
[1] Except the British inset of Walfish Bay.

her imperialists was almost realized. But for German East Africa she controlled a belt of continuous territory from Cairo to the Cape.[1] Her South African and Rhodesian provinces carried her to Lake Tanganyika and the southern frontier of German East Africa. British East Africa, the Uganda Protectorate, and the Anglo-Egyptian lands extended her sway to the Mediterranean. In addition, her holdings in other parts of Africa comprised on the east coast part of Somaliland, on the west Gambia, Sierra Leone, the Gold Coast, and the large province of Nigeria.

The somewhat complicated story of British South Africa [2] has been left at the point when, in a mood of reluctance to undertake further responsibilities, the British Government granted independence to the two Dutch republics of the Transvaal and the Orange Free State. With the latter republic Great Britain remained on consistently good terms; it was the conflict with the Transvaal which filled most of the years to the end of the century. In 1877, owing to the turbulence and disorder within the state, and to the prospect of its extermination by the Zulus, Great Britain annexed the Transvaal, as a result of which she immediately became involved in war first with the Zulus [3] and then with the Boers. After a short conflict Great Britain in 1881 revised her policy once again, and granted the Transvaal independence under a vague British suzerainty. This seems to have been interpreted by the Boers as an indication of weakness, and under the leadership of Paul Kruger a strong Boer nationalist movement grew up. This in its turn aroused a similar British nationalist movement, headed by Cecil Rhodes, an Oxford man who had made great wealth in the diamond-fields of South Africa.

There developed therefore an intense struggle for racial ascendancy. Rhodes' activities were dynamic. A British South Africa was only part of his dreams. He strove to extend British control from the Cape to Cairo. Under his energetic guidance a chartered company was formed which acquired and settled the uplands of Mashonaland and Matabeleland, now called Rhodesia. The British settlement of Rhodesia and the establishment of the Bechuanaland Protectorate had the result of hemming in the two Dutch republics of the Orange Free State and the Transvaal. Moreover, the situation in the Transvaal was considerably modified by the discovery of diamond- and gold-fields, and the consequent inrush of 'uitlanders,' mainly British, to work the mines. The relations between the 'uitlander' miners and the Boer farmers, an expression of the larger racial conflict, grew more

[1] After the Great War this dream was realized through the transfer to a British mandate of German East Africa.

[2] See p. 472.

[3] It was during this war that the tragic death of the Bonaparte Prince Imperial occurred.

acute from year to year. At the end of 1895 the 'uitlanders' themselves, with the support of Rhodes, then Prime Minister of Cape Colony, made an abortive attempt at a *coup d'état* against the Transvaal Government by means of an armed raid led by Dr Jameson. The attack merely fanned the heat of the conflict, and in 1899 the Boer War broke out, a struggle between the two Boer republics (for the Orange Free State finally decided to support her sister-state) and the British Crown. The Transvaalers put up an unexpectedly good fight. They invaded Natal and Cape Colony and inflicted a series of initial reverses on British arms. But they could hardly compete with the resources of the British Empire, and in the end Boer surrender was inevitable. Peace was made in 1902, and the two Boer republics were formally annexed to the British Crown.

The British policy leading to the war was widely condemned at home, and more especially abroad, but it was substantially redeemed by the policy adopted after the peace. Responsible self-government was granted to the two provinces within five years; within eight they had joined in a federal union under the Crown with Natal and Cape Colony, and provided the first Premier, Louis Botha, of the united South Africa. In 1914 Boer contingents, under Smuts and Botha, undertook the conquest of German East Africa, and in 1939 South Africa again came promptly to the help of the mother country.

The establishment of British control over Egypt forms a curious chapter in the history of British empire-building. Its origin was financial. The enterprises of the ambitious Albanian Mehemet Ali—among them was the conquest of the Egypt. Sudan—and the reckless extravagance of his successors had led Egypt into serious financial embarrassment. The Government was on the verge of bankruptcy. In 1875 the Khedive Ismail gained money by selling his Suez Canal shares, which were bought for £4,000,000 by Disraeli on behalf of England. For Great Britain, at one time so hostile to the Canal, had not only come to have a great share in its trade, but had realized its strategic value as a short passage to India. In 1876 the threatened financial collapse occurred; the Khedive Ismail suspended payment on the large foreign loans which he had raised. England and France, the greatest creditors, then conducted an inquiry into the state of the Egyptian finances, which led to the establishment of a dual Anglo-French control over Egyptian financial affairs. For six years—except for a short interval—the two Powers tried to co-operate with native ministers to introduce order into the chaotic and corrupt economic life of the state. The system of dual control failed. The rivalry between the European and the native authorities was intense; each militated against the power of the other. The European countries secured the deposition of Ismail, but the system worked hardly more successfully. In addition the employment of some 1400 Europeans aroused bitter national antagonism, and in 1882 Arabi Bey effected a *coup d'état* and led a revolt to the cry of "Egypt for the Egyptians!" European lives and property were in great danger; Egypt herself was threatened with political dissolution as great as her economic breakdown. The two Powers decided upon armed intervention, but at the last moment France drew back; England intervened alone, and the rebellion was suppressed by Sir Garnet Wolseley. That was the beginning of the British political control in Egypt, undertaken, it should be noted, on the authorization of Mr Gladstone, one of the least imperialist of British statesmen.

After the rebellion Great Britain began to reorganize the political and economic life of Egypt, but it proved to be a gigantic task, and the British occupation was prolonged. Then there broke out in the Sudan the fanatical rising of the Mahdi, which destroyed the Egyptian armies and overthrew Egyptian rule. British statesmen were thus confronted with the problem of whether to allow the Sudan to fall away from Egypt or to undertake its reconquest. After some delay it was decided not to undertake further responsibilities, and that strange, enigmatical figure, General Gordon, was sent to withdraw the remaining Egyptian garrisons. Gordon's story is well known. Having allowed himself to exceed his instructions, he was caught and killed by the Mahdi in Khartum; a relief force reluctantly sent to his help arrived too late, and was then withdrawn. The Mahdi, triumphant in the Sudan, set up a reign of terror and devastation. For some years Great Britain abstained from action, while Lord Cromer in Egypt conducted some of the finest administrative work of the century. At length the ferocity of the Mahdi rule made intervention inevitable, and in 1899 and 1900 General—later Earl—Kitchener, carried out the conquest of the Sudan. The district was placed under a joint Anglo-Egyptian control, the English occupation in Egypt was further prolonged, and in 1914 Egypt was formally declared a British protectorate.

The partition of Africa was concluded without a war between the Powers, but it was not to be expected that it should not have been the source of much international jealousy and friction. The proceedings bristled with agreements and delimitation conventions. There was Franco-Portuguese rivalry on the Congo. The French annexation of Tunisia roused, as Bismarck, who encouraged it, had hoped it would, the bitter hostility of Italy, who consequently gave her adherence to the Triple Alliance. There was acute ill-will for more than a decade between England and France, and when in 1898 a French expedition hoisted the French flag at Fashoda, on the White

Nile, it seemed likely that actual war would break out between the
two Powers.   It was not until 1904, when a mutual arrangement re-

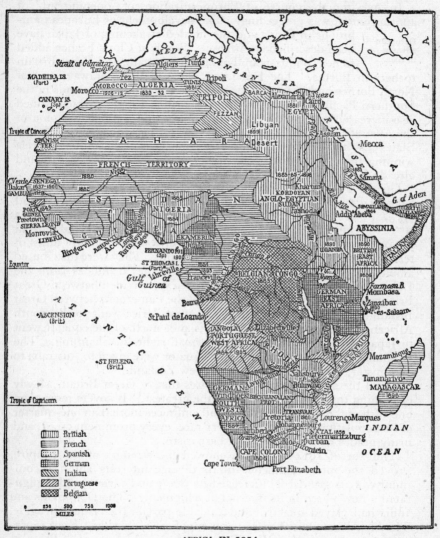

AFRICA IN 1914

garding French and English claims in Morocco and Egypt respectively
was made, that a real reconciliation was brought about.   A little

later, in 1906 and 1911, European crises arose out of the Moroccan Question.

In Asia too the course of Europeanization, of 'opening up,' of appropriation, was proceeding. The development of European am-
European advance in Asia. bitions in China and the startled awakening of Japan have been described elsewhere.[1] South of China France added to her conquests in Tonkin and Annam, and Great Britain to hers in Burma. The Federated Malay States, Sarawak, part of North Borneo and of New Guinea, and a few groups of islands in the Southern Pacific were annexed to the British Empire, which gained also increased moral strength in this quarter by the federal union of the Australian provinces in 1900. France, Germany, and the United States also took their pickings from the Oceanic islands, America winning from Spain the group of the Philippine Islands. Holland already held possessions in that part of the world.

On the eve of the Great War of 1914–18 the leading world and colonial Powers were Great Britain, Russia, France, Germany, and
The Great War. the United States. As a result of the War Germany was eliminated as a colonial Power. She was forced to cede all her overseas possessions, consisting of over a million square miles of territory and about fifteen million inhabitants. They were distributed among the victorious Allies, to be ruled under mandates from the League of Nations. German East Africa was divided between Great Britain and Belgium, and Togoland and the Cameroons between Great Britain and France. German South-west Africa went to the South African Union; the German Pacific islands north of the equator went to Japan, who inherited also the German rights in Shantung. The German Pacific islands south of the equator were given to Australia to administer, and German Samoa to New Zealand.

Of all the surviving colonial empires that of Great Britain, slowly expanding through the century, is the greatest. It covers more than one-fifth of the world's territory, and embraces more than one-quarter of its population. It includes every race, every prominent creed, and many grades of civilization and barbarism.

The war of 1914–18, which showed the strength of the Empire, proved the interdependence of its diverse interests and the community of its standards, increased its range and variety, and inaugurated a new phase in its internal development. The Dominions and India had played an active and valuable part in the critical struggle. They had contributed troops and supplies. They had been represented in the Imperial War Cabinet, at the Conference of Paris, in

[1] See Chapter XI.
[2] Certain Turkish territories were also handed over to French and British administration—Syria (received autonomy 1936) to France, Iraq (received autonomy 1927, member of the League of Nations 1932) and Palestine to Great Britain.

the ratification of the Peace Treaties, and in the League of Nations. Their new status within the Empire was recognized in 1925 by the

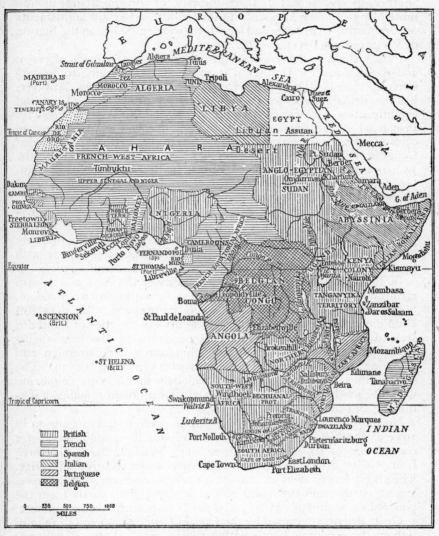

AFRICA IN 1940

creation of a new Secretaryship for Dominion Affairs. It was recognized also in the famous definition by the Imperial Conference of 1926 of the Dominions as "autonomous communities within the British Empire, equal in status, in no way subordinate, one to another, in any respect of their domestic or foreign affairs, though united by a common allegiance to the Crown." Certain adjustments of administrative practice and legal form were embodied in the Statute of Westminster (1931).

India's share in the War had also given her a new pride of place, and the demand for Dominion status in India too came to be persistently raised. The complexity of the Indian problem, however, led the British Government to formulate a programme of gradual evolution toward Dominion status. An All-India Federation, with Provincial Autonomy and responsible self-government, subject to certain safeguards, was established in 1935; but the Nationalist Congress Party continues to demand independence, and, though the Indian Princes have supported Britain in her second conflict with Germany, Congress India is disposed to make her help conditional upon the grant of full Dominion status.

In 1922 the British Protectorate over Egypt which had been declared in 1914 was terminated. Certain administrative and military privileges were retained until 1936. In 1927 the British mandate over Iraq was surrendered. Treaties of alliance were made with Egypt and Iraq which proved their value in the test of 1939.

In Palestine the apparent irreconcilability of the Arab and Jewish claims has prevented the abandonment so far of the British mandate.

Ireland has continued to be a thorny problem. In 1922 full Dominion status was granted to the twenty-six counties of Southern Ireland. They have used their independence to dissociate themselves further from Great Britain, repudiating her Sovereign and declaring themselves neutral in her war with Germany in 1939. The six counties of Northern Ireland jealously guard their connexion with the mother country, and the partition problem remains, a disturbing and mischievous fact.

No more than passing reference can be made to the suspension in 1933 of the Newfoundland Constitution and the appointment of a commission of six members, three from Newfoundland and three from Great Britain, with full legislative and executive authority. The object was to avert an imminent financial and economic collapse, arising partly from the world economic depression, partly from the poor fishing winter of 1932–33, and partly from local mismanagement.

Great Britain attempted by the Ottawa tariff agreements of 1932 to tighten the economic bonds within the Empire. These agreements indicated a definite change of economic policy, the abandonment of Free Trade principles and the adoption of points from the Imperial Preference programme of Joseph Chamberlain.

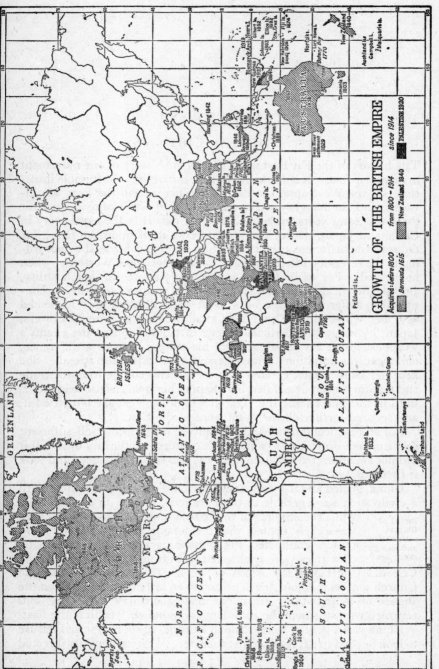

GROWTH OF THE BRITISH EMPIRE

Acquired: before 1800   from 1800 – 1914   since 1914

Bermuda 1615   New Zealand 1840   PALESTINE 1920

CHAPTER XI

THE FAR EAST

THE history of the Far East from 1800 is the history of one movement in many aspects. It is the history of the intrusion—the forcible intrusion—of the West upon the East. Against its will the East was invaded, and the haughty seclusion in which it had wrapped itself for three thousand years broken down. In part it is the same story in China and Japan, that of the West forcing itself upon the East; for the rest, the histories of the two nations diverge considerably, according to the reception offered by each to the unwelcome Westerner when he arrived. For while China, inviting by her wealth, her hostility, and her defencelessness the spoliation she was unable to avert, continued to suffer the onslaught of Western civilization until it seemed as if her whole empire would be swallowed up by foreign Powers, Japan, by ready if superficial change of front, adopted the enemy's weapons, learnt his cunning, wore his clothes, if with a difference, embraced his ambitions, armed herself, and called him friend. She kept her lands intact, entered into the general competition for trade and territory, even demanded her share of her own Asiatic neighbour, until in the end, having the West at a disadvantage, she outwitted it, and secured for herself the dominance of the East.

For all practical purposes, the East lived in seclusion, self-sufficient and isolated, down to the nineteenth century; and of its own will it did not abandon that isolation. It was the West that wooed and took it by force.

China, girded about by sea and desert and mountains, content with a civilization as venerable as the Pyramids, looked on and despised while the empires of the 'barbarians' rose and fell. There was a slight contact with the outside world; Roman luxury traders conducted silk caravans across Asia; diplomatic courtesies were exchanged from time to time between the Celestial Court and the Arabs or Persians; the Roman Catholic Church sent its missionaries to preach to an astonished civilization the Figure of Humiliation; travellers made their way to Cathay, and returned with stories of the abundant and fabulous wealth of the East.

Period of Chinese seclusion and foreign exclusion.

China was a golden legend which Europe, as soon as it had leisure to look beyond itself, resolved to translate. Western cupidity directed

Western enterprise, and when the opening of the seas provided easier pathways the ships of the oceanic nations set their sails for the East. Slowly but doggedly European traders broke into the iso- The wooing lation in which China had held herself. They fastened of China like leeches upon her southern shores, the Portuguese at by Europe. Macao in the sixteenth century, a hundred years later the Spaniards, the Dutch, and the English at Canton. The Chinese Empire, while it did not want them, could not shake them off. It degraded them with indignities and burdened them with restrictions; it made them kotow before the image of the Emperor, it limited their power of domicile, interfered with their private life, confined their trade, taxed them, forbade them to learn the Chinese language, treated them as inferiors, and ignored their petitions, but it could not get rid of them. They pressed increasingly for relaxations, but they accepted the restrictions and the indignities, and continued to trade.

In the meantime another nation, aspiring to be European, had been advancing by land upon the north—Russia. Russia also desired trading relations, but her Asiatic territories were contiguous with those of China, and there were border wars. With Russia, therefore, the Celestial Court so far condescended as to make a treaty at Nerschink in 1689—the first Sino-European treaty that was concluded. Trading concessions were granted, but rigidly limited; Russians were not allowed to trade by sea; they had come by land and must keep to the land; they must make obeisances; their caravans, when after many months they reached the Chinese frontier, were met by Chinese troops who escorted them to their caravanserai in Peking; there they were closely confined until they had disposed of their goods to the few traders who were allowed to trade with them, and secured in return such scourings of the Chinese shops as they had been able to pay for at high prices; then they were escorted back again to the frontier. There were subsequent treaties in the eighteenth century between China and Russia, but no expansion of Russian commerce was allowed, and, being unremunerative, it dwindled to insignificant proportions.

Thus, in spite of the superior recognition given to Russia, the sea-faring nations held the advantage. The coasting trade of the south, in tea, silk, and opium and other articles, proved profitable enough to ensure its continuance and its growth, and European traders came to have interests too great to be left with no better guarantee than the goodwill of the remote Peking Government and the corruptibility of local officials. The British East India Company in particular had built up an important trading connexion, and as its commerce expanded its demands grew for the relaxation of restrictions, for treaty guarantees, and for equal treatment. The British Government took up its cause, but neither private endeavours nor the efforts of the

Company's agents nor Government missions [1] availed with the Celestial Court. The presents of King George III and the Regent were called tribute, and accepted by the Chinese Emperor out of a lofty consideration for the English monarch's feelings, but all requests for a commercial treaty were resolutely declined. China would enter into no treaty relations with the nations of the West; she would admit their traders only as merchant adventurers, as tributaries of a vassal Power. She did not want them or their trade; if they came they must come on her terms. "As your ambassador can see for himself, we possess all things. I set no value on objects strange or ingenious, and I have no use for your country's manufactures." [2] That was the answer of the Emperor Chien Lung to George III, a hundred and thirty years ago. Partly from contempt, partly from lack of economic reciprocity, the door of China remained closed to Western commerce. Sino-European trade would, in fact, have remained one-sided but for one article, opium, which China began to demand in increasing quantities, and out of the opium-trade a new era arose in the history of China.

The issue between East and West was to be put to the ultimate test of force, and Great Britain took the lead. From the time of Lord Amherst's mission in 1816 the ill-feeling between China and England

[1] Two missions were dispatched by the British Government, under Lord Macartney in 1793 and Lord Amherst in 1816. Lord Macartney's expedition was only allowed to proceed to Court on condition that it accepted the title " Ambassador bearing tribute from the country of England."

[2] The following are further extracts from the Chinese Emperor's mandate:

" You [George III], O King, live beyond the confines of many seas, nevertheless, impelled by your humble desire to partake of the benefits of our civilization, you have dispatched a mission respectfully bearing your memorial. . . . I have perused your memorial : the earnest terms in which it is couched reveal a respectful humility on your part, which is highly praiseworthy.

" In consideration of the fact that your Ambassador and his deputy have come a long way with your memorial and tribute, I have shown them high favour and have allowed them to be introduced into my presence. To manifest my indulgence, I have entertained them at a banquet and made them numerous gifts. . . .

" As to your entreaty to send one of your nationals to be accredited to my Celestial Court and to be in control of your country's trade with China, this request is contrary to all usage of my dynasty and cannot possibly be entertained. . . . If you assert that your reverence for Our Celestial dynasty fills you with a desire to acquire our civilization our ceremonies and code of laws differ so completely from your own that, even if your Envoy were able to acquire the rudiments of our civilization, you could not possibly transplant our manners and customs to your alien soil. Therefore, however adept the Envoy might become, nothing would be gained thereby.

" Swaying the wide world, I have but one aim in view—namely, to maintain a perfect governance and to fulfil the duties of the State : strange and costly objects do not interest me. If I have commanded that the tribute offerings sent by you, O King, are to be accepted this was solely in consideration for the spirit which prompted you to dispatch them from afar. Our dynasty's majestic virtue has penetrated into every country under Heaven, and kings of all nations have offered their costly tribute by land and sea. . . ."

had increased. During the same years British trade with China had considerably expanded, and with the abolition in 1834 of the East India Company's monopoly a flood of new competitors had entered the market. On the one hand it became evident that the growing British trade needed regulation; on the other Chinese restrictions and antagonism grew more irksome as British commerce expanded. In 1833 Great Britain appointed a Trade Superintendent, a ' barbarian eye,' as the Chinese dubbed him, in the person of Lord Napier, who proceeded to China with the determination to take a firm line and assert the equality of British subjects. From the first he encountered from the Chinese authorities insuperable obstacles; a spirit of subservience was demanded which he was not prepared to show; a deadlock ensued, and a stoppage of trade which was only ended by Napier's premature death in 1834. He had achieved nothing except the further exasperation of the Chinese Government.

The forcing of China by Europe (1830–61).

In these circumstances of intense strain the opium question produced a crisis. The opium drug was known in China before the arrival of the Portuguese, but its greater use during the late eighteenth and early nineteenth centuries arose principally from the fact that in 1773 the English began to import Indian opium into China. It was a convenient article of merchandise, practically the only one for which there was a Chinese demand. With the growing supply the demand was stimulated, and the import of the drug doubled and quadrupled within fifteen years. Repeated Imperial prohibitions from 1729 onward against its use and importation were fruitless. In 1800 trade in the drug was categorically forbidden, but the trade continued to flourish, largely owing to the connivance and venality of the local Chinese officials, who assisted its import and made their profits from it. A Chinese commissioner sent to Canton in 1833 to enforce the prohibition found his efforts frustrated as much by native as by foreign opposition, and the boats nominally engaged in preventing the commerce turned out to be the main carriers of the drug.

The First China War (1839–42).

In 1839 a new commissioner, Lin, was appointed, and a fresh attempt made to exterminate the traffic. He demanded the surrender of all stocks of opium in the possession of British traders, and accompanied his demand with a blockade of the British community which brought it to the verge of starvation. Under duress Captain Elliot, the Superintendent of the day, a man who had been making previous efforts on his own account to stop the opium-trade, persuaded the British merchants to deliver up twenty thousand chests of opium. The opium was then burnt, under protest from Elliot, who announced that he would petition the Queen of England to seek redress.

Commissioner Lin then proceeded to demand guarantees against the future resumption of the trade, ordering the British merchants formally to bind themselves never again to engage in it, and in case of infringement to submit themselves to the "extreme penalties of the Chinese law"—that is, death.   The whole course of the negotiations had been conducted in a very high-handed manner on the Chinese side; neither side had, in fact, shown any leaning toward conciliation. Acts of violence on both sides complicated the question and exacerbated the temper of British and Chinese alike.   In short, the situation locally was rapidly drifting toward war.

The first shots were fired by two ships of the British navy lying in the mouth of the Canton River.   Twenty-nine Chinese junks drawn up in battle order against them—apparently prepared to enforce Lin's peremptory summons to the British merchants—were scattered and put to flight.   The engagement was reported to the Celestial Court as a Chinese victory, whereupon the Emperor promoted the admiral for his skill and success and issued orders that the British trade was to be ended once and for all.

The war lasted for nearly three years, and consisted of a number of easy victories for the British, interrupted by abortive negotiations for peace.   The island of Cherson was captured and the towns of Ningpo and Amoy; the wealthy port of Shanghai fell to the foreigner and the island of Hong-Kong was occupied.   A squadron was dispatched to threaten the existing capital of Peking, and an assault was made upon the ancient [1] capital of Nanking, which at last brought the Emperor to terms.   For on the Chinese side the military defences were futile and wholly inadequate.   Nanking alone possessed any serious fortification.   The safety of China seemed to be committed chiefly to Imperial edicts and primitive native courage.   Edicts continuously appeared ordering the "rebellious barbarians" to be exterminated from the sacred soil of China, commanding the recall of Commissioner Lin and numerous successors, who were to proceed "with the speed of flames" to Peking, there to be disgraced and punished.   Chinese courage showed itself in extravagant suicide, and, in the taking of the forts of Nanking, far more natives fell by their own hands than by the weapons of the enemy.

The success of Great Britain was the success of modern methods of warfare and of Western civilization.   On that victory was founded the whole Far Eastern policy of Europe in the nineteenth century, the opening up of China, the entry of Japan into the ranks of world Powers, and the Pacific problem.   It proved to China that Europe could enforce her demands and to Europe that China could not resist her.   It is true that the immediate cause and result of the so-called

[1] Readopted as the Chinese capital by the Kuomin-tang party (1928).

Opium War was to force upon China traffic in the drug. There was, however, more at stake.[1] The whole position of foreign commerce and the status of the foreign trader was bound up with the opium question, and the war was an emphatic demand from the West for the legalization of external trade, for the regularization of European contacts, and the recognition of the equality of the foreigner. Had these concessions been granted it is improbable that the opium dispute would have led to war. On the other hand, had China been victorious in the war it can hardly be doubted that the British trader—and perhaps the European—would have been totally excluded from her ports.

By the Treaty of Nanking in 1842, in which were embodied the terms of peace, China was for the first time bound by treaty to a Western Power.[2] She agreed to cede Hong-Kong to Great Britain, to open five ports, Canton, Foochow, Ningpo, Amoy, and Shanghai—that is, practically the whole of South China—to European trade. She paid an indemnity, pledged herself to observe "equality of status in official intercourse," agreed to the enactment of a "fair and regular tariff," and to the abolition of the Co-Hong [3] monopolies. *The Treaty of Nanking (1842).*

The British guns had opened China to Western trade, and other nations hastened to enter the breach that they had made. A series of treaties, on the lines of the Nanking peace, was made with America and France in 1844, and with Norway and Sweden three years later, while Belgium secured some of the benefits of the British treaty.

It was beyond the bounds of historical possibility that the situation in China should remain as it was created by these treaties, or that Europe should not seek to develop the advantage she had gained. She had secured admission to China, but little more than admission. Her position was irksome and in many ways indeterminate. Equal status in official intercourse with the Imperial Court at Peking gave no guarantee of fair dealing at the ports. There was no organized means of diplomatic intercourse, no Chinese Foreign Office, no

---

[1] *Cf.* the following extract from a Chinese point of view : " The foreigners embroider their case by asserting that, in this war, the Western Powers were demanding from China diplomatic and commercial equality. Equality. When China was allowed no freedom to prevent the importation of poisonous drugs. Equality. But, worse yet, even in our own school text-books and lectures, Chinese writers attributed, as the cause of this war, the severance of commercial relationships with England. Even more terribly than opium itself has the poison of Imperialism corrupted our people " (Wong Ching-Wai, 1927, *China and the Nations*).

[2] Excluding Russia.

[3] The Co-Hong was a group of Chinese merchants with whom alone the European trader could do business. Having a monopoly, they could demand high prices. The European trader had, moreover, no protection against such a contingency as the bankruptcy of one of the group.

embassies. The Orientals maintained and plainly revealed a galling sense of superiority, and there were not infrequent demonstrations of hostility to the 'foreign devils.' The Cantonese resisted the opening of their port according to the terms of the treaty, and put up placards threatening "if the barbarians made a single move . . . to take them and kill them absolutely, and not leave a blade of grass an inch high, nor allow the creepers to spread." Nor was amity promoted by Palmerston's talk of the "consciousness of superior strength," of chastisement and retaliation upon the town of Canton, until "if occasion required not a single house should be left standing."

The British traders arrived speedily at a state of dissatisfaction with the benefits they had already won, and began to demand a revision of the treaty and an increase of privileges. Their gains seemed meagre. What were five treaty ports when they wanted the whole Yangtse valley? And any attempt to secure revision was resolutely frustrated by China.

In short, a perfectly natural psychological development had taken place. The European trade with China was a progressive concern; the small concession that had been made was merely a stimulus to further demands. There was no finality whatever about five treaty ports—if five, why not ten, or any number within the limits of the Chinese Empire?—and in the last resort there was the "consciousness of superior strength," the ready apprehension that the arms which had achieved the benefits of the past were always accessible.

In the Second China War Great Britain had the alliance of France.[1] Several incidents supplied provocation. In February 1856 a French **The Second China War (1857–58).** Catholic missionary was executed by the local Chinese authority of Kwangsi for "departing from the treaty ports and exciting rebellion." The French envoy protested that this was an invasion of the rights of French subjects to be tried and punished solely by their own tribunals. In the same year the *Arrow*, a lorcha flying the British flag, but apparently engaged in a coasting smuggling trade, was seized by the Chinese authorities. It is not necessary to enter into the merits of the two cases; the one incident afforded as good an occasion to England as the other to France, and Napoleon III proposed that the Anglo-French alliance of the Crimean War should be renewed in a joint campaign against China. War was declared, and although the outbreak of the Indian Mutiny at the beginning of 1857 delayed the actual opening of hostilities a short campaign in 1858 brought China to terms. She who could not hold her own against England alone twenty years earlier could still less contend with the combined Anglo-French forces. She was, moreover, stricken with civil war by the serious Taiping Rebellion, which for thirteen

---

[1] Other nations also made certain hostile demonstrations.

years, from 1851 to 1864, divided China in the interests of a counter-dynastic movement.[1] Before the terms of peace were ratified, however, war broke out again. It was during these hostilities that the beautiful Summer Palace of the Emperor was destroyed by British orders in retaliation for the torture by the Chinese of British and French prisoners. The allied advance upon Peking led to the resumption of negotiations, and peace was finally ratified in what are known comprehensively as the Tientsin Treaties of 1861.

By these treaties [2] the desired revision of Sino-European relations and the extension of privileges were obtained. Kowloon was ceded to Great Britain, and eleven new ports—making sixteen in all—were opened to foreign trade. A large indemnity was paid to France and England, and rights conceded to foreign missions to reside in Peking, and to foreign nationals to travel in China under passport. **The Tientsin Treaties (1861).** Protection for missionaries was promised, and a guarantee given of freedom of contract in commercial transactions. An explicit recognition was given of what is now held in China to be one of the most obnoxious privileges possessed by foreigners, the right of 'extra-territoriality.' By this concession the subjects of the foreign countries concerned in the treaties were to be subject not to the laws of China, but to the laws and jurisdiction of their own states.[3]

By 1861 China may be said to have been fully though grudgingly opened to the Westerner. He had gained freedom to trade, extra-territorial rights, and a practical control over the Chinese tariff system. He had penetrated to the interior, to the Yangtse valley. The foreign merchant had even come to take a part in the domestic politics of China, and the "Ever-victorious Army," raised on the initiative of European traders at Shanghai in the interests of foreign trade, and officered by Westerners, was collaborating with the Imperial Chinese army in the suppression of the Taiping Rebellion. For it was to

[1] The Taiping Rebellion resembles in some ways the rising of the Mahdi. It was a semi-religious, semi-political movement directed against the Manchu dynasty. Its chief strength lay in the south, and Nanking was proclaimed as the capital. It was suppressed with the help of General Gordon in 1863–64.

[2] Russia took the opportunity of China's embarrassment to make her own terms and secure her own spoil.

[3] The demand arose from the untrustworthy condition of Chinese law and the unfamiliar legal principles on which it is based. It is a right hardly ever conceded between Christian states on an equal footing, and is therefore all the more humiliating to the Chinese, who regard it as a concession of sovereign power. " Extra-territorial rights are the first instrument of the Imperialists for encroachment into foreign countries. Their function is not only to rob us of national pride, but also to enable the foreigners to regard Chinese sovereignty as nothing " (Wong Ching-Wai, *op. cit.*). However embittered and biased, this is a current Chinese view of the question. It is largely on the grounds of extra-territoriality that the 'unequal treaties' are denounced. Extra-territorial rights were originally conceded by Japan also, but were subsequently rescinded by the foreign Powers.

Europe's advantage to maintain the Manchu dynasty, which had guaranteed its privileges.

China had been compelled to acknowledge—formally, if in her heart she withheld it—not only the equality of the barbarian, but in some measure his superiority. Slowly the Chinese Government was awakening to the fact that it must enter into permanent relations with the outside world. In 1861 the Tsungli-Yâmen, or Foreign Office, was founded, a feeble, invertebrate body which entangled foreign relations for forty years, but an indication of a changing outlook. The Celestial Court went so far as to bestow its congratulations upon "Chinese Gordon" for the suppression of the Taiping Rebellion, to offer him a sum of money, which he refused, strike a medal in his honour, decorate him with the highest order of the Dragon Empire, and invest him with the yellow jacket and the peacock's feather. It is true that Gordon was a different type of Englishman from some of the buccaneering opium-traders with whom China had become familiar. In 1873 foreign ambassadors were received for the first time at the Court of Peking and granted an audience of the Emperor. Four years later the first Chinese envoy was sent to London, and the next year Chinese agents were established in most of the capitals of Europe.

After the Second China War the Far Eastern Question entered on a new phase, which in certain aspects has been prolonged considerably into the twentieth century. It will be convenient, how-

The Far
Eastern
Question,
1861–95.

ever, to fix a halt at the Sino-Japanese War of 1894–95. From 1793 to 1860 the interests of the West in the East consisted mainly in a single issue, the opening up of China to foreign trade. Europe had up to that time thought little of anything but trade, or of any Pacific country but China. From 1860 onward, however, the Far Eastern Question began to grow more complex, to reveal new developments. To trade was added empire; to China Japan; to commercial gain political aggression.

Thus while on the one hand the economic tentacles which had fastened upon China were multiplied and strengthened, by the entry of new countries into the competition and by the acquisition of new privileges, on the other hand there was a new European impulse toward empire and political annexation, which, though it so far respected the integrity of China herself, struck at her outlying dependencies, and brought Europe through a series of fresh conquests to the very frontiers of the Celestial Empire.

Moreover, in the East the situation of China and the whole future of Pacific lands was fundamentally modified by the entry of a new candidate for world-power and for Eastern influence, not a Western nation, but one from the very heart of the East itself, Japan.

The period therefore from 1860 to 1895 is marked by three pre-

dominant and parallel developments.   First, the expansion in volume
and the extension in scope of the economic interests of the   Economic
West in the Pacific countries of China and Japan; second,   expansion.
the growth of a new spirit of political aggression, which   Political
resulted in the annexation by Europe of the outlying de-   aggression.
pendencies of China; third, the remarkable development   Japanese develop-
of Japan as a formidable Power.   ment.

The first two developments can be briefly summarized.   Foreign,
and especially British, trade, which was practically ten times as great
as that of any other nation, increased by leaps and bounds.   Economic
New countries, awakening to the immense possibilities that   expansion.
were unfolding in the East, rushed to make treaties with China.
Prussia was the earliest in the field, but the Chinese declared they had
never heard of the state, and were reluctant at first to conclude an
agreement with it.   Eventually they formed a modified convention.
Then followed rapidly the ambassadors of other countries.   At the end
of the Second Chinese War five Powers only had concluded treaties
with the Imperial Government—Great Britain, the United States,
France, Russia, and Norway and Sweden.   During the next thirty
years eleven other states—eight European,[1] two South American,[2] and
one Asiatic [3]—made terms with China and entered into her commerce.

It was through the murder of a British Consul, Mr Margary—which,
like the ill-treatment of missionaries, was found to be so useful a lever
for forcing concessions out of China—and the Chefoo agreement in
1876, by which England received reparation, that the most notable
extension of privileges was won.   By this convention, besides con-
ceding an indemnity and an apology, China agreed to the abolition
of *likin* [4] in foreign concessions, and to open four more ports and
six calling-stations on the Yangtse.   In addition Great Britain
strengthened her diplomatic position, received a promise of greater
security for her travellers, and made certain judicial arrangements.
Her greatest gain was, however, the consolidation of her economic
position on the Yangtse River.

Next to Africa, it was at the expense of China that the great impulse toward expansion which animated Europe in the second half
of the nineteenth century found its satisfaction.   Thus   The loss of
Russia, checked in the Black Sea by the Crimean War,   China's de-
began her great advance in Asia, southward toward Persia   pendencies.
and Afghanistan, eastward into China.   In the south she quickly
came into conflict with British interests; in the east she met only
the comparative weakness of the Chinese Empire, and by a steady

---

[1] Prussia, 1861 ; Denmark and the Netherlands, 1863 ; Spain, 1864 ; Belgium,
1865 ; Italy, 1866 ; Austria-Hungary, 1869 ; Portugal, 1887.
[2] Peru, 1874 ; Brazil, 1881.   [3] Japan, 1872.   [4] Internal transit duty.

progression she pushed her way toward an ice-free coastline on the Pacific. In 1853, by the Treaty of Aigun, extracted from China amid the embarrassments of the Taiping Rebellion and the war with the Western Powers, Russia secured a large piece of territory down to the Amur River. Two years later, posing as China's friend against France and Great Britain, she secured a long line of coast which gave her the harbour on which she built Vladivostok, the "Conqueror of the East." By these acquisitions she was brought into touch with Korea, and was half-way toward the encirclement of Manchuria, where she saw the ice-free port on which she had set her heart. In 1875 she annexed Sakhalin after a long-continued conflict with Japan, who disputed the island with her, while a series of border wars gave her in 1881 the western part of Ili, on the Turkestan frontier.

The next state to desire to enlarge her empire was France, who, like Russia after the Crimean War, looked round for compensation after the defeat of 1870. Again new colonial expansion was achieved at the expense of China, and by a gradual encroachment the French Republic established its authority over Tonkin and Annam during the last two decades of the nineteenth century. Great Britain had no wish to enlarge her colonial possessions, and always pursued in the East trade rather than empire, but the recent French annexations seemed to threaten the Balance of Power and British interests in India. She therefore made war on Burma and annexed it and Sikkim in 1886 and 1890. Small parts of Siam were also annexed by both Great Britain and France, and the remainder was declared a neutral state between British Burma and French Annam. Germany and Italy also entered the ranks of empire-builders, but not yet. It was not only the Powers of Europe, however, who denuded China of the protection which her outlying dependencies afforded her. Japan signalized her conversion to Western civilization by an aggressive attitude toward her neighbour, and the annexation of the Loochoo Islands in 1881 was only the beginning of an encroachment which has come to be the greatest menace to Chinese security and the most significant factor in the Pacific problem.

In certain respects the early history of Japan followed that of China, whence she drew her civilization, and until the nineteenth century she

Japan to 1867.

maintained a seclusion even more rigid than her neighbour's. Traders of Portugal, Spain, and the Netherlands had made their way to her islands before the end of the sixteenth century, and were followed by Catholic missionaries. But native hostility was quickly aroused against foreign missionary enterprise, behind which was seen the threat of political conquest such as had befallen parts of America. It is reported that the master of a Spanish galleon pointed to a map of the world marking the lands which were held by Spain.

When he was asked how the territory had been acquired he replied, "It is by the help of missioners, who are sent to all parts of the world to preach the Gospel of Jesus Christ, for as soon as these Religious had gained a sufficient number of proselytes, the King followed with his troops, and, joining the new converts, made a conquest of the Kingdom." The foreigners, moreover, gave little observance to Japanese laws, and their position was weakened by quarrels among themselves, between the subjects of different nations and the members of different Churches. From the beginning of the seventeenth century Christians and Christian missionaries were forbidden the country, and in 1637 two edicts were issued which effectively closed Japan to the Western world. All foreigners were forbidden on pain of death to enter the Japanese islands, excepting only the Chinese and the Dutch, who were held to be neither Christian enough nor militaristic enough to be dangerous. On the same penalty the Japanese were forbidden to leave their own shores, and no ship was allowed to be built of more than fifty tons burden. For two hundred years Japan lived behind a veil, pierced only by a dwindling contact with Dutch traders. The importunate merchants who besieged the shores of China passed by a country not rich enough to reward the perils of approach. Her own maritime enterprise decayed, her people died of repeated famines that a less exclusive economic policy might have averted.

With the nineteenth century something of the backwash of the new European movement in the Pacific reached her. There were Russian ships in the Sea of Japan; the Dutch reported the growing English trade in the China Sea. Japan wrapped herself the closer in her seclusion, seeking to protect herself by an order issued in 1825 that all foreign ships should be fired upon. Then came the First China War and the defeat of her great and venerable neighbour. The threat to her own empire was too near to be ignored. She imported a few Dutch guns and introduced a slight revision of her military system, but she still strove to avert the danger by maintaining, though with growing uneasiness, her national isolation.

It was, in fact, not from Europe but from America that she received the summons from the West, and what the Opium War was to China the demand of an American admiral was to Japan. The United States had long ceased to be merely a fringe of seaboard states on the Atlantic coast. From the second decade of the nineteenth century America had turned increasingly to the West. In 1848 she had acquired California and San Francisco; the gold rush had given her a population with interests on the Pacific and an outlook toward Asia. The drift of a continuous westward expansion brought her to the shores of Japan. Her whaling-ships were wrecked upon its coasts; in 1846 a ship of the American Navy had sought its ports in difficulties and had been denied its hospitality. As the Pacific interests of the United States increased, the need of a friendly calling-station on the other side of the ocean grew imperative; she began also to desire trading relations.

In 1853 Commodore Perry of the United States Navy appeared with four warships in the bay of Yeddo,[1] with a request that Japanese ports should be opened to American ships. He presented two models of Western telegraph and railway systems, and with them a letter to be delivered to the ruler of Japan. He promised to return for an answer the next year. At the stipulated date he reappeared with eight warships, with four thousand soldiers on board. A hurried debate was held in Yeddo, for no reply had in the interval been prepared. The old anti-foreign arguments were revived. "At first," it was contended, "they will give us philosophical instruments, machinery, and other curiosities, and will deceive ignorant people. Trade being their object, they will manage bit by bit to impoverish the country; after which they will treat us just as they like, perhaps behave with the greatest rudeness and insult us, and end by swallowing up Japan." Others replied that Japan's true policy would be to accept treaties with the Western peoples and strengthen herself by learning their arts and sciences that she might hold her own against them. In the end these arguments prevailed, for they were fortified by the sight of eight American warships in the harbour. A treaty was made; two ports were thrown open to American ships, for provisioning rather than for trade, although commercial privileges were implied.

A beginning had been made in the opening of Japan, and as in the case of China the other nations of the West rushed to secure their places. Great Britain, engaged at the time in war with Russia, speedily realized the advantage of a friendly Japanese harbour in the Pacific, and the first Anglo-Japanese treaty conceded refitting but not trade facilities. Commercial relations quickly followed, and Japan entered on a decade of treaty-making with the chief countries of the West. In all fifteen countries signed agreements with her, and by 1867 she had granted to the foreigners commercial relations and open ports, extra-territorial rights, tariff powers, and general diplomatic and consular privileges. She had guaranteed the free exercise of religion and conceded rights of travel within her empire.

So far the general history of Japan had followed that of China. They were both bound by 'unequal treaties' to the Westerner. Alien peoples had invaded them for their own profit, and the

The Japanese revolution (1867)

future of both empires lay in the issue of a conflict between two civilizations—a conflict without adequate historical parallel in the annals of Greek colonization or of Roman, Spanish, or British conquests.

[1] Afterward renamed Tokio.

It is in the emergence from that conflict that the development of the two nations has diverged so considerably. China had been defeated by Western civilization, but not convinced; Japan was convinced in order to save herself from defeat.

One of the first results of Western contact in Japan was to cause a political upheaval. In the middle of the nineteenth century the Empire of the Rising Sun was still essentially feudal, militaristic, and clannish. The power-holding class in the state were the Damio, or great feudatories, together with their numerous retainers, forming the large body of warriors, or Samurai. The rule of the Mikado, or Emperor, had been from the twelfth century merely nominal. He was a shadowy, semi-sacred figure living in seclusion at Kyoto. The real ruler was the Shogun of Yeddo, whose title literally meant nothing more than 'general.' Theoretically he was the Mikado's agent, but like a Frankish Mayor of the Palace he held all the power in his hands, and it was with him that the foreign countries, in ignorance or contempt of the Emperor, concluded treaties. He was the head of one of the chief clans, but, owing to the strong position of the feudatories, although he transacted all the business of the State for the Mikado he never succeeded in fully establishing his power over the other clans.

The admission of the Westerner and the concession of treaty rights produced the usual anti-foreign movement, and there were constant violent incidents directed against foreign subjects. The anti-Western agitation, drawing strength from the general *known as* discontent incidental to a decaying feudalism, and from *"the Restoration."* class rivalry, turned into a political movement for the deposition of the Shogun and for the restoration of the power of the Emperor, with a view to the exclusion of the foreigners. In 1867 the Shogunate was overthrown to the cry of "Exalt the Emperor and away with the barbarians!" The Mikado was, nominally at least, restored to full power. In reality, when the disturbance and feudal fighting subsided, the "Restoration" was found to be largely a transference of power from the clan of the Tokugawa to the Satsuma and Choshu clans. Nevertheless a real revolution had been accomplished, for the new *régime*, showing a complete *volte-face*, began to introduce a host of Western measures. In the words of a Japanese writer, from 1868 Japan "began to run after Western ideas as fast as she could." She threw away her old works of Ukioye art, and imported lithographs and cheap tin products. She burnt her five-storied pagodas to save the cost of demolition. She did everything she could to reshape her military, political, industrial, and scientific life on Western ideas.

Feudalism was abolished, the nobles were either pensioned or bought off; the clans were dissolved. The former elaborate classification of society was replaced by three new divisions; and local administrative units were set up on the pattern of French *préfectures*. The Samurai were deprived of their military privileges, and a new conscript army was formed on German principles. The navy was refashioned as near to British nautical ideas as possible. British industrial and engineering practices were introduced. Railways, telegraphs, lighthouses, and dockyards were built, coal-mines and silk-mills set up. A Japanese steamship company was founded; a Stock Exchange and a Chamber of Commerce established. There was even held a National Industrial Exhibition.

Public compulsory education was introduced only two years after Gladstone's Education Act of 1870. Universities and technical schools were founded under State supervision. Foreign teachers were invited to the country; the English language was made compulsory in schools, and it was proposed to make it the national language. There was even talk of introducing Western blood into the Japanese race.

The anti-Christian edicts were repealed, as well as those forbidding Japanese subjects to go abroad; delegations were dispatched to foreign countries to learn the newest Western ideas on all subjects. Shinto was reduced from the position of a State religion to that of a religion of the Court, and the Gregorian calendar was adopted.

A land-tax was imposed, and a land survey and valuation authorized. Legal reforms were also introduced and a new criminal code framed with the help of foreign jurists; and since all progressive states had constitutions a constitution was set up in 1889 on the model of that of the Prussian kingdom. For European thought entered Japan in three waves. In the first decade the predominant influence was that of the English utilitarians; in the second decade French democratic writers grew fashionable, and Rousseau was translated into Japanese. Lastly came the German nationalistic and political influences.

Within the remarkably short time of twenty years the outward form of Japan was entirely changed. It has now been realized that the extent of the transformation was exaggerated; that the essential spirit of Japan has remained Oriental. Certainly from the end of the eighties the tide of Europeanization began to ebb, and except in military, scientific, and industrial matters it has tended to be replaced by an articulate nationalism, crying " Back to Japan! "

With other Western features the Japanese Empire began to develop an active foreign policy. Her primary aim was to secure a revision in Foreign her favour of the treaties she had signed with the Western policy. Powers, in ignorance, she protested, of the principles regulating international relations. In 1871 she dispatched the Iwakura mission to Europe to achieve the desired modification, but although it returned with abundant information on Western civilization it

failed to secure the revision of the 'unequal treaties.' This failure
brought home to her the realization that only by making herself a
Great Power would she ever achieve her ambition.   In other words,
it was force that had proved itself from the beginning the only potent
factor in the Far Eastern Question. It was force which had humiliated
China and bound her with the 'unequal treaties'; it was the threat of
it which had imposed the same degradation upon Japan. She began
therefore deliberately to turn herself into a military Power, partly, no
doubt, in satisfaction of a natural martial tendency, largely in the spirit
of self-defence.   She began to adopt a vigorous and assertive policy
toward her neighbours.

In 1872 she demanded treaty relations with China like a veritable
Western Power, and when Korea refused to open its ports to her trade
she bombarded its harbours. She quarrelled with China, and in 1874
invaded Formosa, but subsequently withdrew from the island.   In
1877 she was temporarily handicapped by a feudal rebellion in her
own states, but its suppression by the conscript army, which thereby
proved its efficiency, gave her greater confidence than ever, and in
1879 she seized the Loochoo Islands.

The Powers of Europe, however, still refused to revise the treaties
they had made with her—although Great Britain in 1884 went so far
as to accord her a promise of revision.   Japan therefore resolved upon
a further demonstration. She had already challenged Chinese predominance in Korea; she was now to extinguish it.

The interest of Japan in the Korean peninsula was of long standing,
and in the sixteenth century she had already engaged in a prolonged
war with China for its control, in which she had been
defeated.   Its geographical propinquity gave it an integral   The Sino-
share in the destiny of the Japanese islands, and its inde-   Japanese
pendence was more vital to Japanese security than that of   War
Belgium to the national safety of Great Britain. Such was the   (1894-95).
Japanese point of view.   Korea in hostile hands was "a dagger thrust
at the heart of Japan."

The peninsula had been recognized as a Chinese dependency since
its conquest by the Manchus in the seventeenth century, and the
Dragon Empire had proved neither a harsh nor exacting taskmaster.
But the very laxity of China's rule was raising fresh perils for Japan,
to whom, in view of her new ambition to become a Great Power, the
independence of Korea was of greater importance than ever.   China's
policy of *laissez-faire* and the disorders which were a perpetual feature
of Korean politics were allowing, even inducing, the intervention of
Western Powers.   They had already entered into treaty relations with
her; they had also shown every willingness to annex Chinese dependencies; already Russia, advancing from the north, had put one foot

into Korea, although the jealousy of the other Powers had forced her to withdraw it.   Japan therefore saw the prospect of the establishment of a European overlordship in Korea which would be infinitely more menacing than even a resuscitation of the moribund Chinese suzerainty.   The Sino-Japanese War was an assault upon China; it was not less a challenge flung to the Powers.   "This at least I can tell you for certain," said a Japanese diplomatic representative in Europe, "we neither can nor will leave Korea again until our aim has been obtained in one way or another.   We are fighting in Korea for our own future—I might almost say for our independence.   Once let Korea fall into the hands of a European Power, and our independence will be threatened." [1]

For twenty years before the outbreak of the Sino-Japanese War Japan had meddled in Korean politics, here stimulating the independence and reform party, there curtailing Chinese influence, swinging from the intention of helping Korea to strengthen herself against foreign invasion to that of supplanting Chinese influence in the Hermit Kingdom.   In 1876 she covenanted with Korea to recognize her independence of China.   After the riots of 1884 she entered into a treaty with China that neither Power should send troops to the peninsula without giving formal notice to the other.

In 1894 another rebellion broke out, led by the Tonghaks, a political party with a programme of reform and expulsion of the foreigners. The Korean Government appealed to the Chinese Empire for help, and 2500 Chinese troops were dispatched to Korea.   Japan protested that such an act constituted a breach of faith, and sent on her own part 8000 troops to the peninsula.   The Tonghak rebellion had in the meantime been suppressed, but a far graver issue had been raised. Chinese and Japanese troops were face to face in the kingdom.

For a time the imminent conflict between them was postponed by negotiation.   China suggested a mutual withdrawal of troops and a common agreement not to interfere in Korean affairs.   Japan rejected the suggestion, but proposed that the two empires should co-operate in a joint programme of internal reform in Korea.   China in her turn rejected the Japanese proposal.   The diplomatic *pourparlers* were, however, nothing more than a preliminary skirmishing for a *casus belli*.   Japan was bent upon war.   "She needed a demonstration of her military prowess, so that she could convince the rest of the Powers that she was entitled to a complete recovery of her judicial and tariff autonomy." [2]

In August a transport-ship bearing more Chinese troops to Korea was stopped by Japanese orders, and since it refused to surrender was

[1] Quoted in Bau, *The Foreign Relations of China*, p. 33.
[2] Bau, *The Foreign Relations of China*, p. 32.

fired upon and sunk with nearly every Chinaman on board. Upon this incident both sides declared war.

The war lasted for nearly nine months, and by land and by sea the Japanese were overwhelmingly victorious. They were beyond comparison the better prepared. In Japan nothing was overlooked; the army of 150,000 men was efficient, well trained, regularly paid, officered by capable generals, accompanied by experts in every branch. The mobilization worked easily; ammunition and supplies were adequate; the merchant and convoy service efficient; the navy was as well equipped and as well trained as the army. In every department the organization was excellent.

The Chinese army, except for Li Hung-Chang's small regiment, was an unarmed, untrained, unpaid rabble. Her navy on paper was stronger, and the battleships were of a modern design; but the officering of both army and navy was ruined by incapable commanders, by careless provincial governors, and by the corruption [1] which prevailed in every branch, so that even the shells for some of her largest ships turned out to be wooden dummies.

In such conditions the defeat of China was inevitable, and from beginning to end of the war she had nowhere a gleam of success. By the end of September her troops had been driven from Korea and her navy defeated in the battle of the Yalu River. A Japanese army invaded Manchuria, another landed on the Liao-tung Peninsula. Kingchow and Takin fell, and in November Port Arthur, the strongest port in China, was taken.

In the beginning of the new year the Japanese crossed to Shantung, the opposite tongue of land which, with the Liao-tung Peninsula, encircled and guarded Tientsin and the approach to Peking. By the middle of February Wei-hai-wei had fallen. Other forts fell in the north; the hostile armies began to close in upon the capital.

The venerable Chinese ambassador, Li Hung-Chang, was compelled to sue for peace, which was finally concluded in April 1895 by the Treaty of Shimonoseki. By its terms China recognized the independence of Korea; she ceded to Japan the island of Formosa, the Pescadores, and the Liao-tung Peninsula, and paid a large indemnity. She admitted Japan to commercial relations on the same terms as the Western Powers,[2] and she opened four ports to trade.

[1] The apparently ineradicable corruption which stultifies Chinese political life is often attributed to the excessive exaltation of the idea of the family. The welfare of the family is raised above that of all other social groups, and for its sake a man may cheat his neighbour or defraud the State.

[2] The revised Sino-Japanese commercial treaty was to include a 'most favoured nation' clause. This clause, which was incorporated in all the Chinese treaties with the Western Powers, guaranteed that any privileges granted to one Power should be immediately extended to the others—*i.e.*, each state insisted upon enjoying the privileges granted to the 'most favoured nation.'

The Sino-Japanese War was the critical and decisive event in the modern history of the Far East, and from it followed consequences of fundamental importance. It enabled Japan to revise her own ' unequal treaties.' She had reformed her judicial code and proved her military strength. It was no longer necessary for the Powers of the West to provide exceptional safeguards for the life and property of their subjects. As far as Japan was concerned the 'unequal treaties' were quashed. The extra-territorial rights of foreign nations were abolished; tariff autonomy was restored to her—*i.e.*, the right to impose her own customs duties on exports and imports.

Secondly it revealed as nothing else had done the weakness of China. She had been defeated not by a Western Power, but by the Asiatic nation, the 'dwarfs,' whom she had for centuries despised. She had been compelled to suffer the invasion of her integrity, to surrender not only more dependencies, but a portion of her own territory. In China the revelation led on the one hand to an intense depression and a bitter resentment, on the other to a movement for reform and for the Westernization of the Manchu empire. In Europe and the West it also had its fruits. The Chinese Empire seemed to be falling to pieces; it was about to become another Africa, the booty of the Powers. Thus the idea of the partition of China gained ground; the nations began to scramble for spoil; there followed the struggle for concessions, for leased territories, for spheres of influence, which, disregarding Chinese integrity, seemed to promise only the imminent partition of the empire. There was hardly a European statesman at the end of the nineteenth century who did not forecast its total disappearance.

Thirdly the victory of 1895 stimulated Japanese imperialism on a large scale. For twenty-five years she had been nursing her ambition, forming her army, and accumulating her resources. She had tested her preparations, proved her power, achieved her immediate ambitions. In short, she had been successful, and her success led her to fresh ambitions and fresh victories. Within ten years she had engaged and defeated a European Power. Within fifteen years she had annexed the Korea, for whose independence she had nominally fought. Within little more than twenty years she had advanced still farther.

In the Sino-Japanese War Japan had proved to Europe that she was a Power to be reckoned with, that a new factor had entered into Far Eastern affairs and a new candidate appeared for Far Eastern triumphs. She had also awakened a nascent sense of danger, and the Kaiser's cartoon of the "Yellow Peril" was an early expression of an apprehension of Japanese ambition and Asiatic expansion which has grown with the years.

The Sino-Japanese War was the end of one period and the beginning of another. It ended a period marked by the further opening up of China to Western trade, by the beginning of a political onslaught upon her that resulted in the loss of nine Chinese dependencies and brought France and England to her borders on the south and south-west and Russia on the north. It was finally marked by the opening up of Japan, her swift adoption of Western engines of power, and her sharp, victorious attack upon her neighbour.

It was the beginning of a period in Far Eastern affairs which lasted to the Peace of Versailles, in 1919, a period which may be classified broadly as one of aggression upon China by the European Powers and by Japan. No single generalization, however, adequately covers the period; it was a rich tissue of inter-woven strands. In all directions the Eastern Question was broadening out, and branching into new and unforeseen developments that obscured the original growth. There were European onslaughts upon China's integrity; there were international rivalries among the Powers who were dividing up her skin; there was Russian imperialism to be guarded against, the Balance of Power to be preserved; there was Japan to be regarded, perhaps as friend, perhaps as foe, but always as competitor, and if the Powers of Europe may be said to have possessed any harmony of interests in the face of the yellow race, it was broken by the Anglo-Japanese Alliance of 1902; then there was China changing from smouldering sufferance to active protest; lastly there was the attempt, initiated by the United States, seconded by Great Britain, to substitute international co-operation for international competition, to solve with the doctrine of the 'open door' some of the acute problems that had arisen.

The Far Eastern Question, 1895-1919.

Although it is simplest to treat the development of the Far East during this period chronologically, the pattern of its history is woven about six main threads, European aggression and European rivalry, Russian ambitions and Japanese imperialism, the revolt of China and the attempt on the part of the Western Powers to substitute co-operation for competition.

The new period began with the "Three-Power Intervention," and barely had Japan negotiated the Treaty of Shimonoseki before she was forced to relinquish part of the gains it had conferred upon her. For the Japanese victories had seemed hardly more menacing to China's security than to Russia's ambitions. The cession of the Liao-tung Peninsula, with the strong ice-free harbour of Port Arthur, giving to Japan a strategic command of Peking, brought her into serious rivalry with Russia in Manchuria. "We cannot allow Japan," said Count Witte to the Tsar Nicholas II, "to quit her islands and get a firm foothold upon the Asiatic mainland. That would effectively block our Far Eastern

The "Three-Power Intervention" (1895).

policy of peaceful penetration." Upon Li Hung-Chang's appeal therefore the Tsar determined to intervene ostensibly on China's behalf. A note was dispatched from St Petersburg advising Japan "not to occupy the Liao-tung Peninsula in perpetuity," because such an occupation would "destroy the political balance in the Far East." The summons was repudiated by Great Britain, but supported by France, in the interests of the Franco-Russian alliance which was being consolidated in the West, and by the Kaiser William II, either from a sense of the "Yellow Peril," or because he wished to play a larger part in Pacific affairs, or to make a bid for Russian friendship. In view of the intervention of the three Powers Japan renounced her acquisition. The Liao-tung Peninsula and Port Arthur went back to China in return for a monetary compensation. Japan withdrew with a bitter grudge against Russia. England, who had not joined the other three Powers, found herself sharing with Japan a common apprehension of Muscovite ambitions. The seeds of the Anglo-Japanese Alliance were planted.[1]

However much the retrocession of the Liao-tung Peninsula was to conduce to Russia's advantage it had been made nominally in China's **The scramble for concessions.** interests, and the Powers now proceeded to charge their services to the account of the Chinese Empire. The Peking Government in order to pay the indemnity to Japan was compelled for the first time to have recourse to an external loan, thus inaugurating a new policy of foreign control over her finances which multiplied the bonds about her. The first loan in 1895 was **France.** secured by France and Russia. France also obtained a fresh delimitation in her favour of the boundaries between Tonkin, and China, the concession of mining privileges in Yunnan, Kwangsi, and Kwangtung, the right to extend the Annam railway into **Russia.** China, the opening of new ports. In 1896 Russia won similar privileges in Manchuria, permission to extend the trans-Siberian railway [2] through that province to Vladivostok, mining privileges, and certain military concessions which gave her the right, in case of war, to utilize Port Arthur and Kiao-chau as naval bases. It was a dangerous 'ear-marking' of Chinese territory, and it was obvious that the Dual Alliance had secured a strong position in the north and south of China. Great Britain was disturbed, and Germany reminded herself that alone of the three Powers of the tripartite intervention she had received no reward for her support of China.

In 1897 two German Catholic missionaries were murdered in Shan-

[1] Joseph Chamberlain talked of an Anglo-Japanese alliance in 1898.
[2] The trans-Siberian was rapidly becoming to Russia what the Bagdad railway was to Germany.

tung; Germany thereupon seized Kiao-chau and presented her terms.
A treaty was signed which gave her the lease of Kiao-chau for ninety-
nine years, full jurisdiction within the leased territory, a   Germany.
neutral zone of fifty kilometres outside it in which she
was to have the right of free passage for her armies, concessions for
two railways in Shantung, and the first option on any undertaking in
that province in which foreign assistance was needed.   It signified an
enormous extension of power, and opened a new stage of assault
upon the sovereignty and integrity of China.   The other countries
of the West took immediate alarm.   They could not invoke the
principle of the Balance of Power to compel Germany to disgorge
her gain; they therefore invoked it to justify similar encroachments
on their own account.   They demanded 'compensation,' and a
scramble for concessions began, at the end of which the strongest
points of the Chinese Empire were in European hands.

At the end of 1897 Russia, alleging that Great Britain was about to
anticipate her, seized Port Arthur and Talienwan and demanded a
lease of them, which was granted.   She stipulated that Port   Russia.
Arthur was to be a closed port, accessible only to Chinese
and Russian ships, and she obtained further railway concessions.
France thereupon demanded a lease of Kwang-Chouan and the right
to build a railway from Tonkin and Yunnan, and—for a   France.
distinct ingenuity was shown in finding new handles—she
requested that a French representative should be appointed to the
head of the Chinese Post Office.   All these demands were granted
in 1898.   In the interests of the Balance of Power Great   Great
Britain entered into the competition.   In 1897, in return   Britain.
for France's gains in Tonkin, England had secured a revision of her
Burmese boundaries.   She now asked for the extension of her Hong-
Kong territory, for the opening of inland waterways to steamboat
traffic, and for the lease of Wei-hai-wei "for as long a period as Port
Arthur shall remain in Russian occupation," thus showing very clearly
the direction of her distrust.   As a counter-move to France's control
of the Post Office she stipulated that the Inspector-General of Maritime Customs should be a Briton as long as British trade predominated.

Even Italy put in a claim for a naval base, although "no Italian
missionary had been murdered," but she came too late.   A Court
revolution had placed the control of Chinese affairs in the hands of the
Dowager Empress, Tse Hsi, "Old Buddha," as she was called, a
master-mind of the age.   Tse Hsi determined to show no more
weakness, and ordered the Yangtse viceroys to prepare to resist the
Italian demands.   Thereupon Italy withdrew.

The Powers also secured from China what were known as " declarations of non-alienation," by which the Celestial Empire agreed not to

2 ʳ

'alienate' certain districts from certain European Powers. In other words, the Powers established 'spheres of influence,' or a priority of claims within certain areas of the Chinese Empire. France in this way marked off Hainan and the territory bordering on Tonkin, Great Britain the Yangtse valley, Japan Fukien,[1] while Germany claimed implied priority in Shantung, and Russia in Manchuria, Mongolia, and Chinese Turkestan.

Then there followed an international scramble for the construction and control of strategic railways, for the economic, military, and financial power they would convey. Russia, France, Germany, and Great Britain had already secured certain concessions. They now strove to outdo each other in obtaining further grants. The crucial struggle was concerned with the Peking-Hankow line, which was to connect the Chinese capital with the Yangtse valley. Great Britain, the United States, and Belgium (supported by France and Russia) all contended for the line, but Belgium, with the support of the Dual Alliance, won the concession. Great Britain, much chagrined, demanded compensation against the "overturning of the Balance of Power," and by a naval demonstration she secured a number of important mining and railway concessions. The America-China Development Company had also to be compensated, then Russia and France and Germany. Thus the round of European encroachments went on. China was being parcelled out among the Powers; her strongest forts had been seized; her external trade and her tariffs were under foreign control; and her finances and her internal organization were beginning to fall into foreign hands; the railway lines across her surface were financed and often run by foreign Powers. Her sovereignty seemed to be totally disregarded; and it is hardly to be wondered at that Chinese and Europeans alike should have held the policy of 'spheres of influence' to be nothing more than a mask for partition.

Railways.

Nevertheless China has not been partitioned among the Western Powers, and to-day, if the signs of the times can be read, such a fate is more remote than ever. Three developments arose out of the international scramble, out of the revelation which had been given of European aggression and European rivalry, which were to modify considerably the sequence of Far Eastern affairs. They were the 'open door' doctrine, the Boxer riots, and the Anglo-Japanese Alliance of 1902.

The United States had for some years, owing to a number of actions, been regarded by China as her best friend among the Western Powers.[2] From 1844 the United States had taken a full part in the

[1] And in 1915 Shantung.

[2] To some Chinese, on the other hand, the economic exploitation of China by America seems as dangerous as the political onslaughts of other Powers. In some Chinese quarters, moreover, America has given great disappointment, and won a reputation for giving fair promises unsupported by action. Two among other

opening up of China to trade.   She had not engaged in battle against her,[1] but she had been one of the first countries to enter into treaty relations with the Peking Government after the Opium War, and she had shared in the advantages won by the conflict of 1858–60.   She had secured the same commercial and diplomatic privileges as the other countries.   She possessed extra-territorial, tariff, and 'most favoured nation' rights, like the European Powers.   In 1871 she had forced Korea to open her harbours by a military demonstration, and, as has already been shown, her invitation to Japan was presented by eight warships.   Thus she had fully entered into the competition for the trade of the East, and she had used force, or at least a display of force, to gain her purpose. However, not only had she used force sparingly, but she had made no advances upon China outside the realm of commerce and the judicial and consular safeguards which at the time seemed necessary to it. She had not joined the scramble for concessions, or for 'spheres of influence,' she had annexed no dependency, and her contest for railway grants was purely a commercial proposition.   In short, the policy of the United States in China centred consistently then and since in the pursuit of trade.

The 'open door' doctrine.

The international scramble for concessions, however, and the appropriating of 'spheres of influence' placed her in a difficult position.   In 1898 she had just concluded her war with Spain, which had brought her for the first time in her history a dependency or colony outside her own continent.   The colony, the Philippine Islands, was, moreover, in the East Pacific, well within the Sino-Japanese area.   To many it seemed as if the United States had embarked upon a course of imperialism, and had appropriated a vantage-point for an attack upon China as good as Annam to France, Burma to England, or Primorsk [2] to Russia.   Serious opposition, however, had already been raised in America to so violent a departure from traditional policy as the

instances are commonly quoted : (1) In 1868 Burlingame, the United States Minister at Peking, undertook a mission to Europe to induce more friendly relations between China and the West.   He succeeded in persuading the United States of America to conclude a treaty in which the contracting parties " cordially recognize the interest and inalienable right of man to change his home and allegiance, and also the mutual advantages of the free immigration and emigration of their citizens and subjects respectively from one country to the other for the purposes of curiosity or trade, or as permanent residents.   The High Contracting Parties therefore join in repudiating any other than an entirely voluntary emigration for these purposes." China thinks it inconsistent that the United States of America should have subsequently excluded Chinese immigrants from America.   (2) In 1917 China declared war upon Germany, largely trusting in repeated American declarations of the " rights of nationality," etc.   But in 1919 the United States of America supported the appropriation of Shantung by Japan.

[1] Her ships had advanced to the Taku forts in 1858, but had not taken part in the assault.

[2] The province between the Usuri River and the coast.

annexation of the Philippine Islands had involved, and it was clear that the acquisition of territorial interests in China would not be endorsed by the general will of the republic. On the other hand, with every step taken by the European Powers to tighten their hold upon portions of China it grew more likely that a Power without a territorial interest might speedily be excluded altogether from the empire. The French in Kwangsi, the Japanese in Fukien, the British in the Yangtse valley, the Russians in Manchuria, might easily adopt hostile tariff policies directed against all outside trade, and the United States would thereby be deprived of her markets in China. Therefore America tried to secure a railway concession; therefore she enunciated the 'open door' doctrine. In September 1899 John Hay, Secretary of State to McKinley, dispatched a circular Note to London, Berlin, and St Petersburg, and in November to Tokio, Rome, and Paris, urging the Powers to make a formal declaration in favour of equal opportunity for trade for all nations, of uniform tariffs and harbour dues, which should not discriminate in favour of one nation as against another; and thirdly he pressed them to guarantee the maintenance of the Chinese treaty tariff and the Chinese collection of customs. In other words, Hay required a declaration of an 'open door' policy, that the Powers in their 'spheres of influence' would maintain an open market or an undiscriminating tariff toward all nations.[1]

It was the doors of the Powers, not the doors of China, that were in question. The Celestial Empire had been compelled by force to open her doors to those very Powers who were now proceeding to close their doors against each other. America's demand cannot be regarded as other than self-interested; it undoubtedly recognized, moreover, in its first statement the 'spheres of influence.' But it contained a protest, implied at first, and later definitely formulated, against the dismemberment and appropriation of the Chinese Empire. On the one hand it was a plea for international co-operation, on the other a guarantee of Chinese integrity. "This Government is animated by a sincere desire," so ran the American Note,

that the interests of our citizens might not be prejudiced through exclusive treatment by any of the controlling Powers within their so-called ' spheres of influence ' in China, and hopes also to retain there an open market for the commerce of the world, remove dangerous sources of international irritation, and hasten thereby united and concerted action of the Powers at Peking in favour of the administrative reforms so urgently needed for strengthening the Imperial Government and maintaining the integrity of China, in which the whole Western world is alike concerned.

---

[1] Britain has held the 'open door' policy for half a century.

To this Note all the Powers addressed gave an affirmative answer, as far as the principle was concerned, except Russia, who was significantly silent on the question of the uniformity of harbour and railroad charges. Great Britain in particular had much the same interest in the question as the United States, for although she had, in self-defence, embarked upon a territorial policy in China, she had no wish to acquire new colonial burdens in the Pacific. She too desired to pursue trade rather than empire.

A new principle of co-operation had therefore been affirmed, partly as a remedy against the evils of excessive international competition, partly as a reaction against a crude policy of European encroachment. In China too a protest had been brewing against the same policy.

The Boxer movement was primarily a revolt against the foreigner; it was also partly an Imperial device to preserve the Manchu dynasty. For while there had sprung up on the one hand an intense hatred of the European and a desire for his expulsion, there had been accumulating on the other hand a mood of revolt against the Manchu dynasty, which had by its incompetence and corruption brought the Western degradation upon the Chinese Empire, and which was after all in itself a foreign dynasty that had conquered China in the seventeenth century. Out of the desire to crush or divert the latter antagonism the Dowager Empress determined to exploit the former.

The Boxer Rebellion (1900).

From the Second Chinese War the Protestant and Catholic missionaries of England, France, and Germany had been the object of native hatred. They were distrusted as precursors of political encroachments; they were accused of arrogating to themselves positions and powers to which they had no right, of protecting Christian converts in native courts of justice, of assuming official insignia, and of overstepping their proper sphere. Everywhere, too, the popular charge was brought against them of abducting and murdering children, based, as far as it had any basis whatever, on the fact that foundling children were sometimes brought to their stations. About the time that Mr Burlingame, the United States Minister to Peking, was conducting a mission to persuade Europe and America of the reforming intentions and general friendliness of China, a number of anti-missionary barbarities was showing the nature and intensity of local Chinese feeling. But since a riot was always used by a Western Government to secure further protection and further privileges for its subjects [1] the missionaries did not die in vain.

Previous anti-Western feeling.

---

[1] The advantage was twofold : (1) an 'atrocity' afforded an occasion for demanding reparation from China ; (2) it also provided an excellent political argument to convince hostile critics at home that a 'forward' policy in China was advisable.

The Boxer movement was, however, more than a spasmodic outburst against a local missionary; it was a larger revolt against the whole policy of contact with the West; as far as the north of China was concerned, it may be called national; it was supported by people in high places; it arose during the nineties as the product of three causes—the defeat of China by Japan, the European scramble for concessions, and the Westernizing policy of the Emperor Kwang-Su.

In comparison with Japan, China had remained impervious to Western civilization. In the last quarter of the nineteenth century she had begun to appreciate the advantages of some of its material products. Telegraph and railway lines had begun to be built, the navy and a few fortifications had been remodelled, but apart from a few tentative proposals for the abolition of Chinese examinations and an attempt on the part of one or two foreign societies to spread Western literature, no serious move had been made toward the modification of the Chinese national outlook until the last decade of the nineteenth century.

After the 'degradation' of the Sino-Japanese War a powerful "Young China" movement sprang up in the southern and middle parts of the empire, directed on the one side toward reform and Westernization, on the other toward the overthrow of the Manchu dynasty, "with its benighted conceptions and barbaric leanings." There was a suddenly increased demand for foreign books; fifteen hundred young men of good family presented themselves at the foreign university at Peking; foreign schools and reform societies were founded. The Emperor himself was won over to their point of view, and within a few months a succession of Imperial edicts threatened to revolutionize China as drastically as Japan. The ancient system of examination in the Chinese Classics was abolished; schools were to be set up, a department founded for the translation of foreign literature; scions of the Manchu race as well as the Chinese were to be encouraged to study sciences and travel abroad; a number of useless offices were abolished; even the men's queue, one of the most treasured national features, was threatened.

The Westernizing movement

The result was to arouse a speedy reaction, which took the form of a violent hostility to foreign influences, headed and encouraged by all the vested interests which were affected by the Emperor's reforming edicts. The whole latent force of conservatism and superstition was brought into play. Sacred and religious instincts had been violated; the burial mounds, which render uneconomic so much Chinese land, had been disturbed by the laying of railways; a fire in the Palace was interpreted as the vengeance of the gods.

causes an anti-foreign reaction.

The Dowager Empress Tse Hsi [1] saw her opportunity for reviving her own power and bringing the Manchu dynasty into popularity. By a *coup d'état* she took possession of the Emperor Kwang-Su, and compelled him to publish an edict restoring her regency. She then proceeded to put herself at the head of the anti-reform and anti-foreign movement; the edicts were cancelled, the associations were dissolved, newspapers suppressed. The mustering reaction gathered strength; attacks on foreigners began to multiply, and by the end of 1899 the popular attitude was so menacing that the foreign Legations in Peking appealed for protection. The anti-foreign movement gained its particular violence from the adherence of secret societies, the Society of the Big Sword, the Righteous Fraternity of Fist-fighters, or, as it is better known, the Boxer Society. These secret organizations seem to have been merely groups of malcontents, but the Empress's patronage of the anti-foreign reaction deflected what might have been a revolutionary movement against the Manchu throne into an attack upon the Western Powers, and the banners of the Boxers bore the legend "Exterminate the foreigner and save the dynasty."

In the meantime the Powers protested to the Tsungli-Yâmen and the Imperial Government against the growing frequency of the attacks upon their subjects. But the Tsungli-Yâmen held them up in endless negotiations, and nothing was done.

The movement culminated in June and July 1900 in the incidents of murder, pillage, and incendiarism common to such outbursts of popular violence. Peking and, to a smaller extent, Tientsin were given over to the rioters. In the capital the soldiers joined the Boxers, and the Manchus openly lent their support. Foreigners and native Christians were alike attacked. The German Minister and the Chancellor of the Japanese Legation were among the murdered. Most of the Europeans of the capital took refuge in the Legations, where for six weeks they held out against the Chinese mob, until, in a desperate situation, with food and ammunition at an end, they were at last relieved by an international force dispatched by seven nations,[2] which fought its way through to their help. After the arrival of European troops [3] order was again imposed both upon the Chinese and upon the foreign soldiers, who,

Suppressed by an international force.

[1] When the young Emperor came of age she had been forced to retire (although she had, in fact, retained a great deal of power) with the title of " Tse-hsi-tuan-yu-k'ang-hsi-chao-yu-chuang-shou-king-chin-hsien-chung-hsi-Huang-Tsi-Hou "— *i.e.*, " Kind, auspicious, correct, protecting, strong, deep, bright, satisfied, sedate, sincere, long-lived, revered, respected, ingratiating, noble, splendid Imperial Empress."

[2] British, Russians, French, Germans, Italians, Americans, and Japanese.

[3] At the end of September a German Expeditionary Force of 20,000 arrived under Field-Marshal Count von Waldersee, who by virtue of his rank assumed command of the combined forces.

having got out of hand, had wreaked a terrible vengeance upon the capital.

The Chinese Government had no defence to offer for what had arisen largely through its own actions. The Dowager Empress and the Court fled from Peking. The attempt to exterminate the foreigner had failed, and China had put herself in the wrong; she stood arraigned as a criminal before the bar of the nations for a breach of international law. Her fate was in the hands of the Powers.

There was never a better opportunity for the partition of the Chinese Empire. But partition introduced too many problems. What would be the position of America, what of Japan? In July 1900 Hay again affirmed the principles of the 'open door' policy, and proclaimed that the United States would maintain the integrity of China. But a more serious step was taken in this direction when in October 1900 Great Britain and Germany signed an agreement "not to make use of the present complications to obtain for themselves any territorial advantages in the Chinese dominions," to uphold the 'open door' at the treaty ports, and to consult together on the steps to be taken if any other Power should try "to obtain in any form whatever such territorial advantages."

There is no doubt that this treaty offered the first genuine guarantee of Chinese integrity. Partition was thus avoided, but the Powers **Terms of** demanded a heavy reparation. Normal relations were **reparation.** resumed again only on condition that China paid a huge indemnity [1] secured on the customs duties; that she agreed to the establishment of a foreign garrison in North China, on the Peking-Tientsin Railway, and of foreign guards in the Legations; that she consented to a revision of the commercial treaties, and to the reform of the Tsungli-Yâmen, or Foreign Office.

The suppression of the riots and the conduct of the negotiations had been obstructed by a good deal of international jealousy and rivalry. In particular, Russia, annoyed by the Anglo-German agreement, and hoping to secure more for herself by independent negotiation, presented serious obstacles.

The direction of Russian ambition has already been indicated. In fifty years she had established strongholds in Manchuria, Outer Mon- **Russian** golia, and Eastern Turkestan, sometimes by peaceful pene- **policy.** tration, sometimes by military conquest, more often by posing as China's friend and securing a reward for an alleged service. She had brought her boundaries to the Amur River and to the frontiers of Korea, and she had prepared the ground for the appropriation of Manchuria. Recognizing a rival in Japan, she had turned the latter

---

[1] Over £67,000,000, in addition to special reparations for the murder of the Japanese Chancellor of Legation and the German Minister.

Power out of the Liao-tung Peninsula in 1895, only to occupy Port Arthur herself in 1897. She had secured the concession of her trans-Siberian railway through Manchuria to Vladivostok and to Port Arthur, and from 1895, largely owing to the support of Li Hung-Chang, she had won precedence over all the other Powers at the Court of Peking. The Boxer riots offered her an invaluable opportunity for the furtherance of her ambitions. Using a demonstration of anti-Russian feeling as an excuse, she overran Manchuria, and then, as she had done before, tried to secure a recognition of her position there by undertaking to intervene with the Powers on China's behalf. She managed, for example, to prevent the question of the Dowager Empress's responsibility from being raised. In return she demanded what amounted to a military protectorate over Manchuria, and Sino-Russian negotiations were set on foot to this end. The proposed concession roused, however, so strong a protest from the Powers that China was induced to withhold it, and Russia, complaining that her generous intentions had been misunderstood, withdrew her demands.

The result of Russia's move was to drive the two Powers who most feared her ambitions into each other's arms, and in 1902 the Anglo-Japanese Alliance was signed. The signatories affirmed the principle of the 'open door,' and agreed that if either Power was attacked by two enemies at once the other would come to its aid. Renewed in 1905 and 1911,[1] on terms **The Anglo-Japanese Alliance (1902).** which first permitted and then sanctioned the Japanese annexation of Korea, the treaty lasted until it was superseded by the " Four-Power " agreement in 1923. The alliance has often been denounced, especially in China and America, as a mischievous element in Far Eastern affairs. It was the first time that an Eastern empire had been admitted on equal terms to a European alliance, and it gave Japan a standing that no Oriental state had attained before.[2] On that foundation Japan has built her subsequent policy of imperialism, which has certainly come to be the supreme menace to the peace of the Far East. On the other hand, although the alliance was framed by Lord Lansdowne primarily to check Russian ambition, its intention was also to limit the war between Russia and Japan which was obviously brewing in the East.

Its first result, however, was undoubtedly to precipitate the Russo-Japanese crisis which was expected, and by preventing France, under threat of war with England, from coming to Russia's help it gave to Japan the predominance at sea which made her victorious. **The Russo-Japanese War (1904–5).**

On the conclusion of the Anglo-Japanese Alliance Russia, realizing her peril, had agreed to withdraw her troops from Manchuria, in three

[1] In the meantime Britain had composed her quarrel with Russia in 1907.
[2] Though an obvious comparison is suggested with the Franco-Turkish alliance of the sixteenth century.

stages, at intervals of six months. It soon appeared, however, that she had no intention of relaxing her hold upon the country. At the first stage of evacuation she merely concentrated her troops in another part of Manchuria; at the second she refused to withdraw her forces, and presented to China seven articles in which she demanded satisfaction. They included the non-alienation of Manchuria and the closing of that province to the economic enterprise of any nation but Russia. The Powers protested; China, in fear alike of the Powers on the one side and Russia on the other, prevaricated. In August 1903 a through railway service was opened between Moscow and Port Arthur, and a Russian viceroyalty of the Far East was created which in effect claimed Manchuria as a Russian province. Russian troops were also sent across the Yalu River into Korea, under cover of a licence to cut timber. At this point Japan intervened. She demanded from Russia among other things a mutual undertaking to respect the integrity of China and Korea, an affirmation of the 'open door' principle, a reciprocal acknowledgment of Japanese interests in Korea and Russian interests in Manchuria. To these proposals Russia would give only a one-sided adherence. She insisted on retaining a free hand for herself in Manchuria, while imposing upon Japan serious restrictions in Korea. She therefore practically proclaimed her intention of appropriating Manchuria to herself,[1] an appropriation which would give her a position of advantage in relation to Korea.

She seems to have counted upon Japanese compliance in spite of the English alliance. Japan, however, resolved to choose the issue of war, and in February 1904, after no less than ten draft treaties had been discussed, she broke off negotiations and entered on her first conflict with a European nation.

The war yielded the unprecedented result of the defeat of the European Power at the hands of the Oriental, who fifty years before had been fighting in chain armour with bows and arrows. In resources and size the two belligerents were ill-matched, out of all proportion, and as far as the land campaigns are concerned the war gives the impression of a pigmy hammering upon a giant, and keeping him back by sheer courage and skill. There was the battle of the Yalu River in May 1904, the nine days' battle of Liao-Yang in August, the ten days' desperate struggle of the Sha-ho in October, the long siege

---

[1] Dr Bau quotes the following letter to President Roosevelt from John Hay, May 12, 1903: "I have intimated to Cassini [a Russian agent] that the inevitable result of the present course of aggression would be the seizure by the different Powers of different provinces in China, and the accomplishment of the dismemberment of the Empire. He shouts in reply, 'This is already done, China is dismembered, and we are entitled to our share.'" See *The Foreign Relations of China*, pp. 102–103.

of Port Arthur, and the terrific culminating battle, across a front 140 miles wide, of Mukden in February 1905. They were all Japanese victories, but in most cases the victors were too exhausted to follow up their success. Port Arthur surrendered to the Japanese while there was still a three months' supply of food and plenty of ammunition in the town. After Mukden the land situation was at a deadlock; Japan with the will to win had not the resources; Russia with the resources had not the necessary triumphant purpose.

The decisive event of the war—as far as any event may be held decisive where the stronger Power fell to pieces of its own inherent weakness—was fought on the sea. Russia possessed two squadrons in the Pacific, one at Port Arthur, the other at Vladivostok. Japan's object was to keep the two sections apart, and in spite of Russian sallies she was generally successful in this aim. In October, however, the Russian Baltic fleet, which had been preparing all the summer, set sail for the East, and, after an encounter with some English trawlers on the Dogger Bank which almost brought England into the war against Russia, it reached the China Sea in May 1905. It proceeded to make for Vladivostok by way of the Straits of Tsushima, between Japan and Korea. There the Japanese admiral, Togo, was lying in wait for it, and on May 18 it was defeated and scattered. Tsushima Two-thirds of its ships were sunk, six captured, four only (May 1905). managed to reach Vladivostok, while the rest of the fleet took refuge in neutral ports. There had been no such naval victory since Trafalgar. The breaking up of the Baltic fleet brought the end of the war, and the mediation of the American President was accepted. A few more points were scored by Japan before the actual terms were signed in August at Portsmouth, New Hampshire. By the The Treaty peace Russia ceded to Japan the lease of Liao-tung and her of Portsice-free harbour of Port Arthur, together with the southern mouth half of the Russian railway to Port Arthur; she surrendered (August 1905). the southern half of Sakhalin, which she had annexed in 1875; she promised to evacuate Manchuria, which was restored to China, and she recognized Japanese influence in Korea. No indemnity was paid.

The smallness of the gains, and particularly the loss of an indemnity to cover the expenses of the war, roused great indignation in Japan, who had put forth her utmost strength and had apparently secured a number of brilliant victories. The Japanese leaders knew well enough, however, how heavy were the odds against them. Japan had shown a courage, a strategic skill, a tenacity, and a power of preparation which justified her victory and the pride her victory gave her. But Russia had been her own enemy. She was unwieldy and divided. She misunderstood the character and the resources of the nation against her. Had not one authority pronounced that "Far Eastern affairs were decided in Europe"? In spite of the Moscow-Manchurian Railway, whose effectiveness Japan herself undervalued, her base was far removed from the theatre of war. She was, above all, weakened by division, by revolution among her people, by lack of cohesion and contradictory policies among her leaders.

In Russia, in Japan, in China, in Europe also, the Russo-Japanese War produced its effects. It checked for a time the Far Eastern advance of the Romanov empire, and recalled the Tsar once again to the Balkans and Near Eastern affairs. At home it precipitated the internal revolution in Russia which had long been brewing.

To Japan the result of the war had been a matter of life and death. Had she been defeated her ambitions, her previous achievements, her whole policy, would have been ruined. Her victory gave her the succession to Russia in South Manchuria, an immense prestige, and a special position in relation to China; it gave her the lead in the Far East. From that date she entered openly into competition and rivalry with the European Powers in China, and embarked upon a blatant imperialism which led her to annex Korea in 1910, to seize Shantung, and put forward the "Twenty-one Demands" during the Great War, and generally to enunciate theories and conceive a policy which have made her the supreme problem of the Pacific entanglement.

In China the war gave a double impetus, on the one side to the Western nations, who resumed, with Japan as their serious rival, the struggle for opportunities and powers, who wrangled over railways and loans, who struggled to outdo each other, until once again they were forced to a policy of co-operation as the only alternative to a mutual destruction. On the other hand it gave a profound impetus to the awakening of China. Ten years before, the Sino-Japanese War of 1894–95, together with the international scramble for concessions, had led to the Boxer riots; the Russo-Japanese War and the second period of European encroachments received its answer in the Chinese Revolution of 1911.

The Chinese Revolution can be regarded in a double perspective. Chinese history is made up of a succession of dynasties, each of which reigns for a time, falls, and after a period of disorder is followed by another. Perhaps the overthrow of the Manchu dynasty in 1911 should be put into line with the fall of the Mings, the Yuens, the Sungs, and many others, and the period of disorder which has existed in China from 1911 until the present day viewed simply as a preamble to an establishment of another Imperial dynasty, which in its turn will reign for a time and pass away. The Manchu dynasty was obviously in a decadent state; its corruption and incompetence had brought disaster to China—and in China, however sacred the person of the Emperor may be, there is no right divine to

The Chinese Revolution (1911).

govern badly; only the personality of the Dowager Empress Tse Hsi had kept the dynasty on the throne, and when she died in 1908 its fall was certain. In 1900 she had skilfully directed the threatened attack from her dynasty to the foreigners by leading the cause of reaction; in 1906, seeing the stimulus which the Russo-Japanese War had given to the national discontent, she made another attempt to ward off danger, this time by leading the cause of reform. She modernized the army, converted temples into schools, abolished again the old examinations, and amended the form of government; she even promised a Parliamentary constitution, and while she was alive she succeeded in realizing her aim. It was not until after her death that the dynasty fell.

On the other hand it is obvious that certain factors entered into the Chinese Revolution which entirely falsify any parallels which may be suggested with previous episodes of Chinese history, or with the state of India in the eighteenth century after the decay of the Mogul Empire. In one sense the Revolution of 1911 was to China what the Restoration of 1867 was to Japan—a signal of her awakening and of her transition from a passive to an active existence. It was an announcement to the world that she had begun to take her own affairs into her own hands. For two features of the movement must be emphasized; it was reforming and it was essentially nationalist—that is to say, in so far as the revolutionary movement is represented by the Kuoming-tang, or republican party. For since the fall of the dynasty Chinese history has at times appeared to be nothing but a welter of interests and a bewilderment of names. Undoubtedly the issues have been confounded by the personal ambitions of certain leaders; undoubtedly also the political confusion has been exploited by foreign Powers, but the republican party of 1911, the party which all along has gained its chief support from the South, is the Kuoming-tang, the creation of Dr Sun Yat Sen. From 1895 Dr Sun, or Sun Wen, as he is called in China, was a revolutionary. He it was who succeeded in turning the anti-Manchu Revolution of 1911 into a republican movement, and he was elected the first President of the Chinese Republic. In 1912, however, he resigned his presidency to an Imperial general, Yuan Shih-kai, in the hope that republican unity would be sooner established under Yuan, the 'strong man,' than under himself.[1] To Sun Wen's disappointment Yuan Shih-kai began to turn his power to his own advantage, and, gaining the support of the foreign Powers by offering to guarantee the 'unequal treaties,' he set about the founding of a new dynasty. He had actually been declared Emperor before his death in 1916.

Dr Sun therefore began again the reorganization of a hostile

Sun Yat Sen and the republican party.

[1] Sun Yat Sen was also a Christian.

republican party, and until the end of his life in 1925 he kept up in the South the fight for republican principles, sometimes against the imperialists, sometimes against war lords, who wished to carve empires for themselves out of the general confusion. Dr Sun was not a practical man, nor skilful in co-operation; he was unfortunate in his choice of generals, and he did not achieve in his lifetime the success he desired. But he kept alive the cause by his simple faith and ardent purpose; he gave it an organization, a leader, and, in Communist Russia, an ally, and he provided it with a political faith.[1] After his death, under the leadership of Chiang Kai-Shek, Sun Wen's pupil, the Kuoming-tang began a forward advance from Canton. By 1928 it had captured, with the help of the U.S.S.R., Hankow, Nanking, Shanghai, and Peking, and seemed to have achieved some sort of national unity round the new capital of Nanking.

The fullest exposition of the republican party's faith has been given by Dr Sun himself.[2] It is based on "the three principles of salvation of our country," nationalism, democracy, and socialism—a nationalism based upon faith, self-confidence, and organization, pointing to "peace and internationalism rather than imperialism," but demanding as a *sine qua non* the abrogation of the 'unequal treaties' and equal rights with Powers of the West; democracy in internal affairs, with a representative Government and popular rights;[3] socialism directed toward economic protection, social amelioration, and the encouragement of agricultural and industrial enterprise.

The Chinese Revolution and the ensuing struggle of the Kuoming-tang party introduced many modifications into the Chinese problem. It was followed in three years by the Great War. Together these two factors have altered the whole *status quo* of the Western Powers and have laid China open to the advances of her two neighbours, Russia and Japan. Russia immediately seized the opportunity of the revolution to detach Outer Mongolia from China and set it up as a buffer state under her own military and economic control (1912–14). The other Powers tried to meet the situation and bolster up the weak republican Government by foreign loans, wrangling among themselves for that control which creditorship endows. But the Great War diverted the energies and finance of both Russia and the Western Powers to other fields and gave Japan her chance. The coincidence of disunion in China and war in Europe was Japan's supreme opportunity.

[1] Even after his death Dr Sun's power survived; he left a political will which is regarded by the Kuoming-tang as a sacred political testament.
[2] See *The International Development of China, Three Principles of a People*, etc.
[3] This was abandoned in favour of a one-party rule, professedly adopted for a temporary period during which China was to be prepared for democratic government.

Her first action was, as an ally of Great Britain, to declare war on Germany on August 23, 1914, to send troops to Shantung, to seize Kiao-chau and the German concessions, to occupy the railway from Tsingtao to Tsinan,[1] and to take over the German mining properties along its length. Under cover of war with Germany, she had to China's great indignation violated Chinese neutrality and firmly installed herself in Shantung.

Japanese imperialism and the Great War.

She then presented to China in January 1915 one of the most extraordinary documents in the history of the Far East, the famous "Twenty-one Demands." They were conveyed secretly by night in a personal visit of the Japanese Minister to the Chinese President, Yuan Shih-kai. Every effort was made to conceal their contents from the Powers, but they leaked out. The "Twenty-one Demands" consisted of five groups. The first group related to Shantung, the second to Manchuria and Eastern Inner Mongolia, the third to certain coal and iron concessions, the fourth was a simple and comprehensive demand for the non-alienation of all Chinese gulfs, harbours, and coasts, and the fifth, consisting of six articles, demanded the appointment of Japanese advisers, the purchase of Japanese munitions, the privilege of religious propaganda, police control, and an economic preference, amounting in Fukien to practical dominance.

The " Twenty-one Demands " (1915).

The magnitude of these demands can be readily realized, and pressure of two kinds was brought upon Yuan Shih-kai to accept them. In the first place he was offered 'promotion,' political support for his own imperial schemes; in the second he was threatened with war. On May 7 an ultimatum was presented to China, drafted suggestively on paper watermarked with Dreadnoughts and machine-guns. Yuan Shih-kai therefore accepted the first four groups, giving to Japan all Germany's rights in Shantung, with an added railway concession, completing the Japanese control of Southern Manchuria, granting large coal and iron concessions, and promising the non-alienation of China's coasts. The fifth group, which, as a Chinese writer expresses it, would be "sealing the political annihilation of China," was to be put aside for further consideration.

Japan's gains were enormous, achieved at one blow during the preoccupation of the Powers. Yuan Shih-kai's profit consisted in the founding of the Hung Shien [2] dynasty, which, however, only lasted one year, for the first emperor died in a fit of anger within a year of his promotion. But the treaty, such as it was, has never been accepted by China or the Chinese people.

It was the outcome of a private deal between Yuan Shih-kai and Japan.

---

[1] Replacing not Germans, but Chinese. Tsinan is the capital city of Shantung.
[2] Yuan Shih-kai took the name of Hung Shien.

From a legal point of view it has never been passed by Parliament, and therefore cannot be enforced; from the practical point of view Yuan Shih-kai had at this time already become a criminal traitor to the Chinese Republic, and had no claim to represent the people, who at that time regarded Japan with a universal and bitter hatred.[1]

Perhaps the cleverest part of the Japanese negotiations, however, was still to follow. Those sections of Japan's demands which concerned the rights and possessions of Germany in China stood in a class by themselves, and could only be dealt with by all the Allied Powers. China, for her part, recognized Japan by the treaty as the heir of Germany in Shantung, but the Allies held the view that the final decision on such matters should await the end of the War. Japan therefore set herself to secure separate pledges from the chief Powers confirming her in her demands upon Shantung. The first opportunity came in the spring of 1917, when the Allies, in desperate straits to protect their merchant shipping from German submarine attacks, asked for reinforcements from Japan. Japan agreed to supply the ships [2] on condition that England, France, and Italy would promise to support her claim to Shantung at the Peace Conference. Similarly at the end of 1917 she made with the United States the Lansing-Ishii agreement, in which America recognized "that territorial propinquity creates special relations between countries," and that Japan "has therefore special interests in China"; in other words, the United States was committed to the Japanese claim upon Shantung.[3]

The situation was, however, seriously embarrassed by China's declaration of war against Germany on August 14, 1917. Although Yuan Shih-kai had made a bid for Allied favour by offering to enter the War in 1915—an offer which had been refused by Great Britain and Japan—Chinese sentiment was itself divided on the question. It was largely on the lead of America and on the appeal of President Wilson's circular Note to the neutral states that China broke off relations with Germany.

Her entry into the War was viewed with disfavour by Japan, in fear of what concessions the Allies might grant to her, although Japan had already made her own terms. No specific conditions were actually made between China and the Allies, although the latter undertook to consider the former's claims, to suspend the Boxer indemnity payments, and to revise the customs tariff. Nevertheless the speeches of Allied statesmen in England and America aroused in China full hopes

---

[1] Such is the point of view of a Chinese Nationalist, a follower of Dr Sun.
[2] Japan's part in the War was mainly confined to convoy service. The number of Japanese killed in the War was 300, compared with a total of over 20,000,000 killed or permanently disabled on both sides.
[3] This agreement was subsequently cancelled in 1923, but it had served its purpose.

that the Powers would relinquish their privileges, while President Wilson's "Fourteen Points" seemed to promise her "self-determination."

Then came the Peace Conference of Paris. The Japanese delegation naturally presented its claim for Shantung. The Chinese representatives [1] demanded the restoration of Shantung to China, **The Peace** the abolition of extra-territoriality and tariff autonomy, the **Conference** cancellation of foreign 'spheres of influence,' the with- **of Paris.** drawal of foreign troops, of foreign postal and telegraph officers, of foreign concessions. On all sides China received only disappointment. With regard to Shantung, Great Britain, France, and Italy were already pledged to support Japan; President Wilson, who declared himself ignorant of the Lansing-Ishii agreement, was induced to cast his vote on the same side by Japan's threat to stand out from the League of Nations if she were not satisfied.

So the German rights in Shantung went to Japan. The other demands of China were put aside as not relevant to the **China's** discussion. The Chinese delegates departed practically **disappoint-** empty-handed, refusing to sign the treaty, and China, out- **ment.** witted and betrayed, gave herself over in bitterness to a more violent nationalism.

The Peace Treaty of Versailles in 1919 ended the period which began with the Sino-Japanese War of 1894–95. It marked the peak of the first era of Japanese imperialist expansion.

Since the Peace of Versailles the Pacific problem has grown increasingly acute and increasingly urgent.[2] It may be said **The Far** to present four main aspects, in the establishment of the **Eastern** Kuoming-tang party as the leading power in China, in the **Question** attitude of the Powers to the new China, in the policy of **since the** Russia, and in that of Japan. **War.**

In the disappointment following her excursion into Western politics China fell into increasing confusion and chaos. Chinese nationalism grew more and more hostile to foreign influences—especially, at this stage, to British influence. Treaty rights were infringed with growing frequency. The weak Government could maintain no hold over either riotous nationalists or disaffected provinces. Civil war broke out between rival ambitious war lords. Violence and disorder prevailed, while the resources necessary for

[1] There were two delegations, one from the North, one from the South; and it was the nominee of the South (Dr Wellington Koo, Chinese Minister in Washington) who took the leading part, overshadowing the official head of the delegation.

[2] "The Mediterranean era died with the discovery of America. The Atlantic era is now at the height of its development, and must soon exhaust the resources at its command. The Pacific era, destined to be the greatest of all, is just at its dawn" (Theodore Roosevelt, quoted by Sir Frederick Whyte, in *The Observer*, April 8, 1928).

establishing order or undertaking necessary reconstruction were lacking.

It is true that the Powers from time to time made demonstrations in favour of China and in support of their own vested interests in that country. The years before the War had already seen the beginnings of European financial co-operation there; but in 1920 a new consortium was formed. A group of banks and financial houses from Great Britain, France, the United States, and Japan, known as the "Four-Power Consortium," took over the issue and control of foreign loans to China. The group was to receive official support from the countries concerned, and to consider later the admission of Belgium and Russia. "The object of this, as of the earlier Consortium," writes Sir Frederick Whyte,[1]

> was the protection of China against herself, and against the competitive commercial and financial claims of the Powers; the justification of it was to be found in the weakness of the central Government and the division of the provinces. If there were no Consortium at once indiscriminate and profligate borrowing would revive, and put an end for ever to the financial reconstruction of China, which it is the special function of the Consortium to achieve. The battle of concessions would be renewed. . . . The end for China would be foreign tutelage.

The conference called at Washington in 1921 to consider disarmament also discussed the problem of the Pacific, and came to certain conclusions. The Anglo-Japanese alliance, which had done Great Britain good service in protecting her Eastern ocean routes, was superseded by a Quadruple Alliance between Great Britain, the United States of America, France, and Japan. Further, a Nine-Power Treaty was signed,[2] giving what was described as a "new charter" to China, committing the signatories to maintain the 'open door,' and to respect the "sovereignty, independence, and the territorial and administrative integrity of China."

Discussions were also held on the subject of the Chinese customs tariff, on the revision of the unequal treaties, and on the abrogation of extra-territoriality.[3] But though the Powers were agreed in principle on the necessity for revision in these matters, practical concessions were withheld for some years, in spite of insistent Chinese nationalist demands, on the plea that the disorder in China gave no guarantee of security to European nationals. It was not until 1926 that an international conference at Peking, consisting of thirteen nations, recommended that, with certain safeguards for

[1] *China and Foreign Powers* (1927 edition), pp. 22–23.
[2] Between the United States of America, Belgium, the British Empire, China, France, Italy, Japan, the Netherlands, and Portugal.
[3] Before the Great War, in 1908, several Powers had agreed to abolish their own rights in this respect when other states should do so, but nothing had been done.

freedom of domicile and trade and for civil rights, extra-territoriality should be abolished. Two years later the United States granted tariff autonomy, and Great Britain made a treaty with China relating both to tariff autonomy and extra-territoriality. Further, as a friendly gesture Great Britain gave up her Hankow concession.

This delay, however, together with British and American inability or unwillingness to give any practical assistance in the establishment of internal unity and stability,[1] led China to accept the help of Communist Russia, and a further complication was introduced into Chinese politics. The U.S.S.R. was eager to give help and to get a footing in China. Although Revolutionary Russia had reversed the Chinese policy of the Tsar, her approaches had hitherto been coldly received in China, and from 1919 to 1924 she had remained out of favour. In that year, however, she made a treaty "on equal terms"[2] both with the conservative Peking Government in the North, and with Sun Yat Sen and the revolutionary Nationalists in the South.

In the North Russian popularity was short-lived, and the U.S.S.R. soon concentrated on and apparently captured the Kuoming-tang Nationalist Republican movement in the South. With her help the Kuoming-tang party made during the next few years the progress already recorded, and under her guidance turned increasingly anti-British. By 1927 Russian Communist influence seemed to have become predominant; her propaganda efforts, however, had produced conflicts, divisions, and reaction; the terrorism and counter-terrorism which had accompanied her progress had caused inevitable alienation, and when she showed her clear intention of Bolshevizing China the leaders of the Kuoming-tang turned against their Russian allies.

As the Communist influence receded in China Great Britain and other Western Powers began to recover something of their former position. They began also to give assistance to the Canton Government in the necessary work of reform and reconstruction. The Kuoming-tang had not yet, indeed, overcome all its enemies; opponents to right and left remained to be dealt with; the Chinese Soviet Republic held out until 1936, but most of China had given recognition to the Canton Republic, and a beginning was being made in the work of national consolidation.

The Peking-Canton and other railways were built, communications facilitated by new ground and air transport, education, health, and social welfare services increased or established. League of Nations experts gave advice on irrigation systems, and Sir Frederick Leith-Ross helped in financial reform which gave China in 1936 a

[1] In Britain's case it arose partly from her confirmed belief that China should work out her own destiny.

[2] The first treaty made by China on equal terms was made with the German Republic in 1921.

new currency that opened to her again the prospect of foreign credits. It was at this point that a fresh wave of Japanese aggression broke in upon the work of Chinese national organization.

The most urgent problem of Pacific politics in recent years has been that of Japanese expansion. After the active phase of 1915–19 Japanese imperialism seemed to have become quiescent. It had suffered several checks—in the failure of the Siberian enterprise,[1] in the abandonment of the Anglo-Japanese alliance, and in the distrustful attitude of the Powers shown by the fortification of their Pacific bases and by their declared intention of supporting Chinese integrity. Japanese policy seemed further to be harnessed to the principles of international co-operation by her membership of the League of Nations, and its moderation to be guaranteed by the development of a more liberal *régime* at home.

Japanese imperialism appeared, indeed, to have been abandoned in the twenties. At the end of the decade, however, it was awakened in a more virulent form than ever by the prospect of Chinese consolidation, by the Russian penetration, and above all by the economic blizzard of 1929–31. The economic basis of Japanese expansionism has long been recognized. A very high birth-rate was intensifying the problems of overpopulation in the small Japanese islands. Emigration to the American or Australian continents was forbidden to her by rigid immigration policies designed to protect the American and Australian standard of living from Japanese competition or undercutting. Japanese colonization in China was unprofitable in that it brought Japan face to face with Chinese antagonism and into competition with the still lower standard of living of Chinese and Korean coolies. Economically Japan was becoming increasingly dependent upon the outside world, upon imports of food and raw materials and industrially upon her exports. Her chief export, silk, was a commodity which in itself was dependent upon a high level of world prosperity, and when, under the growing economic depression, the United States and other countries began to protect their own industries and close their markets to Japanese manufactures by high tariffs, her plight became desperate and pitiable. Her own industries had not a sufficient backing of capital to support a period of strain, and her 'economies area' was too small to be protected by tariffs.

It was therefore inevitable—especially as similar theories were being put forward in Europe—that Japan should develop arguments

[1] A Czechoslovak legion of deserters from the Austrian army which, in 1917, tried to reach the Western Front by a long trek eastward through Siberia, fell to fighting with the Bolsheviks. A mixed French, British, American, and Japanese force was sent in 1918 to the help of the legion. Japan attempted to exploit this intervention in favour of Japanese power in Eastern Siberia, but after several vicissitudes her forces were obliged to evacuate Vladivostok in 1921.

in favour of "large economic areas" subject to tariff and financial control. Such arguments fortified the imperialist tendencies of the military classes and strengthened the case for the "Asiatic Monroe Doctrine" by which Japan had already begun to claim dominant, or even exclusive, rights in the North-west Pacific area.

China was her obvious field of action. Japan already had Korea and a footing in Manchuria. Military conquest would give her a large economic area, still slightly industrialized, which under tariff and financial control [1] would provide her with a monopoly of markets and raw materials, which she could purchase without the necessity of free foreign exchange. The existing economic privileges there of Great Britain and the United States aroused her indignation and envy. Increasing Russian penetration aroused her fear. Growing Chinese nationalism, and the imminent consolidation and industrialization of China, prompted urgent action. Chinese weakness offered the opportunity. Economic need and imperialist aspirations provided the incentive and the excuse. Co-operation with the Great Powers had so far done little for her. Japan determined to take her own fate into her own hands.

In 1931 Japan invaded Manchuria, established the puppet state of Manchukuo there under her own power, and began to put increasing pressure upon China.

A nominal truce retarded the Japanese advance from 1934 to 1937, but in the latter year, encouraged by the increasing triumph of the aggressive spirit in Europe, she opened a campaign of invasion and aggression in China whose ruthlessness has shocked the world.

By the end of 1939 Japan had secured a hold over most of the North China provinces, but her difficulties are immense. She is confronted with a hardening Chinese nationalism which is passing from an anti-British, through an anti-Russian, into an anti-Japanese phase. She has not yet overcome Chinese resistance, which is finding new refuges and new centres in the western provinces. She has antagonized the Powers. Nor has she yet secured the desired economic control, even over her conquered areas, and she has seriously embarrassed her own finances at home.

The Powers, occupied with their own economic and political problems, have been able to do little more than deplore Japan's aggression and keep a wary eye upon their own interests in China. Russia alone disputed, in her own interests, the Japanese advance, but without avail. Both China and Japan were members of the League of Nations, but China derived nothing but sympathy from her participation in the League, and in 1933 Japan announced her resignation from it.

[1] By a 'yen block.'

CHAPTER XII

THE UNITED STATES OF AMERICA

I. THE NEW STATE, ITS FORMATION AND EARLY PROBLEMS

ON April 30, 1789, six days before the States-General met at Versailles, George Washington was inaugurated at New York as first President of the United States of America. The one event, like the other, marked a new era in the history of the world. A state was born in the West which within little more than a century was to show a destiny as great and a career as startling as that of any European Power. For while the United States has attained to an influence as vital as that of Republican France, it has grown to empire with a rapidity as remarkable as the development of Imperial Germany.

It was not, indeed, until the conflict of 1914–18, in which America and Germany met for the first time in war, and as enemies, that the international importance of the United States was fully realized. For partly by choice, partly because of her remoteness from what was then the political centre of the world, she had lived aloof during the nineteenth century from the main stream of European politics. By deliberate policy she had kept herself "immune from entangling alliances"; she had refused to allow herself to be drawn into the circle of European wars and European interests. Free from the necessities of military defence, she had been able to turn to her internal development energy which, had she been a European state, would have been expended on her own security. In consequence, however, she failed to play before the twentieth century any decisive or effective part in international questions; her affairs, except in one or two isolated instances, were not considered of more than secondary diplomatic importance; and, if Canning's vision of "a new world which should redress the balance of the old" may be prophetically applied to the United States of America, then the Monroe Doctrine must be held to have postponed the fulfilment of her destiny.

Partly because of this aloofness the United States affords a unique example of uninterrupted as well as of rapid development. She seems to have compressed into one century historical processes which in Europe have extended over more than a thousand years. She has had her *Völkerwanderung* and her conflict with alien races, her war of independence, her civil war, her agrarian and industrial problems, and

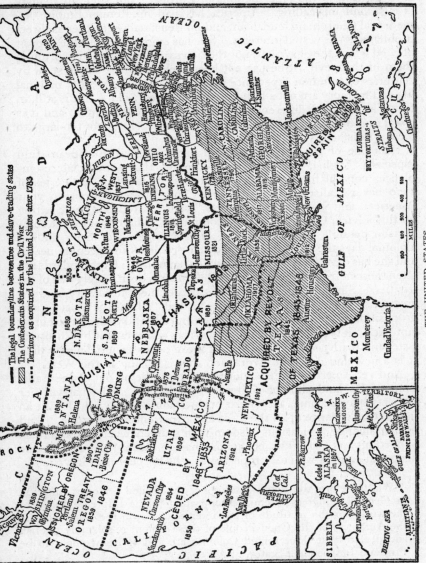

The legend shows:
- The legal boundary line between free and slave-trading states in the Civil War
- The Confederate States in the Civil War
- Territory as acquired by the United States after 1783

THE UNITED STATES

within a hundred years she appears to have placed herself abreast, if not ahead, of the older nations of Europe. But such an analogy is false and misleading. America has had no Roman Empire, no mediæval Church, no feudalism, and no Renaissance, neither as direct problems nor as vested interests. She has enjoyed neither the deposit of good which they have left, nor the rich experience gained in pruning them of their evil. She has not been welded into a single state by centuries of common experience and common suffering; her national life and memory are not a hundred and fifty years old. She is still, in fact, "a mosaic of different stages of social development"; and it is a real question whether, like China and Russia, she is not too large to form a satisfactory political unit.

It is one of the chief sources of error in most European—and especially English—judgments of America that superficial resemblances conceal fundamental differences. It is what the Tories of 1770 never realized. "Do not make any difference between your American and your British subjects," said Dr Johnson, and, acting on this advice, George III lost a continent. There is no valid comparison possible between Europe and America. For from the old Colonial days the latter has had peculiar problems and peculiar needs, and she has developed for herself peculiar solutions. Her standards are often those of frontiersmen, because her life has been largely that of the frontiers. She is the greatest political experiment in history, and the greatest social and economic venture as well. She is the most serious proposition in the world. But between Europe and America is a great gulf fixed; it is not easy to judge American achievement by European taste, and inadvisable to offer to European needs American remedies. It is a new and different civilization that is arising in the West.

And yet American independence came into being out of the traditions of England and the philosophy of France, and whatever her subjects may become, they were born citizens of the world with an indirect inheritance of all the ideas and experiences of Europe. And in that alliance of vicarious wisdom with indigenous energy and fresh opportunity at least one economist has foreseen "the key to the historical enigma which Europe has sought for centuries in vain."

We, therefore, the Representatives of the United States of America, in General Congress assembled, appealing to the Supreme Judge of the world for the rectitude of our intentions, do, in the Name and by the Authority of the Good People of these Colonies, solemnly publish and declare that these united Colonies are and of Right ought to be Free and Independent States. . . .

Thus in 1776 the thirteen colonies of America proudly proclaimed their independence. By 1783 it was achieved and recognized, won by the dogged persistence of a minority and the Fabian tactics of a patient general, by reason of the remoteness and inefficiency of the mother country, and with the help of an ally, France, who gained thereby her revenge for the loss of Canada in 1763. With the conclusion of the war the new republic entered upon years even more critical than those she had just passed through. Peace was accompanied by moral reaction, financial embarrassment, and the inevitable disorganization incidental to a civil war. Washington, having taken farewell of his army and delivered up his commission to Congress, had returned to Mount Vernon to resume the supervision of his estates. The newly disbanded soldiers, discontented, unsatisfied by the pay and lands which Washington had barely managed to secure for them, were thronging westward over the Alleghanies into the territories of the Iroquois, into Kentucky and Tennessee, while nearly a hundred thousand Imperial loyalists, or 'Tories,' as they were called, many of them only passive supporters [1] of the defeated cause, were seeking refuge in the British West Indies, were trailing northward into Canada or southward into Spanish Florida—and not a little of the stability of the country was going with them.

During the war commerce had decayed, and there were as yet hardly any manufactures. The Colonies, which had protested against the British commercial system when they were included within the Empire, found themselves worse off when it was put into operation against them. They could no longer trade with the British West Indies; Spain was closing many ports against them, and France withdrawing privileges which she had previously allowed them. There was a demand for a protective tariff on the model of the English Navigation Acts, but the rivalries of the states and the weakness of Congress were effective barriers to any single code. So the states, freely indulging their mutual jealousies, fell to making tariffs of their own, with, and often against, their neighbours.

Thus the Union, born a twin with Independence, seemed likely to perish. In 1781 the states had, indeed, bound themselves by the "Articles of Confederation and Perpetual Union," but these were rather guarded terms of alliance between jealous equals than a constitutional basis for a single state. Congress, the central authority of the Confederation, was unable to keep the wrangling states in harmony, to frame or impose a common policy, or to deal with the problems which confronted it. It was hardly more than "a mere board of advice about things which had ceased to be interesting." It never had been endowed with any real power. It could only make recommendations, which the Governments of the states put into execution

[1] At one time, however, there were more colonists in the British army in America than in Washington's whole force.

if and when they chose.   It could not exert its authority against the will of a state.   Even its resolutions required a two-thirds majority, and it could not amend itself without a unanimous vote.

It had no power to tax.   It assessed the states for contributions, and upon these it had been dependent for the necessary expenses of the war.   But many of the states evaded their responsibilities, and Congress, having tried to raise increased quotas from the more willing states, having added to the confusion rather than the revenue by contributions in kind and issues of paper money, had fallen heavily into debt at home and abroad.   It could hardly meet the interest on the foreign loans, and the common opinion of the national credit was expressed in the phrase "not worth a continental." [1]

The states also were burdened with debts, and many of them,

Debt and disorder. having multiplied issues of paper money and destroyed their credit, sought by unscrupulous means to evade or repudiate their obligations.

Financial disorder bred social anarchy.   On one occasion mutinous soldiers drove the Congress into flight from Philadelphia, and threatened to break into the Bank, and in 1786 a serious rebellion of debtors led by one Daniel Shays broke out in Massachusetts.

Foreign countries, seeing the difficulties of the now independent Colonies, looked on with contempt and—if they were creditors—irritation.   France, despising her *protégé*, speculated with Spain as to whose lot the provinces would ultimately fall.   England refused to send a diplomatic representative, and maintained forts in defiance of the treaty, as a guarantee for the debts due to her merchants.   Spain intrigued with the Indians for the extension of her American possessions, and made difficulties over the navigation of the Mississippi. "We are held in the same light," wrote a contemporary of their more flattering relations, "as a well-behaved negro in a gentleman's family."

In short, "What indication is there," asked Hamilton, "of national disorder, poverty, and insignificance that could befall a community so peculiarly blessed with national advantages as we are, which does not form part of the dark catalogue of our public misfortunes?"   The time was ripe for a Cromwell, and many thought with Frederick the Great that so vast a country could not remain a republic.   Some plotted to make Washington king.   Others anticipated a dissolution of the Confederation.

Possibly the foundation of a royal Washington dynasty would

Reasons for preserving the Union. have strengthened the Union, but Washington himself repudiated all suggestions of that kind, and it is doubtful whether, had he accepted the title of monarch, he could have preserved the power he afterward enjoyed as President.

[1] A ' continental ' being of course a paper currency note issued by Congress.

It was other considerations which kept the states from falling back into their original separateness or into groups—fear of foreign countries, commercial advantages, and vested interests. It was a Union extorted from "the grinding necessities of a reluctant people." "Let the thirteen states," urged Hamilton, "bound together in a strict and indissoluble union, concur in erecting one great American system superior to the control of all transatlantic force or influence, and able to dictate the terms of connexion between the Old and the New Worlds."

There was a strong vein of democratic idealism running through the political arguments of the day, and a real appreciation of the necessity of guarding by union the measure of liberty and independence which had been won. "With all its imperfections," wrote Jefferson, "our Government is the best existing or that ever did exist." Compared with other countries, he added on another occasion, "it is like heaven and hell—England, like the earth, taking an intermediate station."

Next to commerce, perhaps the strongest impulse to union came from the common lands lying beyond the Alleghanies. These had in 1781 been transferred to Congress largely because the **National territory.** eastern maritime states with fixed boundaries, like Maryland and Delaware, who could not extend their own frontiers, protested against the indefinite westward expansion of more fortunately situated states like Virginia, Pennsylvania, and the Carolinas. They had become therefore the property of the Confederation, and were in a sense colonies of the Union, although the more savoury term 'territory' was substituted for 'colony.' The peace of 1783 had confirmed and extended the appropriations, and by the famous North-west Ordinance of 1787 Congress had assumed over them rights of government. It had authorized a sale and survey of the new lands, prohibited slavery in them, and made regulations for their government, by which, after a term of political apprenticeship, they should be admitted into the Union as fully qualified states.[1]

All these factors worked in favour of union, and, arising out of a movement for the interstate regulation of trade, a convention was called to consider a revision of the articles of Confederation. It met at Philadelphia in 1787, in a straggling, **The Convention of Philadelphia (1787).** nervous fashion, without very much optimism. The delegates arrived tardily, as one state after another decided to send them.

Perhaps a saner group of men never met to frame a political

[1] Without, of course, any suggestion of 'colonial' inferiority. The political equality which was extended to the new territories on maturity is regarded as one of the greatest contributions of the expiring Congress to American political development and to modern political thought. It presupposed, however, a federal system.

document. They were not visionaries, nor had they come together in a mood of revolution. The agitators, the orators and theorists—many of the begetters of independence—were absent—the Adams cousins, Jefferson, who was in France, Patrick Henry, who 'smelt a rat' and, though elected, would not take his seat. They were soldiers, statesmen, and financiers, some of them amateurs, perhaps, but men of experience and affairs, burgesses of their own Assemblies, members of Congressional Committees, convinced of the need of sound government, with a practical judgment and faith in their country. "Let us raise a standard," said Washington, "to which the wise and honest can repair. The event is in the hand of God." Above all they were men who had lived through the decade which followed 1776. They were not met in the first exalted hour of an untested emancipation. Their president, George Washington, was a soldier-planter; their doyen was Benjamin Franklin, the "American Socrates," diplomat, scientist, philosopher, and, in a homely way, a man of letters. He took little active part in the assembly, but he lent it the dignity of eighty years, a wisdom and learning commended in both hemispheres, a high reputation, the record of great public services, and an engaging human simplicity. Robert Morris was there, the financier of the Revolution, who had staked a private fortune on the cause of American independence, and James Wilson, an able lawyer who had emigrated from Scotland in the year of the Stamp Act, and had already served in a previous Congress; and Gouverneur Morris, with plenty of sense, and a good, terse style which found its way into the phrases of the constitution. There were some famous young men too among the fifty-five: James Madison, scholar and political philosopher, a soldier during the war, to whose study of federation the constitution owed most in its construction; Alexander Hamilton, who had been the prime mover in the summoning of the convention, and who, despite his mere thirty years, was to prove himself the greatest statesman among them. He would have liked to frame a stronger Government, nearer the English model, but "though every one praised him none supported him." Nevertheless when the constitution was accepted by the country he did more than Washington himself to make it a practical success.

These were the men who made the new state. Jefferson called them 'demigods,' but they represented, most of them, the solid conservative, commercial, and financial interests of the country. They were bent on practical reforms and on establishing a Government which would be strong enough to regulate commerce, pay the National Debt, solve the currency problems, and defend the liberty and independence which had just been won.

It is natural therefore that the American constitution, the product of such an assembly, should be a simple practical document of less than five thousand words, conservative in its tone, "constructed for safety, not speed," full of compromise and checks, showing an English ancestry.   It is the heir of Magna Charta, with its The reaction from 1776. amendment, the Bill of Rights, of the colonial charters and the state constitutions.   It contains, unlike the Declaration of Independence, no fine generalizations about democracy and equality.   The men of 1776 proclaimed the equality of man; they talked of his natural rights, and believed in his natural perfection. They called George III a tyrant and kingship an oppression. The men of 1786, though some of them were men of 1776 also, guaranteed the rights of property and recognized "natural inequalities."   They had grown sceptical of the philosophy of Rousseau and the creed of popular infallibility, and reverted to the theology of Calvin and the doctrine of original sin.   They held their debates in secret,[1] and the Government they framed, in Patrick Henry's eyes, "squinted towards monarchy."

One delegate, Gerry [2] of New England, ascribed the evils from which they suffered to "an excess of democracy"; another, Mason of Virginia, thought the people as qualified to choose a president as a blind man to choose a colour; Washington himself reflected that they had held "too good an opinion of mankind," and that, left to itself, it was "unfit for its own government."   As for Hamilton, he roundly asserted, "Your people, sir, is a great beast."

Thus the new constitution was to some extent the fruit of a conservative reaction.   And though it was the deliberate composition of a group of men sitting in council it was based on real The constitution. experience, national as well as colonial.[3]

The fundamental factor with which the constitution-makers were confronted was the strong independent spirit of the states.   From this emerged the most serious problems with which they had to deal —how to combine the sovereignty of the states with an effective measure of central government, how to conciliate the natural jealousy of the small states toward the larger, and how to reconcile the interests of those that held slaves with those that did not.

A solution was found in a partial union or federal state.   The essential feature of a federal constitution is the division of sovereign powers between the central and local governments.   There The Federation. is in the United States of America no single omnipotent law-making body like the English Parliament, supreme in all matters and over all persons, competent to override a resolution of any other

---

[1] The first record of their debates was not published until 1840.

[2] From whom is derived the expression ' to gerrymander,' meaning to carve out electoral districts without adequate representation of minorities.

[3] This is an aspect which is apt to be ignored by such descriptions of the constitution as Mr Gladstone's, eulogistic as it is, that it was " the most wonderful work ever struck off at a given time by the brain and purpose of man."

authority within the state, and able, in fact, to do anything except "make a man a woman or a woman a man." On the contrary, there are to-day in the United States of America forty-nine sovereign legislatures, one for each state and one for the whole Union. In 1787 there were fourteen devised by the constitution. Each within its sphere is independent and supreme; outside, each is alike inoperative. The central or Federal Government is alone competent to deal with all matters relating to foreign countries—diplomatic affairs, peace and war, the national defences—and with all matters affecting the states as a whole, or where one state might act against the interests of the others. The central Government must represent the common interest where a common interest exists; it must also be the impartial ruler and the impartial arbiter.

The powers of the Federal Government, broadly stated, under eighteen heads,[1] are express limitations upon the authority of the individual states, who may not make peace or war on their own account, keep a private army, or coin money, nor generally encroach upon the sphere allotted to the central Government.[2]

[1] See the constitution of the United States. A copy may be found in any collection of modern constitutional documents or appended to the chief histories of America.

[2] It has been customary to accept the division of states, made by Aristotle, into monarchies, aristocracies, and democracies. It would now be more appropriate to divide them into single (or unitary) states on the one hand and composite (or federal) states on the other. It is worth while to consider a few of the main principles of federal government, for it seems to offer a solution to most of the political problems of the world.

(1) A federation is suitable for groups of states which are determined to maintain their individual independence, but have enough interests in common to desire a partial union.

(2) A federal Government means a division of powers—i.e., of sovereignty—between local and central Governments. Therefore the test of whether a state is unitary or federal lies in the question of its legislatures. If there is only one sovereign law-making body it is a unitary state, if more it is federal.

(3) The lines of division should be all on the inside, and none on the outside—i.e., as regards foreign countries the federal state must act as a single unit. The central Government must therefore have the control of foreign affairs, peace and war, etc.

(4) Any matters affecting the state as a whole—e.g., commerce—or where it is advisable that the individuals should have uniform rights—e.g., copyright questions—should be entrusted to the central Government.

(5) There will be a residuum of undefined powers which will in a loose federation (where independence is stronger than union) be entrusted to the Governments of the states, and in a tight federation to the central Government.

(6) Experience has proved that it is advisable, if not essential, for the central Government to maintain direct relations with the individual, usually in four respects—by representation and taxation, and through the courts and the army. It is this feature which distinguishes the modern federations (the United States of America, Canada, Australia, Bismarckian Germany, Switzerland) which so far have succeeded from earlier confederations which have failed.

(7) A federal constitution involves almost necessarily a written constitution. This usually leads to a certain rigidity, and to more or less elaborate arrangements for amendment.

In other matters each individual state has absolute independence. Each state may set up any kind of Government, with a one- or two-chambered Parliament, so long as it is generally republican; it may extend the franchise to minors or aliens, and as long as it does not discriminate between black and white,[1] or male and female,[2] it may restrict it to lunatics or millionaires. It may establish Mormonism or Mohammedanism as the state religion, and demand a literal acceptance of the Book of Genesis from all office-holders—for the Federal Government only is bound to respect liberty of belief; it may abolish marriage or motor-cars, and nationalize mines or children. Nine-tenths of the laws to which an American is subject are state laws, and most of the important subjects of controversy in England during the nineteenth century would have been state, not Federal, questions—the whole question of Parliamentary reform, the enfranchisement of women, the Poor Law, the reform of local institutions, Church disestablishment, education, divorce, unemployment, and factory legislation. "The state is the rule, the Federation the exception." It is for this reason that there exists in America so wide a variety in these matters—a variety which would be greater but for a general basis of English common law throughout the states.

It is not so much, however, in the division of authority between the central and local Governments and in the marked independence of the states that the peculiar virtue of the American constitution lies. Partial unions are, after all, as old as the Greeks, and in the mere allocation of spheres of control the new constitution did not differ materially from the Articles of Confederation which it was superseding. It was the nature of the central Government, its composition and functions, that distinguished the new constitution from all federal associations which had preceded it, which made the members of the Convention of Philadelphia pioneers among constitution-makers. *The structure of the central Government.*

In all previous confederations [3] the central body has consisted of a mere advisory or deliberative council, sometimes with committees, but with no executive authority over the individuals of the component states. It is from this custom that a departure was made.

The central or Federal body of the United States is a fully fledged Government, like that of any unitary state. It possesses a two-

---

[1] By the Fifteenth Amendment, passed in 1870.

[2] By the Nineteenth Amendment, passed in 1920, women as such may not be disfranchised.

[3] It is advisable to keep the term ' confederation of states ' for all associations where the central body possesses no executive authority, and the term ' federal state ' for constitutions such as that of the United States of America, where the central body is equipped with executive authority. The Germans have two useful words to express the difference—*Staatenbund* and *Bundesstaat*.

chambered legislature to make its laws, an executive authority consisting of a president to carry them out, and its own courts to judge and punish offences against them. It is largely modelled on the British constitution, except that the executive—*i.e.*, the President—is not answerable to the legislature—*i.e.*, the majority in the Lower House—as is a British Prime Minister. This difference was due to the influence of the theories of Montesquieu, who had wrongly argued that the secret of English freedom lay in the separation of the legislature from the executive.

Into the workings of the Federal constitution it is not possible here to enter. A brief summary of the chief features is all that can be given.

The judicature. The judicature is the exponent of Federal law, the interpreter of the constitution, and the arbiter of all suits to which the Federation is a party.

The executive. The President is, or has become, something between an English king of the eighteenth century, an English Prime Minister of the nineteenth, and a German emperor. He is stripped of the irresponsibility of hereditary succession, shorn of the divinity that hedges royalty, and dressed in republican robes. His prerogatives are restricted; he is elected for four years by the people, to whom he is responsible,[1] and by tradition he may not renew his tenure of office more than once. His salary is too small to enable him to maintain a Court or corrupt a legislature, and he may not seduce the virtue of his people by titles, for they are forbidden. Nevertheless in time of war or of internal disturbance he possesses powers which amount almost to dictatorship.

The legislature. The legislature, consisting of two Houses, embodies an interesting principle which has become one of the most important devices of modern federation. There is much discussion as to the utility of a two-chamber legislature in a single state; in a federal state it serves such a valuable and special purpose as makes it eminently desirable, if not indispensable. For the two Houses ex-

---

[1] No feature of the constitution met with more approval in 1789 than the method of Presidential election, and none has failed so signally to fulfil the intentions of its originators. Theoretically in each state a college of electors is chosen equal to the number of Representatives and Senators to which the state is entitled in Congress. Each elector is intended to exercise his independent judgment in the election of a president. In practice each party runs its complete list of electors, who will vote for the party Presidential candidate, and their election by the people takes place solely on that understanding. Thus the Presidential election is really decided in the November of one year, when the electoral college is elected, although nominally the President is not chosen until January of the next year, and does not take office until March. This often leads to abuses, which have been partly remedied by the Twentieth Amendment of February 1933 (see p. 546, note 2). It is interesting also to observe that, owing to the carving out of the constituencies without adequate representation of minorities, the President has sometimes been chosen by a minority of votes—*e.g.*, in 1876 President Hayes received 252,000 votes less than Mr Tilden, and in 1888 President Harrison received 95,534 less than Mr Cleveland.

press the twofold character of a federal state, its unity and its diversity, as a single and united nation on the one hand, as a number of separate and independent units on the other. Thus the Senate or Upper House of the United States contains two members from each state, representing them therefore as sovereign and equal provinces—for the jealousy of the smaller states insisted upon equal representation whatever the size and importance of the state may be. On the other hand, the Lower House, the House of Representatives, represents the Union as a single entity, voting as one nation according to population. Each state is therefore represented according to its size, except that no state, however small, may remain without a Representative. Thus New York, which sends only two members to the Senate, sends forty-three to the House of Representatives, while Delaware, which is only entitled to one member in the Lower House, sends nevertheless an equal number, two, to the Upper.

But what of the slave states? There was no question of giving a slave a vote, but was he to be counted as one of the population in the apportionment of Representatives? It made a serious difference to the Southern states. It was finally agreed that three-fifths of the slave populations should be counted for representative purposes. It was a compromise for which there is little to be said except that it won South Carolina for the Union, and shelved a problem which the Federation was then too weak to solve. But it contained no seeds of permanence; it merely postponed the issue for seventy years.

One further aspect of the American constitution remains to be emphasized, although it is implied in the distribution of powers and the elaboration of the central Government. It has become a fundamental principle of modern federations which seems to give every promise of endurance, and is the crucial distinction between them and previous confederations which have in the course of time come to an end. By the powers allotted to the central or Federal Government it is able to maintain direct relations with the individual citizen of the state, instead of only with the state Governments. Just as William the Conqueror demanded in the Oath of Salisbury a direct allegiance from the vassals of his vassals, so the Federal Government has an immediate contact with the subjects of the component states. It represents them in the House of Representatives; it enlists them in the Federal army; it judges them in the Federal courts; it taxes them indirectly and, since the amendment of 1913, directly, through its own officials, and in default of payment prosecutes them, and all this without reference to the state Governments. Thus the individual comes as immediately into contact with the marshals of the United States as with the sheriffs of the county or the constables of the town.

Direct contact between the Federation and the individual.

2 M

The constitution of the United States is, of course, not without its critics. A great—perhaps excessive—authority has fallen to the judiciary as interpreter and arbiter of the terms of union. A written constitution always implies some rigidity, and since the modification of its clauses had to be put beyond the chance or captious combination of a group of states amendment is elaborate and difficult. Although some seventeen hundred amendments have been proposed, only twenty-one have been passed,[1] of which twelve were added within five years of the passing of the constitution. Thus the consti-

Criticisms. tutional history of a century and a half is represented by nine amendments alone, and many of the most important political crises in American history have had no bearing on the constitution.

But the United States, like Great Britain, has its unwritten traditions. It too has broadened and developed by usage, by the legislation of Congress and by judicial interpretation.[2] Elasticity is required and proved in a constitution which, constructed for four million inhabitants, can be extended to a hundred million, which can be adapted to the needs of a continent stretching between the Atlantic and the Pacific, between Canada and the Gulf of Mexico. The Union has grown stronger with the passage of time, owing partly to the growth of sentiment and association, and partly to such centralizing forces as railways and telegraphs, controlled by the central Government.

Such, then, are the outlines of the present constitution of the United States of America as it was framed by the Convention of Philadelphia. But the Convention had no authority to do more than submit its proposals to the states. The sanction of at least nine states

[1] *Amendments to the Constitution :*
1791. I–X, based on proposals made at the time of the acceptance of the constitution. They relate to guarantees of individual liberty of speech, Press, worship, etc., and constitute an American Bill of Rights.
1794. XI and XII reverse a judicial interpretation of the constitution and introduce a change in the election of the President and Vice-President.
1865. XIII ⎫
1869. XIV ⎬ relate to the abolition of slavery and the enfranchisement of
1870. XV ⎭ the coloured race.
1913. XVI and XVII empower Congress to impose an income tax and introduce a change in the election of the Senate.
1919. XVIII prohibits the sale of alcoholic liquors.
1920. XIX forbids disfranchisement on account of sex.
1933. XX advances the date of the President's and Vice-President's inauguration and abolishes the lame-duck sessions of Congress. XXI repeals the Eighteenth Amendment.

[2] The method of Presidential election, the restriction of his terms of office to two, the assent of the Senate to the President's Cabinet appointments, the control by a Senator of the appointment to Federal offices (Federal patronage) in his state; the division of both Houses into committees, the work done by them and the importance of the Speaker, who nominates them; the employment of the party engine known as the Caucus; the spoils system—*i.e.* the reappointment to Federal offices by each President; the rule that a member of Congress must reside in the district and state from which he is chosen—all these are matters of tradition and convention, not constitutional law.

was essential before they could be put into execution. Their presentation to the states aroused a memorable storm of pamphlet and discussion, argument and debate. Literature and controversy were pervaded by a majestic eloquence comparable to the spirit of English Puritanism, marking a young nation worthily inspired by ideals. Unsurpassed in the field of constitutional exposition were the cogent and lucid contributions to various New York journals of Hamilton, Madison, and Jay. More than anything else, they turned the scale of opinion in New York in favour of the Union, and they have remained to this day, collected under the title of *The Federalist*, one of the finest sets of commentaries on the constitution.

Ratification by the states.

On July 14, 1788, the following announcement appeared in the *Pennsylvania Packet*, after the report that New Hampshire and Virginia had ratified the constitution, thus bringing up the list of 'ayes' to ten: "Arrived in port, the ship *Federal Constitution*. Her Commander, *Perpetual Union*. In her came the passengers *Flourishing Commerce*, *Public Faith*, *Confidence* and *Justice*." The Union was at last an accomplished fact. The thirteen emancipated colonies had passed with safety through one of the greatest ordeals to which they were ever subjected, and with relief and hope were entered upon a new stage of their history.

There was one man marked out for the Presidency, and he was elected unanimously. Few men of modern times have been to the popular mind so completely merged in a legend as George Washington. His personality seems to have resolved itself into a collection of moral principles and public virtues; his face to have become a mask of grave dignity and calm discipline, and instead of a man there appears a figurehead or a moralist's *mannequin*. There is no dominating ambition nor histrionic trick. He possessed no great learning, nor even supreme genius, and to the end of his life he retained, like more than one English Prime Minister, the tastes of an agriculturist.

George Washington, first President, 1789-97.

Yet, in Henry Lee's unforgettable phrase, he was "first in peace, first in war, and first in the hearts of his countrymen," and when he died the British navy carried its flags at half-mast and Napoleon set up a permanent memorial. And no man was ever more entitled to the national gratitude for his public services, or to the respect of a young republic for his high qualities. Independence and union alike rested upon him, making him, in no sense of mere encomium, the "father of his country."

With the integrity and patriotism of a John Hampden he had taken up arms against what he held to be an intolerable oppression. With a "phantom of a force" he had defied the British army, and his indomitable spirit had disrupted the British Empire. Not by military invincibility—for many of his campaigns consisted of well-conducted retreats—but by personal endurance, self-control, and power of inspiration, by the purest zeal for the public welfare and an unwavering purpose, he had kept together an ill-disciplined, half-naked, half-starved army, through all the difficulties of short-term enlistments, lack of funds, equipment, and ammunition, treason, intrigue, and the half-hearted support of his own people. "If it becomes necessary we will retreat over every mountain and river in America"—these are the words of an enemy who cannot be defeated.

He brought to the Presidency a high endowment. A complete self-effacement before the needs of his country, a "reflecting and virtuous mind" unswayed by fear or favour, personal dignity, invincible rectitude, patience and kindly forbearance, habits of religion and an unquestioning faith, a sense of discipline and order, and a reasonable moderation are qualities that well become the first citizen of the land.

His very impersonalness and elusiveness were an asset to the nation, and the simplicity of his spirit preserved him from the pitfalls of pre-eminence. He was not ahead of his age; he speculated like other men of his time in land and state lotteries, and though with others he emancipated his slaves upon his death he was a slave-holder. He was also no great constructive statesman. In his administration of public affairs he relied chiefly upon his able lieutenant, Alexander Hamilton, but there was ingrained in the Virginian country gentleman a deep good sense and a real political instinct, the fruit of a varied experience and the heritage of a British ancestry.

Washington entered upon his office amid the manifold difficulties which inevitably accompany the setting up of a new state. Initial difficulties. There was no capital, no official residence for the President or meeting-place for Congress. There was no Federal organization and no army; the judges and the Cabinet had still to be appointed, and some of the best men were genuinely unwilling to take office—were, in fact, too poor to do so, for often the salary attached was insufficient to cover expenses. There were the technical difficulties of departmental procedure; every man went to his post without experience or precedent. The constitution had to be worked out in detail, its practical utility tested, the amendments demanded by the ratifying states added.

There were the mutual jealousies of the states, and the divergent interests of a people of four millions which included black, and white, and red races. There were acute financial and economic problems, and the foreign situation was precarious. There was also a by no means unanimous support for the Union. In the states which had ratified the constitution there were large minorities against it, and

North Carolina and Rhode Island were still holding out. The former came in in November 1789, the latter not until May 1790, when she was bullied out of her refractoriness by a threat of commercial boycott.

Washington himself, now nearly sixty years of age, accepted office with real apprehension. "My movements to the chair of government," he wrote to General Knox, before he was inaugurated, "will be accompanied by feelings not unlike those of a culprit who is going to the place of his execution." He appointed as his His Cabinet. Secretary for Foreign Affairs, now known as the Department of State, Thomas Jefferson; as Secretary for War General Henry Knox, who from a Boston bookseller had risen to one of the most important military commands; as Attorney-General Edmund Randolph of Virginia, a lawyer, who proved himself more able than consistent; and, most important of all, as Secretary of the Treasury the President appointed his devoted and intimate friend Alexander Hamilton.

Alexander Hamilton, patriot, soldier, statesman, philo- Alexander sopher, orator, and jurist, the "greatest and most com- Hamilton manding intellect that the New World has produced," (1757–1804). is, next to Washington, the master-builder of the new State.

> Whether we see him as an earnest youth seeking instruction at King's College, in the province of New York, long since become Columbia University, or whether we see him with youthful ardour writing pamphlets in defence of the position taken by the Colonists, or as a brave and competent officer of the Continental army, quickly gaining the confidence and affection of Washington, or as the talented and eloquent leader of the New York bar, or as a persistent and ingenious pleader for a stronger and better Government, or as a secretary of a Treasury whose achievements are yet unrivalled, or as a writer on the philosophy of government who has carved his name by the side of that of Aristotle, there is about Hamilton an infinity of charm and attractiveness that passes all description.[1]

A brilliant financier and statesman, Hamilton was an ardent Unionist, but no democrat. He had argued in the Convention of Philadelphia, and later in his appeal to New York, for a strong executive and a close bond between the states. When he became Secretary to the Treasury he set himself to do everything in his power to strengthen the Union, to cement it by a sound and ambitious economic policy, and to engage on its side the most powerful interests of the country.

Hamilton realized that financial and economic questions lay at the root of the stability of the new Union. The Federal The Government must have a sufficient revenue, and, what was economic more important to its domestic security and its foreign policy of the prestige, a vastly improved credit. Govern- ment.

---

[1] Nicholas Murray Butler, *Master Builders of the Nation.* It should be noted, however, that more recent opinion tends to be much less sympathetic toward Hamilton.

He levied duties upon imports and imposed an excise tax upon spirituous liquors. He passed a Tonnage Act, to encourage American shipping at the expense of foreign. He persuaded Congress to take over the war debts of the separate states; he funded and bonded both the domestic and foreign debt of the United States, and he set up a central financial institution in the form of a national bank.

It was a daring policy for a young state, but it proved successful, largely owing to the growth of a lucrative neutral trade during the wars in Europe. It aroused in the United States, however, a considerable opposition. The new Government, it was alleged, was **Opposition.** unwarrantably exceeding the powers allotted to it. The assumption of state debts was in addition contested by all those states who had made an effort to pay off their own loans. The measure was barely passed, and only by bribing the Southern states with the site of the capital. Thus the new Federal city of Washington came to be built on the shores of the Potomac, a situation on the borders of North and South which proved strategically precarious in the Civil War.

The funding of the National Debt at its face value led to speculation in Government securities, and there was a cry from the Opposition of "favoured interests." The Federal Bank was likened to Montague's Bank of England, the device of an oligarchy to keep itself in power. The national reluctance to be taxed, moreover, still prevailed; a general excise which Hamilton proposed aroused as much indignation as Grenville's Stamp Act, and the limited excise on alcoholic liquors provoked in 1794 a "Whisky Insurrection" of the frontiersmen of Pennsylvania.

The foreign policy of the Government soon became the source of like discord. When the French Revolution broke out a general sym- **Foreign** pathy was felt in the United States for what was easily **affairs.** interpreted as a proclamation of the gospel of American liberty to Europe. Democratic societies were formed, one of which was affiliated to the Jacobin Club, the title of 'citizen' was widely adopted, and banquets and bonfires and the usual demonstrations celebrated the coming of light to the Old World. But as the Revolution proceeded to violence, to the death of the King, and to war with Europe marked differences of opinion began to appear in the United States. There was a strong popular party, which, like the English Radicals, kept its faith in French democracy in spite of its excesses. "The tree of liberty must be refreshed from time to time with the blood of patriots and tyrants." They dwelt on the obligations of the treaty of 1778, and the debt of gratitude which America owed to France, and Citizen Genêt, the accredited representative of the Convention to America, freely ordered French privateers to put into American harbours with any British prizes they had captured. But Citizen Genêt could not understand why, though he was fêted and banqueted by the people, the Government would give him no military equipment. For Washington and the Government party, inclined by intellectual sympathy and social connexions toward Great Britain, alienated by the extremes to which the revolutionary movement had run, had already decided that the United States was not committed to immediate war by the treaty of 1778, and had issued in April 1793, a fortnight after Genêt landed at Charleston, but before he had reached Philadelphia, a proclamation of neutrality.

Proclamation of neutrality (April 23, 1793).

The commercial profit accruing to a neutral country in time of war has been amply demonstrated in this generation. The material advantages of Washington's policy were considerable, though to many Americans neutrality seemed treason. An extensive neutral trade grew up, and America soon became the purveyor of essential products to France. But to Great Britain this trade was but an infringement of the advantage which she had hoped to gain over France by her naval supremacy. Still believing, moreover, that it was only a matter of time until the United States came into the war against her, she put every possible pressure upon American shipping. She extended the list of contraband, and seized vessels in the British West Indies. A bitter hostility grew out of the ensuing hardship to American traders and shipowners; she was freely described as the "robber of the seas," and if Columbian curses had taken effect the island of Albion would now be only "a sandbank for sea-monsters to fatten on, a space for the storms of the ocean to mingle in conflict."

Washington resolutely persisted, however, in his neutrality, a neutrality which, it must be admitted, was friendly to England. He asked for the recall of Citizen Genêt, and sent Jay to England to negotiate a treaty which removed some of the chief grievances of the two countries. It was the first official treaty of the new republic with the Old Country since the recognition of its independence. But it was stigmatized in America as "disgraceful, mortifying, and injurious," and it was carried in the House of Representatives by only three votes.

By this time political parties had grouped themselves round fundamental differences of principle and temperament. It is natural that the controversies which had been waged over the ratification of the constitution should reappear after the Union, and should hinge not upon the passing of the constitution, for that was already achieved, but upon its interpretation. On the one side were the Federalists, the Government party, with Hamilton at their head, aristocratic, conservative, desiring a close Union, a strong executive, and a comprehensive Federal programme, anxious to break down the particularism of the states and to put the broadest and most liberal interpretation upon the powers allotted to the central

Political parties.

The Federalists.

Government.   On the other were the Republicans, or, as they came
later to call themselves, the Democrats, distrustful of the Union,
The   suspicious of Hamilton, seeing in Washington a potential
Republican-   monarch and in the Government a conspiracy to destroy the
Democrats.   liberties of America.   They were 'strict constructionists,' [1]
bent upon confining the powers of the Federation to the narrowest limits
laid down in the text of the constitution.   They were democrats, even
radicals, and, by implication, pro-French.   They wanted Free Trade
because they disliked Federal imposts.   They objected to a navy and
a national university as being destructive of the "true frugality and
simplicity" of democracy.   "Shall we imitate the example of the
nations who have gone from a simple to a splendid Government?"
Patrick Henry indignantly asked.   They denounced Jay's treaty as an
agreement with despotism, and in the Government effort to suppress
the "Whisky Insurrection" they saw an anticipation of tyranny.
"The servile copyist of Mr Pitt thought he must have his alarms, his
insurrections and plots against the Court," said Jefferson of Hamilton.
They criticized the Society of Cincinnati, an hereditary society of
officers of the Revolutionary War, as a forerunner of aristocracy, and
there was a stormy debate on the first Salaries Bill.   They cavilled
at Washington's quasi-royal progresses through the country, at the
Presidential *levées*, at his wife's 'drawing-rooms,' at his four cream-
coloured horses; they deplored the keeping of his birthday as a
national holiday.   On both sides there were many men who believed
that a monarchy would soon supersede the Republic; Adams would
even have liked the head of the state to be styled "his Majesty the
President," and more than once was Washington hailed with the
greeting, "God bless your reign!"

Washington tried hard to keep himself outside partisan groupings.
His own Cabinet was divided, for Jefferson, both from principle and
from personal antagonism to Hamilton, came to be considered more
and more the leader of the Democrats—and Washington would sometimes submit the proposals of one member to the criticism of the other.
But his own tastes and connexions led him naturally to Hamilton's
views and the Federalist side, and when at the end of 1793 Jefferson
resigned from the Secretaryship of State Washington chose his
Cabinet increasingly from the Federalist party.   He came therefore
to be bitterly attacked in the Democratic Press, "in such exaggerated
and indecent terms," to use his own words, "as could scarcely be
applied to a Nero, a notorious defaulter, or even to a common pick-
pocket."   "The world would be puzzled to decide," wrote Thomas
Paine, in a letter addressed to the President, "whether you are an
apostate or an impostor."

I.e., they interpreted narrowly the powers allotted to the Federal Government.

Washington, refusing to accept the Presidency for a third time, resigned in 1797, calling upon the country to abandon its divisions. His retirement was thus announced in the *Aurora*: "The man who is the source of all the misfortunes of our country is this day reduced to a level with his fellow-citizens and is no longer possessed of powers to multiply evils upon the United States." *Washington resigns (1797).*

By a small majority of three electoral votes the Federalists carried John Adams to the Presidency—John Adams of the Revolution, "a man," in Woodrow Wilson's words, "stung by jealousies he strove in vain to conquer, too sensitive, too hasty, too acid in judgment, erratic, intolerant, irascible, irresolute." "No Adams," wrote James G. Blaine in 1875, *John Adams, President, 1797–1801.*

> ever yet headed a party without taking the life out of it. Old John— in many respects the best of them—took the Federal party in 1796, when it had the talent, the character, the culture, the wealth, and the patriotic traditions and prejudices of the country largely in its favour, and in four years he so entirely destroyed it that it never reappeared except as a ghost wherewith to frighten two succeeding generations of statesmen.

In truth, the decline of the Federalist party was already setting in— the Democrats had put in Jefferson as Vice-President—but it was undoubtedly hastened by the blunders of Adams.

To begin with, however, a crisis in foreign affairs caused a temporary cessation of party strife. The military successes and the naval defeats of France had led her to put increasing pressure upon America to come into the war. She demanded the fulfil- *Foreign affairs.* ment of the treaty of 1778 and the immediate repayment of the American debt, and she chose to interpret Jay's agreement with England as an indication of hostility. When therefore Adams's election in 1796 again put the pro-British party into power she abandoned all conciliatory efforts, openly seized American ships, and deliberately slighted her ambassadors. American nationalism was strongly aroused. "Millions for defence, and not one cent for tribute!" became the prevailing cry, and John Adams publicly declared that he would "never send another minister to France without assurances that he will be received, respected, and honoured as the representative of a great, free, powerful, and independent nation." The Government made active preparations for war, conflicts occurred be- *"Virtual warfare" with France, 1798.* tween armed vessels of both nations, and what was afterward described as a state of "virtual warfare" came into being. But war itself was never actually declared, for overtures were made at length by France and confirmed in a convention with Napoleon in 1800, cancelling the obligations of former treaties and enabling the United States to return to its neutrality.

Then the Federalists made a mistake. The Jeffersonians were temporarily submerged in the general excitement of the country. On the plea of military necessity the Federalists sought to gain a political advantage over their party opponents by passing four Acts known **The Alien** as Alien and Sedition Acts. These interfered with the **and Sedition** liberty of the Press, narrowly restricted the immigration **Acts (1798).** of foreigners, and largely increased the powers of the Government. They were a direct challenge to the Democratic party. Had not Thomas Paine called America an "asylum for mankind"? At one blow the principles of the Revolution, the liberty of the individual, and the independence of the states were threatened.

But the Democrats forged a dangerous two-edged weapon in their reply. Jefferson and Madison—who from being one of the most prominent architects of the constitution had come to be one of the foremost members of the 'strict constructionist' party—these two men drew up the resolutions which, from their having been accepted by the legislatures of Kentucky and Virginia, are known as the Kentucky and Virginia Resolutions. There they laid down not only that the Government had exceeded its powers, but that the Union was only a compact, that the states themselves had the right to judge when the compact had been violated, and to seek redress. Thus the states were to become arbiters of the legality of Federal legislation. Immediately, nothing much came of the Resolutions, but they were an attack on the whole foundation of the Union and of American citizenship. They gave authority—though later Democrats and Madison himself tried to disavow it—for the doctrine of nullification (the right of a state to declare null and void an Act of Congress) and for the doctrine of secession (the right of a state to break away from the Union), and they marked the shadow of the coming Civil War. They were prepared by two men, each of whom was to be President for eight years.

The Kentucky and Virginia Resolutions, general dissatisfaction with the "Reign of Terror," a division which arose in the ranks of the Federalists between Adams and Hamilton, the death of Washington, which in 1799 robbed the party of some of its prestige, and brilliant political manipulation, which won all the New York votes for the Democratic-Republicans, all these contributed to bring about the fall of the Federalists. In the new election of 1800, largely owing to the public-spirited attitude of Alexander Hamilton, Jefferson was chosen President. He was the first President to move to the new Federal city, which in 1801 consisted of three thousand inhabitants ; one wing of an unfinished Capitol ; the White House, partially plastered, with a leaking roof and sagging floors, and the principal staircase not even begun; seven or eight crowded boarding-houses, a "tailor's shop, a shoe-maker, a printer, a washerwoman, a grocery, a dry-goods store, and an oyster house"; then a swamp, a few houses, and an unused wharf; another swamp and some public buildings and two or three hundred wooden structures.

Next to Abraham Lincoln there is probably no more popular name in America than that of Thomas Jefferson. He was, like Washington and Madison, John Marshall and Edmund Randolph and Patrick Henry, one of the long roll of great men which Virginia has given to America. Yet he is least typical of the clan of plantation magnates into which he was born. *Thomas Jefferson (1743–1826, President 1801–9).* Long and awkward in appearance, said to be a physical coward, but to many possessed of personal charm and conversational grace, his character and his history are full of contradictions. He was a patriotic American of Scottish and Welsh descent, yet he nourished a bitter antipathy to Great Britain, and approximated in spirit more nearly to a French theorist of the Revolutionary school of sentiment. He was to his family a scholastic hermit of an autocratic bent; to the country he was the *beau idéal* of open-hearted democracy. He was a statesman and a demagogue, a philosopher and a political manipulator, "a dealer in philanthropic notions, and privately malignant and vindictive." He was firmly convinced of the conventional principles of democracy, but he was wavering and uncertain in their application. He proclaimed the Rights of Man, and was, illogically, the founder of the pro-slavery party. His speeches are full both of profound sense and of academic irrelevance, and perhaps the best and worst of him was that he believed in and trusted the people. But he was a man of 1776, untutored by the post-war experience which had modified the democratic views of so many Americans of his time. For from the conclusion of peace to the setting up of the Union he had been in France, watching with eager sympathy the dawning of the French Revolution. And to the doctrines of 1789, as to those of 1776, he was by profession obstinately faithful. For himself, he claimed in his own epitaph a triple title to immortality, as the "Author of the American Declaration of Independence, and of the Statute of Virginia for religious liberty, and as the Father of the University of Virginia."

The advent of Jefferson and the Democrats to office was regarded as a revolution. The term is just, but not in the sense anticipated. It was a revolution not in Government policies, but in party programmes. It is not easy to find in American party politics consistency either of principle or even of nomenclature. The features of one are adopted by the other *The Democratic revolution (1801).* according to its tenure of office, and 'strict construction' becomes the cry of each party when it is out of power. Jefferson was elected to the Presidency as head of the party of economy and strict construction. He was to exceed his predecessors in Federal expense and surpass them in the exercise of Federal power.

In his inaugural speech Jefferson proclaimed "Justice to all men, honest friendship with all nations, entangling alliances with none." **Jefferson's** He advocated the support of state Government as the **inaugural.** "surest bulwark against anti-Republican tendencies," the right of election by the people, the rule of the majority, the encouragement of agriculture and "its handmaid commerce," and public economy. He pointed to the "bright constellation" of revolutionary lights, "the diffusion of information, pitiless publicity, freedom of religion, of the Press and of persons."

He then repealed the Alien and Sedition Acts and set free the prisoners charged under them. He cancelled the hasty "midnight **Party** appointments" of his predecessors, even later going to the **retaliation.** length of an attack on the judiciary, seeking to bring it under party control. He dismissed sixteen Federalist officials without cause assigned, filling their places with Democrats.

Then Jefferson began to be forced by the logic of events into expense, into war, into the building of ships, and into the exercise of unprecedented Federal powers.

First the growing population of the West and the formation in 1803 of the new state of Ohio led Congress to undertake expensive road-**Road-** building, and the old National Road, though it was after-**building.** ward handed over to the states through which it passed, was built at Government expense and under the sanction of a ' strict constructionist ' party.

Secondly the inroads of Barbary pirates drove Jefferson to a vigor-**The Tripoli** ous naval war in the Mediterranean with Tripoli, a war **war (1801-5).** entered into with promptness and conducted with success.

But by far the most important as well as the most romantic event of Jefferson's administration was the purchase of Louisiana from **The pur-** France. One of the most pressing economic problems of **chase of** the day, though it is true that it affected the West more than **Louisiana** the East, was concerned with the navigation of the Missis-**(1803).** sippi. Louisiana to the West and the town of New Orleans at the mouth belonged to Spain, who imposed heavy imposts upon American commerce. She withheld the "right of deposit"—*i.e.*, permission to unload and tranship goods at the mouth of the river without high charges or duties. It was a constant source of irritation and negotiation, throughout which Spain played a vacillating part consistent with the whole of her policy at this date, and varying with the international situation and the amount of pressure exerted upon her by the United States.   In 1801, however, she was bullied into ceding Louisiana to Napoleon.   Whether Talleyrand dreamed of reviving the colonial empire of France, or whether the First Consul sought compensation in the West for the failure of the Egyptian campaign in the East, the transfer of Louisiana from a weak Spain to a strong France entirely altered the situation for America.   "The day that France takes possession of New Orleans," wrote Jefferson to the American representative in Paris, "seals the union of two nations, which in conjunction can maintain an exclusive possession of the ocean.   From that moment we must marry ourselves to the British Fleet."

Jefferson thereupon sent American commissioners to buy the mouth of the Mississippi river, a piece of territory consisting of New Orleans and West Florida.   Perhaps because Napoleon was already tired of his colonial scheme, or was discouraged by the hostility shown toward it in America, or was distracted by the renewal of war with England, or because he was short of money, he suggested the purchase of the whole of Louisiana by the United States.   Jefferson was aghast; ten million dollars for New Orleans and its neighbourhood was one thing, fifteen million for half a continent was another, and against his principles.   He feared that it was outside the scope of the Government, and hesitated; the commissioners insisted that Napoleon would not wait.   He therefore abandoned his scruples with remarkable alacrity before the persuasions of his friends, salving his conscience with the hope of a constitutional amendment.   Thus Louisiana, comprising 800,000 square miles, was bought for fifteen million dollars, one of the biggest bargains in land-buying ever transacted, and the purchase proved so popular that no amendment was necessary.

It was an extension of power undreamed of, and its results were incalculable.   Like the Declaration of Independence and the Ordinance of 1787, it was a landmark in American history.   Six new states have been formed of the land purchased, and it has altered fundamentally the balance of politics, the relation of East to West, of slave- to non-slave-holding states.

So far Jefferson's administration had been brilliant, efficient, and popular, but his next concern was one which, dragged out for half a dozen years, bore fruit in his successor's Presidency in the war with England.   This war, hardly remembered in Great Britain, is one of the most highly illuminated incidents in American history.

It was largely a by-product of the Napoleonic wars.   Napoleon was uniformly successful on land, but while England was equally successful at sea he could not defeat her.   He determined therefore to crush her by economic pressure, to ruin her trade and starve her into submission.   England also sought to use her naval strength to reduce France.   It was a struggle of giants, each putting forth his utmost strength. Edict after edict was issued, like big guns booming at long range, extending the list of contraband, closing enemy ports, threaten-

Incidents leading to the war with England, 1812-14.

ing traders with capture. The restrictions fell heavily on neutral countries, and soon there was hardly a port where an American ship might trade with safety. But though the risks were great and the freight and insurance rates high the profits were large, and the neutral trade went on. Then both belligerents in their death-struggle began to overstep the boundaries of neutral rights, each justifying its action on the grounds of provocation by the other. England since the days of the first Armed Neutrality had had a long-standing quarrel with neutrals over Paper Blockades and "Free Ships make Free Goods," [1] but now both sides indiscriminately seized American ships and searched them for contraband, while British and French ships alike patrolled American shores, invading their territorial waters.

Each side was as guilty as the other, although Great Britain was the more obvious transgressor, as she had more opportunities. But, writes an American historian, "America would have been justified at almost any time during these years in going to war with either France or Great Britain." [2]

The war was, however, finally precipitated by another and independent quarrel which had been brewing between America and England, one which in the circumstances could hardly arise with France. There is no doubt that many deserters from the British navy were finding refuge in American ships, attracted no less by the ease with which they could acquire naturalization than by the deliberate inducements offered to British sailors by American merchants. To this England objected. By her theory of citizenship an Englishman could not renounce his nationality, and in her necessity she could not afford to let him do so. She therefore began to search American ships not only for contraband, but for deserters. The United States bitterly resented her behaviour, and in June 1807, when the *Leopard*, an English fifty-gun ship, fired without warning on the *Chesapeake* and removed four alleged deserters, a climax seemed to have been reached. (One of the deserters was afterward hanged, one died, and two, after five years of wrangling, were returned to the *Chesapeake* and her flag saluted.)

The outrage caused immense excitement in America, and had Jefferson chosen then to go to war with England he would have had a united country behind him. He was, however, reluctant to do so,

[1] These were two of the main grievances of both Armed Neutralities, 1780 and 1800. A Paper Blockade meant that one country should not declare a blockade of an enemy's coasts unless it had the actual naval strength to enforce it. "Free Ships make Free Goods" meant that a neutral flag should cover all goods except contraband, even if they belonged to enemy citizens.

[2] Max Farrand, *The Development of the United States*.

and temporized. A proclamation closing American ports to British vessels seemed to the country a prelude to war ; to Jefferson it was only the first item in a long-pursued policy of "peaceful coercion." It was followed in December 1807 by an embargo which forbade the departure of all vessels in United States ports for any foreign destination. The measure almost ruined the trade of America, especially of New England, and, in spite of successive Acts for its enforcement, which conferred on the Government extensive powers entirely contrary to the Democratic doctrines, it was so frequently evaded that Jefferson in the end repealed it. It was almost the last act of his administration, and spelt the failure of his policy. He substituted for it non-intercourse with either Britain or France, adding, however, a proviso that should either country repeal its decrees trade with it would be renewed. But again America was the greatest sufferer, and again the policy had to be abandoned. Madison reversed the programme, hoping to win with a bribe what his predecessor had failed to win by a threat. Trade with both countries should be resumed, and if either should repeal its orders then non-intercourse with the other should be established.

In pursuance of this Madison let himself be persuaded by a promise of Napoleon, apparently unfulfilled, to send a warning to Great Britain. By this time the party of "War Hawks" in Congress, led by Henry Clay, a Westerner, and John C. Calhoun, a Southerner, were demanding an end to the Government's humiliating inaction. They wanted war and a vigorous defence of the national honour. The Westerners had grievances too against Canada, who they said was stirring up trouble among the Indians. It was the year of the Presidential election, and Madison, it is asserted, as the price of re-election, consented to war. It was in the days of slow communications, and five days before the declaration of war by America it was announced in the House of Commons that the Orders in Council would be repealed.

The war itself falls naturally into three main divisions—in Canada, on the sea, and the two British campaigns in America. **The war (1812–14).**
The desire for the acquisition of Canada was a strong motive for war with many Americans, who believed that they would conquer the colony and then dictate peace. "The militia of Kentucky alone are competent to place Montreal and Upper Canada at your feet," boasted Henry Clay. Several attempts were therefore made, in one of which much of Toronto was destroyed, but all of them proved failures. England could give no protection, and Canada kept herself British by her own resources alone. A Canadian expedition into America was, however, defeated by an American naval victory on Lake Champlain.

On the sea the war consisted mainly of duels between individual ships. Although to English people the best known of these is that between the *Shannon* and the unfortunate *Chesapeake*, there were encounters where victory was carried off by American ships like the *Constitution*, which captured the *Guerrière* and sank the *Java*. The American successes caused great rejoicing in the United States and some consternation in England, and not a little surprise in both countries. They brought a glamour to the war which in American eyes it has never lost. The American ships had excellent sailing qualities, they were often superior in guns and tonnage, and were manned by volunteers. But in the long run the greater weight and numbers of the British navy told, and before the end of the war the American flag had been driven from the seas.

It was not until the end of the Peninsular War that England was able to dispatch troops to America. She then sent two expeditions of veterans, one of which took Washington and burnt the White House. The other tried to seize New Orleans, but was defeated in January 1815 by General Andrew Jackson, a man rapidly rising to fame.

Peace—a peace which has not been broken to the present day—had already been made, however, by commissioners at Ghent. The specific causes of the war were not mentioned in the peace terms, although the end of the Napoleonic wars soon removed the grievances both of the neutral trade rights and of the impressment of deserters. Arising out of the peace there came, however, a settlement of the boundary line between Canada and the United States, an agreement that it should not be fortified, and that there should be disarmament on the Great Lakes—a policy of good augury, which has had the greatest success.

But the war killed the Federalist party. It had strongly opposed the Louisiana purchase; the war and the preceding economic policy nearly drove it to independence. Its strength lay in New England, the area most affected by the embargo and non-intercourse Acts. The militia of the Northern states refused to march into Canada, New England furnished supplies to British troops, and Great Britain exempted three of the states from the blockade. Finally a convention met at Hartford at the end of 1814, which was only saved by peace from putting forward proposals which matched the Virginia and Kentucky Resolutions. The secessionist movement, however, destroyed the party in the eyes of the people.

And so Democrats and Federalists had exchanged programmes. The Federalists had in their turn become 'strict constructionists' and advocates of state rights. The Democrats had become the party of enlarged Federal powers and vigorous Government activities. In 1816 they deliberately adopted Hamilton's policy by re-establishing the National Bank, although in 1811 they had allowed its charter to lapse. They even, like the Federalists, had their insurrection in Aaron Burr's conspiracy in the West. They had survived the Federalists, but only by adopting their programme.

II. THE DEVELOPMENT OF AMERICA, 1815–50

In many ways the war of 1812 was a turning-point in the history of the United States. It was one of many indications that a new stage had been reached, that new conditions were arising which were to modify her life and outlook almost beyond recognition. The old America which had effected the political revolution of 1776 Changing was disappearing—eastern, colonial, dependent, containing America. hardly more than two millions of men and only six "sizable cities," agricultural, with a little fishing in the north, deriving its inspiration mainly from Europe and its impulses from Britain. A new revolution was destroying it, a social and economic upheaval arising out of its own latent forces and virgin opportunities.

Washington was dead, and Alexander Hamilton had been cut off at the age of forty-seven in a duel forced upon him by Aaron Burr, one of the unsuccessful rogues of American history. On July 4, 1826, fifty years to the day of the Declaration of Independence, died John Adams and Thomas Jefferson. The welding of America was left to new men, to Chief-Justice Marshall, one of the best of them, a Virginian of the old school, to Daniel Webster, Andrew Jackson, Henry Clay, and John Caldwell Calhoun. The state which Washington, Hamilton, and Jefferson had launched seemed to have survived its initial dangers, and to be advancing from strength to strength toward the great ideal of "an indestructible Union of indestructible states." Secession, which had reared its head in the Kentucky Resolution and the Hartford Convention, seemed to have been scotched by growing prestige and increasing prosperity. The slavery question seemed to have been given a stable basis in the Missouri Compromise of 1820.[1] Ten new states had by 1821 been born of the Union, and in a confident spirit, which had never seemed more justified, America steered toward an enlarged national consciousness, a greater economic and territorial expansion, and a new democracy. During the war Key had written *The Star-spangled Banner*, and in 1818 the present form of the Stars and Stripes appeared.

The war of 1812 with England is sometimes called the "Second War of Independence." It created a fresh economic opportunity and evoked a new spirit of national self-consciousness. America ceased from that time to be provincial. It self-consciousness. was the first war in which she had been engaged since she sciousness. had won her independence—for the "virtual warfare" of 1798 hardly

2 N [1] See *infra*, p. 576.

counted—and out of the exploits of her seamen she formed a legend to sanctify her unity. Some sectional hostility had undoubtedly been shown, but there had been engendered a real sense of corporate responsibility, and the Federalist party perished because it had committed an offence against the national spirit.

The new tone was quickly marked in foreign affairs. In 1816, over a commercial dispute with Canada, the United States adopted an Foreign almost truculent attitude toward Great Britain, and gained affairs. her will. "Upon a very insignificant subject . . . it was one of the most significant acts," wrote John Adams, "since the Declaration of Independence." [1] It put an end to the sense of inferiority with which her foreign relations had hitherto been conducted, to the period of apprenticeship, of half-achievements like Jay's treaty and the convention with France. She had won a diplomatic triumph over Great Britain.

Six years later came the Monroe Doctrine, in which she was to declare her will to the Holy Alliance. "The American Continents," proclaimed President Monroe, in his famous message to Congress,

> by the free and independent condition which they have assumed and maintain, are henceforth not to be considered as subjects for colonization by any European Powers. . . . The political system of the allied Powers is essentially different from that of America. . . . We owe it therefore to candour, and to the amicable relations existing between the United States and those Powers, to declare that we should consider any attempt on their part to extend their system to any portion of this hemisphere as dangerous to our peace and safety.

Perhaps at the time it meant no more than "Hands off America," signifying that the United States would not permit the exploitation of The Monroe the American continents by European states; that she would Doctrine. resist the establishment of autocracies such as Prussia and Austria in the hemisphere of light; that neither 'legitimacy' nor 'reaction' should find a place in the political life of the Americas; that, in short, she would make the New World "safe for democracy," guaranteeing in return to undertake no political propaganda in Europe. Immediately, she desired to check the advance of Russia from Alaska and the recovery of the Spanish-American colonies by France, and her *non licet* was effective mainly because the power of Great Britain lay behind it.

But the Monroe Doctrine has come to have a more portentous significance; its very ambiguity has enabled it to be elastically interpreted according to America's varying interests. It showed that the United States had already come to consider herself the champion and guardian of democracy in the Western world, and it marked the tendency which

[1] Quoted by Max Farrand, *The Development of the United States.*

she has at other times displayed to identify herself with both halves of the continent. It was the first expression of Pan-Americanism.[1] It was a further severance of the self-made republic from ancestral Europe. It was a manifesto of political isolation, and an appendix to the Declaration of Independence.

The unconscious inspiration of it all was the sense of great unexplored opportunities, the implicit realization that America's "manifest destiny" lay not eastward, but westward. It was an announcement of an intention only half realized, of seeking her fulfilment with her back turned to Europe and her face to the setting sun. The Monroe Doctrine is not therefore in reality as inconsistent as it seems with the great career of expansion on which the United States was about to embark, with the annexation of Texas and the occupation of Oregon, with the appropriation of California, with the assaults on the Spanish colony of Cuba and the British colony of Canada. For it was primarily an assertion of national self-consciousness and, although Europe did not recognize it, a prediction of unrivalled imperialism.

The counterpart of the awakening self-consciousness was revealed in other spheres: in the speeches of the time, in Stephen Decatur's famous toast, "Our country, right or wrong!"; in Daniel Webster's proud identification of America with "free representative Governments, entire religious liberty . . . an unconquerable spirit of free inquiry, a diffusion of knowledge throughout the community such as has been before altogether unknown and unheard-of."

In literature, law, and philanthropy the new spirit was apparent. In 1829 the *Encyclopædia Americana* was published, and Emerson, Hawthorne, Fenimore Cooper, Poe, Whittier, Longfellow, Bancroft, and Holmes were beginning to build up a national literature. John Marshall was strengthening and consolidating the growing unity by a great series of judicial decisions, which have raised the Supreme Court of the United States to the front rank of legal tribunals and justified John Adams's prophecy that in appointing Marshall he had given to his country "a judge equal to a Hale, a Holt, or a Mansfield."

The agencies of commerce, the improved transport facilities, the new roads, the great system of waterways that began with the Erie Canal, the steamboat which appeared first in the year of the embargo and was to revolutionize upstream navigation, the new railway, ridiculed at first, and outpaced by a horse car—all these arteries of the national life were rudimentary but potential forces working for a corporate identity. These were links between East and West, North and South, but the economic factor, nevertheless, was to prove hostile and not friendly to national unity.

The central fact of the middle years of American history is that economically she was developing not nationally, but sectionally.

[1] President Theodore Roosevelt gave official status to this in December 1904.

North and South and West were acquiring divergent interests, which were to bring in their train political divisions and in the end civil war. "We are disgraced beyond help or hope," wrote Daniel Webster. "There is a federal interest, a democratic interest, a bankrupt interest, an orthodox interest, and a middling interest, but I see no national interest, nor any national feeling in the whole matter." He might have added an employer's interest and a workman's interest, a slave interest and a slave-holding interest, a cotton interest and an iron-and-steel interest, manufacturing and agricultural, north and south, east and west.

Economic development sectional.

One of the results of the war of 1812 by stopping the importation of British manufactures had been to throw America upon her own resources. The nascent industries of the Northern and middle states had been strongly encouraged. Factories had sprung up, and a great manufacturing area was in process of development. The return of peace, however, had revived European competition, and a cry of "Protect the infant industries!" came from the suffering manufacturers. Labour troubles had in addition arisen, for slavery had been abolished in the North and free hired labour was difficult to procure in a country where every workman might become a master by going west and acquiring land. Concessions had to be made, wages raised and hours reduced, and the new industries were unable to hold their own without Government protection. Sympathetic Presidents wore homespun garments to encourage native manufactures, and from Madison's "small-clothes from the farm of Chancellor Livingstone" it was only a step to a protective tariff policy adopted first in 1816 and progressively maintained during the next fifteen years. From these import duties there arose in time a surplus of revenue which came to be spent on internal improvements and the development of communications.

The North.

While the North was thus run by manufacturers, bankers, investors, scientists, engaged in manufacture and the profits of manufacture, desiring a high tariff and the opening up of markets, where "the big word was improvements," the South was controlled by planters, slave-holders, buying their manufactures from the North, their cattle and stock from the West, "men on horseback, accustomed to command," where "the big word was chivalry."

The South.

Perhaps there is an inherent antipathy between industrialism and slavery, or it may be because cotton culture acquired too early a hold upon the South that manufacture made little headway there. The wealth, the history, and the fate of the South hung upon the cotton-plant, and upon a small gin or instrument invented in 1793 by Eli Whitney, an ex-Yale student, for removing the adhesive seeds from the fibre.

Few things in this world have so greatly influenced modern life as the fibre of the upland cotton-plant. The development of the demand for cotton goods throughout the world is one of the extraordinary phenomena of the nineteenth century. People left off wearing garments that had been handed down by elder brothers and sisters, and from fathers and mothers, and clad themselves in clothing made of cheap and unenduring cotton fibre instead of the more expensive and longer-wearing flax and wool. Families laid aside their linen sheets for those of cotton, and the sailing-ships of the world—with the exception of men-of-war—ceased the use of linen duck in favour of cotton sailcloth. And whole races of mankind and womankind who before had been innocent of clothing now clad themselves in yard upon yard of cotton cloth.[1]

Behind this social revolution lay the local fortunes not only of Lancashire, but also of the Southern states of North America. Where suitable land could be found cotton was grown. It spread into the favourable Western states, thus forming a 'solid belt' in the South and South-west, bound by one strong economic interest, the cultivation of cotton and its exportation to English and North American markets.

Inextricably allied with it was not only the wealth and prosperity of the South, but its whole social system, and not least of all slavery. In bonds of cotton that proved as strong as steel slavery was tied to the South.

Slavery,[2] which had been regarded as a temporary evil, a disappearing condition, began to assume an entirely different status. It was an easy, and it was believed indispensable, solution to the labour problem. Its importance was magnified; it became a highly valued and in time commercialized asset. It was carried westward with the cotton-plant, and the South, like the North, sought protection for its economic system, not in tariffs, but in Fugitive Slave Laws which guaranteed it against loss of runaway slaves. Thus the economic demands of the North and South were opposed. The North desired cheap labour, the South, which imported its manufactures from the North, wanted cheap goods. It opposed the high tariffs which made them dear. It criticized the application of their proceeds to internal improvements devoted to the interests of the North, and paid for, it alleged, by the South. In time there was to come from it a revival of the theory of state rights, eloquently expounded by Calhoun and Hayne, extended to the length of a logical treatise, and put to a practical test in the Tariff Controversy of 1831–32. In that particular question it was to fail, but the South had realized that the argument

---

[1] E. Channing, *History of the United States*, vol. iv, p. 407.
[2] See *infra*, p. 574 *et seq.*

from the sovereign power of the states was its best weapon of defence. It was to revert to it again in the slavery issue.

The West, on the other hand, desired neither cheap labour nor cheap goods, but cheap land; it was neither manufacturing nor cotton-growing, but land-holding. It was inhabited by **The West.** adventurers, pioneers, settlers, who had gone out from the old states, seeking land for cultivation, for farming, and cattle-rearing, and later for speculation. They wanted small plots at low prices, and so far influenced the Government that in 1820 land was sold in eighty-acre lots at $1.25 an acre. Further, for the purchase and development of their land they required capital, or, still more, easy terms of credit. The West was the debtors' section, and, like most debtors, it came to support a cheap and plentiful currency, a silver and paper standard—which lent itself easily to inflation—rather than gold, and local banks with generous credit terms as against a more rigid National Bank. The East, on the other hand, was the creditor or capitalist section, desiring a stable currency and a well-secured financial system, and, as the manufacturing interest, deprecating cheap land, which attracted its workers away from it.

It is hardly possible to estimate the part played by the West in the development of America. The vast expanse of unexploited, unappropriated territory has entered into her literature, her economics, her politics, and her civilization. The United States has followed for nearly a century an ever-advancing frontier. Its history has been that of the pioneer, the emigrant, and the settler, the story of the breaking in of nature, the mastering of the wilderness, the taming of the prairie, the pushing back of Indians, the clearing of forests, the making of tracks. It has been a record of a rolling tide of expansion, swelled by multiplying streams of immigration from the original states and from across the Atlantic, from Ireland, France, Germany, Poland, the Balkans, as the national tragedies of Europe flung their victims into the wilderness of America. It was a phenomenon without parallel in the history of any civilized country—"swarms of people continually advancing upon the country like flocks of pigeons." "The possession of land," wrote Harriet Martineau in the late thirties,

is the aim of all actions, generally speaking, and the cure for all social evils, among men in the United States. If a man is disappointed in politics or love he goes and buys land. If he disgraces himself he betakes himself to a lot in the West. If the demand for any article of manufacture slackens the operatives drop into the unsettled lands. If a citizen's neighbours rise above him in the towns he betakes himself where he can be monarch of all he surveys. An artisan works that he may die on land of his own. He is frugal that he may enable his son to be a landowner. Farmers' daughters go into factories that they may clear off the mortgage from their fathers' farms, that they may be independent landowners again.[1]

From Virginia and the Carolinas into Tennessee and Kentucky, and thence to Indiana, Illinois, and Missouri; from the South into Texas, along the shores of the Gulf of Mexico, up the Mississippi; from the North into Iowa and Minnesota were the three successive paths of advance. Later a missionary-political movement went north-west into Oregon, and in the south-west the gold-rush stormed California. In the thirties the railways came, webbing the prairies, but by 1860 they had barely threaded their way beyond the Mississippi. The modern civilization of the Middle West is younger than our fathers.

From the ordinance of 1787 the Federal Government had undertaken the surveying, sale, and political regulation of the unappropriated lands. But the zeal of the pioneers ran ahead of the surveyors, and in spite of all attempts to stop them 'squatters' seized the unsurveyed districts, disputing the allotted rights of settlers who had paid for their claim. At last the Government was forced to recognize them, and 'squatting,' which was once illegal, grew to be encouraged.

The histories of nations might be written about their frontiers; that of Rome round her extended lines of defence, that of Prussia round her sandy marshes; and how much of the fortunes of England have hung upon her island security? To the United States the frontier was neither a barrier nor a burden, neither a security nor a defence. It was primarily an opportunity and a treasure, and as such millions have gone forth from the Old and New Worlds to seek it. *The frontier.*

Secondly it was a fringe of humanity "denting the wilderness," throwing like a tide a "layer of scum" before it, breeding a new and different civilization. It was a life of perpetual conflict, with nature, with animals, with Indians, with fellow-settlers. Its domesticity was that of the log cabin, its society too often that of the gambling-saloon, its religion at best that of the revivalist, its philosophy that of pot-luck hunting and rainbow-chasing, its humour of the stables, its discipline the order of the strongest. It was a region where a prisoner might burn down his jail with impunity if he were a good bricklayer, where an election was commonly settled with fisticuffs, where few could read or write, where the parson must be a good chair-maker or a handy man with an axe as well as a brave exhorter, where there was a proverb "The cowards never start and the weak die." That was frontier life. It produced, as would be expected, hardiness and

[1] Harriet Martineau, quoted by Max Farrand in *The Development of the United States.*

resourcefulness, vigour and vitality, individualism, impatience, and that type of democracy where equality is measured by muscle. It bred, too, honesty as well as cunning, kindness as well as cruelty, and the earnest idealism that blossoms from hardship; but it hardly begot respect for tradition, culture, subtlety, or even law. Its view of education might be that of Abraham Lincoln, an object the dearer because unattained, but it was more likely to be that of his father— "Now I haint got no eddication, but I get along better'n if I had." The 'half-horse, half-alligator man' might be strong and shrewd, but his standard of attainment was like to be that of Mike Fink—"I can outrun, outhop, outjump, throw down, drag out or lick, any man in the country, I'm a Salt River roarer, and I'm chockful of fight." Lynch law has left the roadside with "dead men dangling from the boughs of trees" like the native moss of the forest, and the cult of the revolver may be a democratic but is hardly a civilizing force. "In the history of the world there is no example of a society at once dispersed and highly civilized." [1]

"Europe," wrote Emerson, "stretches to the Alleghanies, America lies beyond," and Lord Bryce has confirmed that view. But Eastern America, playing for the vast potentialities of the raw and vigorous West, has herself become submerged in it.[2] What Walt Whitman calls "the dominion-heart of America" has moved inland. Out of the West has come a constant reorganization of social life and political life as men built over and over again from the beginning, an unceasing remeasuring of standards, a new orientation of policy. Thence came the social and cultural differentiation and the political aversion from Europe; the call to territorial expansion, which was the loudest cry of the forties; the new democracy, which "dethroned the Virginia dynasty and revolutionized American politics." In the West too was found that balance of power which saved the Union from disruption.

It is unexpected that America, which condemned unreservedly the imperialism of the *ancien régime*, should have reproduced some of its Territorial main features with almost identical excuses. The Bour- expansion. bons—and the great French Republic after them—talked of "natural boundaries" when they desired a few miles of Belgium or the left bank of the Rhine; America cried "Manifest destiny" and advanced to the Pacific, threatening Great Britain, depriving Mexico of large possessions, occupying half a continent, and shaping an empire larger than that of Rome at its height. The history of the United States is a record of almost continuous territorial expansion, over and above the opening up of the West already mentioned. In

---

[1] Wakefield, quoted by Max Farrand.
[2] It is by no means a forced analogy to compare the influence of Western America upon Eastern with the wearing down of Roman civilization by barbarian influxes.

1803 she acquired Louisiana from France by purchase, and in 1819 East Florida from Spain by treaty. The slave-holding, cotton-growing interests of the Southerners and the friendly indifference of Mexico led to an advance into the Mexican state of Texas, which in 1833 declared itself independent, and nine years later was annexed by the United States. It was the excuse, but not the reason, for a victorious war against Mexico, which, besides creating one or two military reputations, brought to America all the territory lying between Texas and the Pacific, covering more than the present states of New Mexico, Arizona, and California. In exchange the United States gave Mexico fifteen million dollars, and congratulated herself upon her generosity. It is perhaps the worst example in American history of unmitigated imperialism and territorialism. The desire was for California and a port on the Pacific. It was largely a slave-holders' war, barely disguised under the talk of "manifest destiny," and that, said old Parson Wilbur of *The Biglow Papers*, "was one half of 't ignorance and t'other half rum." It was even soberly proposed to seize the whole of Mexico.

The annexation of California at least proved one of remarkable profit. In 1848 one Marshall found there a great lump of soft, malleable metal, which proved to be gold. The story of the gold-rush to California, the luck of the 'forty-niners,' the fortunes made in a fortnight and lost as soon in the gambling-dens which speedily grew up, the misery, squalor, crime, and disappointment that accompanied it, must be left to the romance of history.

A little earlier a missionary enterprise to the Flathead Indians of Oregon had reminded Americans that there too was land worth acquiring. By international arrangement Oregon was open to the joint occupation of Britons and Americans. America, however, bent upon nailing the Stars and Stripes to the Cross, ousted Great Britain by a campaign of colonizing, finally securing a revision of the treaty which extended the Canadian frontier to the Pacific and divided the district between the two countries along the forty-ninth parallel.[1] Again, there were the imperialists with their cry " 54° 40' or fight!" who proposed to make war for the whole of Oregon up to that latitude.

Thus in the four years from 1844 to 1848 the United States had nearly doubled her area, and added, in Oregon and the Mexican Concession, territory larger than her original extent in 1776. There were filibustering raids into Cuba, even into South America. There was a looking toward Canada, and the purchase of Alaska from Russia in 1867 was justified in some quarters by the argument that it would

---

[1] The story goes that a British commission consisting of sportsmen was sent to investigate the district, who, finding that the salmon in the Columbia River would not rise to the fly, reported that Oregon was not worth having.

complete the rounding off of North America, when the whole continent would be united under one flag. Trade-routes began to be opened up with Japan; the valley of the Amazon was explored.

Out of the West came also not only imperialism, but radicalism. **The new democracy.** Up to 1829 the Government of the United States had been in the hands of conservatives; it had been ruled by a class; its democracy had been aristocratic; its Presidents—all but two—Virginians. As the West developed its influence began to be **Andrew Jackson (1829-37).** shown in the increasing democratization of the Governments of the states. But its greatest triumph was the return of Andrew Jackson of Tennessee to the Presidency in 1829.

He came to the White House with the mud of all America's great rivers and swamps on his boots, with records of victories in battles against savage Indian tribes and trained Continental European generals who had fought Napoleon, with shattered ribs and the bullets of Tennessee duellists and gunfighters of the South-west in his body; he knew little grammar and many scars, few classics and many fast horses.[1]

He came

taking the place of John Quincy Adams, who was asking large funds for a national university and a colossal astronomical observatory, " a lighthouse of the skies," a lovable, decent man who knew all the capes, peninsulas, and inlets of New England, who had been across the Atlantic and stood by the Thames and the Seine rivers, and had never laid eyes on the Mississippi nor the Wabach River. Harvard went under as against the Smoky Mountains and the Horseshoe Bend.[1]

With Andrew Jackson a genuine social and political revolution was effected. It was symbolized at the scene of his inauguration.

The buckskin shirts of the Kentucky settlers and the moccassins of the Indian-fighters from Tennessee were seen in the crowd and along with politicians, preachers, merchants, gamblers, and lookers-on, swarmed in to the White House reception, took their turns at barrels of whisky, broke punch-bowls of glass and chinaware, emptied pails of punch, stood on the satin-covered chairs, and had their look at " Andy Jackson, our President." [1]

A new measure of conduct, a new standard of popularity, and a new idea of equality were introduced. "Americans were not equal because Jefferson put it in the Declaration of Independence," it was said, but when Andrew Jackson let the Western crowd into the White House equality, the frontiersman's conception of equality, was won. With "Old Hickory," as his soldiers loved to call him, genuine American democracy, the democracy of the West, came in, and, with the Declaration of Independence and the Monroe Doctrine, Jackson's

[1] Carl Sandburg, *Abraham Lincoln.*

Presidency is the third great stage in the birth and maturing of the real America.

But Jackson, the soldier, the man of duels, of profane speech, ferocious, arbitrary, passionate, was a strong individualist, and in a popular way a despot. His first action was to dismiss all the holders of existing Federal offices, large and small, and replace them with his own followers. "To the victors belong the spoils." His excuse was that they were the corrupt nominees of a ruling clique. Thus the reprehensible 'spoils' system was set going, which has contributed so deplorably to the professionalism of American politics.

The destruction of the National Bank, to which Jackson, true exponent of the West, was violently hostile, was a like piece of autocracy and partisanship. Refusing to wait until its charter came up for renewal, he removed from the bank all the Government moneys and distributed them among local 'pet' banks of the states. He then wiped off the National Debt, and as there happened to be a surplus in the Treasury he determined to divide it in an indirect manner among the states. In the meantime the local banks, encouraged by the Government deposits, had so freely issued paper money, and granted such easy terms of credit to the land-holders of the West, as to create a veritable boom in land speculation. Successive plots of land were bought only to be mortgaged and then sold, payment to the Government being made in paper currencies, which were in their turn placed with the banks. It was a vicious circle of financial inflation, and Jackson, realizing this, suddenly ordered all land to be paid for in specie, at the same moment as he had authorized the banks to distribute the surplus Federal revenue among the states. The result was a hasty calling in of loans, a reduction of credit, a shortage of specie, and in 1837 a financial panic. State Governments which had embarked upon ambitious improvement schemes were forced to abandon them to private contractors. They found themselves unable to meet the interest on the loans they had raised to pay for them, and so many defaulted as almost to justify Dickens's jibe that "the repudiation of debts was a national institution in the United States." The lands of the West, which seemed to have been the source of the panic, began in despair almost to be given away, and—only sure remedy of all—there followed a reform in the conditions of banking.

Not only for his vivid personality, nor for his attack on the National Bank, nor for his contribution to the professionalism of politics, nor for his concentration of executive power in the Presidency, nor only as signifying the triumph of the West, was Andrew Jackson the most notable President between Jefferson and Lincoln. It was his great stand for the Union in the nullification controversy of 1832 that put him into the front rank of benefactors of his country.

In 1828 a high protective tariff had been issued by the Government of John Quincy Adams. It was highly objectionable to the South, who called it the Tariff of Abominations and determined to resist it. A great controversy arose, in which the South, headed by John C. Calhoun of South Carolina, Vice-President until he quarrelled with Jackson, and by Senator Hayne, enunciated and developed the theory of state rights—which had already been broached in the Kentucky Resolutions. The argument was based on the assumption that the Federation was a compact of sovereign states, each of whom retained its indestructible sovereignty. The state therefore possessed the right, the argument proceeded, to decide, in a convention of its chief men, whether its agent, the Federal Government, had exceeded its powers; and, in such a case, as in the Tariff Act in question, which had been enacted for 'protective' and not for 'revenue' purposes, to 'nullify' such legislation and resist its operation within its borders, until such time as Congress could lay the matter before all the states in the form of a proposed amendment and secure the requisite three-fourths majority.

Discussion raged in the Senate, leading to the most famous Parliamentary debate in American history, between Hayne and Daniel Webster. With the writings of Alexander Hamilton the speeches of Daniel Webster must be linked, as the Old and New Testaments of the Union. To the theory of its indissolubility he gave a classic interpretation which not only profoundly influenced Abraham Lincoln, but has become a part of every American's mental equipment.

It was determined to test the views of the President, who had come to office with the solid support of the South, and largely on the re-action against the tariff. He was invited to a Democratic dinner on Jefferson's birthday, at which there were speeches and talk, the burden of which was the glorification of state sovereignty. Then Jackson rose and gave his famous toast, "The Union, it must be pre-served." Calhoun replied with, "The Union, next to our liberties most dear." The challenge had been given, and Jackson had accepted it.

Nevertheless in 1832 South Carolina proceeded to 'nullify' the Tariff Act and to take steps for defending its action. Medals were struck reading "John C. Calhoun, First President of the Southern Confederacy," and a flag devised bearing a palmetto-tree coiled with a rattlesnake and the inscription "Don't tread on me." Troops were summoned, and Governor Hayne made proclamations.

Jackson replied promptly. He called out the Federal troops, introduced a Force Bill into Congress (while preparing to act without it if necessary), and sent a message to South Carolina—"Tell them, if one South Carolina finger be raised in defiance of this Government

I'll come down there, and once I'm there, I'll hang the first man I lay hands on to the first tree I can reach." Privately he let it be known that that man should be John C. Calhoun.

In fact, war was avoided, somewhat to Jackson's disappointment, by a Compromise Tariff negotiated by Henry Clay, the architect of many compromises; but the issue of nullification had been raised, which, over a far more serious matter than a tariff, was to split the Union. "The tariff," declared Jackson, "was a mere pretext. . . . The next pretext will be the negro or slavery question."

The prophecy was realized. In the tariff question the South claimed to have won a victory, but its real significance was that in Andrew Jackson, as again in Abraham Lincoln, the West had spoken for the Union.

About this time there was in American political history a new grouping of parties. The decay of the old Federalists had been followed by an "era of good feeling," when party con- New party troversy temporarily ebbed. It flowed again with the groupings. triumph of Andrew Jackson. On the whole the lingering Democratic party which claimed Jefferson for its founder tended to support Jackson. His enemies therefore formed an opposition group which took the name of Whigs. The Whigs can only be called an episode in American Parliamentary life. They were not the exponents of a natural political division, nor were they a homogeneous unit. They were mainly a coalition of the opponents of Andrew Jackson, and though they survived the termination of his Presidency Democrats they came to an end as a political group in the fifties. They and Whigs. only twice succeeded in putting their candidate into the Presidency, and both times he died almost immediately after taking office. Whether they had any important contribution to make to constructive statesmanship is impossible to say, but it is not easy to see clear lines of principle between them and their opponents. They were neither an aristocratic nor a democratic party; the title of 'Whigs' implied the advocacy of a Parliamentary oligarchy, as against the despotic power of the President. Many of them supported Clay's "American Policy," national improvements, internal developments, and protective tariffs. Many, but not all, were opposed to slavery, and protested against the policy of President Polk, which led to the Mexican War. There were many Whigs in the South, and still more Democrats in the North, but on the whole the former was the party of the North and the latter of the South. On the whole, too, the former dwelt more upon the Union, and the latter upon the rights of the states. As is perhaps natural to a party of opposition and of criticism, the Whigs contained the most intelligent—and perhaps the most public-spirited—men of the day, men like Henry Clay, Daniel

Webster, John Quincy Adams, Abraham Lincoln, and they gained the alliance of distinguished foreign exiles, like Victor Hugo, who fled to America after the unsuccessful European revolutions of 1848.

In political organization the Whigs were soon forced to adopt the methods of the Democrats, who introduced the practice of regional conventions [1] to decide both upon the party programme and the candidates for Federal offices. It is perhaps not forcing the argument to see in the Whig electioneering tactics for President Harrison in 1840 the influence of Western standards, which came in with President Jackson. In reply to the taunt of their opponents that Harrison was a drinker of hard cider who lived in a log cabin, they adopted the slogan "Hard cider and log cabin," and conducted a campaign of "Hurrah and Unreason," in which log cabins and barrels of cider were conducted in tour round the country. [2]

Although a military reputation was an asset to candidates for the Presidency there was a growing tendency to choose nonentities for the post, and to pass over the best men for the highest rank. It was partly due to the complexity of the party programme, and to the increasing professionalism which invaded American politics. The party organization, the spoils system, both witnessed and contributed to it. It seemed as if so much energy was absorbed in the opening of the West and the development of rich native economic potentialities as to leave none over for politics. Thus government was left to those willing to make a business of it, and two classes of men arose, "those interested in business and a smaller class interested in politics: or it might be said that all were interested in business, only some were making a business of politics. It is a fact to be remembered at every stage of American history from that day to this." [3]

III. SLAVERY AND SECESSION, 1850–70

"If destruction be our lot, we must ourselves be its authors. As a nation of freemen we must live through all time or die by suicide," said Abraham Lincoln in an early speech, apprehending justly the direction whence the United States was to be imperilled. Whether

[1] The local party groups would elect delegates to the county conventions, the counties to the state, the states to the National Convention.

[2] On this occasion, when the state of Maine voted for Harrison at its state election, the Whig song-books came out with the famous rhyme :

> " Oh, have you heard how Maine went ?
> She went hell-bent
> For Governor Kent,
> And Tippercanoe and Tyler too."

Tippercanoe was the scene of a military exploit of Harrison's against the Indians in 1810.
[3] Max Farrand, *The Development of the United States*.

the Civil War was fought for slavery or for the right of secession it is not necessary to distinguish. The two were inseparably intertwined. It has been seen that there were two fundamentally diver- gent views of the Union from its formation, that the theory of state rights was one which was constantly reviving, that it was promulgated by all parties, and was the customary weapon of attack adopted by an opposition against the Government in power. On the other hand, only a strong economic interest like slavery would have forced the constitutional issue beyond compromise to civil war. Thus while many people regarded slavery as the end and secession as the means, there were some to whom slavery was but an excuse to assert the right of secession.

Inter- mixture of the consti- tutional and economic issues.

It must always be remembered that at the time of the Declaration of Independence slavery existed in every American state save Massa- chusetts, that it had then flourished for more than two hundred years, since the day when a "Dutchman of Warre" appeared in the harbour of Jamestown, and "sold us twenty Negars," which twenty had with successive importations grown into more than two millions by the end of the eighteenth century. Without entering into the controversial question of whether negroes were intended to be covered by the state- ment "all men were created equal," it is enough to notice that the general opinion of the more prominent Americans toward the end of the eighteenth century was that slavery was an evil— a temporary and disappearing one. In the North it was soon abolished north of the southern boundary of Penn- sylvania, which came to be known as the Mason-Dixon line, after the men who had surveyed it. In the new territory west of the Alleghanies and north of the Ohio River it was forbidden by the Ordinance of 1787, and in the South it seemed to be coming to an end, more by individual emancipation than by legislative enactment. It was common for land-holders like Washington to set free their slaves, and Jefferson proposed a scheme of gradual emancipation to be com- bined with deportation [1] which, had it been adopted, would have rescued America from some of her sharpest difficulties.

Slavery held to be a dying institution

The slave-trade was also being voluntarily forbidden by state after state, although by agreement it could not be abolished by the Federal Government before 1808.

That was the first stage in the history of slavery as a Federal ques- tion. The second opened with Eli Whitney's invention of the cotton- gin and the consequent rapid development of cotton cultivation. It

---

[1] One of the obvious difficulties of deportation was that negroes freed and restored to Africa would most probably be recaptured as slaves by a native tribe, and either be held in slavery in their own country or resold to traders. It was arising out of this problem that Sierra Leone was founded as a ' sanctuary ' state for free negroes.

has already been mentioned that the industry turned slavery into an economic asset too valuable ever to be willingly surrendered. Philanthropic sentiment faded, hastened by the revolt of the slaves of San Domingo and the problems caused by the migration into the South of the free blacks from the North. Self-interest came rapidly to be enforced by argument, and slavery, which perhaps at one time would have been voluntarily relinquished by the South, now came to be an institution to be retained at all costs. It became a growing factor in the national polity, an ever-recurring problem, multiplying in its application, sharpening in its issue. It poisoned the relations between the United States and the liberal countries of Europe; it was the underlying motive in the hastening or retarding of American westward expansion; and from the earliest discussions in Congress to the attack on Fort Sumter it was a disrupting force in the Union. "America entered into the shadow of the Civil War before she had emerged from that of the War of Independence."

until the development of cotton,

Had the mere existence of slavery in the Southern states been the only issue the difference of opinion might have been settled by compromise. But again the West entered in, and behind the existence of slavery lay the vital question of its extension to the new territories. On this development of the problem compromise broke down.

For from the beginning a policy of mutual concession had been adopted on a matter where neither side had been prepared to give way. A clause denouncing slavery as one of the crimes of George III had been struck out of the Declaration of Independence in deference to the wishes of South Carolina and Georgia. The Ordinance of 1787 had prohibited slavery north of the Ohio River, but it had provided for the surrender of fugitive slaves. The makers of the constitution yielded to slavery what the necessity of the case required. Slaves were to count in the allocation of representatives to the states, but only three-fifths of them.

but from the beginning a subject of compromise.

Then in 1820 came the "Missouri Compromise," on which slavery rested for thirty years. It arose out of the colonizing of the lands purchased by Jefferson from Napoleon in 1803. The Ordinance of 1787 had fixed the Ohio River as the dividing line between slave and free states east of the Mississippi; west of that river no arrangement had been made, until the admission of Missouri, part of the Louisiana Purchase, and opposite the mouth of the Ohio River, brought the question up before Congress for settlement. It was finally agreed to admit Missouri itself into the Union as a slave state, but to fix the parallel of latitude (36° 30′) of her southern boundary as the northern limit of slavery in lands west of Missouri. Thus for thirty years, from 1820 to 1850, the slave boun-

The Missouri Compromise, 1820.

dary ran along the Mason-Dixon line to the Alleghanies, then down the Ohio River to the Mississippi, then up along the northern frontier of Missouri, and afterward south and west along the latitude 36° 30'.

In the meantime slavery became increasingly fastened on the South and more and more the fabric of its economic, social, and political life. Romance, which has whitewashed the West, has blackened the South, but the institution of slavery in itself seems on the whole not to have been an unhappy one for the negroes. They were normally well cared for, and not overworked nor hardly treated in old age, and in two hundred years there were only three rebellions. Their economic worth depended upon their physical fitness, and many Southern slave-holders felt a real sense of responsibility, and would no more maltreat a slave than an Englishman would a horse. Often real attachments existed between the negroes and the families to whom they belonged, whom they had often served from childhood as devoted companions. Some emancipated negroes would beg to be taken back again into slavery; some themselves held slaves. There were grades and codes of precedence among them. House negroes looked down upon field negroes, and both despised the 'po' white trash,' the struggling poor whites whom the institution of slavery put into a most difficult economic position.

On the other hand, there were undoubtedly abuses, which most slave-holders deplored as much as the enemies of slavery, and these were bound to recur in a relationship which depended primarily on the decent humane instincts of the owner. There were the evils of the illicit slave importations which grew up under the American flag in defiance of the Government. A fortune might be made in a single journey by packing men and women 'spoon-fashion' in a space between decks three feet ten inches high, the men chained together two and two by the ankles, and so transporting them across the Atlantic. There was the pathos of the slave-market and the scenes of the auction room, where families might be broken up and sold apart. There were the scandals of slave-breeding, and the cruelties of the hunting of fugitives. These things existed, though they were regretted, and the breeder, and trader, and hunter of slaves were loathed as much south as north of the Mason-Dixon line.

Not a few of the slave-holders regarded slavery as based on an abstract evil. But they disclaimed responsibility for its introduction, and justified its retention on the ground that no other The defence relationship between the black and the white races was of slavery. possible, that the negro was reasonably happy, and better off than the white factory hand of the Northern states and than the English agricultural labourer. They believed him to be economically indis-pensable. They depreciated his capacity for intellectual advancement, argued that "teaching slaves to read and write tended to insurrection and rebellion," and made it a penal offence to give a slave a book, not excepting the Bible. It was a measure of safety to forbid the assembly of more than seven negroes without the presence of a white man.

There were apologists of slavery who went farther, like Thomas Rodrick Dew, Professor of History, Metaphysics, and Political Law at the University of Virginia. To those critics who quoted Jefferson's statement that "the whole commerce between master and slave is a perpetual exercise of the most boisterous passions" he pointed out the "slave-holding population," "everywhere characterized by noble and elevated sentiments." To the charge that it was against the rights of nature and of man he replied "it is the order of nature and of God that beings of superior faculties and knowledge, and therefore of superior power, should control and dispose of those who are inferior."

There were some who alleged that slavery was against the law of Christ. To them also he gave an answer:

> We deny most positively that there is anything in the Old or New Testament to show the master commits any offence in holding slaves. No one can read the New Testament without seeing and admiring that the meek and humble Saviour of the world in no instance meddled with the established institutions of mankind. He came to save a fallen world, and not to excite the black passions of men, and array them in deadly hostility against each other. He nowhere encourages insurrection. He nowhere fosters discontent, but exhorts always to implicit obedience and fidelity.

In short, the negro was enslaved for his own good, to save him from his own vile passions of laziness, vagabondage, and improvidence, and to fulfil the divine law.

Though there is much to be said for the contentment of the slaves, there is about the arguments that flavour of sophistry which often creeps into a defence of self-interest. "If slavery is not wrong," said Abraham Lincoln, "then nothing is wrong." Once, however, the conception of slaves as property was granted the demand for the extension of slavery to new territories was logical. It was an unpardonable restriction of liberty to prevent a Southerner from taking his goods with him to his new home. "Why," asked Senator Badger of North Carolina, "if some Southern gentleman wishes to take the nurse who takes charge of his little baby, or the old woman who nursed him in childhood, and whom he called Mammy until he returned from College, and perhaps afterwards too, and whom he wishes to take with him in his old age, when he is moving into one of these new territories for the betterment of the fortunes of the whole family—why in the name of God should anybody prevent it?" To which Senator Wade of Ohio retorted: "The Senator entirely mistakes our position. We have not the least objection, and would oppose no obstacle to the Senator's migrating to Kansas and taking his old Mammy along with him. We only insist that he shall not be empowered to sell her after taking her there." [1]

Behind the ethical controversy there lay the natural indignation of the South against an attempted dictatorship of the North. Many Northerners felt with Abraham Lincoln that slavery was wrong, but that, having been recognized in the terms of Union, having been "nominated in the bond," it must in fairness to the South and as a constitutional obligation be legally preserved. They were determined therefore only to prevent the extension of slavery to new lands, from the conviction that slavery restricted was slavery doomed. On the other hand, there was a strong and growing "Aboli- *Northern Abolitionists.* tionist" party, which demanded the total extinction of slavery. They described the constitution as "a covenant with Death and an agreement with Hell," and were as much enemies of the Union as the seceders. It was the fear of being deprived of their *Constitutional* constitutional safeguard that drove the Southerners to the compact theory of the Union: that each state had compacted with its neighbours for certain ends; that it had surrendered no portion of its sovereignty, nor its right to withdraw from the Union if its ends were no longer served, if its privileges were withdrawn *and economic grievances.* and its inherent liberties overridden. The resistance of the South was further embittered by the knowledge that the North did not pursue its philanthropy at its own expense and by an irritating economic dependence upon Northern manufactures, "from the rattle with which the nurse tickles the ear of the Southern child to the shroud that covers the cold form of the dead." That slavery, the mainstay of the South, should be exposed to the legislation of those who were not economically interested was as galling a piece of tyranny as any in history, and sooner than endure it there were many who would see the Union dissolved.

It was the 'spoils of Mexico' which reopened the political controversy at the end of the forties and led in a crescendo to civil war. Most of the territory won from Mexico lay south of the latitude 36° 30', but the Missouri Compromise, which fixed this boundary, applied specifically to the Louisiana Purchase. The growing anti-slavery sentiment of the North, exacerbated by the conviction that the Mexican War was a slave-holders' war, and seriously perturbed by the reintroduction of slavery into Texas, where Mexico had abolished it, was bent upon opposing the formation of new slave states out of the ceded lands. The "Wilmot Proviso," that slavery should be excluded from all lands conquered from Mexico, was defeated, but threw Con-

[1] Quoted by Max Farrand, *The Development of the United States.*

gress into confusion.   The struggle turned upon California, the most
coveted of the 'spoils.'   There the gold-diggers, in the inaction of Congress, had drawn up a constitution for themselves, which excluded
slavery.   Calhoun called it "a piece of gross impertinence," and the
South, set upon resisting the admission of California to the
Union as a free state, were thus driven by the action of the
'squatters' into the embarrassing and apparently aggressive
position of trying to impose slavery upon an unwilling
community.   A rupture between North and South seemed imminent,
and might even have been precipitated had Zachary Taylor, the Whig
President, lived long enough to force the admission of California.   But
the compromisers prevailed, Henry Clay, the architect of the Missouri
Compromise, and Daniel Webster, who gave him his support.   The
Compromise of 1850, that makeshift of despairing statesmanship, was
passed to save the Union.   California was to be admitted as a free
state.   The remaining territories were to be regulated by their own
inhabitants, and a new Fugitive Slave Act was to be passed, which put
into the hands of the Federal Government the hunting and restoration
of runaway slaves.

The
California
struggle
(1850).

The Clay Compromise was significant.   The South had gained the
principle of squatter sovereignty, as it was called, which might easily
mean an extension of slavery north of 36° 30', and it had won the
authority of the Federal executive for an extremely harsh slave law.

The rupture, however, had been averted.   Men talked of the
finality of the Compromise, and turned to commercial matters—
except that in 1852 a trim, frail, pious little woman of Evangelical
upbringing, Harriet Beecher Stowe, with a delicate husband and six
children, full of care, and penury, and feeling, stirred to indignation
by the exercise of the Fugitive Slave Act, wrote a book
which made her own fortune, and did more than anything
else to turn a political campaign into a popular crusade.   That
book was *Uncle Tom's Cabin*, one of the most potent 'best sellers'
of any age.

"Uncle Tom's
Cabin."

The next step came from an unexpected quarter.   Clay and Webster and Calhoun, masters and creators of an aggressive South, were
dead.   The new men were Seward and Sumner, Jefferson Davis
and Stephen Douglas.   The "little giant," as Stephen Douglas was
called, was rapidly becoming the leader of the Democratic Party.
It is perhaps harsh to call him an adventurer, but, besides his own
advancement, he seems to have been indifferent at this time to everything, even slavery, except the internal development of America.
Later he took active steps to preserve the Union, but at this stage he
moved on the plane of 'expediency,' and when he introduced his Bill
for the opening of the lands west of Missouri into the organized

states of Kansas and Nebraska he made a bid for the Southern votes by proposing the repeal of the Missouri Compromise and the settlement of the slave question on the principle of squatter sovereignty. The Kansas-Nebraska Bill became law in 1854. The first result was that a race took place for the colonization of Kansas between the advocates of slave and free soil, in which fraud, stratagem, bribery, and bloodshed played a large part. Secondly, by the repeal of the Missouri Compromise the friends of emancipation saw themselves deprived at one blow of the advantages they had held for sixty years. They saw slavery, far from being restricted, actually growing; they saw the possibility of its indefinite extension over the whole territory of the United States. They were infuriated by the devices by which the South tried to insinuate or force slavery into Kansas. They were dumbfounded by the Dred Scott decision of the Federal Court in 1857, which not only declared that a slave was a chattel without rights, but that the Missouri Compromise was unconstitutional, and that slavery could not legally be excluded from any soil of the Union.

The Kansas-Nebraska Act (1854).

The Dred Scott decision (1857).

In 1859 a fanatic, John Brown, rifled a Government arsenal and tried to raise an insurrection of slaves at Harper's Ferry, in the valley of the Shenandoah. He was hanged, but he had his supporters. William Lloyd Garrison publicly burned a copy of the constitution, which he had called "an agreement with Hell." It seemed as if it would be the Northerners who would destroy the Union. In 1854, following the Kansas-Nebraska Act, a new Republican party had been formed to resist the extension of slavery. The party programme did not include either the abrogation of the constitution or the abolition of slavery. Its stand was upon Lincoln's phrase, "to put back slavery to where the Fathers had left it," but it undoubtedly included and was bound to be associated with a strong Abolitionist movement, followers of Garrison and sympathizers with John Brown, though men like Lincoln condemned both. It was the fear of the triumph of this section which explains, what seems otherwise inexplicable, why the election to the Presidency in 1860 of the Republican candidate, Abraham Lincoln, should have seemed to South Carolina the signal for civil war. It was the growing consciousness that, as Lincoln had himself expressed it, "the Union could not permanently endure half slave, half free," together with the realization that the North had it in its power to work its will, whether it were abolition or merely restriction. Already its greater population could control the House of Representatives, the numerical superiority of free states was about to give it the Senate, its victory at the polls had put the Government into its hands. In a sense, as Lowell said, the grievance of the South was the "census of 1860," and Lincoln's return had proved that the North could carry a sectional programme by the The census weight of its own numbers. In the election figures the of 1860. South saw the word *finis* writ large, the end of its privileges, perhaps of its liberty, and the certainty of political impotence.

The career of Abraham Lincoln is in a sense as remarkable a phenomenon of modern democracy as that of Napoleon Bonaparte. Abraham It is, however, far less accountable. Abraham Lincoln Lincoln was a great President, but it is no easy matter to take the (1809-65). measure of his greatness, to assign it with sureness to his character, to his opportunities, to the spirit of tragedy which invested his end. It is mingled with wonder that he did so much and with regret that he did not live to do more, and the whole is pervaded by a haunting sense of fortuity.

"Abe" Lincoln was born in 1809, in a log cabin of Kentucky, of migrant settlers. He grew to manhood in the knowledge of the backwoods and the society of the pioneers. He could split rails and build a cabin, pitch hay and cradle wheat, and he could heave an axe deeper than any man. He was a trusty pilot on the Sangamo River, and twice he took cargoes down the Mississippi to the mouth.

Men remembered him as long, odd, and uncouth, flat of foot, of exceptional strength and unusual ugliness, "solemn as a papoose," with "suthin peculiarsome" about him—his strange fits of melancholy, although he was a practical joker, a homely wit, and a *raconteur* and inventor of stories—his shy awkwardness with women—his unusual kindness to animals—his thirst for knowledge and his shrewd common sense. "My best friend," he said, "is the man who'll give me a book I ain't read," but "books weren't as plenty as wild cats in that part of Indiany."

There is hardly anything before the debate with Stephen Douglas which seemed to mark Lincoln as a man destined for distinction, or even success—some unprofitable storekeeping in New Salem, a little soldiering against the chief Black Hawk, in which his main exploit was to protect an Indian from his own men, eight somewhat undistinguished years in the Illinois legislature, a bare unrepeated two years in Congress, then, having considered whether blacksmithing or carpentering were not more needed, some honest but not very remunerative legal work as solicitor and advocate. His only experience of Federal administration was that of a local post-office, which he carried about in his hat. His domestic life was not happy, the Whig party, which he supported, rarely achieved power, and when it did it denied him the post of Commissioner of the General Land Office, which he wanted, and offered him the Governorship of Oregon, which he refused. He learnt something of politics and of political opportunism, showed a taste for party management and a capacity for solitary thinking, picked up much odd knowledge, and mastered the first six books of Euclid. But at the time when the disputes of the fifties were reopening he seemed to have retired from politics as a failure and to have settled down to an esteemed but by no means brilliant legal practice in Illinois.

The repeal of the Missouri Compromise and the formation of the Republican party, the Dred Scott decision and the threatened extension of slavery, brought Lincoln again into politics. In 1858, on the occasion of a contest for a vacant Senatorship of Illinois, he engaged in a prolonged political debate with Stephen Douglas, which placed him prominently before the nation as a logical and powerful exponent of the principles of the new party. He was nevertheless comparatively an unknown man when he was nominated by the party convention for the Presidency. A split in the Democratic ranks gave him the seat, on the suffrages of the free states alone, and with a minority of the popular votes.

Six weeks after his election was known, South Carolina, a second time leader in disruption, hauled down the Stars and **South Carolina secedes.** Stripes and ran up the palmetto flag in its place.

Thirty years before secession had been averted by the vigour of Jackson and the compromise of Clay, but Buchanan, who had still three months of office to run, was no Jackson. His reply to the action of South Carolina was an ineffective speech, proving, in the words of Seward, the Republican leader, "first, that no state has the right to secede unless it wishes to, and second, that it is the President's duty to enforce the laws unless somebody opposes him."

Compromise too was attempted by Crittenden, a disciple of Clay, but broke down before the opposition of Lincoln himself. Crittenden proposed that the line of 36° 30' should be re-established as the division between slave and free states, except **The Crittenden** for California, which should remain a free state. Owing **Compromise** to the Dred Scott decision, however, this measure could **rejected.** no longer be effected by Congressional legislation, but would have to be incorporated in the constitution as an amendment. Thus slavery would obtain a recognition hitherto denied it; it would become part of the fundamental law of the land, a clause in the political testament of the new democracy, and a crumbling structure would take on a new lease of life, propped up by the flying buttresses of constitutional sanctions. It was for this reason that Lincoln took the responsibility, grave as it was, of causing the rejection of the Crittenden Compromise.

Its failure was followed during January 1861 by the formidable secession of the solid belt of cotton states—Alabama, Florida,

Mississippi, Louisiana, Texas, and Georgia, in order of withdrawal
from the Union.   They formed under the presidency of
Jefferson Davis a new Confederacy, based on the recognition
of the principle of state sovereignty, and on a constitution
not otherwise unlike that of the United States.

The secession of the cotton states.

The volcano was in full operation.   In the North there was bewilderment, until the firing on the flag caused indignation.   Some,
like Horace Greeley, editor of the *New York Tribune*, were for "letting
our erring sisters go."   Garrison, the Abolitionist, advocated the
same policy.   "When I called the constitution 'a covenant with
Death and an agreement with Hell' I did not expect to see Death
and Hell secede from the Union."

But Lincoln was determined to preserve the Union at all costs, and
when on April 12, 1861, South Carolina opened the war by bombarding the Federal arsenal, Fort Sumter, which lay in Charleston
Harbour, Lincoln issued an appeal for volunteers.   Upon this intention of using armed force against 'sovereign' states there took place
the second secession of the border states of Virginia, Tennessee, North Carolina, and Arkansas.   So important was
the adherence of Virginia that the Confederacy thereupon
moved its capital to Richmond.   Thus the sides were
formed for civil war.   The three remaining border states, Missouri,
Kentucky, the President's native state, and Maryland, on whose
decision hung the fate of Washington, were preserved to the North
by the prudence and diplomacy of Lincoln.

The secession of the border states.

With the North and West, for the loyalty of the West was the determining factor, were twenty millions of inhabitants, the organization,
arsenals, capital, and prestige of the Federal Government, the navy,
half the army, and resources which were later to prove valuable
in the manufacture of armaments.   With the South were five and a
half millions, a greater unanimity than ever existed in the North, a
superior capacity for valour and endurance, better generals, and, at
the beginning, better discipline, the chance of foreign support, and
trust in a wide frontier and a good cause.

The odds against the Confederacy seemed heavy, and were to prove
so in the long run.   But it was the Yankees of the North who ran
away in the first battle of Bull Run, in July 1861, and the
offensive campaign in Virginia of the Northern general
McDowell that was defeated.   Except for the clearing of Western
Virginia, and the capture of some strategic points in the West, which
exposed the line of the Mississippi, no successes fell to the Northern
arms before the battle of Antietam, in September 1862.   Even this
battle can only doubtfully be claimed as a Unionist victory, but it
had its importance in the triumph of the North.   It marked the end

War.

and the failure of the Maryland campaign of the Southern general Robert E. Lee, causing him to withdraw (whether against his will or not) into Virginia. It signified the abandonment of what might be called a political offensive, the attempt to gain the adherence of Maryland to the Confederacy.[1]

Secondly, it gave Lincoln the excuse for issuing his famous proclamation emancipating the slaves in all states which were in rebellion against the Union on January 1, 1863. Lincoln's position must be clearly understood. That he disapproved of slavery and heartily desired freedom is undoubtedly true. That he believed that the Union could not permanently endure half slave, half free, is also true. But he held slavery to be a dying institution which if left to itself would be crushed by natural, economic pressure, as long as the slave-trade was forbidden. Its extension he therefore opposed at all points. *Lincoln's proclamation of emancipation.*

On the other hand he bound himself to a rigid observance of the constitution, and to a pledge not to abolish or interfere with slavery in those states where it had previously existed.

When the war broke out Lincoln, to the disappointment of the Abolitionists and of foreign liberal Powers, fought not for the emancipation of the slaves, but for the preservation of the Union. The seceding states must be treated as rebels, and as rebels forcibly brought back into the Union. "My paramount object in this struggle," he wrote to Horace Greeley in 1862,

> is to save the Union, and is not either to save or to destroy slavery. If I could save the Union without freeing any slave I would do it; and if I could save it by freeing all the slaves I would do it; and if I could save it by freeing some and leaving others alone I would also do that. What I do about slavery and the coloured race I do because I believe it helps to save the Union, and what I forbear I forbear because I do not believe it would help to save the Union.

The emancipation proclamation of 1862 was therefore, although fully in accordance with Lincoln's principles, primarily a military rather than an ethical measure. He confiscated the slaves of the South as he would any other piece of enemy property which might have been of military use.

The measure had profound results. In the first place it sealed the

[1] The Southerners believed, or professed to believe, that Maryland was at heart Secessionist, and only prevented from becoming so by Unionist force. This idea gained expression in the soldiers' war-song, " The despotic heel is on thy shore, Maryland ! " which ended :

> " She is not dead, nor deaf, nor dumb ;
> Huzza ! she spurns the Northern scum !
> She breathes ! She burns ! She'll come ! She'll come !
> Maryland, my Maryland ! "

doom of slavery, and before the war was over even the Confederacy was enlisting slaves as soldiers and freeing them on enlistment.

Secondly, it won the sympathy of foreign Powers, and especially of England. Though the English working classes were generally friendly to the North the attitude of the governing powers was by no means sympathetic. There was a greater feeling of kinship for the Southern gentleman, and a realization that a divided America was a more comfortable political proposition than a strong and united one. The incident of the *Trent* [1] on the one side and of the *Alabama* [2] on the other aroused ill-feeling between the Governments of Great Britain and the United States. Whether England would have given to the South a support similar to that given by France to the American colonies in 1778 is an idle speculation, for the proclamation of emancipation made it impossible for a liberal country to go to war on behalf of slavery.

From this time the war became a siege of the Confederacy. Lee's attempt to break through the Northern ring by the invasion of Pennsylvania met with failure at Gettysburg in July 1863, often considered the turning-point of the war. Grant's capture of Vicksburg gave the North strategic control over the Mississippi and the Western Secessionist states. The death of "Stonewall" Jackson a month earlier had deprived the South of its ablest general after Robert E. Lee, while the naval advantage which the Confederacy had gained by the first use of ironclads was lost almost immediately by their adoption by the North.

The campaign of Sherman and Grant in the heart of the Confederate country in 1864 was a record of devastation which wore Defeat of down the resistance of the Secessionists. The hunted the Con- "Lion of the South" fought bravely and suffered long, dying federacy. with the Northern refrain in its ears, "John Brown's body lies a-mouldering in the grave."

The end came on April 9, 1865, at Appotomax Court House, where Northern and Southern generals vied with each other in magnanimity. The terms were generous. After the surrender Grant posted off to see his son settled in at school. The stately Lee turned to his men. "We have fought through this war together. I did my best for you." With these words one of the most chivalrous generals of any war abandoned the profession of arms for the comparative obscurity of a college headship.

---

[1] Two Southern envoys on their way to England in an English ship, the *Trent*, were seized and carried off by Captain Wilkes of the United States Navy—a breach of international law for which Lincoln finally made reparation.

[2] The *Alabama* was an English ship, built in Liverpool dockyards, which was allowed, through the connivance or negligence of the English Government, to sail for America. She took service under the Confederacy, and was responsible for serious depredations against Northern ships.

In the number of men engaged and the area over which operations were extended, the war had been conducted on a scale without parallel until 1914. Within twelve months a professedly peaceful people had raised an army of 500,000 men by voluntary enlistment, which after the war melted back again into the civilian population, leaving only 25,000 men under arms, and falsifying all anticipations of Bonapartism and militarism. It had been feared, too, that the defeated states would never completely coalesce with the victorious North, yet in spite of the humiliating treatment they received during the decade after the war the disunion party came to be entirely discredited. One of the most justifiable experiments in nationalism that was ever made had failed; that few Southerners now regret that failure is a reflection which might well be borne in mind by the reckless nationalists and the optimistic nation-makers of to-day.

Five days after Lee's surrender, on Good Friday, April 14, Abraham Lincoln was shot through the head in a theatre by John Wilkes Booth, an actor-fanatic. *Sic semper tyrannis.* So perished the most generous of tyrants, simple, great, and indomitable. *The assassination of Lincoln.*

> The kindly-earnest, brave, foreseeing man,
> Sagacious, patient, dreading praise, not blame,
> New birth of our new soil, the first American.[1]

He had wielded an unrivalled power, he had withstood alike the pusillanimity of the North and the dogged resistance of the South; he had preserved the Union. Growing in greatness as he had grown in power, in self-reliance and devotion to his country, he had dedicated himself resolutely to the enduring vision and the great task before him, "that this nation, under God, shall have a new birth of freedom, and that government of the people, by the people, for the people, shall not perish from the earth."

His firm and generous statesmanship was never more needed than after his death. He had already envisaged the problems of reconstruction in the spirit of the second inaugural:

> With malice toward none; with charity for all; with firmness in the right, as God gives us to see the right, let us strive on to finish the work we are in; to bind up the nation's wounds; to care for him who shall have borne the battle, and for his widow, and his orphan—to do all which may achieve and cherish a just and lasting peace among ourselves, and with all nations.

He had drawn up a practical scheme for the full readmission of Louisiana into the Union, upon her nullification of the ordinance of secession, her repudiation of the Confederate debt, and her ratification of

[1] James Russell Lowell, *Ode* (1865).

the Thirteenth Amendment to the constitution, which had been passed
in 1865 to confirm the emancipation of the slaves.   But his assassina-
"Recon- tion left the inheritance of reconstruction to Andrew John-
struction." son, a man ill-equipped for a very difficult position.   As
a Southerner and a Democrat he lacked the support of the Republican
North; as a Unionist during the war he was execrated by the Secessionist South.   Pugnacity and faults of temper further weakened the
hold of one who had not the prestige either of popular election or of
having carried through and won the war.   Bitter quarrels quickly
broke out between the President and Congress.   In the latter the
Republicans obtained a majority large enough to override the President's veto; they even went to the length of impeaching him.   He
was acquitted, but at the end of his term of office he was superseded
by Ulysses S. Grant, the victorious Northern general, who put off
his greatness with his uniform, and became little more than a tool
of the Republican party.   "Black Codes" passed by the legislatures
of the Southern states to discriminate against the negro played into
the hands of the radical section of the party, which quickly gained
the upper hand, and proceeded to impose upon the South its own
schemes of reconstruction, the basis of which was the enfranchisement and exalting of the former slave.   Two amendments (XIV and
XV) to the constitution were passed, giving to the negro the full
voting rights of an active citizen and disqualifying Secessionist leaders
from office.   The rejection of the Fourteenth Amendment by certain
of the Southern states provided an excuse for laying the South under
military rule.   Carpet-baggers of the North aided by scalawags [1] of
the South, in league with negro adventurers, and supported by a
black militia, began to exploit the ignorance and corruptibility of the
newly emancipated and enfranchised slaves, and to establish over the
whites a political tyranny and a social oppression which was known
in the South as the "Black Terror."

The "Black Codes" which had been passed by the state legislatures
were of course repealed.   Governing bodies were filled by the negroes
or their agents, and became hotbeds of corruption.   It could hardly
be expected that the ex-slave should regard his vote as anything but
a commercial asset.   "It's de fifth time I's been bo't and sold,"
observed one negro, "but, fo' de Lord, it's de fust time I eber got de
money." [2]   State debts grew rapidly where every Government official
held the public finances to be fair spoil.   Social anarchy, looting, and
crimes of violence accompanied political corruption.   In short, as sang
the negro rioters who paraded Charleston, "De bottom rail's on top
now, and we's gwine to keep it dar." [2]

[1] Carpet-baggers and scalawags were political agents.
[2] Quoted by C. Chesterton, *History of the United States*, p. 222.

The South took its protection into its own hands. Suddenly there appeared over the countryside horsemen clothed from head to foot in white, "ghosts of the Confederate army," who began to mete out justice and punishment to the offending negroes and their agents. One evil had begotten another. The Black Terror had raised up the Ku Klux Klan [1] and the secret society.

An end came when the Republican North, to secure the election to the Presidency of its candidate, Rutherford B. Hayes, agreed to withdraw the soldiery from the Southern states. Left to itself, the South was rapidly restored to the control of the whites. It was natural that they should build up a social and legislative wall to protect themselves from the negroes. They could not openly defy the Fifteenth Amendment, which declared that no one should be deprived of a vote on account of race, colour, or previous condition of servitude. But they disfranchised them indirectly by tests of literacy and property, while protecting the whites who might fail before the tests by the famous "grandfather clause," which gave a vote to anyone who had been enfranchised or whose father or grandfather had been enfranchised in 1867. They excluded and isolated the blacks by social codes.

In the meantime many of the freedmen, deluded by dreams of the millennium or indulging native indolence, refused to work, and, becoming thriftless and restless, drifted into the towns. The large cotton plantations began to decay, and the South turned to industrialism, losing as it did so not only its own distinctive economic and social life, but that dependence upon the manufactures of the North which had hitherto given it an almost provincial character.

IV. The End of the Frontier

The two questions which had concerned the United States since her origin had received an answer—whether final or satisfactory posterity alone can decide.

Slavery was not to be extended or tolerated, but abolished. America was to be a country of citizens with free and equal political rights, according to the underlying principles of the Revolution. Negroes were to be counted as men with full opportunities to enjoy the powers and privileges their own capacities could achieve, or the prejudices of the whites allow them. Before the law of the constitution they had as good a right to "life, liberty, and the pursuit of happiness" as any Southern planter or New England manufacturer.

[1] A secret club or circle (Kuklos), founded first, in May 1866, at Pulaski, Tennessee, but which rapidly spread all over the South. Kindred societies sprang up, such as the " Knights of the White Camelia," " Pale Faces," " Constitutional Union Guards," the " White Brotherhood," and so on.

Secondly, America's political structure was to endure as an "indestructible union of indestructible states." The compact theory of the sovereignty of the separate states was discredited, and the secession of any one of them was to be held as much an act of rebellion as the separation of the county of Kent from England. The attempt of the Southern Confederacy, which, if successful, would probably have been hailed as a laudable piece of nationalism, was to be relegated to the failures of history, as an unvindicated cause. Democracy and federalism had won the future.

With a constitution secured and a frontier unthreatened it was natural that America should turn her attention to developing her immense natural resources and to growing rich. In these two pursuits and their consequences is written much of her history for the next fifty years. At the end of the Civil War she entered upon a phase of rapid material expansion, which has brought of itself world-power and world-recognition. It has also completed the transformation of American civilization which began when colonizers set up states on the far side of the Alleghanies. "I believe that from our European point of view the United States of seventy years ago was far more mature than the United States of to-day." [1] The words are those of an English political writer, and point to that new civilization which seems to the Old World to be dominating America, a civilization which, although based on certain political assumptions taken from Europe, is being built up from fresh foundations by a new people growing ever more confident of its own taste and its own solutions to the problems which confront it.

Until the beginning of the twentieth century America kept her face averted from Europe. The opening up of undeveloped lands continued, and six states were added to the Union in the two years 1889 and 1890. A railway was built to the Pacific, and then followed the rapid construction of subsidiary lines, which filled the American seventies with a mania like that of the English forties. The Government adopted a lavish policy of land endowment toward both individuals and corporations. A hundred and sixty acres of free territory was offered to anyone who would work it for five years, and broad lands became a Government bribe or the easy reward of state enterprise—as long as there were any unappropriated. With the extermination of the bison cattle-ranching sprang up on such a scale that the cowboy became the symbol and hero of the West. As the population spread westward, however, cattle-ranching began to give way to wheat-farming, which in its turn has fallen on evil days before the all-absorbing industrialism.

Advancing Americanism revived the old problem of the red race,

The internal development of America.

[1] *The Times*, March 13, 1928.

and opened the new one of the yellow. At the time of the purchase
of Louisiana the Indians had been driven into the West, where, it was
promised, they should remain undisturbed. The promise was not
fulfilled, and a series of petty conflicts accompanied the march of the
white man westward. After the Civil War President Grant, announcing that it was cheaper to feed than to fight the Indians, adopted the
policy of concentrating them in great reservations. The disappearance of the bison, which had formed a large part of the food-supply
of the Indians, forced them to submit. Even then, however, they
were not left in peace. As the unoccupied land became scarcer the
reservations were encroached upon, and in 1887 they were definitely
broken up, under pretext of allotting to each Indian a liberal measure
of land. Although the Indians still congregate largely in group settlements the fairest lands have been taken up by the whites.[1] The reds,
like the blacks, have been admitted to full political citizenship, and
during the Great War more than ten thousand of them were on
military service.

Whatever claims to America might be made by the Indians, none
outside common philanthropy could be advanced by the Chinese, and
later the Japanese, who began to swarm on the Pacific coast, The
introducing cheap competitive labour and a conflicting Oriental.
civilization. It is a problem common to all Europeanized peoples of
the Pacific coasts. Successive Acts were passed by the United States
rigidly restricting yellow immigration, and in 1892 a Federal statute
excluded from the United States all Chinese who had not already
acquired the right of residence. "Yet the Chinese," declared President Wilson, "were more to be desired, as workmen, if not as citizens,
than most of the coarse crew that came crowding in every year at
the eastern ports."[2]

With the twentieth century the Japanese Question became more acute
than the Chinese, and from 1905 to 1913 exclusion laws were especially
directed against the subjects of the Empire of the Rising Sun.

---

[1] President Wilson describes the rush to enter the Indian Territory : " In 1889
the Government had purchased of the tribes even a part of the Indian Territory
which lay within the circle of Kansas, Arkansas, and Texas, to be thrown open
to white settlers—the fairest portion of it, Oklahoma, the Beautiful Land, which
lay almost at its heart ; and all the country had heard how mad a rush there had
been across its borders to secure its coveted acres. A host of settlers fifty thousand
strong had encamped upon its very boundary lines to await the signal to go in
and take possession. At noon on the 22nd of April, 1889, at the sound of a bugle
blown to mark the hour set by the President's proclamation, the waiting multitude
surged madly in, and the Territory was peopled in a single day. It was the old,
familiar process of first occupation and settlement carried out as if in a play, the
story of the nation's making in a brief epitome. Its suddenness, its eagerness, its
resistless movement of excited men marked in dramatic fashion the end of the day
of settlement." (*A History of the American People*, vol. v, p. 212.)
[2] President Wilson, *ibid.*, p. 213.

For the great possibilities of wealth and the comparative political freedom attracted the discontented of all nations. From the middle to the end of the century an ever-broadening tide of immigration swept upon the eastern shores of America; and whereas to begin with the majority of immigrants came from Germany, Great Britain, Ireland, and the Northern and Western nations, the greater number soon came to be drawn from Russia, Poland, Italy, Austria, and South-eastern Europe. This is no occasion to discuss the relative capacity for colonization, citizenship, and adaptability of the various European nations. In such matters as literacy, technical skill, and general cultural qualities the standard of immigration rapidly deteriorated. Moreover, the later immigrants, inexperienced in self-government and unfamiliar with the traditions of early American constitutionalism, could be —and were—exploited both by the great industrialists and by the party bosses, to the inevitable deterioration of both industrial and political life. At first the new immigrants were tolerated "because they occupied no place but the very lowest in the scale of labour," [1] but the undesirability soon came to be realized and measures were soon taken to regulate and check indiscriminate immigration. A quota has now been fixed, and tests of literacy have been imposed, one effect of which is to exclude the agricultural classes while admitting those from the towns. But with an immigration of 40,000,000 aliens within a century it is inevitable that the life and civilization of America should show the marks of the heterogeneous character of its population.

If the primary feature of the half-century following the Civil War was the national growth and expansion, the second and no less prominent one was certainly its remarkable industrial development. Up to 1880 the United States may be called primarily agricultural; from that date she has become primarily industrial, and so far have American trade and manufactures advanced from the dependent days before 1812 that she is now an exporting nation. In her industrial growth she has grasped and combined the two unprecedented opportunities of place and time that have been offered her—a vast market that is both internal and continental, and the unequalled mechanical efficiency of the age, which she has improved by a large expenditure on scientific research. Her manufactures have become the wonder of the world. Highly efficient organization, elaborate specialization of labour, mass production— features attendant upon the large-scale market which dominates America—have resulted in a maximum of economy.[2] They have

(Marginal notes: *Immigration.* · *Industrial growth.*)

[1] President Wilson, *op. cit.*, p. 214.
[2] The tendency to monopolies or 'trusts' has of course modified this result.

also tended to produce a minimum of diversity and individual artistry.

A further by-product has been the increase in the consuming power of the people, and a large part of industrial profits are now everywhere allocated to the fostering, by art and artifice, of habits of spending. This has among other things created an exalted standard of material comfort among all classes, and, together with the real scarcity of labour, has led to high wages for the workers. Among the considerations affecting the labour and industrial conditions of America, however, must be included the high cost of living, the excessive use of the instalment system, which mortgages the possessions of the poor and reduces the economic elasticity of the workers in times of industrial depression, and finally the variations and abuses due to the fact that commercial and economic law is a matter for state and not Federal legislation. From this it arises that there are still one million children between the ages of ten and fifteen working in factories, and that there are no national systems of old age pensions or health and unemployment insurances at present.

The European War of 1914–18 not only gave a great impetus to the export trade of America, but enabled her to take the fullest advantage of what may be called the Second Industrial Revolution, which resulted from the development of electricity just before the War. It allowed her, therefore, to secure dominant control of some of the more recent industries, such as that of the motor-car and the new art-form of the cinema, and Detroit and Los Angeles have enjoyed a world pre-eminence which was, however, being assailed before the outbreak of the war of 1939. Moreover, since America is as yet economically self-sufficing, except in one or two commodities such as rubber, she has been well able to afford to protect her own industries from foreign competition by a high tariff wall.

Great wealth and an immense financial power have come to America from her industry, and during the War of 1914–18 the position which England had long held as creditor of Europe passed from her to the New World. One of the consequences of this was that in practice the United States became the chief recipient of German reparations.

The foreign policy of America was comparatively unimportant until the end of the nineteenth century, since when it has been marked by a growing prestige and a continued expansion. Foreign policy.

After the Civil War a section of the Republicans would have been not unwilling to provoke a foreign war in order to bring home to the country the consciousness of its unity. An opportunity seemed to offer itself in the Mexican expedition organized in the early sixties by Napoleon III. The French Emperor, like his uncle, was drawn to the prospect of the revival of French colonial power in the West, and,

2 P

in contravention of the Monroe Doctrine, he attempted to set up the Archduke Maximilian of Austria—Napoleon was anxious to conciliate Austria at that time—as Emperor of Mexico. The expedition was a disastrous failure. As soon as the Civil War was over the United States adopted a high tone, and summarily ordered Napoleon to withdraw from the New World. The French Emperor, unwilling to go to war with the United States, ordered his troops to retire. The unfortunate Archduke, victim of Bonapartist ambition, was left behind to his death. His wife, driven mad by grief, lived on in insane and merciful oblivion until 1927.

On the question of the *Alabama* claims against England America also took up a firm position, securing from Gladstone's Government, by a notable arbitration, three and a quarter million pounds sterling.

In 1867 Alaska was bought from Russia for seven million dollars. It proved a lucrative purchase. In gold alone many times more than the purchase money has been taken out of the province, which has also rich reserves in timber, coal, agriculture, and fisheries.

In 1895, by an elastic extension of the Monroe Doctrine, the United States interfered in a boundary dispute between Great Britain and Venezuela, and forced a settlement by arbitration.

Two years later a war broke out between America and Spain over the misgovernment of the Spanish island of Cuba. The United States was successful, securing for Cuba independence under an American protectorate, and for herself Porto Rico, the Philippine Islands, and the small island of Guam. In the same year, at the request of the inhabitants, the Hawaiian Islands, two thousand miles off the coast of California, were also annexed to the United States. The Republic had entered on a new stage, that of holding colonies or territory outside the Union.

The Spanish-American War opened a new stage in American history. After a long period of absorption in internal affairs incidental to reconstruction after the Civil War and to the development of national resources it marked a return to an active foreign policy and to the imperialism of the forties and fifties. For the first time it brought to America colonies and colonists outside the Union. It introduced her into the Caribbean Sea, the control of which she rapidly secured during the next few years. It brought her into contact through the Philippine Islands with the advancing power of Japan. In short, it set her on the path toward taking her place in international affairs as an imperialistic world Power.

It is not possible to indicate more than the stages by which, largely under the ambitious and even aggressive leadership of President Theodore Roosevelt (1901–9), whose accession was as significant as that of King Edward VII in the same year, the United States assumed a position of increasing importance not only in the American continent, but in Asia and Europe.

The development of relations with Japan brought America into world affairs from the Pacific side, for it became increasingly evident that wholly outside the European system there was arising in the Far East a Power which would have to be reckoned with as a great empire. In the Russo-Japanese War of 1904–5 the United States acted as mediator, allowing something of a diplomatic defeat to be inflicted upon the Japanese Empire in spite of her military victory. There was in consequence some ill-feeling between America and Japan, fostered further by immigration disputes with California. In 1907, therefore, President Roosevelt went to the length of ordering his fleet to embark upon a voyage round the world, and to call at Japanese ports with a view to impressing her with the might of the United States.

Another marked demonstration of the growing world consciousness of the United States, and a serious departure from the Monroe Doctrine, was the part taken by America in the wholly European question of Morocco in the Algeciras Conference of 1906.

Perhaps the most important development of the new foreign policy, however, was seen in the Caribbean Sea and in Central America. One of the immediate consequences of the entry of the United States into this area was the revival of the project of the canal between the Atlantic and Pacific Oceans. Control of sufficient territory for its construction was secured from Panama by the somewhat high-handed method of encouraging, by a military demonstration, the secession of the state of Panama from the republic of Colombia. An even bolder step was that adopted by the United States of intervening, on behalf of the Monroe Doctrine, between bankrupt West Indian islands and European countries who sought to enforce the payment of debts to their own nationals. Such protection was of course welcomed by the insolvent state; it was only when America, in an attempt to prevent financial disorder by ensuring political order, began to interfere in internal affairs that Latin America began to look askance at its powerful northern protectress.

By one means or another, often by war or warlike menace, the United States has secured practical control over what is called the area of the larger Canal Zone. It has set up protectorates, established financial supervision of some of the islands (and even the administration of Haiti), ensured a monopoly of canal routes, exercised powers of policing disorderly countries, and acquired naval and coaling stations.

Some of these measures were defended by the doctrine of Pan-Americanism, which has become almost as fashionable a creed—and threatened at one time to be almost as aggressive—as the Pan-

Germanism and Pan-Slavism of Europe. Even though it is now mainly directed toward the establishing of closer relationships between all parts of the American continent, it still induces restiveness in some of the South American states. A series of Pan-American Conferences has been inaugurated, consisting of delegates from all the independent nations of the New World, and a Pan-American Union exists at Washington to spread information about the natural resources of the two halves of the continent, and to promote friendly sentiments between their inhabitants.[1]

In the European War of 1914–18 the divided sentiments of the American people, of whom one-fifth are German, prevented the participation of the United States for three years. At length, however, popular opinion declared itself on the whole in favour of the Western Allies, and in April 1917 America, wholly abandoning the Monroe Doctrine, threw her strength on to that side. For nineteen months she was at war, and for five her soldiers were in the fighting-line. The War has been alleged to have strengthened the centripetal forces in the country.

The entry of the United States into the war of 1914–18 was regarded by many people as the sign of her abandonment of that tenaciously held ideal of national isolation implicit in the Monroe Doctrine. But the sign proved false. The United States emerged from the War with a clear determination "never again" to repeat such an intervention in European problems. She detached herself from the League of Nations which her President, Woodrow Wilson, had done so much to bring into being. She refused responsibility for the execution of the terms of peace, and withdrew from participation in most of the post-War reconstruction problems. Her disillusionment was accentuated by Great Britain's inability, on account of her own debtors' having defaulted, to pay the debts to America which the United States had gone to war so largely to protect; and when the Italo-Abyssinian war broke out the United States further reinforced her isolation by neutrality legislation designed to prevent her becoming involved in European conflicts through the export of munitions of war. The rise of the Nazi menace and the outbreak of war between the chief democratic Powers (Great Britain and France) and Germany led President Roosevelt and the Democratic Party to try to repeal legislation which would obviously handicap the democracies. The first attempt in August 1939, on the eve of war, was defeated by the Isolationists. The second, initiated three weeks after the outbreak of war, was successful.

---

[1] The most recent expression of Pan-Americanism is President Franklin Roosevelt's statement that the United States will lend the protection of its armed forces to any state of the two Americas against external aggression.

A reference must be made to American politics, which have since the Civil War been marked by corruption, professionalism, and increased organization.   Except for one or two abortive attempts to form a third party, the two-party system has Politics. continued to this day.   The titles of Republican and Democrat have been retained, although the slavery issue has disappeared.   The Republican party, closely identified as it always was with the interests of the North, has been generally allied with the big business interests, and has stood for a protective tariff.   For fifty years after the Civil War it commanded for the most part a majority in the Senate and the House of Representatives, and with one or two exceptions returned its candidates to the Presidency.

After a long interval during which no legal change was made in the constitution six amendments have been added in the second and third decades of the twentieth century.[1]

A distinct reaction from the materialism which seemed to be dominating America has been noticeable in the new century, and a real idealism has entered again into the social and political, internal and external, life of the country.   It has shown itself in educational, economic, and social experiments at home, in direct intervention in European affairs in the war of 1914–18, in volunteer action in the Spanish war (1936–39), in a wide interest in the moral issues of international politics, and in efforts to promote international arbitration and (as in the Briand-Kellogg Pact of 1928) international peace.

Perhaps, however, the most important feature of recent American history is the 'passing of the frontier.'   The vast territory between the Alleghanies and the Pacific has now been appropriated.   The last states have been carved out and admitted to the Union.   The 'frontier,'[2] which for more than a century has been pushed ever farther west by pioneers or exiles seeking fortune or adventure or escape, has now reached its geographical limit, and the dominant factor in the remarkable development of the United States during the first century of its history has been eliminated.   Its consequences for the future of America must prove incalculable.

The entry of the United States into the European War in 1917 was perhaps in itself a sympton of a redirection of American energies hitherto absorbed in westward expansion.   But the effects of the passing of the frontier, which no longer offers an outlet for surplus energy, nor a safety valve for economic and social lawlessness, which no longer invites a reckless exploitation of lavish and apparently limitless resources, are still greater in home affairs.   It was unfortunate for the United States that the closing of expansion in the West should immediately precede the world economic, social, and moral disintegration which followed the Great War. It is not, however, fortuitous that this event, which compelled the United States, like other nations with closed frontiers, to stand and face her economic and social problems, should be followed by the most comprehensive and radical programme of Federal legislation since the emancipation of slavery.

It is not possible here to describe President Roosevelt's measures to deal with the economic and social depression and disorder which he found on his entry into office in 1933. He checked financial panic, saved the banks from collapse, instituted vigorous Federal police action to suppress the crime which had passed far beyond State resources, and passed a number of laws [1] through Congress to check depression, to promote trade and industry, help farming, relieve and reduce unemployment, and improve social and economic conditions. His measures brought a vast, unprecedented accretion of power to the Federal authority, and it was inevitable that they should therefore be challenged in the courts as unconstitutional by those opponents of the programme (and there were many) who were interested in its suppression. In consequence during 1934 and 1935 three-quarters of the Roosevelt legislation was disallowed by the Supreme Court as *ultra vires*.

This in its turn raised the question of the status of the Supreme Court, which, originally appointed as guardian of the constitution, seemed to the Democrats to have become the guardian of property and privilege and the enemy of progress. Its position lay, indeed, outside ordinary legislative amendment, but President Roosevelt did what he could by introducing into Congress an age-limit for judges of the Supreme Court (most of whom had long passed it) which would have enabled him to appoint a more sympathetic *personnel* to the Bench. His proposal was defeated, but its intro-duction seems to have frightened the Supreme Court into more favourable judgments on the Roosevelt programme, and some of its measures have been allowed to stand. But great constitutional as well as great economic questions have been raised.

[1] The whole programme is comprised in the New Deal. The National Industrial Recovery Act and the Agricultural Adjustment Act are the best known.

PRESIDENTS OF THE UNITED STATES OF AMERICA

1. George Washington (March 4, 1789–March 4, 1793)
2. George Washington (March 4, 1793–March 4, 1797)
3. John Adams (March 4, 1797–March 4, 1801)
4. Thomas Jefferson (March 4, 1801–March 4, 1805)
5. Thomas Jefferson (March 4, 1805–March 4, 1809)
6. James Madison (March 4, 1809–March 4, 1813)
7. James Madison (March 4, 1813–March 4, 1817)
8. James Monroe (March 4, 1817–March 4, 1821)
9. James Monroe (March 4, 1821–March 4, 1825)
10. John Quincy Adams (March 4, 1825–March 4, 1829)
11. Andrew Jackson (March 4, 1829–March 4, 1833)
12. Andrew Jackson (March 4, 1833–March 4, 1837)
13. Martin van Buren (March 4, 1837–March 4, 1841)
14. William Henry Harrison (March 4, 1841–April 4, 1841)
15. John Tyler (April 4, 1841–March 4, 1845)
16. James K. Polk (March 4, 1845–March 4, 1849)
17. Zachary Taylor (March 4, 1849–July 9, 1850)
18. Millard Fillmore (July 9, 1850–March 4, 1853)
19. Franklin Pierce (March 4, 1853–March 4, 1857)
20. James Buchanan (March 4, 1857–March 4, 1861)
21. Abraham Lincoln (March 4, 1861–March 4, 1865)
22. Abraham Lincoln (March 4, 1865–April 15, 1865)
23. Andrew Johnson (April 15, 1865–March 4, 1869)
24. Ulysses S. Grant (March 4, 1869–March 4, 1873)
25. Ulysses S. Grant (March 4, 1873–March 4, 1877)
26. Rutherford B. Hayes (March 4, 1877–March 4, 1881)
27. James A. Garfield (March 4, 1881–September 19, 1881)
28. Chester A. Arthur (September 19, 1881–March 4, 1885)
29. Grover Cleveland (March 4, 1885–March 4, 1889)
30. Benjamin Harrison (March 4, 1889–March 4, 1893)
31. Grover Cleveland (March 4, 1893–March 4, 1897)
32. William McKinley (March 4, 1897–March 4, 1901)
33. William McKinley (March 4, 1901–September 14, 1901)
34. Theodore Roosevelt (September 14, 1901–March 4, 1905)
35. Theodore Roosevelt (March 4, 1905–March 4, 1909)
36. William H. Taft (March 4, 1909–March 4, 1913)
37. Woodrow Wilson (March 4, 1913–March 4, 1917)
38. Woodrow Wilson (March 4, 1917–March 4, 1921)
39. Warren G. Harding (March 4, 1921–August 3, 1923)
40. Calvin Coolidge (August 3, 1923–March 4, 1925)
41. Calvin Coolidge (March 4, 1925–March 4, 1929)
42. Herbert Hoover (March 4, 1929–March 4, 1933)
43. Franklin D. Roosevelt (March 4, 1933–   )

GENEALOGICAL TABLES

THE HOUSE OF BOURBON IN THE OLDER AND YOUNGER (ORLÉANS) LINE

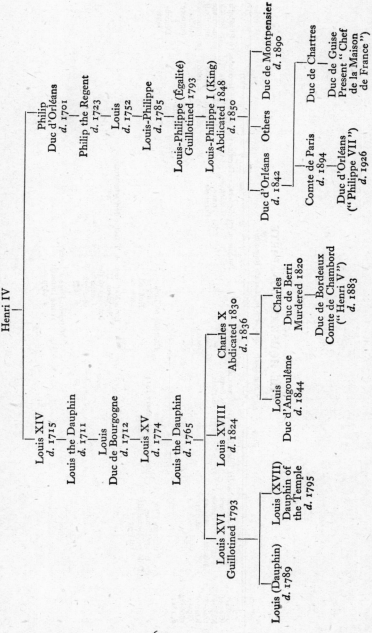

Henri IV

Louis XIV
d. 1715

Louis the Dauphin
d. 1711

Louis
Duc de Bourgogne
d. 1712

Louis XV
d. 1774

Louis the Dauphin
d. 1765

Louis XVI
Guillotined 1793

Louis (XVII)
Dauphin of
the Temple
d. 1795

Louis (Dauphin)
d. 1789

Louis XVIII
d. 1824

Louis
Duc d'Angoulême
d. 1844

Charles X
Abdicated 1830
d. 1836

Charles
Duc de Berri
Murdered 1820

Duc de Bordeaux
Comte de Chambord
("Henri V")
d. 1883

Philip
Duc d'Orléans
d. 1701

Philip the Regent
d. 1723

Louis
d. 1752

Louis-Philippe
d. 1785

Louis-Philippe (Égalité)
Guillotined 1793

Louis-Philippe I (King)
Abdicated 1848
d. 1850

Duc d'Orléans
d. 1842

Others

Duc de Montpensier
d. 1890

Comte de Paris
d. 1894

Duc d'Orléans
("Philippe VII")
d. 1926

Duc de Chartres

**Duc de Guise
Present "Chef
de la Maison
de France"**

THE HOUSE OF BONAPARTE

Carlo Maria Bonaparte *m.* Letizia Ramolino

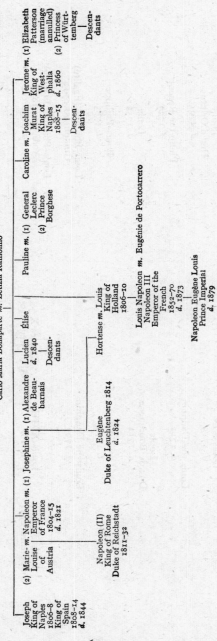

Joseph King of Naples 1806–8 King of Spain 1808–14 *d.* 1844

Napoleon *m.* (1) Josephine *m.* (1) Alexandre de Beauharnais

(2) Marie- *m.* Napoleon *m.* (1) Josephine
Louise of Austria

Napoleon *m.*
Emperor of France 1804–15 *d.* 1821

Napoleon (II) King of Rome Duke of Reichstadt 1811–32

Eugène Duke of Leuchtenberg 1814 *d.* 1824

Lucien *d.* 1840 Descendants

Élise

Hortense *m.* Louis King of Holland 1806–10

Louis Napoleon *m.* Eugénie de Portocarrero Napoleon III Emperor of the French 1852–70 *d.* 1873

Napoleon Eugène Louis Prince Imperial *d.* 1879

Pauline *m.* (1) General Leclerc (2) Prince Borghese

Caroline *m.* Joachim Murat King of Naples 1808–15

Descendants

Jerome *m.* (1) Elizabeth Patterson (marriage annulled) King of Westphalia *d.* 1860 (2) Princess of Württemberg

Descendants

602

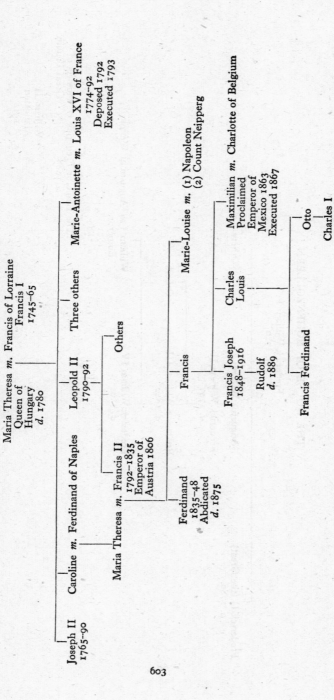

THE HOUSE OF HABSBURG-LORRAINE

THE HOUSE OF HOHENZOLLERN

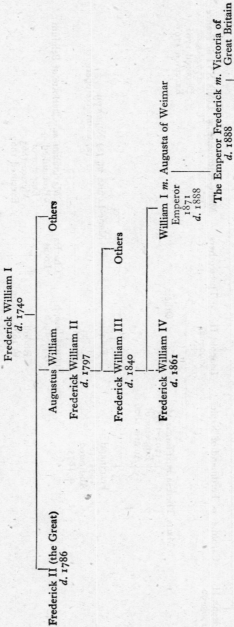

Frederick William I
d. 1740

Frederick II (the Great)
d. 1786

Augustus William

Others

Frederick William II
d. 1797

Frederick William III
d. 1840

Others

Frederick William IV
d. 1861

William I *m.* Augusta of Weimar
Emperor
1871
d. 1888

The Emperor Frederick *m.* Victoria of
Great Britain
d. 1888

William II
Abdicated
1918

THE HOUSE OF ROMANOV

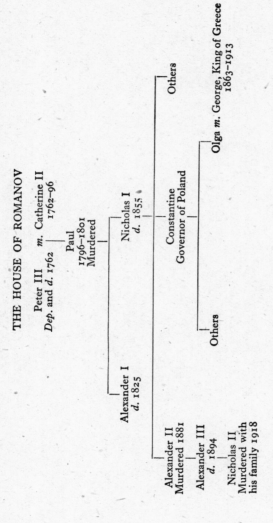

Peter III *m.* Catherine II
Dep. and d. 1762   1762–96

Paul 1796–1801 Murdered

Alexander I *d.* 1825

Nicholas I *d.* 1855

Alexander II Murdered 1881

Alexander III *d.* 1894

Nicholas II Murdered with his family 1918

Constantine Governor of Poland

Others

Others

Olga *m.* George, King of Greece 1863–1913

A FEW SUGGESTIONS FOR FURTHER READING

GENERAL

BEAZLEY, C. R. : *Nineteenth-century Europe and Britain.*
FISHER, H. A. L. : *The Republican Tradition in Europe.*
FYFFE, C. H. : *History of Modern Europe.*
GOOCH, G. P. : *History and Historians in the Nineteenth Century.*
HERTSLET, Sir E. : *The Map of Europe by Treaty.*
LAVISSE, E., and RAMBAUD, A. N. : *Histoire Générale.*
OAKES, Sir A., and MOWAT, R. B. : *Select Treaties and Documents.*
PHILLIPS, W. ALISON : *Modern Europe.*
ROBERTSON, C. GRANT, and BARTHOLOMEW, J. G.: *An Historical Atlas of Modern Europe, 1789-1914.*
ROSE, J. HOLLAND : *The Development of European Nations* (new edition, 1922).
The Cambridge Modern History.
Articles in the *Encyclopædia Britannica* (13th edition).
" Nations of To-day " series (edited by John Buchan) : *Belgium ; France ; Italy ; Japan.*

SPECIAL SUBJECTS
(in order of treatment)

STEPHENS, H. MORSE : *Revolutionary Europe.*
—— *The French Revolution.*
MADELIN, LOUIS : *The French Revolution.*
—— *Danton.*
DE TOCQUEVILLE, A. : *L'Ancien Régime.*
GAXOTTE, PIERRE : *La Révolution française.*
AULARD, A.: *The French Revolution.*
SOREL, A. : *L'Europe et la Révolution française.*
FAY, BERNARD : *The Revolutionary Spirit in France and America.*
SEELEY, J. R. : *Life and Times of Stein.*
ROSE, J. HOLLAND : *Life of Napoleon.*
—— *Napoleonic Studies.*
ROSEBERY, LORD : *Napoleon : the Last Phase.*
LUDWIG, E. : *Napoleon.*
FISHER, H. A. L. : *Napoleon.*
—— *Bonapartism.*

FORTESCUE, Sir J. W.: *History of the British Army*.
—— *Wellington*.
WARD, A. W.: *History of Germany*.
WEBSTER, C. K.: *The Foreign Policy of Castlereagh*.
—— *The Congress of Vienna*.
—— *The European Alliance, 1815–25*.
TEMPERLEY, H. W. V.: *The Foreign Policy of Canning*.
METTERNICH: *Memoirs of Prince Metternich*.
BISMARCK: *Reflections and Reminiscences*.
PHILLIPS, W. ALISON: *The Confederation of Europe*.
HEADLAM, J. W.: *Life of Bismarck*.
ROBERTSON, C. GRANT: *Bismarck* ("Makers of the Nineteenth Century").
LUDWIG, E.: *Kaiser Wilhelm II*.
DAWSON, W. H.: *The Evolution of Modern Germany*.
KING, BOLTON: *History of Italian Unity*.
TREVELYAN, G. M.: *Garibaldi's Defence of the Roman Republic*.
—— *Garibaldi and the Thousand*.
—— *Garibaldi and the Making of Italy*.
—— *Manin and the Venetian Revolution*.
SIMPSON, F. A.: *Louis Napoleon and the Recovery of France*.
GUEDALLA, PHILIP: *The Second Empire*.
DE LA GORCE, P.: *Histoire du Second Empire*.
MARRIOTT, Sir J. A. R.: *The Eastern Question*.
SETON-WATSON, R. W.: *Racial Problems in Hungary*.
—— *The Rise of Nationality in the Balkans*.
MILLER, W.: *The Ottoman Empire*.
WALLACE, Sir DONALD MACKENZIE: *Russia*.
BEAZLEY, C. R., FORBES, N., and BIRKETT, G. A.: *Russia from the Varangians to the Bolsheviks*.
WHYTE, G. F.: *A Century of Spain and Portugal*.
GOOCH, G. P.: *History of Modern Europe, 1878–1919*.
GREY, VISCOUNT: *Twenty-five Years*.
HANOTAUX, G.: *La France Contemporaine*.
BODLEY, J. E. C.: *France*.
RUSSELL, BERTRAND: *Roads to Freedom*.
SHADWELL, A.: *The Socialist Movement, 1824–1924*.
GOOCH, G. P., and TEMPERLEY, HAROLD (editors): *British Official Documents on the Origins of the War, 1898–1914* (in course of production).
"*The Times*" *Documentary History of the War*.
BUCHAN, JOHN: *History of the War*.
POLLARD, A. F.: *A Short History of the Great War*.
(The official publications of the belligerent nations should be consulted, and much evidence can be obtained from contemporary memoirs.)
DICKINSON, G. LOWES: *The International Anarchy*.
MOWAT, R. B.: *A History of European Diplomacy, 1914–25*.
GOOCH, G. P.: *Recent Revelations of European Diplomacy*.
TEMPERLEY, H. W. V.: *A History of the Peace Conference of Paris*.

KEYNES, J. M. : *The Economic Consequences of the Peace.*

TOYNBEE, A. J. : *Survey of International Affairs, 1920–25.*

STURZO, LUIGI : *Italy and Fascismo.*

GIBBONS, H. A. : *Europe since 1918.*

SLOSSON, P. W. : *Twentieth-century Europe.*

RAINE, G. E., and LUBOFF, E. : *Bolshevik Russia.*

MUIR, RAMSAY : *The Expansion of Europe.*

HERTSLET, Sir E. : *The Map of Africa by Treaty.*

JOHNSTON, Sir H. : *The Opening Up of Africa.*

LUCAS, Sir C. : *The Partition of Africa.*

LIVINGSTONE, D. : *Missionary Travels.*

—— *Researches in South Africa.*

STANLEY, Sir H. M. : *How I found Livingstone.*

—— *In Darkest Africa.*

CROMER, EARL OF : *Modern Egypt.*

MORRIS, H. C. : *A History of Colonization.*

EGERTON, H. E. : *A Short History of British Colonial Policy.*

KEITH, A. B. : *Imperial Unity of the Dominions.*

—— *War Government of the British Dominions.*

WHYTE, Sir A. F. : *China and the Foreign Powers.*

BAU, J. : *The Foreign Relations of China.*

DOUGLAS, R. K. : *Europe and the Far East.*

WONG CHING WAI : *China and the Nations.*

GOLOVIN : *The Problems of the Pacific in the Twentieth Century.*

YEN, E. T. : *The Open Door Policy.*

MCLAREN, W. W. : *A Political History of Japan.*

HARA, KATSURO : *An Introduction to the History of Japan.*

BLAND, J. O. P. : *China, Japan, and Korea.*

League of Nations publications.

Statesman's Year-book, China Year-book, Europa Year-book, etc.

BANCROFT, G. : *History of the United States.*

FARRAND, MAX : *The Development of the United States.*

RHODES, J. F. : *History of the United States since 1850.*

CHANNING, E. : *History of the United States since 1850.*

BEARD, C. A. : *An Economic Interpretation of the Constitution of the United States.*

WILSON, WOODROW : *A History of the American People.*

MORISON, S. E. : *The Oxford History of the United States.*

PERKINS, D. : *The Monroe Doctrine.*

ADAM, R. G. : *A History of the Foreign Policy of the United States.*

BRYCE, LORD : *The American Commonwealth.*

CHARNWOOD, LORD : *Abraham Lincoln.*

SANDBURG, CARL : *Abraham Lincoln.*

BEVERIDGE, A. S. : *Abraham Lincoln.*

GARRISON, G. P. : *Westward Expansion.*

POLLARD, A. F. : *Factors in American History.*

2 Q

The opportunity afforded by the new edition has been taken to add the following:

BERLIN, I.: *Karl Marx* ("Home University Library").

LINDSAY, A. D.: *Karl Marx's "Capital"* ("World's Manuals").

ENSOR, R. C. K.: *England, 1870–1914.*

VON BÜLOW, PRINCE: *Memoirs.*

BRANDENBURG, E.: *From Bismarck to the World War.*

OXFORD AND ASQUITH, EARL OF: *The Genesis of the War.*

HART, B. H. LIDDELL: *A History of the World War.*

CRUTTWELL, C. R. M. F.: *A History of the Great War.*

NICOLSON, HAROLD: *Sir Arthur Nicolson, Bart., First Lord Carnock.*

—— *Peacemaking, 1919.*

—— *Curzon: the Last Phase.*

CHURCHILL, WINSTON S.: *The World Crisis.*

WHEELER-BENNETT, J. W.: *Brest-Litovsk.*

GATHORNE-HARDY, G. M.: *A Short History of International Affairs, 1920–38.*

ADAMS, J. T.: *The Epic of America.*

FREEMAN, D. S.: *General Robert E. Lee.*

INDEX

2 R